I0132043

Anonymous

Report of the Select Committee on Reform in the Civil Service

relative to Charges against the United States Civil Service

Commission

Vol. 5

Anonymous

Report of the Select Committee on Reform in the Civil Service relative to Charges against the United States Civil Service Commission
Vol. 5

ISBN/EAN: 9783337296285

Printed in Europe, USA, Canada, Australia, Japan

Cover: Foto ©Suzi / pixelio.de

More available books at **www.hansebooks.com**

REPORT

OF THE

SELECT COMMITTEE ON REFORM IN THE CIVIL SERVICE

RELATIVE TO

CHARGES AGAINST THE UNITED STATES CIVIL SERVICE COMMISSION

UNDER

RESOLUTION PASSED BY THE HOUSE OF REPRESENTATIVES
JANUARY 27, 1890.

WASHINGTON:
GOVERNMENT PRINTING OFFICE.
1890.

REFORM IN THE CIVIL SERVICE.

JUNE 13, 1890.—Referred to the House Calendar and ordered to be printed.

Mr. LEHLBACH, from the Select Committee on Reform in the Civil Service submitted the following •

REPORT:

The Select Committee on Reform in the Civil Service, who were instructed by the House, by resolution passed January 27, 1890, to investigate charges against the United States Civil Service Commission, and the workings and results generally of the civil service law, respectfully submit the following report:

On the 27th day of January of the present year the House passed the following resolution:

Whereas it is openly and repeatedly charged by persons of responsibility and by prominent journals throughout the country that the law pertaining to the civil service is being extensively evaded by the Civil Service Commissioners; and

Whereas charges of partiality shown by said Commissioners in making selections for appointments have caused uneasiness in the minds of many, and to such an extent that new legislation as to the manner of making appointments is advocated; and

Whereas it is deemed expedient that the acts and doings and practical workings of the said Civil Service Commission and the results thereof, and also the practical workings and results generally of the present law relating to the civil service, should be thoroughly investigated: Therefore,

Be it resolved, That the Select Committee on Reform in the Civil Service is hereby authorized and directed to investigate said charges, and to examine and report the practical workings of the system, and to report the evidence and the conclusions thereon to the House, and that said committee is hereby authorized to send for and examine persons, books, and papers, and administer oaths to witnesses, and to employ a stenographer; the expenses of said investigation to be paid out of the contingent fund of the House.

It was the judgment of the committee that the investigation should be conducted in two branches: the one to embrace the charges against the personal actions of the present and former Commissioners; the other branch of the inquiry to examine into the workings of the civil service law. Your committee has completed its examination relating to the first branch of the inquiry, going as far as seemed necessary to obtain a practical conclusion.

The charges against the Commission affecting the personal fitness of the present Commissioners were deemed proper by your committee to be investigated at once and a report submitted to the House as speedily as possible, the same to be accompanied by a resolution.

The committee have examined twenty-four witnesses, and have come to the following conclusions, deduced from the testimony of those witnesses:

On the first charge, affecting the conduct, retention, and promotion of Alex. C. Campbell, the committee recite the following facts and conclusions which they have reached in the case:

It appears that the said Campbell (a brother-in-law of Commissioner Lyman), some time during the fall of 1887, copied certain arithmetical questions of the general examination series for departmental service, together with their answers, at the request of a Mrs. Isabella Smith, to whom he gave them. These papers came into the hands of one Flynn, a person engaged in coaching applicants for office about to take the civil service examinations. It appears from the evidence of Miss Emily M. Dabney that Flynn offered to sell these questions to her, she being about to take an examination. She refused to purchase them, attended the examination, and failed. She recognized the questions as being the same shown to her by Flynn, and consequently these questions were used in the examination held December 3, 1887.

The attention of the Commission was called to the conduct of Campbell.

Mr. Oberly, Mr. Lyman, and Mr. Doyle severally investigated, to a greater or less extent, the charges preferred against Campbell, found him guilty of a breach of discipline, and he was reprimanded. But these gentlemen, as it appears from the testimony, failed to ascertain definitely whether the questions copied by Campbell and given Mrs. Smith were obsolete or not. They gave it as their belief, however, that the questions were obsolete. It occurred that they directed their inquiry to ascertaining whether the copy of the questions was in the handwriting of Campbell—an inquiry that was of little consequence if the questions were in fact obsolete.

The real offense consisted in copying and giving out questions that could be used in the examination to take place thereafter, and not in copying questions that were obsolete, and hence worthless to Mrs. Smith to use or sell. And it is not probable that Mr. Campbell copied questions and answers merely to give Mrs. Smith an idea of the character of the examination, since, if that was so, it would have been quite enough to have copied the questions only. The omission to ascertain whether the questions were for use or to be used at an ensuing examination was a palpable neglect of duty, since the fact not inquired about was obviously the one controlling fact essential in determining the degree of Campbell's culpability.

Obsolete questions are published now. They might have been published then without injury to the public service. Not only is M Dabney clear and explicit in her statement that she recognized questions shown her by Flynn to be the same that confronted her the examination, but all the circumstances confirm her statement. M Smith could have no use for questions and answers unless they w such as she could use for some purpose. Flynn could hardly h hoped to find a market for questions and answers that were obsol and it was not so important whether Campbell did the copying, whether what was copied was of consequence as pertaining to su quent examinations.

It is clear to your committee that Campbell copied the questions, that they were not obsolete. An investigation properly conducted w have disclosed the fact. If the administration of the Civil Service not to fall into disrepute Mr. Campbell should have been dismissed. retention indicated gross laxity in discipline and shows that the administration of the Commission was not such at that time as to receive or merit public confidence.

One of the charges against the Commission was that Mr. Campbell was not only retained, nothwithstanding his offense in the matter of copying and giving out the questions, but that he was promoted. In view of the fact that Campbell had been guilty of conduct which was calculated to destroy confidence in the integrity of the administration of the Commission, his promotion would seem not to have been defensible. Mr. Lyman, however, implies that the conduct of Campbell in giving out questions cut no figure in the matter of his promotion ; that that matter had been disposed of long prior to the promotion, by Mr. Oberly, to whom the charges against Campbell had been referred for investigation and such further action as the facts disclosed might warrant.

It was stated that Mr. Oberly did make the investigation and condemned Campbell's conduct and reprimanded him and there was an end of the matter, and when the question of his promotion came up Commissioner Lyman seems not to have regarded Campbell's conduct with reference to the giving out of the questions he had copied as being an item worthy of consideration. It is admitted that it was a question for the Commissioners to determine what punishment should be visited upon Mr. Campbell in case he was found guilty of a breach of discipline, as he was; but your committee can not avoid the conclusion that either the investigation was very superficial, and hence failed to disclose the gravity of the offense, or that the administration of the affairs of the Commission was not such as to commend it to favor; possibly both. It is submitted that if the Commission had discharged its duty with proper vigor and regard for the public, it would have become manifest that Campbell's retention was not defensible, and it would seem to follow that if his retention was not proper his promotion was not warranted.

Your committee can not accept as satisfactory the answer of Messrs. Oberly, Lyman. and Doyle, that they believe that the questions Campbell copied were obsolete. The facts disclosed to your committee convince them that the omission to ascertain the truth was as reprehensible as to have disregarded it after it had been ascertained, and is little less culpable; and whether they failed through indifference or partiality to learn the facts, or, knowing them, failed to take such action as the public service obviously demanded, is not a matter of great consequence; the neglect of duty in either case is condemned.

It has been suggested that Commissioners Roosevelt and Thompson are deserving of censure for not having taken action in the Campbell case. Your committee do not share in that view. On the contrary, there is nothing in their conduct to challenge criticism. When their attention was called to the matter by the newspaper reports, they called the parties concerned before them, separately and without the opportunity of their conferring with each other, and there was a concurrence of statement that the matter had been fully investigated and Mr. Campbell punished ; and it being, as to them, *res adjudicata*, they did not take further action in the matter, and in that we think they were thoroughly justified.

Your committee has further investigated certain charges against the Commission in relation to the promotion of Edwin D. Bailey, another clerk of the United States Civil Service Commission, to the position of stenographer, and in relation to the appointment of Thomas Mitchell, of Connecticut, to a position in the Pension Office. They have found that the action of the Commission in both these cases was not contrary to the law and rules of the Commission, and in no way are they censurable.

A charge was also preferred against the Commissioners reflecting against the course pursued by them in the case of one Shidy, who was an employé in the post-office at Milwaukee. It appears that Shidy was employed in the post-office at Milwaukee, and was charged with the duty of conducting examinations, or at least in preparing the list of eligibles from which appointments to positions in the Milwaukee office were made; that gross irregularities occurred in the preparation of the list of eligibles and the certification of names therefrom. It seems that Shidy acted under the direction of the postmaster in facilitating the appointment of certain applicants for position in controvention of the plain letter and spirit of the civil-service law.

The Civil Service Commission learning of these irregularities reported the same to President Cleveland, who immediately directed a thorough investigation. An investigation was prosecuted by Webster and Doyle, employés of the Commission, and in the investigation it was made clear that the irregularities complained of really existed. Subsequently Messrs. Roosevelt and Thompson, who had been appointed members of the Commission, had their attention called to the violations of law in the Milwaukee office, and proceeded at once to make a searching investigation. They summoned Mr. Shidy, who appeared before them and expressed his willingness to testify fully as to what had taken place in the Milwaukee post-office, but feared that it would result in his losing his situation, and as a consequence his means of livelihood, as he depended upon his salary for the support of himself and his family.

The Commissioners desired to have him state fully and in detail every fact essential to the exposure of the irregularities that had taken place so far as the violation of the civil-service law was concerned ; and they further stated to him that they would use their influence to protect him and prevent his losing his situation as a result of his disclosing the truth He did testify fully and at length, and was useful in exposing the frauds that had been practiced in the Milwaukee office and vindicating the law. He was discharged by the postmaster for so doing; at least there seems to have been no other ground for his discharge. The Commissioners felt, and it was apparent, that Shidy was being punished for disclosing the truth and felt it to be their duty to aid him by their influence in securing employment, and thereupon recommended him for appointment in the Census Office, and he was appointed.

This recommendation for appointment was made the ground of criticism against the Commissioners, Messrs. Roosevelt and Thompson. Their conduct in this behalf is not exceptional, nor does it tend to the demoralization of the service. It would have been ground for criticism if instead of keeping faith with the witness they had permitted those who concealed the truth and assisted in the frauds to escape and retain their positions, and had suffered Shidy, who had been instrumental in exposing the fraud and bringing the truth to light, to be punished for so doing. The Commissioners insisted that the man who told the truth and assisted the Government in unearthing a fraud and vindicating the law should at least fare as well as those who did the reverse. For that reason they recommended the appointment of Shidy as aforesaid.

Your committee is unable to find anything to criticise in that behalf. They did nothing in their official capacity in the matter of giving or securing Shidy employment, but as individuals, in view of his efforts to aid them, they recommended his employment to Mr. Porter, who gave him a clerkship.

It is proper to say that the investigation of the alleged irregularities in the Milwaukee post-office, conducted by Doyle and Webster, disclosed an utter disregard of the civil-service law in this office, and the failure to submit the result of that investigation to the President indicates either a disinclination to discharge an obvious duty or a fear that such a report would subject the Commissioner to censure. If the former, it argues unfitness for the position; if the latter, it shows the administration of the Commission to have been unworthy of public confidence. On the reorganization of the Commission by the appointment of Roosevelt and Thompson the investigation into the abuses and the irregularities in the Milwaukee post-office was had at once and was thorough.

With regard to the conduct of the Civil Service Commissioners in the matters submitted to your committee for investigation we find, first, that Commissioners Roosevelt and Thompson have discharged their duties with entire fidelity and integrity, second, that the official conduct of Commissioner Lyman has been characterized by laxity of discipline in the administration of the affairs of the Commission and is therefore censurable.

Your committee will proceed at once to investigate the workings of the system and present a subsequent report when said investigation shall have been completed together with a report of their conclusions.

We submit the following resolution:

Resolved, That a copy of the report and testimony taken before the Select Committee on Reform in the Civil Service in the investigation of charges preferred against the United States Civil Service Commission be forwarded to the President.

CIVIL SERVICE INVESTIGATION.

COMMITTEE ON REFORM IN THE CIVIL SERVICE,
Wednesday, February 19, 1890.

The Committee on Reform in the Civil Service, having been authorized and directed by the House, under resolution of January 27, 1890, to investigate all charges against the United States Civil Service Commission and the practical workings and results generally of the civil service law, met at 7 o'clock this evening, Mr. Lehlbach (chairman) presiding.

Hon. Hamilton G. Ewart, and Hon. Frank Hatton of the Washington Post, were present and prosecuted the investigation of charges against the present Civil Service Commissioners, Charles Lyman, Theodore Roosevelt, and Hugh S. Thompson. The following charges were presented:

The following charges are preferred against the Civil Service Commission as now constituted, consisting of Messrs. Lyman, Roosevelt, and Thompson, viz:

1. That on the —— day of April, 1889, without authority of law, Charles Lyman, when acting as sole Commissioner of the said Commission, promoted one Alexander C. Campbell, a brother-in-law of the said Charles Lyman, to a $1,200 clerkship in the Civil Service Commission.

2. That the said Alexander C. Campbell, about the month of January, 1888, had secretly abstracted from the files of the Secretary's division a list of questions that had been used in the examination of applicants for positions in the departmental service, and gave them to a copyist in the Pension Office, preparing for promotion to the position of clerk, who turned them over to one Flynn, principal of the Ivy Institute, of this city.

3. That the promotion of the said Campbell was made by the said Charles Lyman, Commissioner as aforesaid, with the full knowledge that the said Campbell had abstracted these questions from the files of the Secretary's division.

4. That on the appointment of Theodore Roosevelt and Hugh S. Thompson as Commissioners, the attention of the said Commissioners was called to the fact of Campbell's abstraction of examination questions, but that the said Commissioners refused to investigate the matter any further than to examine the party charged with the offense and the Secretary of the Commission, who stated that he (Campbell) had been investigated and censured for the offense.

5. That the said Alexander C. Campbell is still illegally retained as a clerk in the said Civil Service Commission.

It is further charged against the Commission as now constituted—

That one Edwin D. Bailey, in violation of the civil service law, which inhibits the promotion of persons in the classified service until examination, was promoted by the Commission without any examination to test his fitness, as required by law, from a clerkship to the position of stenographer, an important place in the said Commission, when it was notoriously known at the time that the said Bailey was not competent to fill the said position of stenographer.

2. That this promotion was made when there were several other clerks in the said Commission who were expert stenographers, and, under the principle governing promotions, undoubtedly entitled to the said position.

It is further charged against the Commission as now constituted—

That with the knowledge of its members, on the 19th day of September, 1889, Thomas Mitchell, of Connecticut, was appointed to a position in the Pension Office, as

1

a copyist; that the said Mitchell was on September 30, 1887, dismissed from the service *for cause ;* that the said Mitchell failed in his examination held prior to his last appointment, and that this failure becoming known to the parties desiring his restoration to the service, his papers were re-marked and he was raised from the ineligible to the eligible list.

It is further charged against the Commission as now constituted—

That Theodore Roosevelt, a member of the Commission, secured the appointment of one Hamilton Shidy to a place in the Census Bureau, when it was notoriously known to the said Roosevelt that the said Shidy, an officer of the Civil Service Commission as secretary of the board of local examiners of the post-office at Milwaukee, had persistently and repeatedly violated his oath of office in making false certifications and in not reporting violations of the civil service law by the postmaster at Milwaukee to the Commission at Washington.

That this action on Roosevelt's part was made with the full knowledge and consent of the other members of the Commission.

It is further charged that the Civil Service Commission, since its organization to the present time, has, by the manipulation of the rules and regulations, brought about results in violation of the spirit and the letter of the law.

2. That by collusion with departmental officers, appointments have been made in violation of the "merit system," as provided by the law, and that favorites have secured places with little reference to their qualifications.

3. That persons, relatives of officers of the Commission, have been attached to the Commission, gaining a knowledge of the secrets of the Commission, handling the records of the Government—a privilege denied Senators and Representatives—without compensation and in direct violation of law.

4. That offenses which resulted in the dismissal of officers of one political party were condoned when committed by officers of the other political party.

TESTIMONY OF CHARLES LYMAN.

Mr. CHARLES LYMAN, sworn and examined.

Mr. EWART. Before Mr. Lyman is examined I would like to introduce a copy of a letter from Mr. A. P. Edgerton:

WILLARD'S HOTEL, *Washington, April* 24, 1889.

To the PRESIDENT:

Referring to my note to you of April 20, and to your request through Secretary Halford that I should send to you in writing the information referred to, I now do so, stating that I was put in possession of it only on the evening before my note was written.

The case is this, and it shows that watchfulness is a necessity to exact justice in all civil service matters, and that where wrong-doing is brought to light, it should not be condoned by retention in office.

Mr. Campbell, a clerk in the Commission, and a brother-in-law to Commissioner Lyman, several months ago when Mr. Oberly and Mr. Lyman were both members of the Commission, copied a set of examination papers prepared for an examination and gave them to a friend, Mrs. Isabella Smith, who sold them for $25 to a Mr. Flynn, the principal of the Ivy Institute in this city. The papers came into the possession of a Miss Dabney, who went to the Commission to ascertain if they were the questions to be used at the examination. Investigation showed that the papers were in the handwriting of Mr. Campbell, but the result of the investigation was his retention in office by Commissioners Oberly and Lyman, because disclosures would have an injurious effect upon his sister, Mrs. Lyman. Mr. Campbell has since, and recently, been promoted by Commissioner Lyman, sole Commissioner, from $1,000 to a $1,200 salary.

There are matters connected with the office of chief examiner which would not bear a close examination, and to such an extent are they known that the integrity of examinations is questioned. There is altogether too much left to the discretion of the Commission, for through regulations which the Commission itself has power to make and by simple orders and varying opinions almost any desired result can be secured.

I do not give you this information for the purpose of inviting any action upon it, but that you may be advised that there are ways of wrong-doing it is well for the President to understand.

Very respectfully,

A. P. EDGERTON.

By Mr. EWART:

Q. Please state your name, and official occupation.—A. My name is Charles Lyman; I am president of the Civil Service Commission.

Q. How long have you been connected with the Commission?—A. Since shortly after its organization in 1883.

Q. In what State do you reside?—A. Connecticut.

Q. What is your political status?—A. What am I to understand by that question.

Q. What is your political party?—A. I am a Republican.

Q. Did you cast your vote at the last Presidential election?—A. I did.

Q. Are you acquainted with Alexander C. Campbell?—A. I am.

Q. What relation is he to you?—A. He is my wife's brother.

Q. When was he employed by the Commission?—A. I think in 1885.

Q. In what capacity?—A. As laborer.

Q. Was he required to pass any examination when he was first employed by the Commission?—A. He did not pass an examination before he entered the service of the Commission. He had however, passed an examination by the Commission, and was at that time on the eligible list.

Q. When was he promoted to the position he now holds?—A. I can not state from memory the precise date; but I have a memorandum in my pocket, if I may be permitted to refer to it.

Mr. EWART. Certainly.

The WITNESS (after referring to memorandum). From this, I see that the date of his last promotion was April 2, 1889.

Q. What was the date of his first promotion?—A. I think I have the date of his first promotion, but it is not far from the 1st of July, 1886. I do not give that as the precise date, but it was near that time.

Q. Who constituted the Commission when Mr. Campbell was promoted?—A. The first time?

Q. At the time he was promoted, who constituted the Commission?—A. I think the Commission at that time was Mr. Edgerton, Mr. Oberly, and myself.

Q. That was when he was first appointed?—A. When he was first appointed, the Commission consisted of Mr. Eaton, Mr. Gregory, and Judge Thoman.

Q. Can you say as to whether or not he was promoted when you were the sole Commissioner?—A. Yes, sir; he was.

Q. What was the date?—A. I have given it as April 2, 1889.

Q. Was he required to pass any examination at that time?—A. He was not.

Q. Why not?—A. The civil-service rules which apply to the office of the Civil Service Commission, did not require an examination for promotion, and it has not been the practice of the Commission to require any examination for promotion in any case, the promotions being made on the personal knowledge of the Commissioners as to the qualifications of the person promoted.

Q. Is that the case now?—A. Yes, sir.

Q. Have you ever seen the handwriting of Mr. Campbell?—A. I have.

Q. You are familiar with it?—A. I am.

Q. Was it ever called to your attention as a Commissioner, that at any time when Mr. Campbell was clerk, that the examination questions were improperly furnished to any outside parties?—A. It was called to my attention when I was Commissioner, that examination questions, believed to be questions of the Commission, had been furnished to an outside party.

Q. I will ask you to give, as near as you can, the exact date when this matter was first called to your attention, and by whom?—A. I am not able to state the precise date, but approximately, I should say the date was in January or February, 1888.

Q. By whom was your attention called to it?—A. By Mr. Oberly, then a Commissioner.

Q. Will you state what Mr. Oberly said to you, and what your reply was?—A. Mr. Oberly handed me some papers and stated in substance that the papers had come into his possession through a person whom he did not then name, and asked me if I would look at them and state whether I thought they were questions of the Commission.

Q. What was your reply?—A. After an examination of the questions, I said that I thought they were questions of the Commission.

Q. Do you recollect saying to Mr. Oberly on that occasion, that " whoever the guilty party is, man or woman, he or she should be punished?" Did you use that language?—A. I do not remember the precise words which I used on that occasion. I did say something to this effect, that if the questions of the Commission were being given out by any one in the office of the Commission, it was a serious matter, and that the person who was guilty of giving out the questions should be punished.

Q. In other words, whoever the guilty man or woman was, he or she should be punished?—A. I say that I stated in substance what I have said, without pretending to recall the precise words, that if the questions given out were the questions which had not been used in an examination (my remark referred to that state of things), it was a serious matter.

Q. You made that remark before the questions were shown to you?—A. I do not remember whether I made it before or after.

Q. Your recollection is not clear upon that point?—A. It is not perfectly clear upon that point.

Q. The list of questions was shown to you, was it not?—A. The list of questions was shown to me.

Q. At the same time was a copy-book or any book of record shown you?—A. No sir.

Q. When you first saw the questions, in whose handwriting did they appear to be?—A. The handwriting did not attract my attention at that time. I did not recognize the handwriting when I first saw the questions.

Q. I understand you to say that you are perfectly familiar with the handwriting of Mr. Campbell?—A. I am.

Q. Was it in the day-time or the night?—A. The day-time.

Q. Did you make any examination of the list of questions?—A. Yes, sir; more especially with reference to determining in my mind whether they were prepared in the office of the Commission.

Q. Had you any suspicion that Mr. Campbell had written these questions?—A. I had not.

Q. You did not notice the questions close enough to say whether or not the handwriting was that of Mr. Campbell?—A. My mind was upon the questions themselves and not upon the handwriting. I did not pay attention to the handwriting.

Q. Were you at all excited upon that occasion?—A. No, sir.

Q. Were you indignant at the party, when the list was shown you?—A. I am not in the habit of getting excited; I am not in the habit of showing it even when I feel so. I am more apt to be quiet than demonstrative.

Q. Being perfectly cool on that occasion, do you recollect whether or not you asked Mr. Oberly whether he recognized the handwriting?—A. I have no recollection of having asked that question at the time.

Q. Did you have any discussion on that point with Mr. Oberly?—A. My recollection is that the question of the handwriting was not considered at that meeting.

Q. Did you suspect any one?—A. My suspicions were not fastened upon any one in the office at that time.

Q. How long after that was it before you discovered that the questions were in Campbell's handwriting?—A. I think the next day; that is my recollection.

Q. In what way did you make this discovery and by whom was your attention called to it?—A. Allow me to state connectedly what occurred. My recollection is, and I think I am positive in that recollection, that I handed the questions to the chief examiner, with the request that he should examine the questions which had been prepared for the Commission and ascertain whether those were Commission questions or not, and what series of questions, whether they were new questions, or had not been used, and to report to me. It was ascertained that they were questions which had been used by the Commission.

Mr. BUTTERWORTH. Had been used or were to be used?

The WITNESS. Had been used. I so reported to Mr. Oberly. The papers were then placed in the hands of the Secretary by Mr. Oberly with the request, as he stated to me (I did not hear this conversation), that he would compare them with the handwriting of the clerks in the office for the purpose of determining in whose handwriting they were. Soon after that, just how long I do not remember, Mr. Doyle brought the papers to me and attracted my attention to the handwriting, and stated that he had no doubt as to whose handwriting it was; and, upon inspection of the papers with reference to the handwriting, I myself had no doubt in whose handwriting the papers were.

By Mr. EWART:

Q. Please state to the committee what Mr. Oberly said to you when he ascertained the fact that the questions were in the handwriting of Mr. Campbell.—A. If you will put the question in another form I can state the facts better; if you will ask me what I said to Mr. Oberly.

Q. I will ask you, then, what you said to Mr. Oberly and what reply he made to you?—A. I told Mr. Oberly that they were in the handwriting of Mr. Campbell; that I was satisfied of that. I sent for Mr. Campbell.

Q. Immediately?—A. Immediately; and had a conversation with him concerning those papers and repeated that conversation in substance to Mr. Oberly.

Q. In the course of that conversation, do you recollect Mr. Oberly using this language. Did he not say, "I leave you to reflect over this matter?"—A. No, sir; he did not.

Q. Did you not know, when you referred the case to Mr. Oberly, that the questions were in the handwriting of Mr. Campbell?—A. At this time I knew they were.

Q. When you referred the case to Mr. Oberly you knew the questions were in Campbell's handwriting?—A. A direct answer to your question might give a wrong impression as to the order of events. You remember that I stated that Mr. Oberly first called my attention to the matter that there were examination papers of that kind, and to determine whether they were questions of the Commission or not. That they were afterwards referred to the chief examiner to settle that point, and that subsequently they came into the possession of Mr. Doyle, through Mr. Oberly, and came back to me from Mr. Doyle, the question of the handwriting having been determined.

Mr. BUTTERWORTH. Who is Mr. Doyle?

The WITNESS. Secretary of the Commission. After the question of the handwriting had been determined, it was then that the papers were handed back by me to Mr. Oberly.

By Mr. EWART:

Q. I understand that you sent for Mr. Campbell?—A. I did.

Q. And Mr. Oberly was present?—A. He was not.

Q. I understood you to state a few moments ago that you sent for Mr. Campbell and he came?—A. Mr. Oberly was not present.

Mr. BUTTERWORTH. Is there objection to stating the interview?

By Mr. EWART:

Q. Please state to the Committee exactly what occurred between yourself and Mr. Campbell.—A. I laid the papers before Mr. Campbell and asked him if he had ever seen them before.

Q. You refer now to the examination papers?—A. Yes, sir. Mr. Campbell, after a brief examination of the papers, said that he had seen them before. I asked him if they were in his handwriting, he said they were. I think I said in substance this—I do not pretend to reproduce the precise words, but I think they are very nearly, if not exactly, the words which I used: "Campbell, this is a serious matter, and I do not know what will come of it; but I want you to tell me frankly the history of these papers."

Mr. EWART. I would like to know whether the witness is giving his recollection of the matter exactly, or whether he is reading from a written memorandum.

The WITNESS. I am stating the facts, Mr. Chairman, and I am refreshing my memory from a memorandum which I prepared some time ago.

The CHAIRMAN. I understand that the witness is stating the facts.

Mr. BUTTERWORTH. You are giving your independent recollection, after refreshing your memory?

The WITNESS. After refreshing my memory, I am giving my recollection.

The CHAIRMAN. I do not think there is any objection to that. The witness is refreshing his memory.

By Mr. BUTTERWORTH:

Q. When was this memorandum prepared?—A. It was prepared some time last fall.

Q. How long after these events took place of which you are speaking?—A. I think in October last.

Q. Does the paper give a complete record of what took place?—A. It substantially gives a record of what took place.

Q. Do you rely upon what took place on an independent recollection of that matter?—A. I rely upon an independent recollection of the matter. I have used this memorandum.

The CHAIRMAN. What were you going to say?

The WITNESS. I think I had finished the statement. The statement I was making was that I relied upon an independent recollection about these matters. After these charges were made I went over this matter, called up the facts to my mind, and carefully wrote out my recollection of those facts.

By Mr. EWART:

Q. I would like to ask this question: Do I understand the witness to say that he regarded this of sufficient importance to himself that at that time he made the memorandum?—A. Not at that time.

Q. Now, having made them several months afterwards, it does not occur to me, as a lawyer, nor do I believe it would to any lawyer, that a witness in court must speak from his recollection without consulting any memorandum as to dates and names.

By Mr. STONE:

Q. This memorandum was prepared in October last, and when was it you held this conversation?—A. Probably in January or February, 1888.

Q. Then it was nearly two years afterwards?—A. Very nearly two years afterwards.

Q. Who prepared that memorandum?—A. I prepared that paper.

Q. How did you happen to prepare it?—A. Because of the public statements in the newspapers concerning this matter.

Q. With what view did you prepare it?—A. Am I required to answer that?

Mr. STONE. I do not insist upon it.

A gentleman in the room. Answer it.

The WITNESS. I prepared this paper for the information of the President of the United States.

Mr. EWART. At his instance?

[No answer.]

Mr. EWART. I think this is inadmissible for him to read from a written memorandum.

The WITNESS. I have no objection to stating my recollection without the memorandum.

The CHAIRMAN. Suppose you give a history of how that memorandum was made, and what it was made for.

The WITNESS. Mr. Campbell replied in substance this: "I wrote those papers for a lady, a friend of mine, a clerk in the Pension Office, who has some idea, at some time in the future, of taking an examination for promotion. She asked me if I could assist her in any way in preparation for that examination. I told her I did not know of any way in which I could help her. What she wanted was something that would give her an idea of the general character of the questions that were asked in the examinations for promotion. I finally said that I might give her an old set of questions that had been used in former examinations, and that in their general features would embrace the same subjects that were embraced in the examinations for promotions. I therefore copied this set of papers and gave them to her with the understanding that when she looked them over they were to be destroyed. I know nothing of the papers since that time until you now show them to me. I supposed that they had been destroyed."

Mr. GREENHALGE. Were they printed?

The WITNESS. The questions then were printed. I said, "This matter will have to be investigated. You tell me that these are the facts." He said, "Yes, they are the facts." I said, "This matter will have to be looked into, and I propose to have it investigated for the purpose of ascertaining whether you have told me the truth about these papers." I then took the papers to Mr. Oberly, and in substance repeated to him what had taken place between Campbell and myself, and said to Mr. Oberly: "These are the facts, as Campbell states them to me. In view of his relationship to me, I do not think it proper that I should conduct this investigation. I prefer that you should do it; and my wish is that you should ascertain the exact facts, and find out just what there is in it." He took the papers, and at once began the investigation. I had no further connection with it until he had completed it, and reported to me what he had discovered.·

Mr. BUTTERWORTH. Was the report in writing?

The WITNESS. It was a verbal statement. That is all the conversation that took place.

By Mr. EWART:

Q. Just before you had that conversation, was Mr. Oberly there? He was in the room a few minutes before?—A. Whether he was in the room a few moments before or not, I do not remember. I had seen him that morning.

Q. When your attention was called to the fact that it was in Campbell's handwriting, as soon as Mr. Oberly left, you sent for Mr. Campbell?—A. I do not know that Mr. Oberly left that morning. Nothing took place between us.

Q. How long after you had the conversation with Mr. Oberly was it until you satisfied yourself that the list of questions was in the handwriting of Mr. Campbell, before you sent for Mr. Campbell?—A. I did not become satisfied of it in consequence of any conversation with Mr. Oberly. The conversation with Mr. Oberly occurred on the afternoon or on the morning of the next day.

Q. At the time that you had the conversation with Mr. Oberly you knew that the questions were in the handwriting of Mr. Campbell?—A. I do not know. I have stated that I became convinced of that fact when the papers were brought to me by Mr. Doyle on the morning after the conversation with Mr. Oberly.

Mr. BUTTERWORTH. Before you saw Mr. Campbell?

The WITNESS. Yes, sir.

By Mr. EWART:

Q. When you referred the matter to Mr. Oberly, you knew positively that the questions were in the handwriting of Mr. Campbell?—A. I did.

Q. You say the questions were obsolete, or that Mr. Campbell told you they were obsolete?

Mr. GREENHALGE. He said they were an old set.

The WITNESS. They were questions that had been used in a former examination.

By Mr. EWART:

Q. Mr. Campbell in this conversation told you, in explanation of his giving these questions to this lady in the Pension Bureau, that they would probably be of some advantage to her in an examination to be held at some ·subsequent date?—A. It was to give her a general idea of the questions that might arise. I suppose the general character of the questions.

Q. Did he mention the name of this lady?—A. He did.

Q. She had a position, and desired a position in some other bureau?—A. No, sir. She had been appointed in the Pension Office upon an examination.

Q. And desired promotion?—A. Her purpose was to obtain promotion at some time in the future.

Q. And to aid her Mr. Campbell had furnished her this list of questions?—A. He had given her this list of questions, as they stated to me, because they might afford her a general idea of the general scope of the examination.

Q. Did Mr. Campbell state how he got possession of the examination papers?—A. He did not. I did not ask him how he got the questions. I was satisfied that they were questions of the Commission. I had no doubt of that.

Q. You did not ask him whether or not he took them from the files?—A. I did not.

Q. Was it not a very improper thing for any employé in any Department or in the Civil-Service Commission to take questions from the files and give them to outside parties?—A. I should say it was a serious breach of discipline.

Q. It was such a serious breach of discipline as would cause you to dismiss any employé whom you found guilty of such an act. In other words, do you not consider the taking of those questions from the files a very disreputable act?—A. I think such a characterization of it as I have given, it properly deserves. I think it was a serious breach of discipline.

Q. Then you think the taking of questions from the files and letting outside parties have them with a view of enabling them to post themselves for an examination to be held at some subsequent date was only a breach of discipline?—A. I have answered that question.

Q. Would you regard it as an offense calling for punishment?—A. I regarded it as an offense calling for punishment.

Q. Is this the view the present Commission would take of it?—A. The other Commissioners are present and they can speak for themselves.

Q. Was this breach of discipline, as you characterize it, followed by any punishment?—A. Yes, sir.

Q. What was the punishment?—A. A reprimand.

Q. That was all?—A. That was all, except the suffering imposed upon the young man in consequence of his act.

Q. How long after the reprimand did the promotion follow?—A. Something over a year, I think.

Q. I will ask you this question: At what time was the rule altered changing the age from eighteen to twenty?—A. The 1st of March, 1888, I think.

· Q. Before that rule went into effect did any connection or relative of yours make any application for any position in any bureau?—A. I suppose I know what you want, and, if you will allow me to state the rule without questions, I have not the slightest objection to telling it. My daughter some time before that (I do not remember the date) filed an application for examination and subsequently took an examination, which she passed, and her name was entered upon the eligible list of the Commission.

Mr. STONE. What date was that?

The WITNESS. I think the rule was changed on the 1st of March 1888.

By Mr. GREENHALGE:

Q. What was the date of the application?—A. I can not state the date of the application, but my recollection is that the date was some time before the change of the rule. Let me state all the facts.

Q. How long was the rule made before it went into effect?—A. I think two or three weeks, probably.

Q. Not longer than that?—A. That is my recollection.

Mr. BUTTERWORTH. Is there a charge or suggestion that there was any irregularity?

The WITNESS. There was an insinuation in the Post to that effect.

Mr. GREENHALGE. Insinuations are not charges.

The WITNESS. I want to state the facts about this case.

Mr. BUTTERWORTH. Unless some irregularity is suggested, there is no reason for it. I have no objection.

The WITNESS. My daughter made application for examination at a time when she had a right to make that application. She made it on her own motion and without any suggestion from me. She was not then twenty years of age, but the application was filed before the change of the rule. The Commission held, and has always held, that the filing of an application is the beginning of the examination. The actual written examination did not take place until after the change of the rule which fixed the limit at twenty years of age, it having previously been eighteen. But under a rule, made long before that, she was allowed to take the examination notwithstanding that she was not then twenty years of age. Several other cases of the same sort occurred at the same time.

By Mr. EWART:

Q. The application was made before the rule was changed and before it went into effect?—A. Yes, sir. I could not give the date.

Q. Have you any memorandum of it? A. No, sir; it would not make any difference whether the rule were changed or what time it went into effect. The rule went into effect on the 1st day of March, and any application filed by any person prior to that date would have been good.

Q. Did she receive an appointment before the expiration of the year?—A. She did not.

Q. Was she re-examined before the expiration of the year?—A. About the time of the expiration of the year. I do not remember the precise date.

Q. Why before the end of the year? A. I do not know whether it was before or after the expiration of the year.

Q. Was her name placed on the eligible list a second time?—A. Yes, sir.

Q. Who composed the Commission then?—A. I think I was the only member of the Commission.

Q. At the time she passed the last examination you were the acting Commission?—A. Her case was not the only case of that sort. If gentlemen desire to make favoritism out of that they will have to look pretty close. It was done in this case and it would have been done in other cases.

Q. Do you know a party by the name of Charles McCaffery, clerk in the city post-office?—A. I do not know that I do.

Q. Do you recall that he made application for examination?—A. I do not.

Q. Do you know whether he made any application?—A. I have no recollection of ever having heard the name.

Q. Do you know of an instance of this kind, or can you recall an instance, where a party by the name of McCaffery was examined and it turned out that it was some other party and that his name was not McCaffery?—A. I have heard of cases of substitution. I have heard of such cases, where one person took an examination for another.

Q. You know of no instance of that kind, except as you have heard of it?—A. One or two instances occurred in New York.

Q. Do you know of any instances that occurred in Washington?—A. I do not recall any in Washington.

Mr. GREENHALGE. I would like to know whether the questions which are propounded to the various applicants are printed?

The WITNESS. They are.

Q. You have a set of questions which are printed ?—A. Yes, sir.

Q. And submitted to the applicants ? Now, after an examination has taken place, what becomes of those questions ?—A. The questions are not again used. That is the rule of the Commission, that a set of questions once prepared and used for an examination then becomes obsolete, and the Commission, I may state, now publishes these questions, after they have been used, for the information of the public.

Q. Is there any secrecy about questions which have been propounded in a given year, after they have been propounded and the examination has taken place ?—A. Absolutely no secret.

By Mr. EWART:

Q. If there is absolutely no secret, why should it be considered a breach of discipline to take them away ?—A. To take out any set of papers would be a breach of discipline.

By Mr. BOATNER:

Q. I understand you to say that after your interview with Mr. Campbell, before he acknowledged that he had furnished these papers, you turned the matter over to Mr. Oberly ?—A. Yes, sir.

Q. Were there three members of the Commission at that time ?—A. There were.

Q. Was Mr. Campbell's action considered by you, or taken care of by other members of the Commission ?—A. It was investigated by Mr. Oberly.

Q. Was Mr. Campbell reprimanded ?—A. He was.

Q. What I want to get at is, whether or not you acted upon the matter, or whether you turned it over to your associates on the Commission ?—A. I turned over the investigation to Mr. Oberly, then Commissioner, and Mr. Oberly, in the absence of Mr. Edgerton, conducted the investigation. The question was asked as to what had taken place when Mr. Oberly returned the finding to me and with the permission of the committee I will state it. Mr. Oberly reported to me the state of facts, which corresponded substantially with Campbell's statement to me. He stated that he had examined the lady in question separately, and that he had examined Campbell separately; that he brought the two together, and questioned them together, and that he had seen the lady who obtained the questions from Mr. Flynn; that he had probed the matter, as he believed, to the bottom, and the statement which Campbell had originally made to me had been substantially confirmed, showing that Campbell had told me the truth about it at the start. He said, " My conclusion about it is, inasmuch as these questions were not questions of the Commission to be used again, and the integrity of the Commission's examinations is in no manner touched by this matter, and as this lady obtained no information which she could have used, no one else had been wronged, and no harm had been done, the offense is not a serious one, though it is a serious breach of discipline; but it did not involve serious moral delinquency, and my judgment is that all that is necessary is to reprimand Mr. Campbell and drop the matter." I agreed with him in that conclusion, and that course was taken.

By Mr. EWART:

Q. What was the character of this reprimand, and where and how was it administered ?—A. I do not remember the precise words used.

Q. Was he called up before the Commission and reprimanded ?—A. My recollection is that it was done by Mr. Oberly.

Q. Do you recollect his words?—A. I do not remember the words used.

Q. It was such as to impress Mr. Campbell that the matter must not occur again, as it was a gross breach of discipline?—A. A serious breach of discipline.

By Mr. BUTTERWORTH:

Q. By whom are these questions prepared?—A. They are prepared under the direction of the chief examiner.

Q. By whom?—A. They are prepared by a number of persons. A certain number are prepared by the examiners, and occasionally members of the Commission prepare questions. I have prepared them myself.

Q. What I desire to know is this: For instance, a gentleman applies to be appointed in the Treasury Department or the Pension Office: are questions prepared by the members of the Commission or by the clerks under them, or are they prepared outside?—A. Questions for the general examinations of the Commission, those of a non-technical character, are prepared in the office of the Commission. Many of the technical questions are prepared there; but for certain classes of examinations a number of questions are prepared by the particular officer that has to do with those examinations.

Q. The questions in the main are prepared either by the Commission or by heads of bureaus?—A. Yes, sir. All questions are submitted to the Commission for approval before being adopted.

Q. Are any questions prepared by any persons not connected with your bureau?—A. No, sir.

Q. How many persons are connected with the preparation of questions—I do not want a schedule—say from a dozen or half a dozen?—A. I should say six or eight are connected with the office of the Commission. Then other questions are prepared by the board of examiners that are not in the office of the Commission, but work under the directions of, and are responsible to, the Commission.

Q. Where are those persons; are they in Washington?—A. In the boards of the eleven custom-house districts, and there are local boards of examiners at each. Most of the questions are prepared in the office of the Commission. The same is true of the questions used in the post-office examinations. There are now forty-four classified post-offices, and the questions used in all these post-offices are prepared in the office of the Commission, except as to the locality in the States where the examinations are to be held.

Q. Under the supervision of the Commission?—A. Always.

Q. How is it with reference to the questions to be propounded here in Washington?—A. They are prepared generally in the office of the Commission by those acting under the directions of the Commission.

Q. How long prior to this are the questions prepared?—A. Long enough to admit of their being printed; sometimes it is very close.

Q. Are they ever used more than once?—A. In exceptional cases they are used more than once; but as a rule, no.

Q. Illustrate what you mean by "exceptional cases."—A. I mean this: Under a general examination the questions are never repeated, but I dare say that a set might be used which had previously been used if we were satisfied that the person never had any opportunity of seeing them.

Q. What disposition is made of them after you get through?—A. We keep them for sometime; and those that are of any consequence or that may give no information are destroyed. The reason for destroying them is that if they were cut up and made into tablets for reasons of economy they might get scattered around and might excite suspicion.

Q. Where are they printed?—A. In the printing office of the Department of the Interior, which is a branch of the Government Printing Office.

Q. You print different sets of questions for each grade?—A. Yes, sir.

Q. The lowest being what?—A. The copyist's grade; one grade lower is that of printers' assistants in the Bureau of Engraving and Printing.

Q. How long have you been connected with the Commission?—A. Since its organization; first, as chief examiner.

Q. Are you able to, or will you, supply the committee with a list of the questions used at examinations during the last two or three years of the different grades?—A. You mean the questions?

Q. I mean copies of the questions?—A. Certainly.

Q. And indicate to what grade they belong?—A. The questions are headed so as to show that.

Mr. BOATNER. Are not the questions preserved for sometime?

The WITNESS. Questions used by the applicant and the answers are always preserved.

By Mr. BUTTERWORTH:

Q. Have you in any wise changed or modified the system within a year or two?—A. The system is undergoing evolutions constantly.

Q. What is the nature of the evolutions?—A. You mean as to the character of the examinations?

Q. Yes, sir.—A. The whole question of the state of the Departments, the needs of the service, and the adaptation of the questions to the general scheme and requirements.

Q. Is there any effort made on the part of the Commission to so prepare questions as to determine whether the applicant is fit for the particular duty he is called upon to discharge?—A. It is the object the Commission has in view. It has no other object in view.

By Mr. LIND:

Q. Are the questions for the several Departments, the Interior and the State, War and Navy, and the Agricultural Department, not the same?—A. The clerks' and copyists' questions are the same for every Department, except the Department of State. Examinations for the Department of State have more especial reference to the requirements of that Department, in addition to the general subject embraced in the examinations for the other Departments. They contain questions in international law and diplomatic history, and also in general geography. The regular examinations are confined to the United States.

Q. What you call "clerks' examinations" include the eligible places by subsequent promotion up to $1,800?—A. Yes, sir.

Mr. GREENHALGE. When examiners start out on a work——

The CHAIRMAN. I would like to call attention to the fact, before going into those outside questions, that the committee have decided to examine, first, the charges against the present Commission; second, the charges against prior Commissions, and then as to the general method of proceeding, going into the questions of the workings of the Commission,

By Mr. BUTTERWORTH:

Q. How long had Campbell been in the employ of the Commission?—A. I think since 1885.

Q. What were his duties?—A. He was then appointed as a laborer, but the Commission has never been able to use a laborer as such. The duties were clerical, and have always been so.

Q. I understand the Commission itself, in the matter of making promotions, is not controlled by the law in force and applicable to the other Bureaus and Departments?—A. The Commission did not require examinations for promotions in the Commission. The rules for promotion have been applied to the War Department only.

Q. In the matter of the promotion of Mr. Campbell, was it in accordance with the rules?—A. It was in accordance with the rules. He has done his work under the immediate supervision of the Commission, and under their daily supervision. Perhaps I do not make myself perfectly understood on one point. I think I said in answer to a question here of Mr. Butterworth, or Mr. Greenhalge, that after the questions have been once used, they are never used afterwards. That is now the practice, but it has not always been the practice. There have been times in the history of the Commission when it was not practicable to have new questions for every examination.

By Mr. GREENHALGE:

Q. What year was that?—A. That year was 1888.

By Mr. BUTTERWORTH:

Q. Is there anything else in reference to the Campbell matter that you desire to state?—A. I do not know that I have anything else to state.

By Mr. EWART:

Q. You say that the promotion of Campbell was not an unusual thing. I would ask you this question: were there other employés in your Bureau who were equally as competent as Mr. Campbell?—A. Oh, yes.

Q. Had any of them been guilty of any breach of discipline?—A. Not of a similar kind; but we have breaches of discipline occasionally.

Q. But none as serious as the abstraction of examination papers from the files?—A. I think not.

Q. How do you explain why other parties were not promoted?—A. They were promoted. Allow me to state that the Commission exercises its best judgment as to promotions, the first consideration being seniority, then other considerations, such as questions of fitness, adaptability to this kind of work, or that, and then the exigencies of the office are considered. He was next in line of promotion, and a failure to have promoted him at that time would have been a marked thing. In my judgment (and I say it wholly independent of his relationship to me) it would have been an outrage not to have promoted him.

Q. Notwithstanding this breach of discipline?—A. A punishment for that offense was meted out at the time.

Q. What constituted that reprimand?—A. That, in the judgment of the persons concerned, was sufficient punishment for that offense at that time. It was not considered necessary to continue to pursue him ever afterwards.

By Mr. BUTTERWORTH:

Q. Was this matter, with reference to Mr. Campbell, called to the attention of the full Board?—A. I do not know whether Mr. Edgerton's attention was called to it or not. I have reason to believe——

Q. Was there any criticism of your course in that matter in the Board? A. No, sir; 1 never heard criticism on that until I read this Edgerton matter in print.

Q. Did you meet in full Board afterwards?—A. We met for nearly a year afterwards, almost daily, when the Commissioners were in the city.

Q. And you never heard of it?—A. The matter never was mentioned at any meeting of the Commission afterwards, to my knowledge.

Mr. EWART. You were the sole Commissioner at that time?

The WITNESS. Yes, sir.

Mr. BUTTERWORTH. It seems that these questions passed into the hands of some gentleman named Flynn, who sold them for a money consideration.

The WITNESS. I do not think he sold them for a money consideration; but, on the other hand, his statement was that they had not been sold.

By Mr. STONE:

Q. How old is Mr. Campbell?—A. I think he is about forty-eight or forty-nine years old; I think that is about his age.

Q. What was your connection with the Commission at the time he first entered the service?—A. I was chief examiner.

Q. How did .Mr. Campbell happen to be employed as a laborer; at whose instance?—A. I believe the facts are something like this: The Commission always having more work than workers, needed some extra assistance when they were located in the Agricultural Department, and the Commission asked the Commissioner of Agriculture to loan them somebody to help them. Mr. Campbell had been employed in a subordinate position in the Agricultural Department, and he was sent to the Commission by the Commissioner of Agriculture, and assigned to temporary duty as a per diem clerk. He remained there until Congress appropriated for a laborer for the Commission, and then the Commission appointed him to that place. I had no agency in his getting into the Commission, nor in his appointment. I was absent at the time he was detailed to assist the Commission. I had no agency in it.

Q. Were his duties at first those of a clerk?—A. Yes, sir.

Q. But he was there as a laborer?—A. Yes, sir.

Q. What salary did he receive?—A. He was paid by the Department of Agriculture.

Q. Was he a clerk in the Department of Agriculture?—A. He was employed in the seed division at that time.

Q. Had he made application for examination?—A. He had made application, had been examined, and was on the eligible register.

Q. How long was it before he was appointed?—A. I think he was appointed in July. That was in March or April, and the appropriation which provided for a laborer took effect on the 1st of July, and he was shortly afterwards appointed to that place.

Q. You were the sole Commissioner at that time?—A. I was not.

By Mr. EWART:

Q. By whom was he examined?—A. By the Commission.

Q. By whom was his examination conducted?—A. I can not recall whether it was by the chief examiner, or whether it was conducted by some other person.

Q. Is there any memorandum of it?—A. I might find one by getting the papers. Let me make this statement, that I never participate in the marking of the examination papers.

Mr. BUTTERWORTH. Explain how examinations are conducted.

The WITNESS. Examinations were at that time generally conducted by the chief examiner when he was present in Washington. The papers are printed, and the applicants are seated in the room, sheets are given out to them, the questions are answered in writing, and the sheets are turned in at the desk and turned over to a number of examiners for marking. The applicant is not permitted to put his name on any but the declaration sheet. That sheet is inclosed by him in an envelope, which he seals. The practice is to retain them in that condition until the papers are graded. In the process of marking the only identification of papers is a number.

Mr. STONE. The questions I was asking a moment ago were intended to reach not only the facts connected with this particular charge, but to develop the method of this Commissioner himself; that is, his public acts as a Commissioner.

The WITNESS. I am perfectly willing to go into that.

By Mr. STONE:

Q. If you were present and superintended the examination of Mr. Campbell, it was conducted in this way, as you have indicated, by giving him some printed questions?—A. Yes, sir.

Q. He wrote out the answers on the same paper, folded them, and sealed them?—A. No, sir.

Q. What did he do with the paper when he completed it?—A. The paper came back to the examiners. The written answers to the questions came back to the desk. The paper that was folded and placed in the envelope is what is known as a declaration. The name of the candidate is inclosed in another envelope and does not appear except by the other papers.

Q. What becomes of the examination papers?—A. They pass into the hands of the people who mark them.

Q. Did you turn them over to the markers?—A. Yes, sir.

Q. I will ask you the direct question whether you remember seeing those papers after that examination was completed and before Mr. Campbell's grade was fixed?—A. I have no recollection of ever having seen those papers.

Q. Do you know who the markers were who examined those papers?—A. I do not.

Q. Did you ever have any conversation with any of them about it?—A. No, sir; I have no recollection of any conversation with the markers about those papers.

Q. Was Mr. Campbell appointed under this examination before you went on the board?—A. He was not appointed under an examination. He was simply appointed as a laborer in the office, which did not require an examination. The office of the Commission was not at that time a classified office. Appointments might have been made in the office of the Commission to any grade without examination. The office was not classified until afterwards.

Q. What was the salary of Mr. Campbell when he was first employed?—A. He was a laborer at $660 a year.

Q. I mean when he was first employed as a clerk.—A. Nine hundred dollars.

Q. What was the salary of the office to which he was subsequently promoted?—A. One thousand dollars.

Q. Is he in the service now?—A. Yes, sir; at $1,200 a year.

Q. Then he was promoted three times?—A. Yes, sir.

Q. When was the last appointment?—A. I think it was the 2d of April, 1889. That was the promotion made by me when I was the sole Commissioner.

Q. How was it discovered that these papers about which Mr. Ewart questioned you, had been furnished to this lady, or whoever they were furnished to?—A. I think the lady brought the information to Mr. Oberly that she had reasons to believe Mr. Flynn had in his possession certain questions of the Commission.

Q. This charge, as I remember, states that Mr. Campbell sold these papers to some one. Do you know anything about that?—A. He denies that he sold them, and the investigation did not show that he sold them.

Q. What was the name of the lady receiving them?—A. Mrs. Smith.

Q. Was she examined by any of you in regard to it?—A. She was examined by Mr. Oberly.

Q. Did she take an examination soon after that?—A. No, sir.

Q. Has she ever taken one since?—A. No, sir.

Mr. EWART. Has she been promoted since?

The WITNESS. I think she was.

By Mr. STONE:

Q. Did Mr. Flynn subsequently state, or at any time state, to you or any member of the Commission that he did not purchase the questions?—A. I have never seen Mr. Flynn.

Q. Did he write letters to that effect?—A. I have seen it published that there was no consideration whatever paid.

Q. I understand you to say that your daughter was eighteen years of age when she made application for examination?—A. Yes, sir.

Q. And that the minimum limit was eighteen years of age?—A. Yes, sir.

Q. And you afterwards changed the rules so as to make the minimum twenty years?—A. Yes, sir.

Q. She was not examined until after you made that change?—A. I think not.

Q. You say the Commission has ruled that where an application is filed, that would establish a right in an applicant to any benefits under the rules at that time?—A. Yes, sir. In other words, the rules are not retroactive; that the applicant was legally entitled to file an application at the time it was filed.

Q. If you had a rule fixing the minimum age at eighteen, and a person examined was put upon the original list under those rules, and subsequently the rules were changed so that no person should be appointed under the civil-service rules who was under twenty years of age, would that person be eligible to appointment?—A. We have so construed it. I want to give you the theory of the law adopted by the Commission. An examination is in three parts, the application, the written examination, and the period of probation, and after the probationary period a permanent appointment. When an application is filed the examination is taken by the applicant in accordance with the requirements of the rules.

Q. Has your daughter been appointed?—A. No, sir.

3117——2

TESTIMONY OF THEODORE ROOSEVELT.

THEODORE ROOSEVELT sworn and examined.

By Mr. BUTTERWORTH:

Q. What do you know about this Campbell affair?—A. All I know is that some time early in the fall—I have no memorandum with which to refresh my recollection—but I should say——

Q. When did you become a member of the Commission?—A. About May 10 last.

Q. When did you first learn officially of this Campbell matter, and what do you know about it?—A. About the 1st of October last—of course I can not give the date exactly—but about the 1st of October last there were two or three articles in the Washington Post concerning the conduct of Mr. Campbell, who was then charged with "stealing" examination papers and giving them out to some woman who wanted to pass an examination. I think the articles first appeared as preliminary, and then grew to two or three columns on the subject. Mr. Lyman at the time was away; I think he was making some investigations. It was early in October, and Governor Thompson and myself at first disbelieved the story, but on making some inquiry—I think of Mr. Doyle—we found that there was a foundation for it. We also found, for the first time, that Mr. Campbell was Mr. Lyman's brother-in-law. We had never known of that before, at least I had never known of it. We then examined Mr. Doyle, and summoned Mr. Campbell and Mr. Doyle (the secretary of the Commission) before us, and also questioned Mr. Lyman as soon as he came back to the city. We found that the offense had been committed two years before or thereabouts, and that at the same time the acting president of the Commission, Mr. Oberly, had carefully gone into the charges and had investigated the case and had decided that he should not ask for Mr. Campbell's dismissal, and the Commission had accordingly retained him.

We made up our minds that, whatever might be our personal judgment upon the equities of the case as far as we could get at them, we were not willing on secondary evidence two years after the event to reverse the decision of the Commission of two years before when it had all the facts before it. Governor Thompson and myself discussed the question at length on more than one day—I should say probably on five or six different occasions. Of course it annoyed us very much, and we could not get the story in a satisfactory shape so as to tell exactly what had happened. It was two years after the event. It was *res adjudicata*. We knew the custom was that one administration does not criticise the acts of a preceding one, and we were reluctant, unless on the strongest evidence, to reverse the decision made by the previous Commission, and that previous administration of a different political faith, with primary evidence, while we would reverse on secondary evidence. We did not feel that we would be justified in adopting such a course. To dismiss Mr. Campbell would mean a severe reflection upon our colleague, and a much more serious reflection upon the gentleman who had investigated the case two years before, and who was the acting head of the Commission, Mr. Oberly, and we did not feel that we ought to take such action. Governor Thompson suggested to me, or I to him, that I should go home and write a statement of our views of the matter to be spread on the minutes, and that we should also urge Mr. Lyman to write down from recollection a full statement of the facts to be spread on the minutes. I was called back to my home at Oyster Bay, Long Island, where I wrote out a statement and submitted it to Governor Thompson. When I came back I found that the President had called for a full statement from Mr. Lyman, and we thought that that was a further reason why we should take no further action in the matter, and we did not spread our memorandum on the minutes. With the permission of the committee I will submit that memorandum, or would you like for me to read it? This is simply a rough draught of what we decided upon, but which was not used nor put on the minutes:

OYSTER BAY, LONG ISLAND, *October* 14, 1889.

Memorandum of course pursued by Governor Thompson and myself in reference to the Post's charges against Campbell.

As soon as we heard of the charges, and found out that they had some basis, we called Campbell himself, and afterwards Doyle, before us, and later on questioned Mr. Lyman. We found that the offense was committed two years before; that at the time Mr. Oberly, acting president of the Commission, had fully investigated it, and that, with all the evidence fresh before him, he had decided that it did not call for Campbell's dismissal, and had accordingly continued the latter in his position, with the express or implied approval of his colleague or colleagues. This was the first time that either Governor Thompson or myself had known that Campbell was Mr. Lyman's brother-in-law, or had known that there had been any charges against him. We decided that, whatever might be our opinion as to the original equities of the case, we could not venture to decide, on secondary evidence, two years after the event, about a matter which had already been adjudicated by the former acting head of the Commission, with all the facts fresh at his disposal. An adverse decision on our part would have been a condemnation of the entire old Commission, including that member of it who is at present our colleague.

T. R.

P. S.—November 23.—We were confirmed in our ideas as to the proper position to take by the fact that the President had requested from Mr. Lyman a full statement of the matter, which is now before him.

(The first date was put down from memory at the time I wrote the appendix.)
I have read this paper, and I concur in the statements.

H. S. T.

During the reading of the memorandum Mr. Roosevelt made the following explanation:

I was present in Mr. Campbell's room when a former lady clerk of the Commission—I think Mrs. Lockhart—was in there speaking to him. As well as I can now recollect it, she said that Mr. Oberly had told her that he had told Mr. Edgerton of the matter and that Mr. Edgerton had pooh-poohed it. I do not know anything about that.

Some weeks after writing the first part of this I added this about the President. Governor Thompson put on this paper: "I have read this paper, and I concur in the statement. H. S. T."

Q. On the statement appearing in the daily press that the conduct of the Commissioners with reference to this action of Campbell was reprehensible, and on that being called to your attention the subject of making a suitable investigation seemed to you proper, and at the conclusion you thought you were not justified in opening up the case?—A. Precisely.

Q. That it was *res adjudicata* and should rest there?—A. Yes, sir.

Q. He has been continued in office?—A. Yes, sir.

Q. What is his character?—A. He receives the mail and sorts out the different letters. He brings in the mail to my room every day.

Q. Is he regarded as a faithful employé?—A. He is, as far as I know.

Q. There is nothing (and I put it in a leading form) in the course of the investigation which required any action other than that which you have taken?—A. No, sir; none whatever. There were all kinds of conflicting statements as to what had been the exact facts of the case. From the evidence we can not find out whether there was any danger of the particular examination paper ever being used again. It was just about the time the Commission stopped using examination papers twice. Nowadays every man who comes in and wants to look into the system there can do so. I will take down any old papers and hand them over to him. That has been the policy. I think several of you gentlemen on this committee have been shown examination papers. Of course that was never proper while there was any danger of the papers being used a second time. We made up our minds that all those facts must have been fresh in Mr. Oberly's mind. That he must have known all the facts, and that we could not on secondary evidence overrule a decision he had made when the thing was fresh in his memory. For that reason we took no action in the matter.

By Mr. GREENHALGE :

Q. I will ask you whether this promotion came while you were in office ?—A. No, sir.

Q. You stated to the committee your chief reason for accepting the decision of the former Commission was that it might reflect upon them. Was that your chief reason, or was that one of the reasons ?—A. The chief reason was the fear lest we might do injustice in the case. It is a pretty serious matter to turn a man out on as grave a charge as that, and discredit Mr. Oberly and Mr. Lyman for keeping him in, and I was not willing on the secondary evidence before me to take that ground.

By Mr. EWART :

Q. You did not investigate any further to find out if it was *res adjudicata*?—A. The exact course followed, as well as I can now recollect, was to find out who in the office knew anything about the matter. I found that Mr. Campbell himself and Mr. Doyle did, and I believe one or two other employés had heard rumors of it, but nothing definite. All the evidence that amounted to anything was from Campbell, Doyle, and Lyman.

Q. Did you examine the matter to ascertain if it was *res adjudicata*, or did you simply rely upon the fact that Commissioner Oberly had decided the matter ?—A. Not entirely on that fact. I decided that, on the evidence that we had before us, we did not think it was sufficient to justify reversing his action.

Q. Did you examine Mr. Campbell ?—A. Yes, sir.

Q. What statement did he make ? I presume he admitted that he was guilty of the charge ?—A. Yes, sir.

Q. Did you consider it a gross offense; did you attach any importance to it ?—A. I certainly did.

Q. Would you characterize it as a breach of discipline or a quasi-criminal offense ?—A. I can not answer that question, because I could not find out definitely what the offense was.

Q. The Commission as at present constituted—whom we all admit are able and distinguished gentlemen—suppose that one of your employés in the bureau abstracts questions, conceding the questions are obsolete, how would you characterize that offense, and what terms would you apply to it ?—A. Gentlemen of the committee, in answering that question, I am afraid that I may answer—I will state perfectly frankly that I should certainly move to dismiss any employé of the Commission who gave any special advantage to any one.

Q. Would you follow it with immediate and instantaneous dismissal ?—A. Yes, sir. I am not saying this with reference to Mr. Campbell's offense, because I can not be aware of what Mr. Campbell's offense was.

Q. Any employé who would be guilty of such an act as Campbell had been guilty of; would you follow it with immediate and instantaneous dismissal?—A. I have heard six or eight allegations about it.

Q. We find the only allegations that have been made are that he abstracted papers from the files and gave them to individuals on the outside. Suppose you ascertained that an employé in your bureau had been guilty of that action; would you not follow it with instantaneous dismissal?—A. It is a hard thing to answer that question. These were old papers, and I do not know but circumstances might come out that would favorably incline me to forgive the man.

Q. Then you do not consider it any offense to take papers from the files?—A. Yes, I do.

Q. How do you consider it?—A. I want to answer the question, but I would say I want to know all the circumstances of the case.

Q. Suppose his guilt was proven beyond any sort of question or doubt?—A. Guilty of what?

Q. Abstracting these questions from the files.—A. I would want to know all the circumstances of the case before I could pass judgment upon it.

Q. Suppose an employé had given questions out with a view of assisting a party, what would you say about it as a Commissioner?—A. Well, as I say, it would depend upon the circumstances of the case. I am inclined to think I should dismiss the offender. I want you to understand that it is embarrassing to be asked these questions. I can not answer any more definitely than I have done.

By Mr. BUTTERWORTH:

Q. It was the question of intent?—A. Yes sir, it was the question of intent. For instance, if it was a man who had just come in and was ignorant of the rules, I would not have dismissed him immediately.

Mr. EWART. That case was not given you. I am putting a plain simple case where the party had given out papers.

The WITNESS. You are supposing, I know, how Mr. Campbell acted. I do not.

Mr. LIND. Is not this argument?

Mr. BUTTERWORTH. I understand him to say this: That when these charges were made he looked into the matter to see if there was anything that called for further investigation, but he found it *res adjudicata*. There was nothing which prompted him to make a further investigation.

Mr. EWART. Then I followed that statement with this: Did you stop with the investigation when you ascertained it was *res adjudicata*, and he replied, I brought Mr. Doyle and Mr. Campbell before me.

Mr. DARGAN. You do not know whether the act was immoral or not?

The WITNESS. I do not. If you ask me whether I consider Mr. Campbell's act improper or not, I say I do not know. Mr. Ewart is asking hypothetical questions. The thing occurred months ago as well as I can recollect, and I am not perfectly certain even now that I am getting it straight. I should like to hear what Governor Thompson says about it. We examined Mr. Campbell for some time before we found that Mr. Oberly had adjudicated the matter. I am inclined to think, though I do not recollect, that we had Mr. Campbell in and that he said something about Mr. Doyle's knowledge of the case, and that from Mr. Doyle we got the idea (I think, though I may be incorrect, but I think it was from Mr. Doyle) that Mr. Oberly had adjudicated the matter. I think we had Campbell in twice and Doyle in once, and that we went all through the thing and talked it all over ourselves.

By Mr. EWART:

Q. You got the idea from Doyle that Oberly had adjudicated the matter?—A. I believe so. I remember we first examined Campbell and Doyle in Governor Thompson's room, and saw Mr. Lyman in his own room. I think we brought up Mr. Doyle again on the consecutive day.

Q. How did you become satisfied that the matter had been adjudicated by Oberly?—A. It was the unanimous statement of Campbell, Doyle, and Lyman.

Q. You became satisfied that the matter was adjudicated?—A. I became satisfied from the statements of Doyle and Campbell.

Q. Campbell had been charged as the guilty party and Lyman was charged with being his brother-in-law?—A. And the damaging fact had been admitted.

Q. You became satisfied of it from the evidence of Doyle?—A. Yes, sir; corroborated by the statement of Lyman. The witnesses we examined were Campbell, Doyle, and Lyman, and the one whom I spoke of in the person of Mrs. Lockhart who was in Mr. Lyman's room early in October. There were four witnesses. One was Mr. Lyman, one was Mr. Campbell, and two were disinterested outsiders. Their statements agreed entirely with what Mr. Oberly had investigated, and he had continued Mr. Campbell in office.

I did not say I only investigated it until I found it was *res adjudicata.* I do not think we definitely decided it until the witnesses had left and we had consulted with one another. I think my statement will show that, and then as for the evidence on which I was convinced, it was the examination of the three people and subsequently the testimony of Mrs. Lockhart as to the statements made by two or three people as to what they had heard.

By Mr. HATTON:

Q. Mr. Lyman under oath testified that Mr. Campbell had confessed to stealing these questions; also the questions stolen and furnished Mrs. Smith. Did Mr. Lyman make that statement to you?—A. I can not now exactly recollect what Mr. Lyman said. I certainly have no recollection of his making statements of that kind.

Q. You say that you decided not to look into the offenses committed before you came in as a Commissioner?—A. I said that we were very reluctant to take that up. Of course if we felt parricide had been committed, we might have taken it up.

Q. Have you not as a Commissioner recommended the removal of Democratic office-holders because of offenses committed before you became Commissioner?—A. Yes, sir.

Q. This offense has been condoned?—A. No, it has not. This offense had been investigated by a former Commissioner and a decision reached.

Q. You have recommended dismissal for offenses committed before you became Commissioner?—A. Yes, sir; but never where the previous commission had examined into the alleged offense and acquitted the alleged offender. We would not reverse such a decision unless new evidence showed beyond all doubt that the original decision was wrong. Of course, we would have to look into offenses which had never been investigated or where the investigation was still pending.

By Mr. STONE:

Q. On political grounds?—A. For collecting political assessments.

Q. I understood you to say you recommended the dismissal of Democratic officials?—A. Both Democratic and Republican officials were found guilty of violating the law. We have recommended the prosecution of certain gentlemen in New York. We learned they were making collections to elect Mr. Cleveland. We have also recommended the prosecution of Virginians who were making collections to elect Mr. Mahone in 1889. We have meted out justice on each side.

Q. What I want to know is whether you based these recommendations on the fact whether the incumbent was a Democrat or a Republican?—A. Of course not. All the recommendations I made were concurred in by Governor Thompson. I presume it is hardly necessary to answer a question like that of Mr. Hatton's.

Mr. BUTTERWORTH. You do not want to punish a man for being a Democrat; his punishment will come hereafter?

The WITNESS. My main object is to keep Democrats in office.' I do not punish a man for being a Democrat; our aim has been to get Democrats to come forward and be examined for civil-service appointments.

The CHAIRMAN. Your knowledge of this Campbell matter—was it derived officially or through the newspapers?

The WITNESS. Merely through the newspapers.

By Mr. EWART:

Q. What statement did Campbell make to you when you interrogated him as to those charges; can you give his exact statement?—A. I could not give his exact statement; I could tell you probably what he said. He said that he had been asked by a woman who wanted to take a promotion examination, and that he took out his paper and copied the questions and answers. We publish the questions at the end of the year. Campbell not being a bright man, did not want to work out the answers himself, and he took some papers where the answers were already worked; if the papers had been used they would have been of no use to this woman. He took a set of questions that had been already worked out, and he copied them off. Otherwise he would have had to work out the answers.

Q. Would those questions, from the statement that he made, have assisted an applicant in an examination?—A. From the statement that he made I should have thought not, for one of the things that struck me was the aimlessness of the act; I could not see where the great advantage to the woman came in.

Mr. ANDREW. Could not the woman get an idea of the scope of the questions?—A. She could examine the printed lists precisely similar to these questions.

Mr. DARGAN. The printed lists were not given out?

The WITNESS. Samples of the questions are from time to time printed in the paper. I do not believe that they had been printed at the end of the report, but they certainly had been in the papers, all kinds of printed sample papers.

Mr. EWART. Did it occur to you to ask Mr. Campbell what purpose he had in taking the questions out of the office?

The WITNESS. Yes, sir; his reply was she wanted them and he gave them to her. I believe he said she bothered him until he gave them to her.

The CHAIRMAN. How are appointments made in your office, by promotion or otherwise?

The WITNESS. I can only speak of the time the governor and I have been in. The settled policy is to commence at the lowest grade and promote them steadily up to the highest. There are seven grades. Three of those grades have but one man in them and four have two each. We can not hold competitive examinations where there is only one. Even where there are two in a grade they are usually engaged in such different occupations that no common test could be applied to them; for instance, one may be a stenographer or copyist and the other a man skilled in docketing the different letters or answering applications. Whenever capacity warrants we promote in the order of seniority. We take them in the order of their certification. For instance, we wanted a messenger and we found there was a vacancy in the North Carolina list and we wrote to one man from North Carolina named Bunn to take the position. We had originally signified that we would give him the appointment. He is now serving as our messenger. He can not be promoted for a year under the rules because he must serve in the $900 place for a year.

Mr. EWART. The next charge is, appointments are said to have been made in utter disregard of the law.

The WITNESS. That is absolutely false. I am going to ask the committee what the charges are against us.

Mr. HATTON. I charge this, and if I can get a chance I can prove it, that the present Commission have manipulated the rules. It charges the present Commission, and I charge it here and now, and am perfectly willing to formulate those charges. I did not formulate the charges here. I say, and I will prove it, that there is a clerk in the city post-office who was personated by another clerk. We will prove that the present president of the Commission was notified of that fact.

TESTIMONY OF HUGH S. THOMPSON.

HUGH S. THOMPSON, sworn and examined.

By Mr. BUTTERWORTH:

Q. You are one of the Civil Service Commissioners?—A. Yes, sir.

Q. When were you appointed?—A. I was appointed on the 7th of May and took the oath on the 9th of May.

Q. Will you state, if you please, what you know and what connection you have had with this Campbell matter?—A. I read an editorial in the Washington Post which charged Campbell with stealing questions and selling them. I did not believe it, and I thought if there was any foundation for it it was a gross exaggeration. We decided to look into the matter. We examined Doyle and Campbell, and as soon as Mr. Lyman returned to the city we had a conversation with him, and asked him to make a full statement about it. We asked him to submit a statement in writing. The testimony of Lyman and Campbell, whom we examined separately, agreed completely, and they confirmed each other. Mr. Doyle was totally disinterested. We found that the matter had been settled after Mr. Oberly had investigated it, though there was no record of any action having been taken. Campbell had been retained in the service, and it seemed clear that Mr. Oberly had decided that the offense did not deserve dismissal, but only called for a reprimand. Mr. Roosevelt agreed with me that, while it was painful to him to find that such a charge was made and to have a man of that sort in the office, he thought we could not under the circumstances re-open the question, since Mr. Oberly had practically decided the man was not to be dismissed.

Q. In your best judgment the public service did not require any other act?—A. Precisely; I thought it would be going too far to re-open the case. Mr. Campbell I found to be diligent and faithful. I only regretted that such charges could be made against an employé of the Commission.

Q. At the time you began this examination, you did not know the subject had been investigated?—A. No, sir.

Q. You had examined carefully these four witnesses?—A. We had examined three witnesses.

Q. And you found the matter had been given such an investigation as you would give to it if you had been in Mr. Oberly's place?—A. There was the testimony of Doyle that Oberly had investigated it. What conclusion Oberly had come to Doyle could not tell us. The fact remained that Campbell was still on the force and there was no record that Oberly desired his dismissal.

Q. Were any formal charges preferred?—A. Never, except this editorial in the Post. I should say that this man Flynn, whom I have never seen, in an interview, as I recollect, and in a letter purporting to be signed by him, stated distinctly that he had never paid anything for the papers.

Mr. STONE. Does Mr. Oberly live here?

The WITNESS. I do not know whether he does or not. I saw him on the street some little distance away. I do not think I have seen him twice in a year.

Mr. BUTTERWORTH. Have you seen Mr. Edgerton?

The WITNESS. Mr. Edgerton did not confer with me a great deal. I did not know Mr. Oberly was here. However, the non-action of the Commission indicated that we thought it had been settled to suit them in some way.

Mr. ROOSEVELT. Mr. Oberly was one of the people charged. Charges were made with great looseness.

The WITNESS. We made a full inquiry and examined Doyle and Campbell and had several conferences and came to the conclusion that the matter was not one we could properly re-open. We took this ground, that if Campbell was morally entitled to remain, he was morally entitled to promotion, and if that was the case, he was morally fit for an $1,800 clerkship.

By Mr. EWART:

Q. Under the rules would Campbell have been promoted?—A. It is a question of efficiency. I do not know; it would depend on who was in competition with him.

Q. Suppose he had abstracted papers from the files?—A. If morally fit to stay, he was morally fit for promotion. It is simply a question of efficiency.

Q. Would you deem it an offense to abstract papers?—A. I would regard it as a breach of discipline.

Q. You would not have promoted a man guilty of that?—A. I see the President only this morning disapproved the finding of a court-martial in the case of a man guilty of a grave breach of discipline. He is going to allow the man to be promoted in the Army. Under the circumstances I think it is right.

Q. That is not a breach of discipline such as Campbell was guilty of?—A. It depends on what Campbell did. If he took an old set of papers I would not think it a serious breach of discipline; otherwise I would. Something was said here just now in regard to an investigation and Democratic dismissals at Milwaukee. In regard to that matter, as a Democrat I would hang my head, but as a Civil Service Commissioner I would invite an investigation.

Adjourned.

WEDNESDAY, *February* 26, 1890.

The CHAIRMAN. Before calling any witness, Mr. Lyman wishes to make some corrections or explanation as to his former evidence.

Mr. LYMAN. In the testimony which I gave at the last sitting of the committee, I stated, as I remember, that these questions were brought to my attention on the afternoon of one day, and that the handwriting was not discovered until the following day. Circumstances have been brought to my attention since, that indicate that a longer interval may have elapsed between the time the questions were first brought to my attention and the time of the discovery as to whose handwriting they were in. I know I have now reason to believe that several days, possibly three or four days, may have elapsed. I am not certain as to the number of days. The facts that impressed this on my mind, and which have become fixed there, are that apparently questions of the Commission had been copied and that they were in the handwriting of a relative of mine, and that an investigation was needed and should be had. I wish to state further, as I recollect the testimony, that I used this expression: " Commissioner Edgerton being absent." There are some circumstances which lead me to believe that several days may have elapsed between the time the questions were first brought to my attention and the time when they were discovered in the handwriting of my relative, and that Mr. Edgerton may have been present at the office of the Commission during this time. I am not prepared to state positively that he was or was not, but I correct that expression " being absent," because I am not prepared to say whether he was absent or present.

TESTIMONY OF JOHN H. OBERLY.

Mr. JOHN H. OBERLY sworn and examined.

By the CHAIRMAN:

Q. You were formerly one of the Civil Service Commissioners. Will you please state how long ?—A. From April, 1886, until October, 1888.

Q. Do you know a man named Campbell, a brother-in-law of Mr. Lyman ?—A. I do.

Q. Do you remember that charges were made against Mr. Campbell for having abstracted examination papers from the Bureau at one time?— A. No charges were ever made to me against Mr. Campbell of abstracting questions from the Civil Service Commission files at any time.

Q. It has been stated here before this committee that Mr. Campbell had abstracted papers or copies of papers from the files and furnished them to an outside party. That offense was examined into by yourself and the conclusion was reached by you that Mr. Campbell should be retained in office. Will you state as briefly as you can your connection with the matter ?—A. In the first part of 1888, I think it was, information reached me that examination questions of the Civil Service Commission were being copied by some person connected with the Commission and were being sold to a civil service coacher of this city. Believing that if that statement were true the party guilty of the offense of copying and selling such questions should be known to the Commission and dismissed from the service, I concluded that it was my duty to ascertain as much concerning the matter as possible. I thereupon asked the person who brought that information to me to procure for me the copies of the questions which it was said had been called to the attention of this person by Mr. Flynn, of the Ivy Institute.

The person who gave me the information stated, as I remember, that Mr. Flynn proposed to guaranty her passage of the clerk's examination upon the payment of $15 for the entire examination, or $10 for the arithmetical examination. Understanding by that statement that he desired $15 for the questions, I told the lady that if she would get the questions and had to pay $15, I would re-imburse her out of my own pocket. At that time I had an impression that possibly Mr. Flynn had procured the questions of some examination and had them copied or printed and was selling copies of them. In the course of a week or so probably the lady (who is present here) came to me with a roll of manuscript saying that this roll of manuscript was a copy of certain questions of the Civil Service Commission, and that she had been informed that some person connected with the Commission had furnished that copy to Mr. Flynn. She stated to me that I might have the questions to examine upon condition that they should be returned to her within a certain specified time—I have forgotten the time fixed, but it was a week or so, that they might be returned to Flynn—and that I should not in my investigation do anything that would give Mr. Flynn information concerning the fact of the transmission of the questions to me at that time. I think she stated the questions had been furnished without any condition on his part. I agreed to these conditions, and immediately after her departure from my room I went into the room of the president of the Commission, Mr. Edgerton, and the Commission being in session, I laid the manuscript upon the desk and stated the charges that had been made and said: "I believe we should make an investigation to ascertain whether what has been said concerning the manuscript is true, so that we may see if any person is copying or selling questions and making a traffic of that kind." Mr. Edgerton immediately said that he would have nothing to do with any such investigation as that; that it would amount to nothing, that there was nothing in it, and pushed the manuscript aside with his hand in a very determined manner.

When I put this roll of manuscript on the desk and stated the conditions on which I had received it, I said if the Commission would accept this copy upon the terms on which I had received it, that they could have it. Commissioner Lyman, after Mr. Edgerton refused to have anything to do with it, said he thought an investigation should take place; that we should accept the questions, and proceed to an investigation to ascertain if any person had made copies of questions and had sold them; stating that any person who would do so ought to be punished, and he would be in favor of the punishment of such a person whoever he might be. Thereupon he examined the questions. He took up the manuscript and examined it. After he had completed his examination, I said: "Gentlemen, what do you want to do with this matter? Shall we go on with the investigation and accept this manuscript on the terms proposed by me?" Mr. Edgerton again said he would not do so. He said he would not enter into it. Mr. Lyman said it was a serious matter and required consideration. Then I pressed for an explicit answer to my inquiry, whether the manuscript should be accepted upon the conditions I had stated. Some conversation took place between the Commissioners, Mr. Edgerton continuing to deprecate the proposed investigation. The Commissioners talked together. The secretary of the Commission, Mr. Doyle, being present and also saying something in reference to the matter, as I remember. Finally, I said, "Well, the Commission does not appear to be ready to settle this question to-night;" and turning to Mr. Doyle, I continued: "Mr. Secretary, you take this manuscript and lock it in the safe and allow it to remain there until the Commission determines whether it desires to go into an investigation." Thereupon Mr. Doyle took the manuscript from me and went into the certification room where the safe was and put the manuscript in the safe and locked it, he having the combination. I accompanied him and noticed him do this. Then the question was dismissed from the consideration of the Commission.

After a number of days, I have forgotten how many, I sent for the secretary and stated to him that it did not seem that the other Commissioners were ready to go on with the investigation, and I said : "I think I will make an investigation of my own for the purpose of satisfying myself, and I would like you to aid me in it." It may be in the meantime Mr. Edgerton had gone away. Mr. Edgerton may have left the city after the meeting to which I refer. Mr. Doyle told me he would be very willing to aid me in any way. I said to him, "You get specimens of the handwriting of every person employed in the Commission, and let nobody know what you are doing it for. Get them without creating suspicion on the part of anybody." I wanted them for the purposes of the investigation. Mr. Doyle said he would do so, and proceeded to obtain specimens of the handwriting of every person connected with the Commission. Having done this he compared the handwriting with the manuscript that he had taken from the safe, and having completed his investigation he brought to me the manuscript with the copy of a letter that had been copied by Mr. Campbell a couple of years before, and a book in which the letters received were registered, which book was kept by Mr. Campbell at that time. Mr. Doyle laid this copy of this letter and manuscript before me and said, "I think I know the person who made the copy." Then I looked at the three writings and said, "The person who wrote any one of these wrote the other two, and I see from the book, letter, and manuscript that the writing is Mr. Campbell's, Doyle, he having stated that the copy of the letter was in the handwriting of Mr. Campbell."

I then said to the secretary, Mr. Doyle, "Take this manuscript and copy of the letter to Mr. Lyman, and say, as coming from me, that I have investigated this matter, and that I am convinced that Mr. Campbell copied the questions." Mr. Doyle went into Mr. Lyman's room, at least he left my room with the book, letter, and manuscript, and in a short while afterwards, half an hour or so, I went into the room of Mr. Lyman, having ascertained that Campbell had been in .there with Mr. Lyman. I said to Mr. Lyman, "Well, Mr. Lyman, what of this ?" He replied, "I have compared the writings, and have had Mr. Campbell with me and have gone over the matter, and there is no doubt that the copy was made by Mr. Campbell. He has confessed all about it and told me all about it." I asked Mr. Lyman to make a statement to me of what Mr. Campbell had said about it, and Mr. Lyman stated to me that Mr. Campbell had told him that he made the copy of those questions for a lady acquaintance of his who was then in the Pension Office, holding a copyist's place at $900 a year, and who desired to have a promotion as soon as she could have one under the rules ; that after having been appointed from the copyist's register she would have to remain in that position for a year before she could be promoted, and even then could not be promoted after the expiration of a year unless she passed the general examination now called the clerk examination ; that being very anxious that she should pass the examination, and it being evident that she could get a recommendation for promotion, she desired to know what kind of an examination she would have to pass. She said she would coach herself, or be coached, or study the different subjects in order to pass the examination; that she was rusty, particularly in arithmetic, and desired to know what the arithmetical questions would be. He stated that he had no printed questions to give her, but finally was persuaded, and did copy the questions outside of office hours, and gave them to her with the understanding that she should use them for her purpose she had intended and then destroy them, and some other details concerning the matter of this kind.

Then Mr. Lyman said to me, "Now, Mr. Oberly, this is rather a delicate position that I am placed in. I do not wish to do Campbell an injustice, but I am of the impression that he has done a serious wrong. I wish that you would take this matter into your hands and make an examination and investigation, and ascertain whether he is culpable and what should be done. I will be satisfied with whatever report you make."

Thereupon I called Mr. Campbell into my room and asked him to make a statement of the circumstances under which he had copied these questions. He did so, stating to me almost exactly what Commissioner Lyman had informed me was the statement of Mr. Campbell to him. Then it occurred to me that I ought to see the lady in question before Mr. Campbell should see her, so that I might ascertain whether she, without collusion with Campbell and without having an opportunity to discuss the question with him, would tell the same story that Campbell had told, and immediately I went to the Pension Office and requested the Commissioner of Pensions to have this lady called into his room. She came in response to that call, and I then stated to her in simulated anger that she had been procuring questions from the Civil Service Commission. I looked at her very severely. I told her that, in an improper manner, she had lately obtained from Mr. Campbell a copy of examination papers and that she had taken them to a Mr. Flynn and had sold them to him, and that I understood she was making a traffic in such things, and that having discovered her in the matter and also Mr. Campbell, that both of them were to be discharged from the service immediately. I pretended that I knew a great deal more than I did for the purpose of frightening her into a confession.

The lady had seemed much pleased to see me at first, but when the conversation occurred she was changed in her demeanor. I saw at once after I had spoken that she was sorry I had come, and was rather anxious I should go away, but she became indignant and declared I was making charges I had no right to make. I had something of a wrangle with her at that time. Then I said, "Now, Mrs. Blank, tell me exactly how this matter happened, and if my impression is not correct tell me what is the truth." Thereupon she made a statement to me almost identical with the statement Campbell had made to me so far as her intended examination for promotion, and the taking of the questions was concerned, how it had come about, and how the questions were found in the hands of the coacher. She said, "I had a good education in my youth, but I have forgotten a great deal of what I knew, and if I am dull in anything it is arithmetic;" and she said, "when I looked over these questions I was satisfied I could not pass the examination until I had freshened up on this subject." She said, "When I took these questions to Mr. Flynn, they were simply copies of questions which had been used." She said to him that she would have to pass an examination if she got a promotion, and she wanted him to instruct her in the arithmetical part of the questions, and wanted to go over that branch of the examination.

I said, "Did he pay you anything for these questions when he received them from you?" She said no, but on the contrary, she paid him for the lessons. I said, "How many lessons?" I think she said three. I said I thought she ought to quit it. After some other conversation, in which she desired me to undertand that she and not Mr. Campbell was to blame, for she had persuaded him, etc., I left.

I then investigated the matter of the questions. I sought to ascertain and did ascertain whether the questions had been used after that time. The investigation that I made led me to believe that at the time the questions had been furnished they had never been used in any examination except the one. Then I ascertained that no person who was an applicant for a civil service examination for admission to the service had been injured by this act of Campbell. I satisfied myself that the public service had been in no manner injured by this act; that no wrong had been done to any individual or any public officer in the public service, and I concluded, after taking into consideration all the facts, it would be too severe a punishment to dismiss Mr. Campbell from the service. I was led to that conclusion by other considerations which I wished to mention to you gentlemen, so that you may know why this lady applied to Mr. Campbell and not to other persons for copies of questions. Mr. Campbell was a clerk in the office when I became commissioner. He was then, I presume, performing the same duties he is now. It was his duty as a clerk, a duty had been imposed upon him by the Commission to take all letters containing requests for blank applications for examinations and reply to them by sending to each applicant for examination a blank form and accompanying the blank form with a pamphlet which contained specimen copies of examination papers of the Commission, marking the particular examination that the person desired to take, as, for instance, if a request was for blank applications for copyist examination, he would mark what we then called the limited examination and turn down the leaf there, and in other ways call attention to that particular examination; so the party might be informed as fully as possible the character of the examination he would have to take when he came before the board of examiners. It was also the custom almost every day for persons in the city who desired examination blanks to come into the office and get blank applications and information concerning the examination which they proposed to take, and they were always referred to Mr. Campbell.

Mr. GREENHALGE (in the chair). In whose charge were these particular questions which Mr. Campbell copied?

The WITNESS. They were in charge of the secretary, and Mr. Campbell was under him. The secretary had charge of Campbell's books and all examination papers of persons who had become eligible by reason of having passed examinations. Persons who came into the office would be referred to Mr. Campbell. The secretary and the Commissioners would refer them to Mr. Campbell. We would say, "If you want specimen questions go to Mr. Campbell and he will give them to you." It was Campbell's duty to speak to the applicant and call the person's particular attention to the specimen questions printed in the book, and answer all questions which he could, and they generally asked as many as they could. As far as the Commissioners had printed five editions of one of the reports for the simple purpose of supplying the demand for sample questions. We meant to print another edition, but the Commission had run out of money and it had gotten into some controversy, I think, with the Secretary of the Interior, or a clerk of the Interior Department who had some peculiar ideas about printing, and we could not print any more; so that persons who made personal application to the Commission were met with the reply that copies of the book containing specimen questions had been exhausted, and we had no money to print more and could not furnish them. Some of them thought it was a hardship that they had to be ignorant of the scope of the examinations, and it was suggested to the applicants sometimes when they came in and they were told that they could sit in the room and read, and if they wished to even copy, the papers of the last examination made by the person who had passed the highest and given the most satisfactory answers to the questions; that in this way they could see exactly what kind of questions were being asked, and what was necessary in order to pass an examination. We would tell them, "You can sit here and read and even copy these papers."

Mr. HOPKINS. To what point is the witness directing his testimony?

The WITNESS. I was asked when this matter was investigated, whether I investigated it, and whether I arrived at certain conclusions, and if I did, why and how, and I am stating it. I consider this charge made as much against me as against anybody, because I had charge of the whole matter and took the whole responsibility.

By Mr. BOATNER:

Q. I understand you to say that according to the best of your judgment you did investigate and pass upon this matter on your responsibility and upon your best judgment upon it as an officer?—A. Yes, sir.

Q. What punishment, if any, was inflicted upon Mr. Campbell for this breach of discipline?—A. I do not agree with Mr. Lyman that he was guilty of a gross breach of discipline.

Mr. HOPKINS. The point I was making was that he was dwelling on some matters which might be very interesting as a matter of reminiscence, but I did not see the revelancy of it.

Mr. GREENHALGE. State the material facts.

The WITNESS. I am endeavoring to do that. It was Mr. Campbell's duty to give out specimen questions. Questions were taken from the files of the office by Mr. Doyle, Mr. Campbell, and myself. People were sometimes told that they might, if they wished, copy them and carry them away. Because Campbell was in that position it led the lady to make application to him, I presume. Anyhow, he was in that position and it was his duty to furnish specimen questions. I thought he had no right to copy those questions. The fact that they had gotten into the possession of a person who was using them in his business showed that it was an improper thing for him to do. I made this report. I did not think that Campbell as a clerk ought to be dismissed. I think probably I said, "I will see him and talk with him and tell him what I think about this thing." I did not after this insist on the Commission making any investigation.

Mr. HOPKINS. Was it anything that in your judgment required disciplining or speaking to on the subject?

The WITNESS. Yes, sir; it was, under the circumstances. If I had found these questions in Campbell's hands, I never would have thought anything of it. I would have thought Mr. Campbell was doing a good deal of gratuitous work, but I would not have thought there was anything wrong in the mere fact that he had copied the questions.

Mr. GREENHALGE. You did not know of any like practice of an employé of the Commission furnishing copies of examination papers?

The WITNESS. No, sir; I never did. I would frequently hear that persons had questions of the Civil Service Commission, and had boasted of it.

By Mr. HOPKINS:

Q. How did you hear that they had boasted that they had questions of the Commission?—A. There was a case in the post-office.

Q. Who was the person?—A. I can not tell the names.

Q. From whom did you learn it?—A. I learned it by an anonymous letter.

Q. Was that all your information?—A. That was all.

Q. Did the writer of the anonymous letter make such boasts?—A. He did.

Q. Do you remember what the boast was?—A. I do not.

Q. Where is that anonymous letter?—A. I do not know.

Q. What did you do with it?—A. I destroyed it.

Q. You made a statement about certain persons making these boasts.—A. I would frequently hear such rumors.

Q. Can you give the name of any person?—A. They never made any such boast to me.

Q. Can you name any person that did?—A. I can not. I have seen it published in the newspapers, but I can not tell you now what papers.

The CHAIRMAN. Was anything said to you by your colleague, Mr. Edgerton, as to the examination that you were conducting?

The WITNESS. No, sir; because the examination that I was conducting did not last long, and my impression is that at the time Mr. Edgerton was out of the city, but I do not know that that is a fact.

Mr. EWART. Mr. Chairman, before I enter upon the cross-examination I desire to make a brief statement.

There have been intimations made by members of the committee that at the last session of the committee a great many unnecessary and useless questions were asked. I have no desire whatever to detain this committee unnecessarily. I am perfectly aware of the fact that we can not be bound by the hide-bound rules of evidence. As an instance, I may state that legally we are not allowed to contradict our own witness, but in this investigation we will be compelled to do that. I should be glad to see the Commissioners vindicated, and I say frankly that when this evidence is all in, and a perfect case has not been made out by our side, I shall frankly state that, not only to this committee, but on the floor of the House when the report is brought before the House.

By Mr. EWART:

Q. You say that no charges were ever made against Mr. Campbell to you?—A. No, sir.

Q. When you first heard it, you did not call the attention of Mr. Lyman or Mr. Edgerton to the matter?—A. On the same evening I called the attention of the Commissioners to the matter while they were in session.

Q. You say that Mr. Edgerton ridiculed the idea of having anything to do with it?—A. I do not know that he said that. He said he would have nothing to do with the proposed investigation.

Q. Did he assign a reason to you why he considered there was nothing in it?

Mr. GREENHALGE. The witness represented him as saying that an investigation would not amount to anything.

By Mr. EWART.

Q. Did he assign a reason at that time why he was unwilling to go into an investigation?—A. No, except that he would not have anything to do with it; that he did not believe it amounted to anything.

Q. Did he assign any reason whatever ?—A. He said he would have nothing to do with it.

Q. At that time you regarded it as a serious matter ?—A. I did, and so stated to the Commission.

Q. You have read Mr. Edgerton's letter, have you not?—A. I have.

Q. You are aware of the substance of that letter?—A. I am.

Q. You recollect, do you not, that Mr. Edgerton's charges are that the questions were taken out by Campbell ?—A. I do.

Q. And that he was re-instated by you without any investigation either by yourself or Mr. Lyman ?—A. He said Campbell was retained in the service. Nothing was said about re-instatement because he was never dismissed.

Q. I understood you to say that you submitted a copy of a manuscript, or whatever it was, to Mr. Lyman ?—A. It was a roll of manuscript.

Q. Did Mr. Lyman examine that closely ?—A. He took the manuscript up and turned the sheets over and examined it to ascertain what it was.

Q. Did he examine it a sufficient length of time, in your judgment, to enable him to tell the handwriting of the party?—A. I should think he did.

Q. Did he tell you at that time that he had any suspicion as to who wrote it?—A. After that he did.

Q. How long after that?—A. It was after the matter had been taken to his room by Mr. Doyle a week or so, I can not remember how long. He told me, and I think he told the same to Mr. Doyle, that at first he thought the handwriting resembled that of a member of the board of examiners. After looking into it further he ascertained it was not. I think he said he had an impression that it was Campbell's writing.

Q. How long after this conversation were you apprised of the fact that it was Campbell's handwriting?—A. Not until I was informed by comparison that it was Campbell's handwriting.

Q. The comparison made by Mr. Doyle ?—A. Yes, sir. I had no idea it was Campbell's handwriting until then. In my recollection it was a week or ten days, though I may be mistaken. It was several days after I laid the questions before the Commission.

Q. Did you know at that time that these questions were obsolete ?—A. "Obsolete questions" is a term that I do not exactly understand. It is generally used, but it does not mean much. No questions are obsolete entirely, because the Commission can take them and use them at any time it wishes.

Q. Had this particular set been what is called obsolete?—A. Not entirely. They were obsolete in the sense that they were never used again. They would not have been used again.

Q. Were they used at any other time?—A. Not within my knowledge.

Q. They had been used in Washington ?—A. They had been used in Washington,

Mr. HOPKINS. Mr. Ewart's point is as to whether they were used in any other part of the country. They were used in Washington. Were they used in Baltimore, Buffalo, New York, Chicago, or in any other place ?—A. Not within my knowledge. I will state what was the custom of the Commission. Formerly we used to have examinations frequently and we had no one in the Commission who had time to prepare questions for each examination, and therefore we would have to use the same questions more than once. Then we postponed examinations to once a week, and then to once a month, and finally we got so that we would have them only once every three months. Then we adopted the rule that we would never use the same questions twice at the same place, but questions used, for instance, in Washington might be used again in different parts of the country. It was not presumed that anybody could know where the questions would go.

Q. Are you perfectly familiar with the questions that were propounded to applicants?—A. I can not say that I was perfectly familiar with them.

Q. The question is whether or not you were familiar with the character of the questions?—A. All questions prepared by the chief examiners were submitted to the Commission and the commissioners read, criticised, and changed.

Q. When your attention was first called to this list of questions, I asked you if you did not recognize that they were the list of questions that had been used by the Commission.—A. I think I recognized them as new questions, as questions that had been used by the Commission lately.

Q. Why did you attach importance to an investigation?—A. I wanted to see if any person in the Commission was making copies of questions and selling them.

Mr. GREENHALGE. We do not care particularly to know the frame, of mind of these Commissioners. We want to get at the facts.

Mr. EWART. I sincerely hope that it is not the opinion of gentlemen of the committee that we desire only to make an attack upon Mr. Thompson or Mr. Roosevelt. We want to state frankly at this stage that we desire to get at the whole facts in this matter, no matter whom it hurts. Here is a witness, Mr. Oberly, who says Mr. Edgerton, when this matter was called to his attention, distinctly stated that there was nothing in it. Here is a letter of that Commissioner in which he distinctly says that those questions were stolen, and that this man Campbell was re-instated to his position or appointed to an important place in the Commission without any examination.

Mr. GREENHALGE. If you desire to contradict this witness by some other witness, would not it be well to wait until you produce the other witness?

Mr. HOPKINS. That is not the point. It is an old saying that a witness takes his character in his hand when he goes upon the stand. Mr. Oberly has made certain general statements, but the good faith of his testimony is one of the elements in this case. I have faith in Illinois men, for they are all good men. If Mr. Ewart desires to examine him on that point, I think he ought to have the right do so.

The WITNESS. If Mr. Ewart understood me to say that I called the attention of Mr. Edgerton to the fact that Mr. Campbell had done this, he is wrong. I never did. I did not know then who it was that gave out the papers.

By Mr. EWART:

Q. You regarded it as of sufficient importance to investigate it at that time, and I want to know whether you ascertained that the questions were a list of questions that had been used in an examination?—A. I would have considered it just as important if it had been questions a year old.

Q. Why so?—A. Because, as I said before, the charge was not particularly that he had copied specimen questions and given them to any person, but that he had sold them.

Q. Suppose he had given them away?—A. He had a right to give them away under certain conditions.

Q. Under what conditions?—A. If a person had gone in and asked for them, he would have had a right to give them out.

Q. Then the investigation was directed to whether or not he had sold the questions?—A. Yes, sir. I wanted to know whether he was selling them.

Q. You did not consider it an offense to give them away?—A. I considered it an indiscretion.

Q. An indiscretion merely?—A. In one sense—if it was done without informing the Commission.

Q. Did you hear that Mr. Lyman characterized this as a serious breach of discipline?—A. It was a breach of discipline in a person to copy something out of office hours without the knowledge of the Commission, which he [Campbell] had no authority to do at that time.

Q. Did Campbell in his conversation tell you why he had instructed or requested this lady to destroy the questions?—A. No, except that they would be of no further use. He told her either to destroy them or return them to him. The manuscript was in an undisguised handwriting.

Q. Did you ever at any time administer a reprimand to him?—A. I talked to him.

Q. The evidence was that you administered a reprimand.—A. It was called a reprimand.

Q. What was the character of that reprimand?

The CHAIRMAN. Was it as severe as the one you gave the lady in the Pension Office?

The WITNESS. I was more serious with Campbell than with the woman because I was sorry he had got into the trouble. I called his attention to the fact that such actions might lead him into something that would be worse than that. I scolded him some.

Q. When you administered that reprimand you seemed to have regarded it a little more than an indiscretion.—A. It was an indiscretion that amounted to a breach of discipline, of course, but that it was so serious as to demand his expulsion and dismissal from the Commission, I did not believe.

Q. It has been charged by a journal having special facilities for obtaining news from the Commission that you furnished the information upon which these charges are based.—A. I understand that charge has been made by the Evening Post of New York, that I was the person who had been furnishing Mr. Hatton the information on which these charges are based. I wish to say I never furnished Mr. Hatton any information on which he based his broadsides or any of the editorials in his paper or otherwise, and I consider this as a matter against myself because I had the Campbell matter in my hands and acquitted Campbell. I did think then I was right and I now think I was right. I never furnished any information.

Q. Did you ever recommend the promotion at any time of Mr. Campbell after this investigation?—A. No, sir; I did not.

Q. As to the act of Mr. Lyman in appointing Mr. Campbell when he was the sole Commissioner, will you give us your views upon that matter?—A. As to the propriety of it or the legality of the act?

Mr. EWART. This is a matter of strictly legal construction. We desire to invite the attention of the Commission and of the committee to section 1 of the act which distinctly provides that the Commission shall be composed of three members. We take the position that Mr. Lyman's act was illegal because there was only one Commissioner.

TESTIMONY OF WILLIAM J. VICKERY.

WILLIAM J. VICKERY, sworn and examined.

By the CHAIRMAN:

Q. Please state your name.—A. My name is William J. Vickery; I reside in Evansville, Ind.

Q. State as briefly as you can any personal knowledge you may have in the matter of this copying of papers in the Civil Service Commission by Mr. Campbell.—A. I have no personal knowledge of the matter at all. The only knowledge I have is hearsay of the case obtained from one or two persons, which was a garbled account of the statement Mr. Oberly has just made.

Q. Was any statement made by Mr. Lyman or by either of the Commissioners to you ?—A. To me there never has been such statement or admission made. I never conversed with either of the Commissioners or the ex-Commissioners about it. It came to me in a shape in which I was asked not to mention anything about it. It came to me in a way that was misleading in two or three particulars.

Q. Were you employed by the Civil Service Commission ?—A. I was with them from July 25, 1885, until July 1, 1889.

Q. You say you have no personal knowledge of this transaction ?— A. It would be hearsay all the way through.

By Mr. EWART:

Q. Please state exactly what you heard about this matter. You were in the office of the Commissioners as an employé. State whether or not this report of Campbell's taking these questions created any excitement, and if so, what it was.—A. I was told in a conversation some time early this year, perhaps the chief examiner gave the information to me, that it had been charged that questions of the Commission were leaking out and had been furnished to Mr. Flynn. It led to the idea that some of the members of the board of examiners were under suspicion. As I had read the proof sometimes of the questions, I naturally supposed that I was under suspicion. This was early in the year. Early in March I left Washington on a tour of examination and I did not get back until the 9th or 10th of June. Soon after getting back I asked some one, perhaps the chief examiner, whether they had found out who had given out the questions. I never knew what kind of questions they were that were given out, but the charge came in a general form that questions had been given out and that Mr. Flynn was coaching people on questions. As I say, I had taken an interest in it because I had access to the questions before they were printed. I knew of no excitement, but one of the employés told me the story somewhat in detail, not perhaps in full detail, but somewhat -misleading and not as full as Mr. Oberly has given it here to-day. I will say these questions were furnished in advance of their use, and the fact is I think that at the time I did not put very much belief in the story because it seemed to me improbable. It came to me under promise of secrecy. The person seemed to have obtained his facts from Mr. Oberly.

Mr. HOPKINS. Did the person who conveyed this information to you make the statement that these questions were given out and being used ?

The WITNESS. I could not say; the statement was made in that way. My impression was from the chief examiner first that the examiners had given out the questions. It was found that a woman had furnished them to Mr. Flynn. I was not aware it was the last set of questions. Afterwards, the charge was that the woman referred to had obtained them from Mr. Campbell and had furnished them as a regular thing for pay.

By Mr. EWART:

Q. Was it regarded as an offense in the office?—A. Certainly; no member of the board of examiners would have given out any questions used or unused.

Q. Do you know of any instance, while you were clerk in the Civil Service Commission, of any one giving out questions?—A. While I was clerk with the Commission, the Commission used to publish specimen sets of questions. For some reason the supply of specimen questions ran short, and I know that for a long time there was great impatience because the applicants were not furnished with an idea of the kind of examination they would have to take. I think that afterward provision was made by which certain persons could see the whole sets of questions down-stairs.

Q. Do you recollect whether, about this time, just before this investigation, Campbell showed any special interest about the time new sets of questions were to be out?—A. After hearing the story, I did recall the fact that at one time this man Campbell perhaps asked me how many times we used questions, and when we would have a new set of questions out.

MR. J. H. OBERLY—Recalled.

By Mr. HOPKINS:

Q. I desire to ask Mr. Oberly a question or two. Were you a member of the Commission when Mr. Campbell was promoted?—A. No, sir. He was promoted once while I was a member of the Commission.

Q. Was he promoted on a civil-service examination?—A. At the time he was promoted the Civil Service Commission was not under the rules that required him to be examined.

Q. Was he examined for promotion, or was he promoted without an examination as to fitness for promotion?—A. He was promoted at the time. I think, without any examination.

Q. Then he was promoted from one position to another without any questions being put to him to see whether he was qualified for the place?—A. Yes, sir; he was taken from one place and put into another.

Q. The Commission itself was not then under the rules required to examine him?—A. Not under the rules.

Mr. HATTON. Did the rules and regulations require an examination before promotion at any time when Mr. Campbell was promoted?

A. I think the rules did require an examination. The Commission violates the rules when it makes promotions without examination. It is not a fair construction of the law and the rules.

Mr. BOATNER. Do you give this opinion as an expert?

The WITNESS. I give my views because the Commission itself has determined so. The Commission has repeatedly decided that no promotion can be made without an examination in any department.

Mr. ROOSEVELT. You think every promotion should be accompanied by any examination in every department?

The WITNESS. Section 7 of the law says that no promotions to the classified service shall be made and no promotions therein shall be made without examination.

Mr. LYMAN. I think it is due to the Commission and due to Mr. Oberly that I should read the statutes and the rules.

Mr. Lyman here read section 7 of the civil service act.

Mr. EWART. There was one question I failed to ask you in the cross-examination and it was whether or not you regarded this list of questions furnished by Mr. Campbell to this lady as of importance and would they have improved her chances of promotion?

A. No more than similar questions furnished to any person and any person was entitled to get similar questions.

Q. Was that information given as special information or as a secret?—A. I do not know.

Q. What conclusion did you reach about it? Certainly you reached a conclusion upon it at that time.—A. The information that was given was information given in an irregular way that might have been given in a regular way. He did not furnish anything for pay, and that is the reason he was not condemned and blamed.

TESTIMONY OF MISS EMILY M. DABNEY.

Miss EMILY M. DABNEY, sworn and examined.

By the CHAIRMAN:

Q. Please give your name, residence, and occupation.—A. Emily M. Dabney. I reside at 1015 Twentieth street, and am employed in the Department of Labor.

Q. Have you personal knowledge of this matter of obtaining copies through Mr. Campbell of examination papers, and if so, will you state to the committee what that knowledge is?—A. I will. I had a mother and three sisters to take care of. I was earning only a small salary, and I naturally wished to get as much as I could. My mother is in delicate health and doctors' bills were coming in. I wished to pass an examination,' as I thought that would be the only way by which I could be promoted. I asked a friend to advise me. There was a friend of mine in the Second Auditor's Office and she advised me to undergo an examination, saying that she and her daughter would help me. She had passed a good examination. She told me to get a book of reports of what the examination would be and told me to study hard. I found that I was backward in what was the hardest part of the examination, and I went to see Mr. Flynn and studied under him. I have a receipt here for the money I paid him for coaching me. I went to him in August, but my mother was ill and I told him I could not come regularly. I asked him if I might come later, and he said I could do so. I commenced taking lessons in November and took them twice a week.

Just before the examination, which was in December, on Tuesday before the examination was to come off I said to him, "I feel nervous about this examination." He said, "I do not think you will have any difficulty. I think you are fully prepared; but if you are not, I have examination questions which are those to be asked." He said, "If you will promise not to say anything about it, I will give you these examination questions for $25." I said, "I have no money, and do you think it is right for me to buy these questions?" He said, "Other people buy them. I have these questions, and if you will pay the money for them you can have them." I said, "I have no money, but I might borrow it. That is a temptation. I will think over it." He said, "I will keep the questions for you." I said, "Then I will think over it." Afterwards I said, "This thing is not square, and I will not buy these questions," and I did not. I went to the examination room of the Commission. I had to be up until 4 o'clock, and I was feeling very badly, as I say. When the question was asked if I felt badly, I made no reply to it, not because I did not feel well, but because I wanted to get through with it. I did not get through. I did not do some of the sums. There were five examples.

In about three weeks after, I met Mrs. Lockhart on the street and I told her I did not get through. I said to her, "Well, if I did fail, I had the consciousness of knowing that I did not buy the questions." She said, "What do you mean by that?" I said, "Professor Flynn offered me some questions concerning it, but I did not buy them." She said, "It is a fraud, and you ought to mention that you had been offered these questions." I said, "It is none of my business, and I do not wish to get mixed up with it." I saw Mr. Oberly, and he asked me if Flynn had offered me these questions. I told him he had. He said if I did not have the money and I could get these papers for $15 he would pay the money himself. I thought I would ask Professor Flynn if he would let me see the questions. I went to Professor Flynn and told him I did not get through on the examination; and I told him I was sick. I said, "By the way, will you let me look at those questions?" He said, "Well, if I can find them, I will;" and finally he produced the questions. I said, "Are these the ones you were going to sell me?" He said, "Yes, those are the ones." I said, "Would you mind working some of the examples?" And he did so. I then said, "Do you mind my taking these home?" He said, "No; but I would like to have you bring them back." I met Mrs. Lockhart and I told her about it. I said to her, "Would you be willing to take them down to Mr. Oberly?" She said, "No;" that she was on the examining board, and she did did not wish to be implicated in it. I then told her to tell Mr. Oberly I would be down after office hours. Mr. Oberly waited and I saw him.

I said, "Mr. Oberly, before I give these questions to you I want to say to you that I do not want to have my name mentioned. I do not care to have anything to do with telling that the questions were being bought. I went at once with the questions and gave them to him, and told him I wanted them back on Thursday. I went down on Thursday and he gave them back to me. He said he had copied them. I did not see Mr. Campbell. Mr. Oberly said Mr. Campbell had broken down and had confessed that he had given the question out, and Mr. Oberly said he had condoned the offense.

Q. Were these arithmetical questions?—A. They were. I know they were the questions asked me.

By Mr. Hopkins:

Q. You think they were the identical questions that were propounded to you?—A. I know they were.

Q. Do I understand that you learned they were in the handwriting of Mr. Campbell?—A. I know nothing about it. I did not know who gave them to Mr. Flynn. I knew they were the same arithmetical questions asked me.

By the Chairman:

Q. What was the date of the examination that you underwent?—A. December 3, 1887.

Q. Did you have any conversation with Mr. Campbell yourself?—A. None whatever. Mr. Oberly knows I did not. I did not know he had anything in the world to do with it. I merely knew the questions were offered to me.

By Mr. BOATNER:

Q. They were offered to you before the 3d of December, and they were the questions asked you on the 3d of December. If you had been posted by them you could have passed the examination?—A. I could have passed the examination on the 3d of December if I had known the answers to the questions.

Q. How many days after your examination was it before you went up there?—A. It was about three weeks afterwards.

Mr. CHAIRMAN. Did you state that to Mr. Oberly?—A. I did. I went to him with the questions and told him I knew they were the questions I was asked.

Mr. ANDREW. Did you remember them?—A. I did.

By Mr. HOPKINS:

Q. What did Mr. Oberly say to you when you told him you knew they were the identical questions asked you?—A. He said, " I will go and show these to the other commissioners."

Q. Did Mr. Oberly say anything about the impropriety of Campbell giving those questions out?—A. He did. He said it was wrong, and Campbell should not have done it.

Q. Did he condemn Campbell to you?—A. He did.

Q. Did he state in your presence at that time that the questions were in the handwriting of Campbell?—A. He did not, because he did not know.

By Mr. ANDREW:

Q. What kind of an examination was that? Were there a number of questions, or was it only the arithmetical questions?—A. It was a general variety of questions.

Q. This copy which Flynn presented to you contained all the questions, did it?—A. No, sir; only the arithmetical questions. Those were the only ones I was afraid of.

Q. How many questions were there?—A. All the arithmetical questions on the examination, also on his paper.

Q. And none of those questions you answered?—A. I answered some of them.

Mr. LYMAN. Did you take the clerk or copyist examination?—A. I took the general examination.

Mr. OBERLY. How long was it after I returned them to you?—A. It was Thursday that you returned the papers to me.

The CHAIRMAN. Could you state precisely any one of those arithmetical questions now?—A. I could say they were the same.

The CHAIRMAN. I would like to know who has possession of the questions which were alleged to have been copied by Mr. Campbell, and whether they can be identified?

Mr. BOATNER (to Mr. Oberly). Did I understand you to say that they were questions that had already been used?

Mr. OBERLY. They were questions that had already been used.

Q. I understood you to state in your testimony that you found at the time that Mr. Campbell gave out the questions that they were questions that had already been used?

Mr. OBERLY. Yes, sir.

Q. This witness states they were questions to be used and were actually used in an examination occurring thereafter.

Mr. OBERLY. The witness states that Professor Flynn told her they were to be used, but she says she said she did not come into possession of the questions until three weeks after the examination.

Mr. BOATNER. The witness says she went to Mr. Flynn to be coached; that Flynn proposed to her that if she had any doubt about passing that he would sell her the questions which would be used at the coming examination; that she declined to buy them; that she found they were questions asked at that examination, and that if she had been able to answer them she would have passed. I understood you to say that in your investigation you discovered that these questions were obsolete; that is to say, they had been used at a previous examination.

Mr. OBERLY. My recollection is the questions had been printed only a day, and therefore they could not have been furnished to Mr. Flynn by Mr. Campbell any time before that. These identical questions had been used in an examination. My investigation showed that the questions had been copied after the examination in which they had been used and had been furnished this lady, who had taken them to Mr. Flynn after that examination.

Mr. BOATNER. Campbell had given them out before and not after?

The WITNESS. He confessed to have given them out to Mrs. Smith, who was in the Pension Office.

Mr. THOMPSON. How many examinations did you take?

The WITNESS. I took one in December, 1887, and I took one in February.

Mr. THOMPSON. For promotion or entrance into the service?

The WITNESS. Entrance into the service.

Mr. THOMPSON. Was it competitive or non-competitive?

The WITNESS. Competitive.

Mr. ANDREW. What became of this set of questions which the witness said she received from Flynn after she got done with them? Where are they now?

The WITNESS. I took them back to Mr. Flynn. I told him I would carry them back, which I did.

Mr. OBERLY. You gave me to understand that I was not to mention it.

The WITNESS. I did. I did not wish my name to appear in that case, and I did not care to be mentioned in it. I had brought proof to substantiate what I said.

The CHAIRMAN. Are you in office now?

The WITNESS. I am in the Department of Labor.

TESTIMONY OF WILLIAM E. MORGAN

WILLIAM E. MORGAN sworn and examined.

By the CHAIRMAN:

Q. What is your name and where do you reside?—A. William E. Morgan; I reside at 906 Fourteenth street northwest.

Q. Are you in the Government employ?—A. Yes, sir.

Q. In what capacity?—A. I am a stenographer in the Bureau of the Mint, Treasury Department.

Q. State to the committee what you know about this Campbell matter.—A. Of my own knowledge I know nothing except what was told to me by Commissioner Oberly.

Q. State what it was.—A. Mr. Oberly told me that information had reached him that questions were being given out and that he had obtained a set of questions from Miss Dabney. That he had laid the matter before the Commission, and that Mr. Edgerton had refused to investigate it; that Mr. Lyman had told him it was a serious offense, and he said that Mr. Lyman said that any person in the Commission who had been guilty of such an offense should be punished. He said that Mr. Lyman was inexorable. Mr. Oberly finally found that it was Mr. Campbell who had given out the questions, and told Mr. Lyman, and that Mr. Lyman then said that his wife was in bad health, and if this thing was made public it might result seriously. Mr. Oberly said Mr. Campbell was a good clerk, and he did not think the matter amounted to much and the offense had been condoned by Mr. Ewart.

Q. Were you employed by the Commission at that time?—A. I was.

Q. Did the abstraction or taking of these questions cause any excitement?—A. It was a secret.

Q. You say it was a secret?—A. We were told not to make it public. I guess it was a secret.

Q. Why was there so much secrecy about it?—A. This I could not answer; I do not know.

Q. Who told you not to say anything about it?—A. Mr. Oberly.

Q. And Mr. Lyman, too?—A. No, sir.

By Mr. EWART:

Q. Could you give the reason why?—A. No, sir. An investigation was then being made.

Q. Did he state that these questions were worthless?—A. No; he did not.

Q. Did you know what the questions were?—A. I did not know, and I never saw the questions. I heard they were questions that had been taken from the files.

Q. Would you have given out those questions if any one had called for them?—A. I should not. I would have thought that I had no right to, and besides my sense of honor would not have allowed me to do so. I would say further that Mr. Oberly's statement coincides substantially with what he told me. He said on the stand about what he told me.

Mr. OBERLY. I told you not to say anything about it.

The WITNESS. Yes, sir.

By Mr. EWART:

Q. There was a great deal of secrecy about the transaction, was there not?—A. Oh, yes. I understood that he took the questions surreptitiously from the files of the Commission.

Q. He did not let you know anything about it?—A. No, sir.

Q. Did any of the employés in the office know anything about it?—A. I think not.

Q. Do you know how or when he took these questions?—A. I did not see him take the questions, and therefore I can not say, but I understood that he took a set of questions of an eligible in the files. Mr. Doyle had supervision of the room. Campbell, I think, had the run of the room, and he could have taken out whatever he saw fit.

Q. Do you know why he copied them?—A. I do not.

Mr. BOATNER. Were these questions copied by Mr. Campbell before or after they had been used?

The WITNESS. That I do not know.

Mr. ROOSEVELT. They must have been used.

The WITNESS. In this way; I understand the questions were copied from a set of papers of an eligible, and therefore the questions must have been used.

The CHAIRMAN. You always speak of them as questions. Were they not questions and answers on the same paper?

The WITNESS. Yes, sir; the questions and answers both were copied from the same paper.

Mr. ROOSEVELT. The answers were answers made upon an examination of a man which had already taken place?

The WITNESS. Yes, sir.

Mr. BOATNER. Had you seen the questions and answers, and did you see them after they were brought back?

The WITNESS. No, sir.

Mr. HOPKINS. Do you know whether they were questions, or questions and answers?

The WITNESS. I only know what I was told by Mr. Oberly, that they were questions and answers.

The CHAIRMAN. This witness is simply stating what Mr. Oberly said to him, which is that these questions had been taken.

Mr. OBERLY. Mr. Morgan has said that if he were guilty of that offense that he thought he would have been dismissed from the office of the Commissioner. (To Mr. Morgan) Do I understand you to say that if you had been guilty of that offense and I had investigated into the facts and the facts were similar to the offense under consideration that I would have insisted upon having you put out?—A. Judging from that action in Mr. Campbell's case I do not think you would.

By Mr. LYMAN:

Q. You had charge of the certification room?—A. Yes, sir.

Q. While this list of eligibles were in your possession, did you ever show any of those papers to any people who came into the office?—A. To no one except the eligible himself, and then it was the practice. I was allowed to do so, but to no others.

Q. Did you show papers to others?—A. No, sir; except on the order of the Commission or the Secretary.

Mr. OBERLY. Have you, under my directions, allowed persons to see papers as to the general drift of questions?

The WITNESS. I think only to the eligibles themselves.

Mr. OBERLY. Don't you remember the practice was to allow persons to sit down in the room and to see the scope and character of the questions, but that they must not take them away?

The WITNESS. I do not recollect that, sir.

TESTIMONY OF S. WALTER FLYNN.

S. WALTER FLYNN sworn and examined.

By the CHAIRMAN:

Q. Please state your name.—A. My name is S. Walter Flynn.

Q. Where do you reside?—A. I reside at the southwest corner of Eighth and K streets northwest.

Q. Do you know the handwriting of Mr. Campbell, the gentleman referred to in this investigation?—A. No, sir; I do not know that I ever saw it.

Q. Did you ever offer Miss Dabney any set of questions?—A. No, sir.

Q. Therefore you did not make any representation to her about a set of questions or let her have a set of questions to be used in a future examination?—A. No, sir. I would like to explain myself.

By Mr. HOPKINS:

Q. You listened to the evidence of Miss Dabney?—A. Yes, sir.

Q. Did you give her a receipt for the money she paid you?—A. Yes, sir.

Q. Is that the receipt?—A. Yes, sir; that is my handwriting.

Q. How long did you instruct her prior to the examination?—A. Miss Dabney came to me in August, 1887. She continued lessons for one month. She discontinued for want of means to pay me further. She called upon me three or four times, and she repeatedly spoke to me of her want of means and her little pay and of her sick mother. She worked up a certain kind of sympathy in my mind for her. She would occasionally bring questions for me to work out, and I would work them out for her. I did it as a matter of charity and I thought her a worthy object of charity.

About Christmas Mrs. Smith came with some questions to the institute. I remember these matters very well because something occurred to impress it upon my mind. She stated she wanted them explained to her. They were questions that had been asked at a previous examination. We place no importance upon the questions. I supposed from her manner that the questions had been given her by some one who had passed an examination. I explained these questions to her. Miss Dabney came to me for the last time about New Year's. She asked about undergoing an examination in arithmetic. I showed her these questions. She immediately begged me for them. I consented to give her a copy of them and I did not consent to give her the original. I said to her, "It would be a great indiscretion for me to give out those papers in an unknown handwriting." At that time Miss Dabney left immediately. The matter went out of my mind. But in three or four days after this I remembered I had promised to copy these questions for her. When Miss Dabney failed to return immediately I suspected she had taken the original copy when I saw her name in connection with it. This matter has been explained, but the lady that got the questions from me was represented to me as a clerk in the Treasury Department. The newspaper reports did not verify my suspicions. I never saw Miss Dabney until last spring, when she applied to me. This is all I know about it.

Q. You are in the habit of coaching people for civil-service examinations; that is your business?—A. Yes, sir; that is part of my occupation.

Q. What was wrong in your giving Miss Dabney the original questions?—A. I placed no value on them.

Q. Why did you decline to let her have the original?—A. I think any business man would decline to give out those papers, not knowing in whose handwriting they were.

Q. What was there about the unknown handwriting?—A. Nothing at all. It was to me an unknown handwriting.

Q. Was there anything that led you to believe that it would give you or anybody any trouble if Miss Dabney took the original papers?—A. No.

Q. Why did you object?—A. On the ground of ordinary discretion. If you asked for a paper and I did not know the handwriting I would not give it to you.

Q. That is a practice of yours?—A. I never had any experience of the kind before.

Q. How many days after Miss Dabney left did you discover the original questions were gone?—A. Three or four days, or two, may be.

Q. Did you go to Miss Dabney and ask her if she had taken them ?—
A. No, sir; I placed no particular value upon them. I never supposed
she was going to make use of them.

Q. You say you discovered somebody had taken them and you inferred she was the one ?—A. Not necessarily. I suspected her because
she was the last person I had shown them to.

Q. Did you follow them ?—A. No, sir.

Q. Where did you say you got those questions ?—A. From a lady by
the name of Mrs. Smith.

Q. Where did she get them ?—A. I supposed she got them from
some one who had passed an examination.

Q. You did not know where they came from ?—A. No, sir.

By Mr. BOATNER:

Q. You heard Miss Dabney's testimony ?—A. Yes, sir.

Q. She stated that you offered to sell these questions for $15 or for
$25 ?—A. That is not true. I considered Miss Dabney too poor to pay
for them. I never offered to take one cent for them. That is the whole
matter.

Q. Was that after she failed to pass ?—A. I suppose so. She said
she had taken the examination on December 3, and this was later than
that.

By Mr. HOPKINS:

Q. How much later ?—A. I could not say.

Q. You did agree with Miss Dabney to coach her ?—A. Yes, sir.

Q. You agreed with her that if she was poor and unable to pay for
her instructions that you would wait upon her ?—A. Yes, sir.

Q. You also agreed in December that if she took an examination
and failed you would give her these questions ?—A. No, sir; I did not
know anything about it.

By Mr. LIND:

Q. I believe you stated that you considered the questions of no
value ?—A. Yes, sir.

Q. You have also stated that you gave them to Miss Dabney as a
matter of charity ?—A. I told her they were questions that had been
asked at an examination, hence they were more or less important to her
in so far as the questions would be of the same general kind.

Q. I understand you to say she came and asked you to work out
some examples for her ?—A. Yes, sir.

Mr. HOPKINS. When did she come and ask you to work out examples ?

The WITNESS. Her month expired in September. After that several
times she came to see me, and came to take instructions again about
New Year's. She took the examination in December.

By Mr. EWART:

Q. Did you ever see those questions again ?—A. No, sir. It is false
that Miss Dabney brought back those questions.

Q. Were your sympathies at work when you charged this lady $8 for
instructions ?—A. No, sir; not at that time.

Mr. THOMPSON. Did I understand you to say that you left the room,
and that Miss Dabney had left when you came back and the questions
were missing ?—A. I left the room, and immediately upon my return
Miss Dabney left, and afterwards I found the questions were missing.

Q. Have you seen the questions from that time to this ?—A. Never.

By Mr. HOPKINS:

Q. Did you make any investigation about it?—A. No, sir; such would not be my practice.

Q. Did you ever speak to anybody about your suspicions of Miss Dabney?—A. I did not suppose this investigation referred to Miss Dabney until I saw her name in the Star. The lady was spoken of as a clerk in the Treasury Department, and I supposed Miss Dabney to be a clerk in the War Department.

By Mr. LIND:

Q. Did you ever have a sign in the windows of your institute, or about the door, stating that civil service questions were accessible there?—A. I never had such a sign on my house.

Q. Did you ever have anything of that tenor?—A. No, sir.

By Mr. HOPKINS:

Q. Did you advertise in any manner to the public, or those who were seeking civil service examinations, that they could get questions from you?—A. I have a standing advertisement in the paper. I suppose you have seen that advertisement.

By Mr. ROOSEVELT:

Q. What is the wording of it?—A. "Civil service questions. Send 10 cents. S. Walter Flynn, Ivy Institute," etc.

Q. Did that advertisement say that you furnished special questions that were to be used in future?—A. No, sir.

Q. Those questions were such as were printed every year in our annual report?—A. Yes, sir.

Q. You have a little pamphlet of questions and answers?—A. Yes, sir.

Mr. BOATNER (to Mr. Oberly). Please state whether or not the examination papers which were brought to you were questions which were to be asked or had been asked and answered.

Mr. OBERLY. My conclusion and investigation was that they were questions that had been used in a preceding examination, and the examination had been given by a certain candidate who had passed.

Recess until half past 2 o'clock.

At the expiration of the recess the committee resumed its session.

Mr. ROOSEVELT. I should like to make a statement in the nature of a question of privilege, and it is more to avoid a misapprehension of the remarks of Mr. Oberly, which you will recollect, Mr. Chairman, in reference to promotions being illegal than anything else. As I understood Mr. Oberly, and I invite correction if I make any misstatement of what Mr. Oberly said, it was that the law required examinations in all cases of promotion. Am I stating it accurately? If not, correct me at once. As a matter of fact it was not a charge against the present Commission by Mr. Oberly, as I understand, because what he referred to has been the practice steadily from 1883, when the Commission was first organized, to the present time, the practice under all the preceding Commissions, with the full knowledge and approval of Presidents Arthur, Cleveland, and Harrison. The present Commission construed the law as the preceding Commissions construed it, with the knowledge and assent of Presidents Arthur, Cleveland, and Harrison. And the law was so construed by the Commission of which Mr. Oberly was a member and acted upon by that Commission without, so far as we know, any formal protest or anything but acquiescence on Mr. Oberly's part.

It is a question of the construction of the law which Mr. Oberly now says has been misconstrued by all the preceding Commissioners, including himself, and by the Presidents. But it is something that reflects in no manner on the present Commissions, for we have simply construed the law and followed the precedents of all preceding Commissions under preceding administrations.

In the present force of the Civil Service Commission we follow exactly the course pursued in the other Departments of the Government like the Navy, the Interior, the Post-Office, etc.—we follow the same course in promotion in all these with the exception of the War Department.

TESTIMONY OF ALEXANDER C. CAMPBELL.

ALEXANDER C. CAMPBELL sworn and examined.

By the CHAIRMAN:

Q. What is your full name?—A. Alexander C. Campbell.

Q. Are you now employed by the United States Government?—A. Yes, sir.

Q. In what capacity?—A. As a clerk of the Civil Service Commission.

Q. How long have you been an employé of the United States Government?—A. I first entered the Agricultural Department. I think it was in the year 1883. I remained there until the spring of 1885. Then I was detailed from the Agricultural Department to the Civil Service Commission. I think it was in January or February, along in the spring. The same year, in July, 1885, I was appointed as laborer in the Civil Service Commission.

Q. Were you promoted after that time?—A. I was on the roll as laborer until—I could not tell you the date. A year or more after that I was promoted from laborer to a position of $900.

Q. What was that position?—A. The same position that I have always held in the office.

Q. Messenger?—A. No, sir; clerk. I was first appointed as laborer and assigned to clerical work. I did the same work when I was appointed as laborer as I am now doing as clerk.

Q. Although you are receiving a higher salary?—A. Yes, sir. I was appointed from laborer to a position at $900, but I can not tell you the date, and from that I was appointed to a $1,000, and on the 2d of April last I was promoted to a position of $1,200, which I now hold.

- Q. It has been charged here before this committee that you at one time abstracted papers from the files of the office, copied the papers, examination papers, together with the answers, and gave them to a third party, for to be used in preparing for an examination?—A. No, sir.

Q. You know what the nature of this investigation is ; you know what you have been charged with. Will you give the committee a full account of what transpired; what you did in relation to these examination papers that have been spoken of here?

The WITNESS. Is it necessary for me to state what my duties have been heretofore?

The CHAIRMAN. You can state that, but that is not the question. The question is "Did you ever copy any papers?"—A. Yes, sir; I did copy a set of papers, but——

Q. What purpose had you in copying them ?—A. I copied them for my own use; that is, I copied them simply because I wanted a copy.

Q. What did you want the copy for?—A. I did not copy them for any particular purpose at the time.

Q. What reason had you in copying them?—A. I had no particular reason at first for copying them. I admit that I did make a copy of the questions with the answers.

Q. Do you know what year and what month that was in?—A. I am not sure whether it was in December, 1887, or January, 1888. But I am confident, and I will state under oath, that the papers I did copy were papers which had been used in the previous examination and that I thought at the time that they would be of no use to anybody. In fact, I told the party to whom I gave them at the time that they would be of no use to them, and they simply wanted them in order that they might see what the questions were.

Q. What is the name of the party?—A. Mrs. Smith.

Q. When did she ask you for a copy of those papers?—A. I can not tell you the date.

Q. Before you copied them?—A. No, sir; it was afterwards, but I can not tell you the date. It has always been by instructions ——

Mr. LIND. We are not talking about instructions.

By the CHAIRMAN:

Q. The committee wants to know why you took the trouble of copying these papers, and for what purpose they were delivered to a third party. Who was this party who asked you for these papers?—A. The party who asked me for the papers was Mrs. Smith. She is the only one who got the papers.

Q. Did she ask you for them for the purpose of aiding her in an examination to be had thereafter?—A. No, because I told her at the time that the papers would be of no use to her in any future examination. She so understood it; that the papers had already been used and would not be used again, and she so understood it when I gave her the papers.

Q. When was the examination made on the part of Mr. Oberly and Mr. Lyman concerning your conduct in copying these papers?—A. I can not tell you the date of that.

Q. Did you give them a full statement of the facts?—A. I did.

Q. When you made a copy of these papers you had no particular object in view?—A. Not when I made the copy.

Q. Did you ever make any copies of any other papers, except these?—A. No, sir.

Q. The questions and answers were copied?—A. Yes, sir.

Q. Do you remember whose examination papers they were?—A. I do not.

Q. How did you happen to tell Mrs. Smith that the papers would be of no particular use to her?—A. I knew they were old papers and would not be of any use.

Q. She expected they would?—A. No, sir. She understood when I gave her the papers that they would be of no use to her in any future examination. All that she wanted was to get at the nature of the questions.

By Mr. BOATNER:

Q. She wanted to get the general scope of the examination?—A. Yes, sir.

By Mr. EWART:

Q. What did you copy this set of questions from?—A. I copied them from an old set of examination papers.

Q. In what office ?—A. Well, in the secretary's office, in the certification room, adjoining. I got the papers from the certification room.

Q. Where did you find them ?—A. I found them lying with other papers in the room.

Q. Who was in charge of those papers ?—A. I do not know that there was anybody particularly in charge. Mr. Morgan was certification clerk.

Q. Did you ask him to be allowed to copy them ?—A. I do not think he was there.

Q. Was any one there ?—A. No, sir.

Q. Was there any one there at all when you copied these papers ?—A. I would not say whether there was or not.

Q. Let me refresh your recollection about that. What time of the day did you go into the room to get the papers ?—A. Late in the afternoon.

Q. After office hours ?—A. We had no office hours at that time.

Q. After 4 o'clock ?—A. It might have been 4 o'clock, but we seldom got away before 5 or 6 o'clock.

Q. After 5 o'clock ?—A. I can not tell you.

Q. Now, can not you give the committee some recollection about the hour ?—A. I will say that I do not think I made a full copy at the same time. I think it was on two different occasions that I made the copy.

Q. From a printed list ?—A. From the set of application papers that were lying in the certification room.

Q. Printed ?—A. Yes, sir.

Q. How many copies did you find in the room ?—A. I can not tell you.

Q. A dozen copies ?—A. I do not know. There might have been a dozen or there might have been fifty.

Q. How was it that you did not get a copy of these printed questions and give it to this lady? What was your object in copying them? Why was it when you found that number of printed copies that you went to the trouble of copying them ?—A. As I have already said, I copied those long before Mrs. Smith made any request for them.

Q. How long ?—A. I can not tell.

Q. A month before ?—A. I can not tell you.

Q. Two weeks before ?—A. I will not say whether it was two weeks or not.

Q. Can you not give the committee some idea ?—A. I will simply say that I copied these papers before Mrs. Smith made the request.

Q. What object did you have in copying those papers when it was no trouble to secure a printed copy ?—A. I could not have obtained a printed copy.

Q. What object did you have in copying them ?—A. I copied them just simply for my own satisfaction.

Q. How did you propose to be satisfied by copying them? What object did you have, Mr. Campbell?—A. I had simply the object of copying them.

The CHAIRMAN. He has already stated that he had no object in view when he copied them.

By Mr. EWART:

Q. Is it your habit, Mr. Campbell, to copy questions in that way just as mere pastime ?—A. No, sir; I do not have time.

Q. How did you have time in this particular instance ?—A. I can only say this, that I had leisure time and made the copy.

3117——4

Q. Where did you make the copy?—A. At the office.

Q. It is impossible to give to the committee any idea as to the day?—A. Yes, sir.

Q. The copy was made one evening, and there was no one in the room?—A. I would not say there was no one in the office. The secretary may have been there, and there might have been some one in the other room.

Q. At the time you took the copy of these questions you say you had no object in doing so. Did you inform any one that you intended to make a copy?—A. No one.

Q. Why did you keep it a secret?—A. I did not think I needed to tell any one about it. As I was giving out instructions to applicants, giving out information to applicants, I did not think I needed to tell any one.

Q. You made the copy of these questions three or four weeks before Mrs. Smith asked you for them?—A. I will not say as to the time.

Q. At the time you made a copy of those papers they were not being used in the examination-room?—A. No, sir.

Q. You swear to that positively?—A. Yes, sir.

Q. Did you occupy a position in the Civil Service Commission that enabled you to know what questions were being used?—A. No, sir; I will state here that during the whole time I have been in the Commission I have never yet seen a set of questions that have not been used in some examination. I have had no way and no desire to see any questions.

Q. How was it that you had a desire to copy these questions?—A. As I have already stated, I copied them for my own satisfaction; that was all.

Q. Who first apprised you of the fact that there were some harsh comments being made as to the abstraction of these papers?—A. Mr. Lyman.

Q. In what way was your attention called to the matter?—A. He called me into his room one evening late after——

Q. Can you fix the date?—A. No, sir; I can not tell you. He produced the papers and handed them to me and asked me if I had ever seen them. I looked at them and told him I had. He then said he wanted me to make a full statement of the facts; how I came to give out the papers. I made a full statement to him and we had quite a lengthy conversation. Then he started for home, and that was the only interview that I had with him before seeing Mr. Oberly.

Q. Please let the Commission have that statement,

The WITNESS. I do not quite understand you.

Mr. EWART. State the conversation that occurred between yourself and Mr. Lyman when your attention was called to the fact that these papers had been abstracted and Mr. Lyman wanted an explanation.—A. Mr. Lyman handed me the papers and asked me if I had ever seen the papers before.

Q. You have been over that. State the rest of the conversation.—A. He then said—I can not remember the exact words—but he said in substance that it was a serious matter and that it should be investigated.

Q. "A serious matter and that it should be investigated"?—A. Yes, sir.

Q. What was your reply to that?—A. My reply was that I made a copy of these papers and that I had given them to—giving the party's name—and that I supposed that the papers were destroyed.

Q. Did you instruct this Mrs. Smith to destroy these papers?—A. She told me she would.

Q. Did you request her to?—A. I did.

Q. Why?—A. Because I did not want the questions to go any farther than they had.

Q. Why?—A. I can not give any reason for that.

Q. You had some object in telling her to destroy them?—A. Because I did not think that they would be of any use to anybody at all, and I did not want to have them spread out in my handwriting. No doubt the same questions had been published in one of the reports.

Q. Did Mr. Lyman appear to be agitated when he called your attention to this matter?—A. He seemed to feel it very much.

Q. He was very much disturbed about it?—A. Yes, sir.

Q. Very indignant?—A. He felt very much hurt about it.

Q. Do you not know that Mr. Lyman used some pretty strong language on that occasion?—A. I can not tell you what language he used.

Q. I ask you if he did not use some very severe language to you on that occasion?—A. I do not know but what it might be considered strong language by some.

Q. Did he not reproach you bitterly for taking the papers from the files and copying them?—A. Yes, sir.

Q. Did you tell him then that you had no object whatever in copying those papers?—A. I think I told him this——

Q. I ask this question: Did you tell him then that you had no object in copying the questions?—A. I do not think I told him——

By Mr. LIND:

Q. What did you tell him?—A. I think I told him this, that in copying the questions and giving them to the person I did it with no wrong intention at all.

By Mr. EWART:

Q. Did you tell Mr. Lyman at the time when he was using this reproachful language to you that you had no object in copying the question, except merely to satisfy your curiosity, or to satisfy yourself?—A. I do not know whether I did or not.

Q. You must recollect what you told him?—A. Well, I do not.

Q. You did not feel very comfortable that day yourself?—A. No, sir; and I have not since.

Q. You felt agitated?—A. Yes, sir; I felt agitated, because I did not know what the result would be. At the same time I did not feel that I had violated the law at all. I had no such intention, and I did not feel that I had committed any violation of the law.

Q. Was your attention ever called to these sections of the civil-service law, which forbid any employé in the service to give out any special, general, or secret information to any person who would probably be an applicant for examination?—A. Never.

Q. At the time you abstracted these questions and gave them to this lady in the Pension Office, you did not think you were violating any law at all?—A. No, sir.

Q. Nor any rule of the Commission?—A. No, sir.

Q. Mr. Campbell, I will ask you this question, going back to the destruction of these questions: Did I understand you to give any reason why you requested this lady to destroy these questions?—A. I will state that I did not want the questions to go any further, because they were in my handwriting. I did not know what might come out of them. The questions were given to her confidentially, and she was to destroy them.

Q. Why did you give them to her confidentially?—A. Because she asked for them. I gave them to her with the distinct understanding, as I have already said, that the questions would be of no use to anybody at all in any future examination. After she had looked them over and got through with them she was to destroy them.

Q. Do you recollect giving a set of questions to any one else?

The WITNESS. A copy?

Mr. EWART. Yes, sir.

The WITNESS. No, sir.

By Mr. EWART:

Q. At any time?—A. No, sir.

By the CHAIRMAN:

Q. Either the original or a copy?—A. No, sir, no further than this. I will state that I have been always instructed to give an applicant as much information as I could concerning the examination. When we have had reports that contained specimen questions, I have given them to applicants, such as a set of questions in arithmetic, dictation, or any particular subject that they thought they might fail on. I would mark the specimen questions in blue pencil and turn down the leaf.

By Mr. EWART:

Q. Did you ever furnish any copy of questions?—A. No, sir; never in my life.

Q. Did you hear Mr. Oberly's evidence?—A. I did.

Q. Were you reprimanded by Mr. Oberly?—A. I was.

Q. Can you give the committee about the substance of that reprimand?—A. No, sir; not any more than about Mr. Lyman. He told me that he had made a thorough investigation of the case, and he did not think that I had committed any wrong.

Q. And hence did not reprimand you?—A. He did reprimand me.

Q. He told you he did not think you had done any wrong, and then proceeded to reprimand you?—A. No, sir; I will not say that. He told me that he did not think I had done any wrong at all, only he thought that I ought to have consulted him or the Commission before I gave out the questions, or something to that effect.

Q. What did he rebuke you for?—A. I can not recollect what his reprimand was any more than that he called me into his office, and I was there quite a while.

Q. He told you that he did not consider that you had been guilty of any serious offense?—A. He did not think that I had been guilty of anything that would cause my dismissal.

Q. When Mr. Oberly had this talk with you did he show any indication of being indignant?—A. I do not know.

Q. At any rate you did not feel very much reprimanded?—A. Yes, sir; I felt a good deal reprimanded.

Q. Did Mr. Oberly seem to be at all indignant in any way? Did he exhibit any indignation in admonishing this good-natured reprimand to you?—A. I think after he made the full investigation he was convinced that there was nothing in it.

Q. Did he not regard it as a serious breach of discipline?

Mr. LIND. It strikes me that that is rather immaterial.

Mr. BOATNER. I would like to have the resolution under which we are proceeding read. The testimony of this witness has been a recapitulation of conceded and admitted facts, and this examination can have no object except to humiliate the witness, and I do not think that this committee ought to lend itself to anything of that sort.

The CHAIRMAN. I think this witness has been charged with taking papers illegally and copying them, and giving the copies to outside parties, and the question directly before this committee is whether he did an illegal act, and whether the Commissioners were justified in condoning that act; and I think the examination in that regard is perfectly proper, so as to show fully the character of the witness. I think that ought to be gone into very thoroughly.

By Mr. STONE:

Q. I wish to ask one or two questions which may not be entirely appropriate on this branch of the inquiry, but while the witness is here I will ask him. I understand you to say that you had been employed in the Agricultural Department before going to the Commission?—A. Yes, sir.

Q. In what capacity were you employed?—A. I was in the seed division.

Q. You were transferred as a laborer to the Civil Service Commission?—A. While in the Agricultural Department, before the Commission had any funds to appoint anybody as a laborer, I was detailed from the Agricultural Department to the Commission.

Q. As a laborer?—A. Yes, sir.

Q. And you were put to work at a desk at clerical work?—A. Yes, sir.

Q. At a salary of $660?—A. Yes, sir.

Q. How long did you continue in that capacity?—A. I continued in that capacity for about a year; I should think it was about a year.

Q. Then you were promoted under the rules then in force to a permanent clerkship?—A. Yes, sir.

Q. At $900?—A. Yes, sir.

Q. You continued then under the $900 salary at the same desk and in the performance of exactly the same duties you had been discharging at the $660 salary?—A. Yes, sir.

Q. You have since been promoted to a $1,200 place?—A. Yes, sir.

Q. Do you still occupy the same desk?—A. Yes, sir; and do the same work I did when I originally entered the Commission. I have always been in the room of the secretary.

Q. What is the general character of your employment; the work you are required to do?—A. My work is giving out application papers and the reports. I give applicants such information as I have time to give them as regards specimen questions, which are printed in our reports.

Q. Let me go back a moment. When you were promoted from the $660 place to the $900 place, did some other person take your place?—A. No, sir.

Q. When you were promoted to the $1,200 position, did some other person take the $900 place?—A. No, sir; I am doing the same work now that I did when I first entered the service, in 1885. It is merely an increase of salary and an increase of work.

Q. Do I understand that there was a $900 clerkship provided for in that bureau?—A. Yes, sir.

Q. And you filled that place?—A. Yes, sir.

Q. Has that clerkship been abolished?—A. No, sir; it has been filled by promotion.

Q. Well, then, it was filled when you passed beyond it?—A. When I was appointed to the $1,000 position somebody else, I forget who, got the $900 place.

Q. Now your duties as a clerk require you, among other things, to furnish applicants for examination with such information as the board authorizes you to give out?—A. Yes, sir.

Q. What is that information, and in what form does the board permit it to go out?—A. In the report there are printed specimen questions of all examinations held by the Commission.

Q. The annual reports of the Commission?—A. Yes, sir.

Q. The information you furnished then, or were authorized to furnish, was simply to deliver a copy of the report to applicants?—A. Well, if an applicant should come in, if anybody in town, for instance, should come into the office and make a request for a set of application papers and a report and ask me to give him information concerning the examination, I would turn to the report, and, as I have already stated, mark the questions and give him such information as I had time to give about what the examination would be, and also furnish him the necessary papers.

Q. The papers containing an examination already passed by some applicant were put on file and are constantly kept on file in the rooms of the Commission?—A. Yes, sir.

Q. Who has charge of those papers?—A. The certification clerk has charge of those papers; they are not in the room I am in.

Q. You are not, then, in the room where those papers are kept; you are not employed there?—A. No, sir.

Q. Have you any official connection with that room?—A. Yes, sir; I very often have to go in there, if a person comes in and wishes to look at his papers.

Q. Does the character of your employment authorize you to examine those papers to which I have just referred—the examination papers?—A. No, sir.

Q. Was it a breach of the rules of the Commission for you, on your own motion, to go and examine any of those papers?—A. No, sir; I did not consider that it was.

Q. Did you consider it within the range of your authority to look at those papers whenever you pleased?—A. I did.

Q. You state it as a fact that you did have that authority?—A. I had that authority as much as any clerk.

Q. Well, the certification clerk had charge of them.—A. I know he has charge of them, but if a person should come into our room—the secretary's room—and wish to look at his papers, I have always had authority to go and get the papers for him, take them from the files, instead of asking the certification clerk to do it.

Q. Do I understand you to say that if any person who has passed an examination, who has been examined, and whose papers are on file in the room of this certification clerk, comes to you and desires to examine those papers personally, that you have authority to go and get them and let him look at them—A. I think I have, but I should not take that authority on myself; I should first ask the certification clerk for the papers, and nine times out of ten he would tell me to go and get them.

Q. When you got the papers of which you made a copy, did you do it secretly?—A. No, sir.

Q. Did you go into the room and abstract them from the files when no one else was present?—A. No, sir.

Q. Then who else was present?—A. I could not tell you who was present.

Q. When you took them from the files what did you do with them?—A. I took them to my desk and made the copy.

Q. But I understood you to say that you did not make the whole copy in one day?—A. No, sir.

Q. You took them from the files and copied some of it?—A. Yes, sir.

Q. And then you got them again on some other day and finished them?—A. Yes, sir.

Q. And put them back?—A. Yes, sir.

Q. Now how long was it between the first time you got them and when you got them again?—A. The next day or the day after that.

Q. The next day or the day afterwards you returned to the certification room and got those papers again?—A. I would not swear that I had the same papers.

Q. Well, the same class of papers?—A. Yes, sir.

Q. What did you do with them?—A. I kept them in my possession until I gave them to my friend.

Q. The original papers did you take them to the desk and complete the copy?—A. The copy was all made at my desk.

Q. Did you take the original papers from the house in which the Commission hold their sessions?—A. No, sir; I never took them from the building.

Q. After you made this copy, what did you do with it?—A. The copy I retained.

Q. Where did you keep it?—A. I kept it in my desk.

Q. Did you examine it?—A. No, sir.

Q. Were you expecting to take an examination yourself?—A. No, sir.

Q. Were you expecting, at the time you made the copy, to permit any person to examine it?—A. No, sir.

Q. I understand, then, that you had absolutely no motive in making the copy?—A. No, sir.

Q. Who was this lady to whom you gave these papers?—A. A clerk in the Pension Office.

Q. By the name of Mrs. Smith?—A. Yes, sir.

Q. Were you acquainted with her at the time you made this copy?—A. Yes, sir; I had known her for a long time.

Q. Intimately?—A. She was a friend of mine, and I was a friend of hers; there was no great intimacy that I know of.

Q. Were you connected with her in any way?—A. No, sir.

Q. She had never spoken to you up to this time about procuring her a copy of these papers?—A. No, sir; I do not think she had.

Q. Had she been consulting you up to this time touching an anticipated examination?—A. When she first took the examination and went into the service she came to me and I gave her a set of blanks and the report which contained the specimen questions. She took what is called the limited examination. I marked the questions and turned down the leaf, and gave her the necessary papers.

Q. How long was that before she was expecting to take an examination for promotion?—A. I do not know.

Q. Had she said anything of that sort to you?—A. I do not remember that she had.

Q. About the time you made this copy?—A. No, sir.

Q. Had she been discussing the question of her promotion with you before that time?—A. No, sir.

Q. But you remember the fact that she desired or expected a promotion.—A. I knew that she would probably expect to take an examination for promotion whenever her time expired so that she could.

Q. How long after you made the copy was it before you had any con-versation with her about it?—A. I could not tell you.

Q. How long?—A. I could not tell you.

Q. A long time or a short time?—A. I should think it was some time.

Q. In the mean time this copy was lying in your desk. How long did it lie in your desk?—A. I could not tell you how long the papers laid in my desk.

Q. How did Mrs. Smith find out that you had this copy at all?—A. I think I told her I had a copy.

Q. How did you happen to tell her?—A. I could not tell you how I happened to tell her, any more than that we had a conversation and she said she wanted to see a set of questions. I told her, if I remember rightly, that I had a copy of the questions which I had copied from an old set, but that they would be of no use to her or anybody else; that they had already been used and would not be used again.

Q. Right in that connection, unless there is something more you wish to say——

The WITNESS. No, sir.

Q. Do you know how long before the date of your making the copy the questions had been used?—A. No, sir; I do not.

Q. Do you know whether they had been recently used?—A. I could not tell anything about the time. I only know that they were questions which had been used, and I knew, at least I had every reason to think, that they never would be used again. I told Mrs. Smith so when I gave them to her.

By Mr. LIND:

Q. At that time those seeking promotions in the Department were required to pass a written examination?—A. Yes, sir.

Q. I believe you stated awhile ago that you knew nothing about the questions prior to the time they were printed?—A. No, sir.

Q. You knew nothing about the formulation of questions?—A. I have never seen a set of questions——

Q. You knew nothing about the formulation of questions?—A. No, sir.

Q. Did you know anything about the regulations as to how questions were to be used?—A. No, sir.

Q. Did you at that time know that questions used in a general exami-nation might be used in a promotion examination?—A. No, sir; I did not.

Q. What did you think about it?—A. I had no knowledge about it at all.

Q. I did not ask you for any knowledge. What did you think about it?—A. I did not think they would, from the fact that I had been told that the questions once used were not to be used again.

Q. I thought you said a moment ago that you knew nothing about the regulations in regard to questions?—A. I knew nothing further than what I say now.

Q. You had been told that they would never be used again?—A. Yes, sir.

Q. Never again for a promotion examination?—A. No, sir.

Q. Were these questions of such a character that you could have made the answers yourself?—A. Yes, sir; I think I could.

Q. Without any coaching or assistance at all?—A. Yes, sir.

Q. Have you ever passed a written examination since you have been in the service?—A. Yes, sir.

Q. When?—A. I took an examination in 1883, I think it was, while I was in the Agricultural Department.

Q. I had reference to the Civil Service Commission.—A. No, sir; but I was on the eligible list when I was appointed in the Civil Service Commission.

Q. Since then you have never taken a written examination?—A. No, sir.

Q. Do you remember whether the answers in these papers and questions that you selected for copying were graded high or not?—A. No, sir; I do not remember anything about it.

By the CHAIRMAN:

Q. You never looked as to that point?—A. No, sir.

By Mr. LIND:

Q. You did it simply mechanically?—A. That is all. I took the first set of questions that I came to. I could not tell whether the grade was high or low.

By Mr. ANDREW:

Q. When you copied that set of questions what was in your mind?—A. When I made the copy of them I made it after the business of the office was over. At that time I had to remain there to do the copying of the letters, and very frequently I would not get out until 5 or 6 o'clock. When the business of the office would be closed the Commission would be in session and I would have to wait for the letters. As I have already stated, I had no particular object in copying them.

By the CHAIRMAN:

Q. Did you have access to the room where those papers were kept after 5 or 6 o'clock?—A. Yes, sir.

Q. And you returned the same night?—A. Yes, sir.

By Mr. LIND:

Q. I believe you said that you cautioned this Mrs. Smith to destroy the questions?—A. Yes, sir.

Q. Well, if you were so careful about your handwriting why did you not ask their return?—A. Because I had confidence enough in her to believe that she would do as I requested.

Q. Why have them destroyed instead of having them returned?—A. I did not want them. "Why I requested that they should be destroyed," because I did not want that anybody else should see them but her.

By Mr. ANDREW:

Q. Do you want the committee to understand that you copied that set of questions because you had nothing else to do—merely as a pastime?—A. Yes, sir.

By the CHAIRMAN:

Q. Is it for this reason, that they might be taken advantage of hereafter, that you wanted them destroyed?—A. Yes, sir.

Q. In what way?—A. They would have been of no use to anybody.

Q. Were you afraid that anybody might get hold of them?—A. The papers being in my own handwriting, I did not want anybody else to see them.

Mr. OBERLY. Do you mean to say that you made to Mr. Lyman and myself the statement, in substance, which you have just made to this committee?

The WITNESS. No, sir.

By the CHAIRMAN:

Q. In what way do your statements differ?—A. I have not thought that I was making the same statement. I am simply stating the fact to you about how I came to copy the papers.

Q. Were you not called upon to make the same statement to Mr. Lyman and Mr. Oberly? You were examined by Mr. Oberly and Mr. Lyman; were you not called upon to tell the truth and the whole facts in the case?—A. Yes, sir.

Q. You say now that your statements differ; in what way do they differ?—A. I do not know in what way they differ.

Mr. OBERLY. You stated to this committee that you made a copy of the questions before you were requested to do so by Mrs. Smith. Did you state that to Mr. Lyman and myself, that Mrs. Smith asked you for a copy of those questions after you had made them and that you did not know at the time you made the questions that they were for Mrs. Smith?

The WITNESS. I do not know as I said that.

Mr. OBERLY. Did you not tell me that you made them for Mrs. Smith at her request?

The WITNESS. I will state this, that Mrs. Smith had asked me previous to that if I could not get her a set of questions.

Mr. OBERLY. As a specimen of the questions to be used in the examination that she might take for promotion.

The WITNESS. I told her that I could only get her a set of the questions which had previously been used and which would be of no use to her.

Mr. OBERLY. You mean no use to her in the sense that those identical questions would not be used in any examination that she might take for promotion?

The WITNESS. Yes, sir.

By the CHAIRMAN:

Q. If what you stated at the time to Mr. Lyman and Mr. Oberly is true, how did you come to make this statement before the committee, that you made a copy of these papers before anybody ever asked you to make a copy? You certainly made that statement, did you not?—A. If I did I did not understand the question.

Q. You have been examined here. You have made the statement here repeatedly. You make a positive statement that you made the copy, and that at the time you did not make it for any particular object; you had not been asked by anybody to do so. You made that statement here, as the evidence will show. You say now you did not understand the questions.—A. Yes; I did not understand them in the light you put them now.

Mr. LYMAN. I would like to ask if you did not say to me, when I questioned you about this matter, that Mrs. Smith had asked you for the questions, had asked you for any information or questions that would give her an idea of the character of the examination, and that you had taken these questions to her?

The WITNESS. Yes, sir; I think I did.

Mr. LYMAN. In your statement to me it may have been my fault in not questioning you on that point. In your statement to me at that time you stated that you copied these questions for Mrs. Smith, leaving the impression on my mind that you copied them after she had asked you for them. You have stated to the committee that you made the copy before Mrs. Smith asked you for them.

The WITNESS. When Mrs. Smith asked me for the questions I think I had the copy then.

By the CHAIRMAN:

Q. Are you positive?—A. I think I am. I think I told Mr. Oberly and Mr. Lyman both that Mrs. Smith asked me for the questions.

Q. I understood you to say just now that you told ex-Commissioner Oberly at the time that the way you came to make a copy of these papers was that Mrs. Smith asked you for a copy of the papers.—A. Mrs. Smith asked me for a copy of the questions that she might see the nature of the examination.

Q. The whole point is this, Mr. Campbell, we do not want to get you to make any misstatements here before this committee. We take it for granted that you intend to tell the truth——

The WITNESS. I do.

Q. To give the facts just as they are, but you certainly have made two statements before this committee within a half an hour. You have stated to this committee that you took those papers and copied them without having any object in view.

Mr. ANDREW. For a pastime.

The CHAIRMAN. He did not use that word.

Mr. ANDREW. I put a question to him that way, and he answered "yes."

The CHAIRMAN. Then you stated in reply to a question put by Mr. Oberly that at the time the investigation was going on before the Commission you told both him and Mr. Lyman that the way you happened to copy these questions was because you were asked for the questions by Mrs. Smith. We want to reconcile those two statements if we can before you get off the stand. Have you any explanation to make?

Mr. OBERLY. Did you not state to me that you made this copy of the questions and gave them to her and that you did it in accordance with her request?

The WITNESS. I will not deny it.

Mr. OBERLY. She did not ask you for these identical questions?

The WITNESS. No, sir.

Mr. OBERLY. She did ask you for such questions as she would have to answer when she asked for promotion, which would take place probably two or three or four months afterwards?

The WITNESS. Yes, sir.

By Mr. ANDREW:

Q. Was the statement that you made to Mr. Lyman and Mr. Oberly true?—A. Yes, sir.

By Mr. LIND:

Q. Then what you have stated here is untrue?—A. I do not know what you refer to.

Q. The statement you made to the committee to-day is untrue to the extent it conflicts with the statement you made to Commissioners Lyman and Oberly?

Mr. OBERLY. I do not think the witness understands the question.

By Mr. LIND:

Q. Now, as we understand your evidence, Mr. Campbell, we understand that you went before the Commissioners and explained to them that upon the repeated requests of Mrs. Smith you copied certain questions and answers and gave them to her at her instance. As we understand your testimony given here to-day it is, in substance, that having leisure one evening and believing it not to be wrong, not having been cautioned against it, you stepped into the certification room on two or three different evenings as your time permitted, copied certain questions, put them away in your desk, and afterwards, Mrs. Smith having asked you for sample questions of the character of examinations, you gave them to her. Now, which one of these statements is right, and which one is misunderstood by the committee?—A. The evidence that I gave to Mr. Oberly and Mr. Lyman are the facts in the case, whatever testimony I have given here now ——

By the CHAIRMAN:

Q. Is incorrect so far as it conflicts with the statement made to Mr. Oberly and Mr. Lyman?—A. Yes, sir.

Mr. ROOSEVELT. Mr. Campbell, you recollect being called before Governor Thompson and myself in regard to this matter, do you not?

The WITNESS. Yes, sir.

Mr. ROOSEVELT. Some time last fall. Did you not then tell us, in substance, that you had copied these questions at the request of Mrs. Smith? You remember coming before Governor Thompson and myself last fall? It is my understanding—and I think I may say Governor Thompson's—that you then testified to us (correct me if I am misstating the facts) that you copied these questions at the request of Mrs. Smith. Is our understanding correct?

The WITNESS. I do not remember whether it was put in just that way or not. I think I told you at the time that I copied the questions and gave them to Mrs. Smith, and that you thought best that she should be summoned——

Mr. ROOSEVELT. You testified that you copied the questions and gave them to Mrs. Smith.

The WITNESS. Yes, sir.

Mr. ROOSEVELT. Now, did you copy them a long time ahead for your amusement?

The WITNESS. No, sir; I do not know as I did.

Mr. ROOSEVELT. I do not recollect, and I believe I am correct in stating that Governor Thompson does not recollect, that you said anything to us about a request to destroy those papers.

The WITNESS. I think I did.

Mr. ROOSEVELT. I do not recollect it.

Mr. THOMPSON. I do not either.

The CHAIRMAN. I will ask at this point if the Commissioners have decided to examine any one? Mr. Doyle is here and ready to be examined.

TESTIMONY OF JOHN T. DOYLE.

JOHN T. DOYLE sworn and examined as follows:

By the CHAIRMAN:

Q. What is your name?—A. John T. Doyle.

Q. You are now in the Government service?—A. I am.

Q. In what capacity?—A. I am secretary to the United States Civil Service Commission.

Q. Will you state to this committee, briefly, all that you know in relation to this abstraction of a copy of papers which you have heard discussed here?—A. My first knowledge of the matter was obtained at a meeting of the Commission at which I was present as secretary, and of which I made minutes of the proceedings. Messrs. Edgerton and Lyman were present. It was at a meeting, as nearly as I can remember, early in February, of 1888; either a few weeks before or a few weeks after that time. Commissioner Oberly came into the room with a manuscript, which he laid before Commissioner Edgerton, who was president of the Commission, and stated that they were a copy of questions which had come into his hands upon the promise that he would return them. He laid them before the Commission for its investigation. Commissioner Edgerton showed a disposition not to go into the matter to investigate whether the questions had been written by some one connected with the Commission for an improper purpose. Mr. Lyman took the manuscript from the table, examined it, and I think, in answer to a question by Mr. Oberly, stated that they were questions that had been used in examinations of the Commission.

Q. In order to save time I would like to put this question to you. Have you been present during the examination to-day?—A. I have.

Q. Did you hear the statement made by Mr. Oberly?—A. Yes, sir.

Q. Do you agree with him in all points?—A. I agree with him in all points of which Mr. Oberly stated that I had cognizance, with one exception.

Q. Give the exception.—A. I can not recall distinctly the interval of time that elapsed between the meeting of the Commission at which Mr. Oberly brought the attention of the Commissioners to the fact of his having this manuscript and the time when the questions were taken from the safe for the purpose of comparing the handwriting of the questions with the handwriting of a clerk to the Commission.

Q. What is your recollection about that?—A. I can not state the length of time further than it was certainly not more than a few days. It may have been the following day, or two or three days subsequently, or four days subsequently. I know it was a short interval of time.

Q. With that exception do you agree with Mr. Oberly?—A. With that exception, and in all matters in which Mr. Oberly stated that I had personal knowledge, I agree in his statement.

The CHAIRMAN. Are there any other questions to be asked?

By Mr. LIND:

Q. Did you know Campbell's handwriting?—A. Yes, sir.

Q. Did you know it at that time?—A. I had not examined the manuscript——

Q. Did you know his handwriting at that time?—A. When I first took up the manuscript for the purpose of ascertaining in whose handwriting it was, it occurred to me it was in the handwriting of Mr. Campbell.

Q. Had this manuscript been in the hands of Mr. Lyman previous to that time?—A. It had. It was in the hands of Mr. Lyman at the meeting of the Commission at which Mr. Oberly brought the manuscript to its attention, and it was at 5 o'clock in the afternoon on a winter day——

Q. I simply want to know whether it was in his possession?—A. He saw the manuscript.

Q. He did not recognize it or comment upon whose handwriting it was?—A. I have no recollection now of his saying so at that time.

Q. What has become of those papers?—A. At the time I brought Mr. Lyman's attention to the handwriting, and said that I believed the handwriting was that of Mr. Campbell, Mr. Lyman made a remark in turning over the manuscript that it had occurred to him when he had first seen the papers that it might have been Mr. Campbell's handwriting—that the possibility had occurred to him then.

Q. Do you know what has become of those papers?—A. I do not.

Q. It is your duty as secretary to keep the files of papers of the Commission, is it not?—A. It was; but this was a manuscript copy of questions.

Q. We know what it was very well. You did not place it on file.—A. No, sir.

Q. You do not know in whose possession it went, do you?—A. I parted with the paper. It was left with Mr. Lyman.

Q. Can you tell us, from your recollection, as to whether the handwriting was natural or at all disguised?—A. It did not occur to me that it was disguised.

By the CHAIRMAN:

Q. Did you examine the paper in such a way as to mark the questions and answers that were on the paper for the purpose of knowing whether these questions had been used at that time for an examination?—A. No, sir.

Q. You did not look at the questions and answers for the purpose of determining whether the Commission at that time had examined persons on questions similar to those?—A. No, sir.

Q. Was that examined by any one in the Commission at that time?—A. I understood that it was the subject of investigation by Mr. Oberly; and the chief examiner.

By Mr. OBERLY:

Q. Did you hear Mr. Campbell's statement to me, made at that time, in regard to the manner in which, and the reason why, he made this copy of the questions?—A. No, sir; I was not present.

Q. Did you ever have any conversation with Mr. Campbell on that subject?—A. No, sir.

Q. Did he explain to you the reason?—A. No, sir.

Mr. STONE. That does not seem to be a subject of controversy any longer.

By Mr. BOATNER:

Q. Does this witness recollect whether the answers were upon those papers as well as the questions?—A. It is my recollection that the answers were copied.

Q. These lists of questions were printed, were they not; I mean this list which Campbell copied?—A. The list that he made the copy from?

Q. Yes.—A. I did not make an investigation; it was usual for the questions to be printed.

Mr. LIND. He does not know whether these questions were printed or not?

Mr. BOATNER. He knows that all the questions are printed.

By Mr. EWART:

Q. Do you know how many copies are generally made?—A. The number of copies printed of any series will vary according to the number of applicants to be examined.

Q. Just give us an idea of the number of copies generally made?—A. From three to five hundred copies as the exigencies may require.

Q. At the time that this list of questions was abstracted from the files by Campbell did you know whether there was a large number of copies on file?—A. I did not. The copies were in the possession of the chief examiner. Mr. Campbell would not have had access to them.

Q. Would it be possible for you to procure for us a list of those questions printed?—A. Not without consulting the chief examiner.

Q. Upon consulting the chief examiner could you furnish this committee with a list of those questions?

Mr. LIND. Let me understand what questions you refer to.

Mr. EWART. The identical list of questions copied by Campbell.

Mr. LIND. I understand the copy is not in existence.

Mr. EWART. I do not mean the copy which Campbell made, but I mean the printed copy. There are a number of printed lists of these questions always on file with the Commission.

By Mr. LIND:

Q. Do you know what list these questions were copied from? Could you go to your file and take out the list of questions copied by Mr. Campbell?—A. If I knew the series.

Q. Do you know the series? That is what I asked you. Do you know what list of questions was copied?—A. No, sir.

Q. Who examined that?—A. Mr. Commissioner Oberly, and I think Major Webster examined it.

By Mr. EWART:

Q. Say, in December, 1888; could you not procure a copy of the questions used in that month?—A. If the Commission would have on its record unused examination questions printed of that series.

Q. What disposition is generally made of those printed lists; are they destroyed?—A. They are destroyed, but we reserve a small number of copies. It is the practice to preserve ten or fifteen.

Mr. LIND. The witness has already said that he has no knowledge of where those questions are.

Q. I am asking this question for my own information, to ascertain if it would not be possible to get a copy of these printed lists. He says that they always kept on file fifteen or twenty copies.

Mr. LIND. He has stated that he did not know what series it was.

Mr. EWART. He says that you can ascertain the fact. December, 1887, is the date.

Mr. LIND. What purpose would they serve if we had them?

The WITNESS. It is absolutely impossible to identify the papers. I can not get them.

Mr. LIND. The written questions are lost and it is impossible to tell which set of printed questions were used, as I understand it.

By Mr. ANDREW:

Q. You saw this manuscript copy of questions which was presented?—A. Yes, sir.

Q. What was the examination on?—A. I did not make an inquiry into what the examination was or what the questions would cover. It was a matter left to Commissioner Oberly.

Q. Have you any idea as to about what subjects were embraced?—A. I have understood that it was ——.

Mr. LIND. Of your own knowledge?

A. Of my own knowledge I can not state.

Mr. LIND. The witness has already stated that he does not know the subject-matter of the examination for he did not examine the manuscript paper.

Mr. ANDREW. It has been said here that this manuscript contained only questions on arithmetic. Can you state whether or not that is true?

Mr. OBERLY. The lady said so.

Mr. ANDREW. Miss Dabney stated to-day in answer to me that there was nothing upon the manuscript which was given to her and which was brought to the Commissioner except questions upon arithmetic, as she was weak in that branch and wanted the questions on arithmetic.

Mr. LIND. Can you state whether, according to your recollection, that is correct?

A. According to my recollection the portion of the questions which I examined with a view of determining whose hand-writing they were in were questions in arithmetic. I do not know whether the manuscript contained questions upon other subjects of examination or not.

Mr. LIND. Did you notice whether the questions and answers on the manuscript were in the same handwriting?

A. To the best of my recollection they were.

Mr. ROOSEVELT. Do you remember being called in by the governor and myself to state the facts about this case last fall?

A. I do.

Mr. ROOSEVELT. Your testimony then was substantially to the same effect as the statement of Commissioner Oberly to-day, was it not?

A. It was.

Mr. THOMPSON. You stated to us that Mr. Oberly had investigated the matter and decided that nothing more than a reprimand was necessary?

A. Yes, sir.

Mr. ROOSEVELT. And Mr. Campbell has been retained accordingly?

A. Yes, sir.

Mr. ROOSEVELT. The only people in the office who knew of this in the sense of taking personal part in the investigation were Commissioners Oberly, Lyman, Mr. Campbell, and yourself?

A. And Mrs. Smith.

Mr. ROOSEVELT. But Mr. Smith was out of the office when you came in?

A. Those were the only persons connected with the Commission who had knowledge of the fact at that time and knew of the occurrence.

The CHAIRMAN. Mr. Ewart wishes to obtain information as to whether or not the papers copied by Mr. Campbell were delivered to the Commission. Is that true?

Mr. LYMAN. The manuscript copy.

The CHAIRMAN. Where is that manuscript?

The WITNESS. I don't know.

The CHAIRMAN. What became of it?

Mr. LYMAN. The last knowledge I had of it was that it was in the possession of Commissioner Oberly.

Mr. OBERLY. Now that manuscript has been traced further than that this morning, when you were out.

Mr. BOATNER. The lady who testified this morning said that she took the manuscript from Ex-commissioner Oberly and returned it to Mr. Flynn. Mr. Flynn testified that that was false. That is as far as it has been traced.

Mr. LIND. Now I ask that this be stricken out.

Mr. OBERLY. I have made several statements concerning that paper. I never delivered the manuscript to the Commission because they would not accept it from me upon conditions. The condition as imposed by Miss Dabney was that I would return them to her.

Mr. LIND. I understand that perfectly well; and now I ask that these questions and answers be stricken out, simply because it encumbers the record.

The CHAIRMAN. There is no harm in allowing it to remain. Is it the pleasure of the committee to go on with the second charge at present?

Mr. EWART. That is all the evidence on the first charge with regard to the abstraction of the questions.

The CHAIRMAN. Let Mr. Morgan take the stand.

Mr. EWART. Before the charge is read let me briefly call the attention of the committee to the section of the statute which we insist was violated.

The said section says as follows:

SEC. 3. That said Commission is authorized to employ a chief examiner, a part of whose duty it shall be, under its direction, to act with the examining boards, so far as practicable, whether at Washington or elsewhere, and to secure accuracy, uniformity, and justice in all their proceedings, which shall be at all times open to him. The chief examiner, shall be entitled to receive a salary at the rate of three thousand dollars a year, and he shall be paid his necessary traveling expenses incurred in the discharge of his duty. The Commission shall have a secretary, to be appointed by the President, who shall receive a salary of one thousand six hundred dollars per annum. It may, when necessary, employ a stenographer and a messenger, who shall be paid, when employed, the former at the rate of one thousand six hundred dollars a year, and the latter at the rate of six hundred dollars a year.

The CHAIRMAN. Now read the charge.

The charge is as follows:

It is further charged against the Commission as now constituted, that one Edward Daniel Bailey, in violation of the civil-service law, which inhibits the promotion of persons in the classified service without examination was promoted by said Commission without any examination to test his fitness, as required by law, from a clerkship to the position of stenographer, an important position in the said Commission, when it was notoriously known at the time that said Bailey was not competent to fill the said position of stenographer.

That this promotion was made when there were several other clerks in the said Commission who were expert stenographers, and under the principle governing promotions undoubtedly entitled to the promotion.

Mr. EWART. I should have stated that, in addition to this statute, there is a clause in the appropriation act which provides that the Commission shall have the power to employ a fourth-class clerk, who shall be the official stenographer.

Mr. ROOSEVELT. Who shall be a stenographer.

Mr. EWART. Yes, sir; that is right; " who shall be a stenographer." We would like Mr. Lyman examined first on that charge.

TESTIMONY OF CHARLES LYMAN.

Commissioner LYMAN, recalled and examined.

By Mr. EWART:

Q. Mr. Lyman, who is the official stenographer of the Civil Service Commission at that time?—A. There is no official stenographer in one sense, and in another sense there is. Mr. Bailey is the stenographer appropriated for, as such, by law.

Q. When was he promoted?—A. He was appointed in September last.

Q. In September, 1889?—A. I think it was; I have the date of his appointment here.

Q. Was he required to pass any examination?—A. At the time of his promotion he did not pass any examination.

Mr. EWART. What are the duties of the official stenographer?—A. The duties of the stenographer to the Commission are various in their character. If it is desired by the committee I will make a general statement, which will bring out just what the situation is in the Commission with reference to the employment of a stenographer.

Mr. BOATNER. I suggest that we will get through a great deal more quickly if counsel will ask specific and pointed interrogatories.

Mr. EWART. I can not ask any more pointed question than that.

Mr. BOATNER. Let the counsel ask specific and pointed questions and then, when the examination is finished, if the witness desires to make any explanation he may make the statement on re-examination.

The CHAIRMAN. Suppose you answer the questions directly as you can and afterwards make such explanations as you desire of any answers you may have given to a direct question.

Mr. EWART. I repeat the question. What are the duties of the official stenographer?—A. Such duties as may be assigned to him by the Commission.

Q. Taking the testimony in this case ?—A. The Commission exercises its own judgment as to who shall take the testimony in this case.

Q. Is this the official stenographer who is now taking this testimony ?—A. He is one of the stenographers of the Commission.

Q. Is he the official stenographer ?—A. He is a stenographer. He is not the fourth-class clerk appropriated for as a stenographer.

Q. Why do you use this gentleman as a stenographer ?—A. Because it suits our convenience.

Q. In what respect; why does it suit your convenience ?—A. Because he is a stenographer and available.

Q. Is he an expert ?—A. I think he is.

Q. Mr. Lyman, you are certainly in a position to know.—A. I think he is; I supposed you were inquiring about Mr. Holtz.

The CHAIRMAN. You were referring to Mr. Bailey in your question ?

Mr. EWART. No; I am referring to Mr. Holtz. Is Mr. Bailey an expert stenographer ?—A. Yes, sir.

Q. Was he at the time of his promotion ?—A. I think he was.

Q. You think he was ?—A. Yes, sir.

Q. Do you know the fact that he was ?—A. I know that he was a stenographer.

Q. Do you know the fact that at the time of his promotion he was an expert stenographer ?—A. What do you mean by that?

Q. A man who can take evidence rapidly, quickly, and accurately.—A. He was a stenographer.

Q. Was he an expert stenographer ?—A. If you will define to me precisely what you mean by an expert I will answer the question.

Q. I will ask you this question: Did you take any steps to satisfy yourself that he was an expert stenographer ?—A. I did sir.

Q. Was he subjected to any examination ?—A. Not before his promotion.

Q. Did you subject him to any examination to test his fitness and accuracy as an expert, before his promotion ?—A. He has been repeatedly tested as to his fitness.

Q. Did you take any steps to test him ?—A. Yes, sir.

Q. Was it in the form of an examination ?—A. It was in the form of dictations.

Q. Was it in the form of an examination such as is prescribed by the Civil Service Commission ?

Mr. BOATNER. Let him state what kind of an examination it was.

Mr. EWARTS. Did you satisfy yourself in conducting his examination that he was expert enough to take down evidence rapidly and accurately ?—A. I satisfied myself that he was such a stenographer as might be put in that place in conformity with the requirements of the statute.

Q. Was Mr. Holtz a clerk in that Bureau at that time?—A. Yes, sir.

Q. Did you regard him as good a stenographer as Mr. Bailey?—A. I think he is.

Q. Do you regard Mr. Bailey as a better stenographer than Mr. Holtz?—A. I do not.

Q. How then do you explain his promotion?—A. Because he was Mr. Holtz's senior.

Q. Then you promoted him because he was an older man?—A. Not because he was an older man.

Q. You did not make the promotion then on merit?—A. I did.

Q. I just understood you to say you made the promotion on account of his seniority in the service.—A. That is a part of it, sir.

Q. I will ask this question: I will ask you whether at the time you made that promotion you did not know that Mr. Holtz was a better stenographer in every respect than Mr. Bailey, the gentleman whom you did promote?—A. I don't know that I specially compared the two men in that respect.

By Mr. STONE:

Q. Inform me, if you please, who Mr. Bailey is and who Mr. Holtz is— I mean officially?—A. Mr. Bailey is a fourth-class clerk with the designation of stenographer.

Q. Was he appointed under this appropriation act?—A. Yes, sir; he was promoted.

Q. Who is Mr. Holtz?—A. Mr. Holtz is a third-class clerk employed in the office of the Commissioner, at this moment taking notes at the table.

Q. Is he acting as as a stenographer in the Commission?—A. Yes, sir.

Q. Have you what you term your official stenographer?—A. We do not term any one the official stenographer.

Q. What are the duties of Mr. Bailey as stenographer?—A. Mr. Bailey, as stenographer, takes dictation from the Chief Examiner and from the Commissioners.

Q. What are the duties of Mr. Holtz?—A. Mr. Holtz performs a variety of duties.

Q. I mean as stenographer?—A. Mr. Holtz frequently takes dictation for letters and he does other stenographic work in the Commission as the Commission requires.

Q. Both of these gentlemen have been appointed to the position of stenographer?—A. No, sir.

Q. Either of them?—A. Mr. Bailey has.

Q. Mr. Holtz then is simply drawing a salary as a third-class clerk?— A. Yes, sir.

Q. Does Mr. Bailey draw the salary of stenographer?—A. He draws the salary as a fourth-class clerk.

Q. He was a fourth-class clerk before?—A. No, sir; he was a third-class clerk at the time of his last promotion.

Q. Then he gets no additional salary by reason of being a stenographer?—No, sir.

Q. What I want to get at is the matter which Mr. Ewart was examining you about as to the appointment of this man Bailey as a stenographer and concerning your examination of him?—A. I think I can give you the information you want and economize the time of the committee if you will allow me to make a statement.

Q. I wish you would.—A. The civil service law provided that the Commission might employ a stenographer when needed. Mr. Doyle, the present secretary of the Commission, was employed as that stenographer at that time and subsequently, in the appropriation act from year to year, a clerk is appropriated for, "who shall be a stenographer." One is now so appropriated for at a salary of $1,800 per annum, the appropriation being for one clerk of class 4, who shall be a stenographer. Long, long ago the business of the Commission demanded more than one stenographer, and the gentleman who has been employed in the position of stenographer according to the statute in this particular case, has never been, in the history of the Commission, exclusively employed in that work but has been assigned to various other duties from time to time. As business has increased it has become necessary to have other stenographers, and at the present moment, in addition to Mr. Bailey, there are employed Mr. Holtz, who is a stenographer and is used as such ; Mr. Swank, who is a stenographer and is used as such ; Mr. Culver, who is a stenographer and is used as such, and Mr. Doyle is occasionally used as a stenographer when his other duties will permit. I am not certain but what Mr. Leadley is a stenographer also. There are at least five stenographers in the employ of the Commission, all of whom are used to do such work as occasion may require. No one of them is regarded or treated by the Commission as the official stenographer, that is, as the man to do that kind of work, for no one man can do the whole of that work.

Q. Stenography is a branch of learning that is made the subject of a special examination under your rules ?—A. Yes, sir.

Q. Do you understand that this clerk, who is to be a stenographer, authorized to be appointed by the appropriation act, should be examined as to his qualifications before appointment ?—A. If a man were appointed directly from the outside to this place, unquestionably the law and the rules of the Commission would require that the person should be certified from the register of the Commission from the persons who have been examined as stenographers.

Q. If he is already in the employ of the Commission, then, your idea is that he would require no examination ?—A. It is a question of promotion, and his fitness for the position is a matter to be tested by a written examination or the knowledge of the Commission on his qualifications for the place.

Q. You appointed this man, then, not upon an examination, but upon personal knowledge ?—A. By promotion, because of our knowledge of his qualifications for that place.

Q. Did you have personal knowledge touching his qualifications as a stenographer prior to his promotion ?—A. I did, sir.

Q. How had you obtained that knowledge ?—A. Because I had seen him write stenography.

Q. You said in answer to Mr. Ewart that you had examined him in some way by dictation.—A. I had tested him.

Q. You tested him by dictation ?—A. Every stenographer is tested by dictation.

Q. Did you do that before or after the promotion ?—A. He was tested before in practical work.

Q. By you ?—A. By me.

Q. In that way you satisfied yourself before the promotion of his qualifications ?—A. Before his promotion I satisfied myself thoroughly that he was a stenographer.

Q. Could he have passed the examination in stenography at the date of his promotion ?—A. I think he could.

Q. And obtained the grade that would have entitled him to go on the eligible list?—A. I think he could.

By Mr. STONE:

Q. There is one additional question which I desire to ask. I understood you to say that where a clerk was promoted, who was already in the employ of the Commission, that then a special examination in stenography was not required?—A. The rules do not require a special examination where the Commissioners have knowledge of the qualifications.

Q. Is that the practice in the other Departments?—A. I think it is.

Q. In other words could the Commissioner of Pensions promote a clerk of the third class, as you did in this instance, to a higher class—requiring among other qualifications that the employé should understand stenography—could that promotion be made by the Commissioner of Pensions without the person receiving the promotion having been first examined?—A. If you substitute for "the Commissioner of Pensions" the "Secretary of the Interior" I will say yes.

Q. Making that substitution you would say yes?—A. Yes, sir.

By Mr. BOATNER:

Q. You have just stated, Mr. Lyman, that the appointing officer in any department might promote a clerk from one grade to another without an examination or without any additional examination to show his fitness for the place to which he is promoted.—A. I mean to say that the Commission has prescribed regulations which apply to the War Department, under which promotions take place; but the Commission does not attempt and the rules do not attempt to regulate promotions in the other Departments, except so far as to regulate the promotion of those who have been appointed from the copyist register to the thousand-dollar grade.

Q. What rule, if any, have you for appointment in the clerical force of the Civil Service Commission?—A. The rules which apply to the other Departments apply to the Civil Service Commission.

Q. I do not mean in a general way. I mean have you any special rules which apply to the appointment of clerks?—A. No special rules. We are bound by the same rules which apply to the other Departments.

Q. What I want to get at is this: Suppose there is a vacancy, do you call in a new man from the outside, or do you fill that vacancy by promotion, and by taking in a new man at the bottom?—A. The general practice of the Commission is to fill vacancies in the higher grades by promotion, and to make the original appointments at the bottom.

Q. Is there any rule which regulates the appointments in the office, or is that merely at the option of the Commission?—A. It is the matter wholly within the discretion of the Commission except in so far as it is controlled by the departmental rule.

Q. I want to get at this: Suppose it becomes necessary, or you have an opportunity, to promote one of your clerks from an inferior to a superior position, and you have two or more men in the service and in the same grade who are competent to fulfill the duties of the position to which the promotion is to be made, and one has been in the service longer than the other, or they have been in the service different lengths of time, is there any rule which would require you to select one which has been longer in the service?—A. There is no rule; but other things being equal, the Commission would undoubtedly give the preference to the man who was the senior in the length of service. It is a matter of judgment, however.

Q. You said that the Commission, all things being equal, gave the preference to the employé who has been longest in the service?—A. That would be my personal opinion.

Q. Is there any regulation to that effect?—A. I may say that has been the general practice of the Commission. It has varied in individual instances; but it is the general practice of the Commission.

The CHAIRMAN. In making this appointment of Mr. Bailey, in point of fact was he entitled to it by being the longest in the service?—A. Yes, sir.

Mr. STONE. Would he be qualified to come here and take this testimony, in your opinion?—A. Well, gentlemen, I think he could come here and take this testimony. But I wish to impress upon the committee one fact, that the Commission employs five stenographers and that the gentleman who is designated by his appointment as stenographer is not now and never has been exclusively employed as stenographer; that the Commission has been obliged, I may say, by the stress of its work to utilize in the best possible manner the employés to accomplish the work, and in doing that sometimes what you would call an official stenographer would be doing stenographic work and sometimes he would not.

Mr. EWART. Which one draws the $1,800 salary?—A. Mr. Bailey.

Mr. LIND. I would like to ask right here one question, which is this: Does your stenographic work consist principally of taking letter dictation or have you much taking of evidence to do?—A. The greater part of it consists in taking letter dictation and dictation for the minutes and of ruling and of decisions, and all that sort of ordinary current office work,

Mr. LIND. Office work?—A. Yes, sir; occasionally when the Commission makes investigations it takes one of the stenographers, or they employ another stenographer who is not connected with the Commission at all, as has been done in several instances.

By Mr. HATTON:

Q. When was Mr. Bailey originally appointed to a position in the Commission?—A. I can give you the exact date by consulting a memorandum I have.

Q. How long was it from the time he was promoted?—A. I think it was 1886 when he was appointed.

Q. When was he promoted?—A. He was promoted two or three months ago.

Q. Was he a stenographer of any kind when he entered the Commission?—A. I have no doubt he was a stenographer when he entered the Commission.

Q. In making an examination of a stenographer would you ask how long he had been a stenographer?—A. No, sir.

Q. The appropriation bill provides for a fourth-class clerk, "who shall be a stenographer?"—A. Yes, sir.

Q. Has that fourth-class clerk ever been recognized as the official stenographer? You say that he has not been recognized as the official stenographer?—A. He has never been exclusively so, nor exclusively used for that purpose.

By Mr. EWART:

Q. I see in your fourth report here the name of William E. Morgan, of Pennsylvania, given as stenographer. Was he regarded as the official stenographer and the only one?—A. He was appropriated for as stenographer.

Q. As the official stenographer?—A. You may use that word, but I do not.

Q. As a fourth-class clerk?—A. Yes, sir.

Q. His name is the only stenographer's name which appears here?—A. His is the only name which appears there, but at that time there were others in the employ of the Commission.

Q. After the publication of this report and before you issued your fifth report, you decided to strike this official from the list?—A. That is simply a matter of publication of names.

Mr. LIND. Is Morgan still there?—A, No, sir.

Mr. STONE. Is that the place Bailey has now?

By Mr. HATTON:

Q. Mr. Lyman, at the time this report was issued Mr. Morgan was occupying the place which Mr. Bailey has now; is not that so?—A. Yes, sir.

Q. When the report was issued his name was the one that was embraced in the list of the officers of the Commission?—A. After the fifth report was issued Mr. Morgan's name was left out.

Q. You give it as your opinion that, if you had put Mr. Bailey to a test examination, he would have passed?—A. Yes, sir.

Q. Do you give it as your opinion that he would have passed at a higher grade than Mr. Holtz?—A. I am not making comparisons, as that can be determined only by examination.

Q. You can give an opinion with regard to Mr. Holtz as well as with regard to Mr. Bailey. I am only asking for your opinion.—A. Mr. Holtz is a good stenographer.

Q. You will not say then that, in your opinion, he would pass any higher grade than Mr. Bailey would have passed at the time he was promoted?—A. I think it quite likely that at that time and very probably now Mr. Holtz is a more rapid stenographer than Mr. Bailey.

Q. When the Commission has any very important and rapid work which they want done, like taking the testimony in any investigation of a post-office case, does Bailey do that work?—A. He has not been doing that work because he has been charged with another kind of work which takes his whole time.

Q. If you had to choose stenographers there at this time and had to choose between Holtz and Bailey to take this testimony, I would like to ask which one of the two you would select to take it?—A. That is a matter which would be governed by the convenience of the office.

The CHAIRMAN. The witness has said that Mr. Bailey does other work which occupies his time.

Mr. HATTON. That is all.

The CHAIRMAN. Are there any other questions?

Mr. LIND. I would ask, under these specifications, if you have any testimony to offer which differs from this?

Mr. HATTON. The testimony we have to offer is to the effect that this man was promoted without an examination, and to show that at the time of his promotion, and by men qualified to judge better than Mr. Lyman, because they are stenographers themselves, he was utterly incompetent as a stenographer and could not possibly have passed an examination. That is the opinion of stenographers, experts in the business.

TESTIMONY OF WILLIAM E. MORGAN.

WILLIAM E. MORGAN sworn and examined :

By Mr. EWART :

Q. Please state your place of residence and your occupation?—A. I am now living at No. 906 Fourteenth street, Washington, D. C. I occupy a position in the Bureau of the Mint at the Treasury Department, as stenographer to the Director of the Mint.

Q. Were you ever connected with the Civil Service Commission?—A. Yes, sir.

Q. In what capacity?—A. As stenographer. I hold here my commission as such dated February 18.

Q. You were not under the Commission at that time?—A. Yes, sir.

Q. How long have you been employed here as a stenographer, in Washington and other cities?—A. Ever since I have been in Washington, and that was in the latter part of 1885. I was employed before that in Philadelphia for three or four years.

Q. I presume you would consider yourself an expert?—A. Yes, sir.

Q. Did you know Bailey at the time he was appointed as stenographer?—A. Yes, sir.

Q. What is your opinion, as an expert, of Mr. Bailey as a stenographer?—A. Well, in the sense that the stenographers are named in the Civil Service Commission, under the appropriation act, which means that he shall be competent to take testimony in any investigation the Commission is empowered to make, I do not think that he was competent to perform that work. In fact I never thought of calling him a stenographer any more than a man who could play a scale on the violin could call himself a violinist.

Q. Do you know Mr. Holtz?—A. Yes, sir.

Q. Was he in the service of the Commission at the time you were employed there?—A. Yes, sir.

Q. What do you know of his knowledge of stenography?—A. I think he is a man of considerable ability in his line.

Q. What comparison would you make of Mr. Holtz and Mr. Bailey?—A. Mr. Holtz is infinitely superior. They can not be compared at all.

Q. There is no comparison to be made?—A. No, sir.

The CHAIRMAN. Mr. Morgan, when did you leave the Civil Service Commission?—A. I went to the Treasury Department on September 12, 1889.

By Mr. ANDREW :

Q. Last September?—A. Yes, sir.

Q. How long were you a stenographer to the Commission; how many years?—A. From September, 1886, to September, 1889; about three years.

Q. Why were you transferred to the Treasury Department?—A. I left the Civil Service Commission because I felt that I was not treated properly by the Commission. My work was taken away from me and I was assigned to correspondence up stairs at a type-writer, and persons who were not designated as stenographers in the Commission were assigned to stenographic work in making investigations. I was put in such a position that I felt that I was doing work that was not commensurate with my salary, and that it would be a question of but a very short time before I would be asked to leave. I forestalled that by getting transferred.

Q. You resigned ?—A. I resigned.

By Mr. LYMAN :

Q. Mr. Morgan, when were you appointed as stenographer to the Commission ?—A. I think it was on December 18, 1886.

Q. Who signed that commission ?—A. John H. Oberly, Commissioner in charge.

Q. What was your occupation at the time you were promoted ?—A. I was the stenographer in the Bureau of the Mint.

Q. Was this place appropriated for a stenographer in the Commission at that time?—A. Yes, sir.

Q. When you were employed at Washington did you take an examination ?—A. No, sir; at the time I was appointed all stenographers in the classified service were exempt from examination.

Q. How did Mr. Oberly, when he signed your appointment, know that you were a stenographer ?—A. Because I was examined for that position in the Bureau of the Mint, and he questioned me as to my ability as a stenographer ; whether I was competent to take investigations.

Q. Did he test you in any way?—A. He did not.

Q. So that when you were appointed stenographer to the Commission you were not examined?—A. I was not examined. I took an examination when I was transferred this last time.

Mr. ROOSEVELT. That was after you left the Commission ?—A. Yes, sir ; I passed the examination when I was transferred.

By Mr. LYMAN :

Q. While you were stenographer to the Commission, and so designated, did you do stenographic work steadily ?—A. No, sir; in connection with my duties there I was certification clerk.

Q. Did that require stenography ?—A. No, sir.

Q. That was your main work, was it not?—A. Yes, when I was not engaged in stenographic work.

Q. What proportion of your time while you were employed as stenographer was devoted to stenography?—A. I was called in right along, for a long while, as stenographer to the Commission, to take the minutes.

Q. That only took from a quarter of an hour to a half of an hour ?—A. Some days it took from 2 o'clock till 5.

Q. That was only occasionally. Generally it was for a short time?—A. Not always; always more than ten minutes.

Q. Sometimes the Commission had long discussions and you did not have very much to do while waiting. During the last year and a half or two years of your connection with the Commission did you do very much stenographic work?—A. Not towards the latter part, because other stenographers were assigned to do my work.

Q. What do you mean by the latter part ?—A. When you were sole Commissioner.

Q. Did you not do as much stenographic work then as you had done before that?—A. No, sir.

Q. How much stenographic work had you done six months before that or a year before that?—A. I could not say. A year before that I took the Philadelphia investigation.

Q. Is that the only investigation that you took?—A. That's the only one I took.

Q. How many investigations did the Commission make during the time you were stenographer?—A. They made several. You made several in New York.

Q. I am speaking now of the old Commission and not of the time when this Commission was formed.—A. I do not think there was any other investigation excepting the one in the New York custom-house by Mr. Oberly. I did that while I was there.

Q. Was there an investigation made in Chicago?—A. Yes; there was an investigation made in Chicago, and I was assigned to go there; but Mr. Edgerton objected on the score of economy and said that he did not think a stenographer was necessary. When the Commission arrived there they found it was necessary to have a stenographer and I suppose they employed one out there.

Q. You were regularly employed as a stenographer. That was not your main business?—A. I went to the Commission with the intention of being a stenographer and I was informed that that was my position there.

Q. How long was it after you were appointed stenographer before the promotion of Bailey took place?—A. Mr. Bailey swore in before I resigned. I came back and found that he had taken the oath of office. I went up-stairs and said that I thought he was a little premature, that I had not resigned and would not until the next day.

By Mr. EWART:

Q. What was the date of that?—A. That was on the 30th of August, I think.

Q. Of what year?—A. Last year.

Q. When were you appointed?—A. September 18, 1886.

Q. Then your resignation was about three years afterwards? -A. Yes, sir.

By Mr. ROOSEVELT:

Q. Were you appointed by Mr. Oberly when he was the sole Commissioner?—A. Yes, sir; but he had telegraphed to Mr. Edgerton for his concurrence and received that.

Q. But you were appointed by Mr. Oberly when he was the sole acting Commissioner, having received the concurrence by telegraph of the other members?—A. So I understood; yes, sir.

Q. He did not test you by examination when you were appointed?—A. No; he did not.

Q. Had you made your entry into the service by examination?—A. As I told Mr. Lyman, examinations were not required by the Civil Service Commission at that time for stenographers, although I was examined by the Director of the Mint as to my competency to take that position as stenographer.

Q. But you have not had any civil service examination?—A. No, sir.

Q. What was your salary just before you were promoted by Mr. Oberly?—A. I was a $1,400 clerk, appropriated for as stenographer.

Q. You were then promoted from a $1,400 position to an $1,800 position?—A. I was not promoted. I was transferred.

Q. You were transferred from a $1,400 position to an $1,800 position without examination?—A. Yes, sir.

Q. By Acting Commissioner Oberly, with the concurrence of his colleague or colleagues?—A. Yes, sir.

By Mr. THOMPSON:

Q. Do you remember a conversation you had with me about two months ago?—A. Yes, sir.

Q. Do you remember of saying in that conversation that you had a grievance against any member of the Commission?—A. Yes, sir.

Q. What did you say to me?—A. I said I had a grievance against the Commission, inasmuch as they had not treated me properly. Mr. Lyman and Mr. Webster were both very courteous to me personally.

Q. Did you state that you had any grievance against Mr. Roosevelt and myself?—A. No, sir.

Q. You did not say that?—Yes, sir; I said that I had not.

Q. Did you say that you did not propose to make yourself prominent in this matter, but if called upon you intended to testify?—A. Yes, sir.

Q. In that conversation did you tell me Bailey was, in your opinion, not a stenographer?—A. Yes, sir.

Q. And that he was improperly appointed?—A. Yes, sir.

Q. Did you tell me that Holtz ought to have had that place?—A. Yes, sir.

Q. Is it your opinion now that Bailey is not a stenographer. You said just now that you were an expert?—A. Yes, sir; I think he can act as an amanuensis.

Q. Do you think that he could pass the examinations that are required for stenographers in the Civil Service Commission?—A. I don't think he could.

Q. Did you ever tell Holtz that you thought he was entitled to this promotion and ought to have it?—A. I don't recollect. I may have told him that.

Q. I would be glad if you would remember.—A. I could not say; there was a great deal of discussion, and he spoke in strong terms against the promotion of Mr. Bailey to the position of stenographer.

Q. You don't remember whether you ever told Holtz that he was entitled to it and ought to have it?—A. No, I don't; but I think he was entitled to it. I do not recollect of saying it to you; but I would just as soon say it now.

Q. What I want to bring out is whether you did not say so to Holtz?—A. If Mr. Holtz will testify that I did, I will not deny it.

Q. It is important to know whether Mr. Morgan did not say so to Mr. Holtz.—A. I have no recollection on that subject.

Q. Did you ever tell Mr. Bailey that you thought he was entitled to this place and ought to have it?—A. No, sir.

Q. Did you ever tell Mr. Johnson that you thought Bailey was entitled to it and ought to have it?—A. No, sir.

Q. Nothing like that?—A. No, sir.

Q. Do you know Mr. Wallace?—A. Yes, sir.

Q. Did you ever tell him you thought Bailey ought to have this place?—A. No, sir.

Q. I propose to contradict you on this point and I want to give you fair notice. I ask you again if you did not, in one of the rooms in the second story of the Commission, call Bailey to one side and say to him, I am going to resign and am going to the Treasury, I am going to get out of the way, and I hope you will get this place?—A. I recollect of speaking to him.

Q. One day in going to lunch and returning from lunch in company with Mr. Johnson and Mr. Wallace did you not tell them that Bailey was entitled to this position and ought to have it?—A. I have no recollection.

Q. I would like to have you answer the question directly yes or no?—A. How can I answer it yes or no when I have no recollection about it?

The CHAIRMAN. Might you have said so?—A. I might have said so; but I do not think I did and I have no recollection on the subject.

By Mr. THOMPSON:

Q. I understood you just now to say that you did not say so to John-son?—A. I would not be positive.

Q. Do you positively say that you did not say so to Bailey?—A. I am pretty positive on that point. Mr. Bailey, being the oldest clerk there, was entitled to the next promotion; but not to the position of stenographer, unless he was qualified for it.

Q. That was only the $1,800 place?—A. Yes, sir.

By Mr. ROOSEVELT:

Q. Do I understand you to say that Mr. Holtz had told you that Bailey was not entitled to the promotion?—A. Yes, sir; there was a conversation on that promotion and we both concurred in that idea.

Q. Your statement was that Mr. Holtz told you that Bailey was not entitled to the promotion?—A. Yes, sir; he felt aggrieved himself, and thought that he was entitled to it and I thought so too.

Q. You say that was what Holtz told you?—A. That is the sum and substance of it; yes, sir.

By Mr. LIND:

Q. Mr. Morgan, were you acquainted with the relative capacity of these two men, Bailey and Holtz, as clerks?—A. As clerks?

Q. Yes; for ordinary office-work.—A. Well, I thought they were on an equality in that respect as ordinary clerks, outside of their steno-graphic qualifications.

Q. I asked you whether you were acquainted with them?—A. Yes, sir; I have been with both of them. I have seen them both at clerical work in the office.

Q. Did you work in the same room?—A. Yes, sir.

Q. And handle papers alongside of them?—A. Yes, sir; with Mr. Holtz, but not with Mr. Bailey. The only information I had of Mr. Bailey was that I was detailed upstairs, and they assigned me to act as stenographer for him to take down his dictations and correspond-ence. I objected to that.

Q. I do not care about that; you were more familiar then with the capacity of Mr. Holtz than you were with the proficiency of Mr. Bailey for ordinary clerical work?—A. Yes, sir.

Q. And your general information is that they were about the same?—A. Yes, sir.

Q. As a matter of fact much the larger portion of your time and the time of any one who acts as a stenographer or is known as a stenog-rapher in the Civil Service Commission is occupied in performing other duties?—A. A great portion of the time.

Q. The greater portion?—A. Yes, sir; the major portion of it.

By Mr. STONE:

Q. Is this paper which I hold in my hand the original commission given to you by Mr. Oberly?—A. Yes, sir; I think that is the one.

Q. Have you a copy of this?—A. No, sir; that is the original.

Mr. STONE. I will read this and ask the stenographer to take it down.

UNITED STATES CIVIL SERVICE COMMISSION,
Washington, September 18, 1886.

William E. Morgan, of Pennsylvania, is hereby appointed stenographer of the Civil Service Commission, as provided for by section 3 of an act to regulate and improve the civil service of the United States; this appointment to take effect, as soon as he shall file the oath of office, for the probationary period of six months.

JOHN H. OBERLY,
Commissioner in charge.

Mr. BOATNER. I understood you to say awhile ago, in answer to a question about the competency of Mr. Bailey, that you considered him competent as an amanuensis.—A. Yes, sir; I think I saw him take dictation from Major Webster. That is the only stenographic work I ever saw him do.

By Mr. LYMAN:

Q. Just in that line, what opportunity had you for knowing whether Mr. Bailey was or was not a stenographer?—A. During my sojourn upstairs I was in communication with Mr. Bailey every day and I saw him do stenographic work on several occasions and I sat down and saw Major Webster dictating to him. I took the dictation myself to see whether Mr. Bailey was a stenographer or not. He took a good many notes and filled out his letters in his own language, which Major Webster approved; but I do not think he ever took it down verbatim.

Q. That is your only means of knowing?—A. That is my only means of knowing; yes, sir. I never saw him do any stenographic work and never heard of him doing any.

Mr. OBERLY. Mr. Roosevelt asked the question evidently with the intention of showing that Mr. Morgan was transferred from the Treasury Department by transfer without examination. I want to bring out that point.

Mr. LIND. That is immaterial on this specification.

Mr. OBERLY. No examination for transfer was then necessary or could be made.

THURSDAY, *February* 27, 1890.

TESTIMONY OF CHARLES LYMAN—Recalled.

Mr. CHARLES LYMAN, recalled.

Mr. EWART. I want to recall Mr. Lyman in order to examine him in reference to the appointment of Mr. Bailey.

Mr. LYMAN. I was not on the stand yesterday when the testimony closed.

By Mr. EWART:

Q. I believe I understood you to say yesterday that Mr. Bailey was appointed without any examination?—A. I said that Mr. Bailey was appointed without the usual examination.

Q. Then that appointment was made by yourself under Rule 6, which prescribes that no promotion shall be made in any Department without a test of fitness?—A. The appointment was made by the Commission.

Q. Under Rule 6?—A. Under Rule 9.

Q. Rule 6 prescribes that promotions may be made upon any test of fitness?—A. In the last report it is Rule 9.

Q. That being the case, how do you reconcile that action in the case of Mr. Bailey with the language used in the report of July, 1887, where you say the test of fitness is required? Please explain that apparent variation in your appointment of Mr. Bailey, and the language used as a Commissioner in making that report?—A. I will say that the appointment of Mr. Bailey was made in conformity with the general practice of the Commission, both before and after that time.

Q. That is not an answer to the question. I am asking you to explain the variance between the language used in making that report and the action in the appointment of Mr. Bailey without requiring him to pass the examination.—A. If I may be allowed to answer the question in my own way, I will say that I am stating the fact that the promotion of Mr. Bailey was made in conformity with the practice both before and after his promotion—a practice pursued in the office of the Civil Service Commission, and a practice which was in effect at the time this report was written, and a practice which has continued since that time, not only in the office of the Commission, but in the Departments. My understanding of this language is that every promotion must be made with the provisions of the rule referred to. My understanding of what the Commission means to say here is that every promotion must be made in accordance with the requirements of the statute under the provisions of the rule referred to, or any rule which is made to apply to the subject of promotions; and that the law and the rule require that some test should be made. The rule itself says (and the rule must be construed to be in harmony with the law) that it may be upon a test of fitness determined by the promoting officer. That test of fitness, according to this language, should be an examination. That examination may be a written examination made at the time, or it may be an observation of the fitness of the candidate for promotion made from day to day, from week to week, and from month to month, under the direct supervision of the promoting officer. Either of these methods would be in harmony with the law, the rule, and the practice.

Q. Then what you had reference to when you said in your report, the test of fitness required by the rule must be made in accordance with what is quoted there, that the test of fitness must be an examination, had reference to such examination as the promoting officer might choose to make?—A. Yes, sir.

Q. How many stenographers were in the office at the time this promotion was made?—A. Five, at least.

Q. Was your personal observation of these stenographers such as to satisfy you that Mr. Bailey was a superior officer to any of them?—A. I have not taken that position.

Q. Was your personal observation of these five stenographers such as to convince you that Mr. Holtz was a better stenographer than Mr. Bailey?—A. I think I said so yesterday. Let me state, once for all, that under this language of the rule which vests the power and responsibility with the promoting officer to make promotions upon any test of fitness determined upon by him, the Civil Service Commission in the matter of Mr. Bailey's appointment made such an examination as to satisfy it that his promotion would be in conformity with law, and with the best interests of the service.

Q. That is not an answer to my question.—A. That is a statement of the fact, and the Civil Service Commission rests its responsibility, so far as I am concerned, upon that statement.

Q. There were five stenographers in the office. I ask you if your personal observation was such as to satisfy you that when Mr. Bailey was appointed to this position, with a salary of $1,800, he was a superior stenographer, or more expert than Mr. Holtz, Mr. Morgan, Mr. Williams, or Mr. Culver?

The CHAIRMAN. I think Mr. Lyman answered that fully yesterday.

Mr. BOATNER. He said there were other duties than stenographic duties. That Mr. Bailey was appointed, and while this gentleman referred to (Mr. Holtz) was probably a more rapid stenographer, he regarded the young man Mr. Bailey as competent and worthy to fill this place.

By Mr. EWART:

Q. In other words, a more competent one. I ask him if his personal observation was such as satisfied him that Mr. Bailey was a more expert stenographer than Mr. Holtz, Mr. Williams, Mr. Morgon, or Mr. Culver. He can say yes or no.—A. I have answered that several times, but I have no objection to answering it again. I think that Mr. Holtz was a more rapid stenographer than Mr. Bailey was at that time. I have no doubt on that subject.

I think it is due to myself and to the Commission—I have stated it it in part before—but yesterday I said that the Commission had five stenographers. I said also that long ago the work of the Commission became such that more than one stenographer was needed. It frequently happens that three or four are in requisition at the same time. One man can not possibly do all the work required in the commission. The stenographer who was appropriated for as such has never been employed exclusively as a stenographer, but has been assigned to other duties such as the requirements of the office demanded, The work has increased rapidly, and is of such a great variety that it has been impossible to make an accurate division of the duties—to assign one man to this particular line of work, and keep him at it. A man may be doing one work to-day, and another to-morrow, He may be doing stenographic work one day, and in entirely different kind of work another day. The pressure upon the Commission has been such that this great variety of work has been demanded of the employés, and it has been a question of judgment with the Commission, in view of the necessities of the public work, whether this man or that or the other man should do this, that, or the other kind of work. Mr. Bailey has been several years in the Commission. He has proved himself to be an exceedingly valuable clerk. He has been trusted with very responsible work in the office of the Commission. He has performed that work to the entire satisfaction of the Commission. He was, at the time this promotion was made, the senior clerk of the office, and had been for a long time. In view of all the circumstances, in view of his position in the office, in view of the work he had performed, in view of the fact that he was a stenographer, and that his appointment would satisfy the requirements of the law, and in view of every consideration of right and justice, and the interest of the public service, he was fairly and justly, in my judgment, entitled to this promotion. His promotion did not violate any law, rule, or precedent. It did not in any way do violence to the public service or the public interest. A failure to have promoted him at that time would have been, in my judgment, not only a great outrage upon him, but a detriment to the public service.

By Mr. HATTON:

Q. The appropriation act says that the clerk shall be a stenographer?—A. Yes, sir.

Q. Has the Commission at any time made any degree of rank as between the various stenographers?—A. No, sir.

Q. When Mr. Doyle was a stenographer, did his office appear as such in the report?—A. I think that might have been the case.

Q. When Mr. Morgan was a stenographer, did his name appear?—A. I think so.

Q. I think it has always been inserted, until the last report.—A. No importance was attached to that.

Q. Mr. Morgan was the stenographer at the time of the last report, was he not?—A. Yes, sir.

Q. That was a short time before Mr. Bailey had been appointed?—A. It was some time before.

By Mr. BOATNER:

Q. Was Mr. Bailey promoted by law, or by the Commission?—A. By the Commission.

Q. Did he undergo a civil service examination at any time before he was appointed?—A. He took the clerks' examination. He was appointed in the War Department, and was subsequently transferred to our Commission.

Q. I understand that he did not undergo any other examination at the time of, or after, his promotion, and the only test of fitness applied was the observation of the Commission as to his fitness and qualifications for the position?—A. I have not said that. I said that at the time of his promotion no written examination was required of him.

Q. I understood you to say just now, in answer to the question of Mr. Ewart, that you considered that the law was complied with?—A. Yes, sir.

By Mr. EWART:

Q. I asked you, in view of the fact, whether or not Mr. Bailey had a written examination with reference to this promotion, either before or after the promotion, and you said he did not.—A. I did not say that. My testimony has been to the effect that at the time he did not have such a written examination. He did have it after.

Q. How long after?—A. Some little time after this question came up.

Q. What was the result of that examination?—A. He passed the examination.

Q. As a stenographer?—A. Yes, sir.

Q. Before his promotion?—A. No, sir.

By Mr. STONE:

Q. I understood you to say yesterday that Mr. Morgan was receiving, while in the employ of the Commission, a salary of $1,800, and that he was appointed under the authority of the appropriation act. Mr. Oberly said that he was appointed official stenographer under authority of the third section of this act of January 16, 1883, known as the civil service act?—A. Yes, sir.

Q. I find on reference to that third section that the Commission has authority to employ a stenographer who shall be paid, when employed, at the rate of $1,600 a year.—A. Yes, sir.

Q. Do you say that he was appointed under authority of that act?—A. I have never seen the letter of his appointment. I was not in Washington at the time it was made, and I am in no way responsible for it.

Q. I was simply asking in order to understand whether that was a mistake, or how it was.—A. I should say that it was a mistake.

Q. Did the appropriation act authorize the appointment of an additional stenographer?—A. No, sir; I think not.

Q. There was no appropriation then for any appointment under this act?—A. Not under the terms of that act.

Q. Was there any appropriation for more than one stenographer for your Commission?—A. No, sir.

By Mr. HATTON:

Q. Do you remember, on the examination of Mr. Bailey as a stenographer, at what grade he passed ?—A. I think at the grade of 72 and a fraction.

Q. Do you remember whether it was higher or lower than the grade of the other gentlemen examined as stenographers ?—A. I do not remember the different grades. It was a higher grade than the grade attained by Mr. Holtz on his examination. It was a lower grade than was attained by some others.

Mr. EWART. As I understand it, the heads of bureaus in other Departments can make promotions from their personal observation ?

The WITNESS. They are doing it every day.

Mr. BOATNER. I would like to ask some questions as to the general scope of the civil-service law.

The CHAIRMAN. Would it not be better to postpone that until we are through with these charges ? This witness will have to be recalled.

TESTIMONY OF W. S. STURGES.

W. S. STURGES, sworn and examined.

· By Mr. EWART:

Q. Please state you name, residence, and occupation.—A. W. S. Sturges; my legal residence is New York City; I am a clerk in the office of the Adjutant-General.

Q. Were you ever in the employ of the Civil Service Commission ?— A. Yes, sir; from the 1st of August, 1888, to the 1st of February, 1890.

Q. Do you know Mr. Bailey ?—A. Quite well.

Q. At present stenographer in the Civil Service Commission ?—A. Yes, sir.

Q. What position does he hold?—A. I believe he is stenographer, and an $1,800 clerk.

Q. Did you occupy a desk in the room with him ?—A. I occupied a desk in an adjoining room for a year previous to his promotion.

Q. Did he do any stenographic work at that time ?—A. Not to my knowledge.

Q. Were you in a position to know if he had ?—A. I am quite sure of it.

Q. State if he was ever called upon to do any stenographic work of any kind.—A. Not for a year preceding his promotion.

Q. Do you know that Mr. Bailey was not called upon as a stenographer ?—A. He was not, to the best of my knowledge.

Q. You say you know he was not?—A. I had a good opportunity to know it.

Mr. ROOSEVELT. Do you know that Major Webster frequently used him as a stenographer?

The WITNESS. No, sir.

By Mr. BOATNER:

Q. If Major Webster had used him as a stenographer, you would have known it ?—A. I know that he wrote a great many letters, but I do not think that Major Webster used him as an amanuensis. He told Mr. Bailey what he wanted written.

Q. Were you ever present ?—A. After he was appointed stenographer.

Q. You say you *know* that he was not called upon to do stenographic

3117——6

work. Were you present at any time when Major Webster dictated to him?—A. No, sir.

Q. Did you occupy the same room Major Webster did?—A. I occupied the adjoining room.

Q. Are you aware that Major Webster frequently used him as an amanuensis during that period?—A. No, sir.

Q. Do you know that he frequently wrote letters for Major Webster?—A. I know that he wrote a great many letters.

Q. You say Major Webster did not dictate letters to him, but frequently told him what he wanted him to write?—A. That was my observation.

Q. Were you present on any occasion when Major Webster told him what he wanted him to write?—A. I think I have been.

Q. On how many occasions?—A. On some; I don't remember how many.

By the CHAIRMAN:

Q. Did you observe whether he was taking down notes when he wrote letters?—A. He may have taken notes, but I don't think that he took them in short-hand.

Q. You don't know whether he did or not?—A. I do not think he did.

By Mr. GREENHALGE;

Q. Where was Major Webster's room, as regards yours?—A. It was adjoining.

Q. Do you undertake to say what Major Webster and Mr. Bailey were doing when they were in an adjoining room?—A. My work was quite closely connected with theirs.

Q. How closely was it connected with theirs?—A. I had charge of all the applications and everything in reference to an examination, and Mr. Bailey had general charge of the examinations and wrote letters.

Q. You mean that you worked together in the same room?—A. I do not say that we worked in the same room,

Q. Did the work which you did in connection with the work of Major Webster and Mr. Bailey enable you to tell what they were doing, and the manner of their work, when you were in a different room?—A. I had to go into their room quite often.

Q. Do you mean to say with any distinctness that you can remember as to the employment of Mr. Bailey with the work of Major Webster—whether it was dictation, copying, or otherwise?—A. I do not think he ever copied anything for Major Webster.

By Mr. ROOSEVELT:

Q. Have you any personal feelings against Major Webster?—A. Yes, sir; I have.

Q. On what grounds?—A. I don't think he treated me fairly.

Q. Have you any feelings against Mr. Bailey?—A. None at all.

Q. You were formerly with the Commission?—A. Yes, sir.

Q. For what were you dismissed?—A. Making mistakes in marking examination papers.

Q. On the report of Major Webster to the Commission?—A. On one of his reports to the Commission.

Q. Reports which the Commission investigated?

Mr. EWART (interposing). I want to know what connection his feelings have with this matter.

Mr. ROOSEVELT. I want to show that the witness has an animus.

Mr. EWART. He has just testified that he has no feelings against Mr. Bailey.

By Mr. ROOSEVELT:

Q. Your connection with the Commission was severed in consequence of certain errors repeated on more than one occasion?—A. I do not think so. They were errors made in one set of papers.

Q. Do you not know that you were twice reported to us by Major Webster for errors committed?—A. I was reported twice.

Q. When you were first reported by Major Webster, and the matter was investigated, and we determined to remove you, you came down and entreated to be allowed to stay, did you not?—A. I did not entreat to be allowed to stay.

Q. You saw Governor Thompson, and you said that you hoped the fault would be forgiven?—A. I did not confess to any fault.

Q. You asked to be allowed to stay and see if you could not do perfectly satisfactory work?—A. Yes, sir.

Q. And about a month afterward you were again reported as doing unsatisfactory work?—A. I was transferred to the War Department on the request and recommendation of Commissioner Roosevelt.

Mr. ROOSEVELT. And we told the Secretary of War all the facts.

Mr. EWART. This is entirely irregular.

By Mr. ROOSEVELT:

Q. You were transferred to the War Department. Do you recollect coming to Govenor Thompson and myself and admitting frankly that you had committed these faults, and that you had nothing to say about it?—A. I had something to say about it.

Q. You admitted that you had made the mistakes, and you made no complaint against the justice of the action of the Commission?—A. I can not say that.

Mr. ROOSEVELT. I can.

By the CHAIRMAN:

Q. You have no recollection of that?—A. No, sir.

Mr. ROOSEVELT. And you requested that you should be given a couple of weeks to see if you could not arrange for a transfer at a lower salary.

The WITNESS. The Commission stated that I would have until the 15th of February in which to resign.

By Mr. THOMPSON:

Q. Did you not make a special request that the reasons should not be given out?—A. I did not want them to be put on the minutes until after I had been transferred.

Q. What did we say about that?—A. The last time I saw you, you said you had not come to any conclusion about it; but they were not put on the minutes.

Q. Don't you remember coming and making a request after your first offense that those reasons be not given out, for if they got out you could not get employment? You came to me and made a request, or an appeal, for mercy. Did I not say to you that it had always been my practice to help and not to hinder young men; that I could for myself, and I believed I could say for the Commission, that we would give you another trial; that I would report to them and ask that you should be allowed another trial?—A. You also told me that it was reported that the papers were three months behind. I suggested that I could not be responsible, because I had only been six weeks on the board.

Q. Do you not know that you came back to me and said that you had a sister depending upon you, and that it was important for you to have some employment, and that you would like to get transferred?—A. I told you that I would like to get transferred.

Q. Did I not say that we would be willing to exchange you? I suggested to you that possibly we could get a place in the War Department for you?—A. Yes, sir.

Q. I think I told you that I did not know the Secretary of War, and did not have much influence with him; that I felt Mr. Roosevelt would be glad to help any young man, and would probably go to the Secretary of War in your behalf?—A. Yes, sir; that he would certify that I was of good character.

By Mr. EWART:

Q. Do I understand that, after you had been given several trials in the Civil Service Commission to test your capacity, and after you had been pronounced comparatively incompetent, you were recommended by Mr. Roosevelt for a clerkship in another Department?—A. I was given several trials. They said I could not mark examination papers to their satisfaction.

Q. And a member of that Commission recommended you to a position in the War Department?—A. He recommended me to a position in the War Department, stating that it was very likely I would satisfy them. In addition to the first report, I was charged by Governor Thompson with having sneered at the Commission.

By Mr. STONE:

Q. What position did you hold?—A. A $1,600 clerkship.

Q. What were your duties as a $1,600 clerk?—A. I had charge of all the applications made by persons for examinations.

Q. Was any objection ever raised to your accuracy when you were at work as a clerk?—A. None, whatever; if so, it was never brought to my attention.

Q. What work was it which was objected to?—A. I was in charge of the clerical work from the 1st of August, 1888, to the 19th of July, 1889, when I took a vacation. I came back on the 18th of September, and I was told by Major Webster that I would not be put on again. I made five complaints to the Commissioners. The Commissioners finally assigned me to the board of examiners.

Q. You were first appointed to a clerkship?—A. Yes, sir.

Q. And you were afterwards appointed to the board of examiners. What work did you do on the board of examiners?—A. I marked papers.

Q. You graded papers?—A. Yes, sir.

Q. This, then, was the work which was not satisfactory to the Commission?—A. Yes, sir.

Q. What were the duties of an examiner?—A. The board of examiners marks all the papers for examination in the Railway Mail Service.

Q. You were appointed on the board of examiners when?—A. I was appointed on the 21st of October last.

Q. Are appointments made to that board under civil service rules?—A. The appointments are made by the Civil Service Commission.

Q. What was the salary?—A. I had the same place on the pay-roll.

Q. Sixteen hundred dollars?—A. Yes, sir.

Q. You spoke of Major Webster not treating you fairly. Was it on account of the reports made or the character of your work?—A. It was his refusal to give me regular duties for a whole month.

Q. How did you happen to get out of the place you were in at first?—A. Major Webster told me that I could not come back.

Q. How long were you on your vacation?—A. Thirty days. The morning after I came back, Major Webster came to me with some messenger work.

Q. Why did he not let you come back?—A. He never gave any reason to me.

Q. Did you complain to the Commission?—A. Yes, sir.

Q. What reason did you give?—A. I told the Commissioners that I did not care about doing that work.

Q. Why were you not permitted to come back, and what reason was assigned?—A. Major Webster never gave any reason.

Q. Did anybody?—A. I was copying this report. He said the work had never been done by a person graded as high as I was. He said my penmanship was bad, and that a $900 clerk could do my work.

The CHAIRMAN. As an examiner?

The WITNESS. My work as a clerk.

By Mr. STONE:

Q. Where did you come from when you entered the Civil Service Commission?—A. I was a clerk in the Treasury Department.

Q. And you were transferred to a $1,600 place in the Commission?—A. Yes, sir.

Q. And you held it only a few weeks?—A. I held it for eighteen months.

Q. You did not do the work of the place for eighteen months?—A. Yes, sir.

Q. Did you do the work for eighteen months before you went on the vacation?—A. I was transferred to the place in August, 1888, and I staid there until the 15th of this month.

Q. You were really removed from that position as examiner on account of incompetency?—A. The charge made was that I was careless.

Q. No fault was found with you as a clerk?—A. Not to my knowledge.

By Mr. ROOSEVELT:

Q. Your last instance of carelessness was the marking of a series of papers for printers' assistants?—A. Yes, sir.

Q. You overlooked a number of errors made in those papers?

Mr. BOATNER (interposing). If the purpose is to show the bias of the witness, I think this has gone as far as it is necessary. I do not consider it as pertinent.

The CHAIRMAN (to Mr. Roosevelt). You may ask the question.

By Mr. ROOSEVELT:

Q. I would like to prove to the satisfaction of the committee what he was dismissed for. (To the witness:) You made errors in marking these papers. Do you not remember that all those errors being in favor of the applicants, in consequence those applicants were entered on the eligible list at higher averages than they were entitled to, and they were notified of the fact that they had passed? When we came to look over those papers we found those errors, and found that those persons lowest on the list, instead of having passed, failed, and we had to notify the applicants that they had failed. This was after you had been once reported to us for removal, and your offense had been passed over by the Commission.—A. I never acknowledged that I was incompetent.   Major Webster reported that I was inefficient.

Q. Those are the facts?—A. Yes, sir.

Q. You came to me, or rather you came to Governor Thompson and he came to me, and stated that so far as he knew your past character and capacity were good; that you were careless on the Commission and that that was probably due to the fact of the circumstances connected with your appointment, which was said to be due to Mr. Edgerton, and it was alleged (with what truth I do not know) that your appointment was a piece of favoritism on the part of Mr. Edgerton; that you were, therefore, brought into continual clashings with the other members of the force.—A. I did not have any clashings with anybody except Major Webster.

Mr. EWART. After that you were recommended to the War Department?

The WITNESS. The Commission wrote to the Secretary of War about me.

Mr. ROOSEVELT. State fully why we did not want you. I did simply. as a favor to a young man and stated to the War Department the facts.

Mr. EWART. I object to this form of procedure.

By Mr. THOMPSON:

Q. You said that I charged you with sneering at the Commission?— A. Yes, sir.

Q. Think a moment; did I not say sneering at the whole civil-service law? Did I not say that the report was that you were speaking contemptuously of it?—A. You did not give me to understand so.

Q. Did I not say to you to go on and do your duty, and the Commission would forget what was past?—A. Yes, sir; I think you did.

Q. To go along and do your work?—A. Yes, sir.

By Mr. HATTON:

Q. Mr. Roosevelt wanted you to state what you were dismissed for. Were you dismissed?—A. They said they would dismiss me with two week's leave.

Q. But you were not dismissed?—A. No, sir.

TESTIMONY OF EDWIN D. BAILEY.

EDWIN D. BAILEY, sworn and examined.

By Mr. EWART:

Q. Please state your place of residence, occupation, name, etc.—A. Edwin D. Bailey. I am forty years of age. I reside in the city of Washington, and am a clerk and stenographer in the office of the Civil Service Commission.

Q. What salary do you receive?—A. Eighteen hundred dollars a year.

Q. Do you hold the position of stenographer provided for in the appropriation bill?—A. Yes, sir; clerk and stenographer.

Q. When did you commence to study stenography?—A. When I was a boy I made some progress in it, but had very little occasion to use it except in some work as a reporter for newspapers. When I was appointed to a place in the office of the Civil Service Commission, I found that my duties would be to take dictations of letters, and in view of that fact, I took a full course in stenography; employed a private teacher.

Q. When did you receive your appointment?—A. July 19, 1887.

Q. Were you appointed as a clerk?—A. Yes, sir; a clerk at $1,600 a year.

Q. Did you do any stenographic work there?—A. Yes, sir; from the very first I was required to take dictations.

Q. From the Commissioners or from the chief examiner?—A. From both. As I say, when I entered the office of the Civil Service Commission, I at once commenced the study of stenography and I continued the study which I had left off years before. I have continued it up to the present time.

Q. Would you consider yourself as an expert now?—A. It would depend on the definition of the word "expert." I do not think I could take two hundred and fifty words a minute.

Q. Could you take this testimony?—A. I did take it at the first session of the committee.

Q. Would you be willing to take it now?—A. Yes, sir; I would be willing to take it.

Q. Would you be willing to take it and turn your notes over to an expert?—A. Yes, sir.

Q. Would you take this testimony and get your notes up next morning?—A. If the committee required it, I should probably be compelled to.

Q. Would you be willing to do it?—A. I have no apprehension but what I could successfully do it. I would do the best I could. I think I could do it.

The CHAIRMAN. When were you appointed stenographer?

The WITNESS. I should say I have been stenographer of the Commission for three months. I have not refreshed my memory on that point.

By Mr. EWART:

Q. Were you examined when you were first promoted?—A. No, sir; I was not.

Q. Your promotion was made by Mr. Lyman?—A. It was made by the Commission.

Q. You afterwards passed an examination, did you not?—A. Yes, sir; I afterwards passed an examination.

Q. What was the date of that examination?—A. Probably the first or second week in January. I do not remember the date exactly.

Mr. ANDREW. How long have you been in your present position?

The WITNESS. I presume about three months. I did not fix the date.

By Mr. EWART:

Q. After receiving this appointment as stenographer, why was it necessary for you to have any examination?—A. I did not suppose it was necessary. I had fitted myself and I thought I was a competent stenographer. I did not make a request for an examination, but I remember expressing to one of the Commissioners a wish that I had been examined before I was appointed in order to quiet the apprehensions of certain gentlemen.

Q. Did you first call the attention of the Commissioners to the fact that you desired to stand an examination, or did the Commissioners first call your attention to it?—A. I first suggested it to one of the Commission. I have said that on one occasion I said to one of the Commissioners that I regretted that I had not been examined.

Q. To which one of the Commissioners?—A. Mr. Lyman.

Q. Did Mr. Lyman advise you to stand this examination?—A. No, sir, I think not.

Q. Did you request him to fix a date for an examination?—A. No, sir, I did not.

Q. How was the matter brought about?—A. I was examined before the Commission. I knew nothing about the discussions of the Commission on the matter.

Q. How did you come to decide to stand this examination?—A. I did not decide to stand the examination. If you will permit me, I will state the facts. I was examined before the Commission sometime after I had expressed this desire to be examined. No reasons were given me why I was to be examined. I was simply asked to come before the Commission and stand an examination. I did so and they dictated the matter to me, and I sat there and wrote out in long hand what they had given me, and I passed an examination. I do not know what the reasons for it were. I do not know whether they expressed a wish in regard to it.

By Mr. STONE:

Q. Who graded ·that examination?—A. I have understood that a member of the board of stenography and typewriting, Mr. Shively, graded my papers. I have never seen the papers and merely know from hearsay that Mr. Shively marked them.

Q. Since you passed that examination, have you been doing the work in the office as a stenographer?—A. My work has not been very materially changed. Really I was correspondence clerk. I was continued in that position with some miscellaneous duties in addition. I have one class of work which I did not have before. Some of the Commissioners had given me regularly their official correspondence, and I have done other work. I could not do it all, as my other duties would not permit, and there are several stenographers in the Commission. One takes the minutes of the board, and occasionally some are sent out with investigating committees. So far as the work of the Commission is concerned, I do not know that I did as much as any other one man.

Q. Have you ever been out with any of these investigating committees?—A. No, sir. Do you mean out as a stenographer?

Q. Yes.—A. No, sir; I have not. My duties were of such a character that it was very difficult for me to be away constantly.

Q. How long have you known Mr. Holtz?—A. I think I have known him ever since he came upon the Commission. It is probably over two years.

Q. Would you consider him an expert stenographer?—A. I should want to have the word "expert" defined.

Mr. LIND. The law and regulations of the Commission do not require an expert, and I think this is wholly immaterial.

Mr. EWART. All I want to know of this witness is, does he consider himself as good a stenographer as either Mr. Holtz, Mr. Williams, or Mr. Culver?

The WITNESS. I have never had any opportunity of comparing my work with theirs. I have done all I was required to do.

Mr. GREENHALGE. Are you any relation to any member of the Commission?—A. No, sir; I was a stranger to the Commission when I took my first examination.

By Mr. THOMPSON:

Q. Have you not duties in addition to that of stenographic work?—A. I have.

Q. In the absence of Major Webster are you not the acting chief?—A. Yes, sir.

Q. And when he is present you are his principal assistant?—A. Yes, sir.

Q. Did you hear Mr. Morgan's testimony yesterday?—A. No, sir, I did not.

Q. I will ask you if Mr. Morgan ever told you he hoped that you would get the promotion to the place of stenographer in the Commission? I will ask you to state whether Mr. Morgan ever said that to you?—A. In answer to that I would like to state the circumstances. Mr. Morgan came to me one day ——

Mr. STONE. This is that irregular sort of testimony on which I think the rule ought to be enforced. The question was asked Mr. Morgan if, about the date of this appointment, in one of the rooms occupied by the Commission or its clerks, Mr. Morgan said to you that he hoped that you would obtain this appointment, or words in substance.

The WITNESS. He did.

Mr. STONE. I think that ends it.

Mr. THOMPSON. I have two witnesses on that point. One of them is sick.

Mr. HATTON. I would like permission to ask Mr. Bailey one question. Mr. Bailey has been asked in regard to what Morgan said to him, and I want to ask Mr. Bailey one question in regard to what he said to Morgan.

The WITNESS. Would it be fair to state all the circumstances?

The CHAIRMAN. Let the question be asked.

By Mr. HATTON:

Q. Do you remember at any time that Mr. Morgan said he was going to leave the Commission, and you said that you were very sorry and that he had been badly treated? And did you state to him, "This is our hash and we must have charge of the platter?"—A. I remember Mr. Morgan saying that he believed he had been unfairly treated, and I remember saying to him that in my opinion he had not been, and when he stated to me certain facts which he thought were in the nature of grievances, I endeavored to make an explanation of those facts and to show that there was no intentional slight. I said I was sorry he was going. I presume I said it. I had the kindest feelings toward Mr. Morgan, and feeling so, I presume I said this.

Q. Do you remember saying that the reason was that he was a Democrat?—A. I do not think the word "Democrat" was used. I do not think the question of politics was used.

Q. He is a Democrat?—A. I have heard so.

Q. He is a friend of ex-Commissioner Oberly?—A. Yes, sir. I would not be too certain as to what I did say to him. I remember that we talked on that subject. I do not think I could have said it.

Q. Did you say, "This is our hash and the present Commissioners must have charge of the platter?"—A. No, sir; I am not in the habit of talking about hash and platters, and had nothing of that sort to say.

Q. You did not say that?—A. No, sir.

Q. Are you engaged in any business during office hours outside of your duties with the Commission?—A. No, sir, no other business.

TESTIMONY OF THEODORE ROOSEVELT—Recalled.

THEODORE ROOSEVELT recalled.

Mr. EWART. Before this witness goes on with his testimony I desire to state here that I want the rule strictly enforced. I would be glad to hear anything Mr. Roosevelt has to testify to, but anything in the way of a statement is entirely irregular.

The WITNESS. I am pleased to hear that the rule is to be enforced.

By the CHAIRMAN:

Q.—It has been stated that you discharged or were about to discharge a clerk in your Commission by the name of Sturges, and that you afterwards obtained for him a transfer to the War Department. Will you please state how you came to make that recommendation?—A. Mr. Sturges had come to me two or three times during last summer to explain that there was a prejudice against him in the Commission. On the other hand, I had heard from at least four or five employés of the Commission that he was doing bad work in the Commission. He was reported to us twice by Major Webster for dismissal for bad work. The first time he came it was to Governor Thompson, and Governor Thompson came to me. He came to Governor Thompson and spoke in a very humble manner, stating that he was just starting in life, and that it would give him a black eye if he were turned out of the Commission. He admitted that we were justified in our action, but asked that we should have mercy on him. At the request of Governor Thompson I agreed that Sturges should be continued a month longer. We had nothing against his capacity, nothing against his character or his habits. I, for one, and I believe the rest of the Commission felt the same way, thought that he was careless, and that while holding this place he was not doing his work. The case was again brought to our attention. We found that even after our last warning to him another complaint came from Mr. Webster. His mother had been to see me to get me interested in his behalf. I told him that he would have to go. He then came to Governor Thompson, and Governor Thompson spoke to me and said that Sturges had got down on his marrow-bones and hoped that he would not be dismissed without a chance to be transferred, and Governor Thompson said he hoped that no obstacle would be placed in his way. I concluded that Mr. Sturges was a round peg in a square hole. I thought that he might do good work in some other office. Mr. Morgan does good work in the mint, but he certainly was not a satisfactory clerk to the Commission, although personally I always got along with him. Mr. Morgan did not do good work on our Commission. Governor Thompson came to me and stated that Sturges had arranged for a transfer, and wanted to know would I be willing to go to the Secretary of War, explain this to the Secretary and see if they would be willing to take him on my statement. I went there. I did not see the Secretary of War, but I saw a gentleman in the Adjutant-General's office. I stated what the case was. They said they would be perfectly willing to give him a trial. Sturges was exchanged for a man who was detailed as a stenographer in our office.

By Mr. STONE:

Q. Is it the custom of the Commission to visit the Departments with the view of having persons appointed, or see that they have preferences in the matters of transfers, or anything of that sort?—A. In the case of our own employés it is an eminently proper thing, and we always do it.

Q. If this man Sturges had been employed in some other Bureau or Department and was unsatisfactory there, would you consider it a proper thing to go to a different Department and ask that he might be transferred to the Department?—A. No, sir.

Q. Then you make a difference where the employés of your Commission are concerned?—A. Yes, sir; our Commissioners are the only men who can speak for them.

Mr. GREENHALGE. Is there any waiver of examination upon a promotion or transfer to another Department?—A. No, sir; this was a perfectly regular transfer.

By Mr. STONE:

Q. The transfer was regular, but what I was trying to get at was the practice of the Commission in soliciting departmental officers.—A. I will give you a statement on that subject. We have detailed to our Department a number of men from the boards of examiners in the different Departments. They frequently come to me to aid them. In consequence of being detailed from the other Departments they are losing their chances of promotion, especially in the Post-Office Department and the Pension Bureau. If our Commission did not go and speak for those clerks we would be basely ungrateful to them.

Q. I am not criticising your action. I am only inquiring as to the system.—A. That has been the practice in the past and will be in the future.

By the CHAIRMAN:

Q. The fact in this case is that the Commission thought that Mr. Sturges was a competent and efficient clerk as a clerk, but not a man qualified to work as an examiner in your Commission, and therefore they recommended this transfer?—A. That is precisely the case. Those are the terms of our letter. The letter stated he was capable, of good habits and of good character. I think those are the three things mentioned.

By Mr. STONE:

Q. If he was not competent as a clerk in your Commission, upon what theory would you recommend him to the Adjutant-General's office?—A. Because I think in our Commission Mr. Sturges labored under the disadvantage of having been a great protégé of a former Commissioner. It was currently reported that he got his place through favoritism, and he was all the time thinking that he was being slighted. Complaints were made to us by Major Webster that he would smoke and read during office hours, and I thought myself and I believe I expressed that opinion to Governor Thompson, that it was entirely due to his being disgruntled with the Commission. I thought he was a round peg in a square hole.

Q. All this was done out of the purest kindness?—A. It was done out of the purest kindness to Mr. Sturges.

Q. Without reference to his qualifications or efficiency?—A. With absolute reference to his qualifications and efficiency; with direct and studied reference to it.

Q. I want you to state whether or not you said that Sturges had been guilty of serious and gross irregularities?—A. I answer that question by saying that I can not recollect precisely what I stated. I can not answer that yes or no; I do not recollect it. I told him that Sturges was not satisfactory to us. I told him the reason he was unsatisfactory to us I believed to be due to exceptional circumstances connected with his position in the Commission; that it was currently believed his appointment was due to the favoritism of Mr. Edgerton, and that it impaired his service with us; that he was no longer useful to us, but I did not think it would interfere with his being useful in the War Department.

I would like to make a brief statement in reference to Mr. Bailey. We have no official stenographer at present. There was one appointed by the old provisions of the appropriation act for the Civil Service Commission. That has been dropped by Congress. Congress now appropriates for eleven clerks and messengers, and makes the stipulation that at least one of those shall be a stenographer; one of the fourth-class clerks shall be a stenographer. As a matter of fact we have three stenographers. At the time of Mr. Bailey's promotion I was away, but I concurred in it fully. We had at the Commission at that time, as far as I know, only three men able to do stenographic work. I had seen Mr. Bailey employed by Major Webster doing stenographic work. Mr. Swank did the bulk of the work, and he is a $900 clerk. I have no means of knowing which of the stenographers is the most efficient. I should say that Mr. Swank is, merely because he has been doing the bulk of the work. I believe Mr. Holtz is a better stenographer than Mr. Bailey. We chose him (Bailey) with reference to his efficiency as a clerk and stenographer, and not purely with reference to his efficiency as a stenographer alone.

Since I have been on the Commission we have tried always to make promotions from grade to grade. We have eleven employés and seven grades.' Unless there was a good reason for it, we would object to jumping a grade. We would object to jumping a $1,600 man over an $1,800 man. If we considered purely the question of stenography, we might have promoted the man at $900 over the head of all the others to the $1,800 place. Mr. Swank is an excellent man. He is well fitted for his position, but he was not the best fitted man for Mr. Bailey's position at all. What we wanted was a clerk and stenographer combined, and it was my belief that it would have been a great injustice to have passed over Mr. Bailey and taken Mr. Holtz from a $1,400 place and given him the $1,800 position over Mr. Bailey. Mr. Bailey was doing a higher grade of work, and had been longer on the force. We have always striven to make promotions according to grade. It is not always practicable to do that. No examination for promotion was required under the law. Now we certify a clerk. He can be appointed to a $1,400, a $1,600, or an $1,800 position. We can appoint him to an $1,800 position right away. There is no rule of law preventing that. A written examination for passing from one grade to another is not required, except at the War Department, where that system has uniformly been tried, and I think it is a failure. That is my private opinion.

In an office like our office with seven grades, where three are filled by only one man and the other four by two each, doing entirely different kinds of work, any competitive system is out of the question. It is like a county fair; you can not make a competition between a race-horse and a short-horn bull, as no common test will not apply. You can have a test for a race-horse and a test for a short-horn bull. Mr. Bailey, as I say, was promoted to this position in my absence. When I came back I was informed of his promotion, and agreed to it. I had seen that he was a stenographer. I had never looked at his examination papers; nor had I looked at those of Mr. Holtz and Mr. Swank. I had taken it for granted that he had passed an examination. Later it was called to my attention—about three months afterwards (I think by Governor Thompson, but I may be in error)—that Mr. Bailey was charged with not being a stenographer. I then made some investigation, and I heard that Mr. Morgan had told Governor Thompson that Mr. Bailey was not a stenographer. Several pieces had appeared in the papers about that time in reference to the Civil Service Commission. I then went to Mr. Lyman and asked him if Mr. Bailey had taken a stenographic examination. I said that I thought we ought to have a man as stenographer who could pass an examination. That was a personal opinion of mine. I think that was the opinion of the other Commissioners also. We talked the matter over, and we agreed that Mr. Bailey should be tested as a stenographer, and I said on my own responsibility I did not know how the other members felt, that I would not be willing to keep a man who could not pass an examination.

Accordingly, we examined Mr. Bailey, Governor Thompson reading in the regular form one paragraph of the stenographic examination and Mr. Lyman reading the next paragraph. We examined him and sent the paper to the ordinary board of markers. They marked the papers and it was found that he passed at 73. Mr. Holtz's grade was 67. Mr. Swank's (the $900 clerk) was 81. It would have been a self-evident absurdity to have given Mr. Holtz the position which Mr. Bailey now holds. Mr. Bailey holds the highest and most important position in our Bureau. Since he passed this examination all of my stenographic work has been given to Mr. Bailey. I have written some letters to the chairman of this committee; I have written some to Mr. Boatner and some to most of the members within the last two months, and those which do not appear in my own handwriting have been written by Mr. Bailey. Every letter in a different handwriting from the signature has been the writing of Mr. Bailey. He occupies the most important position of any member of our force. As an $1,800 clerk, he must be a stenographer. He has been employed for two months doing my work, and I submit that that is more than complying with the requirements of the law.

By Mr. LIND:

Q. Do you think that your personal appeal to the officer in the War Department had the effect of securing this transfer in behalf of Mr. Sturges?—A. Yes, sir; because if we had simply declined to allow him to be transferred, of course he could not have been.

By Mr. GREENHALGE:

Q. The personal appeal was irrespective of competency?—A. Oh, no.

TESTIMONY OF HON. HUGH S. THOMPSON—Recalled.

Hon. HUGH S. THOMPSON, recalled and further examined.

Mr. THOMPSON. Mr. Chairman, I shall detain the committee but a moment, for I shall be brief. In regard to the question that I asked Mr. Sturges, whether or not he was charged with sneering at the Commission, I have no doubt that he meant to say what the facts were; but he is mistaken. When an order was made to dismiss Mr. Sturgis, in January, he came to me and made an appeal for mercy, and I said to him, "Sturges, I have looked into this matter, and I am satisfied that you are not in sympathy at all with this Commission; that you do not believe in the civil service law; and I believe, therefore, that you are not discharging the duties of your place, except in a perfunctory way." I had a great many employés under me in the Treasury (as it will be remembered that I was Assistant Secretary of the Treasury), and I had had some experience in these matters. In the Treasury I promoted some clerks and reduced others. I told Mr. Sturges I am satisfied that you have the capacity to go on with this work, but I believe the reason you are not succeeding is that you are not in sympathy with your work. I advise you to go to work like a man. If you have made yourself objectionable to your fellow-clerks, try to overcome those troubles. I told him that if he would go ahead and do his work, we would give him another trial. He assurred me that there would be no further trouble.

By Mr. HOPKINS :

Q. When was this talk with Sturges ?—A. It was in January. We thought we could not retain him. I got a letter from a friend of mine, a Democrat and a general in the late war, making an appeal for Sturges. I answered that letter, but kept no copy of the reply. I remember stating that Sturges was an unsatisfactory clerk. He had been appointed by Mr. Edgerton, and that after Mr. Edgerton left he seemed to be more careless than ever. I remember that I was a little influenced by this feeling. You may remember that Mr. Cleveland appointed me at that time. I was not confirmed by the Senate, and President Harrison appointed me afterwards. It will be remembered that Mr. Edgerton had published some strictures against me, and certainly he had said some very harsh things about President Cleveland. I think that feeling caused me to lean back a little bit. I did not want to feel in my own conscience that I had been harsh to the friend of a man who had been unfriendly to me. That was one reason why I asked the Commission to give Mr. Sturges this trial.

My colleague reminds me that I felt exceedingly sorry for the young man. I said that Sturges had "come down off his high horse." He claimed that he was there as a law clerk, and that he had passed a law examination. His idea was that he was to write legal opinions for the Commission. I did not think that the Commission needed clerks for that purpose. We did not need any legal opinions anyhow. Whenever we wanted a legal opinion we sent the case to the Attorney-General for his opinion. We did not really need a law clerk. When Mr. Sturges came to me the last time, I think he said that he had no property in the world, and that if he were dismissed from the Commission it would be a "black eye." With that view, he asked to be transferred. We concluded that we would ask for a transfer for him, as we thought he might do his work well in other Departments. I told him that I had no influence with this administration, and I knew but one or two members of the Cabinet. I said that Mr. Roosevelt was a generous, magnanimous man, and I had no doubt that he would speak to the Secretary of War in his behalf. We selected that place because we had a clerk from the War Department detailed to do our work, and he was satisfactory, and we wanted to get that man on our roll. In the Treasury Department I had repeatedly reduced men for similar offenses. One of the last cases I had in the Treasury was to reduce a clerk who was reported to me for neglect of duty and inefficiency. I reduced a $1,600 man to a thousand-dollar place, and he was turned out soon after I left, showing that I was right, and that I did not go quite far enough. I did not want to do any harm to any man.

By Mr. HATTON :

Q. Your impression was that Sturges was a favorite of Mr. Edgerton ?—A. My impression was that he had become soured on the Commission. He would smoke and read papers during office hours and was not satisfactory.

Q. But he was a protégé of Mr. Edgerton?—A. He was a protégé and personal friend of Mr. Edgerton. I do not mean to charge anything improper in his appointment.

By Mr. BOATNER:

Q. You heard the statement of Mr. Roosevelt this morning? Do you differ with him as to the objects and purposes of the Commission in the action he took with reference to Mr. Sturges?—A. No, sir.

By Mr. EWART:

Q. How is it that you did not assign him to a clerkship in the Civil Service Commission?—A. We had no strictly clerical service to which we could assign him.

Q. Could you not assign him to the place of a copyist or some other position in your Bureau?—A. He had been tried in two or three places and had not succeeded. Mr. Sturges is a man of inaccurate mind.

By Mr. BOATNER:

Q. Do you think a man of inaccurate mind can be a good lawyer?—A. He claimed to be a pretty good lawyer, and I thought it possible that the War Department might use him in preliminary examinations of legal questions. I think probably he could examine some character of claims that they have. I think Sturges could make a preliminary report on questions of law, but I would not trust him to make a final report on anything.

By Mr. EWART:

Q. You would not trust him to do any of the work on your Commission?—A. No, sir; not as it is now constituted. On account of the great variety of work that we have, we have to arrange the duties of the different clerks, and he could not perform the services of any one of them.

By Mr. LIND:

Q. It has been stated that he was a poor penman.—A. I do not know as to that.

Mr. ROOSEVELT. When we recommended Sturges to the War Department, we did so on a fair statement of his case, and asked him to give him a trial.

Mr. THOMPSON. I think it was to General McKeever, or a clerk in his department, and it was upon a full and frank statement. He did not go there with a clean bill of health. If we had had a lower place in our force, I do not know but that I would have been willing to have reduced him and given him another trial there.

By Mr. BOATNER:

Q. He does not seem to have reciprocated your kindness?—A. I was surprised myself when I heard what he said. The clerk with whom he exchanged was Mr. Hoyt. Mr. Hoyt came to me and said, "Sturges wants me to make an exchange with him, and I said to him I will make this exchange if you will keep your mouth shut." I said, "He can state anything he knows; our record is perfectly clear. If you choose, you can exchange with him, but let him talk all he wants to. Our record will show whether we are right or not, and make no compact with him. We do not want to drive him from employment."

When the vacancy to which Mr. Bailey was appointed occurred, Mr. Roosevelt was absent from the city. I did not know that the appropriation bill specified that our $1,800 clerk should be a stenographer. I had read the whole law carefully. I must say I have never read an appropriation act in Congress, except so far as it affected my duties. I did not know that there was anything in the appropriation act which required that the place should be held by a stenographer. Mr. Lyman is clear in his recollection of that matter, and I am equally clear in my own recollection. I had a conversation with Mr. Morgan and he surprised me very much in the remark which he made about Mr. Bailey. He said that he did not think Mr. Bailey could write fifty words a minute. I knew that any man who could not write fifty words a minute was not a good stenographer. I said, " I, for one, am not willing to have a man hold the place unless he complies with the spirit of the law." I thought that we ought to examine him, and if he failed we ought to give the place to somebody else. Accordingly, we ordered Mr. Bailey to stand an examination. He did stand an examination and the board of examiners took Bailey's papers. They did not have any means of knowing whose papers they were, and could not possibly know whose papers they were marking. They were not in the Commission, but the papers were sent just as any other papers are, and they reported upon them. Their report satisfied me that Mr. Morgan's opinion as to Mr. Bailey's qualifications was worthless. The stenographic examiners of the Commission testified that Mr. Bailey was a stenographer.

By Mr. EWART :

Q. Do I understand you to say that the reason why you subjected Mr. Bailey to this examination was that there was doubt in your mind as to whether or not Commissioner Lyman had a right to promote him ?— A. No, sir; I did not know that the appropriation bill called for a stenographer until late in December. One day in talking with Mr. Doyle, the secretary of the Commission, he mentioned the fact that the appropriation act required that our $1,800 man should be a stenographer. I said, " I am surprised at that." Mr. Lyman said that he had called my attention to it at the time. I was surprised when Mr. Doyle told me. I was satisfied I had not known of it. Mr. Morgan said Mr. Bailey was not a stenographer. I regarded Mr. Morgan, and I think his reputation was that of being a good stenographer. When he announced this opinion in regard to Mr. Bailey I was astonished, and I determined to see whether it was so. If I had found that Mr. Bailey was not a stenographer I would have opposed his retention and would have voted to put somebody else in.

Q. What is your construction of this rule which prescribes how appointments can be made for promotion?—A. During the three years that I had special charge of appointments, promotions, and dismissals in the Treasury Department, I presumed that I had a right to make them without examination. I did not make them without examination, and could recall where a man of very great influence came to me and appealed to me not to require certain persons to stand examinations. I did not do it because I did not intend to have any special pressure brought about such matters.

Q. Then in your opinion you thought an examination ought to be held ?—A. I think it is expedient in a place like the Treasury Department, where they have so many clerks. I remember one instance, the case of a lady—I suppose there was not another person in the entire country who could do what she could. I knew that an ordinary examination could not test her fitness, and I allowed her a special examination. My construction of the law is that it was within the discretion of the head of the Department to say what the examination should be, and whether there should be any at all. He is the sole judge of that.

By Mr. HATTON:

Q. Were you in the city when Mr. Bailey was promoted?—A. Yes, sir; and consented to it.

Q. Had you any knowledge at the time that he was a stenographer?—A. I was not aware the law required that he should be a stenographer. This clause of the appropriation act I did not know about.

Q. Do you know whether he was promoted as a stenographer or a clerk?—A. I thought he was promoted as a clerk. I thought we were following the precedent. I did not know what the law was about it at the time, and I want to do my colleague justice. Mr. Lyman insists that he told me so. I do not contradict him on that point. The first person that ever I remember speaking to me about it, and making any impression on my mind, was Mr. Doyle.

Q. To whom were these papers referred?—A. The regular board of examiners. They are not clerks of the Commission, but outsiders.

Q. How are those examinations conducted?—A. Anybody about the office may read the dictation exercises. The result is entered upon the report. Then the report is sent to this stenographic board and marked, without their knowing whose papers they are marking.

Mr. EWART. We would prefer not to go on with this charge until we get certain examination papers of T. E. Mitchell.

The CHAIRMAN. Mr. Mitchell's papers are here.

Mr. EWART. I would like very much to have an opportunity to examine into them somewhat before we put Mr. Mitchell on the stand.

TESTIMONY OF H. T. HOLTZ.

H. T. HOLTZ, sworn and examined.

By Mr. THOMPSON:

Q. You are a clerk of the Civil Service Commission?—A. Yes, sir.

Q. What salary do you receive?—A. One thousand six hundred dollars.

Q. What salary did you get when Mr. Bailey was promoted?—A. One thousand four hundred dollars.

Q. Did Mr. Morgan ever say to you that you ought to have the promotion to this $1,800 place?—A. Yes, sir.

By Mr. EWART:

Q. When did that conversation occur, and where?—A. It was last August, or September, when Mr. Roosevelt was out of the city. It was the latter part of August or the first part of September.

By Mr. ROOSEVELT:

Q. Did you ever tell Mr. Morgan that Mr. Bailey was not a stenographer?—A. No, sir.

Mr. HATTON (to Mr. Thompson). Is this [indicating] the regular form of the examination for stenographers?

Mr. THOMPSON. Yes, sir.

Mr. HATTON. Is this the form which was always used?

Mr. THOMPSON. That I can not tell you; I am not present at examinations.

Mr. HATTON. Were these the same dictations that Mr. Bailey was examined upon?

Mr. THOMPSON. Those are the papers he was examined upon.

3117——7

Mr. STONE (to Mr. Thompson). I observe, in looking over these papers, that the dictations given Mr. Bailey were all made from this paper?
Mr. THOMPSON. Yes, sir.
Mr. STONE. Were these read to him by some member of the Commission?
Mr. THOMPSON. Yes, sir; and he wrote them out.
Mr. STONE. Has he been in the habit of dictating from those papers?
Mr. THOMPSON. I do not know.
Mr. STONE. Was he familiar with them?
Mr. THOMPSON. I should say not. He could not have been familiar with them, I think. A man can not take dictation from memory, because he has to follow the words. Mr. Bailey did not know what he was going to be examined upon. You will see yourself that he could not take stenography from memory. Whether he had ever seen the papers or not I do not know. He may have seen them, and he may not have seen them.

FRIDAY, *February* 28, 1890.

TESTIMONY OF HUGH S. THOMPSON—Continued.

Mr. THOMPSON. Mr. Chairman and gentlemen of the committee, I desire to make a statement in regard to some portion of my testimony on yesterday which seems to have been either misunderstood or misrepresented. I distinctly intended to say, and I thought I did say, that there was nothing wrong in Mr. Sturges's transfer to the Civil Service Commission. I never meant to charge that Mr. Sturges has gotten there improperly or that Mr. Edgerton had done anything improper. My understanding was that Mr. Sturges passed the civil service examination at a high grade, and was appointed to one Department, I am not sure which, and transferred to another Department. I have always understood he was a close personal friend of Mr. Edgerton, and that on Mr. Edgerton's leaving the Commission he recommended him, and I never supposed for a moment there was any irregularity so far as Mr. Edgerton's conduct was concerned, and I certainly did not mean to charge it. My own opinion about Mr. Sturges was that in a large office like the War Office, where he would have a chief of division over him to watch the work, he might be made a useful clerk, but I did not think he could be made a useful clerk in our office, a small office where we did not have men enough to correct his mistakes.

Now on another point. A gentleman stated to me that he understood me as using the word " influence" yesterday in the sense of political influence. Now, if the committee will remember, this was simply an exchange of clerks. I stated to Mr. Roosevelt that I did not know the Secretary of War, and I thought it would be better for him to see the Secretary of War, as I, not knowing him, would not receive the consideration which he would receive, from the fact that he knew him very well. If it had been the Treasury Department I am free to say I would have gone myself; I would have gone to see Mr. Windom at his request. He was with daily intercourse with him on important matters, and in a matter not referring to politics I believed those gentlemen would give him their ordinary consideration, and in the case of a transfer to the Treasury I probably should have gone to Mr. Windom and he would have given me the same respectful consideration.

Mr. STONE. The expression used by Governor Thompson, as I remember, was that he said to Mr. Sturges that he "had no influence with this administration."—A. Perhaps I used that expression with the administration generally. The only member of the Cabinet I know is Mr. Windom. I have been introduced to the Attorney-General and Postmaster-General. I would not know Secretary Tracy or Secretary Noble if I saw him. That is, I have been introduced to Mr. Blaine, but I meant I have no personal relations with the Department that would give me consideration at the Department. At the Treasury Department I would be treated with consideration because I am known, but at the War Department I did not know that I would, because I am not personally known.

Now, I want to say directly on that line. In the Sturges matter I want to say this. Hoyt, who was a clerk in the War Department, assigned to the Commission, agreed to make an exchange with Mr. Sturges if it could be agreed upon—I think Mr. Sturgis had some friends there, but I do not know that; but they were willing to make the exchange. Hoyt subsequently handed me a production to be used, stating he was a good clerk and efficient, and had done satisfactory work. I never used that; ignored it; but I wrote and found, yesterday, the Secretary had kept the original which was sent to the Secretary of War. This is a copy of the original letter:

UNITED STATES CIVIL SERVICE COMMISSION, *February 8, 1890.*

The requests for the transfers of G. B. Hoyt and W. S. Sturges are approved and respectfully forwarded to the Secretary or War. Mr. Sturges entered the service under civil-service rules, attaining a high mark at his entrance examination. He is a young man of good habits, character, and capacity. The Commission desires that these transfers be made for the reason that Mr. Hoyt is specially qualified for the duties to which the Commission proposes to assign him, and also for the reasons given orally by Commissioner Roosevelt to General McKeever and Mr. Tweedale. If these transfers are approved by the Secretary of War the Commission requests that they be made to take effect on the 15th instant.

CHAS. LYMAN,
President.

I say, in addition, so far as the action of the Commission was concerned, we did not intend to bring it out, but in his testimony he made such an unfavorable impression upon me after he had gone upon the witness stand, that I turned to Mr. Roosevelt and said to him we had better bring out the whole thing. It was our intention to give him an opportunity to tell the whole story; we had nothing to conceal. He anticipated the very question which we wanted to show, the consideration with which he had been treated. Some persons may think, Mr. Chairman, that I for my part made a mistake in my action toward Sturges. I do not think so, and I never thought so, and whatever errors I may have committed in public life or private life, this is one thing I am perfectly willing to stand by, and I hope no more serious charge can be made against me than that I listened to the earnest request from a young man and I tried to help him when in this difficulty.

By Mr. HATTON:

Q. In that transfer of Sturges to the War Department as originally intended, would it not promote somebody on the eligible list to have done so?—A. Oh, yes.

Q. You referred to the Secretary of the Treasury in your testimony on yesterday and you stated you never made a removal for political reasons?—A. I did not say that.

Q. I understood you to say so.—A. That is true, but I did not say it; I never made a removal for political reasons. I am perfectly willing to say I made a good many and a good many reductions. If that case of Sturges had occurred in the Treasury Department I would have reduced him. I have reduced men in the Treasury Department for just such reasons. I would have reduced him in the Civil Service Commission but the fact was Sturges was not useful, he made mistakes and a lot of trouble and we had not force to correct his mistakes. I never regarded them as offenses of moral character because I thought he was under such influences as rendered him absolutely useless. I thought his neglect of duty was rather due to his mental condition than to any deliberate purpose to do any wrong.

Q. Of course you have made appointments for political reasons ?—A. Very many, but I never made any in the classified service. Outside of the classified service I made appointments myself for political reasons. Let me explain, I made appointments when Democratic Senators and members came to me with proper representations in regard to a man outside of the classified service. I do not remember that I have, I can not say I have appointed Republicans, but I have promoted them. I can grant that. I never was asked by a Republican to make an appointment.

Q. Did you promote any Republican without an examination ?—A. No, sir; never without an examination. There were two cases in which I waived them. One I referred to yesterday was the case of a lady who was an expert in replacing mutilated bills. The other was a case of a young lady who was deaf and dumb and the examination was waived. She was known to be a bright girl who graduated at the institute of Washington. The examination was modified in her case so as to meet her infirmity.

Q. When a clerk is transferred from one department to the other in the classified service, does it require an examination ?—A. If not examined before. For a transfer there is an examination made; for a promotion there is another examination made.

By Mr. STONE:

Q. The impression you made on my mind yesterday was different from that as made in your statement this morning. I will say this, I assumed from your observations yesterday the inference that Mr. Roosevelt was requested to see the Secretary of War because he was supposed to have influence with the administration. I presume it was personal influence ?—A. 1 never meant political influence.

Q. You never meant any thing of that sort ?—A. I meant he had personal influence with members of the Cabinet because he knew them.

Q. I simply wanted to understand distinctly.—A. I repeat, gentlemen, what I stated just now, that if it had been the Secretary of the Treasury I would have gone in person. I would have asked it on reasonable personal influence, but I would not have asked it on account of political influence. I did not refer to politics at all, it was simply a question of exchange of clerks and Mr. Roosevelt being well known to the Secretary of War could go to see him and have a personal explanation about the matter. It was for no other reason——

Q. That was the question in your mind ?—A. I meant to say his personal relations with the administration enable him to reach members of the Cabinet in a way which I could not do. I did not care to go to the War Office and sit for half an hour in the anteroom waiting my turn, when I knew Mr. Roosevelt would be admitted at once or as soon as the Secretary could see him, on account of his personal relations with him. I did not know him at all and Mr. Roosevelt knew him very well. I did not know the Secretary at all.

Now, sir, before I leave the stand, I want to say in reply to the question that Mr. Hatton asked just now whether I ever made appointments for political reasons, I will state that I have no recollection that any Republican ever asked me to make an appointment. I have several times been asked by Republicans to consider cases of promotion, a thing which anybody had a perfect right to ask me and to say, "Such and such a person is up here for promotion and I would like for you to consider it favorably." I have always replied and stated that he or she must stand an examination and that we could not settle it until the examination was taken. Now, as to the matter about politics, I am a good deal of a partisan myself, but I have never appointed a man simply because Senators and members of Congress said he was a Democrat, though I knew perfectly well when Democratic Senators and Representatives recommended a man for appointment they recommended him because he belonged to the party. If they did not I took it for granted more or less. Outside of the classified service I do not recollect that I ever appointed a Republican to office. I am quite sure I never have. Possibly in minor appointments like messengers or assistant messengers I may have done so, but I know in a high office like a chief of a division or places above the classified service I could make affidavit that I never appointed any one but a Democrat.

Q. You do right about that. I just wanted to ask this question. You said you never made a promotion without an examination?—A. No, sir.

Q. Why did you insist upon the examination?—A. Because, as I recollect, there were fifteen to eighteen hundred people in the Treasury Department, and it was impossible for me to know the fitness of all these men.

Q. Because the civil service law required the examination?—A. No; because I thought the examination was the best test for promotion where there were so many clerks. Mr. Fairchild never interfered in these things much at all; he never knew that appointments were made. Sometimes I would tell him about these matters, but he turned them over to me almost entirely. I could not possibly know all these clerks, as I had an immense amount of work to do. I sometimes signed fifteen hundred papers a day—twelve to fifteen hundred a day. I had a great many duties to perform. Mr. Fairchild was absent a great deal and I would be Acting Secretary, and it would be impossible for me to investigate all the clerks and to know anything about the merits of those people—of this man and that man. I could not always trust to the judgment of my subordinates, and when they recommended a man or woman I always insisted upon an examination, and, so far as I can recollect now, I never waived any examination except in two cases. One was the special case of a woman—I do not know her name, I never saw her in my life—which case I have stated here before, where I ordered her to be examined on her work. The other case was that of a girl who was deaf and dumb, appointed in the Treasury, whose knowledge of mathematics was limited.

You gentlemen know that it is very difficult to teach mathematics to deaf-mutes. The work she had to perform was not mathematical, and to have given her a rigid examination in that might have excluded her. So I may say I never promoted clerks without an examination at all, except in these two cases.

By Mr. LIND:

Q. While we are on this subject. While you had charge of appointments to the Treasury Department did you make original appointments
and promotions from the Civil Service Commission exclusively?—A. In
the classified service, sir; outside of the classified service, no. There is
a large number of appointments outside of the classified service. If an
applicant was not in Washington it would be a great hardship for her
or him to come here to be looked at, and then for me to say I am not
satisfied with them. I have to have the recommendations of political
friends in the matter. When I say political friends I mean Democrats.

Q. Were not promotions frequently made from the messenger service,
made in the Second Auditor's Office; I mean were not persons, employed
as messengers and appointed as laborers, frequently promoted to
desks?—A. Yes, sir: that was frequently done until Mr. Cleveland
stopped it. I urged it upon Mr. Cleveland for a long time. I told him
it was a regular violation of law that had prevailed in the Departments
as I was informed from time immemorial to appoint messengers and
laborers and then assign them to clerical work. I first brought the
matter to Mr. Manning, and Mr. Manning consented that I should stop
all that. I mentioned that to Mr. Fairchild, and he looked at me and
smiled, and said, "Have you got that all in writing?" I said I could
get it, and I took the hint and went back to Mr. Manning. It was said
that I would have appeals brought to me by members of Congress and it
was said I would certainly surrender. The appointment clerk laughingly
said, "You have got yourself into a hornet's nest," and I said, "I do
not care what members of Congress do; I will stand by that." For a
week I had appeals made by members of Congress in regard to the messengers and laborers. It was stated that it had been done time out of
mind and there was nothing wrong about it. I stated that in my judgment Congress had made an appropriation for messengers and laborers
and that they must be paid for that work and not for clerical work, and
from the time Secretary Manning issued the order until I left in April,
1889, I never appointed a messenger to do clerical work. I think I can
claim that I induced Mr. Cleveland to do it. He made an order the
29th of June, 1888, that no person appointed as a messenger or laborer
should do clerical work.

Q. Is it not a fact that hundreds had been appointed to desks prior
to that time?—A. Yes, sir; the way would be this: The chief of the
division would have a man assigned as messenger or laborer and then
the chief of the division would assign him to clerical work without the
knowledge of the Secretary. The Secretary has nothing to do with
bringing this about. It was only to stop what I believed to be a bad
practice that I broke up the entire practice at the Treasury.

By Mr. EWART:

Q. Following your invariable rule that you would not make promotions
in the classified service except upon examination, if he had been examined prior to his appointment or promotion, would you have required
an examination to be made?—A. If the Treasury was no larger than
the Civil Service Commission I think there would be no use for the civil-
service law at all. We have eleven clerks in the Civil Service Commission, whereas as from fifteen hundred to eighteen hundred in the Treasury Department it is utterly impossible for a man to know the qualifications of each.

Q. By the same reasoning could not the head of the Department
know who had only twenty clerks under him?—A. There is no such De-

partment that I know of. I know of no Department in which there are only twenty clerks.

Q. Say a chief of division, an officer of that kind who has twenty clerks under him. Why would he not be equally competent to test the fitness by actual observation?—A. The Secretary of the Treasury would be turning over practically the power of appointment to his subordinate and the power of promotion.

Q. That is not the question. I asked if in your opinion he would not be equally competent, being familiar with the parties from actual observation.—A. Chiefs of divisions do not make promotions, the Secretary makes them upon recommendation of the chief.

Q. I understand that.—A. I doubt whether there is. I do not know. I could not say how many clerks they have.

By Mr. HATTON:

Q. What time did President Cleveland stop the promotion of messengers to clerkships?—A. He stopped the appointments on the 29th of June, 1888.

Q. How long was that before he went out?—A. He went out the following March.

Q. If, when you were Assistant Secretary of the Treasury, either a Democrat or a Republican had applied to you for promotion, you thought the best method of getting at his fitness was from an examination?—A. Yes, sir; I think so.

By Mr. STONE:

Q. I understand you to say that this custom or practice of appointing persons or messengers and laborers and assigning them to clerical work was an old practice in the Department which had been pursued for many years?—A. Yes, sir; I do not want to go on record——

Q. What I want to get at is whether prior to Mr. Cleveland's administration this was a fact?—A. This is a direct answer to your question. When Mr. Manning made this order, the Washington Post, the next morning, came out and attacked Secretary Folger. The Washington Post the next morning came out and stated that this practice had grown to be a great outrage, especially under the administration of Secretary Folger.

SOMEONE. Was the Post conducted by our friend, Mr. Hatton, at that time?—A. I do not think it was.

Mr. EWART. Before we go on with this investigation I would like to make this suggestion, and I do it in the most respectful manner to the committee. Now we have been favored with a good many statements in this investigation. We have avoided making any comments upon the testimony, and very properly so. Had we done so it would have been the duty of the chairman or any member of this committee to have promptly stopped us. We think we have no right to comment upon anything and have no right to interject anything in the testimony while it is being conducted—any comments on these Commissioners who are now being investigated. Now I would respectfully suggest that these explanations and statements and corrections of testimony are becoming very alarming every morning. We were favored with a long statement from Commissioner Roosevelt yesterday which was a correction of a statement. We have been favored with another long statement by Governor Thompson, and we are still to be inflicted with another statement, an argument by Mr. Roosevelt. I respectfully submit that we will clearly make little progress in this investigation if these statements are to be constantly made. If these gentlemen desire to correct their evidence, I think they have a perfect right to appear on the following morning, ask the stenographer to read the evidence and correct it, but I think it is not the proper time to make the statements. When the evidence is all in and the Commissioners desire to make any statement I think it would be proper for them to do so, but at this particular time I think we will make better progress by allowing these statements to go over until the evidence is all in.

The CHAIRMAN. Mr. Roosevelt wishes to make a statement concerning the testimony of yesterday.

Mr. EWART. To correct any evidence?

Mr. ROOSEVELT. To make an addition.

Mr. LIND. I think, Mr. Chairman, Mr. Ewart has stated a practical proposition. The committee, I think, would rather hear the bare statement of facts—not an argument. Now, for instance, the statement made yesterday was purely a statement of fact, because it explained the reasons of action to the committee.

The CHAIRMAN. That is what I understand Mr. Roosevelt proposes to give us now. It is merely an addition to the testimony given on yesterday.

Mr. ROOSEVELT. I was asked by Mr. Ewart yesterday certain questions as to what I said to General McKeever and Mr. Tweedale, the chief clerk in the War Department, to whom I spoke about the transfer of Sturges. Of course, I could recollect only the substance of what I said. I went around yesterday afternoon to see the two gentlemen named, to see if their memory coincided with mine as to what I stated, and if I could refreshen my memory. I can now give you substantially what I told those gentlemen. Of course, after a lapse of three weeks, I could only give the substance of it. I went around—this is the statement referred to in that paper read by Commissioner Thompson, as being made to Mr. Tweedale and General McKeever—I went around and told them we had in our office a clerk, Mr. Sturges, whom we intended to dismiss if he could not be transferred; that Mr. Sturges was a round peg in a square hole; that he was reported to have been a special favorite of Commissioner Edgerton; that this feeling produced much friction between himself and other members of the force; that he was insubordinate towards his immediate superiors; that he was a young man, however, as far as I knew, of good capacity, good character, and good habits, but that he had become entirely unfitted for any work in our office; for a small office, such as ours was, with less than a dozen employés, there was no position in which we could assign him where we thought he could do good work; and that the immediate thing we were going to dismiss him for was for an act of gross carelessness which we could not excuse; but we did not think that the faults he had committed were faults of a moral character, or were such as would prevent him making a perfectly good officer in a minor position in a great department where there were several hundred clerks. At any rate the man had made a personal appeal to us, and that if we could show any mercy to a young man appealing like that we would be glad to do it. I told him also—there is one particular I can not recall; at any rate, that is the substance. This is the substance of what I told him. Oh, yes, this is it: I told them it would be a good deal of a lesson to him, anyhow, to be reduced from $1,600 to a $1,200 clerkship, which would probably act as a warning to him, and he might be very willing to take the opportunity to turn over a new leaf and do very well. In other words, I told them frankly all the reasons why we were convinced he would not any longer be of any use to us, why we did not wish him to be dropped out, and prevent him from having another such position in some other Department where he might do good work.

I also want to make a little statement in reference to what the governor spoke about with regard to influence with the administration. Now my understanding was not quite the same as the governor's about that. I had never known Secretary Proctor until he came here, but I have met him since. I have felt that I, going around there and being known as a party Republican, and saying this much for a Democratic clerk appointed under the last administration, that it would show that there was no party bias in what I was asking. Now if it had been the Secretary of the Treasury, where Governor Thompson is well known, I would have suggested that he go himself. If, on the other hand, we had been under the Democratic administration, and either had known the Cabinet officer, I would have suggested that Governor Thompson would go merely because he was of that political faith, and that would give it a certain *locus standi*, and in the same way I would go as I thought I said in answering a question on the subject yesterday by Mr. Stone. I went about Mr. Sturges—I went about two other clerks, Mr. Wallace and Mr. Van Hanken. Mr. Wallace is a Democrat and Mr. Van Hauken is, I know not what. I was undoubtedly influenced in the case of both Mr. Wallace and Mr. Sturges by the fact that as they were Democrats and I was a Republican there could be no possible construction put upon my act except my being interested in a measure of justice given them which I considered as right and proper.

The CHAIRMAN. Are there any questions to be asked?

By Mr. HATTON:

Q. Was Mr. Lyman a member of the Commission when the Commission decided to get rid of Mr. Sturges?—A. Yes.

Q. Did he say to you that Mr. Sturges had been an indifferent and insubordinate clerk during the time of the former administration of the Commission, the one that preceeded your administration?—A. I do not know. I recollect either Mr. Lyman or Mr. Doyle saying that Mr. Sturges had always been a bit of a lame duck.

Q. Did he give any reason why he was retained as a lame duck?—A. I think with great mercy—we were trying constantly to err on the side of mercy towards Mr. Sturges, because of the fact that Mr. Edgerton's relations toward his two colleagues were reported not to have been always pleasant, and we wanted to err on the side of mercy to a protégé of Mr. Edgerton rather than——

Q. As a matter of courtesy one Commissioner will be very lenient where another was concerned?—A. If you feel hostile—you are simply asking my opinion?

Q. Yes.—A. My opinion is, that as an honorable man, if I feel hostile to another man I am particularly careful to do no injustice to any friend of his.

Q. Did Mr. Lyman ever say to you he had ever recommended the dismissal of this clerk because of his insubordination and indifference—that he was a lame duck as a clerk?—A. If Mr. Lyman had recommended his dismissal he would be dismissed immediately.

Q. Did he recommend to his colleagues the complaint made of Mr. Sturges, Mr. Edgerton, and Mr. Oberly?—A. I know nothing about it.

Q. Mr. Lyman never said that?—A. He never told me if he had.

TESTIMONY OF W. T. WALLACE.

W. T. WALLACE, sworn and examined.

By Mr. THOMPSON:

Q. What is your position?—A. An examiner.

Q. In what department are you?—A. Civil Service Commission.

Q. You do not belong to the Civil Service Commission?—A. I belong to the Interior Department, the Pension Office.

Q. Do you know Mr. Morgan, formerly a stenographer of the Commission?—A. I do sir.

Q. Did you have a conversation with Mr. Morgan about the time of his leaving the Civil Service Commission to go to the Treasury as to who should be promoted to fill the vacancy caused by his removal?—A. I did.

Q. Did he state to you any particular person ought to be promoted, mention any name?—A. Yes, sir.

Q. Whom did he say ought to be promoted?—A. Mr. Bailey.

By Mr. EWART:

Q. Did Mr. Morgan at that time make any complaint as to the manner in which he had been treated by the Commission?—A. I think not at that time; he had prior to that, I know.

Q. How did you happen to speak of Mr. Bailey at that particular time; what were you talking about?—A. I brought the subject up myself.

Q. What did you say to him?—A. It was while his transfer was pending; I did not know he would be transferred and I hoped he would be promoted.

Q. Did Mr. Morgan say he was an efficient stenographer?—A. I could not answer to that.

Q. He told you he expected a transfer?—A. Yes, sir.

Q. Did he give you reasons why he expected that transfer?—A Yes, sir.

Q. What did he say?—A. He felt that he was not treated altogether right.

Q. He felt that he had not been exactly treated well by the Commission. Why did he say he had not been treated well by the Commission?—A. I could not answer that.

Q. Certainly he must have assigned some cause?—A. I do not remember if he did.

Q. Did he tell you he felt aggrieved at the Commission and did not make any statement in explanation of why he felt aggrieved?—A. That was a general remark he made, that he had not been treated right.

Q. Did he not give any explanation?

Mr. ANDREW. You should give the witness a chance, you do not give him a chance to get more than half an answer. Let us hear what his answer is.

By Mr. EWART:

Q. Did he assign any reason at all?—A. Yes; he assigned a reason, but what the reasons were now I do not recollect.

Q. He did not tell you then at the time he felt aggrieved at the Commission because Bailey was to be promoted over his head, an incompetent stenographer?—A. No, sir; he never assigned that as a reason.

Q. He did not assign as a reason that he felt aggrieved at the action of the Commissioners at the time was because he was not promoted?—A. That he was not promoted?

Q. That Morgan was not promoted to the position of stenographer.— A. But he held the position of $1,800; there was no promotion——

Q. If he had been retained, 1 should have said. Did he assign that as a reason?—A. No, sir; I think not.

By Mr. HATTON:

Q. Did Mr. Morgan say to you that he thought Mr. Bailey ought to be the official stenographer or would be?—A. No, sir; his exact words, if my memory serves me correctly, and I think it does was that he hoped that Mr. Bailey would get it. He did not say that he was entitled to it, or that he ought to have it, but that hoped that he would get it.

By Mr. EWART:

Q. That is what he said, that he hoped he would get it?—A. Yes, sir.

Q. He did not say he ought to have it?—A. No, sir; he did not tell me he ought to have it.

By Mr. HATTON:

Q. He did not say he ought to have it because he was a sufficiently qualified stenographer?—A. No, sir; we never discussed Mr. Bailey's qualifications at all.

By Mr. THOMPSON:

Q. What State are you from?—A. Mississippi.

Q. What are your politics?—A. I am a Democrat.

By Mr. STONE:

Q. When did you leave the Civil Service Commission?—A. I never left it at all; I am still detailed there.

Q. I thought you said you were at the Pension Office.—A. I am detailed to the Pension Office, but I belong to the Civil Service Commission.

Q. When did you go there?—A. I think it was in 1886.

Q. You have been there ever since 1886?—A. Yes, sir.

Q. And in the employ of the Civil Service Commission?—A. Yes, sir.

Q. That is, actively employed there?—A. Yes, sir.

By Mr. HATTON:

Q. You are practically an officer of the Commission; do you consider yourself practically an officer of the Commission?—A. Yes, sir; I reckon I may consider it such.

Q. You are one of the board of examiners?—A. Yes, sir.

Q. Your duty is to report to the Commission any violation of the law that comes under your observation?—A. I should feel it my duty to do so.

TESTIMONY OF O. N. JOHNSTON.

O. N. JOHNSTON sworn and examined.

By Mr. THOMPSON:

Q. Please state what is your occupation.—A. Clerk in the Civil Service Commission.

Q. What State are you from?—A. Maryland.

Q. What are your politics?—A. I suppose Democratic, or they will be.

The CHAIRMAN. How old are you?—A. Twenty.

Q. You never have voted?—A. No, sir.

By Mr. THOMPSON:

Q. Did you have any conversation with Mr. Morgan about the time of his leaving the Civil Service Commission and going to the Treasury with regard to the promotion of Mr. Bailey to the position of stenographer?—A. Yes, sir.

Q. What did he say?—A. He said he hoped Mr. Bailey would get it.

By Mr. EWART:

Q. Did he say Mr. Bailey ought to have it?—A. No, sir; he said he hoped Mr. Bailey would get it.

Q. At that time did you know he had applied for a transfer?—A. Yes, sir; I knew that.

Q. Did he state to you whether he had any grievance at that time against the Commission?—A. No, sir; he just stated he thought he had not been treated exactly right, but he did not give any reasons at all to me.

By Mr. HATTON:

Q. Did he say he hoped Mr. Bailey would get it on account of his superior qualifications as a stenographer, or why?—A. He did not say why, but he said he hoped he would get it.

Mr. THOMPSON. Some questions have been asked that would intimate that Mr. Bailey was specially favored in his examination as a stenographer, because of his opportunities to examine the papers. I wish to make a brief explanation. The applications of one or more people applying for stenographers are required to go to a desk where written matter is furnished them, and the examiner connected with the Commission may be the Commissioner, or may be any clerk, may be a man who knows nothing whatever about stenography, and generally is. He is required to read from certain exercises, from certain printed exercises, speeches, letters, and things of that sort. These papers when turned in by the applicant are folded up and sent to the board of examiners, who consist of stenographers. They mark these papers without knowing whose papers they mark. Now, I shall show to you shortly whether Mr. Bailey had been in the habit of reading these dictation exercises. We propose to prove that Mr. Morgan had precisely the same examination that Mr. Bailey had, and he had the same opportunity to see the papers; in other words, that Mr. Morgan, who on leaving the Commission complained that he had a grievance, had precisely the same examination, and the same opportunities of knowing what he was to be examined on as Mr. Bailey, who is charged with having special advantages in seeing these papers.

The CHAIRMAN. Examination before his transfer to obtain the position he now holds.

Mr. THOMPSON. Exactly; that Morgan had exactly the same, had precisely the same as Bailey. I really never saw one of the examinations conducted for stenographers.

Mr. STONE. You say you propose to prove. Are you making a statement of proposed proof, or are you making a statement of facts?

Mr. THOMPSON. I can state the fact and prove it. I can not prove that Mr. Morgan had seen these papers directly before the examination myself, but I can prove it by others that he had seen them; that he had the same means of knowing what was in the papers as Mr. Bailey. I will say this for myself; I am personally ignorant of stenography, but

I have always regarded it as an art which a man is bound to take down word for word, and that the exercises of memory would not be of any assistance to him. Stenographers say that when a man is familiar with the subject it gives them an advantage. My experience with stenographers has been generally, gentlemen, that when I ask a stenographer in regard to what has been said, he could not tell. He would have to go and read his notes. I confess I have not had very much experience with them; that is, I have generally dealt with those who are not generally regarded as experts. I have had a good deal of experience with stenographers in my own home. I remember the man who takes the letters in the office never could tell what the letters were, and he was an exceedingly bright and capable young man.

Mr. HATTON. If I am not mistaken, you stated yesterday that shortly following the promotion of Bailey, you had no personal knowledge of whether he was a stenographer or not?

Mr. THOMPSON. No, sir.

Mr. HATTON. Do you know there are cases where stenographers were dictated to by the Commission; is that always the rule that whoever does the examining does the dictating?

Mr. THOMPSON. Not always.

Mr. HATTON. It has often been done before?

Mr. THOMPSON. Yes, sir.

Mr. HATTON. In what cases?

Mr. THOMPSON. For instance, Mr. Lyman has given stenographers examinations. I think Mr. Lyman had taken several trips. I know he asked me to take a trip.

Mr. HATTON. You do not understand the question. Had any other candidate except Mr. Bailey, who passed an examination in stenography, been dictated to by the Commission?

Mr. THOMPSON. Not to my knowledge. I do not recollect it. There were three commissioners present when Mr. Bailey was examined.

Mr. LYMAN. I would say in answer to Mr. Hatton's question that I have repeatedly given dictation to stenographic examinations; any number of them. I do not know how many, but a great many.

TESTIMONY OF E. D. BAILEY—Continued.

E. D. BAILEY, recalled and examined.

By Mr. THOMPSON:

Q. When you were examined in stenography had you received from any one any information what dictation exercises would be submitted to you?—A. None whatever.

Q. None whatever?—A. No, sir; none whatever.

Q. Do you know whether or not Mr. Morgan, while he was clerk in the office, used the ordinary dictation exercises which are generally used in examination of stenographers, for applicants?—A. I know he has. The exercise from which selection was taken on which I was examined was on a sheet which I believe contained the only exercises used by the Commission for about two years past and I know he has dictated many times from the same sheet.

Mr. STONE. Was Mr. Morgan examined for stenographer on the same dictation?—A. Mr. Morgan was examined a little while before I was in stenography. He had never been examined in stenography by the Commission previously.

By Mr. EWART:

Q. Was he examined on the same dictation?—A. I do not know; I could not say certainly about that. There are many selections on the printed sheet.

Q. Then it was different from your examination?—A. It was from the same set of dictations, probably not the same selection; in regard to that I could not say certain. That could be ascertained, however, by examining the papers.

Q. Do I understand you to say you know the fact that Mr. Morgan had been examined on this same set of questions on which you had been examined?—A. The question asked of me was whether Mr. Morgan had dictated from this same set of exercises, and I answered to my knowledge that he had.

Q. How did you know that?—A. Because I many times when acting as chief examiner requested him to get for the candidates the same identical sheet.

Q. This one sheet given you, you recognize as the same dictation given to Mr. Morgan ; how did you recognize it?—A. I recognized it from the appearance of the sheet.

Q. Then you are perfectly familiar with the questions asked?—A. I have some familiarity with the questions; yes, sir.

Q. Then you stood an examination that virtually you had seen before?—A. I had seen these dictation exercises.

By the CHAIRMAN:

Q. Mr. Morgan had access to this paper and he had seen the questions?—A. Precisely the same as I had.

Q. Do I understand you to say Mr. Morgan occupied the position as it was called here of official stenographer, or stenographer to the board, before having passed an examination, and that was only within a month or two before he was discharged that he was examined?—A. That is the fact. Mr. Morgan came into the Commission without any examination in stenography.

By Mr. STONE:

Q. There was no examination in stenography required at that time; it was not in the classified service. The question I want to ask you is this; you had dictated from these same exercises yourself before the date of your examination?—A. Yes, sir.

Q. Did that fact accrue to your advantage when you were examined? —A. Only to a limited extent. It is possible from having read over these exercises it might have been easier to transcribe the notes, but that would only be to a limited extent; it would be a help by that fact. If it had been possible to commit these exercises to memory, in transcribing the notes it would have been an aid.

Mr. THOMPSON. Do you know from memory any one of the dictation exercises?—A. No, sir; that portion of my mental make-up is such that I can not commit to memory anything with any readiness. I have never attempted to commit any of the exercises to memory, and I doubt whether I could repeat successfully a line of any exercise on that sheet.

By Mr. HATTON :

Q. Why was Mr. Morgan examined before his transfer?—A. He had never been examined before as a stenographer, and in order to be transferred under the rules of the Commission he had to be examined.

Q. He was required to pass an examination in order to accept the position of stenographer in the Treasury Department?—A. I believe his position was to involve work in stenography, and for that reason he took what we call a basis examination, either clerk or copyist, I do not remember exactly which.

Q. You were promoted to his place, which involved stenographic work without an examination ?—A. I was promoted without an examination.

TESTIMONY OF WILLIAM H. WEBSTER.

WILLIAM H. WEBSTER, sworn and examined.

By Mr. THOMPSON:

Q. Will you please state your position in the Civil Service Commission ?—A. Chief examiner.

Q. Who made the appointment ?—A. President Cleveland.

Q. When ?—A. In August, 1886. I took the oath of office the 27th of August.

Q. What are your politics ?—A. I am a Republican.

Q. Do you know anything about Mr. Morgan having had access, ordinary access as a clerk would have, to these examination papers in stenography, and whether he had occasion to use them or not before his examination ?—A. He gave dictation from them.

Mr. ROOSEVELT. That is, Mr. Morgan had the same advantages, if advantages they were, in his examination as Mr. Bailey had.

The WITNESS. Certainly.

Mr. EWART. What was Mr. Morgan's grade in his examination ?—A. I do not remember the grade.

Mr. STONE. It was less than 70 ?

Mr. ROOSEVELT. No; Mr. Morgan's grade was 88.

The WITNESS. The papers will show that fact.

By Mr. EWART:

Q. The question was asked, what facilities Mr. Morgan had to ascertain what the dictation questions would be; what facilities did Mr. Bailey have to ascertain that same fact ?—A. He would have just the same facilities in getting the dictation from these sheets. The sheets contained several selections from speeches and letters and they are taken at random here and there.

Q. So when he had an examination by the Civil Service Commission he certainly knew pretty much what the examination would be and he recognized it at once ?—A. He would recognize the sheet, but he would not know at all what the dictation would be; there are a large number of sheets, I think.

By Mr. STONE:

Q. There is a fact I would like to put into the record at this point for whatever it may be worth. When was Mr. Holtz examined ?—A. I think it was 1887. I am not sure about that. He was taken from the eligible register for appointment by the Commission before the force of the Commission was classified and had to pass his examination, having failed on the previous examination.

Q. Then the examination on which he obtained the grade of about 68 was held something like two years prior to the examination of Mr. Bailey ?—A. Yes, sir; two years prior, probably more than that, but I do not know; probably more than two years.

By Mr. Roosevelt:

Q. Mr. Holtz has greatly improved in stenography since ?—A. Very much, very greatly.

Q. I simply bring that out to show in my question to Mr. Webster that the examinations that were given to Mr. Bailey and to Mr. Morgan were precisely such as and was no more advantage to them than the similar examinations in the past two years.—A. No more.

Q. Another question; you had used Mr. Bailey as a stenographer habitually for about a year prior to his appointment as such ?—A. Ever since his appointment I have used him almost every day, sometimes for a short letter and sometimes for a long letter.

Q. During the period Mr. Sturges testified he did not think you had used him as a stenographer, at the same time you had habitually used him as stenographer.—A. Mr. Sturges was across the hall from me and if he had attended to his duties there he would never have known whether Mr. Bailey was being used at all. The hall was between my my room and Mr. Sturges's room.

By Mr. Ewart:

Q. You say you used him habitually as a stenographer ?—A. Every day.

Q. Did you hear Mr. Bailey's evidence ?—A. I did.

Q. Did you hear him testify that the bulk of the work was clerical work ?—A. He was called the correspondence clerk.

Q. That being the case how could he have the leisure or time to do your stenographic work ?—A. To explain in regard to the matter of work, he is my correspondent clerk and writes part of the letters because they are familiar with those duties and one requires about the same answer as another. In answering such others as he is not able to attend to I dictate to him.

Q. Do I understand you to say he does the bulk of the stenographic work of that bureau ?—A. No, sir; my business does not require the bulk of the stenographic work.

Q. What percentage ?—A. I could not tell you that. We have two methods of correspondence there; the correspondence he does is in a great part of that which he can attend to from previous instruction, letters that are of similar purport and that he has written hundreds of times.

By Mr. Hatton:

Q. As a life-long civil-service reformer and a brother in the cause, do you not think it would have been better for both Mr. Bailey and Mr. Morgan if they had been examined on questions which neither had seen and which neither had access to before their examination ?—A. I doubt whether they could have memorized the several papers; there is quite a large number.

Q. Do you not think it would have been more fair and more in the line of the merits of the system ?—A. I do not think it would have made any difference to them. In regard to these questions, they have a large number and they are dictated, and people constantly have opportunities to gain information about these. We know this set of papers may be known, but there are so many dictation exercises, so many selections from different speeches, from different letters that it is hardly practical for any person to memorize all of them. It is like using an arithmetic; if you say to a man, "We will examine you out of an arithmetic," that man will not know on what portion of that arithmetic you are going to examine him. It is no advantage to him to know that you are going to use Davies's Arithmetic.

Q. We are talking about stenography.—A. The same principle applies to stenography. Having several number of exercises it is not practicable for any person to memorize them, not knowing where he is to be struck. I suggested to Mr. Lyman when the report was made — having a large number of questions——

Q. What do you mean by large number of questions ?—A. Series of questions of all sorts of examinations. When we had——

Mr. ANDREW. You are not talking of stenography ?—A. Stenography with the rest.

Q. There are no questions in stenography; there are exercises.—A. There are exercises; they amount to the same thing. We call them question sheets; it is exercises.

Q. It makes a difference in my mind to say you give exercises for dictation and having known beforehand what was to be dictated to a person. I only wanted to know what you meant. One was all right and the other seemed to me ridiculous.—A. We have had forty-one series of questions which have been prepared and furnished. There is such a multiplicity of these questions that a candidate could not memorize them all.

By Mr. STONE:

Q. These examinations in stenography are not all held here in Washington ?—A. Oh, no.

Q. Would there be any advantage to an applicant here for examination in stenography if he had been previously employed in your office and he had been handling these very papers time and time again and dictating from them to be examined himself from those papers ; would he have any advantage over the applicant say for examination in New York or St. Louis ?—A. No, I do not see how he could under such circumstances.

Q. Are the examinations there from entirely different dictations ?—A. We have a number of them and if it were practicable for the candidate to memorize all of those he would have an advantage. We go upon the theory that it is absolutely impracticable for a man to memorize all the series and he would not know which one is to be selected. There are successions of exercises to be selected and the candidate not knowing which one is to be given to him upon that theory that special candidate would not have much advantage. If he was able to memorize the whole thing he would. If it was a competitive examination outside we would take more precaution than in a promotion or transfer.

Q. You say as much advantage ; it ought to be no advantage at all.—A. Not in the competition.

Q. When there is a competition you put them upon the eligible list and certify the same according to the amount of grades.—A. In promotions they are examined without any competition at all.

Q. Well, for promotions ?—A. For original appointments we do ; they are all competitive there.

Q. My question, if it has any force to it, would apply to original appointments as well as promotions.—A. But this case was only promotion.

Q. It would not apply to those cases ?—A. For an outsider we would have dictated ; we would have preferred a dictation that had never been seen by the party, that he had not seen the sheet at all.

By Mr. HATTON:

Q. Would an applicant for examination in stenography in the War Department have any opportunity to get at the exercises before examination?—A. No; not in the War Department.

Q. Would any outside applicant for examination in stenography have any chance to get at the examination exercises?—A. Only those who had been examined before or who had friends who had been examined.

Q. If he had not been examined?—A. If he had not been examined he may have friends who have been examined on these sheets.

Q. If I understand you, you say that it makes no difference whether they had them or not; why would it not be in the spirit of accommodation to furnish the speeches before?—A. They are printed in the——

Q. They have no chance to get at them as Bailey and Morgan?—A. They have only the chance to get at the books or printed matter from which this may have been taken.

Q. Suppose in the annual report were a list of questions and the Commission decided to change it after the annual report was issued and substitute a new set of exercises?—A. He would not see these; he would not have the chance.

Mr. ROOSEVELT. But as a matter of fact we have not changed them?—A. No, sir.

Mr. HATTON. But you could change them if you wanted to.

The CHAIRMAN. The next charge is the Mitchell charge. There are four witnesses here—Thomas Mitchell, A. B. Toner, M. Smith, and Cyrus Bussey.

TESTIMONY OF THOMAS MITCHELL.

THOMAS MITCHELL, sworn and examined.

By the CHAIRMAN:

Q. Where are you employed at present?—A. I am filling the position, the desk, of an examiner at the Pension Office.

Q. How long have you been in the office?—A. Since last September.

Q. Were you in that office before that time?—A. I was a special examiner in that department for seven years.

Q. Were you discharged?—A. I was dismissed September, 1887.

Q. What reasons were assigned for your dismissal?—A. None whatever.

Q. In what manner did you obtain re-appointment?—A. Through a civil-service examination.

Q. When did you take that examination?—A. I first applied in the spring of 1889. Do you want me to give a statement?

Q. Certainly, give a statement.—A. I think it was in May, 1889, I made application to be designated for examination. On the 17th day of June I received notice that I could appear at the regular examination to be held in the city of Washington on the 9th day of July, 1889. I went to that examination; there were some ninety candidates in the room. I presume you are acquainted how these examinations are conducted.

The CHAIRMAN. You can just give a statement.—A. At 4 o'clock the gentleman in charge, whoever it was, I do not know his name, told me my examination was finished, and that I could go home. Ten days after that I received a letter from the Commission asking me to come there. I went there. This letter was signed by Mr. Thompson, one of the members of the Commission. His door was locked, and I then went to see Major Webster and I asked the purport of that letter. He said, "Were you examined in common law at the regular examination on July 9?" I said, "No, I did not know there was a law examination." He said there was, and took the trouble to give me a paper, and suggested then that I take a seat there, and he handed me a paper of printed questions. I should say that that morning I got out of a sick bed, and I was not in a condition to be examined, either physically or mentally. I sat down and endeavored to answer these questions, and handed them back to him. Some time after that, I do not know the precise date, I received notice that my examination had been rated—I would like to have the letter which I wrote to the Commission on appeal from that rating.

Mr. ANDREW. Was the rating too high or too low?

The WITNESS. The first appeal was August 1, 1889, addressed to the Civil Service Commission:

WASHINGTON, D. C.,
No. 805 Tenth Street, Northwest, August 1, 1889.

U. S. CIVIL SERVICE COMMISSION,
Washington, D. C.:

GENTLEMEN: In the matter of my rating in civil service examination, No. 7277. I have the honor to appeal to you for a review of said rating, in relation to paper No, 7, "Questions on Law," or other papers of said examination.

Very respectfully,

THOMAS MITCHELL.

That was refused. 1 then put in a second protest, and this is under date August 3, 1889, addressed to Civil Service Commission, Washington, D. C.

WASHINGTON, D. C.,
No. 805 Tenth Street, Northwest, August 3, 1889.

To the UNITED STATES CIVIL SERVICE COMMISSION,
Washington, D. C.:

GENTLEMEN: In the matter of my examination, No. 19837, of date of July 9, 1889, I have the honor to request that I may be permitted to appear for re-examination before you, in view of the facts: First, that sheet No. 8, on the subject of law, was not given to me at the time of holding said examination, but afterwards upon notice received by me on the morning of July 19, 1889, and without any prior knowledge that a paper of the character referred to, was a part of the examination. Second, I was not in a proper mental or physical condition to be subjected to the ordeal of an examination on the morning of July 19, 1889, when I gave answers to the questions propounded in Sheet No. 8, as designated. The production of this paper, at that time, was a surprise to me, and in the hurry and excitement of the occasion, without time for deliberation, many of the questions were not properly understood.

The original proceedings were irregular, all of the examination not having been conducted at the time indicated in the certificate of rating.

Under all the circumstances I trust that you will grant me a re-examination.

Very respectfully,

THOMAS MITCHELL.

I handed that paper to Mr. Lyman, the president of the Commission. Mr. Lyman told me I would receive my answer in writing. On the 7th day of August I received a communication in writing from the Commission, stating I could go in the next regular examination to be held in the city of Baltimore, Md. I went there and went through an entirely new examination, and on the 13th of September I received a communication from the Commission stating that I had passed the examination of a chief examiner in the Pension Office, which is a high grade of examination. My understanding is, that is, in addition to the classified service, a very stringent examination in common law and in the statute law of the United States Government and administration of the Pension Office.

By Mr. STONE:

Q. What year was this?—A. What year?

Q. That you took this examination?—A. August 12, 1889.

Mr. THOMPSON. And how soon after that were you appointed?—A. On the 23d day of September, 1889.

By the CHAIRMAN:

Q. So you took two examinations, as I understand it, and on the first examination your rating was below the average.—A. A paper was left out. I was notified by the Commission ten days after that that paper had not been given me.

Q. And you were examined on that paper and the result of that examination was you failed?—A. Altogether.

Q. You afterwards took another examination?—A. An entirely new examination.

Q. Were the questions identical?—A. They were entirely different from beginning to end.

Q. And you passed the second examination?—A. I was so notified. I had no communication with the Commission from the date of my notice to appear in Baltimore until I received the notification that I had passed the examination.

Mr. ANDREW. Is this charge true, "That the said Mitchell failed on his examination held prior to his last appointment and that this failure becoming known to the parties desiring his restoration to the service, his papers were remarked and he was restored from the ineligible to the eligible list?"—A. There is not a word of truth in that to my knowledge; there is not a word of truth in it.

By the CHAIRMAN:

Q. Who interested himself in your re-instatement, any member of Congress or Senator?—A. No, sir.

The CHAIRMAN. I think we will turn the witness over to Mr. Ewart at this time.

By Mr. EWART:

Q. Up to the time of your discharge or removal from office you had been in the departmental service for how many years?—A. Thirty years, in various positions.

Q. You were removed under the administration of Mr. Cleveland?—A. Yes, sir.

Q. When Mr. Lamar was Secretary of the Interior, you were in the Interior Department?—A. I was special examiner in the Pension Office in the field.

Q. Were you removed for political reasons?—A. I believe my place was needed for somebody else. That is the only reason I can offer.

Q. You have always been a Republican?—A. Yes, sir.

Q. There was no cause assigned for your removal?—A. No, sir. I will say I was on a thirty days' leave of absence at the time, and it was a mere accident that I knew that such an order had been issued. I came to Washington and went to see the Commissioner of Pensions. He refused to see me, and I then went to Mr. Muldrow and he said that he knew nothing about it, that it was the action of the Commissioner, I appealed to Mr. Muldrow and Mr. Lamar sent his private secretary and made an appointment to see me, but I have never seen him from that day to this.

Q. Did you address a communication to Mr. Lamar on this subject, complaining that you had been unjustly treated?—A. Yes, sir; and asked for a hearing, that I might have a hearing.

Q. Did you at any time give any reason to any public official why you were removed from your position at the time?—No, sir; beyond a political reason.

Mr. ANDREW. I do not think that Mr. Lamar ought to be dragged into this matter.

Mr. EWART. I may say it is immaterial. Do I understand you to say you never addressed any communication to Mr. Lamar?A.—I did not say so.

Q. Or any other person in regard to your removal. I would like to read—1 understand you to swear you have always been a Republican?

WASHINGTON, D. C.,
709 *Twelfth Street, Northwest, April* 2, 1889.

Hon. JAMES TANNER,
    Commissioner of Pensions:

DEAR SIR: I have the honor to state that I was appointed from the army as law clerk in the office of Second Comptroller of the Treasury, in 1869, on the recommendation of Governor Buckingham, of Connecticut, which is my legal place of domicile. In 1878, at the personal request of Secretary Schurz, I resigned my position in the Treasury Department and accepted the appointment as chief of the Indian division of the office of the Secretary of the Interior. I was subsequently transferred to the Pension Office, and there served consecutively for seven years as special examiner in the field, until peremptorily dismissed by your predecessor, John C. Black, without recourse, charge of any character being made against my character as a public officer, or any reason given to me by said Black for his course of action, although I continuously and persistently sought a reason from him.

Afterwards, Mr. Black stated to Mr. Robert J. Vance, then member of Congress, from first Connecticut district, "that he had removed me on account of my Republicanism, and on the approval of Alfred E. Burr, editor of the Hartford Times, the leading Democratic paper of Connecticut."

Mr. James W. Orme, one of the directors of the Washington Gas-Light Company, having recommended me for employment by that corporation, on his own volition, called at the Pension Office to ascertain the cause of my removal from the public service. At that place he met Mr. William E. McLean, First Deputy Commissioner of Pensions, who informed him "that I had been removed from the Pension Office solely on political grounds; that I was an offensive Republican."

Mr. Black also gave currency to the report "that while a special examiner in his office I had made Republican speeches in the field."

In evidence of my efficiency, the quantity and quality of work rendered and a scrupulous regard for the integrity and best interest of the public service, I point with pride to the public records of the Pension Office itself. No charge has at any time, to my knowledge, been made against me personally as to the integrity of my character as an officer of the Government, or otherwise.

My only offense, as far as I know, has been my allegiance to the tenets of my political faith in the principles of the Republican party, which I have held since 1857, and for which I was without a moment's warning summarily and remorselessly thrust out of employment, upon the cold charity of the world with my wife and aged father depending upon me for support. My wife being a sister of General John M. Brannan, U. S. Army, retired, and whose family are certainly entitled to consideration for his services rendered the Republic on many a hard-fought field.

Now, esteemed sir, I pray that I may, through your kindness and by the virtue of your position, be restored to my right on the rolls as an employé of the Pension Office, and detailed for service as a special examiner in the field.

I court any investigation that may be had as to my public or private character, and do not fear that any individual act of my life should see the light of day.

I am, very respectfully,
THOMAS MITCHELL.

Mr. EWART. Did you write that letter?

The WITNESS. I would like to understand your first question.

Mr. EWART. In this letter you stated you had been a Republican since 1857.

Mr. ANDREW. What difference does it make whether he was Republican——

Mr. HATTON. We certainly will not read these letters unless the committee give us the privilege.

Mr. STONE. He has read one, so he had better read them both.

Mr. HATTON. We certainly will have to have a chance to put in a coupling-pin.

WASHINGTON, D. C.,
No. 1104 Maryland Avenue, September 28, 1887.

SIR: While on a leave of absence for the month of September, 1887, I accidentally received your letter, dated September 5, stating "That upon the recommendation of the Commissioner of Pensions my services as a clerk in the Pension Bureau would be dispensed with from and after September 30, 1887."

The cause of this action on the part of the Commissioner of Pensions is unknown to me. It was not ascertained by me upon my personal inquiry at the Pension Bureau, but I was informed by the Chief of Division that my removal was the act of the Commissioner; from him alone could knowledge of the cause be obtained, and owing to his physical infirmities he could not be interviewed by me.

The present incumbent, for some reason, of which I am entirely ignorant, has manifested a personal antipathy to me from the very advent of his term of office.

I pray you, sir, that the order for my dismissal may be revoked and that you will cause me to be transferred, by appointment, to some other bureau of your Department.

Inclosed herewith please find letters in relation to my status, political and otherwise, addressed to you by Hon. A. E. Burr, editor of the Hartford Times, Conn., and from Hon. R. J. Vance, M. C., First district of Connecticut. Others of a similar character will be forthcoming from other members of our Democratic delegation in Congress.

I have, sir, the honor to be, very respectfully, your obedient servant,

THOMAS MITCHELL.

Hon. L. Q. C. LAMAR,
    Secretary of the Interior.

Mr. HATTON. Did you write that letter?

The WITNESS. Allow me to see the letter. That is not my writing; that is a type-written letter.

Q. You say it is type-written?—A. I will state that I wrote a letter of that character.

Mr. STONE. Did you write one of this character?—A. I wrote one of similar character. I do not know whether that is correct or not.

Mr. STONE. Did you write such a letter?—A. I wrote such a letter.

Q. Do you believe it to be correct?—A. In the main, I do.

Mr. HATTON. Did you write any letter in which you stated you inclosed letters of the Hon. Mr. Vance, Mr. French, etc.?

Mr. EWART. I desire now to read the letters inclosed.

Mr. ANDREW. Are these the original letters?

Mr. EWART. These are the copies, type-written.

The WITNESS. Where did you obtain these?

Mr. EWART. I am not on the witness stand. Keep cool, my friend, and you will have fun enough.

The CHAIRMAN. Why are these letters material? We do not desire to take up the time of the committee. We are not investigating the former Commissioner of Pensions. Whether the man was discharged or not, he had a right to use such influence to try to get back in a legitimate way. We are investigating the Commission.

Mr. EWART. He says he was removed for no cause at all. Then in a letter asking reinstatement he says he was removed because he was a Republican, and at the instance of a Democratic member of Congress and editor of a Democratic newspaper; and then he writes a letter to Mr. Lamar, inclosing letters showing that this man whom he had stated had been removed——

Mr. STONE. I suppose the purpose is to show that he was removed for cause.

Mr. ROOSEVELT. Allow me to state that this is wholly irrelevant. If he was removed for cause, after one year elapsed he could make an application for re-examination and enter the service again.

Mr. EWART. I think we have a right to show the character of the witness.

Mr. ANDREW. If they wish to show the character of their own witness, and impeach the character——

Mr. EWART We put some up with that intention.

The CHAIRMAN. If this man was removed for cause, for incompetency, for any reason whatever, he had a perfect right if he was out of office for one year to apply for re-examination and enter the service again provided he could pass the examination.

Mr. HATTON. This letter is a letter written to Mr. Lamar, just to show that in stating in his former letter that he had been removed—which letter has been admitted, that he stated what was false.

The CHAIRMAN. I have no objection personally to allowing the letters to go in, but I did not desire to encumber the testimony.

THE TIMES, HARTFORD, CONN., *September* 23, 1887.

Hon. L. Q. C. LAMAR,
  Secretary of the Interior:

DEAR SIR : Mr. Thomas Mitchell, son of my old Democratic friend, the Hon. Henry A. Mitchell, of this State, a life-long and respected Democrat, and formerly a judge of our county court, has been dismissed from the Pension Office. He informs me that he does not know the reason of his dismissal and that his record of years of service in the Department stands high. As he is a Democrat of a highly respected family of Democrats of this State, and is capable and efficient, the friends of Mr. Mitchell in Connecticut are astonished at the news of his· dismissal without any alleged cause. He is to go out September 30.

If consistent we should esteem it a favor if the Secretary would withdraw his dismissal and transfer him to another position.
    Very respectfully, yours,

A. E. BURR,
    Editor, Hartford Times.

————

SEPTEMBER 23, 1887.

DEAR SIR : The bearer, Mr Thomas Mitchell, son of Judge Mitchell, of Bristol, has been, by General Black, for some reason, recommended for dismissal from the Pension Department. He is well known here and we can conceive of no reason why this action was taken. He now desires to be transferred to another position in your Department, and this is written in the hope that you may see fit so to do assuring that such an act on your part would please many here and give me personally much gratification.
    I am, sir, yours, etc.,

R. J. VANCE.

Hon. L. Q. C. LAMAR,
  Secretary of the Interior.

————

SEPTEMBER 27, 1887.

Hon. L. Q. C. LAMAR,
  Secretary of the Interior, Washington, D. C. :

SIR : I write in behalf of Mr. Thomas Mitchell, a clerk in the Pension Office of Washington, D. C., whose dismissal has been ordered. Mr. Henry A. Mitchell, of Bristol, this State, father of Mr. Thomas Mitchell, has long been an active and powerful factor in the Democratic party of Connecticut, and is entitled to some consideration. Thomas Mitchell has been in Government service off and on thirty years but always a Democrat. His record is first-class; also his letters on file from prominent Democrats of Connecticut. I therefore hope you can see fit to revoke the order of dismissal, and if possible transfer him to some other bureau of the Interior.
    Very respectfully,

CARLOS FRENCH,
    Member of Congress, Second District.

THE TIMES, HARTFORD, CONN.,
October 18, 1867.

Hon. L. Q. C. LAMAR:

DEAR SIR: I have the honor to acknowledge the receipt of your esteemed favor of the 15th. I beg leave to say that my letter requesting a promotion of Thomas Mitchell was so far guarded as to make the request only in case it could be done in the interest of the public service. I was not aware that there were objectionable personal reasons for the suspension of Mitchell, and I thank you for so kindly taking an interest in the case and letting me know the truth. I do not desire any further investigation.

Very truly, yours,

A. E. BURR.

The WITNESS. Do you say I filed that letter?

Mr. HATTON. I say you stated——

The WITNESS. Did you say I filed that letter?

Mr. HATTON. I did not say anything of the kind, and I am not on the witness stand.

The WITNESS. You seem to think you are on trial?

Mr. HATTON. I think that is the difference between you and myself.

Mr. STONE. Now, these letters have been put into this record——

The WITNESS. May I explain how these letters were obtained?

Mr. EWART. Now, I will ask this question. It seems from the letter written to Mr. Lamar by Mr. Burr that you were removed for cause, that there were personal reasons, and you stated in your examination that you were not removed for cause.

The WITNESS. I do not know anything about that letter.

By Mr. HATTON:

Q. Do you deny utterly that you were removed for cause?—A. I do, sir. Now, I would like to state how the letters read from Mr. Vance and Mr. Burr were obtained. They were obtained by my father. My father was an aged man, poor in fortune, and I was supporting him. He was a life-long Democrat, and when I was removed he tried to get me a hearing. Mr. Burr does not know me personally, and all these allegations as to politics were made in regard to my father.

Q. Why did you write Commissioner Tanner you were removed at the instigation of these two men, who attempted a few months before to keep you in office?—A. They did not attempt to keep me in office.

By the CHAIRMAN:

Q. When you said you were not removed for cause, what did you understand by that; for any dereliction of official duties?—A. I understand by that I have no knowledge of any charge having been made against me.

Q. Against your character?—A. In any manner or shape, either my character as a man or as a public officer.

Q. Do you believe you were discharged because you were a Republican?—A. I believe I was discharged because my place was wanted for somebody else.

Q. That is not the question. I asked you, do you believe you were discharged because you were a Republican?—A. Yes, sir.

Q. And you did not consider that a legitimate cause, and that is the reason you have stated you were not removed for cause?—A. Merely political cause.

By Mr. EWART:

Q. Are you connected with any one in the Interior Department?—A. How connected?

Q. Have you any family connection, any relationship, with any officer in the Interior Department?—A. With Mr. Charles E. Mitchell.

Q. What is the relationship?—A. He is a distant relative.

Mr. HATTON. Are you connected with any member of the Commission in any way?

The WITNESS. No, sir; I have no acquaintance with them.

TESTIMONY OF A. C. TONNER.

A. C. TONNER sworn and examined.

By the CHAIRMAN:

Q. Where are you employed?—A. Chief of appointment division, Interior Department.

The CHAIRMAN. I think it would save time to turn the witness over to Mr. Ewart, and let him ask the questions. Will you ask the questions, Mr. Ewart?

By Mr. EWART.

Q. Have you the records of the appointment of Mr. Mitchell with you?—A. Yes, sir; I anticipated the purpose for which I was called here and I thought the best way would be to bring the records, and I have them right here. This is only a part of it. I have the certification papers here.

Q. That is what I want to see more specifically. Just be kind enough to read that.—A. This is a certification, Civil Service, No. 665. (See exhibit A.)

Q. This appears to be a certificate of a copyist.—A. Yes, sir; if you will allow me to state in this connection that upon the request of the Commissioner of Pensions there were—if you will hand it to me I will read directly from the files. Then I will give it to you exactly as we h. .. ... The request was made for fifteen originally from the grade or special examiners.

Mr. HATTON. On what date?—A. September 17. The request was made September 6; the certificates were dated September 17; and the Commissioner of Pensions, I remember, asked for fifteen of the grade of copyists which could be taken from the register of special examiners. Please note that, for it is an important item.

Mr. STONE. I do not exactly understand it.—A. I will explain that to you. As I stated, the request from the Commissioner of Pensions was for fifteen in the classified service as copyists at $900, to be taken from the special examiners' register. Of course I do not know what the motive existing in the mind of the Commissioner was except by inference, unless from this higher grade of service from which he wanted these people called, he could get a better class of people—for instance he will take a $900 copyist and test him in a lower grade until he ascertains his ability, and then promote him in this special examination work. That, I presume, was his motive in it. It is assumable at all events.

By the CHAIRMAN:

Q. I want to understand that. Was the Commissioner in want of special examiners at that time?—A. Yes, sir.

Q. How many?—A. He was in want at the time he wrote his letter of September 6 of fifteen, but he subsequently modified it to eleven.

Q. I understand he called for certifications of persons who had passed examinations as special examiners, and called for those to fill $900 positions as clerks?—A. In the grade of copyists $900 salary. He asked for eleven by a modification of his first order from the register of those who have passed the special examiner's grade.

The CHAIRMAN. I think the committee wanted to understand that, and I did.

Mr. ROOSEVELT. I think I can bring out the question. Was it not presumable that the idea of the Commissioner was that he wished a high grade or men who would be willing to take these $900 places? We have two or three registers which give men specially fitted for the duties of the Pension Bureau, and was it not with that idea of getting men from one of these registers who would be willing to take the pay and do the work of the lower grade until he was able to test them?

The WITNESS. That was the idea I wished to enforce upon you; that by drawing from the special examiners' register, he was getting the highest grade of ability. Very often we will call from the copyist register and put in $600 places, as you will see by the civil service rules.

Mr. BUTTERWORTH. Let me ask a question in that connection. Would not that result, then, in giving the higher appointments to those who passed examinations for the lower grades of labor?

The WITNESS. It might take that direction in time.

Mr. ROOSEVELT. On the contrary it would cause the appointment from the higher grades to the lower position. The special pension examiner examination is very difficult, and these were certified from that examination to a lower place.

Mr. STONE. Well, go ahead, we understand this.

By Mr. EWART:

Q. I find this mark on the papers. Although Mitchell was a certified copyist, it seems by that mark, he was to be appointed to a $2,000 position. "Appoint Thomas Mitchell, of Connecticut, clerk at $2,000 in office of the Secretary of the Interior, to date January 20."—A. I do not know anything about this mark. It is without signature and how it could have gotten upon it I do not know. Mr. Mitchell never occupied a $2,000 position.

Q. Do you know what position he had?—A. I think it was a $1,400 position. He was special examiner in the Pension Office previous to his removal.

Q. I do not find among these papers some papers which I thought you would have brought. I presume you can give some explanation of why they are not here, showing the cause of his removal.—A. There was no cause given. We have nothing whatever on file in relation to his removal except the mandatory order from the Commissioner and the recommendation and indorsement of Mr. Muldrow on the back of it.

Q. Did you hear a letter read written to Secretary Lamar?—A. Yes, sir; I heard that letter read.

Q. In which he alleges that to be a removal for personal reasons, not political?—A. The letter is the only thing we have in regard to his removal. We know nothing of any charges at all.

Q. Do you know of any papers having been recently withdrawn?—A. Yes, sir; I think I have a receipt here for several.

Q. Do you know where these papers are?—No, sir.

Q. Would it be possible to get those papers?—A. They may be in the possession of Mr. Mitchell or the parties who have withdrawn them for him.

Q. Is the receipt in Mr. Mitchell's name?—A. No, sir; the receipt for the letters withdrawn is in the name of Miss Shedd, who, I think, is a phonographic clerk in the office of the Commissioner of Patents.

Mr. EWART. Mr. Chairman, we will have to have those papers.

The WITNESS. They are the legitimate property of Mr. Mitchell, because they are not relevant to the case. They were letters in relation to his re-instatement, as the receipt shows, and they not being the predicate of any action taken, he is entitled to them. If Mr. Mitchell had been re-instated in office none of those letters could have been withdrawn; but under the rule of the office they are allowed to withdraw any papers where no action has been predicated upon those papers.

Q. Can it be possible that the letter of Secretary Lamar or the reasons assigned for his removal are on file?—A. I say frankly the originals of the letters you read here ought to have been in this file, but previous to last fall there was a rule between my division and the Pension Bureau that was very confusing. They held in the Pension Office part of the files, and we held in my division part of the files; and I had an order issued by which everything was brought to my division. I do not know whether those papers there were the papers involved in this receipt or not. If they were, they are in relation to his re-instatement, and they are his property under the rule.

Mr. HATTON. Would not the letter of the Secretary of the Interior ordering the dismissal of the man and giving the reasons for his dismissal be on file?—A. Certainly; you have just read it:

SEPTEMBER 3, 1887.

Hon. H. L. MULDROW,
    Acting Secretary of the Interior:

SIR: I have the honor to recommend most respectfully that the services of Mr. Thomas Mitchell, as a clerk of class 2 in this Bureau, be dispensed with from and after the 30th instant.

Very respecefully,

JOHN C. BLACK,
Commissioner.

(Indorsed.) Approved: H. L. Muldrow, Acting Secretary. September 5, 1887. Dismissed.

Q. You know nothing about the records of the Interior Department, but know what is the general rule of the Secretary of the Interior to keep copies of letters to any outside persons, giving the reasons why a particular person is removed?—A. There is occasionally some correspondence between some outside parties in relation to appointments and removals and re-instatements that might possibly be upon the private files, but ordinarily all that correspondence comes in my custody and becomes part of the files; but as I said before, the originals ought to have been in these files, and perhaps may have been accounted for by this receipt, because he was entitled to them.

Q. When did you say a requisition for this was made?—A. I think the requisition was made on September 6.

Q. When was Mitchell appointed?—A. He was appointed immediately following—wait until I see it—September 23.

Q. Now, when did you send an order to the Acting Commissioner of Pensions for a transfer of the papers on file in that case relating to his removal and attempt to be re-instated? Do you remember the date? You sent an order signed by yourself to the Acting Commissioner of Pensions, requesting that all the papers relating to this particular case, where this man attempted to be re-instated to this office, to be transferred to your office.—A. I presume I signed such a letter—I usually write no letters myself.

Q. This is a copy addressed to the assistant chief clerk of the Pension Office.

SIR: Please transfer to the files of this division all papers in the files of your office recommending the transfer of Dr. Thomas Mitchell to the Pension Office about two years ago to some other bureau.

Very respectfully,

A. C. TONNER,
Chief of Appointment Division.

A. I have no doubt that letter is correct, never having been returned. If there had been any return in answer to that, they would and should have been in here.

Q. Is it not the custom at all times to keep these papers until some officer sends for them ?—A. Certainly. Charges were never returned in regard to the character of the applicant.

Q. I called on you the other day and asked about this. At that time where were these papers ?—A. Which papers ?

Q. The papers in this case.—A. In my possession.

Q. No, you told me at the time there was a receipt.—A. This is the daily file. I hold Miss Shedd's receipt.

One clerk wrote in here : "Re-instatement in Pension Office in 1887." By this he was entitled to——　　　　　　•

Q. At the time these fifteen examiners were called for, how many examiners were at the Commissioner of Pensions ?—A. I could not tell you.

Q. How many is he entitled to ?—A. Several hundred. One hundred and fifty in the field ; any more are clerks detailed.

Mr. BUTTERWORTH. It runs into the hundreds.—A. Of course we keep watch of that, and do not let them go beyond the limit. I do not remember all the data. I would have to be an encyclopedia to do that.

Mr. EWART. One hundred and fifty ?—A. These are in the field. I believe they are limited to that number.

Q. You do not know if any other papers were taken from your office, if any other papers were removed or not ?—A. No, sir ; I do not.

Q. You do not examine them closely when they come to you ?—A. No, sir, I could not take the time to examine the bushels of papers that come in there every day. They are distributed by the various clerks.

Q. Why was the order made to remove these papers and no other papers ?—A. I could not tell upon what motive. I could not tell. I have no recollection, because I would never have known of this case except by its being especially brought out.

Q. Do you know when he made application for restoration ?—A. No, sir ; that was in 1887. He was promoted in 1887.

Q. How long had he been out when he was restored ? Do you know that ?—A. He was removed in 1887, and made application shortly thereafter, as I understand it. No, I do not know whether he made application under rule 10. It was required to be within a year, unless a soldier ; then under rule 10 as amended.

Q. Did you say within a year ?—A. He was, in fact, eligible under rule 10 for restoration and could have made application under rule 10. I do not know whether he applied under rule 10, being a soldier and eligible.

Q. The allegation was he had been removed for cause.—A. He could not possibly come in possession of any cause from our files, because if any charges were on file we would not have permitted him to see them.

Mr. EWART. Suppose I recall the witness at that point and ask why he did not make application under the soldier rule.

Mr. HATTON. In such a case, in such an appointment in the Interior Department where a man is removed for cause and applies for re-instatement, it is customary for the Civil Service Commission to send and ascertain what the cause is ?

The CHAIRMAN. Do you know anything about that ?—A. No, sir.

The CHAIRMAN. You are not acquainted with it ?

Mr. BUTTERWORTH. In the order of dismissal which I understand you to hold in your hand, the order for dismissing Mr. Mitchell, is it usual or not when a man is dismissed for cause to say so?—A. I do not know what rule prevailed at that time, but we have a rule in our office now that no removal from any bureau shall be entertained without cause. We send recommendations back often and ask them to state the cause for the recommendation of removal.

Q. Your recommendations now always declare and state the cause?—A. Yes, sir.

By Mr. THOMPSON:

Q. In our transactions with officials, when there has been a request for re-instatement, the request has always been made to know as to whether there was cause and then we replied requesting you to state the facts?—A. You mean under the meaning of rule 10. Yes, sir; I had a little racket with some of you on that subject. I thought you were too rigid——

Q. We have reached an understanding upon statements being made?—A. Yes, sir. I mean in explanation about rigid that when we referred a case under amended rule 10 to the civil service, I held that we meant that there were no charges of misconduct or delinquency.

Q. And insisted we must repeat that?—A. Yes, sir. I said I did not want so much correspondence. I thought I did enough.

Mr. BUTTERWORTH. Rule 10 certifies only such facts?—A. That there were no charges for delinquency or misconduct, and I refer the case to you.

By Mr. STONE:

Q. Where a removal is made by a Commissioner of Pensions, for instance, do you report that fact to the Civil-Service Commission, that cause of removal?—A. No, sir; we do not.

Q. Do you understand the Civil Service Commission has any charge over the question of removals?—A. No, sir; I do not. I do not know that the Civil Service Commission can compel an appointing officer to keep anybody in the service unless he sees fit to keep them there.

Q. I do not understand you that on that point is where you had the racket?—A. No, sir; under amended rule 10 for re-instatement of soldiers that are eligible for re-appointment, we must state there was no misconduct or delinquency.

Q. Do you think that had anything to do with the appointment of Mr. Mitchell?—A. Nothing; we got this return from the Civil Service. taken from the list of eligibles.

Q. Did you make a selection of Mitchell from those three names?—A. No, sir; I sent that list directly to the Commissioner of Pensions, and he made the selection.

Q. That is practically all you had to do with it?—A. In regard to the selection, that is all.

Mr. ANDREW. Are you in charge of this case about Mitchell's re-instatement?—A. No, sir.

By Mr. STONE:

Q. Do you know what salary Mitchell was to receive when appointed?—A. Not then certainly. Nine hundred dollars I have since understood.

Q. That is what I understood. When was that appointment made?—A. On the back, here it is "appointed September 23, 1887."

Q. Do you know what salary he is receiving now?—A. I think $900.

Mr. EWART. As a special examiner ?—A. He has not passed the probationery period yet.

Mr. STONE. What was the memorandum about $2,000 salary ?—A. That memorandum I do not know anything about at all.

By the CHAIRMAN :

Q. Let me ask you here; this paper certifies three names and one of these three appointed was Mr. Mitchell ?—A. Yes, sir.

Q. He was not the highest in percentage ?—A. (taking paper and looking over it.) 71, 71, 72. That I take it to be a pretty good grade on this examination ; 77, 79, 74, and one at 77.

Mr. BOATNER. You do not know the way the names were appointed ?—A. Here is a list of those selected on the back. They were noted on the back from those selected.

Mr. BUTTERWORTH. He is allowed to exercise his discretion ?—A. Most assuredly ; and if the highest rated man was a man he did not know anything about, and one near it was a man he did know a good deal about, he could exercise his discretion, most assuredly.

Mr. HATTON. Who selected them after the list was sent in ? Who selected Mr. Mitchell ?—A. I could not tell you that; I do not know anything about it at all.

The CHAIRMAN. I would suggest to Mr. Ewart that he ought to bring witnesses here to state what charges were against this man.

Mr. EWART. We have brought our witnesses here, but they have not brought the records. It seems there are no records here.

Mr. ANDREW. This witness says that he has no knowledge of any cause for removal.

Mr. EWART. I expected this witness to bring certain papers which he has not brought.

The CHAIRMAN. You brought the records in your office ?—A. Yes, sir.

Mr. HATTON. The distinguished gentleman from Massachusetts decided that this witness did not know anything about it. I would like to put a member of the Commission on the stand and ask in regard to the promotion and re-instatement of men who have been dismissed for cause. The gentleman from Massachusetts shut me off on this question because he said this witness knew nothing about the Commission, and a minute afterwards some member of the committee asked about the Commission. I propose to be perfectly fair, and I want to be allowed to put a member of the Commission on the stand.

Mr. ANDREW. I am willing to admit the distinguished part, but I am not willing to admit the declaration as to what the witness knows. I asked a question and he said he did not know.

Mr. EWART. He said——

Mr. ANDREW. I asked if he knew anything about——

Mr. HATTON. To be fair, I want to put a member of the Commission on now. [To Mr. Thompson.] Governor, what is the rule of the Commission where a man is removed for cause, and the cause is stated, and there is an application for re-appointment ? Mr. Lyman decided this very year that re-instatement inquiries ought to come under rule 10.

Mr. THOMPSON. The cause of removals is never reported to the Commission. If a removal is made, and there is no statement of cause, this application is made for re-instatement. For example, if the Secretary of the Treasury desires to restore a man who has been discharged from his service—not a woman, and not in case of an honorably discharged soldier, but assuming that the case is without any limit of time—he writes a letter to the Commission, stating he desires to restore Mr. Blank, under rule 10; that Mr. Blank was a clerk in such and such a grade, and resigned or removed without cause, affecting his character or standing at such and such a time. Sometimes the letters fail to make good that statement. There is one case now pending before the Commission where there is a conflict between the Secretary of the Treasury and the Commission, where he asked for the restoration of a lady. We called the attention of the Department to the fact that they failed to state in this letter whether she was dismissed for cause. The Secretary never answered the letter, and we refused to certify her.

Q. Is it the duty of the Commission to ascertain whether a man who makes application for another place was dismissed for cause, and find out the charges?—A. No, sir. If he says he was dismissed for cause, then we can not certify. If he says not, we are bound to certify him. I have certified a man that if I regarded I had the discretion I should have protested against his restoration.

Q. Has there been any rule of the Commission requiring Department officers to give the Commission the cause of removal—was there a rule of that kind adopted by the Commission?—A. I am not aware of any such rule.

Q. I would like to hear Mr. Lyman or Mr. Roosevelt in that respect. —A. I am sure there is not.

Mr. ROOSEVELT. There is no such rule and never has been.

Mr. HATTON. Was a rule of that kind adopted by the Commission?

Mr. THOMPSON. I can not say in regard to rules adopted in the past. Now, I would like to explain to the committee while I am on this subject, that the Post-Office Department has a regular printed form, and it contains these words in stating the cause: that the man was dismissed at such a time, though without cause affecting his standing as a citizen. Now, several times the mail has brought me letters in which these words were stricken out, and it stated the man resigned at such a time. I wrote to the Superintendent of the General Railway Mail Service to state whether these words were stricken out because the man might have resigned under some charge, and they informed me that when they struck out these words they meant that the person's resignation was voluntary and he was not compelled. We do not wish to have any unnecessary correspondence, and since then we understand from the Railway Mail Service that indicates a resignation; that where the words were stricken out that it meant the person resigned voluntarily and not for cause, and we have been very particular in this respect. The Commission has a case in which a distinguished Republican Senator two or three times interested himself, asking the restoration of a man; there was a letter charging he was dismissed for certain acts, and the Secretary in charge of that Department will say he has no evidence, which convinces him he was mistaken in dismissing him and dismissed the man unjustly.

The CHAIRMAN. As far as the Mitchell case is concerned, this question can not come in at all for this reason: Suppose that a man had been removed for cause. If it was a year after he had a perfect right to apply for examination, and if he passed the examination he had a right to be certified by your Commission, no matter what he was discharged for.

The WITNESS. If he was dismissed for murder we could not question it.

Q. He had a perfect character, etc.?—A. I think under ordinary——.

Q. As far as the man is concerned is the question whether he was removed for cause or not.

Mr. HATTON. I am satisfied with this statement.

By Mr. STONE:

Q. Governor Thompson, did you ever hear of Mr. Mitchell at the time you certified his appointment?—A. Well, no, sir; I never heard of him in my life until I heard of him here. I turn to the minutes and read the charges, and I find this entry, which I made myself: "The appeal in the case of Mr. Mitchell requesting a re-rating," and the words inserted "dismissed." Then on another minute I find I recorded this—I will state here that usually I dictate the minutes—but I find on another date I made this entry: "Examination of Mitchell. Read his paper here this morning. Re-examination of Mitchell granted for reasons given in the letter," that he was sick, and not having the proper time. That is all I know of Mitchell. The Commissioners do not ordinarily know; we have a certification clerk who usually answers these letters.

Q. I want a statement of fact. Did you ever hear of the fact of his having been dismissed from the service?—A. Never a word.

Q. Was the Commission—was any member of it to your knowledge—approached by any person in Mr. Mitchell's behalf with a view to certifying his appointment?—A. Positively not in my knowledge. I never heard his name, and as far as I know, none of my colleagues. I know they expressed as much surprise as I did, and we had to look up the records to see what he was.

Q. Would the fact of his having been dismissed, even for cause, from the service two years and a half before he was certified, or before his examination, if you had known it, as a matter of fact influence you in any way?—A. It could not under the law. The rule is that a man dismissed for cause would not be examined within one year; but this is not the question, for the man had been out for two years, and if he came up the Commissioners would be required, under the law, to examine him.

Q. I understand that.—A. We had no right to go behind it at all.

Mr. OBERLY. Suppose this man had made a statement in his application paper that he had been removed for cause, and you had known that there was cause. Would that in any way affect your determination?—A. Yes, sir.

Q. I understood you to say you had no right to know whether he was removed.—A. I did not mean to express it in this way. In several cases men have made statements in answer to question 8: "Have you ever been indicted for offenses?" Sometimes they have said "yes," and we have made further investigation. For instance, the other day a man said he had been indicted for carrying concealed weapons. The case was referred to the Commission, and they ruled out the case of the man who was indicted for carrying concealed weapons, because, if that was held to be true, a great many of the people in the United States might be indicted——

A VOICE. South Carolina.

The WITNESS. I know it is true down there, and I believe it is true somewhere else.

By Mr. HATTON:

Q. In the application for re-rating on the ground that he was examined when he was physically and mentally demoralized from being sick, did he furnish a physician's certificate of that fact?—A. No, sir; we did not require it.

Q. You took his word?—A. Yes, sir. Major Webster remembers the circumstance, and the fact he had made an omission of a paper, and the man complained he was badly treated, and I confess, when I read the letter the other day, I thought his first examination was not a fair test.

By Mr. STONE:

Q. In the application which Mr. Mitchell filed, and all the applications filed, is he required to state whether he had been previously in the service of the Government?—A. Yes, sir.

Q. Did his application show he had been dismissed?—A. I presume it did; but I do not recollect the fact now. I can not recall the fact.

Q. In making the certifications do you examine all these papers beforehand, or simply take the record showing the grade?—A. That cer tification that the witness has just shown is a copy of the examination paper that goes to the Department of the Interior. These officers—the Commissioner of Pensions in this case, and the chief of division, whom he consults in these matters, take these papers and read them over. The chief of division and head of the office take the papers and read them over. I am giving my own experience in the Treasury.

Q. What I want to get at is this: I make application to-day for an examination in the civil service. When I state that I have heretofore been in the departmental service and have at a certain time been dismissed without stating the cause of dismissal or anything of that kind; now, what effect does that statement have—what purpose does it serve?—A. If we had anything that caused a suspicion that he was a man of bad moral character we would make a further investigation.

Q. At what point would you make this investigation?—A. If anything in his answer conveyed the impression he was dismissed on account of bad character we would probably investigate it.

Q. But at what point?—A. When he made application.

Q. That would be done before examination?—A. Yes, sir. We have applicants who come there with application papers, and where they are regular we file them, and where they are irregular we regard them in the commission exactly as in the case of a man carrying concealed weapons. They are referred to a commission clerk who has full jurisdiction to act upon it.

Mr. TONNER resumed.

By Mr. HATTON:

Q. Is it a general rule when ten or twelve appointments are called for in the Pension Bureau do you know who makes the selection?—A. Presumably the chief of the bureau—that is if the request emanates from that bureau.

Q. Is it a general rule when ten or twelve or more are selected for the Pension Bureau they are sent to you?—A. All communications for the Civil Service Commission come directly to my room.

Q. If ten or twelve or more are sent to your room are they generally in one handwriting?—A. That I never observed.

Q. Will it not be pretty much the case?—A. I do not examine the certificates at all.

Q. Well, say of these ten names; were all written in the same handwriting except Mr. Mitchell's? Are you familiar with the handwriting of the officers of the Interior Department?—A. No, sir; not very. This indorsement was not made by the civil service.

The CHAIRMAN. I think that the proof should be entirely in this line: Whether the Commissioners committed an illegal act in allowing this man to be examined, and whether they gave the certification when he was not entitled to it.

Mr. HATTON. With all respect to you I would like to submit this question to the committee: If the charge is that the Commission by manipulation of examination and registry lists and certification lists was influenced by some man in the Department who was supposed to have nothing to do with the selection of the man at all, is it proper for us to show that possibly when the list gave as certified ten names and one blank, that an officer of the Interior Department filled that blank? I submit that to the committee.

Mr. EWART. We would like to recall Governor Thompson to ask a question in connection with this application.

The CHAIRMAN. Certainly.

Mr. EWART (to Governor Thompson). You see the application of the Civil Service Commission and signed Thomas Mitchell, that in answer to the question: "Were you ever dismissed for any cause, and if so, what cause? State it in full;" that the answer is: "Dismissed United States Pension Office, August, 1887." You will note he does not answer the question in full, and does not give the cause why he was dismissed. Now I want to ask you, Governor Thompson, who examines those application papers?—A. They are examined by the clerks in that office.

Q. By the clerks entirely?—A. Yes, sir; and whenever the clerk is instructed——

Q. Suppose the answer is made, as in this case, "dismissed United States Pension Office, August, 1887," which does not answer the question fully, and does not give the cause of dismissal. Suppose that that clerk in the office had informed you that the answer had not been answered fully, and he was in doubt of the cause he was dismissed for, is it the practice of the Commission then to go into an investigation to ascertain what the cause was for which that man was dismissed?—A. I do not think we would do that.

Q. I will follow that with this question: Does it not seem to you that this is a lame place in the law? Suppose you found out on examination made in the Interior Department that this man had been guilty of burglary or rape or something of that sort, and was dismissed for cause of that kind. Does it not strike you as a lame place in the law?—A. Possibly some injustice might be done by that; but I doubt it very much.

Mr. ROOSEVELT. Look at the preceding question. It says: "Not dismissed for delinquency or misconduct."

Mr. EWART. This I understand. These applications as far as the Commissioners are concerned are conclusive, and you never go back of them?—A. No, sir; but wherever we have any ground to believe it is not conforming to the truth then we investigate it.

Q. That is what I wanted to know. In this particular case you took no pains to ascertain in regard to it?—A. Not that I am aware of.

The CHAIRMAN. If the committee desire to know what the practice of the Commission is under the rules I have no objection, but we have an objection to going into the whole subject.

Mr. EWART. I would like to say this in explanation of the question I asked. It does seem to me if it is the practice of this Commission as now stated not to investigate whether or not an applicant for a position in the classified service states over his oath why he was dismissed when he was dismissed from the bureau—it does seem to me that blame would necessarily attach to the Commission for not taking the necessary steps to ascertain for what reason that man was dismissed.

Mr. LIND. That is not a matter to be brought out by testimony. The witness in his application says that he was discharged for no misconduct or delinquency in office. He has sworn here he was not discharged for any cause except being a Republican. That is all.

Mr. EWART. The Commissioners said that they were satisfied and they did not make any other investigation; that the very application ——

Mr. LYMAN. May I say a word here?

The CHAIRMAN. Is it necessary to take up the time to hear Mr. Lyman? I think it is perfectly clear——

Mr. LYMAN. There is only one point.

The CHAIRMAN. What is it, then?

Mr. LYMAN. The statement has been correctly made that the rules provided that where a man has been dismissed for delinquency or misconduct he was not to be examined within one year thereafter. This application is dated more than one year subsequent to his dismissal, and the Commission would not inquire into the cause of his dismissal, and especially in this case, as he was certified to the same office from which he was dismissed. He is making application to come back to the very office from which he was dismissed, and if he was ever certified the official records would be there to confirm it.

Mr. STONE. I will ask you one question while you are on the stand. Do you know whether any member of the Commission was ever approached by anybody in Mr. Mitchell's interests with a view to urging his certification?—A. No, sir.

Q. Did any person approach any member of the Commission within your knowledge in Mr. Mitchell's interest?—A. I will state the fact. Mr. Charles E. Mitchell, the Commissioner of Patents, came to me and stated that Mr. Thomas Mitchell had said to him that he had taken the examination under unfavorable conditions, and had made an appeal from that examination; and that he was fearful that he could not get justice from the chief examiner who would review the appeal, as he thought the chief examiner had some feeling against him. Commissioner Mitchell asked me whether I knew anything about it. I said to him that I did not know anything about the relations between Mr. Thomas Mitchell and the chief examiner, and that furthermore I knew the chief examiner well enough to believe that he would give those papers the full justice which they deserved if he reviewed the case on appeal. Mr. Mitchell, the Commissioner of Patents, said, as nearly as I can remember, "I have no favor to ask, and I know it would not be granted if I asked it. All I ask is that justice should be done." Are you answered?

Q. And that is the only time he approached you on the subject?—A. That is the only time. I saw him but once.

Q. That is the substance of it—what you said?—A. Yes, sir.

Q. And that was in reference to his examination?—A. In reference to his appeal; and incidentally the question came up whether under the circumstances, if they were correctly stated by Mr. Thomas Mitchell, whether he would be entitled to a re-examination.

TESTIMONY OF J. T. DOYLE—Continued.

J. T. DOYLE recalled and examined.

By Mr. EWART:

Q. From the hasty examination I gave to the eligible list in your presence this morning showing the list of those parties who had passed the copyist examination, I noticed there were a large number marked on the eligible list from Connecticut. Can you give the number on the eligible list in September, 1889?—A. From a casual examination of the register this morning in your presence I notice there were a few—I think three or four or five on the male copyist register from Connecticut—eligible appointments, places of $900 and less——

Q. In the month of September, 1889?—A. Yes, sir.

Q. Can you give the committee any idea of the number of eligibles from Connecticut on the same list the preceding months—say a year preceding?—A. I do not know that I could.

Q. Approximately?—A. I forget—there were a few names on the register.

Q. As many as twenty-five?—A. From Connecticut on that same register?

Q. Yes.—A. I doubt whether there were as many as that.

Q. Twenty?—A. I think there were fewer.

Q. Will you please explain to the committee, Mr. Doyle, how it was when there were fifteen or twenty names directly from Connecticut on the eligible list of copyists why the name of Mr. Mitchell, who appears to have passed an examination, should have been certified to the Interior Department for appointment?—A. Mr. Mitchell took the examination proper for the place of special examiner of what is known as the clerical examining force in the Pension Office. From the beginning of the examinations in the Pension Office the eligible register for special examining officers has been treated as available also for filling clerical places in that office without regard to salary. Mr. Mitchell was eligible on the special registry and could be certified to either a special place or to an ordinary clerical place.

Q. Could not any of the other parties from Connecticut also have been certified as a copyist?—A. They might have been.

Q. Those who passed long before he had been examined?—A. If the request from the Department did not state that those particular qualifications were disirable.

Q. They wanted special examiners. Were not there parties on that eligible list from Connecticut who had passed the examination for special examiners?—A. I do not know, sir.

Q. The same examination that Mr. Mitchell passed?—A. I do not remember.

Q. You can give us information on that point by an investigation?—A. It would not be material since the highest, without regard to State, would be certified.

Q. It would be material on this point. Would it not explain how it was Mitchell passed an examination only in the last few months—in September—when many others from Connecticut passed the same examination?—A. The time of the examination is not counted in making a certification, for you must certify the highest.

Q. Was he the highest of those parties?—A. There were two different registers. The register I spoke of to you was the register of copyist and those who had taken examination for an ordinary clerical place.

Mr. STONE. Well, there may have been others from Connecticut on each register. That is a fact, is it not?—A. They do not come in competition with the copyist register from Connecticut.

A VOICE. Gentlemen of the committee, understand that the certification was made from those who had passed the examination as a special examiner, and that Mr. Mitchell was the highest.

Mr. ROOSEVELT. Let me state this——

Mr. STONE. He does not say that. Let us see if he says so.

Mr. ROOSEVELT. Let me state right here——

The CHAIRMAN. Was it not a fact that these men who were certified to the Commissioner of Pensions had passed their examination and were the highest in percentage?—A. They were the highest, and they have received that certification.

Q. If Mr. Mitchell had been certified that he had only received 70 per cent., and another person had passed say at 75 per cent., the other person would have been reported eligible by the Commissioners?—A. Certainly.

By Mr. THOMPSON:

Q. Had the date of the examination anything to do with the certification?—A. No, sir; because in addition to the order of merit was still the apportionment among the States required by the civil service act.

Q. And by that provision you say Mr. Mitchell was certified?—A. Certainly.

By Mr. BOATNER:

Q. It has been stated here that the name of Mr. Mitchell, on a list which was sent by the Commission to the Department, is written in a different handwriting from the other names.—A. Not in the certification made by the Commission.

The CHAIRMAN. Let me call your attention to the fact in regard to this action in the Pension Office. What I want to get at is this: The man was certified from the Commission to the Department without any request from the Department that he should be so certified.—A. There was a request from the Department for filling a certain number of vacancies in the clerical examining force, and the names to be certified were taken from a list of special examiners, and the name of Mitchell at the time was among the three highest on the register in general average, and was entitled for that reason to the certification which he received, having regard, as I say, to the apportionment among the States according to the population.

Mr. BOATNER. The reason I asked the question the name was reported to be in another handwriting.

The CHAIRMAN. That has nothing to do with the civil service.

By Mr. OBERLY:

Q. There were fifteen places to be filled at the time. How did the Commissioner of Pensions make selections for these fifteen places? Upon certifications regularly made out each in its order, or by taking the papers to him and submitting them to him in groups of three?—A. For the convenience of the Department and for the convenience of the Commission they had printed requisitions of the Department for filling these places. The papers of a sufficient number of eligibles from the special register were taken to the Commissioner of Pensions and handed to him in the order of certification, according to the general average, in order that he might indicate in advance the selections he desired.

Q. That is to say, you took the three papers of the eligibles highest upon the list and handed them to the Commissioner in that way saying: "You will please make selection of one of these three?"—A. Yes, sir; and upon his indicating——

Q. And you made a note of that upon the paper, whereupon you took the two remaining papers if still entitled to certification, not having received three certifications before, and you added to these the papers of the eligible next upon the list in grade, and handed these three to the Commissioner and directed him to make a selection from these three?—A. Yes, sir.

Q. Then he having made a selection from these three after he took one of the eligibles whose paper has been certified on his demand you made a note of that ?—A. Yes, sir.

Q. Then you took the two remaining papers and added the papers of the fourth eligible to the list and handed the list to him and he made another selection ?—A. Yes, sir.

Q. And you continued that process until you got to the bottom of the list and had filled the fifteen places ?—A. Yes, sir.

Q. That is the *modus operandi* ?—A. Yes, sir.

· Q. Let me ask you—then you made up the regular certifications from the notes you had taken ?—A. Yes, sir; the formal certifications in the order of standing and States.

Q. And the Commissioner of Pensions in making his selections in that way for appointment selected Mitchell as one of the persons he had determined should be appointed ?—A. At that time he did not. He did not indicate Mitchell as one of the persons to be selected in that informal method.

Q. How, then, and when was Mitchell selected for appointment and by whom ?—A. After the selections for appointment had been indicated in this informal way the Commissioner of Pensions when the formal certifications were made and sent to the Secretary of the Interior, the Secretary of the Interior notified the names of the persons selected from these certifications, and among the persons thus indicated as selected appeared the name of Thomas Mitchell.

Q. The name of one of the persons selected for appointment by the Commissioner of Pensions having been stricken off the list, you added the name of Thomas Mitchell, whom he substituted ?—A. It was not stricken off the list. It did not appear upon the notifications for the reason the name of Thomas Mitchell did not appear——

Q. I understood you took back with you a memorandum of the fifteen whom the Commissioner of Pensions desired to be put into fifteen vacancies and waited until you had ascertained by official notice whether these selections for appointment had been confirmed by the Interior Department by the appointing officer ?—A. Yes, sir.

Q. Now, one of the persons selected by the Commissioner of Pensions, who generally does this thing, was omitted by some person in the Interior Department, and the name of Thomas Mitchell substituted by some person for his own reason ?—A. That might have been the case.

Q. The fact is it was stricken off. Some name was omitted from the selection made by the Commissioner of Pensions and the name of Thomas Mitchell was put in in that way ?—A. That may have been the case. I merely know the name of Thomas Mitchell was selected.

Q. In making out certificates in that way some pressure might have been brought in the Interior Department to have a person selected upon his merits by the Commissioner——

Mr. ROOSEVELT. There is no charge against the Commissioner of Pensions, as I understand.

Mr. OBERLY. You must excuse me for going into this thing, but I do it in order to make it clear to the committee.

Mr. BUTTERWORTH. That indicates a change may have been made in this handwriting, as I understand it.

Mr. OBERLY. This requisition for these fifteen came in on what date ? I think it was the 6th of January.

The WITNESS. No ; September the 9th.

Q. When was the examination in Baltimore held ?—A. The 12th of August.

Q. That was three days after the requisition for these fifteen?—A. No; a month before.

Mr. OBERLY. The requisition was made a month before?

The CHAIRMAN. The requisition was made in September.

The WITNESS. The requisition was not made until September. In the meantime Mitchell's name had been marked and had gone on the register.

Mr. OBERLY. I understand the requisition came in before the examination?—A. No; a month afterwards.

Mr. THOMPSON. I want the liberty of stating this to the committee: The charge is that Mitchell when his friends found that he was on the ineligible list, that he was re-rated and put on the eligible list. I am prepared to prove from the official report of the chief examiner, if desired, that Mitchell's appeal for a re-rating was dismissed; that practically the only thing in the charge these papers prove was not done. . Mitchell swears to that. Here are the official records of the Commission, and I can produce the official minutes showing the appeal of Mitchell for a remarking.

The CHAIRMAN. He was allowed a re-examination?

Mr. THOMPSON. Yes, sir.

Thereupon the committee took a recess until 2.30 p. m.

AFTERNOON SESSION.

The committee met at half past 2 o'clock, pursuant to adjournment.

TESTIMONY OF CYRUS BUSSEY.

CYRUS BUSSEY, sworn and examined.

The CHAIRMAN. Mr. Ewart, will you please ask the questions you desire to have answered by this witness?

Mr. EWART. Mr. Hatton desires to examine the witness.

By Mr. HATTON:

Q. What is your position?—A. Assistant Secretary of the Interior.

Q. Do you make appointments for the Interior Department, for the Pension Office?—A. In part, I do.

Q. Did you appoint Mr. Thomas E. Mitchell?—A. I believe I did.

Q. Did you know at the time his name was certified his relative standing as a clerk, the rating he had as a clerk?—A. At the time I presume I knew from the report of the Commission.

Q. How many names were sent to you? I do not expect an exact answer.—A. I can not remember at this time. I think fifteen or twenty names.

Q. Was Mr. Mitchell's name sent to you from the Pension Office?—A. His name was not sent from the Pension Office. The blank was left, and the Commissioner wrote me to fill in Mr. Mitchell's name.

Q. When did you write it?—A. When they sent the papers.

Q. Do you know why the name was not sent up; for what reason?—A. Because there was some doubt as to whether he was the party who desired to be appointed.

Q. Having Mr. Mitchell on the eligible list, you desired to have him appointed?—A. Mr. Mitchell had been to see me some time before. I had looked into the case, and was satisfied that he was an efficient clerk, and it is a rule of the Department where we know a person who is efficient we would rather give preference to him than to one whom we do not know.

Q. How did you satisfy yourself?—A. From the records in the office.

Q. Did you know at the time he had been dismissed from the service?—A. I did not.

Q. You did not know at the time whether he had been dismissed or not?—A. No, sir.

Q. Would the records of the Department show whether or not he was dismissed for cause?—A. The records, perhaps, in the Pension Office show that fact, but at the time in the Interior Department it showed that he was an old clerk, and had been an efficient clerk.

Q. If you had known you would have inquired into the case?—A. I would always.

Q. Did any of your associates in the Interior Department see you in regard to the appointment of Mitchell?—A. I do not think they did. When Mr. Mitchell first came to me he first wanted a position in the Census Office and brought himself to my notice before that, and I attempted to interest myself in his behalf to get him a place in the Census Office, and told him his name was on the eligible list and as it came up from the civil service he would be selected.

Q. When did you first know Mr. Mitchell?—A. I can not tell you that. Some time, two or three months, perhaps, prior to his appointment. He came frequently to me, as did everybody else who wanted a place.

Q. Who introduced him to you?—A. He introduced himself.

Q. Did he have a letter to you from anybody?—A. No, sir; he did not.

Q. If you had known at the time you made the appointment he had been dismissed for cause, would you have appointed him?—A. I do not think I would without knowing the cause of his removal.

Q. When names were sent up from the Pension Office one on the list was left blank?—A. Yes, sir.

Q. And you wrote Mr. Mitchell's name in?—A. I do not know whether I did or somebody else did. The Commissioner of Pensions informed me that that blank was left for Mr. Mitchell.

Q. Have you got that list?—A. My recollection is I did not write it.

Q. It was written by somebody in the Interior Department?—A. I think I did not write it.

Q. Would the papers come directly to you?—A. Yes, sir; and the name might have been filled in by my direction, and I think probably it was.

Q. You have no idea who probably did write it?—A. I have not.

Q. Was it anybody outside of your office?—A. No, sir; somebody connected with the office; perhaps it was Mr. Allen, the gentleman in charge of appointments in the office.

Q. Do you know any method of obtaining clerks whom they may desire to obtain after they have passed the examination by refusing to appoint clerks certified until they get down to his name?—A. There has never been a list of appointments sent up from the Civil Service Commission that a name has not been selected to my knowledge.

Q. Out of three one is taken?—A. Yes, sir; always, and some times more.

Q. And then another name is added to the two rejected and sent to you again?—A. Yes, sir.

Q. And then they could take also a name again, and reject the other two?—A. Yes, sir.

By Mr. BOATNER:

Q. This is the charge:

That with the knowledge of its members on the 19th day of September, 1889, Thomas Mitchell, of Connecticut, was appointed to a position in the Pension Office as a copyist; that the said Mitchell was on September 30, 1887, dismissed from the service for cause; that the said Mitchell failed in his examination held prior to his last appointment; that this failure becoming known to the party desiring his restoration to the service, his papers were remarked and he was raised from the ineligible to the eligible list.

Do you know anything as to the truth or falsity of that charge?—A. I do not.

Q. You do not know whether Mr. Mitchell was ever on the ineligible list or not?—A. I do not.

Q. Was any influence from your office that you know of brought to bear to have this man Mitchell pass an examination in order that his name might be sent up?—A. I can say positively I never used one word of influence with the Civil Service Commission in connection with Mr. Mitchell or any other man since I have been in office, positively.

Q. Do you know of any other influence having been used?—A. I do not.

Q. Do you know of any parties who were desirous of his restoration to the service?—A. I do not. I think Commissioner Mitchell one day asked me if there was a prospect there would be a call made by the Civil-Service Commission for appointments. I told him I did not know anything about it, that they were likely to call at any time, but I could not tell.

By Mr. STONE:

Q. Do you know whether any person, any Commissioner, head of any Bureau, or Secretary or Assistant Secretary, has attempted to use any influence in any way with the Civil-Service Commission to procure certifications?—A. I do not know of any.

Q. Have you ever advised with any applicants for appointment as to any method by which they ought to proceed to procure certifications?—A. I do not remember that I ever did. I told parties who have applied that they would have to go and take the civil-service examination. Nothing beyond that. I have never advised any one how he could have his name advanced and how certified, because I never have known of any way to have done so.

Q. That covers my inquiry. [To Mr. Ewart.] That completes this charge?

Mr. EWART. Yes, sir.

TESTIMONY OF HAMILTON SHIDY.

HAMILTON SHIDY sworn and examined:

By Mr. EWART:

Q. Have you been connected with the Civil-Service Commission in the last few years?—A. I have been secretary of the local examining board.

Q. Where?—A. At Milwaukee, Wis.

Q. How long since?—A. Until the 1st day of July of the past year, 1889.

Q. When did you become secretary?—A. Shortly after the passage of the act. I think it was in 1883, and I was one of the original appointees under the act.

Q. And you continued to act as secretary of the local board of the Milwaukee post-office until what date?—A. Until the 1st day of July, 1889.

Q. By virtue of holding that position as secretary of the board you were an officer of the Commission?—A. I judge so; to that extent I was.

Q. What compensation did you receive as acting secretary?—A. Abuse and loss of place.

Q. I did not have reference to that.—A. This is all I received. Nothing. Not one penny.

Q. In salary?—A. No, sir.

Q. Did you have any position in the office?—A. My official designation was superintendent of registered mail.

Q. What salary did you receive for that?—A. One thousand three hundred dollars.

Q. Now, Mr. Shidy, I am going to state to you frankly, as it is my purpose to do, as suggested by Mr. Boatner, that the questions I am going to ask you, if answered in the affirmative, will subject you necessarily to more or less disgrace and odium, and will, in my opinion, subject you to a criminal prosecution, and you may answer them or not as you please.

(Objection was raised to this by Mr. Boatner and other members of the committee, and the question was debated.)

The CHAIRMAN. Let the question be asked, and I think this witness is fully advised by this time of what he should do. Let him take the responsibility of answering. He has a right to decline to answer.

Mr. EWART. I make the request of the committee that whenever I ask a question which, in your judgment, has a tendency to criminate the witness let the witness be advised as to his rights. (To the witness.) What were your duties as secretary of this examining board?—A. To keep the books and papers of the Commission.

Q. Did you have entire charge of the books and papers?—A. Nominally I did; really not.

Mr. LIND. That is not a complete answer.

By Mr. EWART:

Q. Explain what you mean by that.—A. Because the books and papers were not always in my possession or absolutely under my control.

Q. Did you keep the books?—A. You mean as a book-keeper?

Q. Yes.—A. Yes.

Q. Were entries made from certifications and so on in your hand-writing?—A. Yes, sir.

Q. To that extent the books were under your control?—A. Yes.

Q. Do you know, Mr. Shidy, if there were any irregularities in the workings of this office in the year 1888?—A. Of the Milwaukee office?

Q. Yes.—A. I wish you would be more explicit, please, in the scope of the question. It seems to me——

Q. I am not going to specify the irregularities now.—A. Just name the kind of irregularities, whether you mean special violations of the civil-service rules and regulations, or general irregularities.

Q. I will say either.—A. There were irregularities in the Milwaukee post-office.

Q. In the year 1888?—A. I think so.

Q. Do you know that to be a fact?—A. If you could specify more particularly some irregularity——

Q. Any class of irregularities, general or special.—A. In a general way, yes.

Q. Did you report these irregularities to the Civil-Service Commission?

Mr. LIND. That is one of the questions you need not answer unless you see fit.

Mr. STONE. That depends somewhat on the nature of the irregularities at least.

Mr. LIND. That is why I suggested the law should be read to the witness.

The CHAIRMAN. Are you ready to answer the question?—A. I want you to distinctly understand I am ready to testify of any matter of fact I may know of in regard to this matter.

The CHAIRMAN. Answer the question.

By Mr. EWART:

Q. Did you report these irregularities you mention in the workings of the office in 1888 to the Civil-Service Commission?—A. I did not, at least I am not aware that I did.

Q. Was it your duty as an officer of the Commission to make a report of these violations or irregularities?—A. Constructively so.

Q. Was it not actually so?—A. Now you are bringing in——

Q. Just answer the question.—A. No; it was not actually so.

Q. Then if there were violations of the law and you were perfectly cognizant of that fact, was it not your duty as an officer of the Commission to report the facts to the Commission in Washington?—A. It was not. But, excuse me, gentlemen, the chief conditions——

Mr. EWART. Make any explanation you want to make.

The WITNESS. The line of questions is a narrow one, and confines attention only to one part of my duty, whereas my duty was double, and in view of the whole situation I will answer according to my judgment which is correct. I owed a duty to the Milwaukee postmaster as well as the Civil Service Commission. They conflicted. I regarded my allegiance as paramount to the postmaster; he paid me and the Civil Service Commission did not. I simply explain it that I may be understood.

Q. You say the postmaster paid you. The Government pays you, of course?—A. That is a question I do not wish to quibble on.

Q. You say you owed a duty also to the Commission as well as the postmaster?—A. Yes, sir.

Q. What was the duty you owed to the Commission? What do you mean by that?—A. The faithful performance of the duties assigned to me.

Q. Do you not think a faithful performance of the duties assigned you would require you to report to your superior officer the violations of law?—A. I do, and would have so reported if there were nothing to prevent, if some higher duty did not prevent.

Q. What higher duty in this particular instance prevented?—A. My duty to the postmaster.

Q. Then the position you take is that being cognizant of these violations of law in the workings of this office, you considered you owed your first duty to the postmaster and not to the Commission?—A. Yes, sir.

Q. As clerk, or secretary, rather, of that board, will you please state to the committee whether or not at any time while you were acting as secretary you made false certifications upon your records?—A. That question is not entirely fair. I made certifications which were not accurate. That is, they did not conform as to date, and they were not in harmony with the civil-service rules; but that false certifications were made, no.

Q. You answer that emphatically, no?—A. Yes, sir; with that understanding.

Q. State whether or not while acting as secretary of the local examining board you ever tortured the records so as to make the list of eligibles come into line?—A. That was made part of my duty.

Q. Answer the question.—A. That was done.

The CHAIRMAN. It was part of your duty.—A. Excuse me——

The CHAIRMAN. You do not mean to say it was part of your duty as an official of the Civil Service Commission?—A. Gentlemen, you forget my dual character. You are examining me purely as being part of the Civil Service Commission, whereas in reality I was a part of the Milwaukee post-office there.

Mr. EWART. But in making these certifications——

Mr. LIND. It was that part that did the torturing.

The CHAIRMAN. You were really acting as an official of the board?— A. No, sir; as an official of the Milwaukee post-office; assuredly as an official of the Milwaukee post-office.

Mr. EWART. When you made this list of eligibles come into line, you did that in your capacity as a subordinate of the postmaster, and not as an officer of the Commission?—A. Assuredly.

Mr. STONE. Would it not be of importance at this point for the witness to explain just what this torturing process was?

The CHAIRMAN. Let Mr. Ewart get it.

By Mr. EWART:

Q. That is a question I was going ask him. Explain to the committee what this torturing process meant. You did that as a clerk in the office under Postmaster Paul, and not in your capacity as an official of the Commission. You became a sort of Dr. Jekyll and Mr. Hyde?— A. Most unfortunately.

Q. Please explain what you mean by torturing the record.—A. I mean that the records did not conform to the rules and regulations of the Civil Service Commission always, and exactly in spirit and in fact; that they were not made at the time when they should have been made; that the dates were not harmonious with the facts, certain records being made after the fact instead of before the fact, as they of right should have been made. These were not purely my own acts, although I recorded them.

Q. In other words, Mr. Shidy, you made certifications on your records after or before appointments, which?—A. They were made in both ways. Those that were made before appointments were correctly made, and where certification was made after the appointment it was incorrectly made.

Q. That was torturing the records?—A. I presume that is what you mean by that word.

Q. In other words, it was a false certification?—A. No, not probably with the construction which you place on the words "false certification." It was a certification and statement of fact, but it was not false except-ing in its date and the time at which it was made.

Q. Now, Mr. Shidy——

Mr. ANDREW. Will you give the witness a chance to explain?

The WITNESS. The course of appointment under civil-service rules is this: When a vacancy occurred in the office in was the duty of the postmaster under the civil-service rules to notify me in writing that a vacancy existed. I then, as secretary of the board, was required to certify the three highest names on the eligible list from which he should make a selection.

The CHAIRMAN. What was done in point of fact?—A. In point of fact, appointment was made sometimes, and these certifications were made to cover appointments previously made.

The CHAIRMAN. Appointments were made before the postmaster notified you?—A. Without notification and without certification.

The CHAIRMAN. And then you made the certification to agree with his appointment?—A. Afterwards I made the certification to agree with his appointment. He would tell me who had been appointed, and I would make the certification to cover the appointment. Sometimes it was long after the fact.

Mr. LIND. Were these appointments made by the postmaster from the eligible list invariably?—A. To places covered by the civil-service rules? I think yes. There was a large class of exceptions claimed——

By Mr. EWART:

Q. Mr. Shidy, did you give Postmaster Paul free access to the list of eligibles?—A. Mr. Paul had free access to the list of eligibles.

Q. Did he have a right to have free access under the law?—A. No, he did not.

Q. Why did you allow him to have access to those lists?—A. I was not in a position to gainsay him.

Q. Why?—A. Because I was his subordinate, and my official life depended purely on his will.

Q. You knew then that his demand to see these lists of eligibles was a violation of law and you could not refuse to allow him access to the list because your position was dependent on his pleasure?—A. I knew that fact, and I called his attention to it. I gave him the printed circular of the Commission, the only copy which I had, and emphatically called his attention to that fact.

Q. You had control of the entire work of this board, did you not?—A. Only as secretary.

Q. But it is generally conceded you did all the work.—A. As secretary.

Q. Did other members of the board have anything to do with it?—A. Assuredly. I was not the Milwaukee board; I was secretary of the board.

Q. I deem it my duty to caution you in making your answer. The question I asked you is, if the other members of the board had anything to do with this work.—A. Assuredly. Now, Mr. Ewart by "this work," I understand you to mean the civil service work in the Milwaukee post-office. You may apply it in some other way, but if you have some special meaning—if you mean to keep the records, I keep the records.

Q. So far as the records were concerned the other members of the board had little or nothing to do with them.

By Mr. ANDREW:

Q. You were a member of the board?—A. The civil-service board? Assuredly, I was secretary of the board.

Q. Does that constitute you a member of the board?

Mr. EWART. It makes him an officer of the Civil Service Commission.

Mr. ANDREW. What I wanted to know was whether the secretary of the Milwaukee board was a member of the board.

A. Certainly; there were three members of the board. They chose 'one president and one secretary, and the secretary keeps the minutes.

Mr. LIND. Were they all employed in the office?

A. Of necessity, the regulation being, or part of the law being, that they must be Government employés.

By Mr. EWART:

Q. From whom did you hold your commission as secretary?—A. From the Civil Service Commission.

Q. Going back to the line of investigation before we were interrupted, do I understand you to say you made these false certifications or that you tortured these records because you were compelled to do so?

Mr. BOATNER. I would suggest that the witness objected to the use of the words "false certifications," and when you put a question in that shape you compel him either to refuse to answer your question or evade it.

Mr. EWART. Well, then, I will use the expression "torturing the record."

A. I will take your question again.

Q. This torturing of the records; was that done because you felt you were obliged to do it?—A. Assuredly.

Q. At the instance of Postmaster Paul?—A. Assuredly.

Q. Your position depended upon it?—A. I had no interest whatever in changing any record in the post-office, or in making a certification out of time.

Mr. ANDREW. I would like to ask what he means by making certifications out of time; is it not merely technical?

The CHAIRMAN. He has explained. The certification should precede the appointment. I understand that the proceeding was that the postmaster made the appointment, and after the appointment of these gentlemen you made the certification?

A. The certification followed the appointment, instead of preceding it.

The CHAIRMAN. Practically the postmaster was the Civil Service Commission.

Mr. ANDREW. They were not competitive examinations?

A. Yes, sir; the results of competitive examinations.

By Mr. LIND:

Q. Did these irregularities in dates prejudice other eligibles? Did this irregular method of doing what you did prejudice the chances of eligibles on your list, if you know?—A. I think not, so far as that fact alone is concerned. The mere fact that an entry was made after instead of before an appointment would not prejudice the condition of other eligibles.

Q. It is your duty—with the permission of the committee; I do not desire to take up the time of this committee unless it is conceded—as I understand it you were required under the rules to report their names to the postmaster when a vacancy occurred, but instead of doing that, he chose a man of his own accord and appointed him, and then applied to you for the certification of an eligible covering that identical case with the name. Now, then, did that practically prejudice the cases of eligibles on your books who should have received the appointment had it been regularly made and reported by you?—A. In some cases it did unquestionably, and others not. For ordinarily the names chosen would fall within the three which would have been certified, and in that case had it been certified beforehand it could not have affected the case at all.

By Mr. Ewart:

Q. Did you not state in the presence of Mr. Johnson, who was a member of the board, and Mr. Paul, the postmaster at Milwaukee, and also in the presence of the three Commissioners, that the reason you had for changing the grades of some of these applicants was to get them out of the way of other men whom the postmaster desired to appoint?—A. Giving that as being my reason?

Q. Did you not state that as a fact?—A. That being my reason for doing so?

Q. As being the reason why it was done.

Mr. Boatner. Did you state that?—A. I stated that that was the reason why it was done, with that understanding.

By Mr. Ewart:

Q. You stated it in the presence of these commissioners?—A. That my reasons——

Q. That it was your reason and Mr. Paul's?—A. That is the reason it was done?

Q. That it was done for the purpose of getting unfortunates out of the way of the eligibles.

By the Chairman:

Q. It was done under the instruction of the postmaster?—A. Assuredly.

Q. He instructed you to do it?—A. I had no possible interest in it.

Q. He instructed you and you merely carried out his wish?—A. Assuredly so.

Q. Even if it was against your duty as an official of the Civil Service Commission, when you were instructed by the postmaster wherever the two conflicted?—A. Where they conflicted my allegiance was to the postmaster.

Mr. Ewart. Whether it was a violation of the law or not in your judgment?—A. Precisely so. I was not making these appointments, and I was not responsible for them. You will understand me, gentlemen, because I am only one of that board of persons, and this was clearly understood between myself and my colleagues. We were in no position to withstand Mr. Paul, and I repeatedly brought these matters to the attention of Mr. Johnson and the other members of the commission, the question being not what we could do about it, but what we should do about it, and I was asked more than once was I ready to fight. It was an absurdity and we could not do it. It was simply to let Mr. Paul have his own way.

Mr. Boatner. It was simply a question of bread and butter against the civil service rules, and the bread and butter prevailed?—A. Precisely. That is the matter in a nutshell.

By the Chairman:

Q. Did you ever mark up the percentage which different candidates had obtained, that is to say, where a man passed only 40 per cent. did you mark it up to 70 per cent. in order to make his standing so he could be selected?—A. There were a few instances in which papers were reviewed for the purpose of changing the rating. In some cases they were raised, and in one case they were lowered.

Q. They were raised arbitrarily. Understand what I mean by that. Was that done for the purpose of correcting errors or done for the purpose of putting a man on the eligible list who had no right to obtain it?—A. It was done for the purpose of finding a reason for advancing the man.

Q. That is no answer to the question. Was the reviewing done for the purpose of having the man marked higher?—A. He was marked probably with a biased judgment. The judgment was biased by the knowledge that the postmaster wanted that man and wanted him badly.

Mr. BOATNER. You considered that case with a decided leaning?— A. That is the size of it, gentlemen.

The CHAIRMAN. Whenever such marking was made it was made at the instance of the postmaster?—A. It was, and with the knowledge that he wanted that man and was bound to have him.

By Mr. EWART :

Q. That is what is called gerrymandering the list?—A. That is what is alluded to by that term.

Q. And that is done for the purpose of producing a stuffed certification?—A. Not exactly that term "stuffed"——

Q. Explain what is meant by stuffed certifications.—A. The stuffing was merely padding so as to make the certification seem round and full. Gentlemen, you have had your laugh too soon. Names were sometimes added to the certification after it was known that the man was definitely and permanently selected and had been at work for some time. Now, when that name was selected, it was wholly immaterial what names went with him. Those names were simply stuffing and padding to the certification. That is the sense in which that word is used in the written paper you have before you.

By Mr. BOATNER :

Q. You knew when you sent three names that of those three one had been already selected and employed?—A. Yes, sir.

Q. And the other two were sent along as a matter of form.—A. That is all.

Q. In order to comply with the letter of the law?—A. Yes, sir.

By the CHAIRMAN :

'Q. To what extent were the records falsified? I should call it a falsification of the record; that is legitimate I should say. In raising the percentage of different persons who were examined, to what extent was that done? Was it done in one case or in two cases, or was it done wherever it was required to be done?—A. It was not done as a general thing. That remedy was used sparingly.

Q. Was it used whenever necessary to use it? That is the point.— A. I presume so.

Q. Whenever it was necessary to use that remedy it was used?—A. I presume so.

Q. You know so?—A. No, I do not know so. Excuse me. Now I recollect one case in which an effort was made to have the grade raised, but no pretext could be found in the papers for raising the grade. In that case it was not raised, so it would not apply in every case where it might have been desirable to have done so.

Q. This was an exception?—A. Yes, sir.

Q. Was that the only exception; only that one case?—A. I think so.

Q. The committee would like to find out how far this matter went, whether the postmaster and the Civil Service Commission as represented by the three members or officials had that matter in charge, whether they evaded the law in every instance where it was necessary to evade it in order to carry out the will of the postmaster.—A. The postmaster had his way in making these appointments, absolutely.

Q. With the exception of one case. In one case he did not have his way ?—A. In that case he did not, but he got his way in another.

By Mr. LIND:

Q. So it was not a hopeless case then ?—A. I do not want the impression to be made here that this class of cases frequently occurred. The cases in which there was a change or remarking of papers were few.

Q. But there were such cases on both sides, in which the rating was raised ?—A. And in which it was lowered, but they were not many. It was not a general practice. These cases did not require anything of the kind.

Mr. EWART. I will ask you if it is not a fact that the official records which you kept as secretary of that board do not show beyond any possibility of dispute that the list of eligibles was twisted and garbled in almost every conceivable manner in order to produce false certifications by which men could be rejected and others appointed who had no rightful claims to the chance ?—A. In answering that question, I want to make a little statement simply calling attention to the facts. When men were found to be at work in the office, and it became necessary to cover their appointment by certification, that is to make their appointment formal it sometimes was quite difficult to do so. The task remained to do it, and to do it in the least objectionable manner. Still, it had to be done, for the men were at work.

Mr. BOATNER. Does it appear they were competent ?

Mr. LIND. What we want is to know just how you did do it.—A. Unless some special case is brought up——

The CHAIRMAN (to Mr. Ewart). Give him a special case.

The WITNESS. Sometimes there would not—for instance, if there were three names on a given register, none of which would include a chosen man, the fourth name on the register being the one chosen, one of those names would have to be dropped out for some reason. He might be marked "objected to."

By Mr. EWART:

Q. Do you recollect the case of a man named Wakeman, who was examined April 14, 1887 ?—A. I remember the name, but not the numbers.

Q. Do you remember the name of Trump ?—A. Yes, sir; I do.

Q. Explain how he was gerrymandered.—A. In Mr. Trump's case, as far as I or any other member of the Commission is concerned, I do not think there was any irregularity at all. This is a typical case. Mr. Trump was examined at a certain date. He was put to work before his examination papers were marked, before the postmaster knew of his——

Q. Let me refresh your recollection here, Mr. Shidy. He was appointed March 1, 1888. He was not examined until March 17, not certified until April 14. Now, explain how that happens.—A. That happens exactly in the manner I was going to state. He was appointed before——

Mr. ANDREW. Will you please give those dates again ?

Mr. EWART. He was appointed March 1 and began work March 23; he was not examined until the 17th of March, and was not certified until the 14th of April.—A. He was not examined until March 17. My

3117——10

recollection tallies with that, exactly. He was put to work on March 23. Now, the interval between the 17th and the 23d day of March was not sufficient for the board to mark and rate those examination papers. Mr. Trump's standing was not distinctly known at that time. Still, he was appointed on the 1st day of March, and on the 23d day of March he went to work. On the 17th day of March he was examined. His record was not known until the 23d of March, but on the 23d day of March he was put to work, and reported as having been at work on the 23d.

By the CHAIRMAN:

Q. Did he draw his pay from the 1st of March ?—A. I should think so.

Q. Do you know, as a matter of fact, he drew pay from the 1st of March ?—A. I know the general custom is that appointees are paid from the day of appointment.

Q. Really he did not go to work until the 23d of March ?—A. He was not connected with the office until then.

Q. Did you certify the papers back to the 1st of March ?—A. I think not. I do not know what the certification in that case is.

Q. Would not the record show that his certification was made either on the day after or the day of his appointment ?—A. It would.

Q. Did you not falsify the records as far as that is concerned ?—A. No, sir; those certifications which I made where they have dates appended—I guess all have dates appended—are true dates on which I submitted those certifications to the postmaster. The date of the appointment would vary in many cases with the date of certification. That is the point of discrepancy between them. If I had falsified these dates then there would have been no room for discovery, but I put in the correct dates.

Q. As far as the dates are concerned, you always put the correct dates, and if there was any change it was made afterwards by some one else ?—A. I think there is only one instance in which the date was changed, and that was by requirement of the postmaster, in which he absolutely insisted on the change.

Q. Who changed it ?—A. I changed it.

Q. Then you changed the date at his request ?—A. Yes; at his request.

Q. If he changed the date so that a falsification of the record was made, you falsified the record at the request of the postmaster ?—A. Precisely so. There was no reason why I should do it of my own volition in any case.

By Mr. EWART:

Q. I will ask you if it was not often the case that the postmaster would cancel certifications ?—A. Sometimes.

Q. Was it the case that these void certifications were employed and used by candidates on the three certifications ?—A. I am not sure now, but by looking over the certification-book I could tell. I do not know that certifications were ever made for that purpose. I do not recollect that it was.

Q. You would not answer positively about that ?—A. I could not answer positively.

Q. Was it the case that men were ever singled out of a higher list and certified in a lower list, and that others were certified from a lower to a higher with superior advantages to the favored one ? Was that done with your assistance ?—A. Men were taken from a higher to a lower list. I do not mean to answer your question in full by this because as to their qualifications and requirements I do not know exactly.

Q. Why were they taken from a higher to a lower list?—A. The reason was that the postmaster where he chose such a man—I never asked him——

Q. That is another question, where he compelled you to do it.—A. I never questioned his choice of a man.

By the CHAIRMAN:

Q. These questions were furnished you by the Civil Service Commission?—A. Yes, sir.

Q. Did you ever know of any of your associates to your knowledge giving questions out to candidates before examination?—A. Never. If they did I never knew of any such case.

Q. Did the postmaster have access to these questions?—A. No, sir, he did not.

Q. Who kept them?—A. The questions only reached me as a rule the day before the examination. Sometimes on the very morning of the examination. They came there under seal and the seal was not broken until in the presence of the class. So these questions were never tampered with.

Q. I did not know but that the postmaster running the whole Commission had the papers as well as doing the marking?—A. He did not have the papers.

Mr. LIND. Show how these disclosures came to be made to the Civil Service Commission, how the Civil Service Commission got notice of this state of affairs.

The WITNESS. Do you ask that now?

Mr. EWART. Yes.

The WITNESS. In answer to the first question, I remained in the office until the 1st day of July, 1889. The Commission made their report public, I think it was the 25th day of June, or about that time; it must have been June.

By Mr. EWART:

Q. Please state to the committee how those disclosures were brought about.—A. I think that would be very competent for the Civil Service Commissioners themselves, for they know how they got it. I know I did not give it to them; I did not bring it to their attention.

Q. You never did call their attention to it at any time?—A. I did not.

Q. To any of these violations of the law?—A. Now you are pinning me down too closely. I hope you gentlemen will understand me when I speak I mean to say just what is the fact. After this matter was opened up and the Commission began to examine into these things I may have called their attention to some of the irregularities, but what I mean is I did not start this investigation or instigate it in any way. That is what I mean to say.

Mr. LIND. You say after the matter was opened up; then have you any knowledge how it was opened up?—A. I can state all I know about it. Along in the midsummer of 1888, Mr. Doyle dropped in on me one pleasant summer afternoon, I think it was late in June, and asked to see the books of the Commission, which he did. I placed them at his disposal and helped him all I could. He made some short-hand notes as this gentleman is doing, and presently took his departure. His visit was followed by a visit some forty or fifty days later by himself and Mr. Webster who came as an investigating committee to examine into the conduct of affairs in the office. I then was quite severely questioned. I made the statements which I think are before the committee. I have the impression I stated then just what was the fact. I meant to state exactly the facts.

By the CHAIRMAN:

Q. Who made the examination?—A. Mr. Webster and Mr. Doyle. Later on in 1889 the Commission as constituted at present paid us a visit—Mr. Lyman, Mr. Roosevelt, and Mr. Thompson; at that time we were submitted to some examination. I do not think my testimony on the two occasions conflict at all. I have the impression I told the facts in both cases as I meant to do. I was reluctant to testify and it was only when I was obliged to do so or when I was called upon to do so that I did so. I knew the results would be just what they were, and I so stated to the Commission.

Q. What was the result?—A. The result would be my dismissal.

Q. Why were you not dismissed in 1888, then?

Mr. ROOSEVELT. The reports were not made public.

By the CHAIRMAN:

Q. Mr. Paul knew what you stated?—A. No, sir; he did not know the statement I made then. He stated to me that he had called for a copy of my testimony, but I think he never got it. I do not know, for he never stated he had got it. Later he probably knew what I had testified to.

Q. Was there any action taken by the Commission in 1888, after you had stated substantially what you had stated to the Commission in 1889, concerning these charges, to your knowledge?—A. I am not aware of any. I do not know what was done in that respect. I think they considered the testimony which was taken at that time and digested it, but what they did I do not know; I mean what the Commission did.

Q. Mr. Paul was not investigated, neither was he removed.—A. No; he was not.

Q. And you made exactly the same statement in 1888 that you made to-day?—A. So far as the ground was covered.

By Mr. BOATNER:

Q. The time you were examined by Webster and Doyle is the time you refer to?—A. Yes, sir.

Q. What time in 1888?—A. It must have been either August or September, probably early in September or late in August.

Q. You were investigated by the Commission when?—A. That was the investigation by the Commission. The Commission must have been there——

Q. You state that after Mr. Doyle and Mr. Webster left that the Commission came on. How long was that after?—A. They were there, I think, in May; I think it was May the following year. These dates can readily be fixed.

Mr. EWART. What was the date of the investigation made by Mr. Doyle?—A. September 4, 1888.

Mr. ANDREW. One was made in September and the other in May.—A. In May, or it might have been June, 1889, the year following.

By Mr. BOATNER:

Q. How long after the second investigation before Mr. Paul was removed?—A. Mr. Paul was not removed until late in August or September. The Commission made a report requesting his removal, which was made public, I think, about the 25th day of June.

Q. How long after that report was made public requesting his removal before you were removed ?—A. I was removed on the 1st of July.

Q. By whom ?—A. By Mr. Paul.

The CHAIRMAN. As soon as these charges became known ?—A. Probably as soon as they became known.

By Mr. EWART :

Q. You do not mean to say that Postmaster Paul did not know of your evidence taken before the Commission ?—A. I do not know what occurred between Mr. Doyle and Mr.-Webster and Mr. Paul. I know Mr. Paul was not present when I gave that testimony.

Q. Do you swear that Mr. Paul knew nothing about it ?—A. No, sir, I do not know at what time he had knowledge of it. I did not mean to intimate that at all.

Mr. LIND. He simply stated so far as he is concerned he did not make his statement in Mr. Paul's presence.

Mr. EWART. He does not pretend to say that Mr. Paul does not know.—A. I know I did not know anything about it.

Q. Are you in Government employ now ?—A. I am.

Q. What bureau ?—A. In the Census Bureau.

By the CHAIRMAN :

Q. This examination was made by the three Commissioners, in 1889. Were not Mr. Roosevelt, Governor Thompson, and Mr. Lyman the three Commissioners present?—A. Yes, sir.

Q. Did you have any conversation with any of these Commissioners before giving testimony in relation to what would be your position if you gave the testimony?—A. Yes, sir.

Q. What was it?—A. The point was brought out that if I should testify it would provoke a collision between myself and my superior officer.

Q. Who brought that point out?—A. I did, I think.

Q. Did you say you would give this testimony provided you would be taken care of?—A. I did make a bargain of that sort.

Q. State what took place.—A. Such assurances of protection were afforded me.

Q. At your request?—A. It followed as a corollary or result of what I had stated. No, I do not know that I had specially requested it. I may have so requested it, but I do not recollect distinctly whether I requested protection, but assured the Commission—I think I did not request protection, but assured them it was necessary. However, the fact remained I was assured protection by the Commission. That I should be protected from the result of my testimony.

Q. Were the Commissioners or any one of them at the time they gave you that assurance aware of what your testimony would be? Had you told them what you could prove?—A. No, I had not. They knew, of course, what I had testified to on the former occasion; that was a matter of record. This was subsequent to when I testified before Doyle and Webster.

By Mr. LIND :

Q. Was the former testimony under oath or merely a statement?—A. It was a statement. I was not under oath, and yet to me it would not have been changed at all had I taken oath. I meant to state the facts just as much as I now mean to state the facts and the oath would have had nothing to do with it. I believe there was no oath administered.

By the CHAIRMAN:

Q. How long were you altogether in this Milwaukee post-office?—A. Thirteen years to the day and hour.

Q. Always in the same capacity?—A. No; I served in various capacities.

Q. What was your business before you went in that office?—A. I was a physician. I am educated as a physician.

Q. After you were discharged from the Milwaukee post-office did you come to Washington?—A. I did.

Q. In what way did you obtain a position in the Census Office?—A. I obtained a position in the Census Office by the friendly office of the Commission. Mr. Roosevelt particularly being friendly and kind to me in that respect.

Q. What position do you occupy there?—A. I occupy—I went in as the very tail to the kite, at a $720 position in the ninth division of the Census Office, my official designation being computer, which ranks lower than a copyist.

Q. What position do you now hold?—A. It is rather an anomalous one. On the records of the Commission I rate as a computer at the pay of $900. I have from twenty to twenty-one men under me, some of whom are drawing $1,200 and more for aught I know to the contrary. I am directing the tabulation of statistics of wealth, debts, and taxation of cities of 2,500 population and over, a somewhat important position.

By Mr. EWART:

Q. You said you had assurances of protection. From which one of the Commissioners did that come?—A. Mr. Roosevelt was the spokesman of the Commission.

Q. What do you mean by that? In what manner were you to be protected? Were you to be protected from any prosecution?—A. Oh, no.

Q. Were you to be protected from any removal from your position you held in the Milwaukee post-office?—A. I judge that to be the object of the protection as far as they had any power to do anything.

Q. Did you infer from these assurances that Mr. Roosevelt gave you in the presence of the other Commissioners that they would not permit you to be removed, or they would take steps to prevent your being removed from the office as clerk in the Milwaukee post-office?—A. Not absolutely; not that they would not permit me to be removed, because I do not think that that was in their power, but that they would exert themselves to prevent my removal.

Q. You were removed?—A. I was removed.

Q. Do you know whether they ever exerted themselves to prevent your being removed?—A. I have reasons to think they did.

Q. What reasons have you assigned?—A. Because some of them have told me so.

Q. Which one of the Commissioners told you so?—A. Mr. Lyman has stated that he——

Q. Mr. Roosevelt never made any such statement to you?—A. He might have done so.

Q. Did he do so?—A. I do not recollect now.

Q. Governor Thompson never made any such statement to you, did he? Just answer yes or no.—A. I want to clear my mind. I am inclined to think Governor Thompson did say something of that kind, but just what it is now I am honestly in a cloud about it.

Q. But you are inclined to think, at any rate, he made that impression upon your mind?—A. However, I have a telegram from the Commission which perhaps might be of interest.

The CHAIRMAN. Let it be read.

The WITNESS. It does not amount to anything.

Mr. BOATNER. It is historical, I suppose.

The WITNESS. That is all. Here is the telegram which reads—it was sent to me at 921 Walnut street:

Commission will bring your matter to attention of proper authorities as soon as possible.

CHARLES LYMAN,
President.

and is dated July 3, 1889, which you will see is three days subsequent to my removal. I also have a letter of the secretary of the Commission from the Commission, which I will read if it is desired. Here is the type-written letter of the Commission, under date of August 15, addressed to me:

UNITED STATES CIVIL SERVICE COMMISSION,
Washington, D. C., August 15, 1889.

SIR: In response to your communication of July 31, stating the circumstances connected with your service as superintendent of the registry division of the Milwaukee post-office and your dismissal from that office, and asking that the Commission will take such action as it may to secure your re-appointment to the place from which you were dismissed, I am instructed to state that the Commission will take all proper steps in its power to remedy the injustice that has been done you.

Very respectfully,

JOHN T. DOYLE,
Secretary.

Dr. H. SHIDY,
Milwaukee, Wis.

Mr. EWART. The injustice done you was your removal?—A. That was the point.

Mr. STONE. It was signed by whom?—A. The secretary of the Commission, signed by Mr. Doyle.

Mr. EWART. The injustice referred to your removal from office by Postmaster Paul?—A. That was the injustice.

By Mr. BOATNER:

Q. Who were your colleagues on this examining board?—A. Mr. Jerome B. Johnston and Mr. Charles Fahsel.

Q. Were either of these parties examined by the Civil Service Commission?—A. Yes, sir; they were.

Q. Did they corroborate your statement?—A. I have not read their testimony, but I do not see how they could do otherwise.

Q. Was either one of them dismissed from the service at the time you were?—A. They were not.

Q. Are they in the service now?—A. Mr. Johnston I think is, but Mr. Fahsel is not.

Q. Did they hold a higher or lower position in the service than you did?—A. That is difficult to determine.

Q. I mean in point of salary.—A. In point of salary, yes. They were both heads of divisions and Mr. Johnston was in charge of the mail, and as such received a higher salary than I did, who was in charge of the registered mail, although I handled a large quantity of very valuable matter.

The CHAIRMAN. How much salary did he receive?—A. I think his salary was $1,600.

Mr. ANDREW. What was yours?—A. One thousand three hundred dollars.

Mr. EWART. What cause did Mr. Paul assign for your dismissal?—A. Mr. Paul assigned in his letter to me the publication of an article in a newspaper. It was not the real cause as understood between him and me clearly. It was understood not to be the real cause.

Mr. LIND. Did you publish the article?—A. The article had been published; yes, sir.

By Mr. HATTON:

Q. You tried to withdraw that article, after writing it, from the printing office?—A. At Mr. Paul's request. Mr. Paul told me, "There is no use to carry this matter further; I have written, here is my resignation," showing me a paper which I did not examine, " I wish you would suppress this matter." I went to the publishing house and made that statement to the editor. He was rather loath to give out my manuscript, but stepped to the usual little hole in the wall and telephoned, and presently returned to me, and of course he did not directly refuse to give up my manuscript but he declined to do so, and requested that I allow it to remain with him, under the assurance that he would not then publish it but he might do so later. It was considered that he simply tabled it. I went from his office to the office of another newspaper, to still another, and the city editor of that paper brought a copy of the Evening News, or the Evening Wisconsin it was called, in which it was stated in flaming head-lines "Mr. Paul has resigned," " It was stated on the authority of Dr. Shidy that Mr. Paul had resigned," and so on. They had agreed not half an hour before when he had that conversation at the hole in the wall. Now, Mr. Paul had made that statement to me, and the editor with whom I was in conversation detained me there and sent his city editor over to the post office, which was but a short distance, to see about Mr. Paul's resignation. He came back and reported that Mr. Paul had not resigned, and that he did not care anything about my publication, and that he would just as soon have it published as not, and so on. I said, " Mr. Coleman, if Mr. Paul has no objection I have no objection, and you can go ahead." The result was the article appeared in the newspaper the next morning. That is the story of the suppression of this article.

Q. And the time you attempted to withdraw the letter you thought Mr. Paul resigned?—A. I was told so.

Q. You still considered your duty greater to him than you did to the public?—A. I did not see there was any object in persecuting him, I had no ill feeling toward Mr. Paul, none whatever.

By the CHAIRMAN:

Q. When was Mr. Paul removed?—A. He was removed, I think, about—I think he hung on until September.

Q. Before you came to Washington?—A. Before I came to Washington.

Mr. ROOSEVELT. His resignation was accepted, that of the Milwaukee postmaster, Mr. Paul. His dismissal had already been determined upon, and he would have been removed if he had not resigned.

The CHAIRMAN. That is immaterial. I want to find out whether he was removed and his successor appointed before you came to Washington.—A. Yes, sir.

Q. How long before?—A. I came to Washington on the 13th day of November.

Q. I am not particular about the date at all. I merely wanted to know. Did you make an effort to get in the post-office again?—A. No; I did not. I did not ask to be reinstated in the Milwaukee post-office.

Q. Why not?—A. Because of the anomalous state of affairs there. Mr. Paul had a life-long friend who, although of a different political complexion, sustained him, I think, for personal reasons, he being Mr. Paul's friend was naturally my enemy. Mr. Paul had further told me that he would see to it that I should not hold a position again under any Republican administration. He told me in so many words that he would persecute me.

Mr. LIND. Have you got that article here that you sent to the paper?—A. No; I have not. It was in reply to an article. I would state that Mr. Paul published a personal article about myself.

Mr. LIND. I do not care about going into this unless the committee desires it.

By Mr. BOATNER:

Q. Was the successor of Mr. Paul in the post-office a friend of Mr. Paul's?—A. I do not know. I know they were acquainted.

Q. What influence could Mr. Paul bring to bear on the succeeding postmaster which would prevent your being retained in the office or being reinstated.—A. The succeeding postmaster was absolutely dependent upon a Congressman for appointment. The friend of Mr. Paul was——

Mr. LIND. What was his name?—A. Van Schaick.

Mr. BOATNER. The postmaster was connected with a friend of Mr. Paul's, and on account of the connection between the three you do not think you had any chance?—A. Precisely so.

By Mr. HATTON:

Q. In the letter of the Civil Service Commission to you they say, "We will take such action to procure your reappointment in the office after you were dismissed." If you had been restored to that office and a new postmaster like Mr. Paul had attempted to violate the law and asked you to make false certifications, would you consider your duty to him higher than your duty to the Commission, and gone on doing as you did before?—A. Now you are inquiring into a state of facts that are simply suppositions, cases that you may imagine. Is this a question of fact?

Q. I will ask another question.—A. I presume I might imagine myself under these conditions and I will answer this gentleman fairly and squarely. After the lapse of many months and after time for amply considering my course and conduct in the matter I do not see I could have done one whit different from what I did do and if I was placed under the identical circumstances I would pursue a similar line of conduct.

Q. If you had been restored and the new postmaster had asked you to make false certifications, you would have gone on making them?—A. If the conditions were the same as before the results would have been the same.

Q. After securing the removal of Mr. Paul through the Commission you would have gone on and made up a case against the next postmaster in the same way?—A. I did not secure Mr. Paul's removal.

Q. It was partly done through your evidence.—A. My evidence was simply the facts. I had nothing to do with that. I was not responsible for the fact. The facts probably removed Mr. Paul. I did not make the facts.

Q. As a civil service reformer and an officer of the Board——

The CHAIRMAN. He does not say that he was a civil service reformer.

Mr. HATTON. Well, as a former officer of the Board—I do not mean to reflect on the Board——

Mr. BOATNER. You mean to say had you been retained in your place that you would have repeated the violation of the civil service law which you have stated that you have been guilty of?—A. That would depend upon the conditions; if they would not be the same it might not be necessary to repeat it. I served under Mr. Payne and he did not compel me to do so.

The CHAIRMAN. If the conditions were the same you would see nothing wrong?—A. I have not stated that I did not see anything wrong. I think my appreciation of right and wrong is equal to most people. I have stated, gentlemen, that if the conditions were the same the results would be the same. I can not see why like causes should not produce like results.

By Mr. HATTON:

Q. Did you report to Commissioners Lyman, Edgerton, and Oberly any violation of the postmaster in which you assisted him? Did you ever make any report?—A. I did not start the investigation.

Q. You stated one reason why you did not was that this was a matter of bread and butter to you.

Mr. BOATNER. He did not say that, it was myself.

Mr. HATTON. He answered you that it was practically so. Could not you, as a sworn officer of the Commission, have taken the chances on one sandwich and sent these Commissioners word without Mr. Paul's knowledge that he was violating the civil service law? Could you not have sent word to the Commission here; had not you many opportunities to do that?—A. I was not exactly disposed to act on that line, although you may think I have done worse. In the first place, Mr. Hatton, you must realize and understand that when these violations of law began they were a very small thing, and if at once I had withstood them, and if I had called the attention of the Commission to them, it would have been to bring down a rebuke, and the Commission would have admonished Mr. Paul to adhere more strictly to the law, and he would have turned on me for calling the attention of the Commission to these matters. Having condoned one of them it is a very easy matter to condone another and another, and by and by there comes to be a mountain. I state the matter fairly.

The CHAIRMAN. You condoned his offense!

A. Precisely so, because——

By Mr. HATTON:

Q. What were Mr. Paul's politics?—A. He was appointed a Democrat.

Q. What are your politics?—A. I am a Republican.

Q. If it was a matter of bread and butter under your present conditions and the Superintendent of the Census should ask you to make false register and false returns, would you comply with him; would you consider your duty greater to the Superintendent of Census than it is to the Commission and President——

The WITNESS. And the public. The Superintendent of Census knows how he wants the reports.

Q. If you were satisfied in your mind you were doing an improper——

Mr. BOATNER. Let him answer.

The WITNESS. If the Superintendent of Census wants a false report he knows that matter. I am his servant, and he can direct me in these matters and in regard to all matters. In regard to the post-office affairs, Mr. Paul was my superior officer, and directed me. In regard to the Civil Service Commission matters, he ought not to have been my superior or directed me in any way; but unfortunately it was impossible to separate the two II's, I being one and the same individual.

Q. But you know the law gives the Civil Service Commission, in which you were an officer, the right to come in and investigate the affairs of the post-office, and to that extent made the Commission superior to the postmaster.—A. Did they do it?

Q. Not through any active agency on your part.—A. If I had instigated this movement and had brought charges while they were small and inconsequential, would not I have been stigmatized as conspiring against my superior officer, and would not it have been alleged that because Mr. Paul was a Democrat and I was a Republican, therefore I was trying to get a Democrat out of office, or some such reason as that? I had no ill-will against Mr. Paul. I did not try to get him out of office, nor do I. What I testify to is simply fact.

Q. Understand that I was assuming that the Commission is above politics, and of course your political influence and his political influence ought to have nothing to do with that.—A. I think not.

Q. You never reported to Mr. Lyman any of these false certifications or any violation of law?—A. I think I have answered that question before.

Q. Did not you consider it your duty to report these violations of law to Mr. Lyman so that he should have an opportunity to make an investigation of the case in order, if this man had violated his duty, to dismiss him?—A. A report to Mr. Lyman would have been a report to the Commission. I do not distinguish between the two. I did not report to the Commission because I was not in a position to do so satisfactorily.

By Mr. OBERLY:

Q. Why were you not?—A. Because my position was wholly dependent upon pleasing my superior officer.

Q. I wish to know why you believe that to be the fact?—A. Events have borne me out.

Q. Did it ever occur to you that you should have informed the Commission that these abuses were going on; that you were in danger of removal; that an investigation and ascertaining of facts might be made without implicating you, and would show you were anxious to do your duty?—A. No, I do not think that state of affairs presented itself to me as being in conformity with the facts; in fact I know it did not. The letter which I wrote to the Commission very hastily, after Mr. Doyle and Mr. Webster's examination there, on the spur of the moment and while suffering from considerable excitement, being afraid of the course which would then be taken—I sat down and wrote a letter, in which I summed up the condition of affairs, and I stated, I think, there were but three courses open to me; the first was to call the attention of the Commission to the existing state of affairs and to take the consequences; the second was to resign and drop the load; the third was to wait until the Commission, through its own motion, should discover the fact and then simply to let them take all the responsibility of the result. The latter was the course I took.

Mr. LIND. Did you mail that letter to the Commission?

A. No, sir; I gave it to Mr. Doyle and Mr. Webster during the examination. I think it was the final act of that afternoon. That was the first examination. I think it is part of the record here.

Mr. ANDREW. Who were the Commissioners then?

A. Mr. Oberly, Mr. Lyman, and Mr. Edgerton.

Mr. LIND. Is that letter in evidence?

The CHAIRMAN. Do you know where this letter is?

The WITNESS. The Commission has that letter.

Mr. ROOSEVELT. It is on the table.

Mr. HATTON. We will wait for that. In the meantime I would like to hear one question. You stated your construction of your duty duty as an officer——

The WITNESS. (Taking up paper, see Exhibit B.) This is marked Exhibit R. Communication to the Civil Service Commission from Hamilton Shidy, secretary of the board of examiners of the post-office at Milwaukee, and dated September 10, 1888, which is also the date of my letter.

Mr. OBERLY. This is an exhibit?

The CHAIRMAN. Yes, sir.

Mr. OBERLY. Of what?

The WITNESS. I think it is part of the evidence.

Mr. ROOSEVELT. It is an exhibit to the report of last July.

Mr. OBERLY. What is the date of the report which Mr. Webster made of which this is an exhibit?

The CHAIRMAN. He is referring to a letter sent to the Commission in September, 1888.

Mr. OBERLY. He means an exhibit to something.

Mr. LIND. This witness is entitled to have this in the record.

The WITNESS. This is a letter which, as I have stated, I wrote after the testimony was taken in the examination conducted by Mr. Doyle and Mr. Webster. The examination had closed late one afternoon. I went home feeling ill at ease at the turn which affairs had taken. I rose early the next morning, it being understood between Mr. Doyle and Mr. Webster that they were going on the 11 o'clock train and I must be at my desk at work before 8 o'clock in the morning, so I sat down and rapidly dashed off this statement, which I had not occasion to read until I read it before that committee.

Mr. ANDREW. What committee?—A. Messrs. Doyle and Webster, who were then the investigating committee, and I put this in their hand as an explanation how it came that I allowed things to be in the condition in which they were. I shall simply read an extract from this:

Three courses only were open to me under the circumstances—.

(1) To resign my position on the board. This I talked of on several occasions with Mr. Johnson, president of board, and even wrote out my resignation, but it was withheld, as we both thought it would prejudice my position in the office, as of course I would be asked for reasons.

(2) To call the attention of the Civil Service Commission to the manner in which the rules were being violated. This would have been to invite an investigation and conflict with the postmaster, with loss of place.

(3) To let matters take their course until such time as the Commission should discover, of its own motion, the existence of irregularities and deal with them as they saw fit. This I have done. I have been loyal to my chief and have done the best I was permitted to do for the Commission, being heartily in sympathy with the reform movement.

Now, gentlemen, you may laugh, but it is a fact nevertheless.

Mr. OBERLY. What is the date of that letter?

The WITNESS. It is dated the 10th day of September, 1888.

By Mr. STONE:

Q. I would like to ask a question or two, in view of getting matters that have been traveled over in a scattered way together again. How many employés of the Government are at Milwaukee?—A. Do you refer only to the post-office?

Q. Well, altogether.—A. I can not say.

Q. Were there any persons employed in the Government service at Milwaukee other than those connected with the post-office?—A. I think so, although I would be at a loss to specify. Yes, assuredly; there is the custom-house; at present they collect internal revenue at Milwaukee.

Q. This board, of which you were secretary, was composed exclusively of persons connected with the post-office?—A. It was for the greater part of the time. In its incipiency there was a member, a Dr. Kane, who was connected with one of the departments, I think the internal-revenue department. The requirement was that they should be Government employés.

Q. From whom did you receive your appointment as secretary of this board; from the Civil Service Commission?—A. From the Civil Service Commission.

Q. And you held you had a duty then to the Civil Service Commission distinct from that you had to the postmaster?—A. Yes.

Q. Did you take oath as a member of this board?—A. I think not; in fact, I understand not. According to my memory it is not required. It is not likely there was any set oath. I am informed a set oath is not required, so I presume I did not take any oath.

Mr. OBERLY. Is not the performance of the duty of the secretary of a board of examiners made by the civil service law part of his official duty; does not the discharge of these duties therefore come under your oath to do that?

By Mr. STONE:

Q. I was going to ask that question, but you can answer it now.—A. I think there is a provision in the civil service law—you will not be surprised if I am not altogether familiar with the manifold provisions of the law—I think there is a provision making it a part of the public work to be done. I believe that to be so.

Q. In certifying persons for appointment as being on the eligible list who were not on it, in changing the grades of persons who were on the list by increasing some and diminishing that of others, did you understand that it was a violation of your obligation, of your duty as a public officer?—A. My duty was twofold. If I could have separated the part of me which was civil service officer from the part of me which was post-office attaché I would not have had any difficulty whatever in discriminating between the two, but unfortunately I could not.

Q. Do you mean to say that you did not regard your conduct as an official wrong and involving any moral turpitude because a different course might have resulted in your removal from office?—A. Because, considering the situation in its entirety, taking all things into consideration, that was right for me which was not right and proper if there was only one cause. I have been taught that of two evils to choose the least, which I believe is a correct line of conduct.

Q. I think we understand that. Now you have explained this whole business, and your connection with the present Civil Service Commission is as you have stated.—A. Yes, sir.

Q. Soon after your removal do I understand you to say that these gentlemen with full knowledge of your conduct recommended you for appointment in another branch of the service of the Government?—A. No; knowing I had been a faithful servant in the place in which I had been placed, no charge being against me, and it can be testified to that in thirteen years I have handled large sums of money, and I am here and not in Canada.

Q. Did you go into your present employment under civil service rules and regulations?—A. I suppose I did. That is, in the early stages of the process I suppose I did, but I learned since that branch of the civil service is not under what is known as the regular civil-service rules.

Q. In other words, the appointment can be made without civil service examination and certification under the provisions of the law?—A. They have a certain form of examination over there which probably they regard as a substitute and equivalent to the civil service examination. It is not the regular civil service examination. I was required to take such an examination, and when I took it I supposed I was conforming fully to the civil service law.

Q. Is it a fact that Mr. Roosevelt or either of the Commissioners went to the Superintendent of the Census, or to whoever makes these appointments, and personally interviewed him in your behalf to your knowledge?—A. To my knowledge, no; because I have no knowledge of that fact whatever.

Q. What is your understanding?—A. I understand that.

The CHAIRMAN. You will see, Mr. Stone, it is a fact that Mr. Roosevelt got this appointment acting for the Commission.

By Mr. STONE:

Q. What were the politics of Mr. Johnston?—A. He is a Republican.

Q. What was your other associate?—A. Mr. Fahsel?

Q. What were his politics?—A. I do not know. He was appointed by Mr. Paul, so I judge he was a Democrat.

Q. He is not now in the service?—A. No, sir.

Q. Mr. Paul is no longer in the service?—No, sir.

Q. He was a Democrat?—A. He was a Democrat; at least he was appointed as a Democrat.

Q. Is Mr. Johnson still in the service?—A. I believe he is; I think he is; I may say I know he is.

Q. What did I understand you to say the place is you are filling now in the Census Office?—A. My position by official designation there is a copyist.

Mr. BOATNER. I thought you stated it was a computer.—A. I was appointed as a computer, which I think is a less grade than a copyist. I have been advanced, and I now get $900.

By Mr. STONE:

Q. Did you say you have now under you fifteen or twenty men?—A. I have, but that does not appear in my official status.

Q. And you say many are receiving a larger salary than you?—A. Many are; the most of them, I think.

Q. What are you engaged in doing?—A. Tabulating statistics of wealth, debt, and taxation of cities of 2,500 population and over.

Q. You are computing or tabulating statistics of taxation?—A. Yes, sir; and of wealth, debt, and taxation, referring to the financial——

Q. You are in charge of that division?—A. I am not in charge of the division, because, understand me, Mr. Copeland is in charge of the division. In the division of wealth, etc., I take the place of Mr. Copeland, in charge of these statistics, Mr. Copeland being in charge of the division.

By the CHAIRMAN:

Q. You have stated that you have charge of some fifteen or twenty men, what are your duties?—A. My duties are to outline the work for them to break the way before them and see they do as I say shall be done. There can no work at present proceed until I map it out. I break the way for their work.

Q. The men who do the work you designate are paid in some instances $300 per annum more than you receive at present?—A. Yes, sir; I have stated that. Understand I am not complaining at all, but that is simply the fact.

By Mr. HATTON:

Q. After you were turned out of the Milwaukee post-office did you ever make application to the Civil Service Commission for a position?—A. I requested them to do what they could for me.

Q. I know that, but what I mean is by examination?—A. To take the regular civil-service examination.

Q. Yes.—A. No.

Q. Why?—A. Because I knew there were a great multitude who were doing that then, so that I would have a very small chance, a drop in the bucket.

Q. Are you familiar enough with the rules of the Commission to say whether or not after having been dismissed from the service you could have been so certified by the Commission?—A. I see no reason why I should not have been certified by the Civil Service Commission. When I made application for this place I stated fully and explicitly the fact that my connection had been severed from the service. I filled out a regular application blank.

Mr. ANDREW. This is a more argumentative question.

The CHAIRMAN. In this way the question comes properly that the witness is asked whether he did not make application, and whether for whatever cause he had been discharged——

Mr. BOATNER. He has stated it. The question is whether his character is good enough to go through, that is a question of opinion. It is unfair to ask a man to stultify himself.

By Mr. STONE:

Did this examination held by Messrs. Doyle and Webster—this was in September, 1888, I believe you said?—A. Yes, sir.

Q. Do you know anything about when these gentlemen made their report to the Commission?—A. No, I do not.

By Mr. THOMPSON:

Q. When Mr. Lyman, Mr. Roosevelt, and myself called on you at your office at Milwaukee and began to inquire of you about these things, did you or not beg to be excused from saying anything?—A. I did; I stated the result would be disastrous to me.

Q. These assurances Mr. Roosevelt gave, which Mr. Lyman and myself assented to, was it not that if you would tell us frankly the whole truth about this matter we would protect you as far as we could from being dismissed for testifying if you told the truth.—A. That was the substance of our first conversation.

Q. Did I not at that time somewhat severely upbraid you for this misconduct you had been guilty of?—A. You asked me some very pointed questions, I know.

Q. Did you not express contrition and repentance and say to the Commission you had been taught a severe lesson and in future nothing of this kind would occur?—A. I do not remember making that statement, although I might have made it; I do not remember it.

Q. Did you not send me after I had left Milwaukee a newspaper in which there was high praise of you by the former postmaster, Mr. Payne?—A. No, I think not.

Q. You recollect that newspaper?—A. Yes, sir. Your question was simply—I brought that paper here, here it is. Do you wish the paper read?

Q. Before your appointment to the Census Office you submitted to us as evidence a fact that you had the confidence of your superior officer, the postmaster, Mr. Payne, the Republican incumbent, who preceded Mr. Paul?—A. I did.

Mr. ROOSEVELT. Will you submit the newspaper marked in evidence here?—A. I have the paper here.

Mr. THOMPSON. I shall read that portion which Mr. Payne testified to his character and capacity.

[From Yenowin's Sunday News, Milwaukee, Sunday, May 31, 1885.]

THE FOURTH DIVISION.

The registry department was separated from the money department in 1878, and is in charge of Dr. Hamilton Shidy. This branch is rapidly gaining in public favor, as will be seen by its great increase. In 1876 but 45,204 pieces were handled, while in 1884 the number reached 266,995. When we consider that every one of these letters or packages is of more or less value, the great importance of this department will be understood. To Dr. Shidy is due the credit of having originated the idea of simplifying the method of doing the registry business by the use of the postal card. Its adoption by the Department was earnestly urged by me, and it has resulted in a great saving of time and labor, and consequently improving the service throughout the entire country.

A. This copy is dated May 31, 1885. It shows the farewell address of Mr. Payne on his turning over the office to Mr. Paul.

By Mr. EWART:

Q. What is the date of that paper?—A. Sunday, May 31, 1885.

Q. Before you were engaged in the certification business?—A. Yes, sir. No, sir; it was not, for the civil-service rules went into effect, if I remember, about the spring of 1883.

The CHAIRMAN. That was before any irregularities were committed?—A. Yes, sir.

By Mr. THOMPSON:

Q. Did you not tell the Commission when we called your attention to this violation of law which we regarded as very gross, did you not tell the Commission that you had done it under duress?—A. I did.

Q. And the duress was that of the postmaster?—A. I did.

Q. Did you not then, in regard to this re-marking—I beg you now to listen carefully to this question—state that you had never re-marked a paper or marked it up where you did not feel there was a justification in marking it up? Just answer this.—A. I so stated.

Q. That you never marked a man up that you did not believe, when the review was made, that you had sufficient justification for re-marking; and where a review was suggested by the postmaster you had never marked a man up higher than, in your deliberate judgment, he was entitled to?—A. Not higher than we could allow him properly. As a rule those cases were only a fraction of a per cent., just enough to change the relative standing of two persons.

By the CHAIRMAN:

Q. You stated that in one or two instances the marking had been made, that the rate of per cent. had been raised?—A. I state so now. I refer to that that there were changes which were not great, as from 40 to 70, but they were generally only a minor change in marking, enough to change the relative position of two persons.

By Mr. THOMPSON:

Q. You stated that day you had never marked a paper that you did not conscientiously believe, on a review, was entitled to be marked up. Did you or did you not say that?—A. I do not remember positively. I know what the effect was, that that marking these papers sometimes caused——

Q. I just want you to answer the question. Did you not tell the Commission while Mr. Paul sometimes called upon the board to review questions, you had never marked a man higher than you honestly believed on a second review he was entitled to?—A. I do not remember, but in point of fact it is so whether I did or did not.

Q. Did not you distinctly say to the Commission you had admitted your faults, your dereliction of duty, and that you deeply regretted it, and that it should not occur again if you remained in the service?—A. I did state to the Commission that I admitted the fault, and I accepted the verdict of censure which they passed upon me as being just from their stand-point.

Q. Did you not tell the Commission in some of these matters where Mr. Paul had ordered you to do things he stated that to be his opinion of the law, and there was a conflict of opinion between you and Mr. Paul, and you yielded to him, being the inferior officer, and it was done upon the responsibility that his construction of the law was right?— A. He did in some instances; many instances.

Q. Did you not tell the Commission that in a decision where you differed that Mr. Paul, the postmaster, said, "I have the right of the law to do thus and so," and that while you were disposed to differ from him in opinion that it was only upon such questions that the postmaster insisted and you yielded your judgment to his?—A. That unquestionably covers some cases.

Q. I only wanted to know whether you did not tell us that; that where you and Mr. Paul came in conflict in regard to the construction of the meaning as it sometimes occurred, you gave your construction and Mr. Paul his, and that you yielded your judgment to his?—A. I have never tried in any way to conceal the state of affairs whatever here. I simply did not bring up the law——

Mr. BOATNER. The question is about fact. Did you tell him these things or not?

By Mr. THOMPSON.

Q. Did not you tell the Commission, at the time you pleaded for mercy, that you were a poor man with a wife and children, absolutely dependent upon your salary for support?—A. Yes, sir; I did.

Q. And did you not, in stating these facts, admit your errors and say that if you were continued in office it would not occur again; that you had consulted your colleagues of the Board, and they knew what the irregularities and the derelictions that you committed were?—A. Whatever was known to me was known to the members of the Board—anything of importance. There may have been some little trifle that occurred which was not known, but there was nothing of importance

3117——11

which was not known. If I thought there was anything of importance that was not known to the other members of the board I reported it to the board, if any discussions especially between myself and Mr. Johnston, until it became to be monotonous.

By the CHAIRMAN:

Q. Did you tell the Commissioners, at that time that you considered the matter, that you were acting in two capacities, and under the same conditions you were then acting you would act in the same manner again?—A. I do not remember that I made that statement.

Q. You made a statement here that you would consider under the same conditions, that under the same conditions you would act exactly as you did act?—A. Yes, sir.

Q. Did you state that to the Commissioners at that time?—A. I do not remember that I stated that; I do not remember that that phase of it came up at all.

Q. Did not you acknowledge you did wrong, and that it never would happen again?—A. I acknowledged I did wrong, just as I now do.

Q. Did you not tell the Commissioners that you would never be guilty of such an act again?—A. I probably did; I do not recollect that particular statement. I do not know, yet I might have said so. I do not seem to recollect at present that I did make use of that particular expression, but that was the frame of mind in which I was in at that time.

Q. You are positive you never stated to those gentlemen that if you were called to a public position again under the same conditions as those, you would do the same as you had then acted?—A. I do not remember that phase was brought up at all. I do not recollect having made any such statement as that. I do not recollect that particular question was brought before me; still, it may have been.

By Mr. ROOSEVELT. Are you not positive you never said anything of the kind?—A. No, I do not recollect that matter positively; from the fact there is a blank in my mind in regard to it I should think I had not made the statement, but it is hard to state in the negative. I simply do not know. It may come to me.

By Mr. HATTON:

Q. Were you a member of the Board when Henry Payne was postmaster?—A. Yes, sir.

Q. He is the author of the complimentary notice about you which has been read.—A. Yes, sir.

Q. Were you ever obliged by him to make false certifications?—A. No, sir.

Mr. EWART. Before the adjournment of the committee, I would put in evidence and read to the committee the report made to the Commissioners by Messrs. Webster and Doyle, especially one part of the report.

The CHAIRMAN. You can put it in evidence, at least such portion of it as you think necessary.

A portion of the testimony was then read to the committee and it was filed in evidence.

(See Exhibit C.)

SATURDAY, *March* 1, 1890.

TESTIMONY OF ROBERT P. PORTER.

ROBERT P. PORTER sworn and examined.

By Mr. LIND (in the chair):

Q. You are Superintendent of the Census?—A. Yes, sir.

Q. You may state briefly what you know in relation to the appointment in your office of Mr. Shidy; also the matters which actuated you in making that appointment.—A. I think the first time my attention was called to Mr. Shidy was by Mr. Roosevelt, who spoke to me about him. Mr. Roosevelt said that he was a man who had been employed in the Milwaukee post-office, and that in consequence of his having given some testimony which rather aided the Commission to find out certain facts they were interested in, he had been dismissed (Mr. Roosevelt thought unjustly dismissed), and he asked me if I could find a place in my office for such a man. I said I was going to employ a good many clerks, and if he would bring Mr. Shidy on, that we would examine him, and if he was found to be competent I would recommend him for appointment. I said as he had been dismissed from the Post-Office Department, as a matter of courtesy it would be necessary to ask the Postmaster-General if he had any objection to my appointing the man in the Interior Department, and I think the Postmaster-General said he had no objection. Mr. Shidy passed an examination and was recommended for appointment. He was appointed and went to work. That is all I know about it.

By Mr. ROOSEVELT:

Q. He was appointed at $720 and has been promoted to $900 since?—A. Yes, sir.

Q. Here is a letter from T. Campbell Copeland, superintendent of the ninth division in your office. This letter says "He is one of our most valuable clerks." This is a letter handed to us the other day in reference to Mr. Shidy.

Mr. LIND. It would be improper to put it in evidence in this connection. (To the witness.) Do you personally know anything about his standing and efficiency in the office?—A. Yes, sir; he has passed a fair examination. It is not what I would consider a first-class one. I think it was about 67 or 70. He had had some experience as an executive man in a small way. He has been found to be a useful man a little above the average. I know exactly what he does.

By Mr. EWART:

Q. I understood you to say that Mr. Roosevelt told you that Shidy had been unjustly dismissed?—A. I understood that from what Mr. Roosevelt told me. That was my impression about it.

Q. Did Mr. Roosevelt inform you at the time that this man had been an officer in the Civil Service Commission, and as such had repeatedly violated the law?—A. No, sir.

Q. Did he tell you this man had been engaged, while a member of the board of examiners, in gerrymandering the list of eligibles and making false certifications?—A. I did not understand that he was in any way connected with the Civil Service Commission. I thought he was an employé of the post-office at Milwaukee in the money-order department.

Q. The only information Mr. Roosevelt gave you was that this man in his opinion had been unjustly dismissed?—A. That was the main idea.

Q. It was upon that recommendation you allowed Shidy to take an examination?—A. Yes, sir. Some responsible person has to make a recommendation; an examination is made and that is graded, and afterwards an appointment follows or does not, as the case may be.

Mr. STONE. Did Mr. Roosevelt state to you the reasons for his dismissal?—A. I think not in detail. I have so many of those cases that I would not be sure about that. I think he simply stated that Shidy was dismissed.

By Mr. EWART:

Q. If Mr. Roosevelt had told you that this man had persistently violated the law, had stuffed the list of eligibles, had mutilated the records and made false certifications, would you have appointed him in your bureau?—A. I certainly should not.

Mr. EWART. I know you would not.

Mr. STONE. You say you know you would not?

Mr. EWART. I say Mr. Porter would not. That is what Mr. Shidy here called an anomalous statement.

By Mr. STONE:

Q. This man Shidy testified on yesterday that he was now receiving a salary of $900 a year, and that he was practically in charge of twenty-odd men engaged in tabulating and arranging statistics of indebtedness on cities of 2,500 and over, and that there were persons under his control receiving much larger salaries. What I want to know is what system is it that gives a subordinate a larger salary than the man in charge, the responsible man?—A. That is easily explained in the census work. It has to be done rapidly. We are just beginning our bureau. I think Shidy has not been in charge of that more than two or three weeks, and some other men may have been in the office longer and perhaps good at figures, and he may have been chosen within the last few weeks, and I think he has been. I do not make any more promotions until the first of April. If we find a man has changed his position, which a great many do in the Census Office, we have no time to wait. I try to equalize it the next time I make promotions.

Q. He occupies relatively the position of the chief of the division?—A. I think he has charge of certain tabulations that they are making.

Q. He simply gives out the work then?—A. He gives out the work.

Q. These persons in the room with him are, in a certain sense, under his control?—A. He might simply be the man that takes around these sheets when finished, giving them to another and keeping the general run of the work.

Q. Is he responsible in that room?—A. No; I do not think he is even the responsible man in that room.

Q. Who is the responsible man?—A. The responsible man is the chief of the division.

Q. Was Mr. Shidy mistaken in saying he had charge of the men in the room?—A. I should think he was. He may give out the work.

Mr. ANDREW. I think he used the expression "gave out the work," and had "twenty men under him."—A. That is hardly a fair statement. I do not think he keeps their time or anything of that kind. That is kept by another clerk. He has not been there more than two or three weeks. The schedules have not been out more than three weeks.

Q. He does occupy some position of control or superiority in the room. It may be of a low order. Who conferred that authority upon him?—A. The chief of the division, Mr. Copeland. To-morrow he may confer it upon some one else.

Q. To-morrow Mr. Shidy may not be in the office?—A. It is a matter that does not necessarily come under the supervision of the Superintendent. We hold the division responsible for its work.

By Mr. ROOSEVELT:

Q. It was some time after I first spoke to you before Shidy was appointed?—A. It was about six weeks.

Q. Protests were made against the appointment by a number of gentlemen; was not that the case?—A. Some protests were made.

Q. The protest was made by Mr. Van Schaick?—A. Yes, sir; he was one.

Q. Then one or more Senators referred to it?—A. Senator Spooner I think did.

Q. So that you told me once or twice that there was great opposition to it?—A. I told you there was some opposition.

Q. And you showed me, did you not, a number of letters from different places?—A. There was one letter and there was another letter inclosing a clipping from a newspaper. I remember two letters, one from Kansas opposing Mr. Shidy in a general way.

Q. Saying he had been treacherous to Mr. Paul?—A. Yes, sir; had committed some fault.

Q. For six weeks the matter was hung up or in abeyance while the protests were made against the appointment?—A. That is true.

Q. And while I was asking for the appointment I told you that this man Shidy had been removed from office in consequence of giving testimony concerning the condition of affairs at the Milwaukee post-office where he and the postmaster had been mixed up in some matters that we had reported upon, my report being at that time public. I had reported in June and that was long after June that I spoke to you.—A. It must have been about the 15th of September.

Q. It must have been after my report was published broadcast, and after there had been a very great deal of discussion about it by Congressman Van Schaick and the Senators, and after the Postmaster-General, with the consent of the President, had notified Mr. Paul he would have been removed if he had not resigned which was done in August. It was after that time?—A. It was in September. I could not give you the facts about the Milwaukee post-office matter.

Q. You knew that I had made a report on the subject?—A. I knew that and that Shidy and Paul were implicated in that report, and the report was public and that the Postmaster-General had in writing indicated to you his approval of Shidy's transfer, he having known all about my report and having acted upon it. That is true, I think.

Q. I sent you a letter of the Postmaster-General approving the transfer and saying in substance that he would be glad if Mr. Shidy could get this position, and I told you that you would receive a formal letter from the Postmaster-General on the subject saying it would be satisfactory to him to have the appointment made?—A. Yes, sir.

Mr. LIND. Shidy having testified that he had been a party to violations of law and the regulations of the Civil Service Commission while in the office at Milwaukee, was asked: "Do I understand you to say that if you had been retained you would have repeated these violations of the civil service law which you stated you had done heretofore?" To that question he answered: "If the conditions were the same, I would see no wrong in it." Suppose that Shidy had been re-appointed under the new postmaster at Milwaukee and the conditions had been the same as they were under Paul, and he had continued in doing what he did. If you had had knowledge of his views (I might call them moral views upon that question) would you have made this appointment?—A. That is rather a hard question because I have not read his testimony, and I do not know exactly what he said.

Mr. STONE. Mr. Hatton asked him if the Superintendent of the Census Bureau should ask him to make false returns, would he comply with that request, and he answered: "If the Superintendent of the Census wants false returns made he knows that matter. I am his servant. In regard to the post-office Mr. Paul was my superior officer. In regard to the civil service matter it was impossible to separate my two IIs."

Mr. LIND. Assuming that the witness was candid in this statement and that those were his convictions in regard to a man's public duty, with a knowledge of those facts before you, would you have appointed him?—A. I do not think I would. But the point is this: If the Superintendent of the Census was a kind of man that wanted false returns, a man that would make false returns would be the kind of a man he would want to have. This is rather a difficult question to answer, directly or otherwise. That presupposes the Superintendent of the Census wants false returns.

By Mr. HATTON:

Q. Did any of these letters recommending the appointment of this man state in any way that he had been guilty and had testified before the Commission that he had made false certifications?—A. No, sir; the letters protesting against Shidy were of a general character; that he was treacherous.

Q. Did anybody interested in his appointment ever tell you how he had committed these offenses?—A. I am sure they did not.

Q. If you had been informed of them would you have appointed him?—A. Really I do not know what he has done.

Q. Believing in Mr. Roosevelt, and his friends do believe in him, if you had heard that this man had been guilty of making false returns, stuffing the eligible list and committing crimes of that character, believing in Mr. Roosevelt, would you have appointed him?—A. You are going back to the same proposition you had up a minute ago. That would be attacking Mr. Roosevelt. If he was that kind of a man of course he would not have said anything but that. The chances are he did not know it.

Q. Who did not know it?—A. Mr. Roosevelt. I told him to send this man in and I would be glad to have him examined and appointed.

Q. Suppose you yourself had known it?—A. The point is this, if I had known he had done what?

Q. That he had testified to false returns, stuffing the eligible list, and violating his oath of office.—A. I do not know whether he has or not. I have not read the testimony on that point.

Mr. LIND. It is on the assumption that you knew the statements were true.

The WITNESS. What I want to express upon the committee is that I do not know anything about the statements. I just read the paragraph referring to the Superintendent of the Census. That is all I have read.

Mr. THOMPSON. If Mr. Roosevelt had stated to you when he came to you with this application for the appointment of Shidy that Shidy was a member of the local board of examiners, and was assigned to this extra work; that he had allowed himself to be improperly influenced by his superior officer who had the absolute power of removal; that he had confessed his fault most humbly, craved for forgiveness, and given assurance that if he was forgiven he would not again be guilty; and, if Mr. Roosevelt had said in addition to that, that he was dismissed not for cause but for telling the truth when he came before the Commission, and saying that "if I testify I will be removed," and he was subsequently dismissed not for misdeeds but for telling the truth; and if Mr. Roosevelt had stated all these facts so far as he knew, and that Shidy was not a corrupt man but yielded to his superior officer, under all these circumstances would you have given him a trial?

The WITNESS. I think under those circumstances I should have looked more carefully into the matter. I do not know that a man in my position has a right to take the word of another man in a matter of that kind.

Q. Suppose that you were satisfied that Mr. Roosevelt was telling the truth?—A. It was one of those cases I should want to pass upon by itself.

Q. If you were satisfied that this man had been removed not for doing wrong but for doing right, under those circumstances, if you had looked into the matter, would you not have been willing to give him a trial?—A. I would not say I would not give a man a trial under those circumstances. I do not think I can answer your question one way or the other. I should prefer not to answer it.

By Mr. ROOSEVELT:

Q. At the time I spoke to you about this man all these facts were made public in my official report and had been published broadcast in the press; and, you were very busy at one time when I went to see you. You said you had received a protest from Mr. Van Schaick?—A. I did not receive a written protest. He had spoken about it but did not go into the details.

Q. I told you I would not go into the details, that they were in my report; that the circumstances were that Shidy and the postmaster had been mixed up in wrong-doing in the post-office; that Shidy had come forward and confessed, and that he was being persecuted for it, and that we were anxious to protect a man who had come forward to tell the truth.—A. That is what you stated to me.

Q. And I referred to that in full in my report. I knew that Paul had been dismissed?—A. I have so many of these cases; some days we have as many as fifty or sixty appointments to look into. My impression was that this man had been dismissed. I did not know that he himself had been mixed up in any wrong-doing. I did not know he had been in the employ of the Commission.

Q. Do you recollect my saying to you that he was mixed up in this wrong-doing, and that he was the only man who had the manliness to come forward and tell about it?—A. That may be true, but I thought you referred to the post-office matter. I did not know that he was a member of the Civil Service Commission in any way.

Mr. ROOSEVELT. I have not jurisdiction in any post-office matters. All I would have a right to speak about was his connection with the Civil Service. I would not have a right to speak of his connection with the post-office, and all my remarks were in connection with the Commission. You will remember once that I came to speak to you with Reporter Dodge, of the Milwaukee Sentinel?—A. I think you did.

Mr. HATTON. Mr. Roosevelt stated to you that this man was mixed up with the Milwaukee post-office, and did he refer you to a copy of his report, or did he send for one?

The WITNESS. I have never seen a copy of his report. I regret to say I have not had time to read a copy of Mr. Roosevelt's last report.

Mr. ROOSEVELT. Do you remember that I told you this man was a weak man, who had yielded to the importunities of Mr. Paul, and that Paul had turned him out in revenge for his testifying to the truth?

The WITNESS. I think that is what you said.

Mr. HATTON. Did he say what offenses had been committed?

The WITNESS. I gathered from Mr. Roosevelt's statement that he had been guilty of helping Paul to make some political appointments that he should not have made. I understood that in a general way.

TESTIMONY OF THEODORE ROOSEVELT—Recalled.

Hon. THEODORE ROOSEVELT recalled and further examined.

The CHAIRMAN. Mr. Shidy has testified how he came to be appointed a clerk in the Census Bureau. Will you state as briefly as you can your knowledge of that matter.

The WITNESS. If you will permit me, I will make a brief statement of the whole case. Mr. Paul, the postmaster at Milwaukee, has been investigated four different times; the first time by Mr. Doyle, the secretary of the Civil Service Commission, under Mr. Cleveland. His report disclosed such a damaging state of affairs that a further investigation was ordered, in which Mr. Doyle and Mr. Webster took part. The papers of that investigation are before you. When Mr. Thompson and myself came into office we found this testimony, and this matter still pending. Our Commission went up there, and made a report upon that office. About that time, or shortly afterwards, the post-office inspector, Mr. Fleming, a Democrat—at least he was appointed in 1887 under Mr. Vilas—also went and examined the office, and reported officially that the postmaster ought to be dismissed, on the ground that he was dishonest, a fraud, and scientific prevaricator.

By the CHAIRMAN:

Q. What was the date of that report?—A. That was shortly after, or before, we made our report. I have forgotten the exact date. It went into all his faults and misdeeds. I think it would be well, and I would request that you send to the Post-Office Department, and get that report. Mr. Paul sent affidavits to the Postmaster-General in answer to the charges that we made, and I believe also in answer to the charges of the post-office inspector. After reviewing in full the matter, the President or the Postmaster-General (I have forgotten which) indicated that his resignation would be demanded, Mr. Paul having resigned, they accepted his resignation, adding that his removal had already been determined upon on the strength of the report made by the Commission and the post-office inspector. This is preliminary to what I want to say about the case.

When we went up there, we found that there had been systematic and repeated violations of the civil-service law, which had been done by the board of examiners acting under collusion with the postmaster. The postmaster, as he himself testified, though he afterwards retracted it, would appoint a man, and then would have an illegal certification made to cover that appointment. There were two parties to that wrongdoing: one was the postmaster, and one the local board. It was the postmaster, and the postmaster alone, who was benefited. It could be of no benefit to the local board. We were anxious to strike at the head criminal, and not at the tools of the criminal. We have always, where possible, tried to get the man who is ultimately responsible for wrong-doing, and not the poor devil whom he coerces into it. The actual labor of the board had been done by its secretary, Mr. Shidy. It was done, however, with the full knowledge of the chairman of the board, Mr. Johnson. Mr. Johnson testified before us. He testified before Governor Thompson, Mr. Lyman, and myself, that Shidy had consulted with him, and told him that he was under the duress of the postmaster, and that he was compelled to make up these stuffed certificates. Johnson being at that time chairman of the board, was fully aware of the wrong, and stands guilty with Shidy in doing it. Johnson would not testify to the facts. He admitted certain things, but would not come forward to testify. As soon as Shidy was given a chance he at once came forward and told all the truth. I think they were there together in the office. They were reluctant to testify, Shidy saying, "If I do testify to this I will be dismissed for doing it." I then told Mr. Shidy we would protect him from the consequences of telling the truth; not from the consequences of the wrong-doing. He then testified. We told the same thing to Mr. Johnson, but Johnson would not testify. Johnson rightly thought it would be to his interest to keep still, for he knew that he would be punished if he certified. We then came back and made a full and complete report, showing the guilt of Paul, Shidy, and Johnson. We also mentioned that Fahsel was guilty, but he resolutely declined to know anything about it at all. Johnson admitted of knowing of the wrong-doing. As soon as the first report was made public Mr. Paul removed Shidy.

Our feeling was this, that we wanted to condemn the man who was the head devil in the deed, and the man who was really responsible for it. Every one knows that if a head of an office wants to go wrong, he can readily place his subordinates under duress. It is a hard thing for a man to fight against. He ought to do it, and if he has character he will do it. Weak men will not do it. Our report was drawn mostly against Paul. We also reported strongly against Shidy and Johnson, and I beg to call particular attention of the committee to this part of the report. It will be noticed that we asked for Shidy the same protection meted out to Johnson and Fahsel. We had no intention whatever of doing anything except to prevent punishment being meted out to him for doing right, and had no intention of protecting him for his wrong-doing. Mr. Paul dismissed Mr. Shidy immediately; and Johnson, who was equally guilty with Shidy, was not dismissed, has never been dismissed, and is now in the office in the same position in which he was then. Whether Fahsel is or is not I do not know. If he has been removed it has been for something entirely unconnected with this.

By Mr. STONE:

Q. Do you speak of your absolute knowledge when you say that if he has been removed it has been for something unconnected with this?—
A. I do not know. I presume I would have been informed if three had been any change; and if he has been removed, it has been for some cause unconnected with this. I do not know that he has been removed. We asked for the removal of Paul. We thought that the facts of the case warranted his removal fully. We felt that his subordinates were less guilty than he was. We were willing to leave the measure of their punishment, as of course we had to do in any event, to their superior officers. Whatever punishment these men should have been found to

have deserved, well and good, let them suffer it. If we had undertaken that investigation without knowing the facts set forth by Shidy, we might not have been fully informed. I can not say that we would have asked for the removal of Mr. Johnson, as he might have been under such duress that we might have thought to reduce him to a half salary might have been sufficient punishment. I am not making that statement absolutely. In Shidy's case the circumstance that he had come forward and frankly confessed when an opportunity was given him, should undoubtedly have weight as a mitigating circumstance, and I should not have been in favor of inflicting upon him an equal punishment with the other man, unless I was absolutely certain that he deserved it. I do not believe in hitting the tool rather than the man who wields the tool and who alone is responsible. Shidy was timid. He was dismissed for no delinquency; but, on the contrary, for having testified to the truth, and under the civil service law he could have been re-instated at any time. He was not dismissed for having done badly. He had tried to atone by doing well. He was dismissed for trying to atone and doing well.

My two colleagues went to the Postmaster-General, as they informed me, and asked that Shidy be re-instated. They had no intention of preventing any punishment that might ultimately be visited upon him for his wrong-doing, but merely to see that he was not punished for having told the truth to us. He was not re-instated. Shidy had come forward frankly and told Governor Thompson, Mr. Lyman, and myself, when we were up there, the circumstances of this case. He did tell us that he had committed the wrong-doing, and that he regretted it extremely. When he testified before us there was no flippancy or levity in his testimony. He did not admit that he would do a like thing under the same circumstances again. On the contrary, he expressed a deep, sincere, and humble regret for what he had done. He said he would hereafter do, or aim to do, as uprightly as any public officer ever had done. He explained that he was a poor man wholly dependent upon his salary, and had a wife and two young children; that Paul had his fate in the hollow of his hand, and could at any time turn him out; that Paul had forced him to do these things and that he had yielded, being in Paul's power; that did not excuse his offense, but it certainly palliated it.

Accordingly, having failed to have him re-instated, I went to the Postmaster-General myself and laid the case before him, the Postmaster-General having before him our full report. The Postmaster-General must have known all these facts. I told him that Shidy was being persecuted for having had the manliness to come forward and tell the truth. I asked him if he could not have him re-instated; would he be willing that Shidy should have a position in the Census Bureau, I laying stress upon the fact that we were simply trying to protect Shidy on this account. I said that Shidy had been punished for doing right, and not for doing wrong. The Postmaster-General said he was willing that Shidy might be given a place in the Census Bureau.

I went and saw Mr. Porter. Our report had been made out, and had been spread broadcast through the press. It contained a full and specific account of all of Shidy's wrong-doings. Mr. Paul had answered it two or three times, and had been answered back. There was a great deal of discussion about it through the press of the country. Finally, after a month or two, the Postmaster-General or the President had acted on the post-office case, and it was a matter of public notoriety. I went up to see Mr. Porter, who was very busy, and I told him that I had a favor to ask on behalf of the Civil Service Commission, stating that it was with the consent of my colleagues; that through testifying in our behalf to the truth Mr. Shidy had been turned out of the post-office at Milwaukee, and we wanted to protect him, and did not want to see a man punished for having told the truth. As Mr. Porter said to you to-day, I told him that Shidy had done wrong under coercion, and that he had repented and confessed. I did not go into the minutia of the case because Mr. Porter was in a great hurry, and I referred him to my report, which I supposed he must have seen. I gave him practically a résumé of the case just as he has testified to it here to-day. The case was hung up for six weeks. Mr. Van Schaick protested against Mr. Shidy's appointment, and Senator Spooner and one or two outside parties wrote letters protesting against it, so that I had every reason to believe that Mr. Porter knew all the facts that he cared to know in reference to it. All that was said against Mr. Shidy was because he had testified against Paul. So far as the facts were concerned I believed they were all in Mr. Porter's possession. Mr. Porter said he would give him an appointment conditional upon his passing an examination.

I had seen the report of the former postmaster at Milwaukee which was in the evidence and it said that Mr. Shidy had been nine years in the post-office and that he was a peculiarly efficient and competent man. Shidy had expressed the deepest penitence for his misdeeds. He admitted that he had yielded to temptation and showed how strong the temptation was and how completely he was in the power of the postmaster. He had aroused our sympathies. To come back to the vital point, he was being punished, not for his wrong doing, but because he had done right in trying to atone for his wrong.

He came on and passed an examination and is now serving creditably, Mr. Porter stated above the average, having been promoted and is now acting chief in his division. In so far as his efficiency and his capacity as a public servant went he justified entirely the opinion of the Commissioners and has made a capable public servant in his new position.

In conclusion I will say this: The Government must protect its witnesses who are being persecuted for telling the truth. I felt that we would be derelict to a public duty if we did not strive to protect him. We have always striven to protect persons under similar circumstances. I again wish to call the attention of the committee here clearly to the intent of our report, which was to ask that no punishment should be visited upon Shidy for telling of these misdeeds and none visited upon Johnson and Fahsel who were equally guilty but had not told the truth. I did not want him punished while no punishment was inflicted upon the others for their wrong-doings.

By Mr. LIND :

Q. Has the Commission compulsory process for the attendance of witnesses ?—A. No, sir ; all our attendants are purely voluntary. They can not be forced to attend if they do not wish to.

Q. Have you tested the question by making application to the circuit court for process in your behalf ?—A. We have always understood that we had not that power. We have embodied a request that we should be given power to subpœna witnesses and to administer oaths. We have power to do neither.

By Mr. GREENHALGE :

Q. Is there anything in the terms of the act providing what shall be done in this respect ?—A. The act provides we shall investigate and report to the President, but makes no provision how we shall follow that out. When I was in New York last summer I consulted the attorney of the Civil Service Commission, who said that we had no power to administer oaths or compel the attendance of witnesses.

Q. Then if a witness did not appear voluntarily, you had no power to compel him ?—A. If a witness does not choose to testify, we can not make him.

Mr. LIND. Have you submitted that question to the Attorney-General ?

The WITNESS. We did not, because the Commission proceeded on the assumption that it could not, and it never occurred to me that we could.

Mr. BOATNER. Did Mr. Paul deny the statement of Mr. Shidy ?

The WITNESS. Mr. Paul has denied every fact and has denied his denial of the fact. He has further denied his denials of the denials. He has denied everything.

By Mr. HOPKINS :

Q. Those are three removals of denials ?—A. He has made complicated denials. I will state that in our report we explicitly say we have taken nothing against Paul on the unsupported statement of Shidy. In two instances we took the word of Jackson and Shidy when both testified to the same state of facts.

Mr. BOATNER. Have you any fear that you may have done Paul an injustice ?

The WITNESS. I have absolutely none.

By Mr. STONE :

Q. When was Mr. Doyle appointed secretary of your Commission ?—A. I believe he was appointed when it was first organized in 1883. Doyle is a Democrat. He was then the stenographer of the Commission.

Q. He has been connected with it a long time ?—A. Yes, sir.

Q. When was this report made by Mr. Doyle and Major Webster filed with the Commission ?—A. The first report of Doyle was filed some time in 1888. The report of Major Webster and Mr. Doyle, which was the first complete statement of the matter, was probably not prepared and put in shape until some time in the fall of 1888, about the time Mr. Oberly went out of the Commission.

Mr. OBERLY. It was after the time.

The WITNESS. It was after the time. I believe Mr. Oberly vaguely knew there were charges against Paul, but never had any specific facts laid before him.

Mr. STONE. Is it a fact that at that time Mr. Lyman was the sole Commissioner and was absent from the city quite awhile?

The WITNESS. Mr. Lyman was not then the sole Commissioner. Mr. Edgerton and Mr. Lyman were both on the Commission. I have understood that Mr. Edgerton was absent quite often at that time.

Mr. GREENHALGE. This is not within your knowledge?

The WITNESS. I am simply answering Mr. Stone's question.

By Mr. STONE :

Q. What I was endeavoring to get at was to see why this matter was not acted upon sooner ?—A. That I can not tell you.

Q. When you went to see the Postmaster-General about Mr. Shidy, did you go alone ?—A. I did, sir.

Q. Were you the only one who visited him upon that subject?—A. Mr. Lyman and Governor Thompson had previously visited him on the subject.

Q. Did you ever in your conferences with him state to him just what Shidy had said about this matter?—A. I told the Postmaster-General that Shidy was penitent in the matter.

Q. Did you state as to what he had done in the matter of making false certifications?—A. This report was officially laid before him and he had acted upon it. I presume he had read it, and I think that is a fair presumption.

Q. Did he discuss it as if he was familiar with it?—A. I do not think he discussed it at all. I think he said he had notified Mr. Paul that his removal had been determined upon.

Q. I understood you to say that the Postmaster-General at your solicitation wrote a letter to the Superintendent of the Census recommending the appointment of Mr. Shidy to a position there?—A. I would not say he recommended him. Mr. Porter got a letter of the usual form. The Postmaster-General wrote two letters, one to me saying he would be glad to do anything in his power—I could not recollect the exact expression he used, but something like this—" to atone for the hardships done Shidy," or some such expression. What we originally wanted was that Shidy should be re-instated, and that whatever punishment was meted out should be visited upon them all.

Q. Do you mean that you wanted the Postmaster-General to have him re-instated?—A. Yes, sir; although I never spoke about it to him.

Q. Can you state to us the reason why the Postmaster-General refused to interfere in Shidy's behalf as requested?—A. Of my own knowledge I can not. I can not recollect distinctly the details of my conversation with the Postmaster-General beyond the general facts I have stated. I think I spoke to him about the hardship it was to us to feel that a man who was equally guilty with Shidy was kept in office because he did not tell the truth, and that Shidy was turned out because he did tell the truth. I had learned that Congressman Van Schaick was hostile to Mr. Shidy on account of Mr. Van Schaick being a warm friend of Mr. Paul, the statement having been made to me that Paul, though a Democrat, had given an active support to Van Schaick. I know nothing of that beyond the fact that it was told to me that Mr. Van Schaick was the champion of Paul, and of his having made the statement that we had interfered with his prerogative, or making some such statement as that.

By Mr. EWART:

Q. In all this time was Shidy secretary of the board of local examiners in the post-office at Milwaukee?—A. Certainly.

Q. And an officer of the Commission?—A. He was a subordinate of the Commission.

Q. Was it not his duty, as an officer of that Commission, to report to you at once any violation of law?—A. I think it was. I have not recently looked into the duties of the secretaries of local boards, but I conclude that any employé of the public service ought to report any wrong-doing he sees.

Q. Whether on account of duress or not?—A. Whether under duress or not.

Q. Did Shidy ever make any report to you or any officer of the Commission while he was under duress?—A. He did.

Q. When did he first make that report?—A. It must have been to Doyle.

Q. Was the statement made under oath?—A. We have his original letter handed to Doyle at that time.

Q. Was it made voluntarily?

Mr. LIND. Why not ask Mr. Doyle that question? It would only be hearsay with Mr. Roosevelt.

By Mr. EWART:

Q. In all this time he had an opportunity or a "chance," as you prefer to call it in your evidence, to make this report, did he not?—A. In a certain sense he always had a chance. There are plenty of weak, timid men who would not volunteer themselves to report a wrong-doing, but who undoubtedly are conscientious enough to report it as soon as circumstances arise where it is possible for them to do so, and there are other men, like Mr. Johnson, who when these circumstances arise would not report it. Mr. Shidy came under the first class.

Q. What is the reason he did not make this report earlier than he did?—A. I can only give my suppositions on that.

Q. Did the substance of his testimony satisfy you that he persistently and repeatedly violated the law?—A. Yes, sir.

Q. That he had made false certifications?—A. We have stated that.

Q. That he had mutilated the records?—A. I do not know that we said that.

Q. That he had tortured the records?—A. Yes, sir.

Q. That, in a word, he had repeatedly violated his oath of office?—A. Precisely.

Q. After you became aware of these facts that he had stuffed the list of eligibles, that he had violated his oath of office, made false certifications, and that he was a weak man, and you claimed he committed these violations because he was forced to do it by his superior officer, you asked for his re-instatement in that office?—A. We did, not with any reference to these violations, but because he was removed for having tried to atone for them.

Q. When a man commits perjury by the violation of the law he has sworn to enforce and when he confesses he has made false certifications and has persistently and repeatedly violated the law, is it your theory as a civil-service reformer that, because he has frankly confessed that he has violated the law, expressing an intention to reform, that he should be re-instated in office?—A. Do you mean in the same position?

Q. The same position or any position in the Government?—A. That would depend on the circumstances of the case.

Q. Take the circumstances in the Shidy case?—A. I mean to say my action was right in the Shidy case.

Q. Then I take it that in any case where the circumstances are the same as in the Shidy case, where if it were called to your attention as a civil-service reformer, that you would unhesitatingly recommend that man for a position in the Government employ or re-instate him in the position in which he had repeatedly violated the law?—A. Not at all, sir.

Q. I ask you if this is your theory, supposing the same state of facts as existed in the Shidy case?—A. I think not. It is the first case of its kind that came to our attention.

Q. I understood you to say that if a similar case arose you could not take the course you took in the Shidy case, although the circumstances might have been identically the same?—A. That I can not answer.

By Mr. BOATNER:

Q. I understood you to say you made no objections to removals on account of these violations?—A. I explicitly stated that.

Q. Shidy was removed because he told about it?—A. That is precisely my statement. I do not want to be misunderstood. Mr. Ewart is evidently wishing me to state that if these circumstances arose I would not act as I did then, giving the impression that I was sorry for what I had done. On the contrary, I think I was precisely right, and I am glad I took that stand.

By Mr. EWART:

Q. Do you mean that you would take the same course with other cases?—A. There has been full and ample warning given now, and we might not behave with such leniency in the future. In this case I felt that we treated Mr. Paul himself with great leniency. One thing I had forgotten. I told you Mr. Paul not only denied this, but denied his denial. When we went to see Mr. Paul he told us his term of office was over and that he was simply hanging on until his successor should be appointed. After we returned I drew up a short and rather scathing report. "Don't shoot at dead ducks," said Governor Thompson. "He has gone. Let us simply make a report that he had been guilty of gross misconduct, and not recommend his dismissal." We wanted to be just strong enough to make his case an example, and yet not be too harsh. Paul was foolish enough to try to fight back. We found he had not been removed nor had he served his time out, but had several months yet to serve, all of which is stated in the report which we then drew up. In future, in any case, if we found a number of persons engaged in wrong-doing and one repents, I say I would regard that as a strong circumstance in his favor, and I say it would be my purpose to practically take it into account when judgment is meted out. I could not hold my head up if I had allowed Shidy to be turned out and persecuted for having told the truth, in spite of his wrong-doing, when other men who had been just as bad were not turned out. I would have felt I was doing great injustice to him.

By Mr. STONE:

Q. This report made by Webster and Doyle was filed, I believe, some time in October, 1888?—A. I think it was filed in November. I think it was after Mr. Oberly left.

Q. Did you or your colleagues of the Commission examine that report before you went out to Milwaukee?—A. The matter was first brought to my attention by Major Webster, on the eve of our departure for Chicago. I believe there was a remark made by Mr. Lyman that there had been a case of a man in Milwaukee, Mr. Paul, and the only account that I read before going there was this analytical statement of Paul, the certification book and other records, and a statement of Paul himself. I did not read Mr. Shidy's testimony at all that I know of.

Q. You had read it somewhat?—A. I had looked over the papers, but how much I had read of them I could not tell you at this moment.

By Mr. EWART:

Q. Why was it necessary to offer protection to this witness Shidy?—A. I do not know that it was necessary for me to do it. When the man came forward and said, "Gentlemen, I do not want to testify; I am dependent on my salary, and I will be ruined and turned out if I do testify," I naturally said (I believe I was the spokesman), "Mr. Shidy, we will protect you for telling the truth." We did not promise him protection for any of his misdeeds. We promised to protect him from any punishment which might be visited upon him by Mr. Paul for telling the truth. Shidy was much afraid, because he knew that Paul had assisted Mr. Van Shaick for Congress, so that he had a "pull" with the Republican Congressman who would undoubtedly name Paul's successor, and so Shidy felt that if Paul got down on him he would be killed, not only with Paul but with Paul's successor. That is the reason why he was reluctant to testify. Johnson did not testify and has been kept in, showing that Shidy's fears were warranted.

Mr. BOATNER. Would you not consider yourself under somewhat of an obligation to do for Shidy what you have done, whether you made any promise or not? Would not the justice of the case warrant it?

The WITNESS. I think I should have. I would be very reluctant to see a man punished who had come forward and told the truth for the Government, even if he had done wrong before. I think Shidy has been greatly punished. He has lost five month's salary and then got an appointment at $720, while his original place paid him $1,300. He has been badly punished for it.

Mr. STONE. For what has he been rewarded by this treatment?

The WITNESS. I did not consider it in the light of reward. I considered it in the light of an injustice, dismissing a man not for dereliction, but for having testified to the truth.

By Mr. BUTTERWORTH:

Q. You wanted to make it equally as advantageous to tell the truth as to tell a lie?—A. Yes, sir. I think it due to myself to say one thing, and that is, that Shidy did not boast of what he had done. On the contrary, he expressed sincere contrition.

Q. He stated here that he would do the same thing under the same circumstances?—A. He did. I now believe him to be unfit for any public position.

By Mr. EWART:

Q. And utterly untruthful?—A. I am not perfectly certain about that. I have not made up my mind about that.

Mr. BOATNER. I suppose that when you examined him you were supposing the sentiment to apply that "so long as the lamp holds out to burn the vilest sinner may return?"

The WITNESS. Yes, sir. I asked him if he did not appreciate what we had done for him, and if he did not appreciate the gravity of his offense, and if given another chance wouldn't he always do right, and he said "Yes." He seemed to feel very sorry about it, and said he would always try to do right. He said this in the presence of Governor Thompson.

By Mr. EWART:

Q. Coming back to your interview with the Postmaster-General, did I understand you to say that you requested him to re-instate this man Shidy as a clerk in the Milwaukee post-office?—A. I suppose I said I was very sorry he could not be re-instated. The Postmaster-General practically refused to re-instate him. I went to Mr. Wanamaker and I think I said to him that I was sorry that Shidy could not be re-instated. I may be wrong in my recollection about that. I think he said something or other about waiting to see Congressman Van Schaick, or expressed some regret. I have explained that already.

Q. Do you recollect saying anything about the removal of Johnson or Fahsel?—A. We simply made this report. We did not make specific recommendations for their removal. We reported the case and laid it before the Postmaster-General for his action. That was the course we took in this case. Paul we wanted removed.

Q. In this interview with the Postmaster-General do you recollect whether or not you specifically stated to the Postmaster-General that this man was guilty of making false certifications, etc.?—A. I am very confident I did not. I may explain that the Postmaster-General had our report before him.

Q. You do not know whether he had read the report?—A. He acted on the report. I did not read it aloud to him, but he had acted on it, and the presumption is fair that he had read it.

Mr. THOMPSON. Mr. Chairman and gentlemen of the committee, I simply want to confirm what my colleague, Mr. Roosevelt, has said about the circumstances of the interview between the Commission and Shidy when he gave this testimony for which he was subsequently dismissed. He was very reluctant to testify, and stated that he thought he would be dismissed if he did so. Mr. Roosevelt gave him this assurance, that we would protect him as far as we could if he made a frank statement. I remember Mr. Roosevelt calling his attention to the fact of his gross dereliction of duty, and asked him what statement he had to make. He said, "I have no excuse to offer, except that I acted under the direction of the postmaster, and I thought he would dismiss me if I disobeyed his orders." I never saw a man more contrite and penitent, or a more humble man than he was at that time; and he touched my sympathies in spite of his misdeeds. I say unhesitatingly that I would have been disposed to help a man, if I could have done it, in any public or private way, who had expressed repentance and promised in the future not to do so again. I never saw a man in my life to whom I was more inclined to say, "Go and sin no more." I sympathized with his condition, and I knew that he was under a powerful temptation. I cannot state that he said it in words, but I think he probably did say it in words, that it was a great relief to him to come before us and to be able to tell this whole thing. He said it had been a burden upon his mind.

[At this point the witness was interrupted in order that the committee might hear the Postmaster-General.]

TESTIMONY OF HON. JOHN WANAMAKER.

Hon. JOHN WANAMAKER sworn and examined.

By Mr. EWART:

Q. I want to ask you with regard to the recommendation of one Shidy to a position in the Census Bureau and in reference to an interview which Mr. Roosevelt had with you on that subject, and whether at any time in the course of the interview he stated that Shidy, for whom he wished to secure a position, had made false certifications of the Civil Service Commission, had repeatedly violated his oath of office, had stuffed the list of eligibles, and had mutilated or tortured the records of which he was the custodian as secretary of the local board of examiners of the post-office at Milwaukee?—A. He did not.

Q. Please state exactly what he did say to you when he came to you and asked you in reference to the appointment of Shidy to a clerkship in the Census Bureau.—A. So far as I can remember, he said that Shidy had aided in an investigation at the Milwaukee post-office, and that the postmaster had taken offense and had dismissed him; that he felt an interest in Shidy, because he did not want any one who had assisted the Civil Service Commission in the exercise of its duties to be punished, and therefore he was interested in securing a place for Shidy, and asked whether I had any objection, to which, of course, I answered that I had not.

Q. Did he state in what manner Shidy had aided in this investigation?—A. He said that Shidy had given the Civil Service Commission all the assistance that he could; and he conveyed the impression to me that Shidy was an excellent man and worthy of the interest he was feeling in him, and that he wanted to help him because he had aided the Civil Service Commission in the exercise of their duties, and he did not want to see him suffer for it.

Q. In the course of that conversation, did he refer to a report he had made, or a report the Commission had made with regard to the workings of the post-office at Milwaukee?—A. It is possible that he did. I do not remember that he called my particular attention to anything, but simply asked whether I had any objection to his being tried, if a place could be found for Shidy.

Q. Do you remember whether or not he called for that report at the time?—A. I am very sure he did not.

Q. Have you read that report?—A. I have.

Q. Had you read it at that time?—A. I think I had—without reference to Shidy, but with reference to the post-office. I was interested in any question in reference to the duties of the postmaster.

Q. You have a great many reports of that kind constantly before you?—A. Yes, sir.

Q. In this particular instance your attention was directed more particularly to his penitency than to the office that Mr. Roosevelt wanted him to have?—A. I took it for granted that Mr. Roosevelt knew the gentleman he was acting for, and the impression he gave me was that he was one of the men who had been badly treated by reason of his testimony.

Q. Did Mr. Roosevelt state anything as to the reasons why Shidy was dismissed from his position in the Milwaukee post-office?—A. I think on a previous occasion he had spoken about it.

Q. Did either of the other Commissioners request you to re-instate Mr. Shidy in his position?—A. Not that I can remember.

Q. You have no recollection as to that?—A. I feel sure they did not.

By Mr. STONE:

Q. I think you are mistaken about that.—A. It may be possible. I have no recollection of having spoken to Mr. Lyman or Mr. Thompson on the subject.

By Mr. EWART:

Q. At any of these interviews, either with Mr. Roosevelt or the other Commissioners, did either of them ever request you to remove Mr. Johnson and Mr. Fahsel, or other members of the board at Milwaukee.—A. I think not.

Mr. BUTTERWORTH. I understood you to say in giving an account of the interview with Mr. Roosevelt, that you did not give the language, but rather the impression?

Mr. WANAMAKER. Only the impression.

Mr. LYMAN. Do you recollect that one afternoon Mr. Roosevelt and myself went to your room and showed to you two telegrams that we brought with us concerning Mr. Shidy's dismissal from the Milwaukee post-office, which you read; and we asked you what, if anything, could be done about it?

Mr. WANAMAKER. It is possible that that might have occurred, but I can not remember.

By Mr. LIND:

Q. There is one question that the committee, perhaps, does not fully understand. Did you recommend the appointment of this man Shidy, or did you simply report that your bureau had no objections to his appointment?—A. My letter will show that. I think I simply said that I had no objection to his appointment. I have the letter. I was looking into a drawer last evening, as it is the end of the month, and I found a letter.

Q. Do you desire to submit the letter?—A. It bears on this point. I understood that Mr. Roosevelt was endeavoring to ascertain whether I would object to his employment, and I simply took the position that I did not object; and I could not object to it.

By Mr. EWART:

Q. The letter stated that he was a worthy and honest man?—A. That he esteemed him as such.

By Mr. STONE:

Q. Were you requested by Mr. Roosevelt to have Mr. Shidy re-instated in the post-office, at Milwaukee?—A. I think not officially. I think that I recall a conversation with Mr. Roosevelt in which he deprecated the condition of things whereby a man who assisted the Civil Service Commission should be punished for it, and that he thought the man ought to be re-instated.

Q. You say that you have no remembrance of a conversation with either of the other Commissioners at that time?—A. I can not recall a conversation with either of the others in this case, except Mr. Roosevelt; though it is possible that I did have.

Q. Did Mr. Paul resign, or was he removed?—A. We accepted his resignation, but notified him that it came at a time when we were considering his removal, which we thought was justified by his conduct.

Q. Did you read, while considering that report, the report made to the President by the Civil Service Commission?

Mr. ROOSEVELT. Do you know that in that letter I say that his removal had been determined upon in consequence of a report of the post-office inspector, and a report of the Civil Service Commission?

The WITNESS. The removal had been determined upon.

Mr. ROOSEVELT. Can you not get that letter?

The WITNESS. Certainly.

By Mr. EWART:

Q. What I wanted to know was whether you were familiar with it by reason of the examination made in that Milwaukee post-office?—A. I knew generally of the matter at the Milwaukee post-office.

Q. You were familiar with the facts which had been developed by the investigation made there?—A. Certainly, and I examined the report of the inspector.

Q. With your knowledge of Mr. Shidy's action in this transaction from the reports made to you would you have been willing, on a request of the Civil Service Commission, to have directed his retention in that office?—A. The question never came before me. The question which was brought before me by the inspector was whether Mr. Paul was a proper man. That was the only question that came before me.

Q. It has been said here in the testimony that you were requested by the Civil Service Commissioners to have Mr. Shidy retained in his place in the Milwaukee post-office, and that you declined to do it. Now you say, that you do not remember about that?—A. I do not remember the telegram which has been mentioned. It is possible that I may have read it. A telegram might not make an impression upon my mind. It is clear to me that if it had been proper to have re-instated Mr. Shidy, that the order would have been given to do so, regardless of the request of Mr. Lyman and Mr. Thompson. We would have considered our way clear to do that.

Q. They having requested it, and you having declined to yield to their request, do you not think your action was proper?—A. I would have considered the request to take up the case, but it seemed to me that if he had been dismissed, the postmaster who had dismissed him was going out, and that it would have been improper to take any action at that time, but let the man who was coming in settle it. We have frequent cases of that kind.

Q. Do you remember stating in your letter to Mr. Porter, Superintendent of the Census, that you would be pleased if Mr. Shidy were appointed to a position in that office?—A. I have not the letter with me. I send four or five hundred letters a day, and it would be impossible to carry in my mind the terms of a letter; but on general principles I would say that I always express myself as pleased if employment is given to a person that Mr. Roosevelt would recommend.

Q. Knowing the purity of your life, public and private, I will put the question in this way: If at any time in the course of these interviews between you and Mr. Roosevelt, or Mr. Lyman, or Mr. Thompson, it had been stated to you that this man Shidy, for whom Mr. Roosevelt desired to secure a position in the Census Bureau, had been guilty of persistent violations of law, and had violated his oath of office—in other words had perjured himself, to use plain English, had mutilated the records, stuffed the list of eligibles, and all that, would you have felt justified in entertaining any request to give such a person a position in any Department?—A. I certainly should not. I should have regarded it my duty to have opposed the appointment of any such a man.

Mr. ROOSEVELT. All these facts which Mr. Ewart speaks of, in so far as he quotes them correctly, are in a report that we made to the President of the United States on this matter. You had that report, and had acted upon it when I spoke to you, had you not?

The WITNESS. We had the report.

Mr. ROOSEVELT. And you had acted upon it, had you not?

The WITNESS. How do you mean "acted upon it?"

Mr. ROOSEVELT. You referred to it as the reasons why the removal of Mr. Paul had been decided upon in your letter notifying Mr. Paul that you had accepted his resignation. If there is any doubt in your mind, you can produce the letter, I presume?

The WITNESS. The determination to remove Mr. Paul would be made upon the report of the post-office inspector. I can not say how much influence the report of the Civil Service Commission had upon me, inasmuch as it was a report made to the President, and I did not feel the same responsibility about it. In receiving a copy of it, I considered it a matter of courtesy merely, in a measure.

Mr. ROOSEVELT. Would you send a copy of the letter that you sent accepting the resignation of Mr. Paul? My memory is very clear that in that letter you referred to this report.

The WITNESS. I will furnish it with pleasure.

By Mr. HATTON:

Q. As a matter of fact, did not you order the removal on the report of the post-office inspector?—A. It was because of the report of the post-office inspector.

Q. Did Mr. Roosevelt ever request you to remove Johnson, a member of the local board, who was a partner of Shidy in the matter of the manipulation of the eligible list?

Mr. LIND (interposing). That has been asked twice of the Postmaster-General.

The WITNESS. I have already answered that question.

By Mr. HATTON:

Q. Of course you have power to order the removal of a clerk in the Post-Office Department?—A. I think so.

By Mr. BUTTERWORTH:

Q. If in your letter accepting the resignation of Mr. Paul you mentioned the fact that your request for his resignation was predicated (if there was a request) upon the report of the inspector, and a report also of the Civil Service Commission, would not that indicate that you were familiar with the fact that this request had been from information derived from both sources?—A. The letter will show what I said upon that point, and I will send a copy of it.

TESTIMONY OF HON. HUGH S. THOMPSON—Recalled.

Hon. HUGH S. THOMPSON, examination resumed.

By Mr. STONE:

Q. Did you go with Mr. Lyman, after Shidy had been dismissed by the Milwaukee postmaster, to see the Postmaster-General and request that Shidy be re-instated?—A. I went with him, I think, about the first of July. My recollection is that it was early in July, at least. My impression is also that it was to prevent the removal of Shidy. There were two telegrams received about it; I think one stating that he was about to be removed, and another that he had been removed, and we wanted to stop it until the whole matter could be gotten before the Postmaster-General. Mr. Lyman and I went to see him one afternoon. That is the only conversation that I had with the Postmaster-General.

Q. Did you discuss the matter of his re-instatement, or recommend the retention of Shidy?—A. Yes, sir; but not fully. The Postmaster-General declined to interfere.

Q. What reason did he assign?—A. I do not know that he gave any reason. I know that he stated, and from his manner he showed rather plainly, that he would not interfere. I think he said he had not seen our report. My recollection is that Mr. Lyman said to him, "We have sent you a copy of our report." We afterwards learned that there was a report sent to the Postmaster-General, but he had not received it.

Q. Did you approve of Mr. Roosevelt's visit to Mr. Porter in the interest of Mr. Shidy?—A. Yes, sir.

Q. Did you desire that he should receive this appointment?—A. Yes, sir.

Q. Why?—A. Because I thought he had been unjustly punished for doing right.

Q. Do you think now, after hearing his testimony, that he ought to be retained in that position?—A. I do not think he ought to be retained in any position.

Q. Why?—A. I think the manner and assurance of the man was something astounding.

Q. Is there any material difference in the substance of what he said here yesterday, and what he said to you gentlemen?—A. Not as to the wrong-doing; but yesterday he undertook to explain, if not to justify, the wrong-doing. Before us he was humble, and begged for forgiveness. Here he practically admitted that under similar circumstances he would do what he had already done at Milwaukee; and said that if called upon to make false certifications, he would do it. That is not the kind of a man that I thought I was trying to help.

Mr. LYMAN. I agree fully with the statements that my colleagues have made this morning.

TESTIMONY OF JOHN T. DOYLE.

JOHN T. DOYLE, sworn and examined.

By the CHAIRMAN:

Q. Did Mr. Shidy put every facility in your way for ascertaining the truth when you were in Milwaukee ?—A. He did. He laid all the books and papers before me at the first investigation, June 29, 1888. He laid the records before me, and fully gave every explanation asked, and offered facilities for the examination. There was no hesitation or concealment.

Mr. ROOSEVELT. His conduct was in marked contrast with that of Johnson?

The WITNESS. I saw Mr. Johnson after I had got from Shidy the records and an explanation of the manner in which the work had been done. My interview with Johnson was brief, and confirmed the statement of Dr. Shidy.

By Mr. STONE:

Q. What was the date of your first visit to Milwaukee ?—A. June 29, 1888.

Q. Did you ascertain on that first visit the facts which have since been developed ?—A. I did.

Q. Fully ?—A. Quite so; all the record disclosed.

Q. Did Shidy make any confession to you at that time ?—A. He said to me at that time substantially what he said to the committee yesterday.

Q. When you returned did you make a report ?—A. I made a report in writing of my investigation.

Q. Did you state the condition of affairs ?—A. I did. An extract from my report appears in these papers.

Q. What was then done about it ?—A. Major Webster and myself were directed to visit the office, take testimony, and make a statement concerning the matter.

Q. How did you happen to go there in the first place ?—A. I was sent out there to visit twenty-eight post-offices and investigate generally into the conduct of the work of those offices.

Q. You had no knowledge of these irregularities prior to that visit ?—A. None.

Q. After your return, when you made this report, you and Major Webster were sent by the Commission to make a full investigation ?—A. We were. The report of Major Webster is here before you. My recollection is that we returned about the 1st of November, 1888.

Q. Was any action taken on that report ?—A. The report was laid before the Commission.

Q. Who constituted the Commission then ?—A. Mr. Edgerton and Mr. Lyman.

Q. When did Mr. Edgerton go out of the Commission?—A. Mr. Edgerton left the Commission, I believe, in February—the 9th of February, 1889.

Q. Do you know from your connection with this Commission why no action was taken on that report?—A. I do not, further than the fact that the Commission had an immense amount of work, far more than the force could admit of its full performance.

Mr. BUTTERWORTH. It had no work more important than this, if this thoroughly rotten condition of affairs existed.

The WITNESS. If the Commission was fully informed of its gravity.

By Mr. STONE:

Q. Were the Commissioners here in Washington at that time, from November to February, when Mr. Edgerton went out?—A. The Commissioners were not all the time in Washington.

Q. They were generally here?—A. Generally, yes, sir; to the best of my recollection.

Q. This matter was laid before them?—A. Yes, sir.

Q. What was the date of the appointment of Commissioners Roosevelt and Thompson?—A. May 10, 1889.

Q. When was this matter laid before them?—A. I do not know, sir.

Mr. ROOSEVELT. I believe it was laid before us the first of June.

By Mr. BUTTERWORTH:

Q. You returned from Milwaukee about the first of November?—A. About the first of November.

Q. And with a knowledge of the disclosures made there?—A. Yes, sir.

Q. And no action was taken until after the advent of Messrs. Roosevelt and Thompson?—A. No action that I am aware of.

Q. Of course it is one of your duties after making a tour to report irregularities that may have come under your observation?—A. It is; and that duty was performed.

Q. That is the end of your duty in that particular?—A. Yes, sir.

Q. Yours ended and theirs began?—A. Yes, sir.

TESTIMONY OF CHARLES LYMAN—Recalled.

CHARLES LYMAN, recalled and further examined.

By Mr. BUTTERWORTH:

Q. I would like to ask Mr. Lyman why no action was taken by the Commission between November and the date of the action by the new Commission?—A. The investigation which resulted in these disclosures was made early in September. I think Major Webster and Mr. Doyle returned from Milwaukee about the 10th of September. I was anxious at that time that the matter should receive prompt consideration, and urged Major Webster for a preparation of his report at the earliest possible date, so that the Commission might have it in order to take action. There was a great pressure of work upon the Commission, and, as you have observed, there was considerable involved in the preparation of that report. I have reason to believe that Major Webster proceeded with the preparation of this report as rapidly as he consistently could, with the performance of his other duties in the Commission. I think this report is dated the 30th of October, the investigation having been early in September. It came to the Commission, if I remember correctly, on the 11th of November, or I will say about the first of November. It was dated the 30th of October. It may have been a day or two after that before it came to the Commission. I left Washington on the day before the Presidential election, to vote. The election was held on the Tuesday following the first Monday in November. On my return, having been gone three days I think, this report was before the Commission. Mr. Edgerton, who was then a Commissioner, did not return until some days after that. He was in Indiana at the time of the Presidential election. I do not remember just how soon he returned, but it was some days after I returned. As soon as he returned, I called his attention to the report and suggested that immediate action was desirable on this report.

In the meantime, between the time when the investigation was made and the time when the report was completed I submitted it to the Commission. Commissioner Oberly having been appointed Commissioner of Indian Affairs had gone out of the Commission and Mr. Edgerton and myself remained on the Commission. At the first opportunity after Mr. Edgerton returned to Washington I brought to his attention this report and asked for its consideration. He said he could not attend to it then but would consider it soon, as I remember, or something to that effect. Some days passed and I felt nervous and uncomfortable about it. I did not wish the report to remain unacted upon and I again called his attention to it. He gave some excuse, and I repeatedly thereafter called his attention to this report with the view of getting action upon it, but I could never secure his co-operation for action upon that report. In the meantime I had received an order from the President which involved a great stress of work and which required not only the utmost amount of labor which I was capable of giving it during office hours but far into the night. In that condition of affairs this report was not acted upon. Mr. Edgerton persistently neglected to co-operate with me in any action upon it.

.By Mr. STONE:

Q. Refusing to do so?—A. If that neglect after his attention was repeatedly called to it was refusal then he did refuse.

Q. Did you carry it to the attention of the president himself?—A. I did not.

Q. Why?—A. I did not feel that under the circumstances the offenses which had been brought to light by the investigation, and the question being a punishment to be meted out to the guilty, that it was my duty, in view of the fact that I was not the sole Commissioner.

Q. Soon after that you became the sole Commissioner, did you not? Did you consider that you had authority then to take action in this matter?—A. I presume I had.

Q. But you did not?—A. I did not.

Q. Why not?—A. I do not know that that matter impressed my mind at that time. I do not think I formulated in my mind the reason why. During all this time the pressure of the work of the office was simply overwhelming. I was burdened with an amount of labor and responsibility which was almost crushing.

By Mr. BUTTERWORTH:

Q. Who was the ranking Commissioner when you came in?—A. Mr. Edgerton was president of the Commission.

Q. And he was exclusively the head of the office?—A. Yes, sir.

TESTIMONY OF HUGH S. THOMPSON—Recalled.

HUGH S. THOMPSON recalled and further examined.

Mr. THOMPSON. Mr. Chairman and gentlemen of the committee, I never saw this report or had an opportunity to read this report until the morning of the day on which I went to Milwaukee with other work. That morning I borrowed the papers from my colleagues for the purpose of reading them. I read, as I recollect, the preliminary report of Major Webster. I did not read the testimony of Mr. Paul or Shidy. I did not know what Mr. Shidy had testified to when we got to Milwaukee.

Mr. LYMAN. One reason why I desired especially the co-operation of my colleague on the commission in the consideration of this report was that in reading it I discovered serious conflict in the testimony itself, and I did not feel that I could take the responsibility of acting upon a report in which there was such serious conflicting testimony.

TESTIMONY OF JOHN H. OBERLY—Recalled.

Hon. JOHN H. OBERLY recalled and further examined.

Mr. OBERLY. Mr Chairman and gentlemen of the committee, I wish to state that at the time my attention was first called to the condition of affairs in the Milwaukee post-office by the report of the secretary, Mr. Doyle, after his return from the investigation of custom-houses and post-offices in the West—that was, I think, in August or before—the statement of the condition of affairs there led me to believe that there ought to be a more thorough investigation than he has been able to make, and I consulted with Commissioner Lyman upon the matter, and we both concluded that an investigation, more thorough than Mr. Doyle had been able to make, ought to take place. Shortly after our consultation we determined to send an examiner who was familiar with such matters to Milwaukee to go into a more deliberate investigation, and make a more thorough report. And I went to see the President of the United States, and reported what had been said of the condition of affairs at that post-office. Mr. Cleveland expressed his astonishment, and said that Mr. Paul had been appointed for one reason, because he was a man who believed in the principles of civil service reform, and a man who was, I think, secretary of some civil service association in Milwaukee.

Mr. ROOSEVELT. I think he was president of a local civil service association. It was a "happy family" up there.

The WITNESS. The President thought Mr. Paul was a man whose character was respected and esteemed in his community, and he was astonished that such reports should be made of the conduct of the office, particularly with reference to the execution of the civil service law and rules. But he said that it was proper a thorough investigation should be made as speedily as possible, so that the facts might be ascertained and action taken. This conversation I reported to Mr. Lyman.

By Mr. LIND :

Q. About what time was that ?—A. That was some time before these gentlemen went out, a week or two, I think. That is my recollection about it. It may have been longer. It was soon after Mr. Lyman and I had this conversation. I remember that at first it was discussed as to which member of the Commission should go, and I had expressed my willingness to do so. About this time I was nominated Commissioner of Indian Affairs, and my attention was divided between the two offices, so I declined.

Commissioner THOMPSON to ex-Commissioner Oberly. Let me suggest what you said to President Cleveland, that there was some one in the office who had the information and was afraid to give it.

The WITNESS. My understanding was that these offenses had been going on for a considerable time. Mr. Doyle had ascertained these irregularities by an examination of the books, and, being an expert himself, the secretary, Mr. Shidy, nor any other member of the board could well have concealed from him the facts. And in the conversation that was had at the time it was said that Mr. Paul was domineering the persons in the office, and they were afraid of their positions if they were not complaisant and obedient to his will. In my conversation with the President, I said there was probably some fear on the part of employés there that testimony given freely might operate to their disadvantage and result in their dismissal. The President said that the investigation should go on, and that no person in the post-office should be disturbed for any performance of duty or the exposure of any wrong-doing that had been done there.

By Mr. EWART:

Q. Did you read Major Webster's report?—A. No, sir; because it was not made. I read Mr. Doyle's report.

The CHAIRMAN. I understand that when Mr. Oberly was in the Commission the investigation was ordered, and before the report was made he was out of the commission?

The WITNESS. Mr. Doyle and Mr. Webster went out to Milwaukee, and returned about the 15th of September. I was still in office. Major Webster went there and found a pretty bad state of affairs—that the law was being systematically disregarded.

By the CHAIRMAN:

Q. When did you leave the Commission?—A. On the 10th of October. We asked Major Webster to prepare this report so that we might formally consider it.

Q. But the report was made after you left the office?—A. It was made after I left the office, and I had no opportunity of acting upon it further. Mr. Lyman had gone away from the city upon an examination tour.

Mr. LYMAN. I left on the 24th of September. Mr. Oberly had been Commissioner of Indian Affairs several days when I returned.

The WITNESS. Before taking that office, I divided my attention between the two places.

By Mr. EWART:

Q. After reading Mr. Doyle's report, did you think that the Commissioners were justified in extending protection to Shidy, he giving no additional evidence?—A. No. I do not think there was any necessity for extending protection to him. He could not have concealed any facts.

TESTIMONY OF HON. T. H. B. BROWNE.

MONDAY, March 3, 1890.

Hon. T. H. B. BROWNE, sworn and examined.

By Mr. HATTON:

Q. Where do you reside?—A. At Accomac Court-House, in the First Congressional district of Virginia.

Q. What is your business?—A. I am a member of Congress and a lawyer.

Q. Are you acquainted with Miss Emily Dabney?—A. I am.

Q. Please state to the committee what is her general reputation.—A. I have known Miss Dabney, I think, since the spring of 1888. I have known the family a long time. She has a sister who resides in my district, and is postmistress of Spottsylvania Court-House. She held the office during Mr. Cleveland's administration and she still holds it. The family is a very old one. The father of this lady was a clerk of our court for a number of years, and, I think, died since the war. From what I know of the character of her people generally, they are as good as any in the State of Virginia.

Q. Do you believe she is truthful ?—A. She is a woman of good character, perfectly good character. Senator Daniels had recommended her for appointment in the Government service, and if he were here I am quite well satisfied he would corroborate my statement. I think that politics has nothing to do with it, but they are all Democrats.

TESTIMONY OF THEODORE ROOSEVELT—Recalled.

THEODORE ROOSEVELT, recalled and further examined.

Mr. ROOSEVELT. Mr. Chairman and gentlemen of the committee, I wish to make a statement in reference to Mr. Wanamaker's testimony before this committee on Saturday, with your permission. So much latitude has been given to the other side and for the reason that I have sent a copy of this to Mr. Wanamaker, I desire to read from this printed matter.

(See Exhibit D.)

TESTIMONY OF CHARLES LYMAN—Recalled.

CHARLES LYMAN recalled and further examined :

Mr. LYMAN. Mr. Chairman and gentlemen of the committee, when the Postmaster-General was on the stand on Saturday I asked him if he remembered of Governor Thompson and myself calling upon him, and he said he may have done so, but he did not recall the incident. I desire to make this statement confirmatory of what has already been said. On Saturday, the 29th of June, I received a telegram from Doctor Shidy stating that he believed he would be removed from office on the next day. On the 1st of July, which was Monday, we received another telegram from Doctor Shidy, I am not certain what was the date, Sunday or Monday, stating that he had been removed. Late in the afternoon Mr. Thompson and myself went to see the Postmaster-General, and found him in his office, and we said to him that we had received two telegrams, and asked him whether anything could be done in this matter. The Postmaster-General replied that he could no nothing at that time ; that the matter having been reported to the President was practically out of his hands at that time. Upon that statement we withdrew. Nothing further of material character occurred at that interview.

By Mr. STONE :

Q. I understand that you went to see the Postmaster-General with the view of having Shidy re-instated ?—A. That was our purpose in case we should be clear on the subject.

Q. You stated your purpose ?—A. We stated that Shidy had been removed, according to the telegrams which the Postmaster-General read, and we asked him whether, in view of the fact that he was evidently being persecuted for what he had told the Commission, he could not in some way be protected either by his re-instatement then or at a later date.

Q. Did you give the Postmaster-General to understand that you desired or thought it was a proper thing for Shidy to be re-instated?— A. The purpose we had in view was simply to call the attention of the Postmaster-General to the matter and leave it to his judgment. We did not press it.

Q. And he declined to interfere?—A. He declined to interfere.

By Mr. BOATNER:

Q. This man Shidy had, at the solicitation of the Commission, testified as to the workings of the civil-service system in that post-office, and had disclosed irregularities which he said had been committed by direction of Mr. Paul. Did you not bring these facts to the attention of the Postmaster-General that Shidy had testified as to these irregularities and in consequence Paul had removed him from office?— A. Several days before the visit of Governor Thompson and myself the report of the Commission had been in the hands of the Postmaster-General.

Q. I want to know whether you verbally called this to the attention of the Postmaster-General?—A. Yes, sir; we did.

Q. Please state whether or not you expressed a desire to the Postmaster-General that Shidy should not be discharged.—A. We understood he had been discharged.

Q. You immediately called to see the Postmaster-General and submitted the matter to his judgment, making no suggestion of your own?—A. We stated that Shidy should not be punished for having given the Commission information.

The CHAIRMAN. Did you practically recommend his re-instatement? The WITNESS. I do not think we made any recommendation.

By Mr. BOATNER:

Q. Was it not your object to obtain his re-instatement?—A. Unquestionably it was our object to call the attention of the Postmaster-General to the matter, and if practicable to secure his re-instatement.

By the CHAIRMAN:

Q. Did you recommend that he be given some other place?—A. We went there to bring this matter to the attention of the Postmaster-General with the view of having him re-instated if practicable.

Q. Did you so state to the Postmaster-General?—A. Not in precisely that form. The Postmaster-General at once impressed Governor Thompson and myself with the idea that this matter at that moment was not in his possession in such a shape that he could act upon it, and we did not press the matter beyond that point.

By Mr. STONE:

Q. Have you gentlemen of the Commission had any conference with Mr. Shidy since this examination began?—A. I have seen Shidy once since the examination began.

Q. Where did you see him?—A. In my office.

Q. Did you gentlemen of the Commission send for him to come to your office, or did you not write a letter to the Superintendent of the Census asking that Shidy be sent down to your office?—A. I have not written such a letter.

Mr. ROOSEVELT. I did.

Q. Did he go down to your office in response to that request?—A. I believe he did.

Q. Did you see him?—A. I think I saw him, but the interview was between Shidy and Mr. Roosevelt and Mr. Thompson.

Q. Did you take part in it?—Not of any consequence.

Q. Did you hear the interview?—A. No, sir; I think not.

Q. Did you know for what purpose he was sent for?—A. I shall be obliged if you will ask Mr. Roosevelt that question, as he sent for Mr. Shidy.

By the CHAIRMAN:

Q. Do you not know?—A. I believe that he was sent for; in fact, I think I may state that I know he was sent for to confer in regard to the Milwaukee matter.

By Mr. STONE:

Q. To ascertain what his testimony would be before this committee?—A. Mr. Shidy desired to read over the testimony he had given at Milwaukee, and he was permitted to do so.

TESTIMONY OF THEODORE ROOSEVELT—Recalled.

THEODORE ROOSEVELT recalled and further examined.

Mr. ROOSEVELT. Mr. Chairman and gentlemen of the committee: After Mr. Ewart had made the attempt to see Shidy's testimony, I wrote at the suggestion of Governor Thompson to Mr. Porter to let Shidy come down there, and he came down and I recollect perfectly what was said to him. I said: "Mr. Shidy, you are certain to be cross-examined and their purpose will be to threaten and confuse you, and we want you to try and give your answers clearly. I want you to testify to the exact truth."

I said to Shidy: "They are going to try to bully and confuse you and try to make you contradict yourself." I said: "Try to be cool and clear and testify to the exact truth." I do not know whether I said "I want you to tell the exact truth" or not, but one or two gentlemen who have been witnesses here have tried to benefit their cases by telling a little more than was true, and making it lean on their side. I think if Campbell had stuck to the exact story, which was undoubtedly the truth as Mr. Oberly repeated it in his testimony, Campbell would have been clear. I do not believe that Campbell ever had prepared those papers in the manner he stated, but I think he had an idea that he was going to get some benefit.

By Mr. HATTON (to Mr. Thompson):

Q. Did I understand you to say that you accompanied Mr. Roosevelt to Milwaukee when he went there to investigate the post-office?—A. I did.

Q. At what time of the day did you reach Milwaukee?—A. About 2 o'clock.

Q. Do you remember what officer you called on first?—A. Mr. Paul, is my recollection.

Q. Did you state to Mr. Paul the object of the visit of the Commission?—A. I really do not remember now; I think we did.

Q. After calling on Mr. Paul and telling him the object of your visit, what other officer did you see?—A. We saw Shidy and Johnson. I do not think we saw any others.

Q. Did you state to those gentlemen the object of your visit?—A. I think we did, sir; this is my recollection about it, but I am not positive. We examined carefully the records of the office.

Q. Did you state to any members of the local board of examiners where you obtained the information on which you proposed to make the investigation?—A. Not at that time.

Q. Did you examine the other members of the local board?—A. We wanted to examine Fahsel, but he could not be found.

Q. Did you examine any of the examining board except Shidy?—A. We examined Mr. Johnson.

Q. Did you examine him fully in regard to it?—A. I think so. We got all he would tell. He was a reluctant witness.

Q. Have you got any record of the evidence that you got from Johnson?—A. We had no stenographer and no attempt was made to take it down.

Q. Why?—A. My purpose was to see whether Fahsel, Johnson, and Paul would confirm the statements which were in the report of Webster and Doyle.

Q. How did you get Shidy's testimony since you did not have it taken in shorthand?—A. No testimony was taken in shorthand by the Commission.

Q. You examined Shidy and Johnson, and did you not examine Paul at the same time?—A. We asked him a great many questions how it occurred, and all that.

Q. Did you object to Mr. Paul making a statement?—A. We made not the slightest objection to that.

Q. When was Shidy's testimony completed?—A. Not until the next morning.

Q. How long were you in Milwaukee during the next day—A. I think we left a little after midday.

Q. Did you speak to Mr. Paul about the nature of the testimony secured from Shidy?—A. No, sir; except in this way: When we called Shidy and Johnson, there was some conflict betwen the postmaster and Johnson as to the re-marking of papers.

Q. At any time before you recommended the removal of Paul did you give him an opportunity to see the testimony on which you based your conclusions?—A. We did not. When we examined him upon the evidence we called his attention to certain statements and he made his explanation.

Q. Has it been the practice of the Commission in cases where charges have been preferred and you have taken testimony and reached a conclusion on the testimony, have you notified the postmaster of the nature of the charges against him?—A. I do not recall anything at all to be the practice. Sometimes clerks have written to us about charges against postmasters, and in that case we would write to the postmaster and ask for an explanation.

Q. I mean in important charges such as this, where it would be such a serious matter, what was your custom?—A. We have never had any of a like gravity. No postmaster has ever been reported by us for removal. In regard to this Shidy matter, he came to my office two or three times before this examination and made some statements in reference to this Milwaukee matter. Mr. Roosevelt wrote to him at my request and asked him to come down. He wanted to refresh his memory about the matters he had testified to in Milwaukee. I told him that all he had to do was to keep cool and tell the truth.

Q. Have you seen him since?—A. He approached me the other day.

Q. Have you any objection to stating whether or not you have seen Shidy since he has given his testimony here?—A. Yes, sir; he called on me next morning. Shall I state what occurred? I told him, "I think your testimony made an impression. I never heard such a lot of fine-spun theories of ethics and morals as you gave to the committee the other day."

Mr. ROOSEVELT. I told him, "I do not care to talk to you alone any more. You have cut your own throat."

By Mr. HATTON:

Q. Have you recommended the removal of Shidy, having recommended him as a very superior man in the first instance?—A. That I deny.

Q. I will withdraw the "superior" part. Have the Commissioners recommended his removal?—A. None whatever, and I do not propose to.

By Mr. BOATNER:

Q. You heard Mr. Lyman's testimony with reference to the interview with the Postmaster-General. State whether or not you concur in this statement.—A. I recall some things. I remember distinctly that we stated that we wanted to prevent the removal of Shidy until the Postmaster-General could have all the facts before him. We informed him that a copy of our report had been sent to him, and we afterwards learned that it had been received at the Department, but the Postmaster-General had not seen it. The Postmaster-General expressed, if not in words, by his manner, that he was not exactly satisfied with the Milwaukee matter. He said: "Gentlemen, how do you know that I am not investigating that matter? You introduce confusion into the service." We told him that the civil service rules and law required that we should investigate all violations of the law. He said: "I have sometimes had as many as five hundred men under me." I think he said the number was five hundred, "and if some outside man came in there and interfered, it would destroy the discipline of the men and I could not carry on my business." I said, "I do not think this is a parallel case." The motive in my mind was to have him hold up this matter until it could be thoroughly laid before him.

TESTIMONY OF GEORGE H. PAUL.

GEORGE H. PAUL sworn and examined.

By the CHAIRMAN:

Q. What is your full name?—A. George H. Paul.
Q. You are a resident of Milwaukee?—A. Yes, sir.
Q. Formerly postmaster there?—A. Yes, sir.

By Mr. EWART:

Q. How long have you been a resident of Wisconsin?—A. For the last forty years.
Q. Did you ever hold any public position besides postmaster at Milwaukee?—A. I have held public positions always continuously.
Q. What positions?—A. I was postmaster at Kenosha, Wis., and was mayor of that city and postmaster for eight years there, and at Burlington, Vt., previously. I have been a member of the legislature for many years.
Q. Have you held any local positions in Milwaukee?—A. Yes, sir;

I was superintendent of the schools and president of the board of regents of the State University for sixteen years.

Q. How were those places selected?—A. Appointed by the governor each three years.

Q. Confirmed by the senate?—A. No, sir; not confirmed by the senate. My appointment was made at the unanimous request of the senate, however.

Q. You have held other places?—A. Yes, sir; many others. I do not care to enumerate all the places I have held. I was railroad commissioner of the State at one time under what was called the Potter law.

Q. Appointed by the governor?—A. Yes, sir; and confirmed by the senate. I was a member of the commission about three years, I think.

Q. When were you appointed postmaster?—A. In May, 1885.

Q. By whom?—A. By President Cleveland.

Q. When would your term of office expire under that commission? I believe you were appointed for four years?—A. The commission commenced after confirmation by the Senate. That commission would have expired in the month of February this year.

Q. Had the four years for which you were appointed expired when you left the office?—A. I took the position on June 1, 1885, and had held the office until June 1, 1889. Preceding that date I practically resigned the office before the visit of the Commission by requesting my successor to be named, and at that time also I made my resignation under an arrangement with the Representative in Congress to forward my resignation at the time he forwarded the name of my successor.

Q. That was Mr. Van Schaick?—A. That was Mr. Van Schaick. That was my volunteer motion. I did not wish to continue in office.

Q. On whose recommendation were you appointed postmaster?—A. On the recommendation of the entire State nearly.

Q. Were you appointed when Mr. Vilas was Postmaster-General?—A. Yes, sir.

. By Mr. STONE:

Q. At the time of your appointment were you not connected with some local civil-service association?—A. Yes, sir; I have always been connected with the civil-service from the origin of the system. I was vice-president, and I think I am still.

Q. Vice-president of what?—A. Of the civil-service association of that locality.

By Mr. HATTON:

Q. Was it State or local?—A. I think it is State, but I am not positive about that. I have always acted with it.

Q. Are you acquainted with Mr. Hamilton Shidy?—A. I do not know whether I know Mr. Shidy or not. I have had plenty of opportunities of knowing him.

Q. He was a subordinate of yours?—A. In one sense he was. He was clerk.

By Mr. BOATNER:

Q. Which part of Shidy are you questioning this witness about? Mr. HATTON. I think the Hyde part.

Q. He was secretary of the local board of examiners?—A. Yes, sir. I would like to bring out the construction of that board of examiners.

Q. I would like you to state what are the full duties of the board of examiners, and I desire to know whether the committee have any objection?

The CHAIRMAN. I do not see any objection to the question.

Q. As postmaster of an office which was working under the civil-service law, I will ask you what were your ideas of the duties of the local board of examiners?—A. I do not precisely understand your question.

Q. As a postmaster, working under the civil-service law (some officers are not under the law), what is your idea of the duties of the local board of examiners?—A. I will say what I think the question intends. I understand the board of examiners of an office to be the representatives of the Commission. That they in fact are the Commission as to that locality. That is my construction. If you will permit me to state, I will say no recommendation or change in the board was ever made by me. Two of the members of the board, both Republicans—Captain Johnson and Mr. Shidy—remained from the beginning until nearly the end of my administration. Their duties were discharged independent of myself as postmaster, as is well known in the city of Milwaukee. The third member of the board besides Mr. Johnson and Mr. Shidy when I came in was Dr. Kaine, of the Milwaukee Sentinel, and after I went into office Mr. Fahsel, superintendent of the money-order division, was suggested in place of Mr. Kaine. He was for a considerable time a prominent member of the city school board. Both Johnson and Fahsel, if the committee will permit me to say it, are men of high reputation. Shidy was a stranger in the city. Johnson had been in the service, at the head of the mailing division, over twenty-five years. He was, perhaps, one of the best known men in connection with the service in the country. Mr. Johnson was president of the board; Shidy was secretary, and Fahsel was the third man.

Q. How many employés were there at the Milwaukee post-office at the time you took charge?—A. One hundred and fifty to 160.

Q. How many post-office employés are subject to the civil-service law?—A. I could not give you the exact figures, but something more than one-half.

Q. At the time you took charge of the office did you make pretty general removals of clerks not embraced in the classified list?—A. No, sir; I have a statement here of the exact number removed since my term began.

Q. How many removals did you make during your incumbency of the office?—A. I think [referring to statement] the Milwaukee office has been found from the records to stand at the head of all of the offices in the country in that respect.

By the CHAIRMAN:

Q. How do you mean?—A. I mean the removals are less than they are in any office of the same size in the United States.

Mr. ANDREW. Do you mean since the organization of the office.

The CHAIRMAN. He means from the beginning of his administration that the removals in his office have been less than in any other office of the same size.

By Mr. HATTON:

Q. From what records did you secure that information that the Milwaukee office stands at the head of the list, so far as the observance of the civil-service law is concerned?—A. I got it from various sources. The reports of the Civil Service Commission are very limited upon that point. The last report, 1888, will show a comparative statement of removals for a year and a half, I think, preceding July, 1887 or 1888. In that case, I think, the Milwaukee office stands at the head, as I construe it, and the New York Times published a statement giving all the offices under the civil, service in the United States, or nearly all, and the Milwaukee office, according to my construction, was the least liable to censure. The changes of clerks in the Milwaukee post-office, not including civil-service places, I mean those not classified, from June 1, 1885, to August 23, 1887, was twenty-seven. Of these changes there were six removals, all for specific causes.

Q. Were there any for political causes?—A. No, sir.

By Mr. ANDREW:

Q. In what length of time?—A. From June 1, 1885, to August 23, 1887.

Q. Was that in the unclassified service?—A. That was in the classified service.

By the CHAIRMAN:

Q. How many clerks did you have?—A. I could give them, but the removals in the unclassified service are generally considered as a basis for an estimate.

Mr. ANDREW. What proportion of the unclassified service is thirty-seven? Is it the entire service?

Mr. LIND. This is only a portion of the number. Would it not be more satisfactory for you to give the changes in the entire number? This is only from June 1, 1885, to August 23, 1887.

Mr. ANDREW. I am talking about the unclassified service.

The WITNESS. There are sixty clerks in the office, of which more than half are classified. They come under the civil service. They are all under the supervision of the civil service.

Q. I thought these thirty-seven were outside of the civil-service rules.—A. The unclassified clerks are not subject to the provisions of the civil-service law. In the case of unclassified clerks, selections are not required. There is a popular impression that clerks are exempt from the provisions of the civil-service law, but that is erroneous, as I understand it.

By the CHAIRMAN:

Q. For instance, a clerk who is selling stamps is not required to be under the civil-service law.—A. He is on the unclassified list.

Q. How many are exempt in your office out of the sixty?—A. There are many men in many occupations. For instance, the register office and the money-order office are not in the classified service because the postmaster is responsible for them. There are some others in the office for which the postmaster is financially responsible, as, for instance, the money-order department.

By Mr. ANDREW:

Q. I understood you to say you have in your office about thirty in the unclassified service; there are sixty in all, and about one-half are in the unclassified service. You say also that in the period you have mentioned you made thirty-seven changes.—A. This includes the period from June, 1885, more than two years.

Q. In more than two years you made thirty-seven changes?—A. I made thirty-seven changes. If you will allow me I will give the causes of the changes and I think it will throw some light on this question. The causes of the changes were, resignations, sixteen—and I wish to make a remark here that the resignations were not invited in any case but one. On one occasion I advised a man to resign for his own sake.

The removals were six, additional appointments seven, transfers three, and offices abolished fourteen.

Mr. ANDREW. That is in the unclassified service.

The WITNESS. That is the unclassified service. I have here also the classified service. The changes in that were, promotions three, resignations twenty-nine, removals six, additional appointments eight, transfers four, and abolished four.

By the CHAIRMAN:

Q. How many resignations were there altogether?—A. Twenty-nine.

Q. Do you mean to state to this committee that during your term of office forty-five gentlemen resigned and left the employment of the Government?—A. Yes, sir.

Q. For business reasons, or what?—A. Yes, sir; for business reasons. I wish the committee to distinctly understand that the compensation of clerks is so poor and the labor so hard, in our western offices particularly, where we have a rapidly increasing population, that the clerks will not remain in those offices for any great length of time. They are generally anxious to get in, but they are soon anxious to get out and go into other business. A qualified man will always resign.

By Mr. HATTON:

Q. During the term of your office as postmaster, did you ever have charge of the record book or certification papers of the secretary of the local board?—A. No, sir; never in any way.

Q. Have you read the testimony of Mr. Shidy?—A. I glanced over it hurriedly as I saw it in your paper.

Q. Are you aware of the fact that he charges all false certifications, and all violations of law that he did as secretary of the examining board to you?—A. I am aware of the fact that he charges all his errors, and I will call them blunders for such they were, upon my intimidation.

Q. Did you ever assist Shidy in making false certifications?—A. No, sir.

Q. Did you ever assist him in remarking examination papers?—A. Never. Perhaps I ought to explain that last answer by saying that on one occasion some papers were remarked. They were remarked, and the occasion of that remarking was a fact unconnected with the public service as everybody knows, and unconnected with myself in particular. That remarking was originally erroneous and I will state further with regard to that, that the matter was considered by the entire board of examiners and a new marking was ordered. I recognize the fact that the marking which had been made was apparently unjust. I will say further in addition to the explanation I gave the Commission at the time with regard to that which I had forgotten at the time, that that marking of those papers as I am now informed, was made not by the board but by one individual alone, and that the board considered it entirely improper. The only real suggestion I made was to Mr. Shidy, and it was to this effect, that if he had ever improperly marked those papers that he should state all the facts as they occurred, to the Commission, and ask its approval, and under no other circumstances.

Perhaps I ought to complete what I have to say about it. The board came together of its own accord to consider the whole question of the original marking by one member of the board. It came to the conclusion, without any suggestion from me, that the marking was not quite right by a fraction. They changed that accordingly, I think, before the marking went on record. I had no part in that remarking at all. When the Commissioners asked me about this case they took me by surprise. Commissioner Roosevelt had great difficulty in remembering the names. I finally ascertained the name of the gentleman. I knew that there was a charge of interference with the proper authority of the board in the case, but there never was. I suggested to Shidy to send immediately to the Commission a statement of the facts of the remarking and ask for its approval under the rules, and he requested me to give him in full a memorandum of what I thought proper to say in such a case on the ground that he assumed I could better prepare such a memorandum than he could, and I did that, and the first sentence, according to my recollection, that I suggested was simply that the board of its own motion entirely had acted on it. I did not want it understood that I had anything to do with the matter in the way of controlling the board.

Q. Did you ever in any way assist Shidy as secretary of the local board of examiners in stuffing the list of eligibles and making them "round and full?"—A. No, sir; I never did in any case influence Shidy and I want to make a full response to that, that I never in any way influenced Shidy in the discharge of his duties improperly in any case. I wish to make that broad denial that the whole thing is purely a fiction and an assumption. I believe that I ought to make a remark, perhaps in that connection, that the Commission were wholly misled by the cunning and want of veracity of this man Shidy.

Q. Did you ever state to Shidy in what way you would like to have certifications made?—A. I have no recollection of having done anything of the kind.

By the CHAIRMAN:

Q. Did you do it?—A. I did not do it. I will say further that this whole question of intimidation or fear of the postmaster by the clerks in the post-office will not bear scrutiny. I never dreamed of discharging Dr. Shidy until shortly after the Commission were up there, and his discharge had no connection with his testimony, but it was caused by another matter.

Q. Did Shidy ever say to you why he violated the civil-service law?—A. Never. The rules make it the duty of the board of examiners to report to the Commission every month. The rules further make it the duty of the secretary of the board to report dates of certifications every month, as I understand it. I had no idea that he undertook to cover the consequences of his laziness and indolence and dilatory habits by making dates really not the true dates on the book.

Q. Did he ever at any time indicate to you before this examination that he expected to leave the office and secure a place somewhere else?—A. He often in a friendly way said to me that his relations with the Commission were such that he hoped to secure a better position at Washington in due time. I think that was the impression he gave me.

Q. What time was this?—A. I think he frequently spoke of his special relations with the Commission, and I am rather inclined to think that he thought he had been of special service to the Commission, and that he deserved from them more consideration than he had received from that body, and that he was the special representative of the Commission in the Milwaukee office. He was inclined to indulge in dreams of that kind, and that he was a special favorite of the Department. He claimed to me that one of the inducements for his retention would be, I do not know how true it was, that he had invented much of the machinery of the Post-Office Department, and that he hoped to be rewarded for it.

Q. Did he ever claim that he invented the machinery of the Civil Service Commission?—A. I think he regarded himself as a special representative of the great interest of the country in that particular.

Q. Is there any truth at all in any of the statements of Mr. Shidy that you in any way assisted him in the violation of the law, or making false certifications or stuffing the eligible list?—A. No, sir, there is no truth in it that I ever assisted him in any way or any manner, or advised or controlled him. I will, in justice to him, say that I do not think he intended to do anything wrong, all the way through. That as an original proposition I think it was mere carelessness and blunders. He was a man who claimed to be in ill health and very poor, and I attribute it to his careless business methods.

By the CHAIRMAN:

Q. Did you ever appoint a man to office as a clerk before he had passed a civil-service examination, in violation of law?—A. That was a point I was coming to. I never did such a thing as that. Any such thing as that could not have been done without making trouble for myself and the entire office. I will state just how those things occurred. The Commission has referred frequently to the record of certifications in its reports, and its blundering record makes all the trouble.

I do not think it is a criminal record. I do not accuse Shidy of criminality in that matter. The charges are perfectly explained by the fact that the Commission did not make an investigation except by Shidy.

It was Shidy's misrepresentation to cover his own faults. He was intimidated by the Commission, and especially by Mr. Roosevelt. Shidy stated in the presence of witnesses that when his errors became known to the Commission, they would recommend his removal at once. Shidy said he was a poor man and could not afford it. That is the explanation he made to me.

Q. Mr. Shidy testified here, and I believe that was one of the charges brought against your office by the Commissioners, that you appointed a man to office, and that he served and drew a salary for some two or three weeks, and that after having made the appointment in the legal way, you set it aside?—A. I think you will find that I am quite right about that. It was the case of Miss Whitehead.

Q. I do not recollect the case. I heard it stated.—A. I have never seen the official testimony of Shidy. I asked the Commission for it but never could get it. I have only been able to guess for many months what that testimony was. The Commission kept it from me and the testimony is still in their possession. I understand the case referred to was the Whitehead case, Miss Whitehead, of the money-order department. Miss Whitehead was examined for a civil-service place. She was appointed to a civil-service position at first, but under the rules and practice of the Department at that time, the post-office was permitted to give partial employment in the money-order service, and she having passed a civil-service examination and standing very high was appointed as a stamper. She entered upon her duties and performed that work. Shidy supposed, because the money-order clerks are not now performing the service, they were not then allowed to do it. The fact is they were allowed.

Q. What year was that?

Mr. LIND. It is August 1, 1885, that Miss Whitehead was appointed.

Q. At the time it was perfectly right?—A. Yes; it was authorized by the Department. Shidy did not know all my arrangements by any means.

By Mr. LIND:

Q. After you called for a name for the appointment of a clerk as stamper, did you know there was a vacancy in the stamper's division which you desired to fill?—A. At that time or subsequently?

Q. Subsequently?—A. Many times vacancies occur.

Q. Do you remember calling for a name to fill one of those vacancies in the stampers' division?—A. I can remember calling for names, but I do not remember special cases.

Q. Did you ever see that before [handing witness a paper]?—A. I do not know.

Q. Is that the slip that was reported to you to fill a vacancy in the stamper's division?—A. I can not tell. I think it was early in March, 1886.

Q. Do you remember whether you called for a report of three names to supply the vacancy that then existed in the stamp department, and whether there was three names sent in as the law required or whether it contained only one?—A. I think on one or two occasions——

Q. I am speaking of this case.—A. I can not speak definitely as to that case. I have no doubt the name was properly certified.

Q. You are not clear as to the facts?—A. I think Dr. Shidy would be a proper witness in that case.

Q. You do not recollect whether, when a vacancy occurred in March, 1886, you requested names to be certified for the purpose of filling that vacancy? Do you know whether the certification contained only one name, and that was Miss Whitehead, or whether it contained three, as the law requires?—A. I can not say. I feel quite confident there were no remaining persons on the list of stampers, which was always short, and they probably certified to me only one name.

Q. Are men as well as women employed in the stampers' division?—A. Not women as a rule. This is the only case of a woman employed in the stampers' division. She was mainly in the money-order division.

Q. Are not men usually employed in that capacity?—A. Yes, sir.

Q. Were there not eligibles on the list at that time?—A. Yes, sir; matters of that kind were continually occurring, and I could not remember particular cases. Dr. Shidy would be a good witness on that. There was no partiality.

Q. Of course you are quite clear upon that point, and I simply want to know the facts. Have you any recollection of making any remonstrances?

AFTERNOON SESSION.

The committee met pursuant to adjournment.

TESTIMONY OF GEORGE H. PAUL—Continued.

The CHAIRMAN. Mr. Hatton, will you proceed to ask the questions of this witness?

The WITNESS. Mr. Chairman and gentlemen of the committee, I would like to give a table I have here in place of the testimony which I gave this morning, this forenoon, as to the number of appointments. I read from my letter-book a record of the proportion of the appointments, but the statement I have here covers the entire period and it is more intelligible by far, and I would like to submit it in place of that given this morning, inasmuch as there might be some interest in it.

. The CHAIRMAN. I understand that covers the entire period during which you filled the office of postmaster.

A. Yes, sir; entirely, and up to the time the Commission was at my office.

The CHAIRMAN. Suppose you give that, so the stenographer may take it down.

The WITNESS. These are statistics of appointments and removals in the Milwaukee post-office from June 1, 1885, to July 15, 1889, complete. The number in classified service, June 1, 1885, since separated: resigned fourteen, removed five, died one, making twenty changes in the classified service in the entire time of four years and a month and a half. Number in unclassified service, as I term it—those not required to pass the examination—June 1, 1885, since separated: resigned six, removed four, abolished one, making a total change of eleven. Number in classified service by my appointment, since separated: resigned eight, removed five, died one, making fourteen changes. Number in unclassified service, appointed by me, since separated: resigned eleven, removed one, died one, making thirteen. The total certification, including of course the dismissed since June 1, 1885, was one hundred and four, and of the total number holding places July 15 was one hundred and forty-one. That does not include stamp agents and special delivery messengers, but it would come practically about as I stated this morning. That would make the total removals by me—it would make the total removals of all kinds fifteen.

The CHAIRMAN. The total of number of removals during your entire service was fifteen?—A. Yes, sir.

Q. That does not apply to the positions of clerks and letter-carriers?— A. For all officials.

Q. All persons?—A. Yes, sir.

Q. Fifteen?—A. Yes, sir; in my four years.

Q. That includes the entire number of removals in four years?—A. Four years, one month and a half, the entire number of removals.

Q. How many resignations were there during that same time?—A. The resignations in the classified service are fourteen in that whole time. In the unclassified it is six. In the classified service of my appointment eight, and in the unclassified service of my appointment eleven; that makes the whole number.

Mr. LIND. But that does not correspond with the number given in the first two years?—A. I do not know; that is correct, I know.

The CHAIRMAN. Mr. Paul has a statement here, to which he is now referring, which gives the entire changes of the office for the whole term of his office, that is, up to the time he was examined.

Mr. LIND. I know it, but it shows less than half the number he reports for the first two years.

The CHAIRMAN. When we come to examine him maybe he will be called to account for it. Is there anything further you desire to add before you begin?

The WITNESS. No, sir.

By Mr. HATTON:

Q. Mr. Paul, you said this morning that you never had access to the records of the secretary of the board of examiners.—A. The question this morning was whether I had any access to the record of certifications, I think.

Q. I understand you had not.—A. No, sir.

Q. These certifications were made by Mr. Shidy, secretary of the board.—A. Yes, sir.

Q. In what way were these certifications made? Will you explain to the committee, if there is no objection on the part of the committee, what way these certifications were made by the secretary of the board of examiners?—A. Well, sir, the way is the one prescribed by the rules of the Commission; simply that the secretary shall submit the highest four names—it was four originally, but it is three now—to the appointment officer for selection.

Q. Have you with you any certifications made by the secretary of the board of examiners?—A. Yes, sir; I have samples.

Mr. HATTON. I would like to ask permission of the committee for Mr. Paul to submit these copies of certification papers made by the secretary of the board of examiners, and that they be left with the committee.

The CHAIRMAN. There is no objection to that.

The WITNESS. That is the ordinary style of a certification.

Mr. LIND. This is blank; there is nothing on this.

Mr. BOATNER. There is something on the other side.

The WITNESS. There is a case of four certifications in the same manner. Sometimes they were made out in full form, but generally without any regular form for making these certifications.

Q. Was there any regular form for making these certifications?—A. There has been regular forms since provided more recently, but not originally. I would like to have the committee understand——

The CHAIRMAN. These are certification papers?—A. Yes, sir. There are some which show the manner in which the work was done.

Q. Who drew up these papers?—A. The Secretary.

Q. Mr. Shidy?—A. Yes, sir; they are in his handwriting.

Q. Have you submitted the certification papers you desired to?—A. Yes, sir.

Mr. BOATNER. Do you submit the samples of certification which you furnish as——

The WITNESS. I think they are good samples. I wish to explain to the committee further that Mr. Shidy, as I understand, in his testimony makes a sort of discrepancy in the certifications as to the date by assuming that the book of record of certifications, as we were in the habit of calling it, was the certification. Up to the time of the visit of Major Webster, I think Major Webster, at my office, Dr. Shidy regarded these papers as the proper certification to furnish me for any name and standing and that it would have been no violation of rules; he furnished me these papers as the certifications and I never understood until Major Webster came there that the book itself, the record of the certification, was intended to be the certification. I think I am right, Major Webster, in that. But in order to prove further that this is Mr. Shidy's construction of the rule, both to the Commission and me, as to what constituted a certification, I have here his letter dated September 1, 1886, addressed to me as postmaster, in which he specifically declares—

I have the honor to certify the following names as being those of the four having the highest standing on the list of eligibles for appointment as stamper.

and then ensues the names. This fixes the fact of that construction.

Mr. LIND. Is that intended to be put in evidence?—A. Yes, sir; if you will allow it; I have no objection.

The CHAIRMAN. There is no objection.

The WITNESS. Under his instruction, having served from the organization of the Commission on the board of examiners, of course I assumed that that was the intended certification, but under the instruction of Major Webster subsequently, in 1888, Dr. Shidy changed his view and practice and after that date the book itself was submitted as the certification. I do not know to this day where the rules for certifications require the submission of the book to the postmaster as the original and primary certification; it may be in the book or in the instructions to the board of examiners. The instructions to the board of examiners, I will explain further, were never submitted to me as a rule by the secretary of that board. I was not supposed to be interested in the duties of the board of examiners. It was a fact understood by everybody that I had nothing to do with its duties in any manner.

By Mr. HATTON:

Q. During the first year of your service as postmaster did you ever receive a notice from the Commission here or through its officer, the secretary of the local examining board, that you were violating the law in any way in the removals and appointments?—A. No, sir. The first intimation, the first criticisms, perhaps, unless something merely technical and informal, that I ever received from any board or any authority during my entire term was after the visit of the Commission itself in 1889.

Q. After the visit of Mr. Roosevelt and Mr. Thompson?—A. Yes, sir; at the time Mr. Roosevelt and Mr. Thompson and Mr. Lyman were present. After they left——

Q. Mr. Doyle and Mr. Webster did not notify you?—A. Mr. Doyle and Mr. Webster were in my office in September, 1888, and I did not understand this from them or infer from anything that occurred that any question had arisen as to the postmaster's duties. I supposed the investigation or examination related almost strictly or entirely to the manner in which the records had been kept and how the duties of the examining board had been performed. There were some minor matters to which perhaps Major Webster called my attention, but I have no recollection of what I regarded as any serious criticism upon the office. I wish to state to the committee further that the duties of the postmaster of an office under civil-service law are very simple and very limited. The duties include simply, on the presentation of the certification to the postmaster, the selection of one of the men certified for the position, and report the appointment to the examining board, so that it may make up its record. I think this is about all any postmaster under the civil service laws is required to do. That is the end of the matter practically, at least, and I have always so regarded it, and I followed implicitly the rules in that respect.

Q. Did Mr. Doyle and Mr. Webster, when they were there, before leaving tell you the nature of the investigation they had made?—A. The nature?

Q. Yes, sir.—A. Only by leaving me to infer from interrogatories relating very largely to the duties of the examining board.

Q. Did they tell you that the testimony taken in that examination implicated you in any way?—A. I did not so understand it in any way. I never heard from it again, and I did not understand that I was implicated in any manner. I stated there perhaps, under those circumstances, to Major Webster that which I would not have stated under the present circumstances. I was rather disposed to apologize and explain for Mr. Shidy. I did not think he had been anything more than technically guilty. I did not know, and when cases were presented to me for explanation relating to his duties I gave the best explanation I could under the circumstances, from my little knowledge of his affairs, and in that way I possibly gave quite a little testimony. I did not suppose it affected my duties in any serious way.

Q. Do you know whether there was a report made of the testimony taken by Messrs. Doyle and Webster?—A. The report?

Q. Yes, sir; by the Commission.—A. No, sir; I never knew there was any report; to the President, do you mean?

Q. Yes.—A. I understand there was no report of the Commission at the time, but from what source I can not now remember. I since understood directly by information, if proper to state the fact, from Mr. Edgarton to this effect, that the report was examined, and its consideration indefinitely postponed at that time.

Mr. LIND. Examined by whom?—A. By the Commission. I think the Commission was not then full; that is my impression.

By Mr. HATTON:

Q. Did he make a statement of that kind in writing to you?—A. I think he has; yes, sir.

Q. Have you a copy of this letter?—A. I have not that letter with me by a mere accident; I intended to have brought it.

Q. Did the Postmaster-General ever notify you a report had been made which implicated you in any violation of the civil-service law in any way?—A. No, sir. The Postmaster-General—no, sir; but I had words of commendation from the Post-Office Department about that time.

Q. At the time the three commissioners were there in 1889 they did not notify you in regard to the object of their visit, you stated this morning. Did you know at that time whom they examined?—A. Yes, sir; I knew it; it was commonly reported that they examined Mr. Shidy, as I understand it.

Q. Did you understand they examined anybody else?—A. No, sir. Mr. Fahsel, who is a member of the board, I remember distinctly I requested to remain in that office until the Commission might want him, and Mr. Fahsel informed me the next morning that he remained until about dark, after a hard day's work, and then he went to his supper.

Q. Do you know whether Mr. Fahsel was notified by the Commission to give any testimony at all?—A. No, sir; he was not; I think not. He was in the office the next day.

Q. Do you know whether Mr. Johnson was notified to give any testimony? A. Only from information from Mr. Johnson to the effect that he was asked one or two questions and that the answers he gave in the case were from information he derived from Shidy and not from any other source; that he gave the answers, not thinking it was an investigation, merely assuming or believing it to be a fact when he gave those replies. That is what Mr. Johnson afterwards told me soon after the Commission left.

Q. What was the first intimation you had that the investigation had taken place, official information?—A. That the investigation was taking place?

Q. Had taken place?—A. It was through the Associated Press, when the report was made to the country by which I was censured and condemned for everything but political errors and mistakes, and crime; that is, for general violation of law without any specification. That report was sent broadcast through this country and was the first intimation I ever had and the first criticism I ever had in any formal manner from that office.

Q. Did you ever make an effort to secure from the Commission the testimony upon which you had been convicted?—A. Yes, sir; I wrote a formal letter requesting a copy of any testimony which affected my official duties, and I never received that testimony to this day; to this day I am ignorant of the testimony except from inference.

Q. Did you ever receive any reply at all to your letter making an application for this testimony?—A. I can not tell, but my impression is I received a brief formal acknowledgment. That is my impression; I can not state positively; no other reply.

Q. You had a conversation with Mr. Roosevelt the morning after Shidy gave his testimony?

The WITNESS. The morning after?

Q. Yes.

The WITNESS. I can not say; it would be after the testimony. I had a conversation on the morning after he came into the office; a short one; a very brief one.

Q. Can you give the nature of that conversation?—A. I presume you refer to the question with regard to the expiration of my term?

Q. Yes.—A. That was the evening before. It occurred on the evening before.

Q. The Commissioners testify you stated to the Commission you had already tendered your resignation.—A. When the Commission first came into the office—Mr. Van Schaick is here and he can confirm what I say as to the facts—I said to the Commission that I was tired of office and had other duties inconsistent with my remaining there; that I had been there over four years and that I had requested the Representative of the district to get his man as soon as possible. That is the substance of my information as near as I can repeat it; and that I regarded my term of office as about up, having served more than four years, and having requested Mr. Van Schaick to select his man and place him in my place, as I wished to be relieved. I did not say, as the Commission seem to have apprehended—there is certainly very great room for misapprehension under such circumstances—I did not say my last commission had expired.

Mr. BOATNER. You considered the election had something to do with your term, didn't you?

Mr. PAUL. No, sir; not much, because there was no intention of removing me at all at that time by any representatives of the administration there that I ever heard of at all. It was my voluntary resignation at that time, and then, when the Commission commenced its charges, the Representative from that district refused to forward my resignation at all until that matter was cleared up.

Mr. HATTON. Who was the Representative at that time?—A. Representative Van Schaick, and he himself applied to the Department for a re-investigation of the facts with many others, which was never had. The Commission published its first report through the Associated Press, and I presume sent it to the President also, and very soon made a very lengthy supplementary report, as it was called. The first report did not recommend my removal at all on the ground that there was no evidence that I had made any political appointments or removals substantially. Then I replied to that by interviews through the local newspapers. The Commission then made a supplementary report and gave as a reason for so doing, and recommended my removal in the supplementary report, that I had falsified facts as to the expiration of my commission as postmaster, which was probably a misapprehension on the part of the Commissioners. I am very willing to concede the Commissioners misapprehended my statement.

Q. In the second report did they assign as one of the reasons why they recommended your removal the part you had taken with Shidy in making these false certifications ?—A. Well, they gave the whole—embodied about the whole of Shidy's testimony.

Q. The report will show the fact itself ?—A. Assuredly.

Q. After you first heard of the report of the Commission, based on their interview, that of Messrs. Thompson, Lyman and Roosevelt, did you have a conversation with Shidy ?—A. Yes, sir.

Mr. HATTON. Is there any objection on the part of the committee to his giving the nature of the conversation ?

Mr. LIND. Not at all ; that is proper.

A. Mr. Shidy came into my office, I think, voluntarily, and I asked Shidy what he had been saying to my discredit to the Commissioners ; that I inferred from what had occurred that he had been testifying to very extraordinary facts, or facts that were not facts. He immediately commenced to apologize and to explain to me how very sorry he was that he could not have seen me before he gave his testimony and had it arranged in some way, I do not know how. He said that he had been caught in a corner by the Commissioners without any method of escape. He said that if the facts had to come out as I understood them, the Commission would undoubtedly have recommended his removal from office, etc. He talked in that strain and expressed very great regret that the matter had occurred. I asked Shidy why he could not be more honest and brave under those circumstances, and I thought it would be much better for him in every way, and he seemed to be very much excited at the suggestion. He stood up in the middle of the floor immediately and addressed me in his peculiar and emphatic manner. "Why," he says, "Mr. Paul, you can be brave, you have resources; you are a healthy, strong man, and I am a poor, sick man here, dependent upon my salary for a living, in poverty," and he says, " I can not be brave ; you have no right to ask me to be brave under these circumstances." That is the sum and substance of his speech to me, and almost the express words as near as I can recollect them.

A day or two after, as this comes in connection, I then informed him distinctly that I should not remove him for any testimony he had given to the Commission, that it was his right to give that testimony, and that in doing so he was not under my jurisdiction but under that of the Commission, that I did not intend to remove him for it or censure him in any way, but I should leave that question entirely for the Commission to judge. But I think it was on the ensuing day, it was on Saturday morning, I took up a German paper, one of the leading newspapers of Milwaukee with a very large circulation—the Herold—and I saw there a statement of Shidy. A great deal of contempt had been expressed for him editorially by that paper on the ground he was a German originally but he ignored the Germans practically. I think there was quite a bitter feeling in regard to Shidy's German nationality, but Shidy made a statement in that paper, a very extraordinary one, many insinuations in it and many untruths in it. I held a special conversation with Mr. Shidy about that article. I have a copy of the article here which can be submitted to the committee if they would like to see it. It is an open letter. He called it an open letter. Shidy confessed to me that he had done me an injustice in that letter. It is not only false, but very disrespectful. I told him I did not see how it would be consistent for us to continue our official relations in that office, that I thought it would make a laughing-stock of me with the public to attempt to do so, and I suggested to him the propriety of correcting it as to those things where he thought he had done me an injustice. Shidy proposed to do so, and also proposed of his own accord to recall that letter from two or more English papers where he had taken it. He said he wrote it under a state of excitement and said more than he ought to have said. I think he undertook to withdraw the letter. I have the impression very strongly now that one paper—the Evening Wisconsin—at least one of them refused to publish such a scandalous statement. One paper did publish it and it had considerable circulation, whereupon I—this is the letter, if any one wishes to see it, published with illustrations.

By Mr. BOATNER:

Q. It that Shidy's letter?—A. That is the letter Shidy wrote for the press.

Q. You say it is illustrated with wood cuts?—A. Yes sir, it is interspersed with wood cuts.

Mr. STONE. Do you wish to put that letter in?—A. I have no objection if the committee think it is proper.

I then wrote to Shidy a formal letter dismissing him, in which I gave him distinct reasons. I have a copy of his letter here, and I have the letter-press copy here somewhere of the letter to Shidy in return. I did not consider it consistent with my own self-respect and the dignity of the office after the publication of that letter to retain him. From the statements in that letter I might call attention to the fact in regard to my having violated the law in the appointment of Mr. Trumpff, who was paying teller in the money-order office to a civil-service position without certification, which he charges in the letter. Mr. Trumpff makes affidavit (I have the affidavit) that he never was appointed to any civil service position at all; that he never was. He was appointed and accepted the position which Mr. Shidy misapprehended and understood to be a civil service position—supposed it was a civil-service position at the time [reading], "Milwaukee, June 30"—this was nine days after the Commission was there and I think very nearly a week after the publication of the report. The letter to Shidy was as follows:

MILWAUKEE, WIS., *June* 30, 1889.

DEAR SIR: Some of the newspapers of this city contain a letter from you, in which you impugn my integrity in the administration of the civil-service law. You have kindly conceded to me that this letter does me injustice in many particulars, and that you regret its publication; but, though afforded a generous opportunity to tell the public what you have told me in explanation of this letter, you have omitted to do so, and leave me to endure the consequences of your injustice or repel them as I can. As I have already said to you, the continuance of our official relations under these circumstances is impossible, and you will accordingly consider those relations discontinued from this date.

Truly,

GEO. H. PAUL, *P. M.*

H. SHIDY, Esq.,
  Superintendent Registry Division.

That had not the slightest or remotest connection with the testimony at all, and I did not intend it should. Mr. Chairman, while on the subject of certifications I might as well, having the document here in my hand—I might as well present to the committee the publication by Shidy of the entire list of eligibles. It has been stated, I think, that when I was asked if I had ever seen the list of eligibles I smiled. I certainly did smile, for there is the whole list, after the examination, published by Shidy in the Milwaukee Sentinel, I think, or in one newspaper, directly in the order of their standing, and I did see it. Here it is if any one wishes it; it is a clear, palpable violation of law, of which I knew nothing until I saw it in the press. I do not think he intended anything wrong about it, but I think it was simply a part of his slovenly manner of doing all business.

The list was as follows:

Clerks.—Arthur S. Howard, Albert L. Trumpff, Frederick J. Weber, Richard J. Hickey, Howard S. Hills, Richard L. Harney, Frank Stockhausen, John J. McGucken, Frank Pepkorn, George J. Holt, Miss Alice McGuigan.

Junior messengers.—Charles F. Hurley, Wm. Gillis, Patrick McCormack, John W. O'Brien, Joseph Holland, Thos. J. O'Neill.

Carriers.—Evan H. Jones, F. J. Meckelburg, Wm. M. Reilly, F. K. Knobel, Edward A. Dittmar, Peter S. Juneau, James P. Mellen, John H. Ryan, Joseph Klein, E. E. Schoenleber, J. R. Nuzem, J. H. Williams, S. T. Tabert, Joseph H. O'Malley, B. W. Lloyd, R. H. Joers, W. Leihammer, Wm. H. Linke, F. C. Ghout, George W. Lindorf, G. S. Joyce, C. F. Strey.

Mr. HATTON. You stated this morning in a conversation that Shidy had said something about being transferred to a position in Washington. Was that conversation before the Commission went to Milwaukee.—A. Yes, sir.

Mr. LIND. Had not the witness better fix the date of that publication? That may be material.

The WITNESS. I think the date is on the paper.

Mr. LIND. If not it will be well to have it.

The WITNESS. (Examining paper.) No, it is not here. I think it was in the original paper; this has been cut out. But that does not affect the fact.

Mr. LIND. But if you could give us the date it would be an aid to the committee, perhaps, in considering your testimony.

The WITNESS. I can not give the precise date of that.

Mr. STONE. Can you give it in reference to the visit of any of this Commission?—A. Yes, sir; it was before any certifications were made or anything of the kind.

By the CHAIRMAN:

Q. Before the certifications were made to you?—A. Before any certifications were made from that list.

Q. And your information regarding the eligibles was obtained from newspapers?—A. Well, sir, I did not ask for any information; I simply was amused at the very lax manner in which he performed his duty in the case, and I cut it out of the paper and pasted it away. I never used it for information.

Q. What I wanted to get at was whether this publication antedated the visit of the Civil Service Commission at Milwaukee?—A. Yes, sir.

Mr. BOATNER. How much?—A. I referred to it in my talk to the Commission.

By Mr. STONE:

Q. Had you any other reason for removing Mr. Shidy other than the fact that he had been disrespectful to you as his superior officer?—A. No, sir. I should not have removed him because of his giving testimony to the Commission at all. I did not intend it, and he had no apprehensions on that point. He never had apprehensions of removal by me or any penalty because of his course in the office.

Q. At the time you wrote this letter dismissing him, did you know then the nature of his testimony, whether it implicated you?—A. Know of its character?

Q. Yes.—A. Yes, sir; I knew of its general character, and I took this view of it: That Shidy in that respect was acting entirely outside of his postal duties, as an officer of the post-office, entirely; that he was acting as agent of the Commission, and I had no control over him, and I could not punish him properly. I think I so stated that whatever he said or did, it was not my province to punish the act myself, because he obeyed the Commission, to whom he was subject. That was my view of the case then. I know others take a different view, but the view that I took of it was that as a subordinate officer of the Commision I thought his conduct was subject to their supervision properly. Of course it was very unpleasant, the whole matter.

Q. I asked you, but I did not get your answer, when your conversation with Mr. Shidy occurred in regard to his coming to Washington, had the Commission visited Milwaukee or afterwards?—A. I did not intend to speak of a definite conversation, but he frequently expressed a desire or expectation that ultimately he would be transferred to Washington. That seemed to be his pet ambition. I wish to say further, perhaps without interfering with your matter, in way of explanation of Shidy's frequent statement that I had examined and controlled the records, I have never denied that occasionally I have seen the record—not the list, but the record of eligibles after an examination—when placed before me by Shidy. I never saw that register of eligibles, as it is properly called, except when he brought it to me directly or by his authority. I never made any use of it. I never expected or wished to see it in any manner whatever; but Shidy was running around the office with that book under his arm very frequently, and when making the certifications there he was likely to come to my table, so that I can say that I have seen it; but that I have seen it for any improper purpose, or that I myself used it or obtained it during his absence, I wish to say that anything of the kind I utterly deny. I have a letter-press copy of an affidavit of one who kept charge of this register, confirming my statement, and also of another, being the only two to whom the register was accessible save Shidy. Shidy kept the register in the safe where these other parties were, his associates in the office, and I could not have gone to that register without their knowledge and consent, and they are ready to come before this committee and testify that I never saw the register in Shidy's absence, for no one else could have given it to me except Shidy or one of these two clerks. .

Q. Was there no excuse given you by Shidy about the publication of this assault upon you personally?—A. Publication of what?

Q. Of that article in that paper.—A. Well, I do not know, except that he said he was excited and inspired to do it, as it was likely to injure him if he did not comply with what he seemed to think was the compulsion of the Commission. In fact, while he was telling the Commission that he was under my duress he was telling me that he was under their duress in the matter. My theory is that the real reason was, that is, the real object in the matter was, a very natural one for a man in his class. I think, in the first place, he was very anxious to conceal the fact as to his own actions, and, as I told him, I did not think those facts implied any actual guilt, any actual intention to violate the law, but simply a laxity and want of order and a want of sense of propriety in the matter. That is about the view I took of it. I think he would have done almost anything rather than confess the real facts in the case, that is, in regard to his carelessness and the looseness of his methods of business. I always felt a sympathy for him and a disposition to aid him as much as I could; but still he says he was coerced by me there through the entire term of four or five years. The universal public understanding in the office and outside the office was that no man would be removed from that office who performed his duties properly, and he understood it more particularly than any other person, for he exhibited more interest in the result. Not only that, but Shidy's young son was on the eligible list and came up on certification, and I offered to make that selection of his son. I think he declined in due form, because he could get a better place. I was very anxious, as far as I could lawfully, to assist him. He never had any reason to complain. He can not bring a single person—I challenge him—who served in that office, or who is in that post-office now under my successor, or my successor himself, or my predecessor—not one—to corroborate any portion of the testimony reflecting upon my official integrity, not one. Of course it is a question as to veracity between Shidy and myself.

Q. Did you ever hear at any time that the Commission or any member of the Commission had brought pressure to bear on the Postmaster-General and the President to compel your resignation?

Mr. LIND. Well, that would be mere hearsay. I do not think that is proper.

Mr. HATTON. All right.

The CHAIRMAN. What is the question?

Mr. BOATNER. Have you any knowledge of that fact?

The WITNESS. No, sir.

Mr. HATTON. The question was, had the Commission or any member of the Commission ever caused or brought pressure to bear on the Postmaster-General and President to compel your resignation?—A. No, sir. My resignation had been continually before the Department ever since my reply to the Commission, to the President. I have intimation of the fact that pretty strong influences were brought to bear upon the President.

Q. You do not know that of your own knowledge?—A. No, sir.

Q. Mr. Paul, in Mr. Roosevelt's testimony he said you made a statement and denied it and then denied your denial. Have you any idea what he meant in regard to that?—A. I might say to him that I did not hold a report nearly a year, and then divide it and make two reports; certainly. I have no knowledge of having denied anything I have said. The committee, of course, will understand and the Commission would naturally understand that the details of an office like mine are very multitudinous; that in referring to individual questions in detail it is very difficult for any person to remember the precise facts bearing upon the case, and it is a very possible fact that I may at times have given one explanation of a state of facts when upon reflection I could give a fuller explanation. I was taken by surprise, and did not understand this was a formal investigation when the Commission came to my office. There was no stenographic reporter.

By Mr. BOATNER:

Q. Excuse me for interrupting you right there, but did you understand when these officers were out there, that they were investigating you, or that they were investigating the local board of civil-service examiners?—A. I had not the slightest idea that that Commission were investigating me. I did not know anything of the investigation and I do not know now. As I said, the duties of a postmaster are exceedingly simple. The Commission came to my office late in the afternoon, about 3 o'clock. They came into the office and I presume I had been in town an hour, and Commissioner Thompson—I had been out the night before to some public duties at Madison, and on reaching my office very soon after, the Commission came into the office, and I explained to them I was very much exhausted physically, and if an examination was to be had and testimony taken, that I was in a very poor condition to give it; but they did ask a number of questions, and I think we occupied about an hour or so about that matter, or perhaps three-quarters of an hour or more and I then asked to be excused. I answered almost at random, not supposing it was a particular examination, because there was no stenographer present at all. I answered off-hand, and the next morning they were there a few minutes longer, but a few minutes; I think they were in the office the entire time about three hours in the examination of myself and Shidy and in other business they had with the records. I think it would not exceed three hours the entire time for an examination covering details of appointments and changes of more than four years. I think to call that an examination—I never regarded it as such.

Q. During that examination of yourself, did they ask you whether you violated the civil-service law ?—A. I do not remember any such question as that and nothing to intimate that I had violated it.

Q. Did they ask whether you assisted Shidy in making false certifications ?—A. They asked me about Shidy's affairs, as I regarded it, about Shidy's method of doing business, and it was all about Shidy, etc., wholly, I think, wholly. Commissioner Thompson very kindly said to Mr. Roosevelt, " What has the postmaster to do with all these matters you are questioning him about ? He says it does not come within the province of the postmaster." That was the extent of his remarks, as I so recollect.

Q. I have but three other questions to ask you. During your four years' term as postmaster did you ever intimate in any manner whatever to the secretary of the local examining board that you would like him to make false certificates ?—A. No, sir.

Q. Did you ever say to him that you would like to have him pad the eligible list ?—A. No, sir; I never knew that he did. I think the records of certification was produced during this visit of the Commission, and I examined it for the first time subsequently. I have no recollection of ever knowing anything of the kind before. I never examined that book before. The Commission is under misapprehension. The Commission stated the book was always brought to me for my signature. That is practically true, that when an appointment had been made——

Mr. HATTON. I do not care about your explaining anything more about the appointments. Did you ever intimate to the secretary of the local board that he could oblige you by marking up or marking down examination papers ?—A. No, sir; never. I would have resigned my office first.

Q. Did you ever assist in any of these offenses of which Shidy has charged you ?—A. No, sir.

Q. In charging you with these offenses, this making of false certification, the stuffing of the eligible list, and by marking the ineligible up to the eligible list, and by marking eligibles down to the ineligible list, did Mr. Shidy tell the truth or did he tell a falsehood ?—A. He told a falsehood if he stated anything about the list in any manner implicating me as to any wrong in any certification.

The CHAIRMAN. Is there anything further ?

Mr. HATTON. I have nothing further. I would like the Commissioners to ask some questions.

3117——14

By Mr. BOATNER:

Q. I would like to ask the witness a few questions. Mr. Paul, for the purpose of bringing the matter in proper shape before you, I will state Mr. Shidy's testimony. Mr. Shidy has stated that you required him, contrary to the provisions of law, to allow you access to the eligible list; is that true ?—A. No, sir; that is not true.

Q. He has stated that you required him, contrary to the provisions of law, to furnish you with the certifications of men who had already been appointed to office, who were already filling their positions; is that true ?—A. No, sir.

Q. He has stated that you required him to furnish you with certifications containing names of men you wanted and that other names which were merely dummies were put there in accordance with law, when in truth and fact the man you wanted had been previously selected and appointed upon certification by your direction; is that true ?—A. No, sir; he never had any direction from me on that subject at all, of any kind.

Q. He has stated that, under your direction and duress, the names of eligibles who stood high, whom you did not intend to appoint, were marked down so that others you did want to appoint could be furnished you on the list of eligibles; is that true ?—A. No, sir; I never did anything of the kind.

Q. Now, when the Commission came out to Milwaukee for the purpose of looking into this matter, did they inform you charges had been made or information had been given by Mr. Shidy with regard to these derelictions of the civil-service examination board ?—A. When they were in Milwaukee ?

Q. Yes, sir.—A. No, sir, not by direct information. Before the close of the day I discovered that Mr. Roosevelt held in his hand the testimony which had been taken the year previous by Major Webster. That is the first time I knew that testimony was in any manner in investigation, and I learned that—I felt positive by mere inference from remarks made by the Commissioners between themselves. I never was formally informed that this question pertained to that testimony of the preceding year, which I supposed was dead and buried. I did not suppose it related to me in any way, but a remark was made, I think, by Mr. Roosevelt towards the close of the matter, when he held in his hand some papers which undoubtedly was that testimony. I was not informed in advance of my answers that that investigation was directed to me. That is about the whole of it. I think the Commission will confirm it.

Q. Please state whether or not the Commission informed you at that time or at any time before they made their report that Mr. Shidy's confession or statement of his own derelictions of duty involved you and that made you a *particeps criminis* in those derelictions ?—A. I never understood that at all; there was, however, in the conversation between the Commissioners and myself reference to some technical, what you might call technical, violations of law, in the later conversation, that might possibly involve me without explanation. I forget now what they were. The main thing relating to me was the question asked with regard to whether I dictated the remarking of the papers of one man on one occasion. I think that is all I considered involving me properly. I thought the Commission were rather overreaching the mark perhaps in endeavoring to involve me on the basis of the facts relating to the secretary. The construction which I——

Q. What I wanted to get at is this, the general tone of your testimony here would indicate that you were not aware that the Commission were investigating you but that they were rather investigating the examining board there?—A. Yes, sir.

Q. And that you endeavored to explain some technical violations of law made by the board?—A. Yes, sir; the circumstances under which——

Q. And did not understand that they were investigating you. Now, I want to know if that is the impression you wanted to create on the committee that you did not know that they were investigating your official conduct and therefore you had no opportunity to defend yourself?—A. I mean to say that I did not realize——

Q. You did not realize that they were investigating you?—A. No, sir; not in any way.

Q. When did you realize or ascertain the fact that they were investigating you as well as the examining board?—A. In the Associated Press, the report containing the expressions of the Commission.

By Mr. LIND:

Q. I want to ask you one or two questions. As a matter of fact you had access—that is, access in the sense that you knew what the names were on the eligible list right along—that is, from newspaper information, and from the fact that Shidy came around with the book and showed it to you?—A. No, sir; I never had knowledge of the list at all, not even from the newspaper list. I voluntarily put that away in my scrap-book there, or some clerk did it, and I never referred to it again and I never saw it from that day to this until I hunted it up.

Q. Do you remember how many changes, the figures differ—do you remember how many changes were made in the office in the aggregate during your term?—A. It is all in this list, the tabulated statement I gave.

The CHAIRMAN. He has already stated that.

Mr. LIND. The figures he gives for the first two years exceeds the aggregate of the entire term and there is a discrepancy somewhere.

The WITNESS. No, sir; I think there is a misapprehension there.

Mr. LIND. Well, we will waive that testimony. To your knowledge, was any Republican appointed during your incumbency?—A. Yes, sir; very many.

Q. How many?—A. Well, sir, I can only say this, that the office was estimated at the time I retired; that the majority of the whole number of employés of each department were Republicans or so classed.

The CHAIRMAN. When you went out of office?—A. Yes, I never inquired the politics of any man.

Mr. LIND. I do not suppose you did.—A. They were so classed and appointed in the office according to the best estimate. Mr. Shidy was one who hung very high on the fence. I think he told that he was directly related to Mr. Cleveland, he is certainly a very rampant advocate of free-trade.

SOME ONE. Well, that is a good sign.

By Mr. LIND:

Q. Now, did you have any private memoranda of names that you desired to appoint?—A. Never any private memorandum, sir.

Q. Well, did you have any public memorandum?—A. I never had any public memorandum of the eligible list.

Q. That is not what I asked for. I asked whether you had any memoranda of names that you desired to be appointed in the service?—A. No other way than this. I do not think I ever had any memoran dum except in my brain, at all. I have no recollection of it. It is not possible—if the list was certified to me it was necessary for me to make some investigation as to the character of the man certified.

Mr. LIND. Yes.—A. And I sometimes inquired of proper men, both Democrats and Republicans, who knew the history of the men as to their qualifications, their relative qualifications. I considered that my duty and right.

Q. Certainly, I did not criticise that.—A. But beyond that I never kept any formal memoranda in any way. I may sometimes have made these memoranda on paper; I naturally would do that.

Q. But what I had reference to—I did not criticise any action of that kind as improper, I think a man should exercise his judgment in regard to appointments. I simply want to ascertain the facts. Now, did you not have any memoranda of persons who desired and who would be proper to appoint that you were familiar with before the vacancies occurred?—A. No, sir; I had only this. I had in my office a file of petitions and recommendations as high as my hat, unquestionably, but otherwise I had no memoranda, I had no choice.

Q. Well, that answers my question completely. You had petitions and recommendations on file.—A. Yes, sir; every appointing officer has them, but I ignored them all, as a rule, except when a man who was sometimes certified as standing high, and nearly all were strangers to me, outside of my associates, nearly all the appointees in the classified service; sometimes I would go back and see what was said about them, as any business man would, but no further than that. If your question is intended to ask this, if ever I went to that eligible list——

Q. No; I do not care about the eligible names. The committee understand by this time that you had public access to the eligible list at any time you had the curiosity to see it; in fact, you had one of them. I mean, as a matter of fact, you could ascertain who was on the eligible list at any time?—A. No, sir; I could not, and that is a mistake to say I could. That eligible list, or register of eligibles we preferred to call it, was kept locked in a safe in the registry department, and I do not know how I could ever know anything of it without consent of parties in charge of it.

Q. Did not you state awhile ago that Mr. Shidy would time and again shove it under your nose, bring it to your table, and show it to you?— A. Yes, sir; he would bring it in the office, it is true, but not at any time. That question implies that I could take that list and examine it at my pleasure.

Q. What I asked, what I say is, that for practical purposes, if you wanted to be familiar with it you had an opportunity to do so?—A. I do not see how I could get it except through Shidy.

Q. Well, that is what I meant. You had every opportunity if you wanted it to get it through Shidy?—A. I think if I had asked Shidy to examine and look at the list that he would, probably, judging from his usual actions and conduct, have brought it all to me, but I purposely avoided that.

Q. Did not you state awhile ago you frequently did see it; that he carried the book under his arm—1 am trying to get this for the benefit of the committee—that he frequently placed it on your table and produced it before you, and that you were in the habit of seeing?——A. Yes, sir; when he took the names from the head of the list, but I never considered it my right to take advantage of that opportunity.

Q. When he was taking the names from the head of the list he would then have to make out the certifications in your presence, did he not?— A. Not very often; only on one or two occasions, I think, altogether;

but this I never did do under any circumstance, and that is examine that list, what you call an examination of the names on the list, because I knew it was an improper thing to do. I think Shidy trusted me as to that when he brought his book to give the names, which accidentally thus came under my observation. I think he is the last man in the world to believe really that I would take that list and examine the names on it. I certainly would not do it, and I never did do it.

Q. Then he really kept the list cautiously and carefully.—A. Yes, sir; I thought he did pretty fairly so far as that eligible list is concerned.

Q. Then this eligible list did not cut much figure in the office, did it?— A. No, sir; I do not think it did. I do not think this whole matter cuts much figure in my office one way or another. I think it is very much of a tempest in a tea-pot, except so far as it involves the technical operations of the civil service.

Q. And if you consider the civil-service principles as applied to the actual working of your office, if there was a vacancy, and you had recommendations on file in regard to a man, you consulted them for the purpose of ascertaining his character.—A. Yes, sir, in evidence.

Q. And you made the appointment accordingly?—A. I would go to the list and get the names.

Q. I mean you consulted for private information?—A. Yes, sir; and it was my private information in part as to qualifications of candidates.

Q. That is all?—A. I think it is proper for me to state to the committee as to the large proportion of the errors in the record of certifications of eligibles, that is as to how they occurred. This is information that has come to me since the Commission was there. I think it explains largely the case of Shidy at any rate, and it certainly explains how he came to get into the difficulty by the testimony of the record. I have handed to the committee certifications showing how they were made. Abundant testimony can be produced in addition to this to show that Shidy in his hurry, in his illness (which he claimed), and in his indolence, or all three together; in his long dinners, and all that—he did not work near as many hours as I did, or half as hard, he often sitting day-dreaming in the office about some speculation or something else, and the actual fact is, as I have positive information, and which I did not know until after the Commission examined me, that when these appointments were made he took these slips of paper and made another copy and entered it against the names selected on the slips, the word "app."; no date on the certification at all, and took these slips into his office and threw them into a drawer of his own desk, and that often these certifications remained there—the dates show from one day to thirty days, one day too many. Now, when Shidy got around to the time when he felt disposed to make his report to the Commission, he entered these certifications of appointments on his record of certification, and brought the open books for me simply to put my signature against the person appointed in due form, but in order to conceal—I will scarcely say conceal—but in order that it might not appear to the Commission that he had been neglectful in making his entry or in making his report (I think the rule requires the report of certifications to be made the same day, but I am not positive, but I think that is the rule), but in order that the Commission should not have any occasion to censure him, he made the date of the certification to correspond with the date of his report to the Commission and not with the date of his certification in fact. Then the result and the natural proper consequence of all that is, that

Shidy's record shows many cases—I think thirty-five are reported by Mr. Johnson, the president of the board—I think thirty-five cases in which the dates of certification were not the dates of appointment by the record. Now, that was no fault of mine, surely. It was simply the laxity in his methods of doing business.

By the CHAIRMAN:

Q. When he sent this book to you, did you notice the date?—A. After he sent the book? no, sir; for the reason that I would not have the dates in my mind. He would come around at the close of the month to make up his record, and made that record often from my record of appointments for the Department from my letter-book. That was his frequent habit, to ask for my letter-book, and from that he would make these entries, having before entered the certifications on the record of certifications. He would make up the record of appointments from my book, and not from his own knowledge of the facts. Now, that in great part explains the inconsistency of the record, according to my theory. Now there is another thing which accounts, possibly in part, to a very limited degree, for the discrepancy in the dates of appointment. It is the practice in large post-offices when a vacancy occurs for instance on the 1st (and the appointment never can be made instantly, for a day or two) to have the succession continuous. There is one annual allowance for clerk hire by Congress, and in order to keep accounts straight at the Department and at the post-office it is necessary that there should be no hiatus in the date.

Q. You said successor; you mean predecessor, continued. You said it is necessary to let the successor continue; you mean the predecessor. —A. No, sir; we do not continue. He resigned, for instance, on the 1st. Now we have an annual allowance for clerks in a certain position in the Department, and the appointment, when made—for instance, when made on the 4th of the month—we would put the date so that it will take effect three or four days before, so as to make the line continuous.

Q. Certainly, I understand; it but you mean the man resigning continues performing the duties until the new man is installed.—A. Not necessarily. We will say the allowance is, for instance, $500 for clerk. Suppose, for instance, he is entitled to the $500, and the Department allows $500 for that position. Say he clears out and goes to Minnesota, for instance, on the 1st of the month, and on the 3d, perhaps, I have had my certification to select a man for the place, and it is dated back and the name reported to the Department, so as to make $500 apply to the whole year upon the annual salary for the place. That is done in all post-offices in the country.

Mr. STONE. One question, if you please, on that, relative to this particular point. When Mr. Shidy testified, he stated a fact concerning one appointment (the name of the appointee I can not now recollect), but this is his testimony upon this: That this person was appointed on the 1st of March; that he was not examined as being in the classified service until the 17th of March, and was certified on the 23d of March.— A. He was entirely mistaken in the facts. I would like to know the name of the man.

Mr. BOATNER. He said it dated back to the 1st, and he received pay from the 1st.

The WITNESS. I think he referred to the fact——

Mr. STONE. Mr. Chairman, I will not press the question. Governor Thompson says he is familiar with the facts.

The WITNESS. He was never in a civil-service position.

By Mr. ANDREW:

Q. That letter published in the newspapers here, I did not have time to read it through. Was that letter written prior to your severing your connection with the post-office or not?—A. Prior to my——

Q. That letter, the picture in it—the illustrated letter?—A. Yes, sir; the examination of the committee was on the 21st of July.

Q. The letter looked to me, from a hasty glance I made, as if it was a reply to some letter written by you after you left the office, but I do not so understand it.

The CHAIRMAN. It was written prior, it was testified here.

The WITNESS. I did not leave the office until three or four months——

The CHAIRMAN. That letter dated January something?

The WITNESS. No; June.

The CHAIRMAN. It was on that letter Mr. Shidy was discharged from the office by Mr. Paul during July.

Mr. ANDREW. Is not that letter a reply to a letter written by you, Mr. Paul?

Mr. PAUL. No, sir; oh, no, sir.

Mr. ANDREW. It says it was.

The CHAIRMAN. This is not a letter in reply?

The WITNESS. This letter is a cold, unprovoked attack, without provocation of any kind.

Mr. ANDREW. I did not read it then.

The CHAIRMAN. Now, Governor Thompson, will you examine the witness, or Mr. Roosevelt?

Mr. BOATNER (examining letter). Let me call your attention to this:

Mr. GEORGE H. PAUL: I am grieved and surprised at the attack made on me by you in this day's Herold, grieved because my sympathies are always deeply excited by misfortune or injustice, and the picture you present of your being led as the lamb to the sacrifice, for my sin strikes me as too pathetic for description. I am surprised that you ventured to misrepresent facts so broadly, when you must know that I still have some papers in my possession, notwithstanding your abstracting certain papers from the files during my absence June the 25th.

This seems to be a reply to some letter in which you attacked him in the Herold on that day.—A. He refers undoubtedly to some statement by the Herold itself, not under my own signature. I made none.

Mr. ANDREW. That is the reason I asked the question. I thought it was a reply to a letter.

The CHAIRMAN. Was it a reply to an interview?

Mr. ANDREW. What I wanted to get at was, what was it a reply to.

The WITNESS. It was a reply to some interview or something of that kind, in which I probably included Shidy with the testimony of the report of the Commission.

The CHAIRMAN. Do you remember that that was an interview, that article in the Herald?—A. I know it was not anything directly from me, signed or authorized by me in any way. Probably it was an interview, and in that way got in the paper.

The CHAIRMAN (to Mr. Thompson). Will you now take the witness?

By Mr. THOMPSON:

Q. Do you remember that on the afternoon when we first began this examination in your office in Milwaukee whether or not I asked you how much longer of your term you had to serve, how much more of your term you had to serve?—A. On the commission?

Q. How much more of you term as postmaster was unexpired?—A. I told you my service was about up. I made no statement——

Q. I just want you to answer the questions briefly.—A. I remember something was said, to whom I do not know.

Q. It is immaterial. Well, now, Mr. Paul, did not you say to the Commission that day substantially this, "1 am already out of office, I am merely waiting for my successor to be appointed and qualified?"—A. No sir, not qualified.

Q. Well, be appointed?—A. Yes, sir.

Q. You said, "my term is out, I am merely waiting for my successor to be appointed?"—A. "My time is out," it was used in that sense, that I had served four years and over.

Q. But you did not explain anything to us, you simply made that answer.—A. I did not suppose the question was formed to indicate any exact information.

Q. But still you undertook to give the exact information and said "my term is out?"—A. I intended to give simply the information that my time of four years of service had expired.

Q. That is all I want, sir. Now your recollection is not that——

The WITNESS. And I was asking my successor to be appointed.

Mr. THOMPSON. Now, I want to read something you said this morning. I take it from the stenographer of the Commission, who is the present stenographic clerk of the Commission. If you do not agree entirely with what he has reported you as saying, 1 will ask the official stenographer to read from his notes.

The WITNESS. Yes, sir.

Q. By this you stated:

I did not know the act committed by Shidy, that would go directly to the Commission if he performed his duty. I do know he undertook to cover the consequences of his laziness and indolence and dilatory habits by making dates that were untrue.

Did you say that this morning?

The WITNESS. I do not understand I made precisely that statement. Where did that come from?

Mr. THOMPSON. It was taken down by the stenographer for the Commission.·

The STENOGRAPHER (Mr. Holtz). Yes; and I compared it with the notes taken by the reporter for the Post, and they are identical.

Mr. THOMPSON. I will call upon the official stenographer to produce his notes.

The CHAIRMAN. The official stenographer who reported this this morning is not present this afternoon.

Mr. THOMPSON. Did you say, this is the material part: "I did know that he [referring to Shidy] undertook to cover the consequences of his laziness and indolence and dilatory habits by making dates that were not true?"—A. I have no recollection of saying it this morning.

Q. I understand two stenographers agree you did say precisely that?—A. That is not my understanding of it. What I intended to say——

Q. You did not say that?—A. I did not say that. I did not say that I did know he undertook to cover the consequences, etc., but that I had no idea at that time that he undertook to cover the consequences of his laziness and indolence and dilatory habits by making dates really not the true dates on the book.

Q. You retract that; that is if you said it this morning?—A. I do not retract at all.

Q. But if you did say it you now retract it?—A. Yes, sir, if I said it.

Q. Do you remember the afternoon of the first day when you were about to leave the office, what you said when we were about to call Shidy in and question Shidy?—A. Yes, sir.

Q. What was it?—A. To whom?

Q. To any member of the Commission about that, when we were about to send for Shidy, when we dismissed you.—A. The question of Sleutz's remarking?

Q. I do not wish to waste time on that, but what you said about Shidy as a clerk and about the examination we were about to make?—A. I do not remember.

Q. I will try to refresh your memory. Did you not say, "Gentlemen, be generous and light on Mr. Shidy"—I am only repeating this substantially—"he is a faithful and obedient man but overworked?"—A. I think I did say something to that effect. I think so still, as to his duties as a postal clerk theretofore.

Q. That was your opinion, I think, on the 20th of June.—A. Of course, I was not then familiar with all the facts.

Q. I simply wanted to call your attention at this time that he was "faithful and efficient, but overworked." Do you concur with me in the recollection that that was on the 21st of June?—A. I knew that from the Associated Press, but whether it was on the 20th——

Q. We were there two days?—A. Yes, sir.

Q. We were there about the 20th. In this letter of Shidy, which is dated Milwaukee, June 27, 1889, "I am grieved and surprised at the attack made on me by you in this day's Herald." And this is six days after you said to the Commission that he was a faithful and efficient man, but overworked. There must have been some allegation or some strictures upon him before that.—A. I think I was interviewed by reporters, and I think I gave the impression that Shidy had betrayed the office.

Q. Betrayed how?—A. By misrepresentation.

Q. What I wanted to get at is when you dismissed Shidy; you dismissed him shortly after that, did you not?—A. The date of that letter——

Q. As to that, we can prove that; before you dismissed Shidy you had information which made you believe he had betrayed your office to the Commission?—A. I wish that particularly understood, by misrepresentation. Yes, sir.

Q. You stated that you dismissed him on account of the newspaper letter, and now you admit you knew when you dismissed Shidy that he had betrayed the office to the Commission. I would like to be sure about that. I do not think I have misrepresented you, sir.—A. I do not like the language limited to "betrayed my office to the Commission."

Q. Say what you think is right.—A. I am very naturally subject to misconstruction in this, and if that is the purpose I protest against it.

Q. It is not my purpose; state what you wish to.—A. I simply wanted to say by that time I knew very well, or supposed and believed, that Shidy had misrepresented the facts in the case to the Commission.

Q. That was before you dismissed him?—A. Yes, sir; before I dismissed him.

Q. That is not the exact point. You said Shidy published a list of eligibles which you cut out of a newspaper, and a copy of which you have shown. How did you know Shidy published that list?—A. I knew it from the fact that the reporter informed me.

Q. The reporter told you Shidy did, and he did not say Johnston may have done it?—A. No, sir.

Q. Well now, Mr. Paul, at that time, under the rules of the Commission, the lists of eligibles were not published, is not that true that they could not be made public?—A. No, sir; they were not to be made public.

Q. You knew the fact that Shidy, a clerk in your employment, had violated the rules by publishing the list of eligibles?—A. No, sir; I did not. Mr. Shidy was in the employ of the Commission,

Q. But didn't you say a reporter told you Shidy had published a list of the eligibles?—A. I think he did.

Q. You knew from the reporter that Shidy had given out this list?—A. That Shidy, who was the secretary of the Commission, furnished this list.

Q. And this man, who, in violation of the rules and in violation of law, had given out this list of eligibles was the same man of whom you spoke to the Commission and said, "Gentlemen, do not be hard on Mr. Shidy; be light; he is a faithful and efficient clerk, but overworked?"—A. Governor Thompson, you are using language I do not remember; that is, as to his faithfulness and efficiency. I never regarded him as an efficient man.

Mr. THOMPSON. I would ask the official stenographer to see what Mr. Paul did say.

The stenographer read as follows:

A. I think I did say something to that effect. I think so still.

Mr. THOMPSON. I did not propose to have a discussion——
The WITNESS. I think so still.

Q. You spoke about Shidy's being under the control of the Commission. What authority had the Commission over the workings of the Milwaukee post-office and Shidy as secretary of the local board? I will ask you, did we pay him any salary?—A. No, sir.

Q. Could we dismiss him from the office?—A. You could recommend his dismissal.

Q. But could we dismiss him?—A. Practically, I think you could. If your Commission recommended his dismissal, I should have dismissed him.

Q. You would, but we could not dismiss him of our own order if you did not concur with us?—A. Not directly, but you had authority to dismiss him from the board of examiners, certainly, and disgrace him.

Q. For which he received no pay for doing extra work?—A. Yes, sir.

Q. So far as the complaint that he was under the duress of the Commission was concerned, the fact is the Commission had no control over him whatever so far as dismissing him or cutting down his salary is concerned?—A. The condition, and fact as I understood it at that time, as expressed by Dr. Shidy to me, was that the Commission could help him or hurt him.

Q. Now I would like the committee to understand, really I did not know it when I was at Milwaukee, you appoint your clerks yourself, does not the postmaster appoint every clerk of the office? They are not appointed by the Postmaster-General are they?—A. I think that is rather a misapprehension existing with the Civil Service Commission. They speak all the while of appointments made by the postmaster when in fact the postmaster has no more say in appointing the man than the man in the moon, and the Civil Service Commission did not know it and did not know anything——

Q. We will be glad to learn if you will be kind enough to tell us?—A. The postmaster can not appoint a boy a messenger, he can not appoint anybody.

Q. Who does the appointing?—A. The Department. The postmaster recommends simply, that is all, and the law is——

Q. Do I understand you to say that in a classified place in that office that the Post-Office Department makes the appointment and not the postmaster?—A. Certainly, even special-delivery messenger boys. The matter is submitted to the Department, the Department makes the appointment, and then he is put to work.

Q. Has not the postmaster in an office as large as the office in Milwaukee what you call lump sum, where he employs so many clerks, all that is necessary——A. Yes, sir; there is a lump allowance made by the allowance division of the Post-Office Department, a lump allowance for running that office for the various expenses, so much for clerk hire, so much for money-order office, so much for carriers, etc.——

Q. I do not wish to interrupt you, but you say the appointments were made by the Postmaster-General?—A. The appointments probably are made by the heads of divisions. In the divisions, for instance, the carriers are all appointed by Mr. Bates. That is, in his name as superintendent of the free-delivery system, and other appointments are made by other divisions of the Post-Office Department.

By the CHAIRMAN:

Q. Right there let us have a fair understanding. Is it not the rule virtually that it is the postmaster that makes the recommendations and his recommendations are always concurred in?—A. No, sir; not always.

Q. Well, as the general rule, with very few exceptions?—A. I have had orders from the Department to remove and I have had——

Mr. ROOSEVELT. Mr. Paul, let me——

The CHAIRMAN. I would like to get at this thing. How many appointments have you made during the four years you have been in office that has not been concurred in by the Department?—A. Very few.

Q. Well, how many?—A. A number.

Q. Can you give us an instance?—A. Yes, sir; I can give you an instance.

Q. Well how many?—A. I can not tell precisely, but I should think several. I can give you one instance and that is the superintendent of the free delivery who was removed on the order of the Department.

Q. In regard to the system of removals and appointments when you recommend for appointment, say, the superintendent of the free delivery or the superintendent of carriers, or any clerk, or any letter carrier, how many were rejected by the Department on your recommendation; how many appointees were rejected?—A. I do not think they ever rejected one.

Q. That is what I wanted to get at.

By Mr. THOMPSON:

Q. Do not the postmasters employ the clerks?—A. They employ them under authority of the Department.

Q. Who dismissed Dr. Shidy?—A. The Department properly.

Q. The Department properly?—A. Yes, sir; in this case the letter was sent to Dr. Shidy, and the facts were immediately reported to the Department, and the act is confirmed.

By the CHAIRMAN:

Q. Did you dismiss him?—A. Yes; just as you——

Mr. THOMPSON. Who gave the order?

The CHAIRMAN. We want to have a fair understanding.

The WITNESS. Certainly.

The CHAIRMAN. In the workings of these offices I think I understand something how appointments are made by postmasters, and how removals are made. They are made solely on the recommendation of the postmasters, are they not?—A. Not solely. I do not think—the Department always reserves the right——

Q. Oh, certainly.—A. But practically the postmaster recommends and his recommendation is ordinarily approved.

Q. Every recommendation that you have made during the four years you have been in office for appointment has been concurred in, has it not?—A. I think so.

By Mr. THOMPSON:

Q. I only wanted to bring out for the information of the committee the point in regard to the statement that Mr. Shidy complained that he was under the duress of the Commission, that really the only authority the Civil Service Commission had over him was to deprive him of his secretaryship of the local board of examiners, which gave him no pay and which only added additional work; that so far as his dismissal from the office was concerned that you had entire control of that matter?—A. Yes, sir; that is as far as recommending process is concerned.

Q. And you did control him virtually?—A. Yes, sir.

Q. In that conversation in the post-office between the Commission and yourself, I think it was on the morning of the second day or possibly it was the afternoon of the first day, did not Mr. Roosevelt make this statement to you in regard to the irregularities of certification and appointments to which your attention was called; did he not say substantially, "Mr. Paul, these are very grave charges and we would like to hear any explanation you have to make?"—A. Not as to myself, according to my understanding, sir; not at all.

Q. But we were speaking of appointments which you alone could make?—A. Well, sir; I supposed the Commissioner referred in general remarks to the methods of the board in examining certifications.

Q. He handed these papers, I remember particularly, and read from them, and do you not know Mr. Roosevelt said, which was concurred in by his colleagues, "Mr. Paul, these are very grave charges and we would be glad to hear any explanation you have to make?"—A. I do not know whether Mr. Roosevelt said it or not.

Q. Do you deny that he could have said it?—A. No, sir; he said a great many things that I can not remember, as he talks very rapidly.

Q. But you do not deny it?—A. I think he did almost the whole talking.

Q. Was your office inspected at any time, a very little before or a little after the Commission was there, by a post-office inspector?—A. It was inspected frequently all through my term of office.

Q. Do you remember an inspection made by a man named Fleming about that time?—A. I do not think Fleming came there until afterwards.

Q. About that time?—A. After that.

Q. Have you ever seen Fleming's report of your office?—A. No, sir.

Q. You say you resigned and your resignation was accepted?—A. Yes, sir.

Q. Do you know what the letter accepting your resignation contained; what was the purport of it?—A. Of my letter?

Q. The letter from the Postmaster-General, accepting your resignation.—A. Yes, sir; I do.

Q. Will you be kind enough to tell the committee about what it was.—A. I treated that letter very lightly for several reasons. After the President——

Mr. ANDREW. Is this the contents of the letter you are giving now?—
A. I am trying to get at it so the circumstances will be better understood. It was intimated to me—published by the Associated Press—
that the President would accept my resignation. Some time afterwards
I received a letter from the Postmaster-General, who was no authority
in the case more than any child in the country, and he said to me after
notifying me of the acceptance of the resignation—he said to me in
substance this: "If you had not resigned, I would have removed you
on the charges of the Civil Service Commission here referred to, and
on account of the report of the inspector."

Q. That is all I wanted, sir. Then I understand you to say that the
Postmaster-General stated in this letter that if you had not resigned
you would have been removed on charges made by an inspector of the
Post-Office Department and you never saw the charges that were submitted by the Civil Service Commission?—A. No, sir; I would not have
the slightest respect for that kind of charges made. The inspector
was not entitled to the slighest respect.

Q. Do you mean to say——A. There were five or six inspectors sent
there in succession in order to trump up charges against my office. The
man you referred to refused to accept any testimony where he could
get it and went about the streets at night and called on persons he supposed or presumed would be hostile to me to try to cook up a case.
Now, I do not fear that kind of testimony from any man living or dead.

Mr. THOMPSON. Mr. Chairman, I would ask permission of the committee for Major Webster to continue the cross-examination of this
witness.

By Mr. WEBSTER:

Q. Do you remember making a statement to me when I was at your
office in September, 1888?—A. Yes, sir; I remember the examination.

Q. You read that statement through carefully and signed it.—A. If I
signed it I certainly did, but I do not definitely recollect. I was trying
to recollect as to that fact whether I did sign that testimony, and my
impression is I finally did it. I will take your word for it, Mr. Webster.

Q. You added a short paragraph at the end of the report and then
signed it?—A. I remember distinctly that report, I added something or
wrote something, declaring my right absolutely to remove so far as the
postmaster has the right to remove the employés under me without investigation by the Commission; that I was not responsible to them.

Q. You have just stated here that you did not have access to the
register of the eligibles, that you did not see them, and that you had no
means of seeing them. Do you remember saying to me ——A. I do
not understand I made that statement. I simply stated the facts as
they were. That Shidy frequently brought the register around where
I could have seen it, but I never made any regular examination, what
you would call an examination of that register, not that I had never
seen the register at all.

Q. Did not you state to me in that examintation that you sometimes
went to that register when Mr. Shidy had gone to dinner to get information from it?—A. That is not my impression as to the fact or statement; the statement would show if it is——

Q. That is the statement that you made.—A. I may have done so by
his authority, but never without his authority.

Q. And when he was gone to dinner, when he was out of the office,
you stated to me you sometimes went there.—A. In his absence the
registry of the eligibles was in charge of his assistant and the two

clerks in that same office, and they declare they never knew of my doing so, making oaths, or they would make oath if summoned before this committee. I do not pretend, I can not say——

The CHAIRMAN. His question is whether you stated to Mr. Webster at the time of the examination that you did examine the register during the absence of Mr. Shidy. Did you make such a statement to him at that time or not?—A. I do not remember making that statement, I think there is some misapprehension about it.

Mr. WEBSTER. You read that statement through fully and made alterations in it, or alterations were made at your suggestion. and you finally signed it?

A. Yes, sir; that was a very long statement and very difficult to read critically.

The CHAIRMAN. Have you that statement here?

The WITNESS. I will not say I did not, but if I did so, I either ought to or should explain that I never examined that register for the purpose of making selections from the register.

Q. Do you remember making this statement to me, that you made a personal investigation in regard to the character, etc., of candidates, to see what men would properly be eligible for appointment soon after you knew they were likely to be certified to you for the next vacancy, and that you endeavored generally to keep well posted in advance. You say you did not have access to the register and did not know the order in which they stood upon that register, then can you explain how you could do that, how you could make this examination in advance of that certification, and how you could keep well posted in advance?—A. Just as all business men do. It is a very simple affair. The applicants for examination were filing into my office always to file their applications, and I usually turned them directly over to the secretary, or else sent them with a clerk of my office directly to the secretary to get the matter out of my hands. Of course these applicants——

Q. That does not seem to be an answer to the question at all. I wanted to know how you were able to make this investigation in advance of the certifications, if you did not know of the certification in advance.—A. Not always.

Q. How were you enabled to do that; how were you enabled to tell of the certification in order to do this in advance?—A. For instance, a man coming to the office and would not be familiar with the civil service——

Q. That has not anything to do with answering the question. I want to know how you were enabled to make an investigation in advance of the certification; how you would know what certifications were to be made, and when or what certification was to be made, for, as you say, you kept well posted in advance in the order of certifications; how could you do this if you knew nothing of the order of certifications?—A. For instance, if a man makes application for appointment, or would seek appointment there, I took it into consideration, and the question naturally would come up in regard to the qualification of the man. It does not mean I have been examining the list of eligibles to see if he was to be appointed at all, and such inference is not in accordance with the facts.

Q. That is your own knowledge?—A. Yes, sir. Such a thing is not in accordance with the facts. Such an investigation as that is proper, I think. I think all this comes from the fact that the Commission has heretofore assumed that every postmaster is a rascal instead of assuming that he is trying to do the best he can.

Q. You are familiar with the rules and regulations of the Civil Service Commission?—A. Well, I can not say that I am as familiar with rules and regulations as I ought to be. I am familiar with many of them, most of them.

Q. Do you know there is a regulation of the Commission, or there was during the time you were in office, prohibiting postmasters from giving out any applications or receiving applications from candidates or would-be candidates?—A. I think I was first made aware of that by yourself. I had nothing to do with it. Men would come in there; Shidy brought applications there in my office and kept them on his desk probably, in all kinds of ways for anybody who came after them.

Q. Shidy brought them to your desk?—A. Personally brought applications and left them at my desk, and they were left at the window of the registry desk and anywhere so they could be circulated and people could get them.

Q. Did you not state in your statement made to me that you frequently sent for these applications to Mr. Shidy and gave them out to the parties?—A. I frequently sent men for them or asked the clerk for them, or to conduct a man to the proper place to get the application. That is what I did, I do not know what I said.

Q. Were these applications returned to you after they had been filled up?—A. Sometimes, a fact for which I am not responsible, and further, Major Webster, an applicant might come in and leave an application on my table and I would send it to the place where it belonged. I am not going to stand there with a club to keep men out of my office.

Q. Did these parties state what they wanted in your office—what position they were willing to have?—A. There was no discussion of that kind.

Q. You stated to me in your examination that all such inquiries naturally came to you about parties who wanted places, that you necessarily knew about these parties before they were certified to you.—A. That is perfectly legitimate. There is no other way to do the business or to keep the stream of office beggars out of that office except by locking the door. You know how many come making application for place, but it is a thing I had nothing to do with, and it is a thing I always said, "It is not my appointment. You must go to Dr. Shidy, fill up your application, and pass your examination, and that not until then will the question come before me."

Q. You admitted to me you knew all about it before they were certified.—A. I admit just that fact, that a man comes here and applies for an office; I know him from that date; at least I recognize that man as an applicant for a place in my office, and I naturally in the course of business know something about his associations and character.

Q. You knew his politics?—A. No, sir; I never inquired as to his politics; I very rarely ever knew his politics.

Q. If you did not inquire his politics you were informed in regard to them?

Mr. BOATNER. You ought to any way.

A. No, sir; unless accidentally. I never in my life asked a man his politics who made an application for an appointment. Never. The record shows I never did; the record shows that. I do not see any occasion for trying to bring up——

Q. Do you remember Thomas F. Keaveny?—A. Thomas F. Keaveny; yes, sir.

Q. He was certified to you for the position of stamper on the carriers' register on the 20th of January, 1888, three other carriers' names being included in that certification, all of whom had higher averages than Keaveny. You made no selections from that certification. Can you explain why you did not make a selection when a vacancy existed at that time in the force of stampers?—A. I think I can, but I must protest, Major Webster, against being asked details on what consideration I have given as to the administration of that office for nearly five years, nearly five years ago.

Q. I want you to explain why you did not make a selection on the certification made to you for the position of stamper, all the names on that certification being from the carriers' register, a higher register of eligibles—I want to know why you did not make a selection, there being a vacancy at that time.—A. I do not believe there is a man in the United States who could answer that from recollection. As to the case of Keaveny, Mr. Johnston, one of the board of examiners, has volunteered an affidavit. I have not the original affidavit here, but Mr. Keaveny himself has made an affidavit affecting the statement directly. If you want these affidavits I will furnish them. After the taxing of my recollection to a mere frivolous matter of that kind I do——

Q. As to whether it is frivolous or not is immaterial. I want to know whether you recollect anything about that appointment and why you did not make that appointment at that time.—A. What was the date of the appointment?

Q. It was certified to you on the 20th day of January, 1888; four carriers were certified to you that time for selection at that time, and no selection was made from that certification. It stands upon the certification book that no selection was made.—A. Do you know the number of the certification?

Q. It is number fifty-four.—A. Well, sir, I can give you the substance of Mr. Johnston's statement to me in regard to the condition referred to. It seems that Shidy for some reason entered the name of Keaveny on the book for certification number fifty-four, and that in his own handwriting he marked opposite there "void." You must ask Mr. Shidy about that, how that record is made.

Q. It appears from the record, after your failure to select a stamper from the certification of January 20, nearly a month afterwards, on the 18th of February, the name of Thomas F. Keaveny was again certified to you from the carriers' register for the position of stamper, and this time three names from the stamper register were certified to you, that all three were higher averages than Keaveny, and the three carriers which were certified on certification fifty-four were left off. On this occasion you selected Mr. Keaveny, with a very low average. Can you explain that?—A. I think I can. I think I have the explanation among my papers. I wish to ask the direct purpose of this inquiry; I am not being investigated. I do not so understand it.

Mr. ROOSEVELT. Who is being investigated, I would like to find out?

The WITNESS. I would like to know if I have got to go through your investigation the second time; if so, I decline to do it.

The CHAIRMAN. Mr. Paul, from your testimony given here to-day your testimony as taken will show that the Commission had acted very harshly with you, to say the least of it, and brought charges against you which they ought not to have brought against you. They are under examination and they have the right to ask you such questions to show they had good reason for coming to the conclusion to which they did. If you do not remember it you can state so, or if you have reasons to give you may state them.

Mr. BOATNER. This is understood as a cross-examination of the witness; it is really a cross-examination.

The WITNESS. I have not introduced Mr. Keaveny. I made a broad statement here, which I have sworn to, that I never made any appointment except upon certification, and the Commission proposes to revise——

Mr. ROOSEVELT. You stated, you made the broad statement that you had never made an appointment except upon certification—— A. Previous certification.

Mr. ROOSEVELT. That you never have made any appointment except upon previous certification?

The WITNESS. Previous certification, certainly, sir; no appointment in the classified service. I think you had better let Mr. Webster get on; if you give me time, that is all I ask—all I ask is time.

The CHAIRMAN. But you state you really never made any appointment at all; that you made a recommendation, according to your statement. You have said no postmaster makes appointments.

The WITNESS. Made any selection, I should say. I deny *in toto* the allegation that I made selection previous to certification. This is a point I want to make quite clear now. If the Commission——

Mr. WEBSTER. What I ask is, why you did not select Keaveny from the certification of January? Now, I ask, how you happened to make a selection of that man with a very low average from a certification containing only one name from the carriers' register with three names thrown in, perhaps to pad, from the stampers' register.

The WITNESS. Let us see what Keaveny says.

Mr. BOATNER. Allow me to ask for information. Has the appointing officer the right to select any from the list, or is he required to select the highest?

Mr. WEBSTER. He is allowed to select one from the list.

Mr. BOATNER. Can he select any one?

Mr. WEBSTER. Any one. It is only in taking these two certifications together that I ask that question.

The WITNESS. What is the question involved in this matter?

Mr. WEBSTER. It appears from the record that after your failures to select a stamper on certification on January 20, that a month after, on February 18, the name of Thomas F. Keaveny was again certified to you for the position of stamper from the carriers' register, together with three others who were taken from the stampers' register, being higher averages than Keaveny.

The WITNESS. What is the date?

Mr. WEBSTER. The first was on January the 20th, and the last was on February the 18th.

The WITNESS. I was trying to get the first certification.

Mr. WEBSTER. January the 20th.

The WITNESS. What evidence have you he was certified?

Mr. WEBSTER. The certification book.

The WITNESS. The certification record shows the whole thing is one of Shidy's blunders. For instance, here is Mr. Keaveny's statement. State of Wisconsin—this is a letter-press copy of his affidavit submitted to the President. The letter gives——

Mr. WEBSTER. I did not ask that. I only want to know about the selection, why Keaveny was not selected from the first certification on January the 20th, when a vacancy then existed, but he was selected from another certification on February the 18th, the first certification being all names of carriers for stamper place, the second certification having three from the stampers' register with higher averages and one carrier with a lower average.

The WITNESS. Does the book show that Keaveny was certified on the 20th of January?

Mr. WEBSTER. Yes, sir.

The WITNESS. Does the book show that?

Mr. WEBSTER. Yes, sir.

The WITNESS. In Shidy's handwriting also that no appointment was made, marked "void."

Mr. WEBSTER. It is in his handwriting, probably.

The WITNESS. He has never reported to me, as a matter of course.

Mr. WEBSTER. The certification book shows that afterwards you did sign certificate for his appointment.

The WITNESS. Subsequently?

Q. On February the 18th you made a selection from that one.—A. January the 20th, No. 54—Mr. Keaveny does not appear at all.

Mr. WEBSTER. His appointment?

The WITNESS. He does not appear, no, sir; he does not appear to certify.

Mr. WEBSTER. The certification No. 54 contained four names of carriers for stamper place?

The WITNESS. I will read you what Mr. Keaveny says.

Mr. ROOSEVELT. Here are the names: Cumming, Smith, Gaulke, and Keaveny. Cumming, 89; Smith, 87; Gaulke, 82½; Keaveny, 82.

Mr. WEBSTER. On February the 18th, No. 55, we have the three highest carriers dropped entirely, and we have three from the stampers' register put on with Keaveny, and Keaveny is appointed.

Mr. STONE. Was Keaveny on both certifications?

Mr. WEBSTER. On both certifications and appointed on the second certification in preference to the three carriers with higher averages who were on the first.

Mr. STONE. What I was trying to ascertain was that on the first certification would it have been proper for the postmaster to have selected Keaveny?

Mr. WEBSTER. Certainly, I was going to ask that very question in in a moment. He was taken from the higher registry, and could not be put upon the lower registry, and could not be appointed to a lower place without his consent, and I was going to ask that question later. I want to know now in regard to his selection. Why it came about that he was not appointed on the first certification, it being all proper, and that a month afterwards he was appointed, the same man was selected, the vacancy existing in the first certification as in the second. I want to find out why you did not make a selection from a certification that seems to be perfectly straight, as far as the book shows, and on another occasion took the name of a lower eligible from that certification?

The WITNESS. You are asking me now about Shidy's matters. Was this certified at the same time Mr. Shidy entered it upon the record?

Mr. STONE. As far as this question is concerned, I would like to understand it while we are going along. Did you have the right on that certification made in January, the 20th, according to the theory of the Commission, did you then have the right to select Keaveny at all, or any man of the four if you desired to do so?

The WITNESS. Not under ordinary circumstances; I certainly would not.

Q. But did you have the right to do it; under the rules had you the right to do it?

The WITNESS. Yes, sir, at the time when there was——

Mr. STONE. The statement, Mr. Paul, is this, on January the 20th, four names were certified to you, of which Keaveny was one, and that he had the lowest standing of the four certified and you did not select either of these names but postponed apparently the selection for a month.

Mr. BOATNER. He says that certification is marked "void."

Mr. STONE. And then four other names were certified to you of which Keaveny was one again.

The WITNESS. At this time four names were entitled to be certified if I understand—I do not see what the question is. In the first place——

Mr. WEBSTER. There was a certification on that book, you could take under the rule one person for the position, you could take any one of the four from the top to the bottom, but you are bound to take one from the certification, and you took no one, it is marked "void." I want you to explain in that special thing.

The WITNESS. I suppose you—I want to know if you intend to hold me responsible for void certifications of Shidy's which were never made at all.

Mr. WEBSTER. The certification was there in the book, you ought to have known why it was marked void. You had the book before you.

MARCH 4, 1890.

GEORGE H. PAUL—Examination resumed.

By Mr. WEBSTER :

Q. You stated yesterday that you remembered making a statement before me, that you read it over carefully, amended it, and then signed it.—A. That is the case.

Q. That statement made by you, as signed, was a true statement?—A. I have no doubt that it was supposed to be true at the time. I think that answer should be qualified. I was talking of things of which I knew but little. Questions relating to the manner of the action of the board of examiners, and my disposition being, as far as possible, and as far as I consistently and properly could, to apologize for the action of that board and the action of Mr. Shidy.

Q. Then every material point of that statement was ratified by you?—A. That the fact was not known to me is the point I want to bring out. I was talking of things of which I knew but little.

Q. I will make the statement which I made yesterday, in a little fuller form, and I wish you would pay strict attention to it. It will state all the points I wish to bring out.—A. I wish to know whether the statement relates to matters concerning my duty, or the duty of somebody else ?

Q. It relates to your action with the post-office, and your duties in that office. The matters appear from the records of the office.

(4) It appears from the records of your office that on the 8th of December, 1887, a vacancy existed in the grade of stamper. To fill this vacancy four names from the carrier register were certified to you on the 20th of January, 1888, certificate No. 54. In your statement before me you said that these carrier eligibles, or at least two of them, had consented to take lower grade (stamper) positions. The name with the lowest average on this certification was Thomas F. Keaveny. You made no selection. The vacancy was apparently not filled at this time. On February 18, 1888, another certification, No. 55, was made for the position of stamper, which contained three names from the stamper register proper, two of them with very high averages, and the name of Thomas F. Keaveny, the carrier eligible from the preceding certification with the lowest average, although there was at least one other carrier on that former certification who had, according to your admission, signified his willingness to accept a lower place, and whose name should therefore have been placed upon certification No. 55 instead of Keaveny's. You selected Keaveny and dated the appointment back to December 8, 1887.

On February 18, 1888, another certification, No. 56, was made to fill a position of stamper, which contained the names of three eligibles for stampers and one name from the carriers' register, not one of those which had been used on the canceled certification No. 54, but one with a very much lower average, only 68, Michael Cramer, whom you selected, and dated his appointment February 1, 1888, to fill the vacancy caused by the promotion of Keaveny to the position of carrier.

On February 18, 1888, a third certification of the same date, No. 57, was made for the position of stamper, on which appeared two names, with high averages, from the stamper register proper, and two names, Raush and Reilly, with very low averages, the eighth and ninth in order, from the clerk's register. The names of the carriers from the unused certification 54, with high averages, being kept out. You selected from this certification one of the clerks, Raush.

On February 18, 1888, a fourth certification of the same date, No. 58, was made to fill a position of carrier on which appear the three names from carrier register left over from unused certification of 54, together with one name from the clerk register—Reilly, the same name, with low average, that was used on certification 57 for stamper place. You selected Reilly.

On February 18, 1888, a fifth certification of the same date, No. 59, was made for the position of stamper, on which appeared one name from the stamper register proper and three names from the carrier register, two of them being names from the unused certification No. 54, and a new name, Weber, with a very low average, which had already been certified as many times as the rules permitted. You selected Weber.

On February 18, 1888, a sixth certification on the same date, No. 60, was made to fill a position of stamper, which contained four names from the carriers' register, three of them being the names left over from unused certification No. 54, one of whom, Louis Smith, was finally selected.

By these seven certifications, Nos. 54 to 60 inclusive, five eligibles for stamper, the most of them with very high averages, and one eligible for carrier, with a very high average, were put out of the way by certification—were used for "padding" in certifications for the positions for which they had actually been examined, while men who had passed for other positions, but with very low averages, were appointed to the places—four carriers and one clerk eligible were appointed as stampers, and one clerk eligible was appointed as carrier. Not one secured the position for which he was examined. Please explain the manner in which these appointments were made.

A. So far as it relates to my duty, I wish to say broadly in the first place, as a broad fact, that in no case have I made any selection from any certification made to me except in the manner provided by law and the rules. If you will allow me, I will state the facts. Major Webster will concede that the duties of a postmaster are simply to make selections from the certifications. I wish to reply to that proposition, that in no case was any selection made by me for any appointment until after the certification came to me and the selection was made. About those certifications, of course I can not know. I have no official knowledge, and I am not permitted to have any.

By Mr. LIND:

Q. The committee is not inquiring for your official knowledge. You have used that term several times.—A. Well, personal knowledge. As to this record I had no personal knowledge, and can not properly have, and that covers a very large proportion of these questions. I have had since some knowledge of the subject from the examiners, knowledge founded on the examination of the testimony. If you will allow me to take a blank certification, I will give the committee to understand how easy it is to introduce confusion into these certifications. The certification made of four names, for instance. There are three now, under the rule of the Board. Then the balance of the names are carried along and selections are made of the new names until each person when not appointed has been certified three times. The introduction of an error, for instance, in certification 145 creates confusion in all the succeeding certifications, does it not?

Mr. WEBSTER. It probably would.

The WITNESS. I wish to say that no testimony in my possession, sworn to by the secretary of the board of examiners, did make in that case an egregious error in a certification, to start with. I, perhaps, ought to read Captain Johnson's affidavit on that point.

Q. I want to get from you an explanation of how you made these appointments. A vacancy existed on the 8th of December, and a certification was made on the 20th of January, 1887.—A. Certification was made on the 20th of January. I want to see if I understand it, since I have stated positively no appointment was made except from the regular certification. Your certification No. 54, Thomas F. Keaveny, was made January 20. The secretary of the board himself, Shidy, on the face of that, says that it is an improper entry. It was, in fact, as I understand it here from the testimony of Captain Johnson, that no such certification occurred. That is all I have to do with that question. In Shidy's own handwriting it stands on the record, which you have seen. It is written "void" all the way through.

By Mr. LIND:

Q. How did the man get the appointment?—A. At the time that certifications was made Keaveny had already been appointed nearly a month, and am I here to be responsible for such blunders as that? Not at all.

Mr. ROOSEVELT. You have said here that when the first certification was made to you, Keaveny had already been appointed a month.

The WITNESS. Certification number 54 marked "void" on the record, and still you assume it to have been made.

By Mr. WEBSTER:

Q. That is your explanation in full of that point. Please go right on to No. 60.—A. That changes your whole group.

Q. No, it does not. There is a group of seven.

The CHAIRMAN. This is a matter between you and the postmaster, and has already been repeatedly explained.

Q. I will leave that point, and go on to the other that will take 55, 56, 57, 58, 59, and 60. Please explain how four carriers and one clerk were appointed stampers, when the original register of stampers, which was put out of the way by these certifications to get rid of them, while these other men, carriers and clerks, were appointed stampers and a clerk was appointed carrier, not one man being selected from the proper register. That is the point I am trying to get at in this question?—A. So far as I know the facts in the case I am willing to give them to you with a great deal of pleasure. You know perfectly well that you are talking of matters of which I can not know anything. I simply know certifications as they come to me. I do not know how they are made. I would be guilty if I did.

Q. You do not know how it happened that these four carriers and one clerk were appointed to stampers' positions? Can you explain this at all?—A. I do not know but what I can, if you will give me the facts. I do not propose to be held responsible for Shidy's certifications at all in that particular. It is full of blunders.

Q. You do not know how it happened that these clerks and carriers were appointed to places below the place for which they were examined?—A. I know the principle on which it may have been done. He was acting under the construction of the letter of 1885.

Q. You do not know anything about it. I want to find out how you made these selections of carriers and clerks; instead of taking the stampers—you made the appointments. Did you take all these men from a higher grade?—A. No.

Q. You selected them?—A. They were selections of yours. You made the appointments by the secretary, in due order. If you wish to have me explain some of the blunders, it is possible that I can do so.

Mr. WEBSTER. Not on this point.

The WITNESS. I think it would throw some light on this whole matter to read Keaveny's letter.

Q. The certification shows that Thomas F. Keaveny was appointed to the position of stamper December 8, 1887, and promoted to the position of carrier February 1, 1888, but not certified to you by the secretary of the board until February 18, 1888. Can you explain how it happened that he was selected from the book as a stamper after he had been promoted to the position of carrier?—A. Keaveny, who was duly certified in December by the secretary of the board, and appointed from the certified list as a stamper, is the first appointment to my personal knowledge and positive recollection.

By the CHAIRMAN:

Q. Does it appear so on the certification book?—A. That I can not say.

By Mr. LIND:

Q. Was it not your duty to sign the certifications?—A. When presented to me. It is not my duty to hunt up the certification book.

Q. Was it not your duty to sign it?—A. No, sir, not until it was presented to me.

By Mr. WEBSTER:

Q. Was it not your duty to sign the certification book?—A. It was, when I was called upon to do so by the secretary of the board. Allow me to make a little explanation: It appears from the statement of Captain Johnson and others, and Mr. Keaveny himself (but especially Captain Johnson), that Mr. Shidy omitted to enter his original certification in its proper place on the record. I am not explaining my action, but Shidy's. He made no certification in the proper form, as I now understand it. It was on one of those little slips, and he carried it off in his pocket, and never entered it on the record. Subsequently, he proposed to enter it on his record, and when he got to No. 54, he proposed to enter this certification, which contained the name of Keaveny as an appointee. His practice was at that time—say at the time of the entering of the record—to enter from slips. Now he got that entry on his record as under date of January 20. Then it occurred to him, without my knowledge at all, that Keaveny had been appointed a month before, on the 8th of December; and then Shidy, supposing he had already entered his certification, and did not wish to make it twice, made this memorandum: "No appointment; void." It is written right across it. This is the way the first and original error occurred in the case. It is clearly by his own negligence, and of course entirely unknown to me. This is a chapter of blunders by Shidy, which the committee ought to see. After having made this entry there, and finding the appointment was made December 8, instead of January 20, he finds on looking back that the certification was made and entered from this little slip which he carried around in his pocket. So he goes and enters No. 55, containing the certification of Keaveny. Who was with him I do not know. He enters against that name on the record, "appointed stamper December 8, 1887." It is in his own handwriting. He brings that to me to sign, and that I did sign. That explains the whole matter, so far as I can.

Q. You did not examine that as to dates?—A. I never did.

Q. As a business man, of the business experience that you have spoken of to the committee, you think you allowed a subordinate to hoodwink you and make false certifications right under your nose?—A. No, sir; I wish to make this point: Is it allowable to ask me to explain the action of the examining board in matters which I can not know?

Mr. BOATNER. Anything you do not know, we do not wish you to state. Anything you do know from information, you can speak of. Of course, no witness is expected to answer beyond what he knows.

The WITNESS. I protest against this commission holding me responsible for any action of the board of examiners.

Mr. LIND. It is the committee who will hold you responsible for your testimony and action.

The WITNESS. Certainly; but I have not the slightest objection to your inquiring into all the blunders of the secretary.

By Mr. LIND:

Q. At the time you signed this certification in February, did you know that Keaveny was already in the service?—A. I knew of his appointment.

By Mr. BOATNER:

Q. Was your attention called to the date?—A. No, sir; I think the dates were made after my signature.

By Mr. Lind:

Q. Did you sign that certification of the record in December?—A. No, sir; no record was made in December.

Q. When did you sign the record?—A. When the book was brought to me.

Q. In February?—A. I presume so.

Q. You say at the time you knew that Keaveny had been in the service for several weeks?—A. Yes, sir; that is the fact in the history of the case.

Q. Did you know that that was contrary to law?—A. I do not know that it is contrary to law. There is no rule that I know of which requires my signature until the secretary makes a report. It is entirely in the hands of the secretary.

Q. You say that you signed this record when it was presented to you in February?—A. Yes, sir.

Q. What I want to get at is whether you knew or suspected that this was an irregular practice?—A. Soon after that I did.

Q. To make papers out after a man had been actually appointed; did you know that that was an irregular practice?—A. It was not an irregular practice.

Q. As a matter of law, as a postmaster discharging your duties you would say that that was a regular method?—A. I think not. I would like to explain.

Q. You can answer my question. I say that this is irregular.—A. I say that my signature was not irregular. If you will allow me to state I will show how the business was done. There was no impropriety in anything that I did.

Q. The question which I was asking was, is it irregular?—not whether it is culpable, or anything of that sort.—A. Shidy entered the certification at the wrong time.

Q. And you signed it at the wrong time?—A. I did not sign it until after it was presented to me.

Q. Was it irregular?—A. No, sir; I signed it when it was brought to me. When the secretary brings that to me it is my duty to sign it.

Q. Did you know that he acted irregularly?—A. Not at that time; I know it now.

Q. Did you know that it was irregular on his part to present the record to you for signature long after that appointment had been made?—A. He did it continuously.

Q. That is not an answer. Did you know that to be irregular?—A. No, sir; I did not.

Q. But it was irregular?—A. It is the secretary's duty to know the law.

Q. I am not discussing what his duty is. I am discussing your understanding of his duty.—A. My understanding of his duty would throw some light upon it, if you will allow me to make a candid explanation. Allow me then to state, as I understand the law, the secretary each month must report to the Commission. Now the practice of the secretary has been in my office, and in other offices also I think, before he makes his report, at such time as he pleases, to bring to me the register for my name. He brings that, and lays it down before me, and points to the place where I am to sign, I look at the name and see if the man is in the service. It is simply a question as to the signature and the appointment. I signed that as a certification that this man is appointed. Now I can not say that the postmaster should compare the dates of the appointment with the dates of the record. That is not the practice. It is impracticable almost.

Q. Did you understand then that it was his duty to report this within thirty days to the Commission?—A. I understand it was his duty to report within thirty days. I do not keep track of his time. The postmaster can not do it, as he has other matters to attend to.

Q. You did not pretend to keep track of his reports?—A. I have no jurisdiction over the civil-service reports, or his books, any more than you have. I could not see his books in any way.

Q. That book you had legal control of as much as he had.—A. The register certification?

By the CHAIRMAN:

Q. The certification book you have a right to examine at any time?—A. No, sir; I do not so understand it. I have no right to examine the records of the secretary, or interfere with the secretary. I do not propose that Major Webster's statement with regard to the rules shall be submitted without furnishing the rules themselves. You intimated that I had some control of the books. The rules prescribe that the secretary of the board shall safely keep, etc., all the books, papers, and records, and make reports.

Mr. LYMAN. Mr. Paul has a copy of the rules not in force when these transactions took place.

The WITNESS. I think that Mr. Lyman's remark gives a false impression, and I think he has given false impressions repeatedly. That is my opinion. I think that when Mr. Lyman rises here and says that these were not the rules in force at that time, he is wrong. Then I wish to present both rules. I think his making that remark gives a wrong impression to this committee.

By Mr. WEBSTER:

Q. You said that the secretary was required to make a report once a month, and that he brought this book to you for signature.—A. You have not got that quite right. The practice of the secretary in making his monthly report was to come to my room and call for my official letter-book with the letter-press copies. From that book he could make a memorandum of the appointments made, and make his entries accordingly. Anything in that book was reliable. Then, when he has made the record of his monthly report, he brings that record with, perhaps, half a dozen names upon it of appointees during the preceding month. He would bring that record to me, and I would sign my name succeeding the names of the appointees. That shows the practice. I wish to have the committee understand that my signature is not made to the certifications by the secretary, but simply to the fact that that man was appointed. The records show the number of certifications, as Major Webster knows; but the name of the appointee is on the face of the certification, and I put my signature opposite that of the name of the appointee; and that is all I have to do with it. That I have always regarded as a proper thing, and I never examined it in my life. I never supposed I had a right to do anything, except to sign my name.

Q. You had to examine it to make your selection. You could not make a selection without that?—A. That has been explained to this committee. Shidy regarded his slip as a certification, and says himself on one of these certificates, "I hereby certify." Shidy regarded this slip of paper as a certification, and it may be well for the information of this committee to show that it is so regarded in many of the principal post-offices of this country, to my personal knowledge.

Q. This certification was made to you two months and a half after you had actually appointed and selected the man?—A. I undoubtedly signed it February 18. As I understand it, Shidy's memorandum in the right hand column of that record, as furnished me by Johnson, is "appointed stamper December 8, 1887." My signature appears against Keaveny's name in each case on that record; and I wish to say further: Suppose that Shidy neglected to bring that record to me in the proper time, I believe my duty would be to sign it when he did bring it.

Q. On the same date, February 18, the certification of three stampers and Michael Kremer, carrier, were made to you February 18, and you selected Kremer for the position of stamper of February 18, his appointment being dated February 1, to take the place of Keaveny, who had then already been promoted to carrier?—A. He was appointed stamper on the 18th of February; the record of Dr. Shidy shows that. The entry of the date of his appointment on my books is February 1. Now whether this is a misdate by Shidy of the certification, like many others, or whether the appointment is dated to take effect from February 1, according to the usual practice, I do not know. Whether it was a blunder or an improper date of the time, that the secretary should confess, I do not know. I guess it is a blunder of Shidy's.

Q. Both these certifications were made on the same date, and signed on the same date.—A. There is no evidence of that. I have shown already that three of those were misdated.

Q. You signed that in blank, did you?—A. I do not know as to that.

Q. As a business man, would you ever sign that in blank?—A. As a person observing the law; and you are at fault if I am required to do anything more.

Q. But you signed it in blank?—A. I signed it as you have required me to sign it.

Q. On the same date you selected this stamper for the position which he had been filling, and he having been promoted, and you also made a certification for the appointment of Kremer.—A. I think that is a misstatement.

Q. Did you on this same day, February 18, sign a certification for the appointment of Keaveny to the position of stamper December 8, he having already been promoted to the position of carrier on the same date; and signed a certification for the appointment of Kremer to the position of stamper to fill the vacancy caused by the promotion of Keaveny?—A. The question is, whether I signed the book with reference to Keaveny and Kremer on the same date. I can not tell on what dates I sign books. I have no doubt, the case occurring, that the copy of the record is correct. My impression about the matter of Keaveny is that Kremer succeeded him as stamper. I think Keaveny was transferred to the duties of carrier on the suggestion of Shidy. That he transferred Keaveny to the duties of a carrier, the place for which he had been examined on the 1st of February. I think that is probably the case. He commenced his duties as carrier at that time, having been certainly selected as a stamper; and Kremer on the 18th of February succeeded him as stamper, these having been properly dated back to the 1st of February. The question of the promotion or transfer of Keaveny to the place of a carrier had been submitted to the board, and was considered by that board.

Q. Now, on that same date, February 18, from certification No. 57, on which there were these two stampers and two clerks, you selected one of those clerks for the position of stamper, and dated his appointment back to February 1.—A. I know the fact that Roush was appointed stamper.

Q. And you signed the certification, and dated it back for him?—A. Undoubtedly I signed the record but dated no certification back, unless you refer to date of appointment instead of certification. I do not know why I should not. I wish to give the facts in the case of Roush. He was regularly certified by the secretary of the board, and selected from the proper number of names at the time. If there is any impropriety about his appointment, I would like to know it now.

Q. He was selected by you on February 18 from the certification No. 57, being a man from the clerk's register, and yet you selected him for a stamper's place?—A. I do not mix him up with selections from the clerk's register. Where a carrier desired to accept a lower position in the absence of any vacancy above, his application was referred to Shidy in precisely the same manner that the law was supposed to permit, and as it is construed by the board of examiners, and by the Commission itself. I had nothing to do with certifications at all. If a man applied at his own request, the circular says he could be transferred from a higher to a lower service, at his own request, and when that request was made by any clerk or carrier, the secretary was supposed, and it certainly was his duty under this construction, to transfer the names to the other register, and certify this name in accordance with that principle.

Q. I will ask you if you did not testify before me in September, 1888, that all those requests for transfer from higher to lower registers necessarily came to you, because all the parties came to you for appointment, and for that reason all such requests came?—A. Unquestionably every candidate for appointment habitually comes to the postmaster, and the postmaster's duty in such case is very clear, which is, if he wishes to have an applicant transferred to a lower register, to refer that applicant to the secretary of the board of examiners, and this was done by me in every instance that I have any recollection of.

Q. You knew every man that wanted to be transferred from clerks to stampers? All such requests came to you?—A. In that way. A man comes into the office and wants an appointment. I say to him there is no vacancy. I want to explain that. I tell him that I can not appoint him, that there is no vacancy until his name comes up in the regular way. He wants to know if there is a lower place that he can have temporarily, or something else, and it is the duty of the postmaster under those circumstances, and I have always regarded it so, to refer the applicant immediately to the secretary of the board for transfer at his own request under its construction. I think that explains my testimony sufficiently.

Q. Did you state to me that where parties came to you and signified their willingness to accept a place in a lower grade, that you told the secretary to send his name to you next time with the other names?—A. I do not know but I may have said that. I think it is possible that I may have said to the secretary, "Give me the best qualified men that you can lawfully certify to." I think that would be my duty.

Q. You directed the secretary to certify these men?—A. Not individual names, not persons. The principle of certification is all I have ever talked to the secretary about.

Q. You said if you found a man who seemed to be qualified who was willing to take a place below his grade, you told the secretary to send that name to you?—A. Not that name except as to be embraced in the principle of a certification from a higher to a lower register.

Q. You have explained about Roush, who was appointed from a clerk to a stamper's place from certification 57, and who had been certified you as a stamper, and you dated his appointment back to February 1.—A. I do not give these as absolute facts except from my theory of the facts. I wish that understood.

Q. Under that provision did you consider yourself at liberty to make selections from higher-grade registers without regard to there being eligibles on the lower-grade list of eligibles?—A. When a higher-grade eligible has expressed his willingness to accept a lower place, I have told him that under the ruling of the Commission he would insert the name of such person in such certification if he would take a lower position, being entitled to the privilege. I told the secretary that, but that does not refer to one individual. It referred to the principle.

Q. We will come to the certification No. 58. This is the same date, February 18. There was in that certification to you three carriers and one clerk with a low grade. You selected that clerk on February 18, and dated his appointment February 15, did you not, three days prior? This is under the head of Riley.—A. This is the case in which Shidy misdated the certification on February 18, and the appointment was made previous. February 15. The letter to the Department accompanying Riley is dated February 15, and the certification was made previously on · the slip of paper. The date, February 18, is unquestionably the date on which he was entered and was reported by the secretary.

Q. The certification No. 59 is of a similar character, where there were certified Weber, from the carriers' list, for the position of stamper, and he was appointed by February 15, three days prior to that.—A. Weber declined, did he not? Weber was certified to me as a stamper previous to February 15, and the appointment dated on the 15th, the date of the record of certification is on the 18th, in the same manner and in the same way as Riley. I would be glad if all these men could speak for themselves, as I can show by the affidavit of Weber that he was appointed and certified on or before the 15th. There is no question about the facts.

Q. Had he not been certified the full number of times prior to that without being selected?—A. That is not a question for me to determine.

Q. Wouldn't you know whether his name had been before you?—A. I may have had his name before me previously, but how many times I can not know.

Q. On the same date was certified to you a list of stampers from which you selected a Mr. Smith?—A. Weber declined the place, and Mr. Smith was appointed from another certification in lieu of Weber.

Q. We have all these five certifications on February 18, signed by you apparently on that date, from which you have made selections; first of a carrier of a low grade, certified with three stampers to you and dated back, and you promoted him before a selection was made February 1; then the appointment of another carrier, Cramer, to the position of stamper, dating his appointment back to February 1, to fill the vacancy caused by the promotion of Keaveny; then on the same date the appointment of Riley, a clerk, to the position of carrier, and dating him back only to February 15; then on the same date the selection of a carrier and promotion to the position of stamper, and dating him back to February 15. On the same date the selection of Smith, a carrier, for the position of stamper, dating and securing the appointment of four carriers to the position of stampers?—A. Securing? You mean resulting. I do not wish you to use words implicating me.

Q. Resulting in four; four carriers having been appointed to the position of stamper, the certification having put out of the way five stampers on the eligible list and at least one carrier?—A. I do not know whether the stampers were on the list or not.

Q. I want you to state what you know about these. Is it a fact that four carriers were appointed to the position of stampers; one clerk appointed to the position of stamper, and one to the position of carrier?—A. I presume so. I can not understand what the criticism is in the case. The board of examiners certifies to me the names of certain parties. Among these parties are the names of those who had been examined for higher positions, and they are certified to me as stampers. Under a construction of the board of examiners at that time, right or wrong, they felt that they had sufficient authority for it, and I knew nothing to the contrary under the letter of 1885. Under that letter every applicant who came to me for a position and expressed his willingness to take another position lower, as I understand, such could be properly transferred to the lower position. For instance, from carrier to stamper. Then the secretary as a rule, if he performs his duties, would certify the names of those belonging to the stamper list, including those examined for carriers, for the place of stamper; and I consider that the service is very much improved by taking a man from a higher and putting him in a lower grade, but I can not understand what the criticism would be under such circumstances.

Q. I will ask you if, when you saw these certifications, it did not look a little strange to you why all these persons were being certified out of the way so that they could have no other chance, and these names picked out?—A. Do not say "picked out."

Q. They were picked out from low down on the clerk's register where they were out of reach, and put in among these stampers and were always selected. Does it not look a little strange that these should be before you and you not notice it?—A. I do not think it will be strange when you hear my answer. I think, practically, I know about as much as the Civil Service Commission in postoffice matters. I hope I do.

Q. You think you know about as much as the Civil Service Commission, you say?—A. I know as much as the Commission ever stated to me. I will state my reply to Major Webster's question. As to the number that was certified and as to the class of persons that were transferred from a higher grade to a lower: We have a vacancy, say, in the place of stamper in a post-office, and a person desires to be transferred—it does not make much difference, the lower the place the more this is true—and the friends of the person are generally informed, through the person who is about to take some other place and the boys in the office, that a vacancy is about to occur. The result is an onslaught upon the postmaster of applications to fill that place. I did not know where they came from. The postmaster is not bound to know. He does not make a distinction about their grade. In this way, when a vacancy occurs in an office at any time, under the old rule of the Commission there would be quite a number of applications for the place. The postmaster does not know whether it is for one place or another. Quite a large number of applications are made, and that accounts for the number that is on the carriers list. Nearly all of them, especially those low down on the list, are willing to accept any place. They are out of business, perhaps. That accounts for the number that flock in about that time.

Mr. ANDREW. Do you remember the question you were asked? Your answer seems to have no bearing on it.

The WITNESS. Mr. Webster asked how I accounted for so many being certified from the upper list.

Mr. WEBSTER. All to the lower list.

The WITNESS. I will explain further. I wish the committee to understand this. In the transfer from an upper to a lower list, the fact was the secretary deemed the rank of a carrier, for instance, when he was transferred to the stamper's place, as being much higher on the stampers' list than on the carriers' list. It was the opinion of Secretary Shidy to me, on which, on consultation with me, I have known him almost invariably to act, so far as I have known anything about the matter, when a carrier went to Shidy to ask to be transferred to a lower list, the grade on the lower list was increased.

Q. All of these requests for transfer first came to you?—A. Not all the requests.

Q. You said they necessarily came to you.—A. I say so now. I do not question the testimony. Naturally they came to me. I do not mean to say I sent for them. When a transfer was made to a lower list, it was the habit, I believe, of the secretary not to change actually the marking, but transfer the name to the stampers' list and put him higher than those of the same mark standing as stampers, and I think that is natural. I think it would be impossible to pursue that system to transfer carriers or clerks to a lower grade without bringing them almost invariably to the top. These are only a few cases. I think that perfectly answers Major Webster.

Q. This is only an illustration. This is one of the cases to illustrate the manner in which it was done. You say there was a rush for these places?—A. Always.

Q. These were apparently made on different dates; one December 8, one February 1, and another February 1; three more February 15, that are certified February 18. When did that rush occur?—A. That is begging the principle as to two or three appointments, but I wish to say to you it makes no difference. In every instance, without exception, without qualification, these transfers and certifications were made by the secretary of the board and without my instigation.

Q. In regard to this certification from a higher to a lower grade place, who was lower upon the register, I want to put a question here to show the effect and ask you to explain it. The records of your office show that Thomas F. Keaveny, who stood much lower than several other eligibles on the carriers' list, was appointed by you to the position of stamper December 8, 1887, and promoted by you to the position of carrier before he was certified to you, and was thus actually appointed to the position of carrier over those of higher average who were entitled to certification and appointment. I will ask you how it was that this appointment was made in violation of the rules?—A. Before he was certified for carrier?

Q. Before he was certified as a stamper he was appointed carrier by you February 1, 1888.

The CHAIRMAN. Do you understand the question.

The WITNESS. I do not understand his statement of facts, because they are not facts.

By the CHAIRMAN:

Q. The question is this: How did it happen that Keaveny was really promoted to the position of carrier, having a lower percentage, in preference to others who were on the eligible list having a higher percentage as carriers; whether it was done by having him appointed stamper and then promoting him, in that way evading the law?—A. That is an intimation of the Commission that there was some violation of the law.

The CHAIRMAN. How do you explain it?

The WITNESS. The question is as to the promotion of Keaveny from the place of stamper to that of carrier. The exact fact was, how long did Keaveny serve as a stamper?

Mr. WEBSTER. He was appointed December 8, 1887, and promoted to carrier February 1, 1888?—A. He served as stamper from December 8 to February 1. Keaveny was a very competent man, and I can give the reason for his promotion. I repel the idea that there is any impropriety in the matter. He served from December 8 to February 1, as I understand it, as a stamper. He is a man weighing 250 pounds. This fact has a bearing on the motive for his promotion. He then applied for promotion to the place of a carrier, and I doubted whether that could be done under the rule. I submitted the question formally to the board of examiners so that they might take that question up and determine it. I looked at the rules and could not determine whether it was proper or not. The board took the question under consideration and examined the rules for themselves. You understand that I always regarded the board as essentially the Commission in the office.

On a certain occasion Secretary Shidy brought to my room, after a full and rather prolix consideration of the whole matter, a book of rules, which I intended to have brought with me, but by a mistake brought the wrong one. He said he thought it to be strictly proper, and he gave me that opinion as the opinion of the board. Under that opinion I consented to it, but had very much doubt whether it was authorized. I thought it was rather an anomalous case, but that perhaps the Commission had made a lapse there in certain cases. They did not make a lapse for the reason that the instructions of 1885 had been changed, as you know. With the instructions of the letter of 1885, a person could go from a clerk's or a carrier's list to a stamper's, and then, under the then existing rules, the board claimed that he could be promoted to a different place from that for which he was originally examined. Now I was in doubt about that. I think it is proper to allow me to state, if the committee have no objection, that the record of that proceeding of the board of examiners was not in existence in any complete shape. The action of the board—I do not know whether it was the action of the board or one of the board—but I think it is referred to in an affidavit by Fahsel, one of the members of the board, which might be read by the committee. I wish to show why the record can not be produced showing the action in that case as to the promotion. Mr. Fahsel has stated to me in explanation of that, that a resolution offered by Shidy himself construing the case, or the principle covering the case, was adopted unanimously by the board, but is not to be found in the records at all. Those really are the facts as to the promotion.

Q. You mean to say that Shidy forced upon you those appointments, notwithstanding that you had a knowledge of all those requests?—A. I do not see why you should not be candid.

Q. Notwithstanding that the requests for certifications for lower places and requests for appointment by applicants were all made direct to you, Mr. Shidy forced upon you the appointment of all these people from the clerks' register, to the lower stamper register, and from the clerks' to the carriers' register, in spite of yourself, and prevented you from getting any man from the proper register, and by his manipulations alone you were forced to take these men from the higher register? You had nothing to do with the matter?—A. Let me state it in my own language. I have not said in any testimony that I have given that applications were made to me by these men for transfer. I was ignorant of applications and transfers as far as I practically could be. I would tell them when they wanted a transfer to go to the secretary. That was my duty plainly. If I wished to make an appointment as stamper, 1 did not care who was appointed as stamper. I knew none of these men personally.

By the CHAIRMAN:

Q. When you appointed this man Keaveny as a stamper, when you signed that certification appointing him as stamper, did you have at the time of it in you mind that you would make a letter carrier of him and wanted him for that purpose?—A. No, sir; I had in my mind this, which I always had in my mind, that certifications from a higher to the lower list were an advantage to the service.

Q. This. man Keaveny had applied for a place as carrier?—A. Yes, sir; and had been examined.

Q. Did you know him personally?—A. 1 never saw the man before, never in my life. I never saw any of these men and I do not think I would know Keaveny. I do not think I would know these men in the street to-day. I would not recognize them. I never allowed myself to know a man in connection with any possibility of his appointment.

By Mr. BOATNER:

Q. Is not this the same man we were asking you about this morning who was certified to in December on a slip, and appointed by you on one of those certifications which was not entered, and that you promoted him on the 1st of February, and after the promotion the book was brought to you and you signed that as an original appointment?—A. It is the same case.

Q. Was it the rule in your office that applicants for promotion had to be re-examined, or was one who was already in the service subject to promotion without re-examination and re-certification?—A. There is a rule for promotion without re-examination.

Q. On the 1st of February, if this man had been duly certified in December and appointed in December, would he have been subject to promotion on his grade under the rule, without re-examination?—A. The question of re-examination is not involved.

Q. The gentleman asked you this question, how it happened that a man on the carriers' list was reduced to the stampers' list and appointed as a stamper; and, having been appointed as a stamper, was promoted to the carriers' list?—A. That was a case of misapprehension. And as to whether such a system would have interferred with the rights of those on the carriers' list, that was the question that was submitted to the board.

Q. At the time you appointed this man Keaveny, had he been certified to you?—A. Yes, sir; when he was appointed.

Q. Then you had appointed him as a stamper?—A. As a stamper.

Q. Was there anything in the law or the rules which would prevent you from doing that legally?—A. 1 do not know. My testimony is this, that Keaveny was regularly certified and selected on his first appointment to the position of stamper. The question of promotion, which was a new question to me, was submitted to the board of examiners and the opinion given that he could be appointed to the position for which he was originally examined. That is the explanation.

By the CHAIRMAN:

Q. The official records show a wrong date.—A. The official records show a wrong date; there are thirty-five wrong dates on that record of one hundred and four.

By Mr. WEBSTER:

Q. You signed this whole group at one time?—A. I do not concede that.

Q. The record was made up February 18?—A. I have no doubt he gave me that report in that way. I have no recollection of signing a batch in that way; but I do not remember. I would like to have you point me to the rule which relates to promotions of appointees to the places for which they are originally examined.

Q. There is no rule which would prevent that, except where there was a detriment to others on the list of eligibles in those cases.—A. Then you mean to say there was no rule?

Q. Where it was to the detriment of others.—A. There are no such words in the rule.

Q. There is not a rule?—A. I think there is a rule. I do not propose to be misled until I know. I have been misrepresented about as many times as I care to be. The provision refers to appointment and promotion under certain circumstances, until special certification may be made.

By the CHAIRMAN:

Q. Suppose there were ten men on the eligible list for letter-carriers and the postmaster desired to appoint a particular man as a letter-carrier, and the party he desired to appoint was found to be ninth on the list. Under the rule, he could not appoint him, because others of a higher percentage would be first certified, would they not?—A. Yes, sir.

Q. If you take a lower grade, and appoint a man as a stamper, and afterwards promote him, would not that be a violation of the law, being a detriment to those that passed a superior examination?—A. That would really be a detriment. I should object to it most positively. But in those cases referred to, you must understand that I got the opinion of the board as to the transfer from the upper to the lower grade. Under present circumstances, it could not be made at all. But this was done under instructions of the Commission in 1885, which was the prevailing rule at our office until instructions were given to the contrary. That could not be done now.

By Mr. WEBSTER:

Q. You said, I believe, that you had no knowledge of the state of the register at the time these appointments were made. You did not know anything about them, and that Shidy made certifications to you, and you did not know how they came, or what the state of the register was at the time?—A. That I so stated, and I never knew anything of the state of the register. There was an absence of names for stampers.

Q. You did not know what was the state of the register?—A. No, sir; I gave that no consideration. I never influenced the rank of candidates in any way whatever.

Q. Do you remember Charles J. Cumming?—A. Yes, sir.

Q. His name was at the head of this certification No. 54, which was void, and at the head of 58, 59, and 60. You remembered the man and the correspondence?—A. Yes, sir; in a general way.

Q. In the correspondence that you had with the Department when you were endeavoring to get his appointment made, you stated to the

3117——16

Commission that Cumming's name stood at the head of the list of carrier eligibles. This is in the correspondence after the appointment. If you did not know anything about the state of the register, how were you able to state that he stood at the head of the list?—A. Mr. Cumming knew his own rank, and probably gave it to me. I think he was informed by Shidy of his rank. It was commonly known in the whole office.

Q. Then you did know the state of the register?—A. Not from the register. I did not know the state of the register. I simply knew of this remarkable case in which Cumming stood high. That is about all I knew of it.

Q. You said he stood at the head.—A. I may have known that fact at the time.

Q. What did you make your statement on?—A. On common notoriety in the office.

Q. Simply on hearsay?—A. I think on his own statement. I think Shidy spoke of it, that he stood at the head.

Q. In this letter of May 30, you stated at the time that Cumming's name was certified to you from the carriers' register when the stamper register was exhausted; how did you know?—A. I got my information from Shidy. He made a very full statement to me. I think it was very proper for him to give me that information.

Q. In your letter of May 30, 1888, in which you speak of the certification of Cumming, notwithstanding that he had twice declined to accept the position of stamper, you say the list of stampers was nearly exhausted, and Cumming's name was merely used to make the certification as to number complete.—A. That is a matter for Shidy to explain.

Q. This is your letter; this letter you wrote officially to the office.—A. Shidy did use his name, whether rightly or not I do not know, and I do not care.

Q. How did you know it?—A. From Shidy; he made that representation in favor of Cumming. He said injustice had been done him. He had declined a specific appointment as you remember, which was offered to him on a regular certification, and then Shidy informed me that he had carried him on his list of eligibles until he had been certified three times without his knowledge. I think it was a peculiar proceeding and Shidy was responsible for it, and I did not approve of it, to the best of my recollection. Then Cumming came and asked for an appointment, and Dr. Shidy informed him, and he also informed me, that his rights had expired, or terminated, and I thought it was a hard case. I thought he should have a restoration under those circumstances.

Q. Were these certifications ever modified by Shidy at any time?—A. No, sir; not to my recollection. I do not recollect that certifications were ever modified.

Q. Let me read a little piece of your testimony in which you say, "in one or two cases the secretary modified the certifications to accord with the rule?"—A. I do not know that that is not correct. I did not recollect about that. Certifications have never been modified by me, or by my dictation in any way. There were frequent conversations in regard to certifications, and frequently Dr. Shidy would ask me as to whether I thought it proper, and I did not answer as a rule, but referred the question to the whole board, and asked him to do that also. I have abundance of affidavits covering all these points from Fahsel, Johnson, and other parties affected. I should be glad, Mr. Chairman, if you would get their testimony. I should like that every man concerned in the Milwaukee post-office should be examined as a witness. There is not one who would not confirm my testimony. I think it ought to be done in a case where it depends upon the veracity of Shidy and myself. I think other witnesses ought to be made to corroborate one or the other.

Q. I. have confined myself to your own official records, without one intimation as to what Shidy has said or done. In the questions I have asked. I have not taken anything from what Shidy has said?—A. Sometimes Shidy was Dr. Jekyll, and sometimes Mr. Hyde; I did not know him as both.

Q. In regard to that Cumming matter in a letter from the Commission to you about Cumming, signed by Mr. Oberly, you were informed that the only circumstances which would justify his certification to the place of stamper then would be the depletion of the stampers' register below the number required for a single certification. In reply to this, in your letter dated June 9, 1888, you said such was precisely the fact in the case of Cumming, and the depletion of the stampers' list could not well have been foreseen. Please explain, in view of the fact that there were five names yet on the stampers' register with Cumming?—A. You say there were five names on the register?

Q. There were five on the eligible register at the date on which he was reported.—A. What is the date of my letter?

Q. The letter to you was in regard to the certification of Cumming as stamper, though he had been certified for stamper, and had lost his chance by being certified and stating to you that he had no right to be so certified. Please explain, in view of these facts, why these were used for stuffing for certifications?—A. My letter was a reply to you to show how it happened to be done, explaining how his name happened to be used. That was precisely the situation at that time.

Q. You say, in answer, that such was the fact in the case of Cumming; the depletion of the stamper list could not have been foreseen?—A. That letter was in behalf of Cumming, on the suggestion of Shidy. I supposed at the time that was the exact fact. I know very well, and have a distinct recollection as to the circumstances, that I was informed that the stamper eligible list was deficient. I am positive of that; and I feel positive now that Shidy told me that that was the fact. You understand the matter at that time was changed. If you will state the five persons perhaps I can recollect.

Q. I can give them to you. Bruno Losh, average 95, was a stamper; James F. Keenan, Patrick J. McCormick, Albert Klotz, jr., and Frank L. Kocejia. Those were all upon the eligible register and were before you.—A. The information was given at the same time, and it may have been that the number was actually less than the number required; but I am positively sure that that was the information given me by the officer in charge of the register, and there may have been some misapprehension about it. I have a positive recollection of these men remaining on that list, although they were unavailable utterly from previous records in my office. One of them—I would not like to make a public charge—but one of them to my knowledge had run away while in the place of messenger. robbing the other people, etc., and had per-

Q. All these certifications bore these names.—A. I never took note of them, except in making my selection. My letter is written to prove that fact. I make a selection without looking to see whose name is on there.

Q. You did not then take notice of it?—A. No, sir; I could not do it in any way at all. I believe I am not in the habit of telling untruths on matters of that kind, especially in writing.

Q. On May 6, 1887, a certification was made to fill the position of carrier, and you received the names of two carriers and one clerk, Alexander H. Wigman, the latter having failed in an examination. You selected Wigman first, and afterwards promoted him as an auxiliary carrier in August, 1887.—A. I do not know about the matter to which you refer; but I will say I have affidavits covering all the cases you have referred to. You do not seem to have the affidavits produced. I wish to say to the committee that I have affidavits here of the other two members of the board of examiners, and of other persons knowing all the facts sworn to, covering practically every individual and the particular charges of the United States Civil Service Commission, and I think it is proper for me to ask you to accept them in evidence. They are letter-press copies of the affidavits sent to the President of the United States. I think that they would explain to the Commission itself, if they cared to examine them, just the charges the Commission has made. It is testimony entirely of disinterested persons in every case.

AFTER RECESS.

GEORGE H. PAUL—Recalled.

Mr. PAUL, recalled and examined.

By Mr. WEBSTER:

Q. Did you explain the appointment of Mr. Benjamin F. Langland to the position of stamper? He was appointed to it July 1, 1887, without a certification.—A. Again, Mr. Webster, I think you continually do me injustice by saying he was appointed such and such a date without certification. If you would state what the fact is, he was appointed, and, according to the registry of certification, without certification, it would probably be precisely according to the facts.

Q. There is no registry of certification; it is the certification itself.—A. Well, I mean the original certification.

Q. There is no original certification for his appointment.—A. But when your state to this committee here and to the public in your reports through the Associated Press, that such a thing did occur absolutely without certification it may not be true, as in this case, and I object to the language which you use under such circumstances. I do not want any false impressions to go out. I am very glad of anything which will bring out the facts in the case, and I rely upon that only.

By the CHAIRMAN:

Q. Was the man certified?—A. The man was certified.

Q. Does it appear by the record that he was?—A. I understand it does not; that no record of it was ever made by the secretary.

By Mr. WEBSTER:

Q. Then, so far as the Commission is concerned, they had no knowledge that the man had been certified?—A. They had no knowledge from the record that he had been certified; but the truth is, the exact truth is, it was one of the most responsible positions in my department, on account of the character of the man. He was certified regularly, regularly examined, from the list, and I think the matter could be determined by an examination of the list showing that he would have been the proper appointee at the time.

Q. He could not have been appointed at the time when you appointed him.—A. He may have been appointed——

Q. No; because he had been certified out before. ·If you remember about his case the records show that he was certified to you four times from the carriers' register for the position of carrier, the last certification being dated May 6, 1887. He was not selected by you from any one of these certifications.—A. What number was that?

Q. Forty-one, I think, or 44, is the certification on which his name appeared; he had four certifications, one more than he was entitled to, which was an error of the secretary, as he explained to me on the fourth certification.—A. Certified four times.

Q. By mistake he was certified four times?—A. Yes, sir.

Q. And you did not take him; and two months later, after other certificates had been made, did you not appoint him, not to the place to which he had previously been certified, that is to a carrier's place, but to a place for which he had not passed an examination, and for which he was certified?—A. Yes, sir.

Q. According to the certification books he was never certified?—A. Well, I know that. That is in the usual form. He was certified to me and appointed from a certification. That much I do know.

Q. Well, where is his certification of any kind?—A. I do not know. There is undoubtedly no record of it. I find other cases of the same sort.

Q. Where is the certification that you had? There should be one somewhere?—A. It should be in the record.

Q. How, then, are you in possession of these scrap certificates that you testified here to-day about?—A. Because they were not always taken back to his desk. My practice in business is to file every paper, particularly whenever the paper relates to a matter of business. If I have only one name especially I would bring this in and get back perhaps a memorandum or record—what we call a record—and leave the paper with him; then I would call for it again. I remember very well that one or two of these laid in my drawer—in the drawer of my desk at my left hand, as I think I showed you. I think I showed you some that remained there that he had not taken away. I do not know that there is any obligation upon his part to take that certification away, but I think it would be the proper method of business.

Q. You can not point to any certification now in regard to this man's appointment?—A. I do not know what you mean by "point." I know the fact that he was certified and selected.

The CHAIRMAN. You mean any regular certification.

By Mr. WEBSTER:

Q. There is no regular certification. There is nothing in existence to show that he was ever certified to you.—A. I examined that with reference to it. You say the date is what?

Q. He was appointed by you July 1, 1887.—A. Yes; 1887.

Q. Well, do you not know of the existence of any certification covering his appointment?—A. I know that there was a certification; but as to its preservation or record I do not know. I know of some other similar cases—one at least.

Q. Do you remember about your explanation to me in regard to that appointment?—**A.** No, sir; I do not. Perhaps that might refresh my recollection.

Q. Did you not suggest to me that you thought Mr. Langland had been selected from one of those four prior certifications by you at a later date, but that in July you took up that old certification and selected his name from it?—**A.** I do not remember.

Q. You stated to me at the time you thought you had selected him from certification No. 44—the last time his name appeared before you; you thought you had recalled that certification and had selected his name from it. I wish you would explain if that was not the case, and why there was no signature attached to that selection.—**A.** Forty-four; now, I can not tell you that case. That was Shidy's, not mine.

Q. If that were the case the certification ought certainly then to have been made up in the certification book, so that there could be no need for any scrap papers about that. It was dated May 6, 1887, according to the book. You had selected this man, Alexander H. Wigman, who failed to pass the examination at all, and then you say you took from this certification—that you think you took from this certification—later on, the 1st of July of that year, there having been a number of other certifications, that you called for that book and took Langland's name for stamper. You would not have needed any scrap paper for that. It was in the book. Then how can you account for your not signing for it?—**A.** I will say generally as to signing, I signed for the selections as they were presented to me by the secretary, as I explained in the forenoon. If a man had been selected, certified, appointed, and reported to the department and the book had never been presented to me, I do not think I should be aware of the fact that he had not been signed for. I had no means of knowing——

Q. Well, if that were the case you would not have selected him from any scrap-paper certification?—**A.** Why not?

Q. He was in the book by an old certification entered in May, 1887, and, if you had drawn his name from that, what necessity was there for any scrap-paper certification?—**A.** I do not know why there should not be a scrap-paper certification the same as in other cases. Will you be kind enough to read my testimony?

Q. Yes; I have it here and will read it in a moment:

The postmaster addressed the secretary of the board. As to the case of Langland, previously referred to in this testimony, the record does not appear to show his selection. I have positive recollection that he was selected from a regular certification in the manner such certificates were usually made. My impression is that his certification, 44—Wigman was first selected for the place of carrier, and in the meantime Langland had consented to take the place of stamper, and that the certification was then recalled and Langland selected as the second man from that certification. My further impression is that the failure to enter on the record of certification the selection of Langland arises from the fact that the second selection from the same certification was not the rule in this office, and that in making up the record, the secretary, having received my signature to the first selection of that certification, deemed the record satisfied and omitted to enter the second selection of Langland, and that I, when such record was made, would have passed over the entry in the same manner and for the same reasons in giving my signature.

And you asked Shidy if that might not have been the way the error occurred?—**A.** He says that might have been the way the error occurred. That is all I know about it. I only know that he was selected from a regular certification. I forget the circumstances.

Q. Would you have selected a stamper from a carrier's certification certified to you for a carrier?—A. No, sir; I would not. I do not think——

Q. Well, but if you did make the selection, why you made it from a certification for a carrier and appointed him to a stamper's place, did you not?—A. No, sir; I do not remember any such case.

Q. Did you not appoint him to a stamper's place?—A. Who?

Q. Mr. Langland?—A. Yes, sir; I think so but I will not be certain.

Q. And the selection was made from certification 44? The selection was made from a carrier's certification?—A. I do not know that I did that. I do not think that I did do so. I do not think it was in that way.

Q. But that is the statement you made to me in questioning Mr. Shidy.—A. Did 1 say he was selected as a carrier?

Q. You said that you first selected Mr. Wigman, and afterwards recalled that and took Mr. Langland. Whether that was not the way?——A. That might have been the way of it.

Q. He says you did that, and that the board concurred.—A. Let me see. As the case now——

Q. Not just now—just simply the appointment of Langland without certification so far as the records of your office go.—A. I am not aware that I ever used the word "recall." there. Langland came back to me, which is probably the meaning of it.

Q. Would you, in your opinion, have the right to recall the certification?—A. No, sir; I never did to my knowledge. If Langland was selected from a carrier's certification it would have been what I call gross misconduct.

Q. But you state in here in substance that you think we concurred by recalling that certification and took the name off of it.—A. There is some construction to be placed on that language. It is barely possible that Langland was certified as a carrier, and subsequently he was selected and certified as a stamper.

Q. That is not the case here at all. You are trying to get away from the statement as to the effect of this certification 44, which was recalled and Langland's name taken off of it, and you go on to explain that it was not the custom at your office to do that.—A. No, sir, it was not. I know——

Q. And that is the way in which it was done?—A. The recall of him by himself or the secretary?

Q. By you.—A. I think there is a misapprehension about that recall by the secretary. It probably means——

Q. No; the secretary would not recall it. It is your recall.—A. He may have made a certification and recalled it. He might have done that for correction or something of that kind.

Q. No, sir; you had made your selection already from this certification.—A. I only know this, that I never knowingly selected a stamper from a carrier's certification in my life. It would be simply——

Q. Well, this testimony is here. I wish you to explain that statement. It says——A. He may have been coming back to me if you use the word "recall" in that sense. It will possibly explain it, but I can not remember that.

Q. You appointed Langland to the position of stamper?—A. I am not certain about that. Perhaps the official record shows that.

Q. Have you the list?

By the CHAIRMAN:

Q. Does it not show here on your list that you appointed him as stamper?—A. No, sir.

Q. What does it show?—A. I think Mr. Langland's name did not appear on the list at all; I think not. I do not think his name appears here at all.

Q. Was he appointed to any position in your post-office?—A. Mr. Langland, as I stated in my original testimony, was certified to me and appointed to a position. I have no recollection of his ever having been a stamper, although he might have been. Possibly he was in the lower department of the office. I do not think his name appears on the list at all. Does he appear on the record of certification?

By Mr. WEBSTER:

Q. He is on the record of certification. He is not on any certification except his certification which you had passed by——A. He appears on no record, as I understand it, of certification, as a selection from any certification.

Q. No; there is no certification upon his selection.—A. The fact of his selection I remember distinctly, the certification to me.

Q. Well, but do not pass this. Here are four of them back here. He was four times certified to you back there. Do you recollect any other certifications than these four in May, or preceding May 6. I think they were in May. They were all in May—May 6?—A. How many did you say?

Q. The four.—A. Yes, sir.

Q. Well, on this one from which the selection was said to have been made there were Langland, Bauch, and Byrne, carriers, and Wigman, a clerk, all certified for carriers' places, and you selected Wigman?—A. Yes, sir. My impression is that Wigman was examined for a clerkship. His percentage was certified by Shidy to be higher than the others.

Q. Yes; he failed to pass, and July 1, 1887 (I have the report here of the appointments in your office), July 1, 1887—the date of this was August 10. He was appointed in the place of Mr. Wines?—A. Stamper in the mailing division. What date?

Q. July 1, 1887.—A. He was certified and selected; there is no question about the fact at all.

Q. You know of no certification to show that?—A. I know of no record of certification; no, sir.

Q. That is the original certification that you call the scrap papers?—A. Those were never regularly preserved.

Q. Nothing that you can produce now to show that fact?—A. Nothing that I could under any circumstances. Nothing that I could produce in here about his appointment. It is not my business to preserve them.

Q. Do you remember that Charles J. Cumming was appointed to the position of stamper May 1, 1888? Can you tell whether he was certified to you and selected from a regular certification?—A. Yes, sir; I think I can.

The CHAIRMAN. What is the name?

Mr. WEBSTER. Charles J. Cumming, who was alluded to in another case.—A. He was the man who was restored by the Commission to the list.

Q. I can give you something of the history of that case if that is what you are looking for there. I will give that if you desire it, or will quote your statement. We have already had him before us here on four certifications—one, No. 54, void—the one that is spoken of as marked "void"—one, No. 58, for carrier; one, No. 59, for stamper, and one No. 60, for stamper; four certifications that have been made. That was on

February 18 on the certification book. You appointed him May 1, 1888.—
A. Whom are you talking about?

Q. Cumming—to the position of stamper.—A. Do you mean that the record says so?

Q. Yes, sir.—A. Oh, well——

Q. Then you appointed him May 1, 1888?—A. 1888—excuse me just a moment. You say that he was appointed on such a date. You have already said that twice, I believe, now.

The CHAIRMAN. He says the record shows all that?—A. Yes, sir. What is the number?

Mr. WEBSTER. The number of certification?—A. On which his name appears?

Q. The number of his old certification—not the one from which you made his selection; you did not select him from any one. They were 54, 58, 59, and 60.—A. Yes, sir. On the receipt of the order of the Commissioner restoring him to the list from the register of eligibles. (After a pause.) I was about to give that testimony, Mr. Chairman. The secretary brought me the name of Mr. Cumming, as per the order, as he understood it, of the Commission as the person who was to be restored to the right of certification, as having been omitted. That was the action of the secretary. But Mr. Cumming was never appointed by me to any classified position in the world, and never held one. That is a fact.

Q. Never appointed to any classified position?—A. To any classified position at all.

By the CHAIRMAN:

Q. Well, what position did he hold?—A. He held an exempted position—an excepted position. He was appointed to one of the excepted positions—excepted by the Department; the position of custody of stamps—for the sale of stamps in the department. I have his affidavit here to that effect. "Charles J. Cumming"——

The CHAIRMAN. He says his affidavit is there to the effect that he never was appointed to any position except the position of stamp-seller.—A. (Reading.) "After I had been certified three times I was restored to the list and made eligible for appointment by order of the Commission, but was never appointed to a civil service or a classified position before or after or since said order, as the place I filled was declared exempt." That is the fact about it.

By Mr. WEBSTER:

Q. Well, you appointed him on May 1, 1887, did you not?—A. He said himself——

Q. May 1, 1888, I mean.—A. (Reading):

STATE OF WISCONSIN, Milwaukee County :

Charles J. Cumming, being duly sworn, deposes and says that he has read a supplementary report of the Civil-Service Commission in which it is stated that after a man has been certified three times and was not chosen and therefore was not eligible, the postmaster truly proceeded to appoint him; and said Cumming further deposes and says that if this statement refers to him, as he believes, from the circumstances, it wholly explained by the fact that after I had been certified three times I was restored to the list and made eligible for appointment by order of the Commission, but was never appointed to a civil-service or a classified position before or after or since said order, as the place I filled was declared exempt.

CHARLES J. CUMMING.

Q. Well, you appointed him May 1, 1888. Did you not recommend or sign that as the date of his appointment?—A. The particular date I can not state.

Q. Well, there is that list you brought with you—this list?—A. What is the number of the certification?

Q. Well, there was no certification for that, unless it was of a very late date?—A. Cumming appears here somewhere, does he not? This is the secretary's record. The certification shows that he was certified September 7. He was appointed to an excepted place, I think, May 1.

Q. To an excepted place. What was the place he was appointed to, then?—A. Custody of the stamps.

Q. What was his grade—what was the name of the place to which he was appointed?—A. Appointed a clerk.

Q. Stamper?—A. No, sir.

The CHAIRMAN. A clerk.

Mr. WEBSTER. But he never served in that way?—A. I think——

Mr. WEBSTER. This report was made August 10, 1888, and shows that Charles J. Cumming was appointed stamper May 1, 1888, and was certified three times without having his eligibility restored by the Commission. Now, that was an appointment as stamper at that time?

The CHAIRMAN. Well, but he says he was never appointed to that position.

Mr. WEBSTER. I want to know another thing [holding a paper in his hand].

Mr. STONE. What is that?

Mr. WEBSTER. That is the report made by the secretary of the board?—A. I will say further, and perhaps throw a little more light on it——

The CHAIRMAN. Just one moment; answer this question so that the committee will understand it. Is this report made to the Civil Service Commission correct in the statement that Cumming was appointed on May 1; eighteen hundred and eighty what—what year is it?

Mr. WEBSTER. May 1, 1888.

By the CHAIRMAN:

Q. May 1, 1888; to the position of stamper. Now, one moment. Answer that; you stated here a few moments ago that he never held a position under the civil-service rules, but he was appointed. Now, was he appointed as a stamper or not? If he was not appointed as a stamper, and this report says he was, is not the report incorrect in so far as it relates to that item?—A. Yes, sir; if you will allow me state my recollection of it I think you will understand my testimony. I think when his name was certified as a stamper he was appointed, that is, nominally, and that he might have declined. He never served as stamper. That is my recollection of it. I think he declined the position very promptly.

Q. I understood you to say——A. It was my duty to make a selection, you understand.

Q. Yes; I understand.—A. And nominally he was appointed; but not actually, because he declined without going into the service.

Q. Well, I understand you; the reason I asked you that question was because I understood you a few moments ago to say that he was never appointed to the position——A. Never held the position.

The CHAIRMAN. Well, I understand you.

By Mr. WEBSTER:

Q. You say he was appointed to the position of stamper, but never performed the duty?—A. Never performed any duties of stamper, I am very positive. I know that he declined.

Q. In your examination before me, I asked you questions in regard to Cumming. "In the report of the secretary it appears that Charles

J. Cumming was appointed May the 1st, 1888, without certification. He had been certified three times without selection. His eligibility was restored by the Commission June 16, 1888. How was he appointed without certification on the date mentioned, June 16?" You say "the question of Mr. Cumming's appointment was referred to the Commission. The letter of the Commission was construed to cover the original appointment of May 1, 1888, and he was restored to his position in the office, his service having been suspended in the meantime, and the record should be duly corrected as to his eligibility, in accordance with the decision of the Commission, in case his eligibility is deemed not to date back to his original appointment." All that is underlined there and corrected as your correction.—A. What is the question about?

Q. The question that I have just read.—A. I do not quite understand what it is.

Q. Well, I ask you to explain about how Charles J. Cumming was appointed in your office to the position of stamper, May 1, 1888?—A. Yes, sir.

Q. There being nowhere in existence any certification for that appointment?—A. Yes, sir.

Q. That can be found?—A. Yes, sir. Mr. Cumming was duly certified and selected for stamper and declined.

Q. And declined, but was duly certified?

By Mr. STONE:

Q. Let me ask that question. You state now, Mr. Paul, that Mr. Cumming never accepted any appointment or performed any service as stamper?—A. Not to my recollection. I am very positive he never did. I think the appointment remained suspended until the instruction of the Commission was received; at one time or another, but the precise date I can not recall.

Q. Your statement a moment ago also was to the effect that when he was offered the position of stamper he promptly declined it?—A. That is what I mean when he declined it; and I think he remained on the books and was understood to be eligible by myself, probably with the consent of the Commission; but he was not improperly appointed as stamper at all. He was selected from the eligible list, and I think subsequently there was some action with reference to Cumming that involved perhaps the appointment to a clerkship.

Q. I understand; but I am trying to get at the point. As I understand Major Webster was speaking a moment ago that when Cumming was appointed in May, it was to a place not excepted from the classified service.—A. It is my impression that he declined the place of stamper, and it was proposed to make him a clerk, and that the whole matter was suspended until the order of the Commission could be received.

Q. That is the explanation which you made in your first examination as read by Mr. Webster just now.—A. Well, I did not know that; I did not recognize it.

Q. But I mean when you were examined a few moments ago you made the statement to which I have just called your attention.—A. Yes, sir.

Q. Now, Mr. Webster read a question which he propounded to you at Milwaukee when he was there in 1888, in substance the same as this that I have just put to you, and your answer then was as it is recorded here.—A. At Milwaukee?

Mr. STONE. Yes, sir.

Mr. WEBSTER. The question of Mr. Cumming's appointment was referred to the Commission.

Mr. STONE. Read this.

Mr. WEBSTER. That is what I am reading from. That is the answer which was referred to the Commission on receipt of the restoration to eligibility. "The letter of the Commission was construed to cover the original appointment from May 1, 1888. He was restored to his position in the office, his service having been suspended in the meantime, and the records should be duly corrected as to his eligibility in accordance with the decision of the Commission, in case his eligibility was deemed not to date back to his original appointment."

Mr. STONE. Now, he says you ought to reconcile any discrepancies, real or apparent, between this statement made in Milwaukee, and the statement you have made here to-day concerning Mr. Cumming.

The WITNESS. What is the discrepancy, Mr. Stone?

Mr. STONE. Well, he calls attention——

By Mr. WEBSTER:

Q. He was appointed there apparently, and you are asked the question about his appointment of May 1, 1888, to the position of stamper?—A. Yes, sir.

Q. Illegally, without certification; and you now explain it by saying that he was never appointed to a classified place. He was appointed to an excepted place there. You were explaining that his appointment was irregular; but that you immediately suspended him as soon as you learned it, and applied for authority to restore him to the eligible register, and that you sought that authority to be given you there.—A. My recollection of the facts as the conversation proceeds are substantially these : Cumming was certified to me the first time as a stamper. He appeared at my office and declined the position, and then subsequently I construed the case of a certain clerkship, that of the custody of stamps at the office, an excepted position. I had some doubt upon the subject, but proposed to give him that position if he would accept it. In the meantime, in order to cover all questions as to the facts the opinion of the Commission was asked as to his position, and a request made to restore him. We received the information or action of the Commission. In the meantime, or about that time, the Department sent him an act of the persons exempted from examination in the office, and that I construed to cover the whole matter. I think that is as near as my recollection goes.

Q. Did you make that explanation to me when I was in Milwaukee?— A. Perhaps not. I do not remember. It is very difficult to remember these details.

Q. Did you not explain to me then that you thought his appointment was all right as stamper and that you were authorized to make it by the Civil Service Commission?—A. Yes, sir; that was so.

Q. And that was to the position of stamper?—A. Yes, sir; that is what I say now, but he declined the position.

Q. When did he decline it?—A. He declined, I think, upon receiving his appointment; that is my impression.

Q. When did he go on duty in the office?—A. Well, he did not go on duty finally until he received information, I think, of the action of the Commission. I am not positive about the exact date.

Q. Well, he did not go on until after you had obtained the information from the Commission?—A. I will not be positive about whether he went on at that time or not.

Q. Did you not state to me that he had been on duty and you suspended him until you could get this information from the Commission?—

A. I think very likely it is a fact that his appointment was suspended, but not his service.

Q. When did he go on duty, then?—A. Well, sir, I can not state the precise date. I have no means of recollecting.

Q. Did he go on duty prior to the time of the investigation that we held at Milwaukee?—A. Well, I can not state that. He went on duty 1 think, permanently, on receipt of the order of the Commission, but I will not be positive about that. It may have been—I do not see what the question really is, anyway.

Q. The question involved the appointment of a man without any certification to you whatever so far as to any record, either informal or formal.—A. Well, I have given my testimony upon that point.

Q. Well, now you say he was appointed to an excepted place, do you?—A. Subsequently; yes, sir.

Q. When?—A. Well, that date I can not give you.

Q. Prior to the investigation that we held in Milwaukee in September, 1888?—A. But he gives it himself.

Mr. STONE. He swore he had never been appointed to any position under the civil service.

The WITNESS. Mr. Cumming does not give it in his affidavit.

Mr. WEBSTER. You made a report to the Commission, did you not, in August of the number of excepted places — gave a complete list? This is a report of that, I believe, of all your excepted places, and the names of persons on duty in excepted places.—A. What is the date of making the appointment, May 1, 1887?

By the CHAIRMAN:

Q. May 1?—A. 1887.

Q. May 1, 1887. Did you find the name of Charles J. Cumming on that list?—A. No, sir.

Q. Not on the list?—A. I find in that place the name of another person holding it.

Mr. WEBSTER. Then Charles J. Cumming's name is not on your list of excepted persons (persons excepted from examination) that you sent to the Commission?—A. What is the date of that?

The CHAIRMAN. The date of the letter is August 6, 1888.—A. What is the date of the letter of the Commission?

Mr. WEBSTER. June 16, 1888.—A. June 16, 1888—it may be an omission from the record.

The CHAIRMAN. Well, now you have just told that. Here is Albert Trumpf. He was appointed stamper March 1, 1888, in place of some one who was transferred. I can not read his name.

Mr. WEBSTER. Wigman.

By the CHAIRMAN:

Q. And you state that this man Cumming was afterwards put in Trumpf's place?—A. Yes, sir; he succeeded him.

Q. Well, but that is considerably over a year after you made the appointment of Cumming.—A. I have already explained that Mr. Cumming did not immediately take possession. Of course the place had been filled.

Q. I did not understand that answer, please.—A. My remembrance, Mr. Chairman, of the fact is that in the first place Mr. Cumming was certified to me as a stamper. He declined the position. In the next place I proposed to transfer in the office Mr. Trumpf from the general delivery, and to put Mr. Cumming in his place.

Q. At that time?—A. Subsequently; then Mr. Cumming was nominally placed in this position until Mr. Trumpf's transfer and finally Mr. Cumming was placed in the position of Mr. Trumpf. Mr. Trumpf went into the money-order office. Now, that is the order of proceeding, but the dates I can not give you.

By Mr. WEBSTER:

Q. Do you mean to say that Mr. Cumming was never employed in your office at all until he took the place of Mr. Trumpf as stamper clerk?—A. I think not.

Q. Which was an excepted place?—A. I think not.

Q. Never had any employment prior to that. Did you not admit to me that he was employed at the time I was in Milwaukee taking testimony about the first part of September?—A. What time was Mr. Trumpf transferred? That may be possible.

Q. You do not state, but up to August 6, 1888, he had not apparently been transferred. He was then stamp clerk.—A. I presume that was the exact case. If I made that statement I think it must be correct.

Q. Was he not employed prior to the time of my investigation in your office, as stamper?—A. I do not think he was there.

Q. You think he never was.?—A. I think he never was. He says himself in his affidavit he never was in any classified position.

Q. Prior to September. I made the investigation between September 4 and 10.—A. Yes.

Q. Prior to that time you say that Cumming was never employed in your office as stamper?—A. I think he never went into the service. No, sir; that is my impression about it.

By the CHAIRMAN:

Q. Do you recollect, Mr. Paul, about the time when Cumming first went into the service in any capacity?—A. I can not give the date.

Q. Was it in 1887?—A. I can not give the date of any clerk in my office without referring to the record. I had entirely too much to remember of that kind to undertake to do it. It is impossible for me to remember these with any degree of certainty, but I can not see the point involved in all this.

By Mr. WEBSTER:

Q. The point is this: I asked you the question at the start, whether there was any certification at any time whatever for the appointment of Charles J. Cumming for the position of stamper on the 1st of May, 1888?—A. The answer to that is: I answered in the affirmative.

Q. That he was certified?—A. Yes, sir; that he was certified and selected for the place of stamper.

Q. When was that certification made?—A. Now you commence to ask me details. It is impossible for any living man to remember——

The CHAIRMAN. The witness has stated that the certification was made, even if it does not appear in the official records.

By Mr. WEBSTER:

Q. You admitted to me when I was up there prior to the coming of the Commission. Do you remember?—A. No, sir. I do not remember.

Q. Let me read this letter of yours. Perhaps it may throw some light upon things:

May 30, 1888.

Perhaps it will be best to go back to the letter of Mr. Shidy, of May 17, 1888.

MILWAUKEE, WIS., *May* 17, 1888.

SIRS: Charles Cumming, an eligible under the civil-service rules, was on the 18th day of February, 1888, certified for appointment as stamper, which position he refused to accept. He was again certified the same day for the same position. This was his third certification, as he had been twice certified previously. He has now reconsidered his refusal to accept the position of stamper, and the postmaster wishes to appoint him. Can he do so? An immediate answer will greatly favor

Yours, respectfully,

H. SHIDY, *Secretary.*

CIVIL SERVICE COMMISSION,
    Washington, D. C.

In answer to that the Commission stated he could not be certified; that he had already been certified. The substance of that it is not necessary to read.

MILWAUKEE, WIS., *May* 30, 1888.

Hon. JOHN H. OBERLY,
    President Civil Service Commission:

SIR: Mr. H. Shidy, secretary board of examiners at this office, has shown me your letter of the 25th instant, in which you give the opinion that Charles Cumming is not entitled to further certification under the rules in force February 18 last, on the ground that "when the position of stamper—the position for which he was examined—was offered to Cumming and declined by him, his rights under his examination were exhausted."

I think the conclusion in this case based on a misapprehension of the facts, arising from an imperfect statement of them by the secretary, and is, therefore, unjust to the person whose privileges are involved, and also to the public service. Referring to the record for verification, permit me to state——

I would like to state here in reference to the record——

The WITNESS. That is what letter?

Mr. WEBSTER (continuing the reading of the letter):

Charles Cumming was not examined for the place of stamper, but for that of letter carrier. At the time he was first certified to me for a stamper his name was at the head of the eligible list for the place of carrier, and, as the stampers' list was nearly exhausted, his name was used simply to make the certification as to number complete. This without his knowledge or request. On the same day (February 18) he was certified three times; first as carrier, when an eligible for clerk was appointed, and twice for stamper under circumstances as above stated. But he was not examined for stamper, did not then desire the place of stamper, and declined the place of stamper simply because he preferred the place for which he was examined. He was not appointed a carrier, because I did not believe him old enough and strong enough at that time for the duty.

Has he thus forfeited his "rights," as expressed by you? In other words, has the Government forfeited its rights to a first-class man, marking 89, by certifying his name to an inferior position without his consent? Can the appointing official sacrifice all the eligibles on the list by calling for their certifications to inferior positions, which he must know they will not accept, without their knowledge or consent?

Mr. Cumming declined lower positions while he thought the opportunity possible for appointment to the position to which he aspired; and now that such opportunity has passed away, is willing to accept a lower place, to the advantage of the service, and I accordingly nominated him for the position of stamper, holding his acceptance subject to your opinion; but I had not dreamed that the Commission had closed the door of public service against an eligible of higher grade.

Respectfully asking further consideration of this case, I am, very truly,

GEO. H. PAUL, *P. M.*

That is your letter in which you state the fact that you had nominated him for the position of stamper on the 30th of May.—A. The 30th of May. That is undoubtedly the fact; the letter so states.

Q. But consent was not then given; and subsequently, on the 16th of June, 1888, it was. I read further:

MILWAUKEE, WIS., *June* 9, 1888.

Hon. JOHN H. OBERLY,
    Acting President Civil Service Commission:

SIR: Replying to your communication of 6th instant, permit me to state that Cumming's name appears at the head of the register of eligibles for carrier at this office, as having been examined October 19, 1887, with an average standing of 89.8, and that the secretary of the local board claims to have duly reported the examination of that date. Your statement of all the facts as to Cumming is accordingly correct, and your conclusion that " he was and is entitled to three certifications for position in the grade for which he was examined " accords with my opinion and action in this particular.

I shall request the secretary of the board of examiners at this office to forward to you at once a duplicate report of the examination of October 19, 1887.

You remark, further, that " the only circumstance which could justify his (Cumming's) certification to the position of stamper, even with his consent, would be the depletion of the eligible register below the number required for a single certification," etc. Such was precisely the fact in the case of Cumming, and the depletion of the stamper list could not well have been foreseen. In fact, the depletion of lists as to competent men can rarely be foreseen, or provided for, without a considerable increase in the number of examinations, much to the inconvenience of the public service at this office, where clerical aid is limited to the last point of endurance.

Moreover, to make certification from a higher to a lower grade is obviously a great advantage to the public service, since it not only provides for the deficiency of depleted lists, but enables the appointing officer to secure a higher grade of service than otherwise.

Furthermore, certifications from higher to lower grades was distinctly authorized at this office, in a letter from the Civil Service Commission, dated September 18, 1885, and signed by Robert D. Graham, secretary, in which he says: "Those who have taken higher examinations as clerks or carriers may, of course, be certified to these lower places, and for this purpose may be transferred to the lower registers on their request." And certifications of this kind have been frequently made to me at this office, under this authority, largely to the benefit of the service, inasmuch as it has in many cases secured a better ability and education in lower places than could otherwise be obtained, and also permitting more convenience in promotions on the ground of qualification and merit. This is illustrated in the case of Cumming, standing at 90 on clerical list and accepting the place of stamper.

Respectfully,

GEO. H. PAUL, P. M.

You say " accepting the place of stamper." Now, the letter of the Commission in reply to that was dated "June 16, 1888," and authorizes the restoration of his name to the eligible list for the purpose of certification to you for a position and appointment. Now that shows the argument that you made in the case to secure his appointment or the approval of the Commission to the appointment that you had already made by appointing him to the position of stamper on May 1.—A. Why not put that letter in testimony?

Mr. WEBSTER. This can go in evidence if it is not in evidence, and as an exhibit. It is a part of this——

The CHAIRMAN. And the appointment was made before you had the authority to make it. That is the way I understand it from the reading of the letter.—A. No, sir; I did not so understand it.

Mr. WEBSTER. The appointment was made before the letter or any of those letters were written. You appointed Charles J. Cumming before you wrote any of those letters, did you not?—A. I selected him from a certification.

By the CHAIRMAN:

Q. When did you appoint him?—A. Well, I can not tell.

Q. Is it not on your list there?—A. How?

Q. Is it not on your list that he was appointed May 1, to date from May 1?—A. Yes, sir.

Q. That is the date of the appointment?—A. That is to an excepted position. Of course I can not give all the dates of my clerks except from the records as they existed at that time.

Q. Well, of course the record shows, then, that the appointment was made May 1, and that the authority for the appointment and the letters in the case were in June, 1888, after the act had been done.—A. But you understand, as I do, when he was appointed it was not on the authority of the letter, but to an excepted position which did not require any authority. That is my——

By Mr. WEBSTER:

Q. He was appointed as stamper, as shown by these records?—A. Yes, sir.

Q. The whole of your letter is in regard to a stamper—asking his appointment as stamper, getting his certification by permission?—A. Yes, sir.

Q. Did he decline the position you offered?—A. Yes, sir; but his declination was made between that time. He at one time declined, and at another accepted. Now, I can not arrange these facts. You will have to give me time to look them up.

Q. Does not this report, which you have in your own handwriting corrected, show that there was a certification to you on September 7 for that appointment?—A. September 7. That is Shidy's record. That is all I know about that.

Q. We commenced our investigation at your office September 4; then he made the certification to you to cover the appointment of a man who was already in your office when we commenced our investigation.—A. If the committee would like a complete record of Shidy's action in the matter I would be very glad to furnish it, but I can not give it from remembrance. I will say, however, that he never was to my knowledge appointed without authority under any circumstances. There were particular pains taken, as my letter shows, and I think he never held a classified position at all—that is, occupied one. He may have been nominated——

Q. You stated to me when I was in Milwaukee that he had been suspended pending this investigation of the committee.—A. That is possible.

Q. And that you thought that that permission covered his appointment; that there was no necessity for any certification; that you did not have any name.—A. Yes, sir; possibly I may have regarded it as covering the appointment. I will say there was no appointment to any classified position without certification. No appointment——

Q. Thomas J. O'Neill was appointed in your office, was he not, as a stamper?—A. I think there was such a man.

Q. August 1, 1888, was the date of his appointment?—A. Thomas J. O'Neill, as stamper; yes, sir.

Q. Was he not actually at work in your office at the time we commenced our investigation there in September, 1888, as a stamper?—A. His appointment was August 1.

Q. Then he was actually employed there in the first part of the fall when we were investigating?—A. I can not say as to that. I presume so.

Q. He had been at work there prior to our investigation as stamper?—A. I think so.

Q. Had he been certified to you at the time when we commenced our investigation in any manner, or even as stamper?—A. The record has him certified on the 7th of September.

Q. Well, we commenced our investigation the 4th of September there, you will remember?—A. No, sir; I do not remember.

Q. He had not been certified to you when we were there—when we commenced our investigation?—A. What is the question about it?

Q. I want to know by what authority you appointed him to the position of stamper.—A. Prior to September 7?

Q. Yes.—A. Undoubtedly to fill a vacancy. I do not think he was appointed then. Let me see. Did you say he had not been certified?

3117——17

Q. The certification as on there is August 7, is it not—according to your statement?

The CHAIRMAN. September 7.—A. September is given as the date on the record of the board as the date of the certification.

By Mr. WEBSTER:

Q. There had been no certification prior to that date, had there?—A. Well, I have a memorandum here that this man was certified as the only man on the stamper list, and that certification was made in July.

Q. In July?—A. In July. It is so here on my memorandum. I think that is from Shidy's memorandum on the back. Whether he put it on afterwards or not I can not tell.

Q. There was nothing upon the back when we reported there, was there?—A. I can not say.

Q. Do you not remember signing for that, and that certification being made during the time we were at your office?—A. I remember something about it, but I can not say.

Q. There was no certification on the book when we came there, was there?—A. Well, that I can not say, Mr. Webster, whether there was or not. If you have any statement by me there I would like to see it.

Q. Do you remember calling in Mr. Shidy and asking him to explain to you what this man was certified from and what he would be certified from?—A. I remember something similar to that as to some man, but I can not tell you anything about this man.

Q. There was no kind of certification when we were there in regard to him.—A. On record, you mean?

Q. Of any kind?—A. No, the record——

Q. Did you not make diligent search at that time to find something to give—— A. Sir?

Q. At that time when we were there is that not true?—A. Well, I can not remember, sir, what occurred in the case at all except this memorandum.

By the CHAIRMAN:

Q. Was this memorandum in existence at that time, or has that been made since?—A. I can not say whether that is a copy or not.

Q. Was that sheet of paper in existence at that time?—A. No, sir; this paper was not in existence.

Q. It was made since?—A. Yes, sir; it was made since. I think I made a memorandum of the facts afterwards. You call attention to the fact that the original certification was made in July. I do not know whether he has an affidavit on the subject or not. There is certainly no evidence of any impropriety on the part of the postmaster that I can see.

By Mr. WEBSTER:

Q. There is one other point here that I want to make an inquiry about in regard to Mr. Trumpf. You state, I think in answer to some questions yesterday by Mr. Lind, that Mr. Trumpf was appointed to an excepted place and never held any other position whatever than an excepted place, as I understood you?—A. Yes, sir; that is what I said myself.

Q. Did you not have him certified to you for appointment?—A. I can not say, sir.

Q. Was he not certified to you on April 14, 1888?—A. I think not, sir; still he may have been.

Q. Well, the record does show that he was certified to you on April 14, 1888, for a position as clerk, and that he was selected and that his appointment dated March 1, 1888. He was not examined until March 10, 1888, and he entered upon the duties of the office March 23, 1888.—A. Certified April 14—appointed March 1?

Q. Yes.—A. That is the way you have it.

Q. That is right.—A. Appointed to an excepted place; was never appointed under that certification.

Q. You had appointed him already to a position which you thought to be excepted, had you not?—A. Yes, sir; I thought so.

Q. You were afterwards informed that that place was not excepted; that you had no right to except it without the authority of the Post-master-General?—A. No, sir.

Q. Did you not write to the Postmaster-General to get that place excepted afterwards?—A. I have no recollection of doing so. Possibly I did, but I have no recollection of it.

Q. Now, in answer to a question which I put to you, you said—I will give you the question:

Q. Albert L. Trumpff was appointed as a clerk on March 1, 1888, on a certification dated April 14, 1888. Explain that appointment.

Your answer was—

Trumpff was appointed to a place regarded by me as excepted, being personally responsible to the appointing officer for funds placed in his possession as stamp clerk at the general delivery window. At that time he was eligible to certification, I think. Subsequently, for the first time my attention was called to the fact that in order that a position should be excepted it should be reported formally through the Post-Office Department to the Commission. This information came from a letter from the Commission, I think, to Dr. Shidy. I immediately called for a certification from the board and appointed Mr. Trumpff under it in addition to his previous appointment until the position could be certified to the Commission through the Department at Washington as an excepted one. Immediately after such action I received from the Department itself a notification to furnish a list of all excepted positions in the office for approval by the Commission, which I did, including the position occupied by Mr. Trumpff.

A. Here is Mr. Trumpff's statement in explanation of the matter, made of his own accord.

Q. I only wanted to ask you whether you did not appoint him to that position without any certification originally.—A. I think I did.

Q. Did you know at that time that he had not been examined?—A. I did not know whether he had a certification or not. I appointed him, as I supposed, to an excepted position.

Q. Did you know at that time that he had not been examined, either?—A. He had not been examined. No, sir. I was very sorry, indeed, that he had not. That is not the fact, but still I prefer to find my own dates [reading]:

STATE OF WISCONSIN, *Milwaukee County, ss:*

Albert Trumpff, being duly sworn, deposes and says that he has read a statement published in the so-called supplemental report of the Civil Service Commission as emanating from one H. Shidy, late of the Milwaukee post-office, declaring that I was appointed to a position in said office March 1, 1888, again about the 23d, and not even examined until March 17, the papers not being marked and listed till the 30th nor myself certified till April 14, 1888. Said Trumpff further states that he has never received an appointment to any civil service position in this office whatever. "It is true that I was duly examined, receiving the second highest mark on the whole list, and was certified and subsequently nominated to a position which was immediately filled by me, but was declared by the Commissioner an excepted position before I began work which fact sufficiently accounts for the misapprehension of the Commission.

STATE OF WISCONSIN, *Milwaukee County.*

Subscribed and sworn to the 22d of July, 1889, before me.

T. B. FAHOEL,
Notary Public, Milwaukee County, State of Wisconsin.

Q. It was not an excepted place at the time you made the appointment?—A. Yes, sir; I regarded it as an excepted place under general law.

Q. It was not in fact an excepted place. It had not been excepted by the Post-Office Department?—A. I think so. I spoke of that as an expression of opinion by the Commission. All places of responsibility to the postmaster under his bond, I think, are considered as excepted places.

Q. You so consider it?—A. Yes, sir.

Q. But he had not been excepted by any authority?—A. No clerk in the Milwaukee ——

Q. Had he been excepted by any authority at that time when you made the appointment?—A. No clerk in the Milwaukee ——

Q. Will you answer the question about this?—A. Yes, sir.

Q. Had he been excepted at the time you made the appointment?—A. Well, if you want me to answer that question you must not allow me simply to make a statement that is only partial in the matter.

Q. I want an answer to that question. That is all I want.—A. I think a statement of the entire fact is simply just.

By the CHAIRMAN:

Q. According to your idea your opinion was that it was an excepted position?—A. Yes, sir; under the law.

Q. That is all that is necessary for you to state. You understood it so?—A. It was a position as much excepted as the chief of the money-order division. It was excepted in the same sense as any other position in my office.

Mr. STONE. There had been, in point of fact, no action of the Department especially excepting this particular place?—A. Not technically according to the law, but the law excepted these positions, and we postmasters always recognize the law in regard to them.

Mr. THOMPSON. This is taken from the National Democrat, but it is said to be a copy of a letter published in the New York Star. Mr. Paul says:

Further and again, I deny that I ever misrepresented to the Commissioners the time when my commission would expire. On the contrary, I gave them the exact date, and can prove it.

Now, Mr. Paul, is that correct?

The WITNESS. Yes, sir; I think it is. The whole statement is correct; if the chairman will allow me——

The CHAIRMAN. Mr. Stone, at this time do you desire to examine the witness?

The WITNESS. I would like to state one word in explanation. I did not ever purposely or in fact in my own opinion misrepresent the time when my commission would expire. I think I gave to one or all the members of the Commission the exact date when my commission would be out, but I did say that my time was about up, because I had arranged for the selection of my successor, and requested that his name be sent on for appointment as early as practicable. Now, the substance of all that is this: I am very certain I did say, "As to a portion of those facts, they can be proven, and I think all of them. If you will give me your attention I think I will prove the entire statement." I can not see that it is essential anyway, because I said very pointedly that my time was about out, and the Commission itself, without such examination, ought to know when the commission of every postmaster expires if they do not. That is all I have to say.

By Mr. STONE :

Q. You were appointed postmaster about the middle of 1885, and held the office until about the middle of 1889, covering a period of about four years one month and a half?—A. Yes, sir.

Q. Who was your immediate predecessor?—A. Henry C. Payne.

Q. That office was under the civil-service law during his administration?—A. Yes, sir.

Q. Indeed, since the law became operative?—A. Yes, sir.

Q. When you entered the office as postmaster what was the total force of all grades employed?—A. I should think that——

Q. I would like to have it accurately if you can give it?—A. I do not know that I can give that, Mr. Stone. Let me see. I can only get at that answer, Mr. Stone, by recollection and a little calculation. I do not carry those statistics in my head. In June, 1885, the number of carriers was very many less than the last of September, 1889, when I went out. There were sixteen carriers added; there were about eighty carriers.

Q. Your answer is rather anticipating some questions that I might ask.—A. Well, I should say there were one hundred and forty-one holding places July 15, 1889, that figure is correct. The total number was placed July 15, 1889, at one hundred and forty-one, exclusive of some agencies, which would be ten, and of messenger boys, which would be five; that would be fifteen and one hundred and forty-one, which makes one hundred and fifty-six. Now, I should think there were as many as that. I would estimate the number of new appointments in the carriers division to be between twenty-five and thirty. There was a large increase of carriers—twenty-five or thirty increase of carriers; the clerks not as many. I should say nearly ten, perhaps, increase of clerks, so that if you will deduct say forty from the total—thirty-five or forty from the total number—I think you will get at about the right number, which will make——

Q. One hundred and fifteen to one hundred and twenty?—A. Yes, sir; somewhere along there; one hundred and ten to one hundred and twenty perhaps.

Q. Of that number how many were in the classified service?—A. I can only give my impression as to that number.

Mr. ANDREW. You said from one hundred and fifteen to one hundred and twenty-five.

Mr. STONE. No; from one hundred and ten to one hundred and twenty?—A. From one hundred and ten to one hundred and twenty. I should say that is in the classified service, if that is the number you wish to know. By the way, that can all be figured out by these statistics, but it would take some little time. I would say that always as a rule in the classified service there were a trifle more than one-half of all the clerical force—say one-half of the clerical force—about 50 per cent.

By Mr. ROOSEVELT :

Q. Mr. Paul, when we went up to Milwaukee and examined you are you positive you told us the date when your commission would expire?—A. Well, sir, that is my very strong impression that I gave you the exact date; at least the date of the month in which it was to expire. I can not say I gave you the exact day of the month.

Q. You told us about the time it would expire?—A. I am very positive I did.

Q. Did you tell it to any one Commissioner or to all three?—A. Well, I can not say I gave it to all the Commissioners.

Q. Because we are all three willing to testify under oath that you never told us anything of the sort; that on the contrary you told us that your term was out, and that you were just hanging on until your successor would be appointed?—A. My time was out.

Q. Your time was out?—A. I am perfectly willing to allow, Mr. Roosevelt, that there might have been a misapprehension on the part of the Commission of the manner in which I spoke of that; but not thinking I was being investigated, and not being asked the direct question in regard to that——

Q. Mr. Paul, in our supplementary report, as I think you call it, of your office, do you recollect that the statement occurs that "we never accepted the unsupported statements of Shidy?"—A. I remember that expression occurs.

Q. It occurs in the report?—A. Yes, sir.

Q. That we base it entirely upon your own testimony.—A. I think not entirely.

Q. We base it almost entirely upon your own statement and upon the analytical statement compiled from the records.—A. Why, sir, the report will show for itself.

Q. You recollect that. Do you recollect in the report that it is also shown that when we went up there to investigate you that we did not try to get out any new facts in that case; but simply (of course I am only quoting from memory) to see if you could disprove the charges made in Major Webster's and Mr. Doyle's report?—A. I remember a reference to that report, but I do not remember that exact statement.

Q. The statement is in the report. You can see it by referring to the report, Mr. Chairman. Now, Mr. Paul, did you not say yesterday, in stating to Governor Thompson that you did not remember my saying to you, "These are very grave charges, Mr. Paul, and we want to see what you can say in answer to them," or words to that effect?—A. I do not remember that, Mr. Roosevelt.

Q. You state you do not remember that, Mr. Paul?—A. No, sir.

Q. I believe you also state that you could not say that it had been made to you.—A. I may be incorrect.

Q. In your memory?—A. Yes, sir. Well, I can say positively, however, that there was nothing said to give me the impression that I was in any manner seriously involved in any investigation.

Q. Well, I propose to contradict you upon that point by the testimony of my colleagues and myself, that we explicitly told you that these were very grave charges against you, and we wanted to hear your defense.—A. You may have made the remark "that they were grave charges." Perhaps in my innocence I did not take the application to myself. I certainly did not——

Q. Now, Mr. Paul, I want to try to call to your mind some of the circumstances of our investigation of you.—A. Yes, sir.

Q. Do you remember how we entered—suppose the room stands like this; the desk is off there in the room [indicating]?—A. Yes, sir.

Q. And you sat down on this side of the desk here which Mr. Lelbach is occupying, as if the desk were behind him, and I sat in a place about like that [illustrating].—A. Yes, sir; you are correct.

Q. And Governor Thompson sat on my left hand and Mr. Lyman on my right.—A. I think Mr. Lyman sat near the desk.

Q. Well, one on either hand, then.—A. Yes; but it does not make any practical difference.

Q. And I did most of the examining of you, and sometimes my two colleagues would——A. Yes, sir.

Q. Assist me.—A. Yes, sir.

Q. Governor Thompson, ever cautious, was the man who asked you specifically when your term of office expired, to which you made that answer?—A. I think there were some words of a social character passed between the governor and myself soon after he entered the office, and if this remark fell from me it came voluntarily, not supposing that it was a matter of any official moment.

Q. You think it was not in response to a question of the governor?—A. I think perhaps he might have asked me when my term of office expired, or something of that kind.

Q. To which you may have answered that your time was about up and that you were hanging on until your successor should be appointed?—A. My time was about up, and until my successor could be appointed—that is about the substance of it.

Q. Then you do not recollect telling us the date, or thereabouts, when your term expired?—A. I think I gave to one of the Commissioners sooner or later the exact date when my commission would expire.

Q. Have you any memory to which Commissioner you gave that?—A. No, sir; I have not.

Q. We are all willing to testify under oath that it never was given?—A. Well, I presume so.

Q. Now, Mr. Paul, we examined you on these two exhibits which I hold in my hand; these two exhibits, A and B, being analytical statements from the record book, and your own statement.—A. Just in that condition?

Q. Precisely as they are now?—A. Yes, sir.

Q. Do you recollect——?—A. That was in the morning, was it not? Did you not have your questions there the first day that you were there?

Q. I had them with me.—A. I think you did the first day.

Q. But at any rate——A. In the morning, I think, you had one of them. I do not think you had both at that time.

Q. I had both, and read from them, and then I would ask you questions about them, and then pass them over to you; and then I think you would put on your glasses and look at them so, and then say: "They refer to Mr. Shidy; not to me."—A. I think you are entirely mistaken about that.

Q. You think I am entirely mistaken?—A. Yes. I do not think I ever saw a single page of that testimony through glasses or in any other way.

Q. I intend to testify under oath that you did, and held it in your hand and looked it over, and have my colleagues testify to the same effect.—A. I think you handed me a copy of that, and I did not know that that was the testimony of the year before until near the time that you left the office finally.

Q. What did you think I was reading from then? but I will quote your statement in the testimony. Did you think I was reading from——A. Well, I suspected that you had taken some memoranda from the Commission in reference to the office, and were asking questions about it; but it never occurred to me——

Q. For instance, if you will wait a minute, when I said to you as I did again and again: "Mr. Paul, you say this; what did you mean by it? You say that; what do you mean by that? You put that statement there; what do you mean by that?" Do you mean to say you thought I was simply referring to memoranda taken in the office?—A. No, sir. That was near the close of your conversation, or examination, as you choose to call it. Near the close you inquired of me if I made such and such a statement, looking at the single document in your hand. That was near the close of the visit. Then for the first time I suspected you had this old testimony, which I understood had been rejected as frivolous.

Q. And you are quite confident, then, sir; that I did not pass them to you, and that you did not look them over and say that they were matters that were for Shidy and not for you to explain, and then passed the book back to me?—A. I am very confident I never had one of those papers in my hand. I do not know now this morning, nor could I tell if I were put upon my oath upon that special subject whether that is my own or any other manuscript. I do not know a thing there is in any of those papers.

Q. I propose to show by the testimony of my two colleagues that what I state occurred, Mr. Paul.—A. I have some witnesses on that subject, too, if it is necessary.

Q. Do you mean to say witnesses who were present at this interview?—A. One or two.

The CHAIRMAN. Who were present at this interview?—A. The chief clerk in the office, and I think one other.

Mr. ROOSEVELT. Where was he?—A. At that time, that morning?

The CHAIRMAN. So the chief clerk of the office was in the room at that time?—A. A portion of the time; yes, sir.

By Mr. ROOSEVELT:

Q. He was not there very much of the time?—A. Not much of the time.

Q. Then the chief clerk would testify that while you were in that room you did not have any of that testimony?—A. I think so.

Q. Who was in the room all the time?—A. I think no one all the time.

Q. Who was there most of the time?—A. I do not think any one was there most of the time. I am very frank to say that.

Q. Then you mean that you would produce witnesses, none of whom were there most of the time?—A. Except at the particular time that you had this manuscript or this testimony. I do not think that the point is very essential, anyway.

Q. It is so essential, that we three Commissioners are going to show that you had this testimony before you; that we asked you on a number of specific points, and that you kept answering that you did not know; that you could not say, or explain what Shidy had done at that meeting; could not give us any more explanation one way or the other; that Shidy was the man who had been doing all that, and that you could not tell us all about it. I would ask you, and then you would say—— A. Yes.

Q. That was a matter for your own judgment; that Shidy was looking after that matter entirely, and we could not get any definite answers from you. However, I pass from that.—A. That is simply your way of justifying the suplementary report. I am perfectly willing to concede that there is a misapprehension on your part if you claim it.

Q. I do not claim any misapprehension at all. Mr. Paul, I believe I understood you to testify to-day or yesterday that you never interfered at all with the work of the board of examiners?—A. I never interfered in any but a proper manner.

Q. Well, you never suggested to them what names to certify to you, for instance?—A. What names to certify? I have no recollection of doing that.

Q. You never told Mr. Shidy to include a certain name in the next certifications?—A. Not by way of instruction or anything of the kind.

Q. Not by way of instruction?—A. I may have possibly said, Mr. Roosevelt, that such a name certified to me on the list of three or four, such as the case might be, would naturally come up in the next certification. Having been certified once I would know, or when in a case like that occurred to my recollection——

Q. In a case, for instance, of a higher-grade eligible agreeing to be transferred to the lowest list you would never tell Mr. Shidy to include that man in the next certification?—A. Not at all.

Q. You would never tell him to include him in the next certification?—A. I did not think that was necessary.

Q. So, as a matter of fact, you did not instruct him?—A. I did not instruct him.

Q. Did you hint to him?—A. Not improperly.

Q. Well, did you do it properly? Then did you properly hint to him to do anything of that kind?—A. Well, as a matter of course, if a man came to me and asked to be transferred to a lower list—I think it would be very natural for either Mr. Shidy or myself to remark about the fact, but never by way of influencing——

Q. That is not my question, Mr. Paul. I want to know if when a man came to you and asked to be transferred to the lower list, if you ever requested that he be certified to you in the next certification?—A. Not by way of influencing the certification in the slightest.

Q. In what way did you do it? Mr. Chairman, I do not want to seem to ask too many questions, but I do desire to get some answers to these questions. Did you or did you not sometimes ask that a given name be included in the next certification?—A. No, sir; not in the sense in which you mean—not in the affirmative; not in the sense that I meant in any way to influence him.

Q. In what sense, then, did you ask him?—A. In the sense of doing his duty; that is all. If I ever said anything of the kind I have no recollection of it.

Q. In the sense of doing his duty?—A. Yes, sir.

Q. Now, I do not quite understand—in fact, I can not understand. How do you mean that you would make the request that he would do it in the sense of doing his duty?—A. In the first place, I have no recollection of ever mentioning any name to Shidy in that connection in any way whatever; and in the next place I say that it is a bare possibility that any man may be referred to who has made application to be transferred. What I mean to say is this: That if any remark or reference was made to any applicant to be transferred it was not made with a view of influencing the rank of the applicant or the selection or anything of that kind.

Q. Well, now, I come to another subject for a moment. I shall come back to that in a minute or two. You never would undertake to oversee and direct the work of the board where it was purely their work, would you?—A. No, sir.

Q. I mean, for instance, you would not write to the board and ask them the reasons for certain markings and otherwise—you would not tell the board how to answer?—A. Of certain markings, or tell the board how to answer? No, sir.

Q. You would not draw out a rough draught of the answer that the secretary was to send to us?—A. No, sir. I know very well what you are getting at. There is nothing in that, Mr. Roosevelt—nothing in the world. You are simply losing your time and wasting the time of the committee. I would be very glad to state what you are driving at.

Q. I will tell it, sir.—A. I think I ought to state it. It is already in the evidence, every word of it.

Q. Well, will you tell it or put it in as evidence?—A. I did voluntarily. There is nothing about that which will inculpate me in any way.

Q. Will you tell me when it was put in evidence?—A. It was put in evidence yesterday.

By Mr. ROOSEVELT:

Q. Now, will you state to me what I am driving at?—A. Yes, sir. I understand your purpose. If I am wrong, of course I would be very glad to be corrected. You are referring now especially to the case which you call "the re-marking case," where papers were re-marked.

Q. Yes, sir.—A. Now, if you will permit me to state to the committee, or restate to the committee, the circumstances of that I would be very glad.

Q. If you will permit me first I will put it in evidence. Here is a letter from ex-Commissioner Oberly of August 4 to Shidy, the secretary of the board of examiners, asking about certain apparent discrepancies in the markings of the certification of a number of men, and here is the rough draught in Mr. Paul's handwriting. I think you will acknowledge that to be your handwriting?—A. Yes, sir.

Q. Of what was to be said in response by the board, and here is the letter of the board on the line of this draught answering the Commission. It was a matter with which the postmaster ought properly to have had nothing to do. It referred purely to the duty of the board, and to judge from these rough draughts, (the outline of the board's reply) was drawn up by the postmaster and then were sent to the local board. —A. Allow me to look at that, please.

Q. I do not notice the first or second or final letters of Mr. Shidy, because they reflect on Mr. Paul, or Mr. Shidy's own statement. We never paid any heed to it. How did you happen to state to Mr. Shidy about what answers the board would make?—A. Because Mr. Shidy was very much annoyed by the whole arrangement.

Q. By the whole arrangement?—A. Yes, sir; with the re-marking; very much annoyed by it. It was his disposition to make a correction in that marking. The board collectively, as I understand, and still understand it, marked the papers, and Mr. Shidy came and said this: "I think that marking ought to be private." It was not with reference to any partiality on my part in any way. There was nothing suggestive of that kind.

Q. Certainly. I am not saying that you neglected your duties to help Shidy. Is it true that you drew up those rough draughts which he was to follow in his letter?—A. The secretary went to the other members of the board of his own accord, and called the entire board together to consult as to that marking. I said nothing to them in any way whatever. I did say this, however, when he had told me the facts, that I thought there was only a very small difference between the two men; that I thought one man did seem to be getting the start in the marking, an unfair advantage, because technically he could answer one question very much better than any other person because of his practical knowledge. That question Shidy told me himself related to the different localities in the city of Milwaukee. That was one of the questions, it appears, in the examination. I never saw the question to my knowledge or recollection; but Shidy said that a man quite ignorant in most respects had received a marking of about 100 on that question, and simply because he had been a street-car driver many years in the city. He subsequently became a candidate for appointment as carrier. There was unanimous concurrence of opinion all around that that was certainly not in accordance with the spirit of the examination, that a man having that technical knowledge should supersede other men of much higher capacity.

Q. Of much higher mental capacity. Now, then, let me see. I stated—— A. That is about what occurred; but I did not interfere with it except——

Q. You advised him to be marked down, did I gather you to say?— A. I did not advise any marking up or marking down. But I simply said if he made any entry upon his records of his marking of the papers (in the permanent record) I would advise him for his own protection and for mine and for the good record of the office to consult the Commission as to the proceeding and give a full and frank account of the facts and submit them to their decision in the case.

Q. I do not quite get the connection, Mr. Paul. What you were saying is that you disapproved of them marking a man perfect simply because he happened to pass a perfect examination.—A. I did not say that I expressed any disapproval; I did not object in that view of the case by any means, because a person naturally would not object.

Q. What did you do then, sir?—A. Well, sir, I will tell you. I had nearly concluded what I had to say. The board reviewed the papers by themselves without dictation, without influence of any kind, without the least care of what they did, and after it had adjourned Mr. Shidy came to me and in pursuance of my suggestion that any action of that kind out of the usual line should be reported to the Commission for consideration, and asked me if I could not suggest some way or form of letter to the Commission giving the facts. I think he requested me twice, but I rather thought it was not well for me to interfere in the matter. Naturally, I did not say anything about it. I did at his request make a suggestion, but not by the way of dictation in the slightest degree, but at his suggestion; and so I did make a little memorandum. It is not a letter.

Q. It is just a memorandum?—A. Of what I presumed to be the facts, for him to change or make just as he pleased.

Q. Now just let me ask you this—you have gotten off from the point of this examination—what was it you said about this letter-carrier who was marked down—what did you say?—A. I know what Shidy said. I said——

Q. I do not care what he said, but what you said. What did you say?—A. I have no recollection of making any remark at all.

Q. You did say when your attention was called to the facts that this man was marked very high.—A. By information from Shidy. He came to me and to advise about it. I think he tangled his records in addition in regard to the examination in some way; but as to that I do not know. That is all.

Q. What right had you to know about the board making these markings or to know the candidates whom the board had marked? How did you happen to know that this man had been a car-driver?—A. I could not know except from Shidy.

Q. You could not know except from Shidy?—A. No, sir.

Q. So Shidy told you?—A. Yes, sir; the members of the board talked in my presence about it.

Q. So that the members of the board told you about the marks of the candidates? This was at the time when the eligible lists were secret. They consulted there with you, or in your presence, about lowering the marking of the candidates whom they, apparently with your consent, deemed to have gotten a higher marking on account of his knowledge of local delivery than his general education would entitle him. Is that so?—A. I think I became possessed of the information casually and partially because Shidy thought I could assist him or some thing of the kind.

Q. Shiddy thought you could assist him by marking the candidates?—A. No, sir; not in marking, but as to the method of proceeding.

Q. As to remarking them?—A. Whether it would be proper for me to do any such thing as that.

Q. And Shidy consulted you as to the propriety of remarking?—A. He certainly asked me something about it.

Q. And must have told you who the man was in order that you should know that he had been a car-driver?—A. Yes, sir; that came out in some part of the proceedings. I do not think I knew his name at that time. I think I simply knew the fact of his business.

Q. The fact of his business? I gather from your words the proposition was to mark this man down because he had a special knowledge of the streets, a knowledge directly in the line of his duty which he had gained as a car-driver?—A. No, sir; it would not be in the direct line of his duty.

Q. As a letter-carrier it was in the direct line of his duty.—A. Not such knowledge as he would have. It would not apply to a mere knowledge of the district.

Q. Oh, I misunderstood you. Just now when you said that it was proposed to mark him down or in some way to offset the high mark he had gained in consequence of his practical knowledge as a car-driver— that was the question that the board was determining?—A. I do not think they had anything to do with it at all.

Q. That is not answering my question. I asked you if they proposed to do that?—A. I do not think it was made by me at all. I did not overhear nor know what the conversation of the board was.

Q. Well, then, you did not remonstrate with the board for any impropriety in their conduct in remarking that man, nor you did not take part in their deliberations, nor write this draught, nor were you present?—A. I took no part whatever. I have stated that repeatedly. I took no part whatever.

Q. You were simply present at their deliberations?—A. I was scarcely present. I was attending to other duties.

Q. How did you happen to know the facts so well?—A. Sir?

Q. That they were engaged in remarking this man, and you were able to outline their letter for them afterward?—A. I knew from what Shidy said to me. I knew something of that kind was going on. I told Shidy in effect that he had better be cautious and not violate any rules of the civil-service law; and whatever he did he had better consult the Commission. That I have told him a number of times. I think there is no——

Q. You wrote that rough draught of a letter that he was to follow at his request?—A. Mr. Shidy came to me after the adjournment of the board and said he wanted to make a proper representation of the facts, and at his suggestion he may have dictated a portion of it; but I do not think that is the letter. I do remember this, that in the course of the letter the particular words that "the board of its own motion" appeared, and Shidy kept that and sent it of his own accord.

Q. You mean that you had first put in "the board of its own motion?"—

A. Yes, sir; I thought it was very important for the Commission to know——

Q. You thought it was very important for the Commission to know that the board had done it "of its own motion?"—A. Yes, sir.

Q. So you put it down in the rough abstract that "the board of its own motion"——A. The board "of its own motion" had done this.

Q. That was put in, then, by your direction?—A. Put in by my direction, I say; no more or no less.

The CHAIRMAN. He came to you for advice and you gave it to him?—A. Yes, sir; I think it should be "that the board at its own suggestion and motion."

By Mr. ROOSEVELT:

Q. This is your statement to Major Webster. You have already spoken about that to-day. You went over it after it was made and underlined it and then signed your name.—A. Possibly.

Q. Did you or did you not?—A. If you will allow me to look at it I can tell you positively. I have to be very cautious what statements I make to you, Mr. Roosevelt, for I expect you misuse them, and the Commission itself misuses them, but for what reason I do not know; I think the Commission has shown that disposition in my case.

Q. Answer my question.—A. Yes, sir; that is signed by me.

Q. Is that the statement you made to Mr. Webster and signed and went over and underlined any corrections you saw and then signed it?—A. I think so.

Q. All right, sir. Was that statement true or was it false?—A. It was true, as far as I knew at that time.

Q. As far as you knew at that time?—A. I may have changed my opinion upon obtaining some additional knowledge of the facts.

Q. Now, yesterday I believe you stated that you knew nothing of the eligible list in advance, did you not?—A. Of the eligible list? I never knew anything of the eligible list in advance with reference to any selections from it.

Q. Well, now you state to Mr. Webster in answer to the question:

Have you generally or at any time known the state of the register; the order in which the names stood before making appointments?—A. Yes; I think I have been aware unavoidably of the list.

Q. Was that the truth?—A. I had reference wholly to this published list.

Q. To the published newspaper list?—A. Yes, sir.

Q. Then a little further on you say as to the list of eligibles: "I think so, and I must say simply as a matter of truth that the secretary has never regarded the list of eligibles on the records as in anywise but a public record."—A. I do not think the secretary was ever very scrupulous in regard to copying his books and records properly; but I was none the less careful as to my own duties and my own relations to the board and secretary.

Q. You regarded the board, then, as public. You think the lists were made public?—A. No, sir; they were not.

Q. They were not made public?—A. My view of the case was as I understood it at the time——

Q. Well, now, just let me ask you one question. I stated to you, "do you regard them as being public," and you said, "No, sir; I do not," and then you told Major Webster "I must say simply as a matter of truth the secretary has never regarded the list of eligibles on the record as in anywise but a public list." That was what you told Major Webster, was it not?—A. Public record? Yes, sir.

Q. That means that it was open to public inspection, does it not?—
A. Not quite that.

Q. What does it mean, sir?—A. Take the books of any office you please, your office or any one's letters. They may be public records and still not be open to inspection to the entire public. I did not mean that, sir.

Q. What did you mean?—A. I thought Mr. Shidy up to that time had not regarded his record as simply an official record of eligibles, and he did not appreciate the consequence of keeping them wholly private.

Q. I see. So that they were not kept private from every person?—
A. There were two or three, perhaps, who had access to them all the time.

Q. But you did not? They were kept private from you, but not kept private from other people?—A. They were generally kept private from me, as a rule.

Q. As a rule?—A. As a rule.

Q. What were the exceptions to that rule?—A. As to others?

Q. As to you. You say they were generally kept private from you?—A. I gave testimony on that point yesterday.

The CHAIRMAN. Suppose you state it again, the exceptions, if there were any.—A. As I said, Shidy would take his register of eligibles, very frequently take it up to my room and open it in my presence and look at the names, and all that kind of thing; but I never would take any advantage of it of course. I never consulted the list.

By Mr. ROOSEVELT:

Q. You never had it in your custody, sir?—A. No, sir; I never had that list in my custody.

Q. Mr. Shidy and Johnson testified before us in your presence that they had seen the books in your keeping, and on your table?—A. If they testified to any such thing it is not the truth. I question very much whether they ever gave any such testimony. Mr. Johnson, I am quite sure, did not.

Q. Mr. Johnson and Shidy both so stated in my report.—A. The majority of the board, I am very sure, will not bear you out on that point.

Q. Now, you stated to Major Webster, in answer to the question: "Have certifications been made to you for appointment prior to appointment in writing?" Your answer is: "The certification"—I hope you will give me your attention, because it is a little difficult to understand— "The certifications have in all cases been made to me in writing or verbally, and I think in all cases prior to appointment, with possibly an occasional variation which may have arisen on a question of construction of the rules, or something of that kind, in which case my impression is that in one or two cases—or a very limited number—the secretary would modify the certification to accord with the rule." Now, what does that mean, Mr. Paul?—A. That is substantially the same testimony as I gave yesterday in the case.

Q. Do you mind telling me what it means? You say: "That certifications have in all cases been made to me in writing or verbally." Do you mean that some certifications were made to you verbally and not in writing?—A. No, sir; I did not. I would not regard anything verbal as a certification.

Q. What do you mean by saying: "Certifications have in all cases been made to me in writing or verbally."—A. It only says that in one or two cases, does it not?

Q. No; it says simply "certifications have in all cases been made to me in writing or verbally."—A. What succeeds that?

Q. "And I think in all cases prior to appointment."—A. I mean just this: I refer to Mr. Shidy's loose habits of doing business; and I think in some cases when I called for certifications that Shidy would come to me in reference to the rule fixing certifications and give, perhaps, the certifications; for it would be under such and such circumstances, or such and such constructions, and there may have been one, or perhaps two or three such cases as that.

Q. And those were verbal certifications to you, as you call it?—A. That is what I call it; certainly.

Q. Now, do you mean, then, that you treated that verbal certification as a regular certification?—A. No, sir.

Q. The question was, then, of having certifications made to you for all appointments prior to appointment in writing? Your answer is: "The certifications have in all cases been made to me in writing or verbally."—A. Yes, sir; that is correct.

Q. I will call your attention to your statement:

I think in all cases prior to appointment, with possibly an occasional variation, which may have arisen on a question of construction of the rules, or something of that kind, in which case my impression is that in one or two cases—a very limited number—the secretary would modify the certification to accord with the rule.

Now, this seems to say that in a limited number of cases you appointed a man before he was certified to you, and that the secretary modified the certification to accord with the rule. I do not know what "to accord with the rule" means.—A. The reference to that circumstance means this: The secretary would bring me, for instance, the names from which a selection was to be made. Perhaps he would have in his mind some doubt about the construction of the rule, or whether he had made the certification properly. Then I would have the names for selection, and I modified one or two cases. I do not remember any such case by which I would know the names. The names came before me for my selection, and he would arrange the certification——

Q. You mean that you would not know the names that would come before you—you would make an appointment and he would modify the certification to accord with that appointment?—A. No, sir; not to accord with that appointment.

Q. To accord with the rule? I am trying to get at what you mean here.—A. I did not say any such case occurred. I remember no such case. In my answer I——

Q. In one or two cases your impression is—it was quite a limited number of cases—you would make the appointment and the secretary would then modify the certification in accordance?—A. Yes, sir; before I ever made the appointment. It would be a name that was entitled to certification, and he would bring the certification immediately to me.

Q. Now the next answer you state is this:

Without a distinct recollection of the facts, my impression is that a vacancy having occurred, upon inquiry as to the character of a man and knowing that he was eligible from previous certification I nominated him, dating his nomination from the time of the occurrence of the vacancy.

A. How is that? I would like to hear that read again.

Q. "A vacancy having occured upon inquiry as to the character of the man, and knowing that he was eligible from the previous certifications I nominated him, dating his nomination from the time of the occurrence of the vacancy."—A. I did not catch the whole of it; but it is substantially correct.

Q. That is substantially correct?—A. It is not quite correct.

The CHAIRMAN. Do you agree with the answer now?—A. Not altogether.

By Mr. ROOSEVELT:

Q. In what way do you differ?—A. I think my words are a little misconstrued there; my idea is misconstrued. I was up the entire night before this testimony was taken.

Q. Before Major Webster took the testimony?—A. No, sir.

Q. This is Major Webster's testimony?—A. Yes, sir.

Q. This is the testimony that was taken by Major Webster that I read from and which you interlined and signed your name to.—A. The question relates to a matter of selecting a man or choosing a man from a former certification.

Q. We do not say anything about a former certification. As a matter of fact, there is only one certification. This is in advance of all certifications.—A. Now, the answer is, not what might have been; I do not know what might have been; but I intended to make these answers, sir, so as to cover the possibility of any informality in an exceptional case. That is all.

Q. You state that you had——A. Allow me to complete my answer.

Q. Certainly.—A. If a certification of certain names had been made to me and was on my table, for instance John Jones and two or three others, the other names would come up subsequently in the next certification under the rule, as I understand it, which allows the selection of more than one name from the certification or did then.

Q. And as a matter of fact you never chose more than one from one certification?—A. Well, will you allow me to answer the question, please. The rule allows that, but Shidy preferred always to have a separate certification, and sometimes, possibly in one or two cases (I doubt whether it ever occurred at all), where the names appeared on the first certification, if the man marked the highest would be higher than any subsequent names that came up I would suggest that man for the place. I did not consider that——

Q. You would suggest that man for the place. Do you mean you would appoint him and then have the certification made for him?—A. Get his nomination ready.

Q. I shall only keep you a very few moments longer. The question was: "You necessarily know all of the candidates before they are examined?" You answered: "Not in the sense of knowing anything about them and their personal history, relations or opinions upon any subject. I purposely avoid knowing anything until after the examination, until such a time that circumstances make it probable they are to be eligible for appointment soon."—A. Yes, sir.

Q. "I then make personal investigation somewhat as to their character and duties."—A. Yes, sir.

Q. Now, what do you mean by that? How did you know "that circumstances make it probable that they are to be eligible for appointment soon?—A. Simply being on the eligible list that is referred to. If you want to know how I know every single man who is examined and on the eligible list I might——

Q. You misunderstand my question. Your answer was: I purposely avoid knowing anything until after the examination, until such a time that circumstances make it probable that they are to be eligible for appointment soon."—A. Yes, sir; that is perfectly correct.

Q. How did you know "that circumstances would make it probable that they are to be eligible for appointment soon ?"—A. Well, our lists were generally pretty short, and the applicants would immediately apply to me for places, and I, being informed as to the number that had been examined (that was no secret), generally knew what would be wanted pretty soon. For instance, you take the case of the sixteen carriers who were appointed at one time. I knew very well from the length of the list that the old list had nearly expired, and Shidy had told me so.

Q. Shidy told you what? That the old list had nearly expired and was not sufficient.—A. I would know very well about that. You could not fail knowing about it.

Q. So that you knew a good deal before you made the appointment ?— A. Only what I got from the list.

Q. But you did not get information from other channels ?—A. No, sir.

Q. You say in reference to the letter about certifications from the higher to the lower grade : "I can not see any conditions except that they should be transferred on the list in their order according to average, and providing their grade was sufficient 'to entitle them to compete in the lower grade." That was your understanding ?—A. That was my understanding.

Q. That they should be transferred according to average ?—A. According to average.

Q. According to their standing ?—A. I do not wish any misunderstanding about that. I presume there is none. The application for transfer for lower places when there were more than one under consideration, or any number of such applications, my idea was that they should be transferred—that is, reported to me for selection on the certification according to their standing or their mark—that is, the highest mark should come first in the certification.

Q. You would think it an injustice, for instance, if there were four carriers willing to be transferred, to transfer the lower mark first and certify that up to you before you certified other higher ones?—A. Oh, it might frequently occur that the one marked lowest would make his request first.

Q. I put this case, that if four were willing to be transferred, all of them of equal height, you would think it an injustice to transfer the lowest one of those four first and have him appointed before the other three had a chance?—A. Yes, sir; that certainly would be an injustice. I never knew that to occur.

Q. It happened in the Keaveney case.—A. I doubt it very much. I do not think it did.

Q. Well, now, when you made that, when you had shifted a man, would you certify a lower carrier above a high-grade stamper? Do you think that that would be the proper way to make certifications ? Do you see the point I am getting at ? If they certified a man who was low on a higher grade above a man who had a high average on a lower grade, now would you think it right to certify him up above those lower grade men with high averages?—A. Well, sir, that is simply asking me my opinion as to that. It is true it was not for me to determine anything in any way, and I never did determine that question in any way. I can give you my opinion about it.

Q. You never did determine it ? Would you not think it unfair if you should see on a certification a carrier of 72 with a stamper of 91 certified for the position of stamper ?—A. I know the practice of the secretary—that is, I think I do. The practice of the secretary——

Q. I do not care about the practice of the secretary. I only ask if you knew?—A. It relates practically to that point, and it was inconsistent with itself.

Q. The practice of the secretary was inconsistent with itself?—A. Yes, sir; according to this information; but my——

Q. And you knew at the time that it was inconsistent with itself?—A. Well, I understood, sir, from him that it was inconsistent.

Q. Inconsistent with itself?—A. I remember remarking to him that I thought he ought to be very careful and follow the rule.

Q. Did you state you knew at the time of the practice of the secretary in making these transfers that he was inconsistent with himself? Did you ever protest any way against that practice?—A. Certainly.

Q. You did?—A. I did make a remark to him once—a pretty sharp remark—that he should follow one rule or another.

Q. Then you knew that you were making appointments upon his certifications when he was now following one rule and then following another?—A. No, sir; I do not think that is so.

Q. Why, did you just say so, sir—what do you mean, then?—A. Well, sir, I think he said to me once that he had not always the same rule in making transfers as to standing. If you will allow me to state where the difference is I think we will make the whole matter clear.

Q. Would it not be better——A. I give this as an impression. Of course this is the construction of the secretary's duty. My impression was at the time—when he made transfers during the early days of my administration that he transferred a man from a clerk's or carrier's list with the same marking without any change, that subsequently he changed the marks to correspond with the standing in the lower degree, increasing the marks——

Q. What did he do? Did you know he did that?—A. I only know that from Shidy himself.

Q. When did he tell you that?—A. Well, I can not give the date at all.

Q. Before this investigation?—A. Before the investigation.

Q. You knew from Mr. Shidy's own statement that he would change the marks of eligibles on the register in shifting them from one list to another to be certified to you.

By the CHAIRMAN:

Q. Let me see whether I understand you correctly. Where he would certify a letter-carrier for the position of stamper, it being a higher examination, he would mark up an average obtained by the candidate for the carrier's position?—A. I think originally he followed the other rule, Mr. Chairman.

Q. Well, I know. But did I understand you aright?—A. You see the examination for a messenger or stamper is very different.

Q. Certainly. It is a lower grade.—A. Than the one above.

Q. Now, suppose he sent in four names for stamper and three of them had passed the stamper's examination.—A. Yes, sir.

Q. Received 80, 75, or 70 per cent. Suppose the party who had been certified on this list as a stamper had passed an examination say at 70 per cent. as letter carrier. He would mark him up to make up the difference in the degree of the examination.—A. He would mark——

Q. How much would he mark him?—A. I do not mean that he would mark him just according to his notion or anything of that kind. I mean simply that he would take the studies or papers that covered the ground of a stamper and adopt that mark instead of the mark——

Q. Is there any such rule made by the Commission to say what percentage would be allowed in these different grades?- A. Well, sir, when he mentioned that matter to me my impression is that he said perhaps he had been doing wrong or doing injustice to those who accepted those lower positions—not a large number of them—and my remark to him was that he must not be guilty of any irregularity, and if he had any doubt about it he should ask the Commission. I always requested him to consult the Commission and not to have two systems of marking That that would not answer. I think I talked to him about it in that way.

Q. Was that when the certification was made for a letter-carrier or as a stamper? Would he appear when the list came to you on a higher average than he actually did obtain as a letter-carrier?

By Mr. ROOSEVELT:

Q. You knew of that.—A. I never knew of it.

Q. That was actually the case, was it not?—A. I only knew from a single conversation, and in that conversation I almost instructed—I certainly advised him very strongly—to consult the Commission and settle upon a rule. I did not investigate the right or wrong of the rules.

By Mr. ANDREW:

Q. What they would do was to mark up a letter-carrier when he was certified as a stamper?—A. It was not a question of advantage any way. It was a question of right or wrong. It did not change the marking very much, you understand.

Q. Could not the letter-carrier get into the certification of a stamper unless these changes were made in the marking? Was not that the object?—A. This is simply a question of knowledge.

The CHAIRMAN. Knowledge. Was there any other object than to give the man knowledge of his certification?—A. No, sir; it was simply on what terms this transfer should be made, what transfer ought to be made, and what standing he would occupy as a stamper.

The CHAIRMAN. I think I understand.

Mr. ANDREW. Well, I do not. I am satisfied of what the witness intends to say. A man is examined as a carrier, he stands low on the list and there are others higher than he is; but he is willing to take a position as stamper.

The WITNESS. Yes, sir.

The CHAIRMAN. He is certified to you, and in order to close the difference between the course of examination he is marked up in his certification to you or has been.—A. Yes, sir, he is marked on this principle—marked on the studies—on the class of questions.

The CHAIRMAN. Certainly.

The WITNESS. It relates to the stamper. Those are included in his examination, as I understand it, as a carrier.

Mr. ANDREW. That part is clear enough; but that has nothing to do with what I asked.

Mr. ROOSEVELT. What possible authority could there have been to do that?—A. I never had anything to do with it.

By Mr. ANDREW:

Q. What I wanted to get at, simply for the purpose of information, is this: What was the object in making that change in the marking? Suppose he had only gotten as a letter-carrier the average of 50, why did you put him on the other force? What was the object of it?--A. Because he possessed more extensive qualifications for the requirements of a stamper than he would for a carrier.

Q. What was the object in changing the mark when you put him on the list?—A. Well, you are asking me now to say what reasons governed Shidy.

Q. No; what would be anybody's reason for it?

The CHAIRMAN. What would the object be, Mr. Paul, to enable the Commission to certify him at all to you?—A. It would be no wrong. There is none on the part of Shidy.

Mr. ROOSEVELT. Could not it be——

Mr. ANDREW. I asked what was the reason?—A. I am answering the question.

Mr. ROOSEVELT. If a carrier passed at 72 and there were stampers on the list at 80, then if you transfer a carrier to the stampers' list at 72 he could not be certified unless you raised his mark?—A. I can not understand the question.

Q. You say here "when a higher grade eligible has expressed a willingness to accept a lower place I have told the secretary, with request, that under the ruling of the Commission of September 18, 1885, he would include such person in his next certification to me for the lower position if entitled to transfer." Now, did you not very distinctly state that you would tell the secretary to include a given higher grade eligible in his next certification to you for the low position? Did you or did you not?—A. Well, sir, I shall have to answer that by stating the precise facts. Generally, the applications for transfer from a higher to a lower grade, or sometimes only one and no more, and sometimes others, and sometimes there might be two or three, but rarely more than one at a time. Now if, for instance, a clerk or a carrier should apply for transfer to the secretary or to myself, or through myself to the secretary, and the list was short in that case, as a matter of course he would go into the next certification. I do not know that I have ever made that remark. I think I did not.

Q. What remark is that?—A. What did it state?

Q. Well, here you state when a higher grade eligible has expressed his willingness to accept a lower place I have told the secretary, with request, that under the ruling of the Commission of September 18, 1885, that he would include such person in his next certification to me for the lower position if entitled to transfer."—A. Yes, sir. The reference was to a case where it would become lawfully in the next certification; but not otherwise.

Q. How could you know it would come lawfully in the next certification?—A. I could know that in many cases that he would be the only person to come in the next certification.

Q. You did not make any such qualification as that in your statement.—A. How?

Q. You did not make any such qualification as that in your statement. You expressed it as a general fact.—A. Oh, no; not as a general fact.

Q. Well, here it is.—A. I did not intend it as such. What I intended was to cover all possibilities. One case I remember——

Q. If you did not know the list of eligibles how could you know what would come up the next time?—A. I did know the man who was transferred, and made the request.

Q. You did know what?—A. I would know when a man made application for the transfer. He came to me——

Q. You would know his standing?—A. No, sir; I did not say that at all; but I would know this, Mr. Roosevelt, that if John Jones came to me and asked to be transferred from the clerks' list, and the stampers' list were exhausted, that he would be certified the next time. As a matter of course I knew that, and would give instructions to that effect.

Q. Well, you again make the statement here: "If in the case of any proper person with whose character and capacity I had become familiar a desire had been voluntarily expressed to me to accept any position in the service lower than that for which he had been examined, I would then request the secretary to include the name of such person in the certification for the place to be filled." You do not say a word about exhausting the list of eligibles or anything of that kind.—A. I think it referred to some other cases.

Q. Well, you do not say it refers to a particular case; you make it as a general statement.—A. If I did, that was my meaning very plainly. I stated it as a fact, it was not a rule at all.

MARCH 6, 1890.

EXAMINATION OF MR. PAUL—Continued.

By Mr. ROOSEVELT:

Q. These certificates from No. 54 to 60, inclusive, show that by shifting one eligible from one list to another and certifying him out of order, to the detriment of those above him, half a dozen eligibles who were entitled to appointment by their standing were certified out of official existence; and that half a dozen men not entitled to appointment by their standing, and who under a proper certification could not have been appointed, were appointed. In each case, however, you chose the particular man for whom the certification was cooked.

The WITNESS. Only one man.

Q. Have you any explanation to give how it happened that in each one of these "cooked" certifications you chose the man for whom it was cooked, while the men entitled to the certification were certified out of existence, and only men improperly certified were chosen ?—A. I think I have sufficiently covered such a question by many answers. I said that in every case I accepted the certification of the board and made my selection from it. There was where my official existence under the law begins and ends. I have my presumption on the subject as to how it happened. I do not remember what explanation I may have made two years ago, but I have my theory of how that was done.

The CHAIRMAN. State that theory.

A. But I do not wish to be held responsible for that theory, nor do I know I am absolutely correct. It is simply theory, and I give it as a theory. That would be that the secretary transfers a certain number of men from a higher to a lower list. Is not that the case, Mr. Roosevelt ?

By Mr. ROOSEVELT:

Q. You are not answering my question at all.—A. I do not know what the point is for me to answer.

Q. My question is specifically if you had any explanation to give how it happened that you choose each particular man on these six certifications and chose the men apparently for whom the certifications were "cooked."—A. I chose the men I considered the first on the three certifications in each case.

Q. You see the point I am trying to get at. You say these certifications are garbled. Each one is cooked for the benefit of one man.
That would require the aid of two parties, the party making the certifications and the man choosing. How is it, or have you any explanation to make "of the fact that in choosing from these certifications
you invariably chose the man for whom the certifications had been
cooked; could you possibly have done so accidentally in every one of
the cases?"—A. When you say certain names are "cooked" I do not
think you refer to my testimony.

Q. I have submitted the record.—A. It is a mere assumption.

Q. Will you look at these certifications Nos. 54 to 60 and say if you
think they are proper?—A. (After examining the certifications.) On
the face of the record as you exhibit those certifications they are certainly improper.

Q. On the face of the record?—A. Yes, sir.

Q. You chose them all, at least as it appears by this they were made
to you in the record book on one day, so that they were all before you
at once.—A. The certifications were never all made to me at the same
time.

Q. This official record was before you on the 18th of February, on
which date you wrote your name opposite each appointee, signifying
the choice of the man, so that the record of that was before you on February 18.—A. I do not think it was.

Q. How did you happen to write your name?—A. Whenever the
secretary presented it I wrote my name opposite the name of the appointee.

Q. Did you look at the date? Each certification is dated, from No.
55 to 60, February 18, 1888, and did you look at that date when you
wrote your name?—A. I have already testified to this committee that
the blanks of the Commission require no date at all. I did not look at
the dates. It was not my duty to do it.

Q. You didn't look at that record at all?—A. Never, in any particular way. The secretary brought the record to me with a designation
of the name, and I signed my name opposite the name of the selection.

Q. Have you never looked over this official record containing these
six certifications and never examined them?—A. With reference to
the practice? No, sir; my presumption is I did not. I do not recollect.

Q. Then what did you mean by saying in your letter of May 30, 1888,
to Mr. Oberly, then president of the Commission, referring to these
very certifications in reference to Cumming, "Referring to the record
for verification, permit me to state," etc.?—A. What record? My own
record or the record of the Board?

Q. "Referring to the record of Charles Cumming, permit me to say
he was not examined as a letter-carrier. As the stamper list was exhausted his name was used," etc. What record did you mean?—A. I
can not say. I may have referred to either.

Q. What is either?—A. If I had taken action I would have referred
to the record of the Commission, and if I had not, I would have referred
to my own record. My recollection is that that letter was written on
information from Shidy, in some shape.

Q. When you say "referring to the records for verification," you referred to what Shidy told you about the record?—A. I should think
so. It may be so. It was supposed that the Commission itself had the
record. It is a very singular fact that if the Commission had that record in its possession a year or more that my attention was never called
after that to my letter referring to these same names.

in the hands of the Commission, and if they showed anything improper in the certifications that impropriety should have been investigated.

Q. What records were in the hands of the Commission?—A. Reports from the local board should have been.

Q. As a matter of fact it was that record that led to the investigation?—A. Yes, sir. I am very glad to know that.

Q. You have no further explanation to give as to saying that you referred to the record for verification. When you told the Commission that you made these statements referring to the record for verification, did you mean that you had referred to the record?—A. No, sir; I did not necessarily. I do not think I ever saw the record.

Q. What did you mean when you wrote that?—A. It is impossible to tell the precise fact. I referred to a record for verification. If the secretary of the local board said the records were so and so, in a letter to the Commission, I would have asked them to refer to the record. I do not see anything involved in that.

Q. You said you referred to the record. You did not ask them to refer to the record at all.—A. I wrote a good many letters. I used most any kind of language that would cover the case.

Q. You used most any kind of language to cover the point?—A. To cover the point.

Q. You say these seven certifications are evidently improper?—A. I said that with this qualification—"as they appear upon your testimony."

Q. As they appear in the analytical statement?—A. As they appear in this statement.

Q. Do you think they are correct?—A. I do not think the certifications would be correct. I do not wish to hold myself responsible for that fact.

Q. I only ask you to state if those certifications which appear by the record you signed on a given day were in your opinion improper?—A. Were they all signed by me on a given day?

Q. I say, as it appears by the record, you signed all those seven certifications on February 18, 1888.—A. There must be some mistake about that. According to my statement of the facts which I have in my hand, no such number is dated in this statement.

Q. What are the dates in that statement?—A. The case of Keaveny here appears to have been entered by the secretary of the Board and stricken out. This is No. 55. Again at No. 54 appears the same explanation. I think it is all frivolous.

Q. All I ask is if this record or analytical statement is correct. All of these are dated on one day, February 18, and to all of them the postmaster has signed his name opposite that of the appointee.—A. I want to make one explanation. The facts as presented by him (referring to Mr. Roosevelt) do not conform with my memorandum of the names opposite.

Q. You can contradict my facts.—A. I have already covered the testimony showing the facts stated, but the statement of Mr. Roosevelt is not in accordance with the facts. Mr. Keaveny was entered upon the record a long time after his real appointment and then crossed out. Keaveny was entered again in order to get my signature, and I did sign it. That was January 20 and it was crossed out for February 18. He made this notation: "Appointed December 8, 1887." There are two instances. Keaveny had been appointed and these are two of the cases to which Mr. Roosevelt refers as being of the six.

Q. Did I understand you correctly to state here the other day that you regarded Shidy as slovenly and careless and a man who did not mean to do anything wrong?—A. I undertook to say the other day that I thought that Shidy in the duties of the Civil Service Commission was slovenly, careless, and dilatory; that I did not think he intended—I state it for the benefit of Shidy, if you please—that Shidy ordinarily was a pretty fair man; that Shidy as a representative of the Civil Service Commission was a man who continually complained that that duty was imposed upon him without pay, and that he was slovenly and dilatory, as I have ascertained since that time in taking care of his records.

Q. You do not think he did anything wrong?—A. I did not think so up to the time he appeared before the Commission in the post-office, or about that time. I do not know what I stated to Major Webster, but at that time I never saw or heard any intention on his part to do wrong. I think he is simply a weak man who was actually intimidated by the Commission in his examination because of his previous errors.

Q. Intimidated by myself and Governor Thompson?—A. He was made to believe that if those errors appeared as his own, and he was responsible for them, he would lose his place.

Q. You say he was a timid, weak man, and was intimidated by Mr. Lyman, Governor Thompson, and myself?—A. That is his statement.

Q. It could not have been retroactive, could it? We examined him in June, 1889, and we could not have intimidated him into making a statement in June, 1888?—A. He was in constant fear of the Commission.

Q. His statement was made in August, 1888, to Mr. Webster and Mr. Doyle. It would have been difficult for us to have intimidated him several months before we ever saw him.—A. I think he had an insane desire to please the Commission and at the same time he was intimidated.

Q. Mr. Shidy never coerced you in any way? He did not force you to choose any particular man from a certification such as appears to be improper?—A. I wish to explain that, if you will allow me. I regarded the local board as a proper portion of the Commission. I perhaps placed too much confidence in them as the representatives of the Commission. That is the only fault I can think of. There was no intimidation, as a matter of course; but if the examining board should present to me certifications and records, I would regard it as a compliance with the spirit of the law and I would raise no question nor go back into an investigation about the propriety of the action of the board. I accepted fully anything they did.

Q. You accepted fully what they did?—A. In the line of duty.

Mr. BOATNER. You considered them the civil service commission in Milwaukee?—A. Yes, sir.

By Mr. ROOSEVELT:

Q. Take, for instance, the certifications you have examined to-day and you say they appear to be improper. Did Shidy force you to take any given man from any one of those certifications?—A. No, sir. He did not force me in the discharge of my duty.

Mr. ROOSEVELT. I would like to submit in evidence the report of the certifications. It covers seven cases. It does not show what grade these different men are from, and we of course would be unable to tell unless by examining them. The point is this: "We certify to the correctness of the report." It is signed by Jackson, Shidy, and Fahsel. This conclusively proves that Johnson and Fahsel were equally guilty with Shidy as far as these certifications are concerned.

The WITNESS. Let me look at that [taking the paper].

By Mr. BOATNER:

Q. There are four certifications here signed by you on the 18th of February, among whom is the name of Thomas F. Keaveny. It seems from the testimony in the case that Keaveny was really appointed to the position of stamper in December.—A. I think so.

Q. I think he was promoted to the position of carrier on the 1st of February following, and that his certification to you does not appear until the 18th of February, at which time you signed for it. I understand from the testimony that Keaveny was really certified to you in December prior to his appointment by one of these slips, samples of which you gave?—A. I think that is the fact.

Q. And that having appointed him as a stamper you considered him as subject to promotion on the 1st of February.—A. I did not consider him subject to promotion. The board recommended him for promotion. I took their opinion on that point.

Q. What I want to know is this: Was this individual a favorite of yours, or was his appointment due to political influence or to any other influence than should have prevailed?—A. Those are precisely the circumstances. I never saw Thomas F. Keaveny at all until he appeared in the certification, and then I had not seen him. Judge Jenkins, of the United States district court, stepped down to my office from the court-room—I forget whether it was before or after the certification, but about the time of the certification—and spoke to me about a man whom he understood had passed an examination, as he explained it, and desired me to consider his case when the name came up for consideration. When the certification did come, of course I remembered what Judge Jenkins had said, but I never knew Keaveny personally until the certification, and then I called him before me to see what kind of a man he was. He was certified, I think, originally as a stamper. I think so. I remember him. He was rather a large man for the place, but Judge Jenkins told me he was a capable, intelligent, reliable man, and I appointed him to the position. There was no favoritism about it. I did not know him or his friends.

Q. As to either one of these who were signed for on the 18th of February, was there any political or personal motive which dictated the appointment of these people?—A. The names appointed, according to my memorandum—I answer it specifically, for if every one of those would meet me in the street I would not know them from Adam. I never saw him.

Q. I do not think that is a full answer.—A. I do not know to-day and never did know what their political ideas are.

Q. Can you state whether or not you considered at the time of appointing these men you were appointing them in violation of the civil-service rules, at the suggestion of some one, or because of some favoritism?—A. There was no favoritism. I never appointed a man on that account. I do not care what the record shows.

Q. Please state whether or not in any of these appointments which have been referred to by the Commission you acted knowingly in violation of the civil-service rules.—A. No, sir.

Q. Now, it was stated by Mr. Shidy that you required him to send up the certifications of people whom you wanted, and you required him to mark down other people in order that he could send up these. Please state whether or not in any instance within your recollection you did require him or any member of the board to send certifications which contained the names of any particular individual.—A. No, sir.

Q. Please state whether or not you ever made an appointment without a previous certification from the board.—A. No, sir; never.

Q. Please state whether or not, having made an appointment, you required the certification to be furnished afterwards to cover the name of the person whom you appointed.—A. At the hour when appointed? No, sir.

Q. State if, having appointed a man without certification, you afterwards required a certification to cover the case.—A. I will answer that in the negative; but I ought to explain that I said in my testimony in 1888 that when I was hurried and Shidy was slow I might have said to him to bring me the names of some one whom the board might select, and I would tell him to make out a slip and bring it to me quick.

Q. You mean you appointed the man and told him to bring in the certification afterwards?—A. Bring in the names.

Q. When you did that, would you knew the man you appointed in advance was on the list properly?—A. Only as Shidy may have made the remark. He may have said the first three are so and so.

Q. Did you in any case appoint any three men in advance?—A. No, sir.

Q. With respect to these dates the books show these people were appointed and signed for February 18. Do I understand you to say that you signed the book as it was brought to you by Shidy without paying attention to the date?—A. I have no recollection of paying attention to the date, because——

Q. Are you aware and did you consider that it was essential under the civil-service rules that you should sign the book in advance for appointments; or that you signed the book after the appointment, provided the party was certified to before the appointment?—A. The secretary always stated to me before that those were reported every month, and that his habit was to report them each month.

Q. Then you considered it necessary for appointment?—A. We understood the slip to be a certification.

Q. What did you consider the object was in signing the book?—A. To complete the record of the certification and appointment.

Q. For what purpose was the record to be completed?—A. They keep a record and certification of the appointment, and a copy was forwarded to Washington.

Q. I understood you to say that Shidy made a report and brought the book to you. What connection did Shidy's having to make a report have with your signing the book?—A. The board is required to keep a record with the signature of the postmaster.

Q. What connection did it have with the questions?—A. I do not know as I understand you.

Q. I understood your testimony to be the other day this: That Shidy would furnish you a certification on slips of paper, samples of which you showed, and that afterwards when he would make his report he would give you the letter and the book to sign.—A. Yes, sir.

Q. Then you say you did not sign the book for the purpose of enabling him to make his report? —A. It was for both purposes.

By Mr. GREENHALGE (in the chair).

Q. I understand from the testimony the appointment of Keaveny was actually made in December?—A. December 8. He has a sworn affidavit to that effect.

Q. The appointment was actually made in December. Now you represent that that appointment was regular and in accordance with the rules of the Civil Service Commission.—A. According to the construction placed upon those rules in our office at that time.

Q. The appointment, then, depended upon the certification by the board, did it not?—A. Yes, sir.

Q. Now I wish to ask you whether there has been or can be produced any record evidence, either by copy or book, or certification, or of any other kind, showing the certification of Keaveny prior to the appointment when you say the appointment was actually made?—A. The only record that I know is Shidy's own record.

Q. And that appears of date February 18?—A. And his memorandum under the head "Remarks." On that record, as Johnson informs me, appears this statement in his own handwriting.

Q. What does it show?—A. "Appointed stamper December 8, 1887."

Q. Is there anything showing the certification?—A. No, sir; it was simply——

Q. They do not appoint, of course. The board does not make the appointment.—A. It is a record of the certification and appointment.

Q. Is there anything showing a record of the certification prior to February 18?—A. No, sir; nothing but the necessary fact that a certification must precede selection. I have my recollection of the fact.

Q. I am asking you now as to what record was made in the case, and whether all the records have been produced that can be, so far as you know.—A. So far as I know, except my letter to the Department. I think all the appointments to the Department of persons in the classified service, or persons not exempt from examination, contain a statement to the effect that they have duly passed and been reported for appointment.

Q. What date was your letter to the Department, and has that been put in evidence here?—A. That is an official letter in the possesion of the present postmaster.

Q. Has any mention been made of it, or has a copy been produced in this hearing? Do you know the date of that letter?—A. I think I could find it if I had time.

Q. At a subsequent meeting, produce a copy of that letter, if you can.—A. I will.

Q. I mean a copy of the letter to the Department containing a statement as to the appointment of Keaveny; it is a public letter.

By Mr. THOMPSON:

Q. I understand you to say——

The WITNESS (interposing). I wish to know if all the Civil Service Commissioners are going to be put against me. I think it is rather unfair—fifteen to one. I wish they would select some one man to examine me.

Q. I understood you to say in your examination day before yesterday that you were quite as familiar with the rules of the civil service as the Commission were. That may be so, for I do not claim to know them all myself.—A. In their practical application to my office. I do not wish to claim anything else.

Q. What course did you take to inform yourself as to the rules when you became postmaster?—A. I took the rules home and read them all night.

Q. Did you make appointments in any case at any one's suggestion? Are you responsible for all your appointments?—A. I am responsible.

Q. You say some five or six were irregular?—A. Apparently irregular.

Q. If those were made to you as they now appear, how is it possible for you not to know that they were irregular?—A. Is there a rule which would require me to examine certifications and know whether they are irregular or not?

Q. If you are familiar with the rules, how is it possible for you not to know that they were irregular?—A. If you ask me how it is possible to know——

Q. It is indifferent to me how you answer the question.—A. It is indifferent to me. I will say, whatever the rules may be, I have not understood that they required me to supervise any certifications of the local board. I have never undertaken to do so.

Q. Did you ever regard your signature as a part of the record?—A. Yes, sir.

Q. You admitted that you repeatedly failed to make that signature when you made appointments?—A. I have made that signature when the secretary of the board brought me the record to sign.

Q. You did not complete the record at the time?—A. I did not keep track of the business any further.

Q. You think that Shidy was slovenly in keeping these papers, and that was the cause of your not signing them at the right time?—A. I think so.

Q. Did you ever report him to the Civil Service Commission as slovenly?—A. No, sir; I did not know it until after the Commission was there.

Q. You knew these certifications were on scraps of paper?—A. I said the other day that this was the general practice in the office.

Q. On slips of paper?—A. I think so. It is the common practice of the postmaster.

Q. Did you ever write letters to the Postmaster-General about this man Cumming?—A. Yes, sir; I think I did.

Mr. THOMPSON. We have asked the Post-Office Department to send us the correspondence on that subject.

Q. When did you resign?—A. I resigned on the 8th of March, 1889, by a verbal arrangement which I have explained.

Q. Did you resign to the Postmaster-General, or the President?

By Mr. GREENHALGE:

Q. (Interposing.) Was it a resignation to take effect at some future time?—A. Not the original resignation.

Q. The question is as to the time of the resignation, not the nature of it.—A. That requires some explanation as to when I resigned. As I say, by the original resignation I resigned in March, 1889, and requested the Representative from my district to send in the appointment of my successor, and that he agreed to it and was engaged in selecting him and in looking up the matter. I gave him to understand that the quicker it was done the better it would suit me. He being rather slow about it, I subsequently wrote my resignation of the place, which was in his possession before, and this was before the visit of the Commission considerable time.

By Mr. THOMPSON:

Q. In whose possession?—A. The Representative.

Q. What I want to get at about the resignation is whether it was sent to the President or the Postmaster-General?—A. My resignation was addressed to the President.

Q. Was it delivered to your Representative in Congress?—A. No, sir; not my last resignation. I resigned three times.

Q. When was your final resignation—the one that was accepted ?—A. The Representative in Congress brought back my manuscript resignation after the Commission visited there. My first manuscript resignation addressed to the President was returned to me by the Representative in Congress immediately after the visit of the Commission, on the ground that they had done me a manifest injustice by misapprehension and he wished me to have an opportunity of defense before I left the office.

By Mr. GREENHALGE:

Q. You did not resign that time ?—A. I was prevented.

Q. Now as to the second resignation.—A. That is the second. The third was addressed to the President of the United States; and he informed me I think originally, I can not say positively, through Mr. Halford, his private secretary, that my resignation would be accepted.

Q. What date was that ?—A. Immediately after the decision of the President. I then sent it to the Postmaster-General, but I can not remember the date.

By Mr. THOMPSON:

Q. Did you not state in the newspapers, notably the New York Star, at the time the investigation was talked about that you hoped there would be a full and fair investigation before a tribunal whose decision would not be questioned ? Did you ever see this published letter of yours in reference to an investigation, and you hoped it would be fair, impartial, etc. ?—A. I think so.

Q. When it was intimated that your resignation would be accepted, you were then under a cloud ?—A. No, sir.

Mr. THOMPSON. I will introduce at this point a letter from the Post-Office Department.

OFFICE OF THE POSTMASTER-GENERAL,
Washington, D. C., August 3, 1889.

SIR: Your letter of July 29, tendering your resignation of the office of postmaster at Milwaukee, Wis., has been received. Before its receipt the Civil Service Commission had submitted a report of an examination of your office, upon which I should have taken action before this but for your request for delay in order that you might submit a statement in your own behalf. After the examination by the Civil Service Commission, a post-office inspector was sent to examine your office, and his report has also been submitted to me. Upon these reports your removal from office has been determined upon, but, as pending action upon them, you have offered your resignation. I will accept it to take effect upon the appointment and qualification of a successor, who will be designated as soon as possible.

Very respectfully, yours,

JNO. WANAMAKER,
Postmaster-General.

GEORGE H. PAUL, Esq.,
Milwaukee, Wis.

By Mr. ROOSEVELT:

Q. I would like to ask one question: Do you recollect in whose handwriting the certifications were that were submitted to you ?—A. I can not tell; I know the handwriting. This is in the handwriting of the secretary of the local board.

Q. Do you know whether those were the certifications submitted to you [handing the witness a paper] ?—A. I believe they were.

Q. Did you ever have submitted to you certifications of this character ?—A. Yes, sir.

Q. You have had certifications similar in most respects to these submitted to you ?—A. Not frequently; once or twice. The certifications gave me the standing of the applicant. In both cases I informed the secretary that although I did not consider it my business, it was my opinion that they were illegally there.

Q. Not "frequently, but once or twice." Do I understand you that certifications of this character were submitted to you ?—A. According to my memory.

Mr. ROOSEVELT. I offer that in evidence. It shows the arrangement and the adjustment by which certain men were brought into line.

Mr. GREENHALGE (in the chair). This is an original paper, and it has not gone in before?

Mr. ROOSEVELT. It is.

The WITNESS. I wish to say that I have never brought anybody into line, nor do I care to.

FRIDAY, *March* 7, 1890.

TESTIMONY OF GEORGE H. PAUL—Continued.

By Mr. STONE:

Q. Mr. Paul, you were appointed June 1, 1885, and retired from office September 27, 1889 ?—A. I took the position at that time, June 1. I was appointed some time before.

Q. You went out in 1889 ?—A. September 27, 1889 ?

Q. Who was your predecessor ?—A. Henry T. Payne.

Q. Was he a Republican ?—A. By common report; yes, sir.

Q. The office had been subject to civil-service regulations for some years before your incumbency ?—A. Yes, sir.

Q. When you entered the office, what number of people were then employed therein in all grades ?—A. I wish to say as to these statistics, some of which I did not have before, have been prepared with some little hurry, but mostly they are data furnished me from the Department on yesterday.

The CHAIRMAN. Can you answer the question, how many ?

The WITNESS. And according to that information I give these statistics, which I believe to be correct. The number of employés of all grades, June 1, 1885, were ninety-four.

The CHAIRMAN. That is, letter carriers and all ?

Mr. STONE. Of all grades. Of that number, how many were in the classified service and subject to be examined before appointment ?—A. The number requiring civil-service examination was sixty-nine, as I have it.

Q. Of the total force of ninety-four, how many were in the excepted places or places below the civil service; that is, how many in the unclassified service ?—A. Twenty-five.

Q. Can you state accurately or approximately how many of the ninety-four people you found in the office were Democrats and how many were Republicans ?—A. Well, sir, I can only give the general opinion, which was the public opinion, which I never heard contradicted, and never knew any reason to change my supposition on the subject; that there were eighty-seven adults, that is, voters, in that office when I went in, all of whom were understood to be, and always have been understood to be, Republicans. There were six minors and one or two women.

Q. When you retired from the office in September, 1889, what was the total number of people then employed therein in all grades ?—A. One hundred and forty-five.

Q. Of that number how many were in the classified service and subject to examination before appointment?—A. One hundred and two. I think that is inclusive of substitutes.

Q. How many were in the excepted places, or places below the civil service?—A. I believe twenty-eight, sir.

Q. How many in the excepted service—the number in the classified service.

The WITNESS. One hundred and two.

The CHAIRMAN. What is the other?

The WITNESS. One hundred and forty-five.

The CHAIRMAN. Then that would leave forty-three?

The WITNESS. There is some below the civil service what you would—for instance, some stamp agencies, etc., so it makes the whole number, the number in the excepted positions, proper would be twenty-eight and fifteen.

The CHAIRMAN. That would be forty-three; that is what it is.

The WITNESS. Altogether.

Mr. BOATNER. It is bound to be if there are one hundred and two in the classified service and one hundred and forty-five in all; it is bound to be forty-three.

The WITNESS. You understand there are men appointed who sell stamps in the city.

The CHAIRMAN. They are simply selling stamps and are not in the office?—A. Yes, sir.

By Mr. STONE:

Q. Of the sixty-nine persons employed in the classified service on June 1, 1885, when you took charge, how many severed their connection with the office during your incumbency?—A. Twenty persons.

Q. Of the twenty persons how many were removed?—A. Five.

Q. For what reason were they removed; I mean were their removals due to political, personal, or official causes?—A. There were no removals on political grounds ever. The only removals made were for violations or offenses under the postal law and regulations generally; a majority, I think, according to my recollection, were for intoxication.

Q. Well, of the twenty who separated from the office five were removed, how did the other fifteen separate?—A. Resignations and deaths. I think they were all resignations. Allow me to examine my memorandum for a moment (looking at memorandum), fourteen of them resigned and one of them died, sir.

Q. That covers the classified. Now there were twenty-five persons employed in the excepted places?—A. Yes, sir; what is the inquiry?

Mr. STONE. One moment. How many of those severed their connection with the office during your incumbency?—A. Fifteen.

Q. Of that number how many were removed?—A. Five of them were removed from the excepted places.

Q. How did the other ten cease their connection with the office?—A. Five of them resigned and the positions of five were abolished by the Department.

Q. Then of the employés in the office at the date of your appointment thirty persons were removed or died or resigned and five places were abolished?—A. Five places.

Q. Twenty in the classified service and ten in the unclassified service were removed, died, or resigned?—A. Yes, sir.

Q. Were those thirty vacancies occasioned by resignations, removals, or death filled by your appointment?—A. Yes, sir.

Q. To what extent and what number was the classified service or classified force of the office increased during your incumbency?—A. Well, sir, I make thirty carriers, adding the other places ten, making a total increase of forty.

Q. But to what extent was the excepted or unclassified board increased during your incumbency?—A. Eleven.

Q. The office force, then, was increased to fifty-one persons during your term?—A. Yes, sir.

Q. Those fifty-one added to the ninety-four employed at the date of your appointment makes one-hundred and forty-five employed at the date of your retirement?—A. Yes, sir; that is the figure. Yes, sir; that makes ninety-four.

Q. It makes one hundred and forty-five?

The WITNESS. I mean makes one hundred and forty-five.

Q. Your appointment, then, covered the fifty-one increased force and thirty vacancies referred to as occurring in the old 1885 force?—A. Yes, sir.

Q. Of the employés, both classified and unclassified service?—A. Yes, sir; the whole number.

Q. Is it true also that persons appointed by you afterwards ceased their connection with that office during your term?—A. Yes, sir.

Q. How many in the classified service of your own appointees retired during your term?—A. Fourteen.

Q. Of these how many were removed?—A. Five.

Q. How did the others separate?—A. Those of my own appointees?

Q. Yes, sir.—A. Nine; eight resigned and one died.

Q. How many in the unclassified service of your own appointees retired during your term?—A. The same number, fourteen.

Q. How many were removed?—A. Two.

Q. How did the other twelve separate?—A. Resigned, eleven, and died, one.

Q. Altogether, then, twenty-eight of your own appointees separated from this office, fourteen in each branch, and their places were refilled by you?—A. Yes, sir.

Q. Now, let me understand——

The WITNESS. Recollect, this is on my best calculation on these statistics.

Q. Where have you made these calculations, from reports in the Post-Office Department?—A. Yes, sir, and from reports I have taken from the official records.

Q. Now, let me understand. There were in your office sixty-nine people under the classified service when you took charge in 1885?—A. Yes, sir.

Q. And you removed only five of them during your entire term?—A. Yes, sir; that was all.

Q. Now, there were twenty-five persons in office when you took charge in excepted positions and not included in the civil service, and who could be removed and their places filled by you at your pleasure.—A. Yes, sir.

Q. You removed only five of them during your entire term?—A. Yes, sir; that is all, sir.

Q. Of the ninety-four persons you found in your office when you took charge you removed only ten?—A. That is all.

The CHAIRMAN. Is it necessary to repeat these questions? He has already stated all that.

Mr. Stone. I think you had better just let me proceed, Mr. Chairman.

The Chairman. All right. I only wanted to get through with the witness as soon as possible.

Mr. Stone. I will get through shortly. (To the witness.) Now, you were responsible for the official integrity of the employés?—A. Yes, sir.

Q. What were the politics of your chief officers—heads of divisions?—A. The answer to that question covers a period of over four years. Shall I answer that question in detail, Mr. Chairman?

Mr. Stone. I simply asked the question what were their politics.

The Witness. Of the chiefs of divisions?

Mr. Stone. Yes, sir.—A. At what special dates, sir.

Q. Well, during your term.—A. I can not answer that question directly as to the entire term. For instance, I will illustrate. The chief of the money-order division was there about three or more years—a Republican; and then Mr. Fahsel of the exa iining-board took his place, being promoted.

Q. He was a Democrat?—A. Fahsel was understood to be so; he was termed a Democrat, I believe.

Mr. Boatner. That is, his politics were not very well defined?

The Witness. No; they were not very well defined. No, sir; he was not a politician.

By Mr. Stone:

Q. Well, as to the others?—A. The superintendent of the mail division, from my understanding, was a very pronounced Republican; not offensively so in his political duties. The superintendent of the stamp division was a Republican. The superintendent of the registry division was Shidy. I do not know what you would call him now. The superintendent of the free-delivery division was a Democrat and a labor man.

Q. Was what?—A. He acted partially with what is called the labor organization of our State.

Q. Well, is that all?—A. The superintendent of the general delivery was a Republican throughout. I think that makes a complete answer to the question.

Q. And these chiefs had immediate control of the men in their respective divisions?—A. Yes, sir; had immediate charge of them.

Q. Can you give me an accurate or an approximate idea of the political affiliations of your office force at the date of your retirement?—A. I have undertaken to state that fact as nearly as possible from my information, but it is an estimate. I was not in politics myself directly, and of course do not claim to be an expert in that matter, but this is my answer. There were eight minors and five women in the force, and of the remainder I estimate there were about seventy persons of Republican proclivities a id associations, and fifty or more of Democratic proclivities, some of whom probably belonged to the labor organization, which is a third party organization. The others are wholly unknown to me of their political associations or ideas.

Q. So then during your term and at its close, practically, nearly all employés in your office were Republicans, having only one Democratic head of division; a large majority of your working force was Republican?—A. Yes, sir; quite a large majority. Of course that included the original force, and I should say that those who entered the office by appointment during my term were very nearly divided with a little preponderance in the favor of the anti-Republican force.

3117——19

Q. Of your own appointees?—A. Yes, sir.

Q. Did that apply to both classes, that is, the classified and the unclassified appointments?—A. Yes, sir; it applied to all classes.

Q. Mr. Paul, what are your politics?—A. My politics, it is almost impossible to state. If you wish me to explain my political views I could do so at length, but it might not entertain the committee.

Q. Were you considered a Democrat or a mugwump?—A. I am classed as a Democrat in my views on Government principles.

Q. A Democratic spoilsman?—A. No, sir; not under any circumstances.

Q. If you were a Democrat in charge of this office why did not you select Democrats at least in the chiefs of divisions, at the head of them?—A. Well, sir, I understand that would have been a violation of the intent of the civil service law.

Q. But those men held excepted places?—A. Yes, sir; but I understand the law to be general, especially the proclamations of successive Presidents have been to the effect to include those outside the rules and regulations, to the effect that political considerations shall not govern any official charged——

Q. You were an officer of the civil service association in the Northwest when you were made postmaster?—A. Yes, sir; and am still.

Q. The object of that association was to inculcate and advance the civil service idea?—A. Yes; the civil service idea.

Q. You were an advocate of civil service reform?—A. I am in a general sense. I have expressed my views in writing and they are published with others in the reports to Congress. I have doubted the practicability of the civil service reform law in its present state. If I am allowed a single remark, I think it restrains an honest man and does not restrain a rascal in this. That is my impression of the law.

Q. Do you contend that you conducted your office along the line and practice of civil service reform?—A. Yes, sir; I do entirely.

Q. Do you contend that you conformed your administration substantially to the requirements of the civil service law?—A. Yes, sir; I do.

Q. Do you contend that your appointments in the classified service were made in conformity with that law?—A. Yes, sir; but I ought to say this, perhaps, that the law and the rules being new are in a technical sense considerably crude; that there is necessarily an insufficiency in the execution of the law because of the inability under that organization to execute such a law. The Commission is not large enough to carry on the machinery throughout the entire country on that account.

Q. I am speaking now of your office, not of the Commission, of your work in your office at Milwaukee.—A. So far as I could understand the purposes of the Commission and its rules and so far as they were applicable to myself as postmaster I executed the law, I think, as correctly and uniformly as can be done by any postmaster.

Q. Do you contend that the local board at Milwaukee observed the law so far as your knowledge extends in examining and marking and certifying applicants to you for appointment?—A. Yes, sir; I believe that the local board acted in good faith so far as that is concerned, as a board.

Q. I understand your legal connection with the civil service is to call for certifications, to make your appointment from same, and then receipt for your man?—A. Not entirely.

Q. What else had you to do with it legally?—A. Yes, sir; there are some reports to make, but practically the duties of a postmaster or appointing officer under the law are limited to the mere selection of his appointees from the certification.

Q. The Civil Service Commission charges and Shidy swears that the local board acted in concert with you, manipulated markings and certifications in order to secure appointments which could not be made in the regular way. I understand you to deny that?—A. I deny that totally.

Q. Mr. Paul, as a matter of fact, can not such things be done, and easily done, by a postmaster situated, for instance, as you were, provided the postmaster is disposed to do it under the law?—A. It is my opinion, in answer to this question, that a postmaster disposed to be dishonest and who is without conscientiousness in the execution of the law, can fill his office from top to bottom with his own political friends. I have not the slightest doubt about that, under the law.

Q. How can he do that without coming into violation of the law, and subjecting himself to punishment?—A. I do not think an open violation of the law would be necessary, nor do I believe, under the present system, that he would be discovered as a rule if he should calculatingly intend to violate the law. While I think it could be done——

Q. Well, how?—A. Well, sir, one answer to that question implies some reference to the process of appointment from the beginning. The examinations are made by the local board. A postmaster and his friends and political committees may stuff the examination class to any extent, is the first criticism I will make. Supposing the local board to be fairly observant of the law in the marking, there was really no penalty that they fear in that, but as a rule they would naturally mark correctly under the instructions of the Commission, but when the certifications are made it is very possible for them to make these irregular certifications in some cases if the Commission does not exercise an immediate and constant practical supervision over the whole matter. Then, again, while I disclaim that my board was ever in any manner subservient to me in any special way, still in that case I think they are very liable to be subservient to the general political character of the office, to the disposition of the appointing officer, and might be under his control. Then, perhaps, lastly and in the most important degree, the discretion which is given the postmaster in the selection from three names now, which was formerly four, is almost sufficient practically to enable him to select men of his own politics in every case. In three names coming to him, if the appointing officer is a politician, he either knows or can easily ascertain what is the political character of these men. If his object is to promote the interest of his political party, he selects in every instance—in every instance he will select a political friend, of course, and in that way nearly all the appointments would go out to a man of his own political faith. I do not see anything to prevent him if the person is not conscientious in the observance of the law. I think, after all, the efficiency of the civil service must depend upon the character of the appointing officer.

Q. Is it not true as a rule, speaking as a man of observation and experience, that more people friendly to the existing national administration apply for civil-service examination than those opposed to it?—A. Yes, sir; the public sentiment is, "after all, I am entitled to appointment because I have served the party." This is the general current of opinion among applicants.

Q. Now, if these certifications could be manipulated so as to secure the appointment of a political friend, could not the manipulation extend a little further so as to secure the appointment of a personal friend?—A. Yes, sir; in the same way precisely.

Q. In other words, can not the postmaster at Milwaukee or New York or St. Louis, if he felt disposed to do so, reach about the same end he desired with this law?—A. Yes, sir; I do not think the law is a necessary restraint except upon a man's conscience and his oath of office.

Q. Mr. Paul, do you think such a course as Shidy swears he pursued is in accord with the civil-service idea of which you are a distinguished advocate and exponent?—A. I do not quite understand the latter part of the question, Mr. Stone.

Q. Do you think that the course which Mr. Shidy swears he pursued is in accord with the civil-service idea?—A. In accordance with civil-service law as I understand it?

Q. Yes, sir.—A. Well, sir, it is my opinion that his course certainly is not in accord with the requirements of the law and rules, but I believe the trouble with the certifications arises largely from the confusion of the board as to the instructions of the Commission, and its many changes of the Commission itself, many changes of the rules themselves, and the crude state of those rules. Perhaps I did not get your idea.

Q. I am speaking of Mr. Shidy's testimony, which you have read. Do you think it would have been a proper thing for Mr. Shidy to do what he swears he did do?—A. No, sir; I do not.

Q. Would you have considered it your duty to report him to his superiors here at Washington if you had had knowledge of such conduct on his part?—A. If I had had an opportunity to have examined his record of certifications and to know just precisely his process of making the certifications, I certainly should have reported it to all mankind without exception.

Q. Would you have a man remain in your employ who was constantly and intentionally violating the law he was specially charged with enforcing?—A. No, sir, I would not.

Q. Did you not know it was improper, even criminal, for Mr. Shidy to publish a list of eligibles and expose the record to your inspection or to the inspection of others in your office?—A. Yes, sir, I did, and I supposed at the time that the Commission itself was perfectly aware of that fact. That was my presumption. But this the Commission ought to know, and it is alone responsible for the discharge of its duties under the Commission or any of its officers, and the postmaster has too many other duties to charge him with the supervision of that portion of the law.

Q. Did you permit these practices of Shidy's to be done with your knowledge and pass without censure?—A. No, sir; in every case known to me I usually referred the matter of Dr. Shidy's to the board and told them they must be more careful in observing the law as well as the spirit of the rules.

Q. As you are an advocate of civil-service reform, why did you not insist on Shidy's obeying the civil-service law?—A. I was not aware, sir, of any violation, mainly, except in a technical way, until this investigation.

Mr. THOMPSON. Will you ask the witness where that list of eligibles was published, whether he regarded that as a technical violation of the law, which was a positive violation of the rules at that time?

Mr. STONE. What do you say to that?

The WITNESS. No, sir; I would not regard that as technical, but at the same time I did not regard and never have regarded it as my especial duty to look after the immediate action of the examining board in my office.

Mr. BOATNER. Has it been offered here in evidence that Dr. Shidy published a list of eligibles in a paper?

The WITNESS. Yes, sir; he published all of the persons——

Mr. STONE. Mr. Paul testified to that. In this connection is it not evident from your statement that the civil-service law was administered loosely, to put it in a mild form, at Milwaukee, without regard now to whose fault it was or the motive. The fact is, it was loosely administered.—A. I do not think that word will apply to the general administration of the law, sir. There were a number of cases referred to as violations of the law, technical violations——

Q. I understand that you claim that it was largely owing to the inattention, indolence, and loose business methods of Mr. Shidy, etc.

The WITNESS. And that the actual violations were limited—there was a small number—out of the number of cases referred to, about one hundred certifications, very few were of this class. I think the law was pretty well observed by the board.

Q. Mr. Paul, you did not remove Shidy from the post-office because of any official irregularities committed by him as secretary of the board of local examiners?—A. No, sir; I did not, because he was at that time in the hands of the Commission.

Q. Did the Civil Service Commission remove him from the local board after his alleged crimes were discovered?—A. No, sir; they did not, or any other member of the local board.

Q. Was he a member of the local board at the time you discharged him from the post-office?—A. Yes, sir; he was as far as I know.

Q. Did the Commission remove Johnston or Fahsel after their visit to Milwaukee in 1889?—A. No, sir; Mr. Johnston served until a week or two ago continuously; Mr. Fahsel until he resigned, I think, from the office, perhaps a month ago or more.

Q. Did this Civil Service Commission permit these three men, after all these alleged irregularities were discovered, to continue there as a local board?—A. They did continue to act as a local board as long as they remained in the office, each and every one, except Mr. Johnston, who resigned, I think, two or three weeks ago.

Mr. ROOSEVELT. This is Mr. Paul's statement; this is simply his statement; I understand this is not a statement of fact. We can be examined on that evidence.

The CHAIRMAN. This is all Mr. Paul's testimony.

The WITNESS. This is my understanding of the facts, sir.

By Mr. STONE:

Q. The charge against you is, you conspired with Shidy to defeat the civil service law so as to make some appointments which would not have been made if the law had been followed in letter and spirit; that favoritism was shown and that some men were appointed who were not entitled to receive appointments. Have any other charges been made against your administration of the office?—A. Not that I know of or ever heard of.

Q. Has any person in authority—have the people or the press ever complained that your office was badly administered?—A. No, sir.

Q. And that the public service suffered by reason of your method of business?—A. Not in any essential particulars to my knowledge.

Q. Did you have any trouble in your office? This list of charges states that rules of the civil service were not observed in these appointments or some of them——

The WITNESS. In these certifications?

Q. Was there any trouble about the actual workings of the office?—A. No, sir; the workings of the office and the office itself generally was commended by the Department repeatedly, by the heads of the Department.

Q. Now, I want to ask this question and I believe I am through. I want to ask you as an experienced civil service reformer——

The WITNESS. I do not claim that, sir.

Q. Whether it is not possible that a post-office even of the first-class might be successfully administered and the work of the office done by men who were never asked, for instance, when the battle of Bunker Hill was fought, but who were equal to the duty of canceling stamps, keeping books, and delivering mail?—A. Oh, yes, sir; I think there is a wide discordance in the nature of the examination to the duties to be performed practically in the office, except in this, that the examinations generally are an evidence of good general information and intelligence somewhat on the part of the candidate. But it must be also understood practically—I have given this information to the committee some time—it must also be understood that this class which apply for examination are those men least fit for entering the public employment as a rule, and they apply because they are out of places. When men get out of places because of lack of qualification they are sure to come into this examination if they have any school education at all.

Q. The men appointed by you to excepted places, were they men of as much capacity for the discharge of the duties to which they were called as those that were appointed under the rules of the civil service?—A. Far better, sir; far better, and their qualifications were far better than those obtained from the Civil Service Commission at the close of my administration, for I made special comparisons in reference to the truth of this matter.

(Here Mr. BOATNER took the chair.)

Mr. STONE. According to the theory that when no examination was to be had he would have in view more especially the particular qualifications of the applicant for the service he was called upon to perform than a general scholastic examination.

The WITNESS. My office is peculiar in that respect.

Q. I am not speaking particularly of your office. I am discussing this with you now as a gentleman who is supposed to have given a good deal of attention to civil service.—A. I am positive of this fact, Mr. Chairman, that an intelligent appointing officer, with the desire to promote the public service to the highest degree and with a familiar knowledge of all the facts concerning his office, can make a better selection, a far better selection, from the applicants examined if the whole list was submitted to him than by a selection from three at a time. I think the examination is a good guaranty of general qualification for the position as far as it goes, but the selection could be very largely improved if he was allowed the whole range of the list, so as to study the special adaptation of applicants to particular places. The qualifications required are very various, which are not recognized in the examination at all. For instance, the stamp clerk requires one qualification, a money-order clerk another, and a stamper another, and so on all the way through. The man who stamps letters, 12,000 before breakfast, ought to be a quick man, for instance, and he must be rapid, must be a light, nervous, quick man. The man who counts money must have some financial ability; and so the man who is a letter-carrier must not be a man in poor health, in poor strength, or lacking in strength, or other qualities that make a man rapid and strong on foot; and so I might go on indefinitely. The examination should have reference to all these things. A carrier who can not speak the German language in our city is utterly worthless; the carrier who comes from the outside of the city can not perform any duty worth while for months and years, and so on. I might enumerate an indefinite number of these qualifications, special qualifications required, which are not recognized in the examination at all. For instance, in our office, which is a large one in the United States, we have Germans, Norwegians, Italians, and every kind of population. You hear, as I once mentioned to the Commission, at least five languages spoken in a street-car at the same time, and what are you going to do? One neighborhood is Italian, another is a lot of Icelanders, perhaps another is entirely German, and all that; still you must take one of the three that is presented for that particular district for which his appointment is to be taken at the time.

Q. Well your idea is this, by submitting the whole list you would be able to secure a man competent for a particular position.—A. Yes, sir; I think the only safeguard is in submitting the whole list as according to law, also in the appointment of the appointing officer or postmaster or custom-house collector, whatever he might be. If a man is a bad man who is taken he will perform bad service and in the case of a good man he will naturally perform good service in that light. The point I make is, that the civil service law and rules as now constructed, of course being somewhat crude, being new and not grown up by any process of evolution, are not a practical restraint upon a man of bad disposition in office except to a very limited degree.

The CHAIRMAN. Are there any further questions of this witness?

Mr. LYMAN. I would like to ask Mr. Paul two or three questions. He has stated, in answer to questions propounded by Mr. Stone, that a certain number of employés then in his office were of two political parties, and as I understood him, in answer to Mr. Stone's question, he stated they were all Republicans when he took charge; is that a fact?— A. Yes, sir; that is what I stated.

Q. On what do you base that statement?—A. Well, sir, I base it partially on a practical knowledge of the relation of the men, partially on the fact that the postmaster himself was an officer of the Republican State Committee; but I dislike to give some evidence of that because——

Q. Do you mean that you yourself were a member of the State Committee or your predecessor?—A. My predecessor, I stated.

Q. Did you make inquiry of the employés of the office to ascertain their politics?—A. I had knowledge from facts in that office.

Q. You can answer the questions directly, can you not?

The CHAIRMAN. He asked you whether you made inquiry of the employés whether they were Republicans or Democrats?

The WITNESS. No, sir. I never did.

By Mr. LYMAN:

Q. Did you make inquiries for the purpose of ascertaining what their politics were?—A. No, sir; but they were publicly known. They were known by conversation, but I had knowledge from other sources.

Q. But you satisfied yourself on that point, so you are speaking now from information you obtained at that time that they were all Republicans?—A. They always were and always had been Republicans.

Q. In answer to Mr. Stone you also stated that of the persons appointed by you while you were postmaster a large percentage were Democrats. How did you know that fact?—A. Appointed by me a large percentage? Not a large percentage; no, sir; I did not intend to say that.

Q. You gave the figures?—A. I did not give definite figures; I did not know exactly how they stood, but I say by estimate——

Q. But you gave certain figures, and all I wanted to know was upon what you based that statement?—A. Not by personal investigation at all, sir. I ignored the political side of the question entirely in the management of the office; entirely.

Q. Then you did not know the politics of these people who were in the office when you came in by personal inquiry, and you did not learn the politics——

The WITNESS. I would like to state to Mr. Lyman personally just how I knew the politics of the men, if it is deemed necessary.

Mr. LYMAN. That is all I wanted to bring out, the basis of your information.—A. I did know the fact. I do not wish to reflect upon my predecessor at all, but I do know the fact that a large portion of the force of that office was practically engaged in politics, in canvassing the city. I knew so from the books and papers left in the office.

Q. Was not that the tendency under the old system of appointment, that they should all be political?—A. Yes, sir; my predecessor was not under the civil service at that time.

Q. For how long?—A. Well, sir, that the Commission can answer. The date I went in was June the 1st, 1885.

Q. I want to know if you can tell how many appointments he made under civil-service law?

The WITNESS. What was the question?

Q. Can you tell from memory how many appointments your predecessor made under the civil-service law?—A. No, sir, I can not.

Q. But a very small part of the force?—A. I presume it would be a very small fraction of the whole number.

Q. Then it is probably true that a large percentage of the force was appointed before the civil-service law went into effect?—A. That is unquestionably the fact.

Q. And you think that probably accounts for the fact that the force was almost unanimously Republican?—A. It may account for the fact that a great part of the appointees were of one political party. I did not comment on it, but stated it in answer to a question.

Mr. LYMAN. I wanted to state to the committee that the Commission may desire to file statements from the official record and the Post-Office Department in connection with the testimony given by this witness this morning—drawn out this morning.

The WITNESS. Is it a question of politics?

Mr. LYMAN. No, sir, it is simply the statistics made up by the official record and Post Office Department.

The WITNESS. The statistics I have are simply verified by me, by the Department reports here mostly and from the official record.

Mr. THOMPSON. I desire to introduce a letter into testimony here from the Assistant Postmaster General, and I will state——

Mr. STONE. Are you through with this witness?

Mr. LYMAN. That is all I desire to ask of this witness now.

Mr. THOMPSON. I understood Mr. Paul to say yesterday or in the course of his testimony that Mr. Cumming had never held any but an excepted place in the Milwaukee Post Office; that he never held a place in the classified service. I understood him to introduce or to offer to introduce an affidavit of Mr. Cumming to that effect. In reply to Mr.

Paul's statement and that affidavit I desire to read the following letter from Assistant Postmaster General Clarkson.

POST-OFFICE DEPARTMENT,
OFFICE OF THE FIRST ASSISTANT POSTMASTER GENERAL,
Washington, March 6, 1890.

SIR: In reply to your letter of the 5th instant, relative to Mr. Charles J. Cumming, a clerk formerly attached to the post-office at Milwaukee, Wis., I beg to state that the records show that Mr. Cumming was approved as a stamper, at an annual compensation of $220, from May 1 to May 15, 1888. From May 16 to July 31, 1888, his compensation was increased to $270 at year; from August 1 to September 14, his compensation was approved at $410 a year; from September 15, 1888, to January 15, 1889, his compensation was approved at $450; from January 16, 1889, to June 30, 1889, his compensation was approved at $500; from July 1, 1889, to December 31, 1889, his compensation, under the classification act, was approved at $600 a year.

The pay-rolls on file with the Auditor show that the quarterly compensation approved for Mr. Cumming was as follows:

From May 1 to June 30, 1888 .... $43.33
Quarter ended September 30, 1888 .... 90.72
Quarter ended December 31, 1888 .... 112.50
Quarter ended March 31, 1889 .... 112.50
Quarter ended June 30, 1889 .... 125.00
Quarter ended September 30, 1889 .... 150.00
Quarter ended December 31, 1889 .... 150.00

Very respectfully,

J. S. CLARKSON,
First Assistant Postmaster-General.

Hon. CHARLES LYMAN,
President Civil Service Commission, Washington, D. C.

I have run this over rapidly, and I understand that he received nearly $800 pay straight along under that appointment.

Mr. BOATNER. What is the lowest salary under the classified service?

Mr. THOMPSON. There is no minimum in a post-office.

The CHAIRMAN. He was receiving payment as stamper under civil-service rules in the classified service?

Mr. ROOSEVELT. From May 1. May 1 was the time he was appointed, and he received this pay right along. I understood Mr. Paul the other day to state that he was not appointed to that place, and then he stated he was appointed and declined, and produced an affidavit to that effect.

The CHAIRMAN. Mr. Paul, the recollection of the chairman is that you stated Mr. Cumming was appointed stamper and declined, and that he never held any but an excepted position?

Mr. STONE. The evidence itself will show it.

By the CHAIRMAN:

Q. Now, one moment. I will ask this question: Here is a letter from Mr. Clarkson, which says that he received pay as a stamper? The WITNESS. Did I put those affidavits in yesterday? Mr. Cumming makes affidavit that——

Q. Have you any knowledge of this? The WITNESS. If you will allow me time to look at this letter I may give you an answer.

The CHAIRMAN. Not referring to the affidavit of Mr. Cumming, have you any personal recollection whether Mr. Cumming served in an excepted position or in a position which came under the civil-service regulations?—A. I think he was confirmed in an excepted position. I think he was first nominated for stamper, but transferred to an excepted position, and I know that nearly all this time referred to in these dates he was serving in an excepted position.

Q. Mr. Paul, I want to call to your mind that you did state here when you were under examination the other day that he was appointed as a stamper and declined to accept that position.—A. Yes, sir.

Q. And you stated then that he never was employed in the office in a position other than an excepted position.—A. Yes, sir; and that is why he was employed all the time referred to.

Q. How do you account for this letter of Mr. Clarkson?—A. I might account for it in this way. He says that Mr. Cummings was approved as a stamper at $220 per annum from May 1 and May 15, etc., and May 16, July 1, and so on. Now the fact is, according to my recollection, that Mr. Cummings was first nominated by the express direction or order of the Commission as a stamper, which would be in the classified or service covering an examination, and that having been nominated under that letter from the Commission to the Department, he declined and then was simply transferred on the record from the position of stamper to that of a stamp clerk in the general delivery, which place he occupies now and is there in the office. I can not see that there is any discrepancy here except in this, that it is true that it has assumed that he was in the classified service up to the present day, which is not the case at all, to my knowledge.

Q. Your statement is, he never was in the classified service.—A. I never knew him to be in the classified service.

Q. The facts are, if this letter is correct, and that appears to be taken from the record, the facts are these, that Mr. Cummings occupied a position in the post-office that was an excepted position.—A. Yes, sir.

Q. And that he was by your report drawing the salary as a classified clerk, was he not, by your report here to the Department; that he was on the pay-roll of the Department in one capacity and doing work in another, was he not?—A. Well, sir, I think he is reported to the Department and occupying another position; I am not quite sure he is. Mr. Stone, did you return those papers?

Mr. STONE. That is the roster?—A. Yes, sir.

Mr. STONE. Yes, sir, I sent them back.

The WITNESS. I examined the roster very rapidly going over it yesterday, but I think he is reported as having accepted the position as a stamp clerk, and Mr. Clarkson, of course, in making this would not have the other before him. I know it to be the fact that he has served continuously in an excepted position and not in the classified service, and I am very positive that he is now reported on the regular roster as being in an excepted position.

The CHAIRMAN. I understand, Mr. Paul, the affidavits you desire to be an exhibit before the committee. Are there any other papers you wish to go before the committee?

The WITNESS. Yes, sir, I think so. I wish to refer directly in reference to the communication of Mr. Clarkson and the rosters themselves. As it now stands it is disconnected entirely ——

Mr. STONE. I had these rosters you know, and Mr. Scott, chief of that division, requested me yesterday to return them, and said he wanted to use them; I do not know what for, and in accordance with his request I gave them to the messenger to go back.

The CHAIRMAN. Mr. Paul, let me ask you this question, because you want to be set right if you have made any mistake. In case it should appear that he is carried on the roll as in a stamper's position, it is then merely an oversight on your part?—A. Nothing more than that, in that position.

Mr. THOMPSON. He was paid for it——

The CHAIRMAN. I stated if it is so made Mr. Paul says it was a matter of oversight in not notifying the Department.

The WITNESS. Entirely.

The CHAIRMAN. You want it to be so stated?

The WITNESS. Yes.

Mr. BOATNER. Would the pay be better or less for the position which he actually holds, or the position to which he would carry on the roll as shown by this letter?—A. There would be no difference. I think the committee will understand this better when it is understood how clerks are reported. The law requires the postmaster to make a roster of his clerks and report them as he wishes them confirmed. Once in so often. Now it is simply possible that while Cummings was appointed a stamper and that in the report of the entire force of the office, that he was included in the roll in an excepted position and confirmed by the Department. I think that is the exact state of the case.

I wish to introduce into the testimony a copy of the letter of the United States Civil Service Commission, signed by Mr. Graham, the secretary, September 18, 1885. That letter is not addressed to me; it is addressed to the examining board, and the only object in introducing it is to have the committee judge whether that letter was misconstrued as charged by the Commission.

U. S. CIVIL SERVICE COMMISSION,
Washington, D. C., September 18, 1885.

DEAR SIR: In the absence of his colleagues, Commissioner Gregory, now in charge, directs me to reply to your letter of September 16, that the examination for porters, stamp boys, junior clerks, etc., provided for in Regulation 22, implies that the persons eligible under these examinations shall be included on a distinct register of eligibles from which certifications may be made to such positions as you describe paying $360 a year. Those who have taken higher examinations as clerks or carriers may, of course, be certified to these lower places, and for this purpose may be transferred to the lower registers on their request.

Very respectfully,

ROBT. GRAHAM,
Secretary.

Dr. H. SHIDY,
Secretary Board of Examiners, Post-Office,
Milwaukee, Wis.

The CHAIRMAN. Here is Cumming's affidavit.

The WITNESS. Shall I read it?

The CHAIRMAN. It is in evidence, you want merely to refresh your memory and there is no necessity of reading it.

The WITNESS. I think the affidavit explains the matter, the latter end of it.

The CHAIRMAN. You have been examined on it and it is unnecessary to have it go down again.

The WITNESS. He was simply nominated as a stamper, but declined the position of stamper; he was included as stamper, but subsequently the Department or the Commission declared his position exempt, and that is where the transfer was made by the action of the Commissioner.

By the CHAIRMAN:

Q. Did not declare the position of stamper exempt?—A. No, sir.

Q. Then if this affidavit is correct, if it is true, then the records in the Post-Office Department are false in this when they say that he was appointed as a stamper, are they not?—A. I think not, sir; he was appointed as a stamper or rather in the grade of a stamper.

Q. But he was drawing pay as a stamper?—A. Yes, sir. If you will allow me just to state the fact as it is so, there will be no misapprehension. Mr. Cumming was nominated as a stamper in the service, that is to the grade of a stamper. There is no difference in the pay, and subsequently while being put to work in a certain position in the grade of stamper by the Department, or with the concurrence of the Commission, the position he filled was declared to be exempt from civil-service examination, and that transferred him by the action of the Department from a certified to an excepted position.

Q. But, Mr. Paul, one moment; the roster of the department showed that this man was receiving salary as a stamper; that is incorrect, is it not, because he was not doing work as a stamper?—A. The roster does not declare that; the roster declares the actual position. I am very sorry I can not be understood.

Mr. WEBSTER. Will you allow me to ask one question in this connection? This is a matter I brought out on Tuesday evening, and ask if this letter——

Mr. STONE. Just one moment, if you please. I would like to understand this; I have not done so yet.

SEVERAL MEMBERS. And we have not either.

The WITNESS. I gave you the common understanding of it in connection with the affidavit. Mr. Cumming was duly examined; the Commission ordered or permitted his restoration to the service, after having been certified three times; on account of injustice in the matter. He was then appointed a stamper, which would be a civil service position, that is, nominated for that position.

Mr. BOATNER. Do you mean appointed as a stamper or to the stamper grade?—A. Not as stamper, but to the stamper grade. Subsequently the very position to which he was appointed to, the stamper grade, the duties were such that department declared that position exempt from the classified service. Now, can that be understood?

Mr. BOATNER. Allow me to see if I get this idea. Mr. Paul, you say he was appointed to the stamper's grade?—A. Yes, sir; nominated.

Q. What kind of work was he assigned to?—A. To the handling of the stamps.

Q. To the handling of the stamps?—A. Yes, sir.

Q. Which class of work to which he was assigned was declared by the department not to be in the classified service?—A. Yes, sir.

Q. And he still remains in that grade?—A. Appointed at that time.

Q. And payment allowed for that place?—A. Yes, sir; there is no difference in the pay.

By Mr. HATTON:

Q. When the position was declared exempt he was in the registry department?—A. No, sir; the general delivery.

Q. In the stamp department of the general delivery?—A. Yes, sir.

Q. And they declared that place exempt from the civil-service law?—A. Yes, sir.

Q. Would it not be quite a natural mistake to have him still carried on the roster as stamper when he was in the general delivery?—A. But I think it is carried on the rolls as a stamper. I think the name appears there.

Q. In making allowance it would be a very easy matter to carry him on the roll and register as a stamper?—A. They could do it.

Mr. ANDREW. But did they do so?

By Mr. ROOSEVELT:

Q. I want to ask a question. Do I understand you correctly to say that we allowed you to appoint him to the classified service; that the

Commission allowed you to appoint him in the classified service ?—A. That is my impression, sir.

Q. What date does he begin payment there ?—A. May 1.

Q. On June 9 you were still writing to the Commission asking if the man could not be appointed. This shows, therefore, that at the time you were writing the man had been appointed and was receiving pay over a month before you had any permission from the Commission. Your letter of June 9 shows that at that time he was not in any excepted position. It is clear, then, that for six weeks at least he was drawing pay, or you were drawing pay for him while he was not in an excepted position and had been illegally appointed.—A. Let me see, sir. "It is all explained by the fact that I had been certified three times; I was restored to this list and immediately received an appointment by order of the Commission, but was never appointed to a civil service or classified position before or after or since said order——"

Q. It is his own statement. Let me point out to you according to this statement he could not have been restored to the list until after June 9 and he was appointed on May 1. He was not appointed to an excepted position until after June 9. On what date do I understand Mr. Paul stated he was appointed—he says he was appointed and declined at once?

The WITNESS. I did not say at once, but I think——

Mr. ROOSEVELT. Mr. Chairman, what date did Mr. Paul say he had been appointed and declined ?

The CHAIRMAN. He said he was appointed and declined to accept the position.

The WITNESS. My recollection is simply this: That Mr. Cumming was appointed a stamper and declined the position, but was not dismissed at all. This correspondence was had with the Commission. That is my impression as to the facts.

By Mr. ROOSEVELT:

Let me ask you right there what you mean by the fact that he was appointed and declined the position but was not dismissed. What do you mean ?—A. The question is we waited for the Commission to determine that fact in the case and give it consideration.

Q. What do you mean by declining the position ?

The CHAIRMAN. Let me ask this question right there: What was the necessity of writing to the Commission at all if this man was not to be appointed to a classified place and had not been so appointed, but had been appointed by you to an excepted position. What was the use of having this correspondence with the Commission at all ?—A. I will go into all that if the Committee desires.

By Mr. ROOSEVELT:

Q. Let me ask first what you mean by saying that he was appointed and declined the position, and yet was not dismissed. If your words mean anything, if the man was appointed and declined the position, he is not now in the service. Is not that what you understand by declining the position ?—A. I think, sir, he took the matter under consideration further sometime.

Q. He took under consideration; took what, the office under consideration ?—A. Took the position.

Q. Now, as I understand Mr. Paul's words here, they were that he was appointed but declined the position, but was not dismissed. Now, what that means, I do not know.—A. That is not what I said or intended to say, sir.

The CHAIRMAN. It may be perhaps what you did not intend to say.— A. He was offered the position of a stamper. I think the Commission itself can answer this question quite as well as I can. Of course I have

The CHAIRMAN. You have stated everything as nearly as you can recollect?—A. Yes, sir; there was no impropriety in it; the more you investigate it the more you will find no impropriety.

Mr. ROOSEVELT. You have nothing to say in explanation of the fact that he was appointed May 1 and was paid steadily on at the time you wrote us here, and as you state he had declined the position of stamper, and he in his affidavit says that he never was, never held the position, while as a matter of fact he was being paid nearly two months, possibly more, in a classified position?

The CHAIRMAN (to the witness). Do you want to make an explanation?—A. Nothing, but I think the records of the Department and the office of the Commission, in my opinion, together with the affidavit, will clearly explain the entire question involved. I can not recollect the special circumstances of any one case of a very non-essential appointment, certainly not for several years.

Mr. WEBSTER. I called your attention on Tuesday to the statement you made to me in Milwaukee, which was to the effect that you appointed him to this position and then suspended him from that position pending the report from Washington, intimating to me very clearly or gave me to understand at the time, that he was not in office in that interval, while this report from the Post-Office Department hows that he is certified there as being continued. I want you to explain that.

The CHAIRMAN. Did you say so to Mr. Webster at that time when they made the examination?—A. I gave him the impression when he was there, that previously to the pending question which arose as to the propriety of the appointment that he was held on——

Q. Was he suspended?—A. Not substantially, not in an offensive sense; that the appointment was held until the matter could be determined.

Q. How does it happen that you paid him at that time?—A. I have explained that all to the committee once, I think. I can not say positively, but possibly he was one of those persons who being entitled to appointment, and the committee having determined that he was entitled to an appointment at that time, he was also entitled to a compensation.

Mr. ROOSEVELT. Whether he was suspended or not?—A. Yes, sir. I think it is very much like a Commissioner going out for a month on his ranch and still drawing pay. We have those instances.

Mr. BOATNER. You think his position ought to be retroactive, that the pay becomes retroactive?

The WITNESS. Yes, sir.

Mr. THOMPSON. Mr. Chairman, I now desire to make a statement.

The CHAIRMAN. Very well, sir.

Mr. THOMPSON. Mr. Chairman and gentlemen of the committee, just as we were leaving in June, the 15th of June as I recollect, for inspection of some post-offices in Chicago and other places, Mr. Lyman called my attention and that of Mr. Roosevelt to the fact that there were serious charges against the postmaster at Milwaukee, and explained why it was not acted upon before that time and that it would be well for us to include Milwaukee in the trip. We were very busy and investigated three offices as I recollect, including Chicago. The morning of the day on which we were to leave for Milwaukee I got the statement of Mr. Doyle and report of Mr. Webster, all this mass of papers which have been submitted, and attempted as well as I could to get at their contents. I recollect, I know I read the first statement of Mr. Doyle and report of Mr. Webster, but I do not think I had time to read anything else when I left for Milwaukee. We called on Mr. Paul at his

office and examined him as to the whole matter of incorrect appointments in his office. I remember very well what occurred. Mr. Roosevelt would take Mr. Paul's statement and read from it and ask his explanation. Mr. Paul would occasionally glance at it, putting on his
glasses, but always putting it aside and stating, "You will have to
see Shidy about that; I do not know anything about it." Mr. Roosevelt stated, "I am reading this statement, Mr. Paul; we are not talking
of Dr. Shidy, but of what you did. Why did you make this appointment,
why did you make that appointment," and the invariable reply was,
"You must ask Dr. Shidy about that." In the course of the examination I think that afternoon (we examined him one afternoon and one
morning), I asked with a definite purpose in view which I will explain
if the committee desires it, "Mr. Paul how long have you served?"
and the reply was, "My time is out or my term is out. I am simply
waiting for my successor to qualify." The next day we examined him
again.

The WITNESS. I think it would make a good deal of difference whether
I said my time was out or that my term was out. I have granted,
Governor Thompson, and I grant it was very possible for the Commission to misapprehend the fact. I find no fault with the Commission; if
I have, I withdraw any complaint against the Commission in the construction of that language. I stated what the language was and the
purport of it and almost the precise words as I remember it. I do not
see any occasion why the testimony has been important, for on the
basis of their understanding they made the second supplementary report.
It is a fact that has passed and which can not be remedied, and the Commission can not remedy that now. I do not find any complaint against
the Commission making any number of reports if the Commission thinks
it their official duty, whether they make it on one question or another.
That is my view.

Mr. THOMPSON. The next morning we concluded the investigation
and went to Grand Rapids to investigate the post-office there. That
evening, in the hotel at Grand Rapids, Mr. Roosevelt approached Mr.
Lyman and myself with a rough draught of a report of Mr. Paul's case. I
objected to signing the report and we had a discussion about it. I took
the position, in the first place, that the letter which was just introduced
in evidence, and to which we referred fully in our supplementary report,
would explain perhaps some irregularities in the transfer of eligibles
from one list to another. Of course it could not explain the irregular
appointments and could not explain other irregularities except that
point. Secondly, I had not as far as I have been able to observe, thought
that Mr. Paul had been influenced by political considerations. There
seems to be no evidence of that kind; and thirdly I stated he is out of
office, and what was the use of shooting at a dead duck, what was the
use of making up a case against a man out of office, why should he be
brought before the bar of public opinion in this way. I stated if he
could be removed after what has been done I would not object very
much to signing the report. Mr. Roosevelt handed me the report and
said, "What will you agree to?" I took it and made some material alterations in it. My recollection is now I struck out one of two sentences, and
I know I altered several. Mr. Roosevelt and Mr. Lyman went over that
amended report, and they afterwards both said that they could sign
that. We came to Washington and certified the report to the President
and Postmaster-General.

The WITNESS. And to the Associated Press.

Mr. THOMPSON. Oh, yes, to the Associated Press. We wanted them to know it. Then Mr. Paul came out with a statement, which I think was stated to me by him, some parts of which he has omitted. In that, though he stated distinctly that he had told the Commission, he contradicted us positively; that he had not told the Commission that his term of office was out, but he had given up the exact date at which it expired, and he could prove it. I immediately said if that was the case, if he had any unexpired portion of the term to serve, why, it was the duty of the Commission to report it to the President and the Postmaster-General for gross violations of the law, and upon that a report was prepared and signed by all three of us.

By Mr. STONE:

Q. In regard to one question. You say you expressed it as your opinion, in a conversation to which you have alluded, held with Mr. Roosevelt, that Mr. Paul was not influenced in the violation or advising violations of the civil service law by political reasons.—A. I said as far as we had any evidence; we had no proof.

Q. Do you think so now?—A. I have no evidence of it, sir.

Q. What motive, then, did you understand actuated Mr. Paul in violating the civil service law?—A. I will tell you frankly; I think he was governed by personal considerations.

Q. You mean he made appointments for personal motives, personal desires?—A. Or to oblige his friends. That, however, understand me, Mr. Stone, was an inference which I drew. There was no positive proof, and I have never seen it till Mr. Paul's statement here; I never saw any proof that there was. He said yesterday, in regard to the appointment of this man Keaveny, that Judge Jenkins asked him to give consideration to Keaveny's name. That is the first evidence; I had personal evidence of it. I will say I suspected at the time, but the proof was not such as to justify reporting him to the President for it.

Q. It did not make the basis of your report?

Mr. THOMPSON. Not at all.

The CHAIRMAN. Now, Mr. Thompson, I would like you to state for the information of the committee and in order that they may understand at this point that the rule which was enforced while Mr. Paul was postmaster, which prohibited the postmaster from having knowledge of the eligible list, and made it a violation of the rule if he should see this list at any time, that your Commission has changed this rule and the eligible list is now in fact published as soon as the people pass their examination and it is posted up in every post-office with the percentage they receive, and the postmaster and the public has full knowledge. This Commission has changed that rule to that effect, as I understand it.

Mr. THOMPSON. It was changed by the present Commission very soon after Mr. Roosevelt and myself took the oath of office. I have been always of decided opinion that while there was some objection to making the list of eligibles public, there were much stronger objections to keeping it secret, and therefore I advocated earnestly making it public, and my colleagues were unanimously of that conclusion and the lists were made public.

Mr. STONE. Do you think any harm resulted from Shidy's publishing that list?

Mr. THOMPSON. Except the violations of the rules.

Mr. STONE. I will say no actual harm.

Mr. THOMPSON. No, no actual harm.

Mr. STONE. He merely did what you have since authorized.

Mr. Thompson. Yes, but it was a violation of the law.

Mr. Lyman. On this point it seems to be assumed that it is true that Mr. Shidy published a list in the newspaper.

The Chairman. That has been testified to. I merely asked this question so the committee would understand, because I always thought myself it was an unnecessary thing to keep the eligible list from the postmaster, and I learned this morning as a matter of fact they changed the rules, and it was proper to bring it out because we are investigating the system as well as these charges.

Mr. Stone. In addition, outside of the mere violation of a rule of law, there was no harm then according to the theory of the Commission at this date if a postmaster examined the list of eligibles in the book on the register.

Mr. Thompson. I do not think so, sir; I think he was prohibited from doing so.

Mr. Stone. I know he was prohibited.

Mr. Thompson. Distinctly prohibited.

Mr. Lyman. I wish to make a point there. I should say there was a greater harm in the postmaster examining the list unless the public had the privilege of examining it at the same time.

Mr. Thompson. Of course.

By Mr. Hatton:

Q. After you read the report of Messrs. Doyle and Webster that Mr. Lyman gave you, did you make up your mind from the testimony in that report there was sufficient ground for the removal of the postmaster and Mr. Shidy?

Mr. Thompson. I did not read it at the time, I only knew——

Q. But you have read it since?—A. Yes, sir.

Q. Is it your opinion now there was sufficient evidence contained in that report to have removed Mr. Paul and Mr. Shidy?—A. Ample.

Q. Did Mr. Lyman give any reason why he let the matter remain for eight or nine months without making any report to President Cleveland so as to give the President an opportunity of removing these wicked men? Has Mr. Lyman discussed the matter with you?—A. Yes, sir.

Q. What was his opinion?—A. As I remember he told me that Mr. Oberly went out of the Commission about the time of the report of Messrs. Webster and Doyle, and he had no opportunity to confer with him, and that he could not get Mr. Edgerton to attend to it.

Q. Did he give any reason why he did not do so when he was the sole Commissioner?—A. I do not recollect that he did.

Q. When he was not hampered in any way?—A. I remember the time, but I do not remember his saying anything about it.

Q. Did he ever call your attention to this letter of Mr. Graham, secretary of the board at the time he was a member of the board?—A. He mentioned it in our report, sir.

Q. I mean at that time?—A. No, sir, he never went into Graham's case at all, but said it was very damaging testimony there in Milwaukee.

Q. When the Commission went to Milwaukee did they know that the time of Mr. Paul's term had expired?—A. I knew nothing of it then.

Q. You did not know that when you left here?—A. I never have known except from learning from him.

Q. Then the Commission really went to investigate an office when they did not know anything about when the term of the postmaster expired?—A. Entirely so, but I presumed it had expired.

By the CHAIRMAN:

Q. I want to ask this question: The fact that the postmaster was supposed to have access to the eligible list at that time did not govern you in your recommendation for removal?—A. I must say, sir, that the fact that he did have access to the eligible was an evidence of a violation of law.

Q. But that was not the only point on which the Commission recommended his removal?—A. No, sir. Mr. Paul was asked this morning whether Johnston and Fahsel had been retained in that post-office on that board? That was a subject about which my colleagues and myself conferred as soon as we came from Milwaukee as to what we should do. In order to explain to the committee how these boards are appointed, I will state they are appointed as a matter of fact on the nomination of the postmasters, for this reason, that these offices vary so in the character of work assigned to the clerks, and the Commission not knowing any of the force of the postmaster on the books to be put upon the board of examiners——

The WITNESS. Upon the nomination of the postmaster?

Mr. THOMPSON. I will state the fact. We usually wrote a letter of this purport: There is one or more vacancies existing upon a board of examiners at your office. You will please give us several names from which to fill these vacancies, and we desire to have your views as to who shall be on the board.

The WITNESS. What is the law, the exact language of the law?

Mr. THOMPSON. I can not quote exactly the law.

The WITNESS. It makes a great difference.

Mr. THOMPSON. Then after consultation—we consulted of course by letter as we can not go to every postmaster in the country in the classified service—we stated this in regard to the post-office at Milwaukee: We can not make a new appointment there now because we must consult Mr. Paul, and I for one was not willing to take any name which he advised in the matter; I was not willing to consult him after what we discovered to be there—but that we must wait until the new postmaster came in, and then consult him. As soon as the new postmaster did come in, we consulted with him and he made the nominations, and we removed Johnston and Fahsel, stating distinctly in our letter to the postmaster and them that they were removed for their misconduct in appointments—we removed them for their connection with the frauds committed in that office.

The WITNESS. Gentlemen, I made an open publication, reported right to the commission that I would concur in the appointment of any man suggested by the Commission of the entire force.

Mr. THOMPSON. That is my recollection that you did, but of course the committee understands that no man in the post-office except Johnston and Fahsel could possibly be selected for the examining board without consultation with the postmaster.

Mr. ROOSEVELT. I entirely concur in almost all that has been said by Governor Thompson, but there are two or three things I did that he did not. For instance, my attention was first called to this matter by Major Webster. Major Webster called my attention to these reports stating that he had gone up there and that the postmaster was guilty of gross misconduct, and he ought to be removed, and that that was the worst case he had ever seen. I then spoke to Mr. Doyle about it and he also said the postmaster was guilty of gross misconduct, of a gross breach of law, or some such term.

The WITNESS. On the evidence of Shidy.

Mr. ROOSEVELT. It had nothing to do with the evidence of Shidy. This statement is based on the records of your office. I then, two days before I went up there, began to read over the report. I read it carefully through on the train on the way to Cincinnati, from Cincinnati to Indianapolis and Chicago, and I read through all the papers, and I made up my mind that Paul was guilty beyond doubt unless he could explain away his own evidence and the official records. We found that Shidy had testified to the wrong-doing, that Johnston testified that Shidy kept telling him all about the wrong-doing, but he would not take any interest in it; that Fahsel had stated he did not know anything about the thing one way or another. We did not want to have to try Mr. Paul on the evidence of Johnston or Shidy at all, and we agreed to examine him and make our report on the administration upon his own statement and upon the analytical statement of the records and upon what he could say in explanation thereof. The letter of Mr. Graham submitted in evidence here this morning was submitted to me, the letter alluding to the transfer of eligibles from one list to the other. Mr. Paul's own statement was he understood that letter; that the only qualification was that the eligibles should be transferred in their order according to average; I have read that and the report is in evidence. Had he acted only according to what he himself said was his interpretation of that letter we would not have made such a report as we did; but, as a matter of fact, he did precisely the things that he himself testified the letter did not authorize.

The WITNESS. What had I to do with that letter; was the transfers——

Mr. ROOSEVELT. I think the letter does not excuse him at all, simply because the examining board does not affect Mr. Paul one way or another. By Mr. Paul's own statement he would have nothing to do with that letter.

The WITNESS. I never saw the letter until Mr. Webster came here.

Mr. BOATNER. I think it would be better if you did not interrupt the witness who is making his statement.

Mr. ROOSEVELT. I beg your pardon; but you say you did not see the letter——

The WITNESS. Until Mr. Webster came to my office.

Mr. ROOSEVELT. He also testified before Major Webster that he had taken these eligibles from the higher list and told Dr. Shidy to include them in the next certification in the lower list.

The WITNESS. No, sir; that I have disputed in my testimony, and it is entirely false in the sense in which——

Mr. ROOSEVELT. Those are his words. I do not care to get into an argument, Mr. Paul, now. We went up to Milwaukee to the post-office, and we saw Mr. Paul on that afternoon, and we saw him the next morning. We examined also Shidy and Johnston, and Fahsel we tried to find, but he had gone away we were told. Also, Fahsel, in the testimony, had simply said, "I do not know anything about it."

The WITNESS. I have his affidavit on that point.

Mr. ROOSEVELT. We have his testimony here on that point, too. So we only examined Johnston and Shidy and Mr. Paul himself. As Gov-

The CHAIRMAN (to the witness). If you have anything to say in reply to this you will have ample time to state it.

Mr. ROOSEVELT. We examined Mr. Paul. We never got a direct answer from him in reply—a yes or no. We very rarely got an answer that had any logical reference to the question put.

The WITNESS. Simply because you were questioning me about Shidy's duties, not my own.

The CHAIRMAN. Mr. Paul allow Mr. Roosevelt to go on and make his statement and then you can make yours afterwards.

Mr. BOATNER. He wants this testimony to be in a parallel column.

Mr. ROOSEVELT. I would be very glad to have it put in in that manner. As I stated, we could not get a direct answer and we could rarely get an answer having any reference to what the question was. Generally his answer was, "You have got to ask Shidy; this is an affair of Shidy's." We would say, "We are not talking of Shidy. We wish to know about your part in these certifications. How did you happen to choose the man for whom each certification was garbled, and Paul would answer 'I do not know anything about it, you will have to ask Shidy.'"

The WITNESS. No, sir; I gave you a written answer that it was my right to choose a man from the certification, and that nobody had the right to ask me why.

Mr. ROOSEVELT. But I am speaking of this one time. We would ask you if you could explain, and you would say, "No." We would ask you why, and we would get the same answer, that we would have to ask Dr. Shidy, and often Paul would not really answer at all; he would make a long, profuse statement. We became convinced very shortly that Paul could make no explanation of his wrong-doing. Well, now, I believe you want me to tell you exactly what we believed and what our views were.

The CHAIRMAN. I would not waste any——

Mr. ROOSEVELT. We became convinced that Mr. Paul was not telling the truth. We then left him, and went to make up the report. I felt quite strongly that whether Mr. Paul was out or not we ought to recommend his dismissal. It seemed to me a peculiar, gross, and flagrant breach of the law.

The WITNESS. I think you came there with that impression before.

Mr. ROOSEVELT. I recommended that——

The WITNESS. I think you came there with the purpose to see if you could not find a basis for recommending a removal. Mr. Roosevelt, allow me to ask you——

Mr. BOATNER. I think the witness ought to be allowed to make his statement.

Mr. ROOSEVELT. I am perfectly willing to be interrupted, but I do not care to be interrupted——

The CHAIRMAN. Let the witness state it as briefly as he can.

Mr. ROOSEVELT. I think I stated that Mr. Webster and Mr. Doyle reported that he should be removed, but we had to see if he could make any explanation of these reports, but Paul failed to make any explanation of the specific acts of wrong-doing with which he was charged. We then went into consultation about the matter, and, as I stated, I wanted to recommend his removal at once, and drew up a very sharp report, but Governor Thompson stated, as stated here, that we did not want to shoot dead ducks, and he——

The WITNESS. I am not so dead yet.

Mr. ROOSEVELT. That is the opinion of the governor—I am not——

The WITNESS. You may ask my opinion of him.

Mr. ROOSEVELT. We then drew up this report on the statement that Mr. Paul had made to us, basing it on the fact he had stated he was out of office. We had found no evidence that Mr. Paul had been influenced—let me make a correction of what Governor Thompson said. I had found in my opinion sufficient evidence that Mr. Paul had been influenced by "party considerations." Mr. Stone asked Governor Thompson then what he thought was Mr. Paul's motive. If I may be allowed to state, Governor Thompson has stated his opinion and I would like to state what my opinion was. My opinion was that Mr. Paul's case was a perfectly familiar thing in New York, where this explanation has been made to me: "Oh, Mr. Roosevelt, you know there are no politics in politics;" that is, a man in politics has no party affiliations. You will find in New York plenty of offices where Democrats or Republicans have no control, where the subordinates, representing different organizations, control it from having influence in that district, Republican and Democrat, Tammany Hall, County Democracy, stalwart, half-breed, or whatever it is, indiscriminate. That has been my impression. Now Mr. Paul had a great influence with certain Republican politicians there, and he was commonly reported to have helped a certain Republican politician to Congress, and all that. That seemed to me a more than adequate explanation of his motive, but we did not go into that at all in our report. We did not base our report on that line, on anything he had done for political reasons; we did not allude to that in any way or consider it in our report. I did not regard that Mr. Paul was peculiar to one party in the least.

Now, we came back and we found then that we had been misled as to the date of Mr. Paul's removal, and we then drew up our final report. Now, I want to say this, in regard to this which has been brought out. The governor said that letter would excuse a portion of the misdeeds. That letter, of course, would excuse the mere transfer of an eligible from one list to another, and accordingly, as we implicitly declared in our report, we never counted that against him at all. The letter construed, as Mr. Paul states himself it ought to have been construed, was no excuse for transferring an eligible from one list to another without transferring the man above him, without transferring all according to their grade. It did not look for a moment to transferring the man who had passed at 70 as a carrier, when there were a whole lot above him on a lower list, and have him certified up with the stampers with that grade, at 94 and 95, and have the man appointed as a stamper and immediately afterwards promote him to be a carrier again. Of course, that was a clear evasion of the law, and the law gave no authority for anything of that sort, as construed by Mr. Paul himself.

I would also like to state, in answer to the question of Mr. Stone the other day, in reference to these certifications—so called certifications. You recollect asking if it was not technically irregular if a man would be certified up on a little bit of paper with three names. It is, for this reason. It is exactly as if you had requested your agent in business to keep the books, and you should ask him how you stood and he should answer you, " It is no use for me to do that; you have lost $2,000," and when you press him he would say, " I have kept these records on scraps of paper, and I have lost them; there is no book, but you have lost $2,000." The books are part of the necessary record. These are the only things by which we have means to judge anything. I will say this much, it is possible, thoroughly possible under the old system of certification, that the work may have been done honestly, but it is certain if there had been any intention to commit fraud, it would have been done in just this way. Mr. Paul, for instance, in stating the matter the other day, testified here that they had lost one certification; that there was no certification at all; that that so happened on a certain occasion.

The WITNESS. No; I stated that Shidy had lost it.

Mr. ROOSEVELT. That Shidy had lost the certificate; that Shidy had done it.

The WITNESS. Shidy had done it.

Mr. ROOSEVELT. That Shidy had lost this certification; that there was no record to the appointment; that they had no record whatever to show that Mr. Paul complied with the law. We have only his own statement that he complied with the law, no record of any sort. When Mr. Webster and Mr. Doyle went up there they caught Mr. Paul and the examining board in the act; they caught a man appointed a month before and no certification made. Shidy could not recollect any certification and Mr. Paul could not say——

The WITNESS. Is that testimony, Mr. Chairman; what is this?

Mr. ROOSEVELT. I am stating this as the ground on which we made our report.

The CHAIRMAN. He is testifying in regard to what the Commission made their report.

The WITNESS. You are permitting statements here that might take me three days more to contradict. The Commission has had a fair opportunity to make statements. I object to anything that is new being offered.

Mr. ROOSEVELT. This is nothing new. We have a right to make these statements.

The WITNESS. This is a distortion of the facts in a large degree.

Mr. ROOSEVELT. Mr. Paul has had all of his own time and about half of mine. I think he has had a fair chance to be heard. I will simply say that the records of these so-called certifications of appointments we had before us. I mean by so-called certifications the false certifications which we put in evidence here. These certifications on their faces showed that names had been brought by Mr. Paul and furnished and refurnished. It is stated that he only looked at them once or twice, but they were showed to him. By all that evidence it was proved clearly, without a shadow of a doubt, beyond any possibility of a doubt, that this wrong doing was between the board of examiners and the appointing officer or postmaster; that the examining board could get no benefit from it, and that the postmaster who had control of these men entirely must be and could not but be the party to blame. Accordingly we made our report, and that is what you have before you.

Mr. STONE. One question of this witness, looking to the defects in the system. I will ask you the question I asked Mr. Paul, if it is not a fact that a postmaster situated as he was at Milwaukee with a board of local examiners who were employed in his office, and who depended largely upon him for their retention in their places, and were in most cases a majority of that board are in accord with him, is it not a fact that the examination and certification can be so manipulated without any real violation of the law, or such violations as could be reached, in the event he saw proper to do so?

Mr. ROOSEVELT. They can not without a real violation of the law. If you will look at the concluding sentence of our report, we in this case make a recommendation we should be allowed to choose examiners outside of the service entirely.

Mr. STONE. Examiners receive no compensation.

Mr. ROOSEVELT. We could get men to serve voluntarily.

Mr. STONE. I will ask you this——

Mr. ROOSEVELT. Do you object to my going on and answering your direct question just now? What you say is perfectly true. A postmaster under the present condition can coerce the board, as we believe Mr. Paul did, into helping him violate and evade the law, but it is extremely difficult for him to do it without leaving traces of it, and he has got to face the fact that this wrong doing will be found out sooner or later, as we believe we found out Mr. Paul; and he will then be removed for his conduct and the punishment of one person will, we believe, have a great deterrent effect upon others. There is no doubt that since these facts about Mr. Paul have been brought to light, it will deter others more than before, because they know what to expect from us.

Mr. STONE. Is it not a fact it did occur—I believe there is no impropriety in my speaking to you about it, as I think it came to my knowledge through some remark of yours—that during the last administration that a postmaster at Baltimore made changes amounting in the aggregate to 90 per cent., turning out Republicans and putting in Democrats, for instance, without committing such a violation of law he could be reached?

Mr. ROOSEVELT. That would lead me into a much longer explanation than I would care to make now when we are still on the case of Mr. Paul. That is intimated in the public report, and I intended to bring that either before the Commission—but I will explain if you will allow me——

The CHAIRMAN. I think we had better let it go to another part of the examination.

Mr. ROOSEVELT. I can answer you right there if you will allow it.

The CHAIRMAN. This is a general question and it has nothing to do with these charges.

By Mr. BOATNER:

Q. I understood you to say, Mr. Roosevelt, that it was improper under the rules, at the time this removal occurred in Milwaukee, for a postmaster to know anything of the eligible list except the name certified to him by the board of examiners.

Mr. ROOSEVELT. It was, sir.

Q. But since that time the rules are that the eligible list is public?

Mr. ROOSEVELT. Yes, sir.

Q. Now I want to ask this. Is the postmaster, who is generally the appointing officer, under obligation to make selection from the three names which are presented to him?

Mr. ROOSEVELT. They are, except in the case that all three are entirely unfit. He may then send a letter to the Commission detailing the reasons why he thinks them unfit and they, if they choose, can look the matter up and report them. He may give——

Q. Wait a minute; let me ask you this: The law, as I understand, requires the examining board to make examination without reference to the position which the parties are expected to fill?

Mr. ROOSEVELT. Yes, sir.

Q. Then you say the appointing officer has the right, after the examining board has sent up three or four names which they declare, after examination, are eligible and are fit for these positions it is still in the power of the appointing officer to say that they were wrong, that the parties are not fit for the position?

Mr. ROOSEVELT. If you will look at one thing. Probably you do not know that part of the examination is the six months' probation trial of the appointee. His appointment is not made final until he has six months' trial, so as to see practically how he works; so by our examination we believe that in the vast majority of cases they get the best man in the service, but we do not say they do so always. We think there are certain parties, although they pass they will not do well, and it is to provide merely for such accidents. It is an accident that very rarely occurs, not once in five hundred times, that three such men go up and one of them would not be chosen on account of the inefficiency of all three.

Q. I was not speaking of that particularly. I was speaking of any appointing officer.

Mr. ROOSEVELT. Now, sir, if you will let me give an example perhaps it will be made clear to you. Under Mr. Bayard the clerks of the Department of State were examined separately, and it proved to be a very high special standard of clerks, a special standard of qualifications for these clerkship. They were to be proficient in foreign geography and to be proficient in certain kinds of diplomatic history and the like. These qualifications in the men were what the Department of State then needed. Under the present administration there suddenly occurred there a demand for men having good handwriting. They wanted for these particular positions men having very good handwriting. Well, we know the men that know the most about foreign geography and foreign history often do not have good handwriting, and in consequence of his making suddenly that additional qualification we had to send a couple two or three times with certifications who were returned, saying they did not have good enough hands for this purpose.

Q. Then whenever names were sent the examination was passed and the names appear on the certification?

Mr. ROOSEVELT. Yes, sir.

Q. What I want to get at is this: I understand you to say that the appointing officer can not arbitrarily reject the name sent up; that he can only do so for cause, and that the cause must be assigned?

Mr. ROOSEVELT. A cause must be assigned.

Q. Is there anything in the rules, or in the law, which prevents the appointing officer from discharging a man after having been selected?—A. Nothing that is——

Q. Is there any check in the law against the arbitrary power of removal?

The CHAIRMAN. In other words, can the officer remove at any time?—A. He can remove at any time. This case has never come up that I can recollect.

Q. What is your opinion as far as the civil service law is concerned?—A. Mr. Chairman, I would like to look up the matter first as to civil service law before rendering an opinion.

Q. Are you not sufficiently conversant with it now to render an opinion?—A. In every one of these cases that would come up——

Mr. BOATNER. You say you are not prepared to answer that question now?

Mr. ROOSEVELT. Whenever a thing happened like this, and came up to be decided, we would examine it, I will say, in order to see if it is perfectly straight. The theory of the law at present is—I think I ought to make this explanation possibly to clear up the question that has been asked—the theory of the law, as at present enforced, is that no check on removals is required at all except specific cases. A man is not allowed to be removed for refusing to be coerced in his political opinion, etc. Now, I do not believe in that portion of the present law or rule. I believe that whenever a man is dismissed the appointing officer should be required to state in full, minutely, the reason why he has been dismissed without giving him a chance to be heard in his own defense. That is what I believe; but that is in the present law, and neither Mr. Arthur, or Mr. Cleveland, or Mr. Harrison approved of having in that check on removals. It is deemed unnecessary. I do not know whether the former Commission approved of it or not; but I say certainly, when I went to my colleagues, I certainly talked the matter over with Governor Thompson, and Governor Thompson considered me right about removals. We have now no authority on that point.

The CHAIRMAN. I think these questions, of course, are very proper, but they will come up a little later, I suppose when we go into the system, and then we will probably have the Commissioners before us. This is a question that will lead so far that at present it is not necessary——

Mr. ROOSEVELT. I beg your pardon, sir.

The CHAIRMAN. I think we may as well close this case now.

Mr. ANDREWS. I think Mr. Paul ought to reply to Mr. Roosevelt.

Mr. PAUL. I do not wish to make a lengthy reply; if you will allow me a few——

Mr. ROOSEVELT. I would like to make one remark in conclusion of my statement to corroborate what Governor Thompson said about the examining board. There are two examinations in the post-office held a year; one in August and one in February. The August one was held while Mr. Paul was still in the office, and it was our opinion that no change in the board would work any detriment at all while Mr. Paul was in office. The next examination was not held until February, and before that we requested the removal of what force was left in.

The CHAIRMAN (to Mr. Paul). Now state as briefly as you can what you wish to say.

The WITNESS (Mr. Paul). I wish to state from the report being public in a very few days I wrote to the board of commissioners formally that the men they had charged with being unfit as members of that board and whose removals they had recommended, that is Johnston and Fahsel, that I would concur in any proceeding for changing the board that they might suggest. That covers that whole ground. They still remained in office, until recently.

I wish to state further that in all my reference to transfers from a higher to a lower list that I had no other reference or supposition that such transfers should be governed otherwise than by the law which was established in regard to those taking precedence, but the Commission seems to assume——

Mr. BOATNER. A person could not be transferred from a higher to a lower list unless he wanted to?—A. No, sir; it would be at his request. I wish to state further that Commissioner Edgerton—I should say Commissioner Eaton—has given me his opinion as to the construction of the law of 1885 in accordance with my own practice or the practice at my own office by the local board as being correct. Commissioner Eaton I would be very glad to have here as a witness if you can; otherwise I state that as a fact.

Mr. ROOSEVELT. I contradict it on what Mr. Eaton told me. You can examine Commissioner Eaton if you wish it.

The WITNESS. I say I would be very glad to have him as a witness on the subject. I wish to state further Commissioner Edgerton has given an entirely different version of the retention of the testimony and report and his disposition in the Commission from that given by the Commission here. I think Mr. Edgerton ought to be a witness in this case. I wish to state further in regard to the reference by Commissioner Roosevelt——

The CHAIRMAN. I want to say to the witness here that Mr. Edgerton was subpœnaed to this investigation, but has not appeared here on account of illness. He will be here later.

The WITNESS. I wish to state in reference to Commissioner Roosevelt and Representative Van Schaick, of the House, that as to any motive, any political motive, in making these appointments with regard to any Republican and myself, I would be glad to have him appear here as a witness. I think he would be entirely willing to do so. I have not had anything to do with political manipulation by which any Democrat, or Republican either, was chosen to office while I was in this post-office. I wish to state further that I never presumed or supposed that I had anything to do with the construction of the law or of the rules of the Commission in making the certification. The presumption was that that local board was a part or representative of the general Commission, and I accepted its construction of the rules, as I believe it to be my duty to do. Mr. Roosevelt refers to a case where there is no record, in which he caught me in the act, he says. I wish to state as to that case it was simply this, that the record of certification was omitted by the secretary on his books. The fact of the certification is in there.

Mr. BOATNER. You say it had been certified?

The WITNESS. I never made any appointment in my life that had not been properly certified as I understand, until first approved by the local board. Commissioner Roosevelt asserts there is some testimony that I shared in false certification. If there is any such testimony, the fact is that I never did share in any false certifications, as I understand, in any way whatever, not in false certifications at all. Sometimes members of the board would converse with me upon special certifications in case they had a question about the rules, etc., but not otherwise. I wish to say, further, that all this matter, the whole mass of testimony, at least the substance of it, as presented in the report to the Commission, I am informed and believe was presented to the President of the United States, the only authority authorized to act in my case, either for removal or acceptance of resignation or appointment under the laws to the Constitution, and I also submitted to the President by his own permission, as I am informed by his private secretary, all the facts in the case as I knew them, with other testimony, and that he did not, as reported in the press nearly every day now, he did not remove me at all and never has, for which I am very grateful to him under the circumstances.

The CHAIRMAN. Mr. Lyman, now you make your statement, but please make it as brief as possible.

Mr. LYMAN. I will detain the committee but a brief time. I have heard Governor Thompson's statement this morning as to what took place at Milwaukee at the time the Commission was there. I have heard Mr. Roosevelt's statement as to what took place at the time. My own recollection of what took place agrees with these statements so far as they purport to state the facts, except this. It was stated by Mr. Roosevelt in his testimony this morning in calling Mr. Paul's attention to these charges during the conversation with Mr. Paul, as well as I recollect: "Mr. Paul, these are very serious charges and we wish to call your attention to them," or words to that effect. That is the only additional statement I desire to make.

Mr. ROOSEVELT. I ought to have made that statement myself.

Mr. LYMAN. I do not wish to go into any general statement of construction this morning, as I suppose oral argument will be heard on the general aspects of these charges. I certainly have some statements I desire to make, based upon the testimony which has been given in reference to these charges, but I do not wish to make this statement at this time. I have refrained from making argument as the case has progressed supposing there will be an opportunity for argument based upon the testimony.

By Mr. BOATNER :

Q. Mr. Lyman, I want to ask you one question. Are you able to state what opinion the Commission had formed upon the report of Major Webster and of Mr. Doyle, secretary of the Commission, before going out there to see Mr. Paul ?

Mr. LYMAN. I am not able to state. I do not think the Commission had formed an opinion.

Q. Had not formed a conclusive opinion ?

Mr. LYMAN. They had not formed a conclusive opinion before going to Milwaukee. That is my judgment.

Q. The principal object of the Commission going to Milwaukee was to give Mr. Paul an opportunity to explain his irregularities and discrepancies which the records show, was it not ?—A. I think that is the only reason why they went there ; certainly they wished from personal observation and investigation to confirm or disprove the truth of the statement.

Q. Was the examination which was held by the Commission when they reached Milwaukee more searching and full than the examination which had been already made by Mr. Webster and Mr. Doyle ?

Mr. LYMAN. It went over that again.

Q. Did it go over the same ground ?

Mr. LYMAN. Substantially the same ground.

Q. Did they re-examine the same witnesses ?

Mr. LYMAN. They did re-examine the same witnesses except Fahsel, who was absent.

Q. Did they reduce that testimony to writing ?

Mr. LYMAN. No, sir.

Q. You stated you examined Mr. Paul with reference to the discrepancy which the record shows ?

Mr. LYMAN. Yes, sir.

Q. And in the judgment of the Commission Mr. Paul did not make any satisfactory explanation of these discrepancies and irregularities ?

Mr. LYMAN. That is my judgment and the judgment of the Commission as announced in the report of the Commission.

Q. And the Commission formed the judgment that Mr. Paul was actively concerned in the violations of law which you discovered ?

Mr. LYMAN. Yes, sir ; that is certainly my conclusion.

By Mr. HATTON :

Q. During the eight or nine months you held this testimony taken by Messrs. Doyle and Webster, was any outside pressure brought to bear on you to induce you to formulate this report ?

Mr. LYMAN. No, sir.

Q. To let Paul die with the Cleveland administration ?

Mr. LYMAN. No, sir.

Q. Would it have been improper for any outside person to have attempted that?

Mr. LYMAN. The party must be the judge of that. I should be the judge of my own action.

Q. I have asked you to state it and I should like to have an answer; would it be a proper matter for an outside party to come to you in regard to testimony before the Commission, or to attempt to influence you in the time you should make a report; would it be the proper thing for an outside party to come to you in regard to a statement of an examination that had taken place before the Commission?

Mr. LYMAN. As no such influence was used, and as no such attempt was made, I do not know whether I ought to answer a question of that sort. It would be simply a matter of opinion.

The CHAIRMAN. It would be a matter of opinion which any one has.

Mr. BOATNER. You say no one went to you about a matter coming before the Commission, or before it came up for consideration by the Commission?

Mr. LYMAN. Thousands of times.

Q. Will you please state whether or not these charges, or rather the fact, elicited by Chief Examiner Webster and Mr. Paul were made to the President and Postmaster-General before the incoming of this administration?

Mr. LYMAN. Mr. Oberly stated to me that he had acquainted President Cleveland with the situation at Milwaukee at the time of Mr. Doyle's first visit. That is the only basis of information I have on the subject.

Mr. STONE. Mr. Oberly went over all that.

Mr. BOATNER. I beg pardon, I was not here at the time and did not know that ground had been gone over.

The CHAIRMAN. Now, Mr. Paul, do you desire to ask some questions?

Mr. PAUL. Nothing more than this. Mr. Lyman, did you examine Mr. Shidy when there the last time?

Mr. LYMAN. Yes, sir.

Mr. PAUL. To a considerable extent?

Mr. LYMAN. Yes, sir.

Mr. PAUL. Was that testimony in any way reduced to writing?

Mr. LYMAN. No, sir.

Mr. PAUL. Was I in any manner ever furnished with a copy of this testimony so as to see it?

Mr. LYMAN. Not that I am aware of.

Mr. PAUL. Until I saw the result of it in the public report.

Mr. ROOSEVELT. I would ask to be recalled for a moment. I want to——

Mr. LYMAN. You were examined upon this testimony and analytical statement which has been frequently referred to.

Mr. PAUL. You remember, Mr. Lyman, I was asked a multitude of questions in a very hurried manner in my office, and that I said you must ask Shidy several times, where it was a case where I did not consider the questions related to my personal duties.

Mr. LYMAN. I do not know what you considered.

Mr. PAUL. But did not, as a fact, these questions relate mainly to the action of the local board?

Mr. LYMAN. They related to the whole matter of the appointment.

Mr. PAUL. But largely and mostly to the action of the local board?

Mr. LYMAN. To the action of the local board and the postmaster; one is involved in the other.

Mr. PAUL. Is it not a fact, as you understand the rules, that the duties of the postmaster are limited very closely to the simple duty of selecting from certification?

Mr. LYMAN. I think they were at that time, sir.

Mr. PAUL. I have not anything further.

Mr. STONE. How long did Mr. Paul's examination last, Mr. Lyman; how long were the Commissioners examining Mr. Paul in reference to these charges?

Mr. LYMAN. They consumed nearly all one afternoon and probably some of the next morning, probably part of the next morning.

Mr. STONE. I refer to the examination of Mr. Paul himself.

Mr. LYMAN. Mr. Paul was before the Commission in the afternoon and on the following morning.

The CHAIRMAN. Is there anything further? I think a great deal of this is repetition, and we would like to get through.

Mr. ROOSEVELT. Will you let me introduce one statement which I forgot?

The CHAIRMAN (to Mr. Lyman). Have you anything further to say at this time?

Mr. LYMAN. Not in this case, but I have some papers I wish to offer in evidence.

The CHAIRMAN. In what case is that?

Mr. LYMAN. In regard to my authority to act as sole Commissioner. I wish to offer these papers and to state the contents of them.

The CHAIRMAN. The contents may be stated, but the papers will show it themselves.

Mr. ROOSEVELT. Before you go into this will you allow me to make one supplementary statement?

The CHAIRMAN. Let us get through with this statement, then.

Mr. ROOSEVELT. When I was on the stand I forgot a question Mr. Paul had called out. We intended in making our report, the reason the evidence of Mr. Shidy and Mr. Johnson was not submitted to Mr. Paul was because we intended to make no allusion to it whatever in our report. Our intention had been to make the report solely on Mr. Paul's own testimony and on the record, so as not to bring in conflict nor jeopardize Mr. Shidy's position with anything of the kind; we did not intend to bring in any allusion to Shidy's testimony.

Mr. PAUL. What your intentions were are not facts. I oppose——

Mr. ROOSEVELT. You have nothing to do with what I testified to; I am testifying to the committee. We intended to make no allusion to it at all. When we made the supplementary report Shidy had been already dismissed, so we did not see any reason for not using his testimony; but we only used it in two cases where Johnson had corroborated it to us. Those are the only two cases, as you will find explicitly stated in the report as made, and I think that if you will read the report you will see the answers there to many questions that had been put by us. I should say we examined Mr. Paul about nearly two hours one afternoon and something over an hour the next morning, as we explicitly stated in our report, and we examined him on the statements that had been given for this reason, to see if he could explain this evidence that had already been given; we did not try to get any new evidence.

Mr. BOATNER. You did not declare what Mr. Shidy had told you?

Mr. ROOSEVELT. We did not inform him of anything Mr. Shidy told us, and we only used Mr. Shidy's testimony in making up the report on two points.

Mr. BOATNER. And Mr. Johnson's statement?

Mr. ROOSEVELT. Mr. Johnson testified to two cases which we undertook to put in our report; that is as to the fact that Mr. Paul, has as Shidy stated, forced them, or, as he said, merely advised them; they merely corroberated such testimony; and the other case was as to the custody of the eligible record. These are the two cases and the only two ones where we used their testimony at all. We did not use the testimony a bit otherwise in making up our reports.

Mr. HATTON. I would like to ask the Commissioner one question.

The CHAIRMAN. I think we have gone into this far enough.

Mr. HATTON. I have not seen that anybody on the other side has been refused to ask a question. I understood Commissioner Roosevelt to say that they did not rely to a great extent upon Mr. Shidy's testimony. I am correct, I believe, to that extent, and I would like to ask how Mr. Shidy, that being fact, was entitled to a reward or an appointment in a department here?

Mr. ROOSEVELT. I have already gone over that in the Shidy case several times, but I will answer that if the committee wishes.

Mr. BOATNER. I object to this question as being an argumentative question.

Mr. ROOSEVELT. I have stated it several times to him before.

The CHAIRMAN. I am going to rule this question out; I am not going to open the case again.

Mr. ROOSEVELT. I would be glad to answer, but I have answered it a dozen times before.

The CHAIRMAN (to the stenographer). You need not take this now.

Mr. LYMAN. I wish to submit these papers.

The CHAIRMAN. Just tell what the papers are.

Mr. LYMAN. It is part of the first charge that I made a certain promotion in violation of the law, being sole acting Commissioner. I desire to offer in evidence certain papers which will show in full the actions that I took when acting as sole Commissioner. I have here the certificates made by the secretary of the Commission that while acting as sole Commissioner I made not one promotion but three promotions and an original appointment. I promoted Mr. Holtz from a clerkship of class 1 to a clerkship of class 2, that I promoted Mr. Campbell from a clerkship of $1,000 to a clerkship of class 1, that I promoted Mr. Culver from class $900 to class $1,000, and that I appointed Mr. Swank to a clerkship of $900. He was appointed as stenographer and typewriter. On the day that Mr. Edgerton was removed as Commissioner I entered upon the minutes of the Commission a statement to that effect, so that the records of the Commission show that he was removed on the 9th of February and contained a copy of the order of the President removing him, with this comment made by myself as part of the record: "This action leaves the Commission with one Commissioner and two vacancies." That was the record made on the 9th of February.

Mr. STONE. What year?

Mr. LYMAN. 1889, the 9th of February.

The CHAIRMAN. Do you desire to make any statement?

Mr. LYMAN. That is all of that statement I desire to make, but there is another statement I wish to make. I wish to state the contents of these papers. The copy of this paper is simply to show that I assumed the functions of the Commission during this period when I was the only Commissioner. During this period, and the date will be shown by this paper, the Postmaster-General informed the Commission that certain post-offices had reached the number of 50 employés and were proper subjects for classification. I issued the necessary orders for that classification of these post-offices and reported the fact to the President.

Mr. THOMPSON. Which President?

Mr. LYMAN. President Cleveland, on the 21st of February, 1887. On the 1st day of March I submitted to President Cleveland a certain number of requests made by the heads of Departments for examination for promotion under general rule three, section two, class 3. The rules require that these promotions should be made with the consent of the President on the recommendation of the Commission. I submitted that recommendation to the President on the 1st day of March and on the same day he approved them. On the 11th day of March, 1889—these acts took place under President Cleveland——

The CHAIRMAN. Well?

Mr. LYMAN. On the 11th day of March, 1889, I addressed a communication to the President of the United States, Mr. Harrison, stating that the railway mail rules had been approved to go into effect on the 15th day of March; that I would not be ready to put those rules into effect on that date for the reason it had been impossible to complete the necessary arrangements, and recommended that the date be postponed from the 15th day of March until the 1st of May. On the same day the President issued the necessary order approving this recommendation, in which occurs this statement: "Whereas it is represented to me by the Civil Service Commission, in a communication of this date, etc." On the 16th day of April I submitted to the President of the United States the recommendation for the amendment of special departmental rule No. 1, which the President approved. On the 25th day of April I submitted a further recommendation to the President of the United States for an amendment of special departmental rule No. 1, which the President approved. The amendments have been inadvertently omitted, but the letters are here and I will file the amendments which were approved by the President. These papers show that I assumed and performed the most important acts which the rules require to be performed by the commission with the knowledge and concurrence of the President of the United States; and I desire to make this additional statement, that on the day of Mr. Edgerton's removal from office as Civil-Service Commissioner, or possibly on the following day, or within a day or two, I called upon President Cleveland on official business and in the course of conversation that ensued I raised the question of my authority to act. Some conversation took place on that question between President Cleveland and myself, and I think I suggested if he had any doubts as to the matter of my authority to act for the Commission under the law that the question should be referred to the Attorney-General for his opinion. There the matter dropped as between President Cleveland and myself and was never afterward referred to, and I have no official knowledge whether he referred the question to the Attorney-General or not, but subsequent to that time he did approve my official acts as Commissioner.

By Mr. HATTON:

Q. When was the first public notice given that the railway mail service had passed under the civil service law?—A. I do not know——

Q. You say it was to go into effect on the 15th of March; that was the time President Cleveland——

Mr. LYMAN. It was made public at once, early in the year 1889, the fact that the rule had been approved and would go into effect.

Q. At the time President Cleveland went out do you know how

many applications filed with the Commission had passed the examination—had been examined?

Mr. LYMAN. I can not state the number, but a very large number.

Q. After the railway mail service passed under the law of the Commission did these early applicants get the benefit of their early application or not?

Mr. LYMAN. They took the same—they had the same rights which were accorded to all applicants.

Q. No; but were they served in turn and given the same rights? As I understand it there was a thousand or fifteen hundred applicants.

Mr. LYMAN. Let me state that the date of filing an application does not give a person any rights as to an appointment. It simply gives him the right to be examined at the earliest day fixed for an examination.

Mr. HATTON. Does it give them the right of examination?

Mr. LYMAN. They were all examined at the earliest possible moment; every one.

Q. I understood there were one thousand or fifteen hundred applications, and President Harrison extended the time of the operation of Mr. Cleveland's order.

Mr. LYMAN. They were all examined; every one who presented themselves to the board of examiners. They were all notified to appear, and were all examined who offered themselves.

The CHAIRMAN (holding up a letter). Do you wish this letter put in evidence, this letter, Mr. Paul?

Mr. PAUL. I think the letter should go up in evidence in the matter of the Cummings case.

The CHAIRMAN. The case is now closed as far as relates to the charge made by Mr. Ewart against the Commission, and the committee will meet on Monday next at the usual hour to decide what further course to take under the resolution of the House.

Thereupon the committee adjourned.

Exhibit A.

[Certificate No. 665.]

UNITED STATES CIVIL-SERVICE COMMISSION,
Washington, D. C., September 17, 1889.

SIR: Upon your request No. 638, for the names of three eligibles under the civil-service act and rules to a vacancy now existing in class $900, clerical examining force, Office of Bureau of Pensions, Interior Department, certification is hereby made that the following-named persons are eligible to the vacancy specified, and are now entitled to this certification under Departmental Rule VII:

Names.	State.	Examination.	Grade.	Post-office address.
			Per cent.	
Everard C. Brown ...	Nebraska	Special examiner ...	72	410 Boundary street, Washington, D. C.
Wm. W. Watson	Indiana	......do	71	Rensselaer, Jasper County, Indiana.
Thomas Mitchell	Connecticut...	...... do	71	805 Tenth street northwest, Washington, D. C.

You are authorized, under Departmental Rule VII, clause 3, to select and appoint one or more of the eligibles thus certified.*

JOHN T. DOYLE, *Secretary.*

The SECRETARY OF THE INTERIOR.

*The Commission requests that the examination papers sent with this certificate be returned within three days, in order that the applicants not selected may not lose opportunity for appointment in other Departments.

[Certificate No. 666.]

UNITED STATES CIVIL-SERVICE COMMISSION,
Washington, D. C., September 17, 1889.

SIR: Upon your request No. 638, for the names of three eligibles under the civil-service act and rules to a vacancy now existing in class $900, clerical examining force, Office of Bureau of Pensions, Interior Department, certificate is hereby made that the following-named persons are eligible to the vacancy specified, and are now entitled to this certification under Departmental Rule VII:

Names.	State.	Examination.	Grade.	Post-office address.
			Per cent.	
Thomas Mitchell.........	Connecticut...	Special examiner ...	71	805 Tenth street, north west, Washington, D. C.
Wm. F. R. Phillips...	Virginia.........	......do	70	Signal Office, Washington, D. C.
Stephen W. Morris...	Ohio	......do	70	Ironton, Lawrence County, Ohio.

You are authorized, under Departmental Rule VII, clause 3, to select and appoint one or more of the eligibles thus certified.*
Very respectfully,

JOHN T. DOYLE, *Secretary.*

The SECRETARY OF THE INTERIOR.

*The Commission requests that the examination papers sent with this certificate be returned within three days, in order that the applicants not selected may not lose opportunity for appointment in other departments.

[Certificate No. 677.]

UNITED STATES CIVIL-SERVICE COMMISSION,
Washington, D. C., September 17, 1889.

SIR: Upon your request No. 633, for the names of three eligibles under the civil-service act and rules to a vacancy now existing in class $900, clerical examining force, Office of Bureau of Pensions, Interior Department, certification is hereby made that the following-named persons are eligible to the vacancy specified, and are now entitled to this certification under Departmental Rule VII:

Names.	State.	Examination.	Grade.	Post-office address.
			Per cent.	
Thos. Mitchell	Connecticut	Special examiner	71	805 Tenth street northwest, Washington, D. C.
Wm. F. R. Phillips	Virginia	do	70	Signal Office, Washington, D. C.
David E. Buckingham	Delaware	do	72	505 West Twelfth street, Wilmington, Del.

You are authorized, under Departmental Rule VII, clause 3, to select and appoint one or more of the eligibles thus certified.*
Very respectfully,

JOHN T. DOYLE, *Secretary.*

The SECRETARY OF THE INTERIOR.

*The Commission requests that the examination papers sent with this certificate be returned within three days, in order that the applicants not selected may not lose opportunity for appointment in other Departments.

EXHIBIT B.

[Exhibit R.]

Communication to the Civil Service Commission from Hamilton Shidy, secretary of the Board of Examiners at the post-office, Milwaukee, Wis., explanatory of his conduct in connection with the administration of the civil-service laws at that office. Dated September 10, 1888.

MILWAUKEE, WIS., *September* 10, 1888.

In view of testimony having been taken by the Civil Service Commission tending to show irregularities in appointments and mode of certification in Milwaukee post-office, it is but just to me that I be given opportunity for stating how this state of things came to be allowed without apparent protest on my part.

About the 20th day of May, 1885, Mr. George II. Paul was appointed to take the place of Mr. II. C. Payne, postmaster, and an offensive partisan. In the ten days which intervened between the appointment and taking possession of the office, much caucusing between the present postmaster and certain members and followers of his party occurred, having reference to the bestowal of places in the Milwaukee post-office; and resulted in bringing in with Mr. Paul on the 1st day of June, 1885, an almost entire new set of officers. Old and faithful employés, some of whom had served more than a quarter of a century and had grown up in the service, were thrown out of employment without even a single day's notice.

According to Mr. Paul's statement these men were not removed for political or personal reasons; they were entered on the records "resigned." Amongst those whose removal was so contemplated was myself, H. Shidy, superintendent of the registry division; and my place was promised to a young tailor, who probably had never seen the inside of a post-office, much less was familiar with its workings and requirements. I closed my work on Sunday, May 31, 1885, turned over everything in my possession to Mr. Paul, and was left in entire ignorance as to whether it was desired that I should conduct the work of the department the following day or not. However, I went to work as usual, and for some reason the induction of my successor did not at once take place; and I was given to understand, after some days, that it would occur July 1, 1885. In the mean time an examination was held June 30, 1885, with 142 applicants, making over 600 papers to be marked. Mr. Paul showed the greatest impatience at the necessary delay in getting papers. I worked late at night, and Sunday, and all day 4th of July, and on that day he insisted on taking the papers and selecting half a dozen of those which appeared best from which to make an immediate appointment.

The first certificate and appointment from this examination was made July 6, 1885, and was followed by others on the 7th, 8th, and 9th of July, 1885. I had at this time a desire to retain my place, which I felt sure he would see could not be satisfactorily filled by one who had no knowledge or experience of post-office matters, when he himself came to know more of such matters. And such indeed proved to be the case, for when the time for delivery of my place arrived he declined to make the change. Had I in the mean time opposed his methods, or thrown obstacles in the way of the attainment of his wishes, he would certainly have merely informed me that my successor was appointed. He abused me considerably over the markings of "Eviston's" papers, who, he said "was the best man on the list," and who "had the whole Third ward behind him." Tried to induce me to change his marking, but the work was so very poor that no pretext could be found. He was with difficulty induced to wait awhile before appointing him.

One of his first official acts was returning to me his supply of printed forms of "Request for a certification," with the remark, "I have no use for these things." And I very soon discovered he had "no use" for any provision of civil-service law. He had, from the first, kept copies of the list of eligibles, and when the Commission sent a circular (July, 1886) positively and explicitly prohibiting this I was so sure that it could not be enforced that I made it the subject of discussion before the board July 8, 1886. (See record, book p. 4.) I then presented the postmaster with the only copy of the circular furnished me. After reading it, he said to me in a very significant manner, "You can't prevent me keeping copies of the lists," and of course I didn't try. He had frequently asked me in regard to appointments which he had already made, and which were not yet provided for by certification: "What are you going to do about it? This man is appointed and sworn in, and must be provided for."

It was discovered long ago that "no man can serve two masters;" yet in spite of this well-known truth, the Civil Service Commission have been engaged in an attempt to force such state of servitude on their local boards, and especially on the secretary thereof, who is directly the servant of the postmaster from whom he gets his appointment and his pay, and also at the same time is made the servant of the Commission, which loads him with work, all of which is extra and requires much labor outside of business hours, and for which they pay nothing. To which master is it reasonable to suppose such servant will cling; to the one who pays him or the one who does not? I have repeatedly urged to every one connected with the Commission who has come in my way, that the members of local boards should not be Government employés.

Three courses only were open to me under the circumstances.

(1) To resign my position on the board. This I talked of on several occasions with Mr. Johnson, president of board, and even wrote out my resignation, but it was withheld, as we both thought it would prejudice my position in the office, as of course I would be asked for reasons.

(2) To call the attention of the Civil Service Commission to the manner in which the rules were being violated. This would have been to invite an investigation and conflict with the postmaster, with loss of place.

(3) To let matters take their course until such time as the Commission should discover of its own motion the existence of irregularities and deal with them as they saw fit. This I have done. I have been loyal to my chief, and have done the best I was permitted to do for the Commission, being heartily in sympathy with the reform movement.

If I have acted from a selfish motive it is because I have found by forty years' experience that my interests are only looked after when I look after them myself, and I am not called on to immolate myself and family without even the hope of advancing in any way the interests of reform thereby.

To any one who is disposed to criticise harshly the action of the secretary in this matter, I would simply say, "Put yourself in his place," and perhaps you will see things very different.

Yours respectfully,

HAMILTON SHIDY,
Secretary.

To CIVIL SERVICE COMMISSION.

EXHIBIT C.

UNITED STATES CIVIL SERVICE COMMISSION,
Washington, July 17, 1889.
The PRESIDENT:

In making our first report on the management of the Milwaukee post-office, in so far as it was affected by the civil-service law, we were influenced by the statement made to us by the postmaster himself to the effect that his term of office had already expired, and that he was merely "holding over" because his successor had not yet been appointed. This proves not to be the case, and we accordingly report more at length. Our examination was made by the entire Commission, and the conclusions reached were agreed to unanimously. The postmaster was given a full hearing. Every statement and alleged fact on which we base our report was laid before him and every opportunity offered for him to explain them. His assertions recently made, to the effect that he did not know the accusation made against him and was condemned without a hearing and without being given a chance to explain every charge, are simply gross misstatements. In making our report we did not consider a single fact which had not been laid before him.

· In the spring of 1888 certain irregularities in the working of the Milwaukee post-office were reported to the Commission, and in consequence the secretary, Mr. John T. Doyle, was sent to Milwaukee in July to make inquiries. His report (see Exhibit L) showed such a condition of things that the chief examiner, Mr. William H. Webster, was sent the following September to make a full and exhaustive inquiry. The chief examiner's report (Exhibit X) disclosed gross and repeated violations of the law. Accordingly, shortly after the Commission was reorganized, all three commissioners went to Milwaukee, as we deemed the accusations of such importance as to warrant an investigation by the full board. Except in two important cases we did not try to get at any new facts; we simply examined Mr. Paul to see whether he could disprove the statements or give any satisfactory explanation of the charges made in the two preliminary reports. He entirely failed to do so.

That there has been crooked work in the office is admitted by all. It can be shown to exist by a brief examination of the analytical statements compiled from the certification book, and of the pencil memoranda from which the certifications were actually made (see Exhibits A and D). The only question is where the responsibility lies. We examined the secretary of the local examining board, Hamilton Shidy, and the chairman, J. B. Johnson. Shidy is admitted by all to have done the work of the board, the other members doing little save assisting in marking the papers and attending occasional formal meetings, held at long and irregular intervals.

Shidy testifies that he was compelled by the postmaster to give the latter free access to the lists of eligibles, although such access was at that time strictly forbidden; and he further testifies that the postmaster, knowing those who were eligible, as well as their standing, appointed whomsoever he chose, and then forced him (Shidy) to torture the lists and certification book so as to produce a certification which should bear the appointee's name (see Exhibit C, pp. 2, 4, 5, etc.). This the postmaster denies. Johnson (see Exhibit E, pp. 2, 3, 4) testifies that he knows nothing personally of the matter, but that the secretary, Shidy, consulted him from time to time, telling him that the postmaster had access to the records, or insisted upon having men certified out of place, and the like. Johnson resolutely shut his eyes to what was going on, making no inquiries to test the truth of Shidy's statements; apparently he thought that by so doing he could avoid all responsibility in the matter. But this is a wholly improper position. He admits being told of the various matters, and being continually consulted by Shidy; he was derelict to his duty when he failed to satisfy himself as to the work that was done by the board of which he was chairman, and is as much to be blamed for conniving at what went on, as Shidy, on his own statement, is to be blamed for yielding to the postmaster's demands. It is impossible for a man to shift the responsibility from his shoulders in the manner that Johnson has tried to do. Shidy testifies (see Exhibit R) that he yielded to all the postmaster's demands because he knew that a refusal to do so would have entailed the immediate loss of his place, and therefore of his means of support, and that he even consulted the board as to what course he should follow, bitterly lamenting the fact that to obey the commands of the Commission, of which he was nominally the servant, would force him into immediate antagonism to the postmaster, who could turn him out of his position at pleasure. Shidy and Johnson are equally to blame; but of course, if their statements are true, an infinitely heavier load of blame rests on the postmaster.

In drawing up our report we have based our conclusions almost entirely on what is shown by the official records and by Mr. Paul's own statement (Exhibit B). We have never used Shidy's uncorroborated assertions, although in certain instances we add them as offering the only possible explanation of some of the "gerrymandering" of the certifications. But in two important instances Shidy is explicitly backed up by Johnson and here we have accepted the statements of the two men, borne out, as they are, by other facts.

Shidy and Johnson testified before us, in Mr. Paul's presence, that on one occasion he examined the papers of an applicant, which papers they had already marked, and forced them, against their own judgment, to remark them, giving a lower grade. Mr. Paul's explanation was that he had not forced them to alter the marks, but he admitted that he had expressed great dissatisfaction with the marking and that in consequence it had been changed. Shidy in the presence of both Johnson and Mr. Paul, as well as of the three commissioners, stated that the reason for their changing the grade of the unfortunate applicant was to get him out of the way of another man whom the postmaster desired to appoint; Shidy's words were, substantially, "You remember, Mr. Paul, that we changed the marks as a last resort because we had exhausted every expedient to get the lists as you wished."

Again Mr. Paul states that he did not examine and never had in his possession the lists of eligibles; whereas Shidy states that they were time and again taken to the postmaster's room, and Johnson testified before the Commission that he had himself seen them there. Mr. Paul's testimony on this point is not always very coherent, however, for he qualifies his denial by remarking that he "does not think" he ever examined the books "with reference to any appointment except upon application of Dr. Shidy himself" (Exhibit B, p. 2), and adds (p. 31) that he was "unavoidably aware of the state of the register, of the order in which the names stood, before making appointments," and that he does "not think that the register was regarded as strictly private." (See also pages 6, 7, and 8 of Exhibit B, for other admissions of his familiarity with the lists.) Shidy testifies that when in July, 1886, the Commission issued a circular positively prohibiting the postmaster from having copies of or knowledge of the lists of eligibles, he promptly called the attention of the postmaster thereto, and received for reply, "You can't prevent my keeping copies of the lists."

Mr. Paul, in an interview in the Milwaukee Sentinel of June 30, which may be considered authentic, as he forwarded it with a letter to a member of the Commission, admits this charge of Shidy's, and explains it by stating that he considered the prohibition of the Commission "simply humorous," in view of the fact that on one occasion the entire list had been published in the newspapers, which was certainly extraordinary. From all of which it may be safely asserted that Mr. Paul kept well acquainted with the exact condition of the eligible register, of which he was properly supposed to be ignorant.

He was enabled to take advantage of this knowledge owing to the very peculiar and improper construction he put on a letter from the Commission, written September 18, 1885. This was in reply to a request for a special examination for the lowest grade of employés, that of stampers, it being stated by the Milwaukee board that the list of eligibles for such places was exhausted. The letter from the Commission granted the request for a special examination, and also stated that the men who had taken the higher examinations, as clerks or carriers, could be certified to the lower places, and for this purpose transferred to the lower register on their request. The permission thus given was very ill-advised, as it was not clearly expressed that it applied only to a single emergency. But little harm would have resulted, however, had Mr. Paul obeyed the evident intent of the letter, which he certainly clearly perceived, for he himself says (Exhibit B, p. 11) that the letter provided that eligibles should be transferred from the higher to the lower grades "in their order, according to average, and provided their grade was sufficient to entitle them to compete in the lower grade."

Instead of doing this, however, Mr. Paul has chosen any one he wished from the higher lists and then made the secretary certify him immediately with three unfortunates from the lower lists, who were simply put on to complete the certification, thereby diminishing their own chance of appointment, as if not appointed after three certifications their names were properly dropped. Mr. Paul explicitly testified (Exhibit R, p. 12) that he himself was in the habit of picking out a higher-grade eligible who had consented to the transfer and then telling the secretary to "include such person in his next certification for the lower position," especially if "there was an absence on the list certified to me of proper parties," this last being a most extraordinary admission, tantamount to saying that the postmaster illegally declined to take any man from a given certification unless he chose to do so. Thus Mr. Paul explicitly testified before the chief examiner that he himself, and not Shidy, the secretary of the board, chose out the eligible from the higher list who was to be put on the next certification for a lower position. But the first day he appeared before the Commission he equally explicitly testified that it was Shidy who always made the choice and that he himself knew nothing about it. The following day he was confronted with the stenographic report of his statement to the chief examiner, whereupon he calmly admitted that it was true, and that he did make the choice himself; and in a newspaper interview has since again stated that he did not. This may be accepted as a fair test of Mr. Paul's marvelously treacherous memory. It seems certain Mr. Paul habitually usurped the functions of the board, and forced it to act in a manner entirely subservient to his wishes (see Exhibit X, pp. 2, 3, and 4), although he denies this.

Shidy testifies that it was, and Johnson testifies that Shidy kept telling him of Mr. Paul's usurpations and dictations; and the fact that Johnson never dared interfere nor try to find out the truth of the matter is proof positive that he likewise dared not thwart Mr. Paul's wishes. (See, also, his testimony about remarking the paper and about the lists of eligibles.) Moreover, in Exhibit Y are given the rough draughts of letters in Mr. Paul's unmistakable handwriting, from which the board afterwards made smooth copies in corresponding with the Commission, showing that he interfered in what were properly purely the duties of the board and practically dictated the latter's correspondence. In the records of the board (see Exhibit C, p. 26) there is a very remarkable entry, unanimously agreed to, to the effect that the board would enforce the decision of the Commission "so far as laid in their power." This proviso could only refer to the overruling actions of the postmaster, as shown by the context, for it referred to the circular forbidding him to have access to the records. It shows that the whole board knew the facts as well as Shidy did, and makes it clear that its members are all equally to blame; and if the postmaster could by any possibility be considered blameless, Mr. Shidy's two colleagues must still share the guilt equally with him. Their sole excuse lies in the guilt of the postmaster.

Mr. Shidy testifies that Mr. Paul made his appointments first, and then forced him, Shidy, to "gerrymander" the lists of eligibles so as to produce a "stuffed" certification which should contain the name of the already appointed man. Mr. Paul practically admits that he did this in certain cases (see Exhibit R, pp. 5 and 6), stating that the requisitions on the secretary "have always been made as a rule" prior to the appointment or designation of a man, and that the certifications were made to him "in writing or verbally" and he "thinks" they were made "prior to appointment, with possibly an occasional variation," when "the secretary would modify the certificate." In other words, Mr. Paul admits that Mr. Shidy's accusation is true as regards certain cases; it is, therefore, merely a question whether Mr. Paul acted illegally and improperly in all instances or only in some.

A peculiarly flagrant instance (among many others almost as bad) of Mr. Paul's conduct in choosing at will any higher class eligible, when there were others of the same class with inferior averages to the one chosen, may be found in Exhibit A, certifications 54 and 55. On January 20, 1888, a certification was made for stamper which included the names of four carriers; Mr. Paul very improperly refused to take any names from the certification; but February 15 another certification was made, for the same place, and the lowest of the four carriers certified on January 20 was again certified, this time with three stampers, to the exclusion of his companions of higher grade, and was appointed.

For such conduct there can be but one explanation, that given by Shidy, who admitted that the first certification was canceled and the next rearranged "for convenience, to bring the desirable men—the men who were wanted—into, proper position." As Mr. Paul himself canceled the first certification, and chose out the man to be appointed from the second, he of course stands responsible for this piece of dishonest gerrymandering. But this is not the full measure of his misconduct in this particular. The carrier (named Keaveny) selected from the second certification for stamper on February 18, 1888, had actually been appointed stamper on December 8, 1887, two and one-third months before, and had been promoted to be carrier February 1, 1888. In other words, Mr. Paul selected the man whom he desired out of the carrier list, passing over carriers of higher average, appointed him as stamper, and then promoted him to be carrier without even waiting for the "stuffed" certification from which he was nominally appointed. A more outrageous piece of official misconduct it would be hard to imagine.

It is, however, so far from being unique that it is simply a sample of the misdeeds shown in Exhibit A, the analytical statement compiled from the certification book and other records. It is these records, even more than Mr. Paul's own statements, that condemn Mr. Paul. They show the grossest irregularities. which are set forth at length in Exhibit A, and need only be referred to or summarized here. (See, also, Exhibit Y, the supplementary testimony of Shidy, with quotations from the records.)

One man, Wigman, was examined for a clerkship April 14, 1887; he passed very low, just under 70 per cent., yet Mr. Paul immediately appointed him carrier, and afterwards, on May 6, a certification was made to cover his appointment. Again, one Tabert, examined as carrier, was certified as stamper on April 14, 1888, having already been appointed on April 1, and two months afterward was promoted to be carrier. (A worse case still has recently been reported by Shidy, but the Commission has not yet had time to verify it. According to this statement one A. L. Trumpf was appointed March 1, 1888, and began work March 23, although not even examined until March 17, the papers not being marked and listed until the 30th, nor the man himself certified until April 14.) On a number of occasions the postmaster refused to make any appointment at all from certifications, returning them as void, which was entirely improper: How flimsy were the pretexts on which these declarations of "void" were made may be gathered from the fact that what was held to render one certification void was not held to invalidate another, when it contained the name of a man the postmaster wished to appoint (see Exhibit X, certifications 29 and 31). Again, the postmaster would often cancel a certification on the pretext that a man was a non-resident, and yet in one instance he afterwards appointed to office one of these same non-residents (see Exhibit X, certification 25). Sometimes these void certificates were employed to use up a candidate's right to three certifications, sometimes not. It is difficult to discover any reason for such methods of making and refusing to make appointments from them unless we accept the statement of Shidy that they were "cooked" so as to get men who were not desired out of the way (see pp. 5 and 6 and portions of Exhibit A). In a number of instances (see Exhibit A, pp. 2, 3, 4) but one name was certified. Again, it is impossible to see why the postmaster should have accepted such a certification if honestly trying to obey the law; the only possible explanation seems to be that given by Shidy, to the effect that these persons were already "appointed, and more names would not have altered the case at all."

Men were continually singled out from the higher lists and certified on the lower, although there were plenty of others on the higher lists with superior averages to the favored ones, who were likewise willing to be certified for the lower places. Other men were certified for positions on lower lists without their consent and for no conceivable reason unless it was to juggle with the certifications. Once after a man had been certified three times and not chosen, and was therefore no longer eligible, the postmaster coolly proceeded to appoint him. (For a discussion of this case, and of the utterly inadequate explanation of the postmaster see Exhibit A, pp. 9 and 10). Nor was this a solitary instance of the kind (see Exhibit A, p. 15). Sometimes the certifications would be so twisted that of the entire regular list for the lower grade not one would be appointed (see Exhibit A, p. 14). Appointments were frequently made prior to certification in any form (for the last instance see Exhibit A, p. 21). Even after the visit of Chief Examiner Webster last fall the postmaster continued to appoint men prior to any certification (see Exhibit Y, Shidy's statement, corroborated by the formal request for certification, dated January 16, 1889).

In short, the official records show beyond possibility of dispute that the lists of eligibles were twisted and garbled in almost every conceivable manner in order to produce swindling certifications whereby certain men could be rejected although entitled to appointment, and other men appointed although having no rightful claim to the chance. In order to make use of these swindling certifications it was absolutely necessary that two parties should be privy to and cognizant of the whole transaction, viz, the party making the certification, that is, Dr. Shidy and perhaps his colleagues, and the party making the appointment, that is, the postmaster, Mr. Paul. Unless both parties were equally guilty, it follows of necessity that either Dr. Shidy was the tool of Mr. Paul, or Mr. Paul the tool of Dr. Shidy. For Mr. Paul to plead innocence is equivalent to his pleading imbecility, for no sane man could have made appointments from a succession of such certifications without perceiving their character, and it is quite incredible that he could by mere chance have picked out from each certification the very individual to favor whose choice it was designed. Mr. Paul can not plead ignorance of the certification book, for his own signature, as is right and proper, stands therein opposite the name of every man appointed (see Exhibit X, p. 10). Mr. Paul alone benefited by the crookedness of the certifications, for he alone had the appointing power; there could be no possible object in Shidy's conduct unless it was fear of thwarting the wishes of his superior officer. The conclusion is irresistible that Mr. Paul is responsible for the wrongdoing. He has grossly and habitually violated the law, and has done it in a peculiarly revolting and underhanded manner. His conduct merits the severest punishment. His further continuance in the office would be a great misfortune, and we recommend his immediate removal.

As for Shidy, he, equally with his colleagues Johnson and Tahsel, was certainly guilty of grave misconduct in permitting the board to become the tool of Mr. Paul; but he did it under fear of losing his place if he rebelled, being wholly in the power of Mr. Paul; and unlike his two colleagues, who were equally guilty with himself, he had the manliness to come forward and tell what had occurred when the chance was given him. It is manifestly unjust to visit him with any punishment not also inflicted on Johnson and Tahsel. The whole history of the case emphasizes in the most striking manner the urgent need of having at least some members of every local examining board entirely removed from the influence or dictation of the appointing officer. While all the members of the board hold their places at the will of the appointing power there will be perpetual danger that the latter will seek to exercise undue influence over the former. Provision should be made by which at least some salaried members could be added to every local board from outside sources, so that it should contain members removed beyond the possibility of influence from the appointing officers.

We have the honor to be your obedient servants,

CHAS. LYMAN.
THEODORE ROOSEVELT.
HUGH S. THOMPSON.

EXHIBIT D.

Before this investigation goes further I wish to make a statement in reference to the testimony elicited on Saturday in regard to Mr. Shidy. I have nothing further to say as to the wisdom or unwisdom of seeking to protect a man who abandoned his wrongdoing and at the risk of his place turned Government witness. I thought then, and I think still, that it was my duty as a Government officer to protect a Government witness. As to that policy the committee will judge. But there is another point which I wish to make perfectly clear before leaving this branch of the subject. The testimony of the Superintendent of the Census and of the Postmaster-General might give the impression that I had concealed from them the facts in regard to Shidy when I sought their assistance in protecting him. If such an impression was given by Mr. Porter he amply corrected it when recalled to the stand, as appears by the record. The impression of concealment given by the Postmaster-General if it exists may still remain. It is, however, impossible that the Postmaster-General could have meant to convey such an idea, for he was officially cognizant of all the facts in regard to Shidy by the report in the Paul case; the report which he assigns as in part the basis of his action in determining on the removal of Paul. I quote from the report. This sentence occurs at the beginning of the report:

"Shidy testifies that he was compelled by the postmaster to give the latter free access to the lists of eligibles, although such access was at that time strictly forbidden. He further testifies that the postmaster, knowing then who were eligible, as well as their standing, appointed whomsoever he chose, and then forced him (Shidy) to torture the lists and certification book so as to produce a certification which should bear the appointee's name.

A little further on the report says: "Shidy testifies that he yielded to all the postmaster's demands because he knew that a refusal to do so would have entailed the immediate loss of his place, and therefore, of his means of support. * * * Shidy and Johnson were equally to blame, but of course if their statements are true an infinitely heavier load of blame rests on the postmaster."

Again, toward the close of the report:

"In order to make one of these swindling certifications it was absolutely necessary that two persons should be privy to and cognizant of the whole transaction, namely, the party making the certification, that is, Dr. Shidy, and perhaps his colleagues, and the party making the appointment, that is, the postmaster, Mr. Paul.

"Unless both parties were equally guilty, it follows of necessity that either Dr. Shidy was the tool of Mr. Paul, or Mr. Paul the tool of Dr. Shidy.

*   *   *   *   *   *

"As for Shidy, he, equally with his colleagues, Johnson and Fahsel, were certainly guilty of grave misconduct in permitting the board to become the tool of Mr. Paul; but he did it under fear of losing his place if he rebelled, being wholly in the power of Mr. Paul; and unlike his colleagues, who were equally guilty with himself, he had the manliness to come forward and tell what had occurred when the chance was given him.

"It is manifestly unjust to visit him with any punishment not also inflicted on Johnsen and Fahsel."

It may be added that any one who has read the report, even in the most cursory manner, can not fail to understand not only the evidence given by Mr. Shidy before the Commission, but the exact nature of Mr. Shidy's violation of law; for Mr. Shidy's name occurs in almost every sentence of the report, and his testimony both as to his own wrongdoing and that of his colleague is an integral and inseparable part of it.

As the charge against Mr. Paul involved of necessity collusion with Mr. Shidy, it is impossible to read the report in reference to the former without understanding precisely both the testimony and defense of the latter.

The Postmaster-General was also cognizant of the facts in regard to Johnson, who was equally at fault with Shidy, who did not confess, but who is still retained in office by the sufferance of the Postmaster-General. There was nothing inconsistent, therefore, in seeking to protect and give a living to the man who repented and confessed his wrong-doing; we were merely trying to put him in a position where he would not be very much worse off than his equally guilty colleague who had not repented or confessed. Again, at the time I saw the Postmaster-General in regard to Shidy all the facts in reference were matters of public notoriety, for I had stated them in two published interviews and they had been commented on. The Postmaster-General, I am sure, did not mean to convey the impression that anything was concealed from him in regard to Shidy, but in case such a mistake should arise I desire to say that I not only concealed nothing in regard to Shidy from any one, but all the facts in regard to him were publicly and officially known at the time of my suggestion of him for office and at the time of his appointment. Not a fact has been elicited during this investigation as to Mr. Shidy's conduct while in office that we did not clearly bring out in our official report of last July, which was not only formally brought to the attention of the Postmaster-General, but was published broadcast in the press.

EXHIBIT E.

Report of certifications for the month of February, 1888.

UNITED STATES CIVIL SERVICE COMMISSION,
CLASSIFIED POSTAL SERVICE, BOARD OF EXAMINERS,
Post-Office at Milwaukee, Wis.

NOTE.—At each monthly meeting of the board the secretary will submit the report of certifications during the preceding month for the perusal and signature of all the members of the board present at the meeting. The report, together with the monthly report of appointments and the report of the transactions of the board, will thereupon be forwarded to the Commission.

Names.	General average.	Number of times certified.	Selection and date thereof. (Write "Selected" opposite name.)
Certification No. 55, dated Feb. 18,1888, grade of stamper	Albert Klotz, jr.	95.0	3	
	Bruno Lasche	94.5	1	
	Thos. F. Keaveney	81.8	1	Selected.
	Jas. F. Keenan	75.7	1	
Certification No. 56, dated Feb. 18, 1888, grade of stamper	Bruno Lasche	94.5	2	
	Jas. F. Keenan	75.7	2	
	Patrick J. McCormack	73.0	3	
Certification No. 57, dated Feb. 18, 1888, grade of stamper	Mich. Cramer	68.0	1	Selected.
	Bruno Lasche	94.5	3	
	Jas. F. Keenan	75.7	3	
	Marthias S. Rausch	71.3	1	Selected.
Certification No. 58, dated Feb. 18, 1888, grade of carrier	Patrick J. Reilly	70.8	1	
	Chas. Cumming	89.8	1	
	Louis Smith	87.6	1	
	Wm. C. Gaulke	82.5	1	
Certification No. 59, dated Feb. 18, 1888, grade of stamper	Patrick J. Reilly	70.8	2	Selected.
	Chas. Cumming	89.8	2	
	Frank L. Koceja	69.0	3	
	Frederick J. Weber	74.3	4	Selected.
Certification No. 60, dated Feb. 18, 1888, grade of stamper	Louis Smith	87.6	2	
	Chas. Cumming	89.8	3	
	Louis Smith	87.6	2	Selected.
	Wm. C. Gaulke	82.5	2	
Certification No. 61, dated Feb. 18, 1888, grade of carrier	Frank X. Mayer	71.1	1	
	Wm. C. Gaulke	82.5	3	
	Frank X. Mayer	71.1	2	
	John A. Koelsch	69.2	3	
	Thos. J. Murray	67.7	1	Selected.

To the UNITED STATES CIVIL SERVICE COMMISSION,
Washington, D. C.

Post-office at Milwaukee, Wis.—Report of certifications, etc., month of February, 1888.

We certify to the correctness of the within report.

J. B. JOHNSON,
H. SHIDY,
C. D. FAHSEL,
Board of Examiners.

EXHIBIT F.

UNITED STATES CIVIL SERVICE COMMISSION,
Washington, D. C., March 7, 1890.

I hereby certify that the records of this Commission show that on April 2, 1889, Henry T. Holtz was promoted from class 1 to class 2; that on the same day Alexander C. Campbell was promoted from class $1,000 to class 1; that on the same day Frank E. Culver was promoted from class $900 to class $1,000; that on April 23, 1889, Orville S. Swank was selected and employed upon certification under the civil-service rules as clerk class $900; that on April 24, 1889, Otis N. Johnson, upon examination and certification under the civil-service rules, was promoted from class $900 to class $1,000; and that this employment and these promotions were in the clerical force of this Commission.

JOHN T. DOYLE, *Secretary.*

EXHIBIT G.

Commissioner Edgerton appeared at the office of the Commission this morning and stated to Commissioner Lyman, in the presence of Chief Examiner Webster and Stenographer Morgan, that he had been removed from his office of Civil Service Commissioner by the President, and exhibited a letter signed by the President so removing him, of which the following is a copy:

"EXECUTIVE MANSION, *February* 9, 1889.

"SIR: You are hereby removed from the office of United States Civil Service Commissioner.

"Yours, etc.,

"GROVER CLEVELAND.

"Hon. A. P. EDGERTON,
   " *Washington, D. C.*

This action leaves the Commission with one Commissioner and two vacancies.
(Minutes U. S. Civil Service Commission, February 9, 1889, vol. 10, p. 176.)
A true copy.

JOHN T. DOYLE,
Secretary U. S. Civil Service Commission.

(2) Post-Office Department; Dickinson, Postmaster-General, February 14, transmits for the information of the Commission a tabulated list showing the number of postal employés required for the several lines of postal duty in the forty post-offices where fifty or more employés were in the postal service as shown by the rosters submitted to take effect January 1, 1889; also, a list of three post-offices—Atlanta, Ga., Nashville, Tenn., and Grand Rapids, Mich.—whereat the rosters submitted to take effect January 1, 1889, show fifty or more persons in the service in connection with each of said offices; also, a third table showing four offices—Augusta, Me., Nashville, Tenn., Springfield, Mass., and St. Joseph, Mo.—where the number of employés is less than fifty, but is approaching that number.

Will be acknowledged and the Postmaster-General will be informed that, in view of the information contained in this letter that there were employed on January 1, 1889, as many as fifty employés at Atlanta, Ga., Nashville, Tenn., and Grand Rapids, Mich., these offices will be treated as having been classified by the Postmaster-General in accordance with the requirement of section 6 of the civil-service act, and the President will be informed, as required by section 2 of Postal Rule I, that said offices have been included in the classified service and that the Commission will provide an examination for testing fitness of persons employed therein.

(Minutes U. S. Civil Service Commission, February 21, 1889, clause 2, vol. 10, pp. 227, 228.)
A true copy.

JOHN T. DOYLE,
Secretary U. S. Civil Service Commission.

UNITED STATES CIVIL SERVICE COMMISSION,
Washington, D. C., March 1, 1889.

SIR: The cases presented in the following requests for non-competitive examination under General Rule III, section 2, clause (c), are well supported by the accompanying papers, and appear to be meritorious and of a character similar to those that have heretofore been recommended to the President for his approval. They are therefore submitted to the President for his consideration and approval.

REQUEST OF THE SECRETARY OF THE INTERIOR.

A. Request No. 381, Thomas A. Green, from messenger at $840 to copyist at $900, office of the Secretary.

B. Request No. 397, Frank D. Hester, from messenger to copyist at $900, Bureau of Pensions.

C. Request No. 399, Mrs. Louise E. McFalls, from laborer at $600 to skilled laborer at $720, Patent Office.

D. Request No. 400, Miss Daisy M. Carter, from laborer at $600 to skilled laborer at $720, Patent Office.

E. Request No. 401, Miss Lucy Dyer, from laborer at $600 to skilled laborer at $720, Patent Office.

F. Request No. 402, Miss Josephine Luckey, from laborer at $600 to skilled laborer at $720, Patent Office.

G. Request No. 403, William M. Terrell, from laborer at $600 to skilled laborer at $720, Patent Office.

H. Request No. 404, Mrs. Pattie Brown, from laborer at $600 to skilled laborer at $720, Patent Office.

I. Request No. 405, Mrs. Julia B. Banks, from laborer at $600 to skilled laborer at $720, Patent Office.

J. Request No. 406, Rose H. Lord, from laborer at $600 to skilled laborer at $720, Patent Office.

K. Request No. 407, Araminta L. Calvert, from laborer at $600 to skilled laborer at $720, Patent Office.

L. Request No. 408, Mrs. Mary A. Lomans, from laborer at $480 to skilled laborer at $720, Patent Office.

REQUEST OF THE SECRETARY OF THE TREASURY.

A. Communication of February 20, 1889, Frank M. Skinner, from messenger at $840 to class D, office of the Treasurer of the United States.

REQUEST OF THE SECRETARY OF WAR.

A. Communication of October 20, 1888, also communications of October 16 and 23, 1888, and February 18, 1889, with indorsements thereon, for the promotion of Miss Bessie S. Lawton from messenger to clerk class $1,000, office of Quartermaster-General.

I have the honor to be, your obedient servant,

CHAS. LYMAN,
Commissioner.

The PRESIDENT.

Approved March 1, 1889.

GROVER CLEVELAND.

(Letter-book H, pp. 40–43.)
A true copy.

JOHN T. DOYLE,
Secretary U. S. Civil Service Commission.

U. S. CIVIL SERVICE COMMISSION,
Washington, D. C., March 11, 1889.

SIR: On the 4th of December, 1888, the President directed the Postmaster-General to classify the Railway Mail Service under and in accordance with the provisions of section 6 of the act to regulate and improve the civil service of the United States, approved January 16, 1883, and at the same time directed this Commission to prepare and submit to him for his approval rules governing appointments, promotions, etc., in that service.

In pursuance of these directions the Postmaster-General issued his order of classification on December 31, 1888, and on January 4, 1889, this Commission submitted rules, which were, on the same day, approved by the President in the following terms, to wit:

"The above rules are hereby approved, to take effect March 15, 1889, provided that such rules shall become operative and take effect in any State or Territory as soon as an eligible register for such State or Territory shall be prepared, if it shall be prior to the date above fixed.

"GROVER CLEVELAND."

The Commission at once set about the necessary preparations for putting these rules into effect, in accordance with the terms of the President's approval of them, and has pursued these preparations with the utmost diligence to the present time. It is found impossible, however, to complete them so that the rules can go into effect as to all the States and Territories on the 15th instant. Examinations have already been held in twenty-six States and one Territory, and have been or will be arranged for in all the remaining States and Territories at the earliest practicable moment. The papers from these examinations will be marked as rapidly as possible, and eligible registers established; but with the limited force and other facilities at the command of the commission it is believed that this work can not be completed and registers established for all the States sooner than May 1 next. It is therefore suggested that that date instead of March 15 be fixed as the date when the Railway Mail rules shall go into full effect, and to that end approval of the accompanying order is respectfully recommended.

I have the honor to be, your obedient servant,

CHAS. LYMAN,
Commissioner.

The PRESIDENT.

(Letter-book H, pp. 59–62.)
A true copy.

JOHN T. DOYLE,
Secretary U. S. Civil Service Commission.

———

EXECUTIVE MANSION,
Washington, March 11, 1889.

Whereas civil-service rules for the Railway Mail Service were approved January 4, 1889, to go into effect March 15, 1889; and

Whereas it is represented to me by the Civil Service Commission in a communication of this date that it will be impossible to complete arrangements for putting said rules into full effect on said date, or sooner than May 1, 1889: It is therefore

Ordered, That said Railway Mail rules shall take effect May 1, 1889, instead of March 15, 1889: *Provided,* That such rules shall become operative and take effect in any State or Territory as soon as an eligible register for such State or Territory shall be prepared, if it shall be prior to the date above fixed.

B. HARRISON.,

A true copy:
JOHN T. DOYLE,
Secretary U. S. Civil Service Commission,

———

U. S. CIVIL SERVICE COMMISSION,
Washington, D. C., April 16, 1889.

SIR: I have the honor to submit herewith a proposed amendment to Special Departmental Rule I, to include among the places excepted from examination under that rule in the office of the Secretary of the Treasury that of inspector of furniture.

The Secretary of the Treasury, in a communication to the Commission of date April 13, herewith inclosed, states the reasons which induce him to ask that the place named be made an excepted place. Concurring in the views expressed by the honorable Secretary, I respectfully recommend your approval of the proposed amendment.

I have the honor to be, your obedient servant,

CHAS. LYMAN, *Commissioner.*

The PRESIDENT.
A true copy:

JOHN T. DOYLE,
Secretary U. S. Civil Service Commission.

U. S. CIVIL SERVICE COMMISSION,
Washington, D. C., April 25, 1889.

SIR: I have the honor to submit herewith a proposed amendment to Special Departmental Rule I, to include among the places excepted from examination under that rule in the office of the Secretary of the Treasury the following:

Custodian of dies, rolls, and plates at the Bureau of Engraving and Printing, two subcustodians, keeper of the vault, and distributer of stock.

The Secretary of the Treasury, in a letter dated the 18th instant, herewith inclosed, states the reasons which induce him to ask that the places named be made excepted places; and the reasons given seem to me to justify the request. I therefore respectfully recommend your approval of the proposed amendment.

I have the honor to be, your obedient servant,

CHAS. LYMAN, *Commissioner.*

The PRESIDENT.

(Letter-book II, p. 361–362.)

A true copy:

JOHN T. DOYLE,
Secretary U. S. Civil Service Commission.

Exhibit II.

United States Post-Office,
Milwaukee, Wis., June 9, 1888.

Sir: Replying to your communication of the 6th instant, permit me to state that Cumming's name appears at the head of the register of eligibles for carrier at this office as having been examined October 19, 1887, with an average standing of 89.8, and that the secretary of the local board claims to have duly reported the examination of that date. Your statement of all the facts as to Cumming is accordingly correct, and your conclusion that "he was and is entitled to three certifications for position in the grade for which he was examined," accords with my opinion and action in this particular.

I shall request the secretary of the board of examiners at this office to forward to you at once a duplicate report of the examination of October 19, 1887.

You remark further that "the only circumstance which could justify his [Cumming's] certification to the position of stamper, even with his consent, would be the depletion of the eligible register below the number required for a single certification," etc. Such was precisely the fact in the case of Cumming, and the depletion of the stamper list could not well have been foreseen. In fact, the depletion of lists as to competent men can rarely be foreseen or provided for without a considerable increase in the number of examinations, much to the inconvenience of the public service at this office, where clerical aid is limited to the last point of endurance.

Moreover, to make certification from a higher to a lower grade is obviously a great advantage to the public service, since it not only provides for the deficiency of depleted lists, but enables the appointing officer to secure a higher grade of service than otherwise.

Furthermore, certification from higher to lower grades was distinctly authorized at this office in a letter from the Civil Service Commission, dated September 18, 1885, and signed by Robt. D. Graham, secretary, in which he says: "Those who have taken higher examinations as clerks or carriers may, of course, be certified to these lower places and for this purpose may be transferred to the lower registers, on their request." And all certifications of this kind have been frequently made to me at this office, under this authority, largely to the benefit of the service, inasmuch as it has in many cases secured a better ability and education in lower places than could otherwise be obtained, and also permitting more convenience in promotions on the ground of qualification and merit. This is illustrated in the case of Cumming, standing at 90 on clerical list and accepting the place of stamper.

Respectfully,

Geo. H. Paul, Postmaster.

Hon. John H. Oberly,
Acting President Civil Service Commission.

Exhibit I.

[Exhibit A.]

Analytical statement compiled from the certification book and other records showing the manner in which certifications, selections, and appointments have been made at the post-office, Milwaukee, Wis., October 30, 1888.

[The entry at the right of each copy of certification indicates the register from which the name of the eligible was taken.]

	Name.	General average.	Number of times certified.
Certification No. 19, September 26, 1885, for stamper.			
	Clarence E. Chapin	83	4
	Harry Flint	77	3
	John F. Murray	77	2
	William A. Strong	73	1

This certification was marked "void," aud is one of the six referred to by Mr. Doyle, in his report, from which no selections were made. It was properly cancoled, one of the names entered thereon, Clarence E. Chapin, having already been selected from the next preceding certification (No. 18). The mistake is one which might easily be made in the process of "stuffing" a certification to cover an appointment (or selection) previously made, in the attempt to "gerrymander" the eligibles "to make them gee into line," as the secretary describes it.

The secretary, however. made another mistake, and an inexcusable one, on this certification and on his records. Harry Flint, whose name was borne on the certification, passed the clerk examination with an average of 79.3, and his name was entered on the clerk register with that average July 1, 1885. It was also entered on the same day on the stamper register, but with an average of 77 only (the average he obtained on the first two subjects), and was certified three times for stamper with this lower average, but not selected. This mistake might have worked an injustice to the eligible.

Certification No. 21, November 1, 1885, for stamper.	Name.	General average.	Number of times certified.	
	Martin J. Wawezymakowski	89.5	1	Stamper.

This certification contained but one name, next to the highest name on the stamper register. This eligible had already been selected and appointed when the certification (in the book) was made.

Certification No. 22, November 1, 1885, for stamper.	Name.	General average.	Number of times certified.	
	Charles J. Darbellay	90.5	1	Stamper.

This certification contained but one name, the highest on the stamper register. The selection and appointment preceded the certification (in the book).

Certification No. 23, November 1, 1885, for piler.	Name.	General average.	Number of times certified.	
	Albert W. Phillips	81.3	1	Carrier.

This certification contained but one name, which was taken from the carrier register. At the time when the three last-mentioned certifications (21, 22, and 23) were made (all November 1, 1885) there were five available eligibles on the regular stamper (or piler) register. There was, therefore, no necessity for a resort to the carrier register.

Certification No. 24, March 13, 1886, for stamper.	Name.	General average.	Number of times certified.	
	Miss Josie Whitehead	87.7	1	Stamper.

This certification contained but one name, but the only one of a female borne on the stamper register. The certification was, therefore, properly made, provided the requisition of the postmaster called for names of females to be certified. The eligible (Miss Whitehead) was, at the time of the above mentioned certification and selection, already employed in the Milwaukee post-office as a money-order clerk, having been appointed to that position—held by the postmaster to be an "excepted place"—August 1, 1885. She was, however, appointed from this certification (No. 24) to the position of stamper March 13, 1886. The postmaster says that this appointment was made in order to adjust accounts, "in order to adjust the allowance by the Department." (I did not inquire whether she was allowed to draw the salary of both places, as that seemed to me to be a matter entirely between the postmaster and the Post-Office Department.)

Certification No. 25, May 6, 1886, for carrier.	Name.	General average.	Number of times certified.	
	John B. Hasley, jr.................................	85.1	2	Carrier.

This certification, like the four preceding it, contained but one name, and that not the highest on the carrier register. All of those, however, with higher averages had opposite them on the register—after they had been once certified—the note "Objected to and not again certified." There was opposite Hasley's name a similar entry, namely: "Objected to as non-resident; not certified again." The postmaster it seems overcame the objection to this one man and appointed him, and the secretary of the board then made a certification to cover the appointment. These notes of objection appear quite frequently on the registers, sometimes without any reason, and at other times with "non-residence" as the alleged reason. The postmaster says that he thinks non-residence "a fundamental ground of objection." The board so treated all of his objections, and after they were made did not give the eligibles against whom they were made the further certifications to which they were entitled under the rules, except in cases where the postmaster saw fit to remove his objection.

In explanation of his neglect to include the requisite number of names (4) in each of the five preceding certifications, the secretary says that the persons named on the certification were selected (or appointed) before the certifications were made, and that it was therefore useless to include other names. "These persons were appointed, and more names would not have altered the case at all. They were definitely chosen and appointed."

Certification No. 26, June 4, 1886, for piler.	Name.	General average.	Number of times certified.	
	Edward N. Ewer.................................	93.7	1	Clerk.
	Shelton M. Minor.............................	81.3	1	Clerk.
	Alfred W. Traverse...........................	89.5	1	Clerk.
	Alphonse G. Lochemus.....................	79.6	1	Clerk.

This is another of the six certifications mentioned by Mr. Doyle, from which no selection was made. There is entered on the certification-book opposite the name of Alphonse G. Lochemus, "Now in postal-service, second certification made to give four names to select from." Lochemus was appointed December 7, 1885, to a position (clerk south side station, money-order, etc.) which the postmaster held to be an "excepted place." The secretary considered that a sufficient reason for canceling this certification and sending up a new one, which he did do the same date—certification No. 27, which was a duplicate of No. 26, with the omission of the name of Lochemus, and the substitution from the clerk register of the name of Edward A. Graw, average 75.5, who was selected. Although Certification No. 26 was canceled it was erroneously charged up as one certification against each eligible whose name was borne thereon. In attempting to explain the matter of charging certifications from which no selections were made the secretary says: "It was a nominal injustice. They would not have been selected anyway." There were available stamper eligibles when this certification was made.

Certification No. 28, June 4, 1886, for stamper.	Name.	General average.	Number of times certified.	
	Sanford H. McCall.............................	90.7	1	Carrier.
	Luke McCormack.............................	90.6	1	Carrier.
	Willett S. Cossett.............................	89.5	1	Carrier.
	A. C. Ewens......................................	86.9	1	Carrier.

This certification was wholly from the carrier register, although there were then at least two available eligibles on the regular stamper register. The four names on this certification were taken from the top of the carrier register. McCormack was selected, his selection and appointment being dated June 1, 1886.

Attention is called to the fact that there were eligibles of the clerk register with higher averages than the carriers on this certification, who had evidently consented to take lower places, for their names were certified for stamper on the date of this certification (see Certifications Nos. 26 and 27), and as they were not selected they were still eligible and should have been entered on this certification. The secretary says that it was known that Mr. McCormack would take the place and it was intended that he should have it, and the other names were thrown in as "stuffing."

	Name.	General average.	Number of times certified.	
Certification No. 29, Aug. 5, 1886, for carrier.				
	Sanford H. McCall	90.7	2	Carrier.
	Willett S. Cossett	90.6	2	Carrier.
	A. C. Ewens	86.9	2	Carrier.
	Robert L. Cooley	85	1	Carrier.

The four names on this certification were from the head of the carrier register, the first three having been on Certification No. 28 for the position of stamper. Cossett was selected notwithstanding the fact that Cooley's name was on the certification, which fact was considered sufficient ground for canceling Certification No. 31, *post*. Cossett's selection and appointment were dated July 1, 1886. The postmaster says that he dated his nomination (appointment) from the time of the occurrence of the vacancy. He also says that Cossett made a kind of statement accompanying his application (when he handed it in to the postmaster) for carrier with reference to his previous business, and adds: "My attention was directed to him as a candidate through that original statement. Undoubtedly the fact of his having been certified from a higher register was a matter of consideration between us."

	Name.	General average.	Number of times certified.	
Certification No. 30, Sept. 1, 1886, for stamper.				
	Edward N. Ewer	93.7	3	Clerk.
	Alfred W. Traverse	89.5	3	Clerk.
	Sanford H. McCall	90.7	3	Carrier.
	A. C. Ewens	86.9	3	Carrier.

The first two names on this certification were from the clerk register, and the other two from the carrier register. Opposite this certification on the book appears the note "No appointment made." This is another one of the six certifications referred to by Mr. Doyle, from which no selections were made.

It will be noticed that this made the third certification for each man whose name was borne thereon, and the certification, it would seem, was charged to them, for their names do not appear on any subsequent certification, but, instead, others from the same registers with lower averages. This certification (30) seems to have put out of the way four men with high averages, two of whom—Ewer and Traverse—had been on only one certification, from which a selection was made, viz, No. 27. In explanation of charges for certifications from which no selections were made the secretary says: "It was a nominal injustice. They would not have been selected anyway." The postmaster says that one of the eligibles on this certification was offered the place, but declined it. If that was the case, the postmaster should have noted the selection and signed in proper form.

	Name.	General average.	Number of times certified.	
Certification No. 31, Dec. 1, 1886, for carrier.				
	John D. Dropper, jr.	91.3	1	Carrier.
	Robert Schoschon	85.3	1	Carrier.
	Robert L. Cooley	85	2	Carrier.
	William K. Hughes	81.3	1	Carrier.

These names were all from the carrier register. This is another one of the six certifications from which no selections were made. Opposite the certification on the book ap-

3117——22

pears the note, "R. L. Cooley objected to as residing beyond the delivery of the office. No selection." It will be noticed (ante, Certification No. 291) that one selection had been made from a certification on which Cooley's name was borne. No great harm seems, however, to have been done by canceling this certification, except in dropping off one more name (Cooley's) from the register of eligibles, as the first name on this certification (John D. Dropper, jr.) was selected from the next certification (No. 32), which was made up of the names on Certification 31, except Cooley's, in place of which another name was regularly substituted from the carrier register.

Certification No. 33, Dec. 1, 1886, for carrier.	Name.	General average.	Number of times certified.	
	William Paul	84.7	1	Clerk.
	Robert Schoschon	85.3	3	Carrier.
	William K. Hughes	81.3	3	Carrier.
	Lawrence A. Mehan	83.9	2	Carrier.

The first name on this certification was taken from the clerk register, where it stood the tenth name from the top of the list of those then eligible for certification for the position of clerk. The three other names on this certification were taken in proper order from the carrier register. Two of the carriers were out of the way by this (their third) certification, and the other carrier (Mehan) by the next certification. Certification No. 34 was not properly made up, as it contained the names of Schoschon and Hughes, who had been "put out" by this certification. Mehan's was the only name from No. 33 entitled to further certification. * The name of Gustav Ziegler, average 82.5, from the carrier register, was added to make up Certification No. 34, and Ziegler was selected. It does not appear that the eligibles on the clerk register with higher averages than Paul's were ever given an opportunity to consent to certification for a lower place. There was an ample carrier register at this time.

Certification No. 36, February 11, 1887, for carrier.	Name.	General average.	Number of times certified.	
	Burton W. Lloyd	87.2	1	Clerk.
	James E. Bradley	86.2	1	Clerk.
	Anton B. Elblien	81.5	1	Carrier.
	William F. Reimers	81.3	1	Carrier.

The first two names on this certification were taken from the clerk register, but they were not the highest eligibles on that register. The other two names were taken from the top of the carrier register. Bradley was selected, his selection and appointment being dated January 1, 1887. There were four eligibles on the clerk register with higher averages than Bradley's. The postmaster, in attempting to explain why these clerk eligibles were entered on this certification, says: "On the principle already explained, of taking the highest on the carrier list with those of sufficient grade on the clerk list to come into the same certification."

Certification No. 37, May 2, 1887, for carrier.	Name.	General average.	Number of times certified.	
	William Hegner	86.6	1	Carrier.
	Frank C. Ghent	85.6	1	Carrier.
	Eugene A. Sexton	85.2	1	Carrier.
	Evan H. Jones	83.4	1	Carrier.

No selection was made from this certification, valid objections having been made to two of the eligibles named thereon—to Ghent as being over age for a carrier (thirty-six

---

* If Certification 31 was not charged to the eligibles named thereon, both Schoschon and Hughes were entitled to a further certification. Both should have been included or both excluded.

years old), and to Sexton as being physically incapable (having lost his left forearm). This certification appears to have been charged to one of the two eligibles not objected to (Hegner), but not to the other (Jones). See next certification. The error was doubtless due to carelessness on the part of the secretary of the board.

	Name.	General average.	Number of times certified.	
Certification No. 38, May 2, 1887, for carrier.				
	William Hegner	86.6	2	Carrier.
	Evan II. Jones	83.4	1	Carrier.
	Anton B. Elblien	81.5	2	Carrier.
	Frank Van Ells	78.9	1	Clerk.

Elblien was selected from this certification, the selection and appointment being dated May 1, 1887.

	Name.	General average.	Number of times certified.	
Certification No. 39, May 2, 1887, for carrier.				
	William J. Hegner	86.6	3	Carrier.
	Evan II. Jones	83.4	2	Carrier.
	Frank Van Ells	78.9	2	Clerk.
	William F. Reimers	81.3	2	Carrier.

Van Ells was selected from this certification, the selection and appointment being dated May 1, 1887. His was the only name taken from the clerk register, the other three coming from the carrier register.

	Name.	General average.	Number of times certified.	
Certification No. 44, May 6, 1887, for carrier.				
	Benjamin F. Langland	78.4	3	Carrier.
	Emil C. Bauch	75.2	2	Carrier.
	Joseph H. Byrne	74.7	1	Carrier.
	Alexander H. Wigman	69.6	1	Clerk.

Wigman was selected from this certification, and his selection and appointment were dated May 1, 1887. He did not pass the examination under the rules in force at the time, as he obtained an average of only 62.5 on the first two subjects; he was not, therefore, eligible.

It will be noticed that the name of Benjamin F. Langland was entered on the four next preceding certifications (Nos. 41 to 44 inclusive). The secretary explains this error—he admits that it occurred through carelessness in entering the third certification as the second, and then in not examining the book back of that certification when he made the fourth (No. 44). Langland was not selected from any one of these four certifications. He was, however, subsequently—July 1, 1887—appointed to the position of stamper, for which appointment no certification appears on the book. It is not probable that any certification to cover this appointment was ever made. It is evident that no formal one was made after No. 44. It is not claimed that he was subsequently certified in any form. The secretary in his report of appointments (Exhibit M) certifies that he (Langland) was appointed stamper "without certification," and in his statement before me declares that he does not know how Langland was appointed. The postmaster, however, declares in his statement that "he was appointed stamper on regular certification from the carrier list and on his expressed willingness to accept lower place," and precedes this declaration with the general declaration that "no person has ever been appointed to such place without certification." He attempts to explain the matter by suggesting that certification 44 was probably recalled after Wigman had been selected therefrom for the position of carrier, and that, on such recall, Langland was selected for the position of stamper, and that the secretary had failed to note this second selection on the certification book.

Such a hypothesis can hardly be entertained, for several reasons.

First, certification No. 44 was regularly entered on the certification book, May 6, 1887, nearly two months before the appointment was made, and if recalled would naturally have been put before the postmaster in that form, instead of in the form of an informal (memorandum) certification. If so presented the secretary should have had nothing to do with indicating the selection made. It is the duty of the postmaster to make the selections and to authenticate the fact by signing his name under the selection. The book of certifications and the records of appointments do not show a single instance, unless the case of Langland be one, in which the postmaster has failed to comply with this regulation. He did not indicate or sign the book for Langland's selection.

Second. It was not the custom at the Milwaukee post-office to make more than one selection from a certification. The book of certifications does not show a single instance. Even in cases where the selections made on a single day nearly or quite exhausted a register—all the names on several successive certifications of the same date—a separate certification appears on the book for each selection.

Third. Other certifications (and selections) intervened between No. 44 and the date of the appointment of Langland. The postmaster certainly was not authorized to recall and make selections at will from any old certifications. Such a course of procedure would be about as irregular as the making of appointments to non-excepted classified places without any certification.

Fourth. Certification No. 44 was for the grade of carrier and was made from the carrier register, and the postmaster had already selected a carrier therefrom. He had no authority under the rules, even with the liberal interpretation he undertakes to give them, to select a stamper from such a certification.

Fifth. Langland was no longer eligible. He was "out" on certification, and could be restored to the eligible register only by an order of the Commission, or through another examination.

	Name.	General average.	Number of times certified.	
Certification No. 45, May 6, 1887. For piler.				
	Benjamin W. Wines............................	85.6	1	Clerk.
	Albert Klotz, jr................................	95.0	1	Porter.
	Patrick J. McCormack.........................	73.0	1	Porter.
	Frank L. Kocejia.............................	69.0	1	Porter.

The first name on this certification was taken from the clerk register, all of the others from the porter's—the regular register for the position of piler or stamper. Wines was selected, his selection being dated May 1, 1887, and his probational appointment May 6, 1887. The records of the Post-Office Department give the date of his appointment as July 1, 1887. An exceptional case, the appointment not being of an earlier date than the certification.

	Name.	General average.	Number of times certified.	
Certification No. 54, January 20, 1888, for stamper.				
	Chas. Cumming...........................	89.8	1	Carrier.
	Louis Smith....	87.6	1	Carrier.
	Wm. C. Gaulke	82.5	1	Carrier.
	Thos. F. Keaveny	81.8	1	Carrier.

All of the names in this certification were taken from the carrier register. On the book opposite the certification appears the entry " Void." This is one of the six certifications, previously referred to, from which no selections were made. It is admitted that the persons whose names are borne on this certification had consented to take lower positions than that for which they were examined. Their names ought therefore to have been taken up on certifications for lower places (if they were entitled at the time to go at all upon certifications for such lower places) in the order of averages. They were not, however, taken in that order, as will be seen by the five next succeeding certifications, on some of which other names from the same register with lower averages than any of those on No. 54 were substituted, although the certifications were, except No. 58, for a position of the same grade that No. 54 was made to fill. It is evident that these eligibles (on No. 54) had not withdrawn their consent to certification for lower places, as they were all subsequently certified, although not together (on Nos. 55, 59, and 60) for the position of stamper. They were, however, so "gerrymandered" that two of them were "put out" on certifications, without receiving appointments. In regard to the canceling of this certification and the making of the next (No. 55) for the same position, the secretary says: "It was done for convenience so as to bring the desirable men into the proper position—bring in the men who were wanted."

	Name.	General average.	Number of times certified.	
Certification No. 55, February 18, 1888, for stampers.				
	Albert Klotz, jr.	95.0	3	Porter.
	Bruno Losche	91.4	1	Porter.
	Thos. F. Keaveny	81.8	1	Carrier.
	James F. Keenan	75.7	1	Porter.

All of the names on this certification were from the porter's register (the register for stampers or pilers), except the name of Keaveny, which was from the carrier register, and the lowest in average of the four on the next preceding ("void") certification, and therefore not entitled to a place on this certification.

Keaveny was selected, and his selection and appointment were dated December 8, 1887—two and one-third months prior to his certification for the position, as it appears in the book. He was promoted from stamper to carrier February 1, 1888—more than half a month prior to his certification for the position from which he was promoted. The postmaster says that Keaveny was selected from the carrier register in order to get the best qualified man, because he was a thoroughly qualified man and would accept.

	Name.	General average.	Number of times certified.	
Certification No. 56, February 18, 1888, for stamper.				
	Bruno Losche	94.5	2	Porter.
	James F. Keenan	75.7	2	Porter.
	Patrick J. McCormack.	73.0	3	Porter.
	Michael Cramer	68.0	1	Carrier.

The first three names on this certification were taken from the porter (stamper) register. The last name (Cramer's) was from the carrier register. The three carriers with very high averages on void certification No. 54, who had not been selected and who had consented to take a lower place, were passed over and Cramer, who had a very low average, was given a place on this certification. He was selected and his selection and appointment dated February 1, 1888. This selection was made to fill a vacancy created by the promotion of the man (Keaveny) selected from the last preceding certification of even date with this one.

	Name.	General average.	Number of times certified.	
Certification No. 57, February 18, 1888, for stamper.				
	Bruno Losche	94.5	3	Porter.
	James F. Keenan	75.7	3	Porter.
	Patrick J. Reilly	70.8	1	Clerk.
	Mathias S. Raush	71.3	1	Clerk.

The first two names on this certification were taken from the porter (stamper) register, and the other two were from the clerk register, the ninth and eighth in averages, from the top of that register. Raush, one of the clerks, was selected, and his selection and appointment dated February 1, 1888. The three carriers of void certification No. 54 are wholly ignored in this certification, and clerks with lower averages are substituted.

	Name.	General average.	Number of times certified.	
Certification No. 58, February 18, 1888, for carrier.				
	Charles Cumming	89.8	1	Carrier.
	Louis Smith	87.6	1	Carrier.
	William C. Gaulke	82.5	1	Carrier.
	Patrick J. Reilly	70.8	2	Clerk.

This is a certification for carriers, and the first three names are those of the carriers whose names appear on the void certification No. 54. The fourth name is that of one of the clerks, Reilly, which appeared on No. 57 for the position of stamper. His was the ninth name from the top of the list of eligible clerks. He was selected, and his selection and appointment dated February 15, 1888.

	Name.	General average.	Number of times certified.	
Certification No. 59, February 18, 1888, for stamper.				
	Charles Cumming	89.8	2	Carrier.
	Frank L. Kocejia	69.0	3	Porter.
	Frederick Jas. Weber	74.3	4	Carrier.
	Louis Smith	87.6	2	Carrier.

All of the names on this certification, except one, were taken from the carrier register, two of them being names which appeared on void certificate No. 54. The second name, Kocejia, was from the porter (stamper) register. He was the last eligible stamper. When the first (No. 55) of this group of certifications for stamper's place (four in all and all of the same date) was made there were five names—Klotz, Losche, Keenan, McCormack, and Kocejia—on the stamper register of eligibles, two of them with very high averages. Their names were all woven into the four certifications so adroitly as, with former certifications in some cases, to put them all out of the way on certification without making a single selection from the register. The positions for which they were examined were filled by the selection of three from the carrier and one from the clerk register. Those selected were far from being the highest on their own registers (carriers or clerks), and with one exception were much lower than the stampers whose names appeared on the certifications with them. Frederick Joseph Weber, on the last mentioned certification (No. 59), had a higher average than the porter (stamper) certified with him. Weber was, however, not entitled to this certification, it being his fourth, except upon request of the appointing officer (which does not appear to have been made) and not then unless his average would entitle him to a place, and in determining this question not only the names on the regular register for the place but all others who had consented to certification for the lower place should have been taken into consideration. Weber was selected from No. 59, and his selection and appointment dated February 15, 1888.

After Weber had been selected from the carrier register for the position of stamper he was improperly allowed by the board to take the clerk examination. His name was entered on the clerk register of eligibles March 30, 1888, and certified three times, but not selected.

	Name.	General average.	Number of times certified.	
Certification No. 60, February 18, 1888, for stamper.				
	Charles Cumming	89.8	3	Carrier.
	Louis Smith	87.6	3	Carrier.
	William C. Gaulke	82.5	2	Carrier.
	Frank X. Mayer	71.1	1	Carrier.

All of the names on this certification were taken from the carrier register, the first three being the first three names borne on void certification No. 54. One of these—Smith—was selected, his selection and appointment being dated February 15, 1888.

The report of appointments, promotions, etc., at the Milwaukee post-office, made by the secretary of the board (Exhibit M), shows that Charles Cumming, whose name is borne on this certification, after having been certified three times (on Nos. 58, 59, and

60), not including the void certification (No. 54), was appointed May 1, 1888, to the position of stamper. This was nearly two and a half months after his last certification (No. 60), by which he was certified "out." Several other certifications were made after No. 60, prior to the date of the appointment of Cumming. It was finally discovered, but not until Cumming had been in actual service under this appointment for some time, that the proceeding was irregular and the appointment illegal.

More than half a month after Cumming had been actually appointed and assigned to duty—on the 17th of May, 1888—the secretary of the board sent a communication to the Commission (see Exhibit K) in which he stated that Cumming was certified February 18, 1888, for appointment as stamper, "which position he refused to accept." "He was again certified the same day for the same position," which made his third certification. "He has now reconsidered his refusal to accept the position of stamper, and the postmaster wishes to appoint him. Can he do so?" This was a strange communication to come from the secretary of the board, who knew, or should have known, the rules regulating appointments, and who must have known, and his testimony before me shows that he did know, that Cumming had already been appointed and was on duty in the office. His statement was misleading in other particulars. It did not give all of the facts, viz, that Cumming had taken the carrier examination and had been certified three times on the same date—February 18, 1888—once for the position of carrier and twice for that of stamper. (See letter of the Commission in reply, dated May 25, 1888, Exhibit K.) The Commission informed the secretary that Cumming was not entitled to further certification. This brought on further correspondence, in which the postmaster showed that he was better informed than the secretary in regard to the state of the registers of eligibles, and confirmed the secretary in his recent statement in regard to the "stuffing" of certifications.

In a letter dated May 30, 1888 (see Exhibit K), the postmaster says: "Referring to the record for verification, permit me to state: Charles Cummings was not examined for the place of stamper, but for that of letter-carrier. At the time he was first certified to me for a stamper his name was at the head of the eligible list for the place of carrier, and as the stamper list was nearly exhausted his name was used simply to make the certification as to number complete. This without his knowledge or request. On the same day—February 18—he was certified three times, first as carrier, when an eligible.for clerk was appointed, and twice for stamper, under circumstances as above stated. But he was not examined for stamper, did not then desire the place of stamper, and declined the place of stamper, simply because he preferred the place for which he was examined. * * * Can the appointing officer sacrifice all the eligibles on the list by calling for their certification to inferior positions, which he must know they will not accept, without their knowledge or consent? Mr. Cumming declined lower positions while he thought the opportunity possible for appointment to the position to which he aspired; and now, that such opportunity has passed away, is willing to accept a lower place, to the advantage of the service, and I accordingly nominated him for the position of stamper, holding his acceptance subject to your approval." * * *

This communication is stranger than that of the secretary. The postmaster substantially admits that he controls the certifications; that he could sacrifice eligibles on the higher registers by calling for their certification to lower places; that he did sacrifice Cumming by having him certified to lower places until there was no possibility of his securing a higher position and was willing to accept the lower place; that certifications were "stuffed," and that he actually made selections and nominations for appointment without proper certification to him.

That eligibles of higher registers, and with very high averages, were sacrificed by being certified to lower places (whether with their consent does not appear) is clearly shown by several of the certifications reported on this exhibit. (See certifications 26 to 30, inclusive, by which three clerks and two carriers, all with very high averages, were put out of the way by certifications to lower places.) Other illustrations may be found on the records. (See letter of the Commission, dated June 6, 1888, in reply to the postmaster, Exhibit K, in which attention is called to certain apparent violations of the rules and further reports are asked for.)

In his letter of June 9, 1888, in reply to letter of Commission of June 6, the postmaster says: * * * "You remark, further, that 'the only circumstances which could justify his (Cumming's) certification to the position of stamper, even with his consent, would be the depletion of the eligible register below the number required for a single certification, etc.' Such was precisely the fact in the case of Cumming, and the depletion of the stamper list could not well have been foreseen. In fact, the depletion of lists as to competent men can rarely he foreseen or provided for," etc.

In regard to this matter, attention is called to the comments on certification No. 59, in which it is shown that at the time when this group of certifications (Nos. 55 to 60, inclusive) was made there were five eligibles on the proper register for stampers who were "gerrymandered" out by these very certifications, two of whom at least must have been selected if the rule of the Commission quoted in the postmaster's letter had been followed.

There is much significance in the qualified expression used by the postmaster, viz: "In fact, the depletion of the lists as to competent men," where the question as to competency is determined solely by the appointing officer with all of the registers open to him, and without limitation, at least in the descending line, as to the register from which he must make his selection.

(See letter of the Commission dated June 16, in reply to the postmaster's letter of June 9, 1888, Exhibit ——.)

Following the letter of the postmaster of June 9, came one from the secretary dated June 12, 1888, in which he says: "In order to correct the record as to the certification of Cumming in accordance with the views of the Commission, it will only be necessary to direct that his name be stricken off the certification (No. 59) in which his name was used to complete the list, and to allow it to be again presented to the postmaster. Certifi-' cation No. 59 so modified will be satisfactory, as it still includes the name chosen."

This is a peculiar method for solving the difficulties of the situation—strike the name off, as it was only used to complete the list, that it may be again presented to the postmaster, and then the certification so modified will be satisfactory, as it still includes the name stricken off—it includes the name chosen. Evidently what he intended to say was, the man has been chosen (or appointed) and the matter can be fixed by declaring that the entry of his name on certification No. 59 was irregular, but may be left there to cover the selection already made—to save "stuffing" another certification.

In reply to the secretary of the Commission, in a letter dated June 16, 1888, after quoting the secretary's statement only through that part which suggests the striking the name from the certification (No. 59) and allowing it to be again presented to the postmaster, says: "In reply, you are respectfully informed that the proceeding suggested by your board is hereby authorized and directed, and that hereafter the rules and regulations now in force must be strictly observed in all particulars." This action put Cumming in a position for further certification. He was not, however, again certified, but permitted to retain his place without ever going through with the form of "stuffing" a certification to cover his appointment. The postmaster says that after the question of legality of the appointment was raised, Cumming was suspended from duty until the letter of the Commission of June 16, 1888, was received, and that this letter authorizing a restoration to the list of eligibles was construed by him (the postmaster) as an approval of the original appointment, and that he therefore restored Cumming to duty without further certification or appointment. The secretary says that Cumming was at work in the office for some time prior to the receipt of the authority to restore his name to the register of eligibles.

Certification No. 64, April 14, 1888, for piler.	Name.	General average.	Number of times certified.	
	Andrew D. Tabert	80	1	Messenger.
	Charles F. Hurley	92	2	Messenger.
	Patrick J. McCormack.	85	1	Messenger.

The names on this certification were all taken from the messenger (stamper or piler) register. Tabert was selected, his selection and appointment being dated April 1, 1888. He took the examination for carrier, and stood, at the time, the eighth from the top of the list of eligible carriers. His name was, however, regularly transferred to the messenger (piler) register, whether with his consent or not, does not appear. He was not entitled to this certification, there being at the time two others on the messenger register with higher averages than his, viz, Joseph Holland and Thomas O'Neill, each with an average of 81.

Certification No. 72, May 15, 1888, for clerk.	Name.	General average.	Number of times certified.	
	Frank Stockhausen	80	1	Clerk.
	Frank J. Pesskorn	77	1	Clerk.
	Frank Schoenfeld	77	1	Clerk.

Opposite this certification on the book appears the entry "No selection made." The postmaster states that he expected to be able to appoint a clerk at that time, but found that he could not. It does not appear that any appointment of clerk to a non-excepted place has been made since the date of this certification.

	Name.	General average.	Number of times certified.	
Certification No. 73, July 18, 1888, for carrier.	Evan H. Jones	85	2	Carrier.
	Joseph Klein	82	1	Carrier.
	Cornelius E. Smith	80	1	Carrier.

Opposite this certification appears the note "Not used." The secretary evidently made a mistake in entering certain names on this certification and therefore canceled it. The next certification of the following day for the same position contains two names from the same register, with higher averages than two of those on this certification.

	Name.	General average.	Number of times certified.	
Certification No. 74, July 19, 1888, for carrier.	Evan H. Jones	85	2	Carrier.
	Edward A. Dittman	83	1	Carrier.
	Joseph P. Mallon	83	1	Carrier.

From this certification Dittman was selected, his selection and appointment being dated May 1, 1888.

	Name.	General average.	Number of times certified.	
Certification No. 95, September —, 1888, for stamper.	Thomas J. O'Neill	81	3	Messenger.

This certification had not been made, or at least it did not appear upon the book, at the date when I commenced this investigation. It and the selection from it by the postmaster were made just before I completed my examination of the records and witnesses. The last certification appearing on the book on September 4, 1888, was No. 94, dated July 30, 1888. In answer to the question whether any appointments had been made subsequent to the one from certification No. 94, the secretary says: "None to my knowledge. I see persons around me not yet provided for—one, at least." In answer to the question put to the postmaster in regard to this appointment he says: "The record of certifications is only made up to July 30, and O'Neill has been since appointed. He would come on the next certification." The postmaster claimed that this selection was made from among other names on regular [informal] certification; he could not, however, produce the memorandum certification, but called in the secretary of the board and requested him to give the names which should appear with O'Neill's on the certification. The secretary apparently knew nothing of any certification, even an informal one, and found it necessary to examine the registers to ascertain what names ought to go on the certification with O'Neill's. He made the examination in my presence, and informed the postmaster that O'Neill's was the only name on the proper register for this certification. The secretary then made a formal certification to cover the appointment, and the postmaster entered thereon his selection, dating it back to cover the date of the appointment, August 1, 1888, a month and ten days prior to the certification. The secretary in his report of appointments [Exhibit M] says that O'Neill was appointed without certification. This appointment was evidently made by the postmaster directly from the register, and without certification in any form.

The certifications included in this statement are those containing the most positive evidence of violations of the rules. The most of those omitted show irregularities, especially in the matter of discrepancies between the dates of certifications and the dates of selections or appointments. Very few exceptions were found to the rule, that the selection and appointment preceded or antedated the certification, at least on the certification book.

Respectfully submitted,

WM H. WEBSTER,
Chief Examiner.

WASHINGTON, D. C., October 30, 1888.

EXHIBIT J.

[Exhibit B.]

Statement of George H. Paul, postmaster, Milwaukee, Wis., made before W. H. Webster, chief examiner United States Civil Service Commission, September 5 and 10, 1888.

MILWAUKEE, WIS., September 5, 1888.

Examination of GEORGE H. PAUL, postmaster at Milwaukee, Wis.

By CHIEF EXAMINER:

Q. What is your name, residence, and occupation?—A. George H. Paul, 321 Hanover street, Milwaukee, Wis., and postmaster of that city.

Q. How long have you held that position?—A. Since June 1, 1885.

Q. Who are the members of the civil service examining board at your office?—A. When I came in the board consisted of Dr. Shidy, superintendent of the registry department; Superintendent Johnson, of the mailing division; and the third member, whose name I do not recall, was succeeded by Mr. Furlong, a new appointee. Mr. Furlong was succeeded by Mr. Fahsel, on the resignation of Mr. Furlong from the office. The third member has changed with appointments to the money-order office. But the main fact which I wish to appear is that the majority of the board is the same as when I came into the office, and both Republicans. The other member has been changed only by reason of his change in his relation to the office.

Q. Who has been secretary of the board since you became postmaster?—A. Dr. Shidy. He has been the most active member since the commencement.

Q. Who has had the custody of the records of the board, especially the register of eligibles and the certification book?—A. The secretary.

Q. Do you know in what safe place he has kept them deposited?—A. Only incidentally, not officially. I do not think it a part of my official duty to know. I have never seen them but in one place—deposited in the safe in the registry office.

Q. Have these books been accessible to you at all times and have you examined them whenever you wished?—A. I do not think I have ever examined them with reference to any appointment except upon application to Dr. Shidy himself. There may have been some occasion on which I have, during his absence at dinner, got the address of some party, but not on any other occasion of business.

Q. Have you generally or at any time known the state of the register-the order in which the names stood before making appointments?—A. Yes, I think I have been aware, unavoidably, of the last. In fact, they have been published in the newspapers, perhaps on one or two occasions; names only.

Q. The lists of eligibles have been published in the newspapers?—A. I think so, and I must say as simply a matter of truth that the secretary has never regarded the list of eligibles after record as in anywise but a public record. Still that is a matter on which he should speak for himself.

Q. Have these publications disclosed the grades and relative order of eligibles?—A. Reporters are frequently in the different departments of the office for news, and when examinations occur and applications are filed, etc., they get such such facts as they can. It is a mere matter of opinion, but I do not think the register has been regarded as strictly private matter. I do not think the lists have been published frequently. I prefer that Dr. Shidy should give his own statement.

Q. Do you know how the lists of eligibles with averages have been obtained?—A. I do not think the averages have been made public, but simply the names in the order of eligibility, perhaps on one or two occasions. I wish to add to my statement that the list has never been called for by me or shown by him with any reference to any discrimination or deviation from the supposed requirements of the law and rules on no occasion.

If it has been examined at all by me, it has been with reference to what qualifications persons standing near the head of the list and likely to be recommended—coming within the range of immediate appointments—possessed, and with that reference solely.

Q. How have you made requisitions on the board for names to fill vacancies?—A. When a vacancy has occurred I have verbally requested the Secretary to certify to me the proper number of eligibles formally.

Q. You have never made any written request on the secretary for a certification specifying the place to be filled?—A. No.

Q. Have you seen the blank form of requisition prescribed by the Commission?—A. I do not think I have. There would have been no objection to its use on my part if my attention had been called to it.

Q. Have you made requisitions on the secretary in all cases prior to the appointment or designation of the person for appointment?—A. The requisitions on the secretary have always been made as a rule. I know of no variation prior to the appointment of any person, except, perhaps, in a single case—not the case of a single person, but on a single occasion.

Q. Have certifications been made to you for all appointments prior to appointment, in writing?—A. The certifications have in all cases been made to me in writing or verbally, and I think in all cases prior to appointment, with possibly an occasional variation, which may have arisen on a question of construction of the rules or something of that kind, in which case my impression is that in one or two cases—and a very limited number—the secretary would modify the certification to accord with the rule.

Q. Explain the discrepancies in the dates in certification No. 29—the date of the appointment and the certification of Willett S. Cossett.—A. Without a distinct recollection of the facts, my impression is that a vacancy having occurred, upon inquiry as to the character of the man, and knowing that he was eligible from the previous certification, I nominated him, dating his nomination from the time of the occurrence of the vacancy, upon official knowledge based upon the preceding certification. My inference is that the entry of the latter certification at a later date was made under these circumstances. Whether or not these are the exact facts, there was no discrimination or intent of discrimination in his favor otherwise than is provided for by the rules.

Q. State whether you made the same inquiries as to character and fitness in the case of the other persons on certification No. 29 as you made in the case of Cossett.—A. I answer in the affirmative by saying that I never make an appointment from any certificate without previous inquiry as to the relative capacity and fitness of the persons named.

Q. In what form was that certification. before you at the time you made the selection, the book showing that it was not entered until August 5, while the appointment was made on July 1 preceding, it not apparently being then before you in the form of a certification?—A. I unavoidably know in many cases the names of the best qualified candidates for examination. The blank forms of application have been uniformly given out with instructions to return them to the Secretary, but that injunction is almost invariably disregarded, they being handed to me and passed to the Secretary directly. In the case of Mr. Cossett I have a distinct recollection that he made a kind of statement accompanying his application for carrier with reference to his previous business, having had a large business experience in the city, and that my attention was directed to him as a candidate through that original statement. There has never been any partiality exercised in the cases of person eligible for appointment that they may be by their own request taken from a higher register. Under the ruling of the Commission, as we have construed it, I have deemed it desirable that the eligible willing to accept a lower place from the higher register or proper standing should be appointed to the lower place, thereby getting better ability. Undoubtedly the fact of his having been certified from a higher register was a matter of conversation between us.

Q. By whom are the blank forms of application distributed?—A. The rule is that they are to be given out by the secretary, but he is often absent, and sometimes applicants come two or three at a time, and I simply request my clerk to procure the blanks which are in the custody of the registry office, of course constructively in charge of the secretary, and to hand them out. My clerk goes into the registry office, gets the blanks and hands them to the men without even knowing their names or anything about them.

Q. These blanks are returned to you on completion?—A. Candidates are enjoined to return them to the secretary of the board, but very frequently, and probably in a majority of cases, the injunction is utterly disregarded.

Q. You necessarily know all of the candidates before they are examined?—A. Not in the sense of knowing anything about them and their personal history, relations, or opinions upon any subject. I purposely avoid knowing anything until after the examination, until such a time that circumstances make it probable that they are to be eligible for appointment soon. I then make a personal investigation, somewhat, as to their character and duties.

Q. After you know they have passed?—A. Yes; after I knew they are likely to be certified to me, after the next vacancy or within two or three vacancies, I generally intend to keep well posted in advance. This office, as a general rule, has been so liable to depredations that I keep a very rigid account of all complaints to the minutest detail. I have endeavored, and considered it to be my duty to endeavor, to avoid the introduction of any improper person to the affairs of the administration of the office. I do not believe that without such a prior investigation the office would be safe from depredation at any time of the year. I give that as my conviction and as an explanation of the reason for the rigid inquiry and investigation as to the personal character and habits of every person appointed. I will not appoint a man simply on a scholastic examination to take charge of any important portion of the office where he will be subject to constant temptation unless I know that his habits are correct and his moral principles reliable.

Q. Do you understand that names can be taken from any higher register for certification to any lower place without limitation?—A. (Refers to letter of secretary of the board to the Commission, dated September 16, 1885, and reply of the Commission dated September 18, copies of which are annexed hereto as Exhibits A and B* respectively.) I can not see any conditions except that they should be transferred on the list in their order according to average, and provided their grade was sufficient to entitle them to compete in the lower grades, and the Commission has been informed as a matter of course of my action under that construction and has never intimated any disapproval until a recent date when the whole matter was declared void, as being against the rules. I have no recollection of seeing the letter of the board, and so far as the reply relates to my duties I have accepted the statement of Mr. Graham as a general construction of the rule. It certainly is a general statement in terms. Of course, the treatment of the registers is a matter which is not under my observation nor within my sphere of duty in making appointments.

Q. Under that provision did you consider yourself at liberty to make selections for lower grade positions from higher grade registers without regard to there being a list of eligibles for the lower grade?—A. When a higher grade eligible has expressed a willingness to accept a lower place I have told the secretary, with request that under the ruling of the Commission of September 18, 1885, he would include such person in his next certification to me for the lower position if entitled to transfer.

Q. Have you consulted with these persons before appointment?—A. No farther than to ascertain the general facts as to moral character and capacity. If a person has applied to me for a place and was apparently a man of excellent qualifications, and there appeared to be an absence on the list certified to me of proper parties, in one or two instances I may have asked him if he would accept a lower position under proper certification from the examiners, but the number of such instances is very limited, in fact not the practice, always having reference to the rules and the construction of the Commission, as I understood them.

Q. Have written requests been made in any case by eligibles for the transfer of their names to the lower registers, or any written notice of willingness to accept such lower places?—A. I think in a few instances I have received such requests by way of letters begging for place, but they have in all cases been practically disregarded.

Q. Whether made orally or in writing to you, they have have been communicated by you to the board?—A. Generally that is the fact when a formal request for transfer has been made. All talk about appointment naturally and unavoidably comes to me.

Q. Have such requsts been numerous?—A. Quite numerous in comparison with the whole number of eligibles, but no record is taken of them. They are simply expressions of willingness to get anything to do. I refer to office-beggars generally and not to formal applications of eligible parties.

Q. How have you been able to determine in taking a man from a higher register whether certification has been made to you of those highest on that register?—A. I have always so presumed and understood—highest of those requesting transfer and eligible to transfer by examination. If, in the case of any proper person with whose character and capacity I had become familiar, a desire had been voluntarily expressed to me to accept any position in the service lower than that for which he had been examined, I would then request the secretary to include the name of such person in the certification for the place to be filled.

Q. Certification 54 contains the names of four persons standing highest upon the carrier register at its date, January 20, 1888. The vacancy was of a stamper. No appointment seems to have been made. Opposite the certification in pencil is written the word "void." Explain why no selection was made.—A. I think it is merely a clerical matter relating entirely to the secretary of the board. I can not say under what circumstances the names appear as they do upon the register.

Q. The next certification, 55, dated February 18, 1888, for stamper contains the name

---

* Exhibits A and B are both in present Exhibit I, with Mr. Doyle's report.

of Thomas F. Keaveney, also contained in the previous certification. On the first certification his name was certified with three others from the carrier register, but on the second, with three from the porter's register, Keaveney being selected. Why was not his selection made from the first certification? A. I can not say. Mr. Keaveney was one of those who expressed a willingness to accept any position. My impression is that he stood quite high.

Q. Was certification 54 ever before you?—A. I can not say, except so far as that his certification certainly came before me when he was appointed. In what form I can not state.

Q. When was Keaveney selected and assigned to duty?—A. He was employed on December 8, 1887, as stamper, on proper certification under our construction. On February 1, 1888, he was appointed a substitute carrier.

Q. Do you know whether, at the time Mr. Keaveney was certified with the three names from the porter register, he was the only one or the highest of the carriers then eligible who had signified willingness to take the lower place?—A. My impression is that at least two of those certified with Keaveney on certification 54 from the carrier register had signified willingness.

Q. Keaveney being already at work, why was he not selected from the first certification?—A. My impression would be, without a distinct recollection of the facts, that he was selected from the first certification on the ground of supposed superior qualification. Because the appointment is dated December 8, it does not follow that he was in the service at that time. The selection may have come afterwards. Certification was made from the carrier register in order to get the best qualified man, with the knowledge that Mr. Keaveney, a thoroughly qualified man, would accept, and when the second certification was made it was made to include the stamper list. I do not think it comes within the province of my duty to make the explanation. Certification 54, according to the record, is void and probably an error. As to that I have no personal recollection of the facts beyond what the record shows. Certification 55 contains the names of three eligibles, Klotz, Lasché, and Keenan, from the porter register, besides Keaveney who had consented to serve in a lower grade. This certification appears to be regular under the practice of the office. Certifications 56 and 57 also appear to be regular under the same practice and construction. There is evidently a confusion of dates owing presumably to the fact that the entries were not made at the proper time or under some misapprehension as to the dates of appointment and selection not affecting the merit of the selections or the proper order.

Q. Certification 55 contains the names of Albert Klotz, jr., 95, third certification; Bruno Lasché, 94.5, first certification; James F. Keenan, 75.7. first certification, from the porter register, and Thomas F. Keaveney, 81.8, from the carrier register. Keaveney was selected for stamper from this certification. Certification 56 for stamper of the same date contains the names from the porter register of Bruno Lasché, second certification; James F. Keenan, second certification, and Patrick J. McCormick, third certification, average 73, and Michael Cramer, from the carrier register, 58, first certification. Michael Cramer was selected. Certification 57 of the same date for stamper contains the names from the porter register of Bruno Lasché, third certification; James F. Keenan, third certification, and from the clerk register Mathias S. Rausch, 71.3, first certification, and Patrick J. Reilly, 70.8, first certification. Rausch was selected. State whether none of the lower-grade eligibles, who passed with good averages, were competent to fill the position and whether all of the persons who were selected—two from the carrier and one from clerk register—had signified their willingness to take these lower places.—A. First, I presume the Civil Service Commission does not intend to inquire into the exercise of my discretion under the law. On a proper certification to me, of course the right of selection is absolute without supervision, except by the Post-Office Department. Secondly, as to each and every certification referred to, I voluntarily and cheerfully state that the best-qualified man was in each case of the four certified selected and intended to be selected. Thirdly, that the rank of a carrier and that of a porter on the eligible list is not to be determined by the mark appended to his name. The conditions of the standing are not the same under the rules, not only with reference to these special certifications, but as to all certifications from a higher to a lower grade. The actual rank in the higher grade has entitled him to transfer and in the lower grade has entitled him to certification as made. My belief is the standing of the person taken from the higher list has been estimated for the lower list, giving him the privilege of certification, and that no person not so entitled has ever been certified in this office. It is a further fact known to me that the duties of a stamper are determined in a less degree by the rank at the examination than by other qualifications not taken into consideration by the examining board, such as quickness of perception, bodily temperament, and habits of life. Daniel Webster would have made a poor stamper, but undoubtedly would have passed a magnificent examination. I give these considerations entering into my selection for the information of the Commission, because I am never actuated by private, personal, or political considerations, and not because I deem the authority of the Commission competent to inquire as to their merit in determining the measure of my duty.

Q. On certification 57 the names of Rausch and Reilly certified for stamper were nearer the foot than the top of the list of eligibles. Were there any other clerk eligibles who expressed or were given an opportunity to express their willingness to accept a lower place?—A. The rule has been to give to the person of highest rank upon a higher list the first opportunity for certification when request has been made for employment in any grade of service, as far as I know. Personally I have been governed by this rule as to transfers. Often, however, a person on a higher list has signified a disposition to accept a lower grade of service and then withdrawn his assent because circumstances have in the mean time intervened, such as offers of employment at compensation greater than a lower grade would afford, or for some other reasons pertaining to his own judgment, and those changes of disposition have been respected.

Q. Do you know whether there were any other clerks eligibles February 18, 1888, who had signified a willingness to take a lower place?—A. I think not of equal grade. My conclusion as to that is based upon the fact that no others were certified at the time. If others had signified a disposition to accept a lower service they would not have been certified by the secretary probably, unless of equal actual grade with those of the lower grade who were certified, or sufficiently so to come within the certification.

Q. Had any opportunity been given to others on the clerk register to signify such willingness?—A. The opportunity at all times and under all circumstances to signify any disposition of the kind has been equal to all persons whose names were upon the eligible register and unrestrained. In fact it has been deemed by me an excellent policy, as already expressed to the Commission, to encourage appointments from the higher grades to the lower, for the reason that the better ability in respect to grade of service may thus uniformly be obtained, and further, because of the great proportion of poor material which appears uniformly upon the eligible register, a fact due to the low compensation offered for the service on the average, and to the further fact that a large proportion of the applications come from a class which from some deficiency in ability or education or habits of life find it difficult to obtain employment elsewhere.

Q. Explain the discrepancy in the dates on certification 36 for carrier. It purports to have been made February 11, 1887, and the selection and appointment January 1, 1887. As this is illustrative of many such discrepancies make your answer cover all such cases.—A. These discrepancies are a necessity of the circumstances in all offices situated as this is. When a nomination is to be made the secretary is called upon for a certification. He makes that certification in writing. Subsequently the persons certified must be investigated as to relative character and ability. This requires more or less time. Frequently one or more of the parties are absent from the city and can not be personally een. After investigation is made the selection is determined and the secretary is informed. The secretary of the board is chief of the registry department, personally responsible for all the valuables passing through it. The clerical force of the department is notoriously insufficient, and his time is fully occupied by his postal duties and responsibilities. In the case of several appointments they are treated by him oftentimes together from necessity, and the record made up when the time of the appointing officer and that of the secretary will mutually permit. In this way the actual record is oftentimes not made up until a considerable time after the certification, and the discrepancy in every such case appears upon the register. This difficulty can only be obviated by a more liberal provision of law for the execution of the duties of the Commission at offices of this class.

Q. Certification 36, for carrier, contains the names of Burton W. Lloyd, 87.2, and James E. Bradley, 86.2, from the clerk register, together with Anton B. Elblein, 81.5, and William F. Reimers, 81.3, from the carrier register. Lloyd was selected. Explain why Lloyd and Bradley were taken from the clerk register, there being at that time an ample register of eligibles for carrier.—A. On the principle already explained of taking the highest on the carrier list together with those of sufficient grade on the clerk list to come into the same certification.

Q. Do you remember that these parties made requests to have their names certified to the lower places?—A. There is no question about it. I do not know the men. I have treated these men as entitled to certification on request by the instructions of the Commission.

Q. Albert L. Trumpf was appointed as clerk on March 1, 1888, on a certification dated April 14, 1888. Explain that appointment.—A. Trumpf was appointed to a place regarded by me as excepted, being personally responsible to the appointing officer for funds placed in his possession, as stamp clerk at the general-delivery window. At that time he was eligible to certification, I think. Subsequently for the first time my attention was called to the fact that in order that a position should be excepted it should be reported formally through the Post-Office Department to the Commission. This information came from a letter from the Commission, I think to Dr. Shidy. I immediately called for a certification from the board and appointed Mr. Trumpf under it in addition to his previous appointment, until the position could be certified to the Commission through the Department at Washington, as an excepted one. Immediately after such action I received from the Department itself a notification to furnish a list of all excepted positions in the office for approval by the Commission, which I did, including the position occupied by Mr. Trumpf.

Q. Benjamin F. Langland was appointed stamper July 1, 1887, without certification. He was certified four times on certifications 41 to 44, inclusive, for carrier, but not selected. Explain this appointment.—A. No person has ever been appointed by me to such a place without certification. He was appointed stamper on regular certification from the carrier-list and on his expression of willingness to accept a lower place.

Dr. SHIDY. Certification 42 was the second one in which Langland's name was used. In making 43 in the column of "number of times certified" a "2" was erroneously inserted instead of a "3." In making 44 I referred to 43, and finding that was the second time his name had been used, I put it in 44, marking it the third, whereas in reality it was the fourth time it had been used.

By the CHIEF EXAMINER:

Q. To what position was Langland appointed on February 1, 1888, vice Wines? The POSTMASTER. To a position of the same grade, with a slight advance in salary.

Q. In the report of the secretary it appears that Charles J. Cumming was appointed May 1, 1888, without certification. He had been certified three times without selection. His eligibility was restored by the Commission June 16, 1888. How was he appointed without certification of the date mentioned, his restoration not being until June 16?— A. The question of Mr. Cumming's appointment was referred to Commission. On receipt of his restoration to eligibility the letter of the Commission was construed to cover the original appointment from May 1, and he was restored to his position in the office, his service having been suspended in the mean time, and the records should be duly corrected as to his eligibility in accordance with the decision of the Commission in case his eligibility is deemed not to date back to his original appointment.

Q. In the same report the name of William Gillis appears as appointed May 15, 1888, as stamper without certification. Explain this appointment.—A. Mr. Gillis was appointed to the excepted position of money-order clerk at the South Side Station.

Q. Is his grade, strictly speaking, that of money-order clerk?—A. We have only two clerks in that office and he has to take turns with the other clerk in tending the money-order window. He is, strictly speaking, a money-order and a general clerk. He is a money-order clerk for whose fidelity I am responsible.

Q. Is he borne on the rolls as a money-order clerk or stamper?—A. He should be enrolled as a money-order and general clerk.

Q. This report shows that Thomas J. O'Neill was appointed August 1, 1888, as stamper, vice Louis Smith, and not certified. Explain his appointment.—A. The record of certifications is only made up to July 30, and O'Neill has been since appointed. He would come in the next certification.

Q. From what memorandum was the certification of O'Neill made? Can you furnish the group of names from which it was taken?

(After search made for the memorandum without finding it Dr. Shidy stated that the name was the last remaining on the list.)

Q. Certification 24 contains the name of Miss Josie Whitehead, certified for stamper from the stamper register and selected for that position March 18, 1886; but the register shows that she was already in the service, the entry, under the head of "permanent appointment," reading "clerk in the money-order department August 1, 1885." Was that appointment to an excepted place?—A. In fact she was never in any other than an excepted place, but for a time she may have performed some postal duties as a clerk, probably because of the want of a sufficient money-order allowance to cover the compensation.

Q. She is in the money-order division now?—A. Yes; she is the issuing teller.

Q. At that time she was a clerk in the money-order office and withdrew from that place to accept the stamper place?—A. I think there were some changes in the money-order office at that time, and that she was carried on the list and certified as a stamper from her examination in order to adjust the allowance by the Department. I do not know that she ever received any clerk salary. I do not think she was ever classed as a stamper on any report. My rule has been to select for the excepted places from the eligible registers, and my impression is that when she passed the examination she was nominally appointed stamper and soon transferred to an excepted place.

Q. Why was no selection made from certificate 30, September 1, 1886, for stamper?— A. Ewer was offered the appointment, but declined. The record should so state.

Q. On certificate 31 note was made that R. Q. Cooley resided out of the delivery of the office, and no selection was therefore made. Have you always objected to appointing persons residing out of the city?—A. I have done it with the knowledge of the examining board. A person residing out of the city limits is not usually qualified for carrier. He is an entire stranger to our streets and numbers. I have not considered it equitable or within the intent of the law.

Q. In that case you had other names to select from?—A. It seems to me a good ground of fundamental objection. The selection was made from the list as presented to me by the board of examiners.

Q. Why was no appointment made from certification 72, of May 15, for clerk?—A. The probability is that I was not allowed a clerk for the place I expected to fill. I have made no appointment since of a clerk.

Q. Have you examined the circular in the front of the certification book and noticed the requirement that certifications should be entered before any selections were made?— A. This circular has now been shown to me for the first time. I have now examined the circular thoroughly, but I do not understand it to forbid the selection of eligibles for appointment before the record of certifications is made, nor do I understand how in cases of emergency it would be practicable and at the same time maintain the efficiency of the service. In the recent appointment of additional carriers under the eight-hour law, ordered to be provided for without delay, the only manner in which the whole number of appointments could have been made in a safe and satisfactory manner, in my opinion, was to obtain the certification of eligible names at once. Had I done otherwise, separate certification by record and separate investigation as to the candidates would have been required as to every appointment made, thus consuming a large amount of additional time on the part of both the secretary and the appointing officer.

Q. Examine Postal Rule VIII and state whether, in compliance with the requirements of that rule, you have made reports of changes in the force.—A. I have observed the rule (but not precisely in its present form). Notice of all changes has been given orally to the secretary, as required by the rule.

The POSTMASTER. I desire to state that in no instance has any appointment or removal been made at this office on the ground of partisan or personal preference, and in every case any change in the clerical or carrier force has had sole reference to the efficiency of the service. No technical error which may appear upon record or in the administration of the duties, in the testimony I have given upon this subject, is based in any instance upon partisan or personal preference relating to such changes. I ask Dr. Shidy to state fully and freely whether that statement is according to his observation as an appointee under the preceding administration.

Dr. SHIDY. Mr. Paul's statement in regard to the weight that should be given to any clerical discrepancy in the records is a just one, for many of these records are made in haste and under severe pressure. There is room for a certain percentage of clerical error which I believe does not come to any considerable amount. I have not exercised any particular supervision or overexercised my judgment upon the appointments which Mr. Paul has made. I think they have been good appointments and made for the good of the service. I think that has been his object in making those appointments. The mode of making appointments is all shown by our records except as to excepted places, of which I have taken no note. I believe them all to have been made in accordance with the rules.

SEPTEMBER 10, 1888.

Statement by Mr. Paul explanatory of the foregoing testimony.

When the foregoing testimony was taken, until near its close, I had never seen or heard of a circular of the Commission dated March 15, 1885. No copy of such circular has ever been sent me by the Commission from Washington, and no copy of it has ever been shown me by the board of examiners at this office previous to this examination. For more than three years I have been guided in all my actions by the distinct requirements of the laws, rules, and regulations of the civil service, with accompanying instructions and correspondence with myself direct, coming from Washington, and by interpretations placed upon the same in case of doubt by the representatives of the Commission constituting the examining board at this office. I have no recollection of ever receiving information from the Commission itself, or from the examining board, that the record of certifications was the certification itself.

Referring to the circular dated March 15, 1885, now that I have seen it, I discover in it no distinct prohibition of selections from names regularly furnished me by the examining board at this office when called for. I have been unable to find any such prohibition in the laws, rules, or regulations or any document ever coming to my notice. My predecessor received the certifications in precisely the same manner as I have received them, and I have presumed all the facts to have gone regularly to the Commission at Washington and been noted by said Commission. For about three years these facts have been without criticism of any kind. Morever, I find on my files a letter of September 18, 1885, soon after I came in office, signed by Robert D. Graham, secretary of the Commission, in which he states explicitly that the "examinations for porters, stampers, junior clerks, etc., provided for in Regulation 22 implies that the persons eligible under these examinations shall be included *on a distinct register of eligibles from which* (meaning the 'register of eligibles') *certifications may be made to such positions* as you describe," construed by me to mean that certifications should be made by furnishing me names from the "register of eligibles," as the rule of practice.

Having given my previous testimony under this state of facts as to the practice required, I have used therein the word "certification" in a sense quite different from the sense intended by the chief examiner in the questions asked. In all cases he seems to have referred exclusively to the book record of certification, while I referred in my answers to certifications made to me before the record of certifications was made up by the secretary of the board. With this explanation, the reason of the discrepancies in dates upon what this office has regarded as the record of certifications becomes apparent. The certifications have been uniformly made from the "register of eligibles" direct to the appointing officer. The selections have been made when such certifications have been made, and subsequently the secretary of the board of examiners has made up his official record on the book of certifications, the selection dating from the time of actual selection and the record dating from the time of actually making the record.

No one at this office, to my knowledge, has ever dreamed that the Commission ever prescribed or ever intended any other method of certification than that I have described, either before or since my appointment; nor can I find any letter, instruction, law, rule, or regulation enjoining a different method from that pursued at this office, except the circular referred to of March 15, 1885, which I never saw, and which, in my opinion, unconstrued by the chief examiner, would not forbid the construction placed upon the practice by Mr. Graham in his letter of September 18, 1885, and which confirmed me in my impression of the correctness of the manner pursued at this office.

The question of transfer from higher to lower positions was raised in this office early after my appointment in 1885, by myself. The examining board were in some doubt, and the question was distinctly submitted to the Commission, with the reply from Mr. Graham in his letter of September 18, 1885, including these words:

"Those who have taken higher examinations as clerks or carriers may, of course, be certified to these lower places, and for this purpose may be transferred to the lower registers on their request."

Now, I wish to say, broadly and positively, that I know of no law, rule, regulation, or instruction ever seen by me as coming from the general commissioners or the board of examiners which I have not strictly and rigidly obeyed in every particular, in letter and in spirit. In the execution of the law, further, the board of examiners has exercised uniformly an independent judgment, and in questions of doubt as to law or practice I have accepted the decision of that board as the authorized voice of the Commission itself. I have exercised no control of any kind over that board's action, and have never advised such board as to its duties, whether legal or ministerial, and do not suppose it proper for me to do so. If I had supposed, in my own opinion, that the certifications intended a presentation of the record of certifications as the only form of certification that could be made, and the examiners had deemed another course in accord with the purpose of the Commission, I should have unhesitatingly surrendered my own opinion to that of the representatives of the Commission, on the ground of their superior authority in the interpretation of the wishes of the Commission.

I add, further, that I know of no difference made or that could have been made in selections, because of the method of certifications adopted by the examining board at this office. It occasions a discrepancy in dates but not a difference in selections, as far as I can see. The discrepancy in dates is not in all cases by any means explained by the manner of certifications referred to as pursued at this office. Selections for nomination only are made by myself. The appointments are made by the Department, and the dates of appointments are fixed by the Department. As a matter of official comity and convenience these dates are often adjusted with some reference to dates of resignation or removal, so as to make the actual service continuous upon the roster. This is particularly so with reference to substitutes.

As to the blank entitled Form No. 6 *b*, I have never seen a copy of the same until Saturday last, and was not aware that selections were not immediately reported to the Commission.

In case any testimony is taken in this investigation in any manner affecting the statements I have made or impugning my official integrity in the execution of the civil-service law, I ask the privilege of an examination of such testimony and of cross-examining the witness or witnesses before any judgment in the case.

3117——23

By the CHIEF EXAMINER:

Q. Have you preserved the memoranda of certifications which you say have been made in pencil prior to the formal certification on the book?—A. No, for the reason that the certifications have been supposed by me to be a matter of record by the secretary as soon as he could, consistently with his official duties, enter them upon the record. They have been sometimes retained by me for the purposes of investigation of the eligibles as to character and capacity, but oftentimes immediately returned to the secretary for the record. I know of no instance in which the certification made in the manner habitual at this office has varied from the subsequent record made by the secretary, and all selections, I think, without exception, have been made in the manner regarded as formal and regular, and by uniform rule, in accordance with the language of Mr. Graham's letter, as understood and construed by me, and the certifications and selections as made were entered on the book of records by the secretary, as was supposed to be intended.

Q. By what interpretation do you conclude that the letter of Mr. Graham authorized certifications to be made informally by pencil list prior to the formal certification on the certification book?—A. I have understood from the letter and from the previous practice that the furnishing of the names for selection from the register of eligibles constituted the formal certification, the adoption of the written method in ink or pencil being not an informal but a formal certification, and the record of certifications constituting the actual record of the certifications or acts done or certifications "posted up" as described in the circular of March 15, 1885. I think that a careful examination of that circular, now for the first time known to me since this examination, would necessarily lead to the impression that the record of certifications is a record of proceedings and acts done in the matter of certifications. I think, however, that had the circular been known to me possibly a doubt would have been created in my mind by its language as to whether it was intended to regard the record itself as the certification or as merely a record of acts done in the matter of certification.

Q. In furnishing the list of names for certification at any particular time has the list been confined to the four names under the old rule and the three names under the new rule to which you were entitled on a certification, or have you had more names before you for consideration?—A. The number of names certified in each case, according to my recollection, at one time has never varied from the regular number fixed by the Commission as the proper number for certification, either before or since the date of change in the number. In one recent case, when enjoined by the Department to make immediate preparation for carrying into effect the eight-hour law by additional carriers, I requested the secretary to certify to me all the eligibles on the old carrier list at once, but in separate certifications in their proper order, and the selections were made from such certifications, also in their proper order, the certifications each being made according to rule.

Q. Have you always made written requests for certifications upon the blank form furnished by the Commission for the purpose?—A. I have no recollection of seeing a blank form of requisition for certification. I certainly should have used one if one had been in my possession, as preferable. I understand that the secretary has an impression that he received or showed me such a form, but I have no recollection of having seen the form, and if shown me by him it was done in the hurry of other business so that I did not become aware of the nature of it, and I certainly have no such form in my possession or among my blanks.

Q. While it is a fact that the list furnished you on each certification comprised only the number of names authorized by the rules to be certified, is it not also a fact that the entire list of eligibles of all grades was known to you at all times?—A. No; the list was never known to me in any definite way. I have never examined the list with reference to appointments until certification came before me, and then only as to the parties properly certified. I make this answer with the qualification that parties upon the list have frequently applied to me for appointment, often with their notices of standing in their hands. In that exterior way, or by the appearance of occasional names of examined parties in the papers, not including their standing, I have had some general knowledge of parties on the list, but have sedulously avoided any formal knowledge of order and standing beyond the immediate necessities of the case.

Q. On the register of carrier eligibles of names entered July 1, 1885, and certified September 19, 1885, there appears opposite the names of Mathias Roth, John H. Tates, and Charles Buscher the note, "objected to and not again certified." Were the objections in these cases such as came under the provisions of old Regulation 15, and were the objections made in the form required by that regulation?—A. No; I do not know the ground of objection. Talking to the secretary as a representative of the views of the Commission, I have repeatedly objected to the certification of non-residents, unless I deemed such certification necessary under the rules of the Commission, for the reason that I did not deem such persons, in fairness, or possibly in the intent of the Commission, eligible to the places o' carriers in a city like this. I said this much to him with reference to a construction of the law, no limitation being expressed in this particular by the Commission itself as to the eligibility of candidates from any country or clime, but I did not object to any selection under the rule specified.

The POSTMASTER (addressing the secretary of the board). As to the case of Langland, previously referred to in this testimony, the record does not appear to show his selection. I have positive recollection that he was selected from a regular certification in the manner such certifications were usually made. My impression is that in certification 44 Wigman was first selected for the place of carrier and meantime Langland had consented to take the place of stamper, and that the certification was then recalled and Langland selected as the second man from that certification. My further impression is that the failure to enter on the record of certifications the selection of Langland arises from the fact that the second selection from the same certification was not the rule at this office, and that in making up the record, the secretary, having received my signature to the first selection from that certification, deemed the record satisfied, and omitted to enter the second selection of Langland; and that I, when such record was made, would have passed over the entry in the same manner and for the same reason, in giving my signature.

Dr. SHIDY. That might have been the way the error occurred.

The CHIEF EXAMINER. Has it been the practice to make an absolute appointment at the end of six months' satisfactory service by a probationer?

The POSTMASTER. No. I have been in doubt as to the construction of the rule, for the reason that I merely nominate and the appointments are made through the Department. For that reason I have construed the failure to remove to be tantamount to an absolute appointment at the end of six months, and in this conclusion I have been supported by the opinion of one or more of the examiners. An "absolute appointment" means a reappointment by the Department, in this case, of parties already in the service; and such "absolute appointment" would require a renomination by me to the Department and the confirmation of such nomination by the Department, a process which I have not supposed to have been contemplated by the Commission. As to that, I would be glad to receive the specific instructions of the Commission. I would also be glad to receive from the Commission specific instructions as to method of selections, and any other matters as to which the opinion of the Commission differs from instructions of the Commission now on file at this office.

GEO. H. PAUL,
Postmaster, Milwaukee, Wis.

EXHIBIT K.

[Exhibit K.]

Correspondence relative to the appointment of Charles Cumming to the position of stamper in the post-office at Milwaukee, Wis., May 17 to June 16, 1888.

No. 1.

MILWAUKEE, WIS., May 17, 1888.

SIRS: Charles Cumming, an eligible under the civil-service rules, was, on the 18th day of February, 1888, certified for appointment as stamper, which position he refused to accept. He was again certified the same day for the same position. This was his third certification, as he had been twice certified previously. He has now reconsidered his refusal to accept the position of stamper, and the postmaster wishes to appoint him. Can he do so? An immediate answer will greatly favor

Yours, respectfully,

H. SHIDY, *Secretary.*

CIVIL SERVICE COMMISSION,
Washington, D. C.

No. 2.

WASHINGTON, D. C., May 25, 1888.

SIR: This Commission has received your communication of May 17, stating that Charles Cumming was certified on February 18, 1888, which position he refused to accept; that he was again certified the same day for the same position, which was his third certification; that he has now reconsidered his refusal to accept the position of stamper, and the postmaster wishes to appoint him.

The Commission holds that when the position of stamper—the position for which he was examined—was offered to Cumming and declined by him his rights under his examination were exhausted, and he was not entitled to further certification under the rules in force February 18 last. As soon as the position then offered to Cumming and refused by him was filled by the appointment of another person, his opportunity to reconsider his refusal passed from him beyond recall.

This practice is now different, being governed by clause 4, Regulation VII, but this regulation is not retroactive and Cumming can take no benefit under it.

Very respectfully,

JOHN H. OBERLY,
Acting President.

H. SHIDY, Esq.,
    Secretary Board of Examiners, Post-Office, Milwaukee, Wis

---

No. 3.

MILWAUKEE, WIS., *May* 30, 1888.

SIR: Mr. H. Shidy, secretary board of examiners at this office, has shown me your letter of the 25th instant, in which you give the opinion that Charles Cumming is not entitled to further certification under the rules in force February 18 last, on the ground that "when the position of stamper—the position for which he was examined—was offered to Cumming and declined by him, his rights under his examination were exhausted."

I think the conclusion in this case is based on a misapprehension of the facts, arising from an imperfect statement of them by the secretary, and is, therefore, unjust to the person whose privileges are involved, and also to the public service. Referring to the record for verification, permit me to state:

Charles Cumming was not examined for the place of stamper, but for that of letter-carrier. At the time he was first certified to me for a stamper his name was at the head of the eligible list for the place of carrier, and, as the stampers' list was nearly exhausted, his name was used simply to make the certification as to number complete. This without his knowledge or request. On the same day, February 18, he was certified three times—first, as carrier, when an eligible for clerk was appointed, and twice for stamper under circumstances as above stated. But he was not examined for stamper, did not then desire the place of stamper, and declined the place of stamper, simply because he preferred the place for which he was examined. He was not appointed a carrier because I did not believe him old enough and strong enough at that time for the duty.

Has he thus forfeited his "rights," as expressed by you? In other words, has the Government forfeited its rights to a first-class man, marking 89, by certifying his name to an inferior position without his consent? Can the appointing official sacrifice all the eligibles on the list by calling for their certifications as to inferior positions, which he must know they will not accept, without their knowledge or consent?

Mr. Cumming declined lower positions while he thought the opportunity possible for appointment to the position to which he aspired; and now that such opportunity has passed away is willing to accept a lower place to the advantage of the service, and I accordingly nominated him for the position of stamper, holding his acceptance subject to your opinion; but I had not dreamed that the Commission had closed the door of public service against an eligible for higher grade.

Respectfully asking further consideration of this case, I am

Very truly,

GEO. H. PAUL, *Postmaster.*

Hon. JOHN H. OBERLY,
    President Civil Service Commission.

No. 4.

WASHINGTON, D. C., *June* 6, 1888.

SIR: In the case of Charles Cumming, and in reply to the letter of this Commission of the 25th ultimo, you state that Cumming was not examined for the position of stamper, but for that of carrier; that the certification of his name for the former position, on February 18, was without his consent; that at that time his name was at the head of the list for carrier; that the list of stamper was nearly exhausted, and Cumming's name was included in the certification to make the number complete; that on the same day he was certified three times, first as carrier, when an eligible for clerk was appointed, and then for stamper; that he declined the place of stamper, because he preferred the place for which he was examined; and that he was not appointed a carrier because you did not believe him old enough and strong enough at that time for the duty.

Before considering your communication, it is proper to say that the decision of the Commission in the case was based wholly upon the supposition that Cumming was examined for stamper, which was justified by Secretary Shidy's statement as follows: "Charles Cumming, an eligible under the civil-service rules, was, on the 18th day of February, 1888, certified for appointment as stamper, which position he refused to accept. He was again certified the same day for the same position. This was his third certification as he had been twice certified previously." As this supposition was not true the decision of the Commission of course falls.

Cumming's name does not appear upon any report of an examination held at your office on file in this office. The only examination not reported, held before the 18th of February last, is the one of October 19, 1887, which should long ago have been reported, and the Commission desires to call the attention of the board to its dereliction in the matter. It is presumed that Cumming was examined at that time. It would appear from your statement that Cumming was first certified for the position of carrier, which was a proper certification; that he was then twice certified for the position of stamper without his knowledge or consent, and that when offered the position of stamper he declined it. These certifications being made without his consent were improper and should not be charged against him. He was and is entitled to three certifications for position in the grade for which he was examined. The only circumstance which could justify his certification to the position of stamper, even with his consent, would be the depletion of the eligible register for stamper below the number required for a single certification, and such depletion should be guarded against by timely examinations. To make certification in this way is to break down the distinction between the examinations for different grades, introduce confusion, disorder, and uncertainty into the methods of the board, and violate the fundamental principles of equitable competition. It can not be allowed. In this connection attention is called to your statement that Cumming was on the same day certified three times, first as carrier, "when an eligible for clerk was appointed." By what authority was an "eligible for clerk" certified and appointed to the position of carrier? What was the condition of the carrier eligible register at this time? Why this confusion of grades in certification? This communication is addressed to you, but it is intended equally for the board of examiners, and the Commission desires from that board at once: (1) a report of the examination of October 19, 1887; (2) copies of the several eligible registers as they stood before the certifications of February 18 were made; (3) an explanation of why any persons have at any time been certified to positions for which they were not examined. When this information is received the Commission will determine what the rights of Mr. Cumming are and will communicate with you further on the subject.

Very respectfully,

JOHN H. OBERLY,
Acting President.

GEORGE H. PAUL, Esq.,
Postmaster, Milwaukee, Wis.

No. 5.

MILWAUKEE, WIS., *June* 9, 1888.

SIR: Replying to your communication of the 6th instant, permit me to state that Cumming's name appears at the head of the register of eligibles for carrier at this office, as having been examined October 19, 1887, with an average standing of 89.8, and that the secretary of the local board claims to have duly reported the examination of that date. Your statement of all the facts as to Cumming is accordingly correct, and your conclusion that "he was and is entitled to three certifications for position in the grade for which he was examined," accords with my opinion and action in this particular.

I shall request the secretary of the board of examiners at this office to forward to you at once a duplicate report of the examination of October 19, 1887.

You remark, further, that "the only circumstance which could justify his (Cumming's) certification to the position of stamper, even with his consent, would be the depletion of the eligible register below the number required for a single certification, etc." Such was precisely the fact in the case of Cumming, and the depletion of the stamper list could not well have been foreseen. In fact, the depletion of lists as to competent men can rarely be foreseen or provided for without a considerable increase in the number of examinations, much to the inconvenience of the public service at this office, where clerical aid is limited to the last point of endurance.

Moreover, to make certification from a higher to a lower grade is obviously a great advantage to the public service, since it not only provides for the deficiency of depleted lists, but enables the appointing officer to secure a higher grade of service than otherwise.

Furthermore, certifications from higher to lower grades was distinctly authorized at this office, in a letter from the Civil Service Commission, dated September 18, 1885, and signed by Robert D. Graham, secretary, in which he says: "Those who have taken higher examinations as clerks or carriers may, of course, be certified to these lower places, and for this purpose may be transferred to the lower registers on their request." And certifications of this kind have been frequently made to me at this office, under this authority, largely to the benefit of the service, inasmuch as it has in many cases secured a better ability and education in lower places than could otherwise be obtained, and also permitting more convenience in promotions on the ground of qualification and merit. This is illustrated in the case of Cumming, standing at 90 on clerical list and accepting the place of stamper.

Respectfully,

GEO. H. PAUL, *Postmaster.*

Hon. JOHN H. OBERLY,
   Acting President Civil Service Commission.

No. 6.

WASHINGTON, D. C., *June* 16, 1888.

SIR: Replying to your communication of June 9, relative to the certification of Charles Cumming, and calling attention to the letter of the Commission of September 18, 1885, which says: "Those who have taken higher examinations as clerks or carriers, may, of course, be certified to these lower places, *and for this purpose may be transferred to the lower register on their request,*" you are respectfully informed that the practice authorized by this letter is not allowed under the new rules, except where the lower registers are exhausted and it is not practicable to replenish them in time to meet the demands of the service, and then only with the consent of the persons interested. It will be observed from the words underscored that consent was necessary under the old practice. Instructions have been communicated to the board of examiners.

Very respectfully,

JNO. H. OBERLY,
Acting President.

GEORGE H. PAUL, Esq.,
   Postmaster, Milwaukee, Wis.

No. 7.

MILWAUKEE, WIS., *June* 12, 1888.

DEAR SIRS: In response to your communication of June 6, 1888, addressed to the postmaster at Milwaukee, Wis., and calling for copies of "Report of examination of October 19, 1887," and of our register of eligibles prior to certifications of February 18, 1888, and for certain explanations, I herewith inclose the copies desired, and would state that persons have been certified for positions for which they have not been examined, under authority of a letter from the Civil Service Commission dated September 18, 1885, in which it is explicitly stated that those who have taken higher examinations as clerks or carriers may, of course, be certified to these lower places, and for this purpose may be transferred to the lower registers on their request.

In order to correct the record as to the certification of Cumming, in accordance with the views of the commission, it will only be necessary to direct that his name be stricken off the certification (No. 59) in which his name was used to complete the list, and to allow it to be again presented to the postmaster. Certification No. 59, so modified, will be satisfactory, as it still includes the name chosen.

Respectfully, yours,

H. SHIDY,
Secretary.

CIVIL SERVICE COMMISSION,
   Washington, D. C.

No. 8.

WASHINGTON, D. C., *June* 16, 1888.

SIR: Your communication, inclosing copies of report of examination of October 19, 1887, and of registers of eligibles prior to the certification of February 18, 1888, has been received.. You state that persons have been certified for positions for which they have not been examined under authority of a letter of the commission dated September 18, 1885, in which it is explicitly stated that "those who have taken higher examinations as clerks or carriers may, of course, be certified to these lower places, and for this purpose may be transferred to the lower registers on their request," and that in order to correct the record as to the certification of Cumming in accordance with the views of the Commission it will only be necessary to direct that his name be stricken from the certification No. 50, in which his name was used to complete the list, and allow it to be again presented to the postmaster.

In reply you are respectfully informed that the proceeding suggested by your board is hereby authorized and directed, and that hereafter the rules and regulations now in force must be strictly observed in all particulars.

Very respectfully,

JNO. H. OBERLY,
Acting President.

H. SHIDY, Esq.,
Secretary, Board of Examiners,
Post-Office, Milwaukee, Wis.

EXHIBIT L.

WASHINGTO N, D. C., *March* 4, 1890.

DEAR SIR: I did not read the published report of the testimony I gave before your committee February 28 until to-night. As published in the Post I am made to say in answer to the question "if the conditions were the same you would see nothing wrong in it?" "I did not say that I had done anything wrong." I beg to be informed if this is in accordance with the official record. I certainly thought I had said, "I did not say I had not done anything wrong." This it was my intention to say; I think I must be misreported.

Very respectfully,

H. SHIDY,
1607 *Marion Street.*

Hon. HERMAN LEHLBACH,
Chairman Congressional Committee Investigating Civil Service Commission.

EXHIBIT M.

DEPARTMENT OF THE INTERIOR, CENSUS OFFICE,
Washington, March 1, 1890.

DEAR SIR: On returning to the Census Office this morning I made inquiry of Mr. Campbell Copeland, special agent and chief of the division on wealth, debt, and taxation, in regard to a statement made by Mr. Hamilton Shidy to the effect that he (Mr. Shidy) had charge of clerks in the above-named division, some of whom were receiving $1,200 per annum and more, for what he (Mr. Shidy) knew, while he (Mr. Shidy) was receiving only $900 per annum as a copyist, in which capacity Mr. Shidy is employed in the Census Office.

In answer to a question from a member of the committee (his name I do not now recall), I stated that while this might be possible in the Census Office, from the fact that in the rapid organization of the office changes of this kind are sometimes made, but I likewise informed the committee that Mr. Shidy could not have been in the position, as stated by him, many weeks. Upon inquiry I find that Mr. Shidy entered upon this work February 11, that he is not in charge of a room, that he does give out the work for fourteen people, not one of whom is receiving more than $900 per annum, like himself. Mr. Copeland informs me that there was only one instance of a man receiving

$1,200 per annum being placed under Mr. Shidy's supervision, and that was when said clerk was brought in and placed at a desk in order to discover his ability in the direction of the work that was likely to be required of him.

The committee will therefore see that Mr. Shidy's testimony as reported in the Post, and as read to me this morning, is entirely misleading. As a matter of fact, Mr. Shidy has never had, except in the one instance referred to (for two days only), a man or woman under his supervision who received more salary than himself.

Very respectfully,

ROBERT P. PORTER,
Superintendent of Census.

Hon. HERMAN LEHLBACH,
Chairman of Committee on Reform in the Civil Service,
House of Representatives.

www.ingramcontent.com/pod-product-compliance
Lightning Source LLC
Chambersburg PA
CBHW030912270326
41929CB00008B/666

* 9 7 8 3 3 3 7 2 9 6 2 8 5 *